MUSLIM RESI

TO THE TSAR

Shamil (*an artist's impression*)

MUSLIM RESISTANCE TO THE TSAR:

Shamil and the Conquest of Chechnia and Daghestan

Moshe Gammer
Tel Aviv University

FRANK CASS

First published 1994 in Great Britain by
FRANK CASS & CO. LTD.

Reprinted 2004 by Frank Cass
2 Park Square, Milton Park,
Abingdon, Oxon, OX14 4RN

Transferred to Digital Printing 2005

Frank Cass is an imprint of the Taylor & Francis Group

British Library Cataloguing in Publication Data

Gammer, Moshe
Muslim resistance to the tsar: Shamil and the
conquest of Chechnia and Daghestan.
I. Title
947.900882971

ISBN 0-7146-8141-5 (paperback)
ISBN 0-7146-5099-4 (hardback)

Library of Congress Cataloging-in-Publication Data

Gammer, M.
Muslim resistance to the tsar: Shamil and the conquest of
Chechnia and Daghestan/Moshe Gammer.
p. cm.
Includes bibliographical references and index.
ISBN 0–7146–3431–X
1. Shāmil, Imām, 1798–1871. 2. Muslims—Russian S.F.S.R.—
Caucasus, Northern—Political activity. I. Title.
DK511.C2G28 1993
947'.00882971—dc20 91–23436
CIP

Phototypeset by Intype, London

Printed and bound by Antony Rowe Ltd, Eastbourne

Jacket illustration: Shamil rallying his troops
before battle (painting by a later artist)

Contents

To Li-Ling

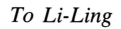

List of Illustrations

Grateful acknowledgement is due to the Institute of History, Language, and Literature of the Daghestani Academic Centre, Makhachgala, Daghestan, and to the Society for Central Asian Studies, London, for permission to reproduce the illustrations listed below.

List of Maps

Acknowledgements

This book is based on a PhD thesis submitted at the London School of Economics and Political Science, University of London. First of all, I am grateful to my teachers and masters – my supervisors Professor E. Kedourie and Dr D. C. B. Lieven – who with infinite patience guided, helped and encouraged me through this lengthy research. I always found their doors open and them more than willing to answer my queries and assist me in overcoming difficulties. No PhD student could have had better and more helpful and responsible supervisors.

I consider myself very lucky indeed to have enjoyed the help, co-operation and encouragement of so many friends and colleagues. Marie Broxup and Dr Paul Henze were a constant source of help and encouragement. Professor Osmo Jussila and Dr Hary Halén assisted me in Helsinki. Professors Michel Lesure and Alexandre Popovic extended a helping hand in Paris. In İstanbul I benefited from the friendship and help of Professor Mehmet Saray and Dr Nâdir Devlet and their assistants. In Israel I enjoyed the advice, encouragement and help of Professor Michael Zand of the Hebrew University in Jerusalem and of all my friends and colleagues at the Dayan Centre for Middle Eastern and African Studies at Tel Aviv University. Dr Butrus Abu Manneh of Haifa University shared with me his vast knowledge of the Naqshbandiyya-Khālidiyya. Dr Maarten Maartinus van Bruinessen supplied me with information on the Nehrī Branch of that order. Daniel Dishon was kind enough to transcribe the Austrian consular reports from Gothic to Latin script in addition to his important comments on the first draft. Massi Torfeh helped me with Persian. A Pakistani friend, who prefers not to be named, helped me with Urdu. Dr Stephen Jones helped me with Georgian and Dr Simon Crisp helped me with Avar. Michael Harpke, who is writing a PhD dissertation on a closely related subject at the University of Wisconsin, Madison, kindly exchanged with me notes and thoughts. Finally, this is the place to pay tribute to the late Professor Alexandre Benningsen, who encouraged me in my research.

This study could not have been done without the assistance of the staff of all the archives and libraries I used. Specifically, I am grateful to Jarmo Suonsyrjä and the staff of the Slaavilainen Kyrjasto in Helsinki, who showed me that librarians in a national library can be friendly and helpful beyond the call of duty or any expectation. Dr Eric Ormsby supplied me with copies of his own photocopies of two letters by Shamil now in the possession of Princeton University Library, after the librarians there had been unable to locate them. Dr Ernst Petritsch of the Haus-, Hoff- und Staatsarchiv in Vienna took the trouble of locating, photocopying, and sending to me the relevant documents. Mr Mathews and Mr Higgins, the librarian and deputy librarian of the London Library, generously allowed me to use the material bequeathed to the Library by J. F. Baddeley. Mr and Mrs Humphrey Brook allowed me to use the Benckendorf archive, and Dr Fr. Hiller von Gaertringen, as an historian himself, allowed me the use of the papers of Leutnant Hiller von Gaertringen, and even took it upon himself to photocopy and mail all the documents I required.

Finally, I am indebted to Eileen Roberts and the other librarians at the inter-library loans department of the British Library of Political and Economic Science (the London School of Economics and Political Science), who performed miracles in getting me from all over the world all those publications with unpronounceable titles in strange languages. My thanks are due also to Jane Pugh and Gary Llewellyn of the cartography unit at the Geography Department of the London School of Economics and Political Science, who taught and helped me to draw the maps.

Financially, this research could not have been undertaken without an Argov studentship from the London School of Economics and Political Science. Further assistance was extended by the School, by the Anglo-Jewish Association and by the Leo Baeck (London) Lodge of B'nai B'rith. My two stays in Helsinki were financed by a Jewish fund which prefers to remain anonymous. My stay in İstanbul was financed by the Society for Central Asian Studies, as was the typing of the thesis. I am especially grateful to Mr Djanogly, who contributed personally towards my research in the archives in İstanbul. Since, unfortunately, this research did not materialise, the money was returned without diminishing my gratitude for this act of personal trust and generosity.

As ever, I am grateful to my friends, Debbie and David Arbiser and Eliezer Yemini, for their constant friendship and support.

Note on Transliteration and Calendar

Since this book deals with people who wrote Arabic, it was deemed proper to use throughout it the Arabic form of personal and place-names rather than the Russian form of these names. (The Russian form is used only in a few cases in which the Arabic is unknown.) However, the first time each place, and some of the names, are mentioned, their Russian form is given in square brackets. The Arabic alphabet used in the Caucasus included several additional letters to signify sounds specific to local languages. The transliteration system from Arabic is as follows:

أ — ’	چ — Ch/Zh	ر — R	ض — Ḍ	ق — Q	لّ — Tl
ب — B	ح — Ḥ	ز — Z	س — S	ق — Ql	م — M
پ — P	خ — Kh	ژ — Ts	ش — Sh	ك — K	ن — N
ت — T	څ — Kh	ط — Ṭ	ع — ‘	ڭ — G	ه — H
ث — Th/Ts	د — D	ظ — Ẓ	غ — Gh	ڶ — L	و — W/V
ج — J	ذ — Dh	ص — Ṣ	ف — F/P	ڸ — L	ي — Y

Russian places and names, with the exception of a few well-established ones like Moscow or Nicholas, are rendered in transliteration from the modern orthography. The transliteration system from Russian is as follows:

А – A	Е – E	Л – L	Р – R	Х – Kh	Ъ – "
Б – B	Ж – Zh	М – M	С – S	Ц – Ts	Ы – Y
В – V	З – Z	Н – N	Т – T	Ч – Ch	Ь – '
Г – G/H	И – I	О – O	У – U	Ш – Sh	Э – Ë
Д – D	К – K	П – P	Ф – F	Щ – Shch	Ю – Iu
					Я – Ia

Names of Russian officials written originally in Western languages (Polish, German, French), are spelled in their Latin form, with the Russian form given in square brackets at their first appearance. Georgian names are transliterated from their Russian form. Their Georgian form is rendered in normal brackets the first time they appear. Transliteration from Georgian is in accordance with the system used in D. M. Lang, *The Last Years of the Georgian Monarchy* (New York, 1957).

Turkish names and places are written according to the modern Turkish orthography. Whenever both an Arabic and a Turkish form exist, the Turkish is used for the areas now in the Turkish Republic and the Arabic for areas now in the Caucasus, or the Arab Middle East. On such occasions, the other form is given in normal brackets on its first mention.

All dates in the text are in the Gregorian calendar, unless stated otherwise. In the notes the dates are given in the original – i.e. Julian ('Old Style'), *Hijri* (Muslim), etc. – with the corresponding Gregorian date following in square brackets. Names, places and dates within quotations were changed wherever necessary, for the sake of uniformity. In the notes some places appear in at least three different spellings, Erzurum, for example, is rendered Erzeroom (English), Erzeroum (French) and Erzerum (German). Also for the sake of uniformity, titles of sources, regardless of their language, have been capitalised as in English.

Preface

The so-called '*Murīd* movement' was but one of a series of similar phenomena, grouped by Bernard Lewis under the title 'The Revolt of Islam'.[1] Indeed, Shamil's struggle has often been compared with that of ʿAbd al-Qādir in Algeria,[2] with that of al-Sayyid Aḥmad Barelvī in India,[3] and with the Ache War in Sumatra.[4] One can further liken it to a series of other fundamentalist Muslim resistance movements to Western encroachment in Asia and Africa.[5] In addition to all their shared characteristics, one common denominator can be found in most of them: with one or two exceptions, none of them has been studied thoroughly. In the case of Shamil and his movement, much has been published, mainly by Soviet and Caucasian expatriate authors, but the best study is still one written at the beginning of this century.[6]

The aim of this book is to be a thorough study of the '*Murīd* movement' and of its main leader, Shamil. However, by no means does it attempt to be a 'definitive' study. In history, as in the humanities in general, there are not, and could not be, definitive studies. Even the most intensively researched subject is always open to revision and reinterpretation, and this book aims at such a reinterpretation. As well as being a thorough study of the subject, it seeks to open the field for further research and to raise further questions.

One such area for further research could be the pursuit of new sources. Until very recently Soviet archives have been practically closed to historians writing on this subject. The prospect of their opening to research raises the possibility of further important information being released. In this context the collection of Arabic manuscripts in Makhachqala, the capital city of the Daghestani ASSR, is of special importance and interest. Other interesting sources might be found in Polish archives and libraries, which have never been thoroughly scrutinised. Turkish,

Egyptian and Iranian archives might add to our knowledge of Shamil's foreign relations.

Fortunately, however, the closure of Soviet archives is to a great extent compensated for by the published material. The centrality of the subject in pre-revolutionary Russian, as well as Soviet, historiography resulted in the publication of thousands of documents and letters, and dozens of diaries, memoirs, notes, travellers' accounts and, most important, detailed summaries of the events based on the archives in Tiflis (Tpilisi). These are especially valuable because they contain very little interpretation and are, therefore, the next best thing to the archives themselves. All these sources, together with contemporary newspaper reports and Western archival material, form a solid and extensive base for the reconstruction of the events and for their reinterpretation.

Finally, it has been claimed that 'history is the verdict of the lucky on the unlucky, of those who weren't there on those who were'.[7] These facts cannot be changed when one deals with events which took place long before one's birth. One can only try not to be smug.

Chronology

1829

December Ghāzī Muḥammad proclaimed *imām* of Daghestan.

1830

January Ghāzī Muḥammad proclaimed *imām* again. Occupies Harakān.

24 February Ghāzī Muḥammad checked at Khunzakh by Pakhu Bike.

March The Russians occupy Chārtalah; Ghāzī Muḥammad declares *jihād* on the Russians.

May ʿAbdallah al-ʿAshilṭī sent to Chechnia; Russian force seizes the herds of Hindāl.

September Shaykh Muḥammad al-Yarāghī declares *jihād* on the Russians.

September–October Ghāzī Muḥammad tours Chechnia.

1831

March–June Ghāzī Muḥammad's campaign in Northern Daghestan.

10 May Paskiewicz leaves Tiflis for Poland.

May–July ʿAbdallah al-ʿAshilṭī's and Ghāzī Muḥammad's campaign in Chechnia.

26 June–11 July The siege of Vnezapnaia.

13 July Russian force defeated at Aghdash ʿAwkh.

August–September Ghāzī Muḥammad's campaign in Southern Daghestan.

1–8 September Derbend besieged.

2 October Rosen arrives in Tiflis.

15–23 October Pankratʿev's campaign in Ṭabarsarān.

October–November Pankratʿev's and Velʿiaminov's campaigns in Kunbut and ʿAwkh.

13 November Ghāzī Muḥammad's raid on Qidhlār.

13 December The Russians take by storm Ghāzī Muḥammad's position at Aghach Qalʿa.

1832

April Ghāzī Muḥammad's raids in the vicinity of Naṣrān and Groznaia.
2–3 July Klugenau takes by storm Ghāzī Muḥammad's position at Yol-Sus-Tawh.
2 July–21 August Ḥamza Bek's campaign in Chārtalah.
24 July–5 August Rosen's campaign against the Galgay.
25 July–9 August Velʿiaminov's campaign against the Qarābulāq and Galasha.
15 August–6 October Rosen's campaign in Lesser and Greater Chechnia.
29 October Rosen storms Ghāzī Muḥammad's position at Gimrāh. The *imām* killed in battle.
November Ḥamza Bek proclaimed second *imām*.

1833

October Ḥamza Bek defeats the united forces of Aqūsha, the *shāmkhāl* and the *khān* of Mekhtulī at Girgil.

1834

25 August the annihilation of the Avār ruling house.
19 September Ḥamza Bek assassinated.
24 September Shamil proclaimed third *imām*.
26–27 September Lanskoi's attack on Gimrāh.
14 October–4 November Klugenau's expedition to Khunzakh.

1836

January The Chirqaṭa agreement between Shamil, Ḥājj Tāshō and Qibid Muḥammad.
2–6 August Réoute's 'patrol' to Irghin.
2–6 September Pullo's attack on Zandaq.
2–15 September Réoute's expedition to Khunzakh.

1837

4–12 February Faesy's campaign in Lesser Chechnia.
16 February–11 April Faesy's campaign in Greater Chechnia.
19 May–24 July Faesy's campaign in Daghestan.
17 July Faesy storms Ṭiliq and holds the upper half of the village.

18 July Agreement reached between Shamil and Faesy.
11 September Faesy arrests Shamil's nephew.
25 September–10 October Klugenau's negotiations with Shamil.
12 December Rosen replaced by Golovin.

1839

21–27 May Grabbe's campaign in Chechnia.
2 June–11 September Grabbe's campaign in Daghestan.
5 June The battle of Burtinah.
11–13 June The conquest of Irghin.
24 June–4 September Siege of Akhulgoḥ.
29 August Second storming of Akhulgoḥ; Shamil sends Jamāl al-Dīn as hostage to Grabbe.
2–4 September Final assault on Akhulgoḥ.
11 September End of resistance to the Russians.
15 September Russian force attacked at Chirkah.

1840

19 February The Circassians storm and destroy fort Lazarev.
March The Chechens rise and ask Shamil to lead them.
11 October Akhbirdi Muḥammad's raid on Muzlik.
8–30 November Grabbe's campaign in Chechnia.
22 November Ḥajimurād escapes from the Russians.

1841

January Ḥajimurād joins Shamil, nominated *nā'ib* of Avāristān.
17 February Bakunin killed during a failed attempt to storm Tselmes.
May–October Golovin concentrates all his efforts on building fort Evgenievskoe.
27 October–13 November Grabbe's campaign in Chechnia.
30 October–4 November Shamil's first pincer attack on Avāristān.
23 November Shu'ayb's raid on Qidhlār.
29 November–7 December Shamil's second pincer attack on Avāristān.

1842

18 February–18 April Faesy's campaign in Daghestan.
2 April Shamil captures Ghāzī-Ghumuq.
11–13 June Grabbe's disastrous campaign in Ichkerī.

30 June Grabbe's attack on Ihali repulsed.
7 December Golovin replaced by Neidhardt.

1843

24 June Akhbirdi Muḥammad killed in attack on Shatil.
8 September–3 October Shamil's first offensive in Daghestan.
11–12 October Shamil's raid on Enderī
6–7 November Shamil's raid on Vnezapnaia.
9 November–28 December Shamil's second offensive in Daghestan.

1844

18 January Shuʿayb assassinated.
16 June–3 July Schwartz conquers and abolishes the sultanate of Ilişū; Daniyāl escapes to Shamil.
18 June–15 July Neidhardt's offensive in Daghestan.
3 September–1 December Erection of fort Vozdvizhenskoe.

1845

8 January Neidhardt replaced by Vorontsov.
15 June–31 July Vorontsov's campaign against Darghiyya.
16 December–5 January (1846) Freytag clears forests along the Goyta.

1846

27 January–11 February Freytag clears forests along the Gekhi.
25 April–9 May Shamil's campaign in Ghabarṭa.
30 June–22 October Erection of fort Achkhi.
20–28 October Shamil's attack in Aqūsha.
25–26 December Ḥajimurād's raid on Jengutay.

1847

16 December (1846)–1 February Freytag's winter campaign in Lesser Chechnia.
13 May–9 June Daniyāl's offensive in Chārtalah.
13–20 June Vorontsov's attack on Girgil repulsed.
6 August–27 September Vorontsov's attack on Salṭah.
30 November–2 March (1848) Russian winter campaign in Lesser Chechnia.
18 December Freytag's raid on the hamlet of Saʿid ʿAbdalla.

1848

17 June–30 July Argutinskii's attack on Girgil.

19 June–1 October Russian summer campaign in Lesser Chechnia; fort of Urus Martan established.

17 September–4 October Shamil's campaign in the upper Samur.

1849

December (1848)–February Russian winter campaign in Chechnia.

17 July–4 September Argutinskii's siege of Chōkha.

21 July–14 August Vorontsov holds discussions with the tsar in St. Petersburg and Warsaw.

2–30 December Nesterov 'pacifies' Galasha and Qarābulāq.

1850

January Sa'īd 'Abdalla's counteroffensive in Galasha.

22 January–7 March Nesterov's winter campaign in Greater Chechnia.

February Hajimurad's counteroffensive in Galasha.

13 August–16 September Kozlowskii clears forests along the Michik.

9 September Sleptsov's raid on Shamil's fortifications in the forest of Shali.

13 October Russians finally seize control over lower Lesser Chechnia.

1851

30 December (1850)–8 February Sleptsov's winter campaign in Lesser Chechnia.

13 January–12 March Kozlowski's winter campaign in Greater Chechnia.

11 March Shamil's *niẓām*, used for the first (and last) time in pitched battle; dispersed by Bariatinskii.

12 July–6 August Ḥajimurād's campaign in Qaytāq and Ṭabarsarān.

25 November Ḥajimurād escapes to the Russians.

1852

11–30 January Buq Muḥammad's campaign in Qaytāq and Ṭabarsarān.

17 January–17 March Bariatinskii's winter campaign in Greater Chechnia.

29–30 January Bariatinskii's and Vrevskii's double raid on the upper Goyta and Roshna.

29 February–1 March Bariatinskii's march across Greater Chechnia.

8 March Meller-Zakomelskii's raid on Talgik's village.

7 May Ḥajimurād killed in attempt to escape back into the mountains.

23 August Baklanov's attack on Gurdali.

26 August Young Vorontsov's attack on the Argun defile.

1853

15 December (1852)–27 April Vrevskii's winter campaign in Lesser Chechnia.

16 January–26 March Bariatinskii's winter campaign in Greater Chechnia.

5–18 September Shamil's campaign in Chārtalah.

5 October The Ottomans declare war on Russia.

1854

March Vorontsov leaves; replaced temporarily by Read.

14 July–11 August Shamil's campaign in the Alazan valley.

September Shamil's attempt to effect a juncture with Muḥammad Amin.

11 December Muravʿev nominated viceroy.

1855

22 March Exchange of prisoners between Shamil and the Russians.

1856

30 March Peace treaty of Paris signed.

17 June Muravʿev resigns; replaced by Bariatinskii.

1857

December (1856)–January Evdokimov's winter campaign in Greater Chechnia.

28 June–28 November Orbeliani's campaign in Salaṭawh.

14 July–3 September Vrevskii's campaign against Dido.

1858

December (1857)–April Evdokimov's winter campaign.
28 January Evdokimov conquers the Argun defile.
31 May–31 July Wrangel's campaign in Lesser Chechnia.
June Shamil's campaign in Lesser Chechnia.
10 July–12 September Evdokimov's summer campaign.
August Shamil's campaign in Naṣrān, following a local revolt.
22–25 December Shamil attempts a counteroffensive in Greater Chechnia.

1859

2 January–13 April Evdokimov's winter campaign.
27 January Evdokimov conquers Tawzen.
8 February Evdokimov takes ʿAlisanji.
19–20 February Evdokimov invests New Darghiyya.
13 March–21 April Wrangel's campaign in ʿAwkh.
26 July–6 September The final Russian assault.
27–28 July Wrangel crosses the ʿAndī Koyṣū.
21 August Ghunib invested by the Russians.
6 September (25 August, Old Style) Shamil's surrender to Bariatinskii.

Introduction: The Russian Conquest of Transcaucasia

Russian contacts with the Caucasus date back to the times of the principality of Kiev.[1] In the Muscovite and early Imperial periods these contacts, mainly with the Daghestanis and Chechens, took place through two separate channels: one was the gradual southward expansion of Russia through the independent activity of the Cossacks, who 'in the course of centuries added belt upon belt of fertile territory to their own possessions, and eventually to the Empire of the tsars.'[2]

The first Cossacks in the Northern Caucasus arrived during the sixteenth century in two separate groups. These settled in the Terek Delta and on the foothills of Chechnia and subsequently became known as the Terek [Terskie] and Grebenskie (or Grebentsy) Cossacks, respectively. The northward expansion of the Chechens pressed both the Grebentsy (in 1685) and the Terek Cossacks (in 1712) to move to the left (northern) bank of the Terek. Here they served as the beginning of what would more than a century later become known as the 'Caucasian Line'.

The second channel of Russia's engagement with the Caucasus was through contacts with Georgia. Surrounded by stronger Muslim neighbours, the Christian-Orthodox kings of Georgia turned to the rising Orthodox power in the north, which in turn was more than willing to intervene in the affairs of the Caucasus.

In 1586 Alexander II, king of Kakhet'i, asked for the assistance of Tsar Feodor (Theodor) against the *shāmkhāl* of Targhū [Tarki, Tarku]. Feodor sent in 1594 a force of 7,000 men under the *boiar* Khvorostin. This force was cut to pieces by the *shāmkhāl*, as were two forces sent ten years later by Boris Godunov.

These were the first engagements of Russian regular forces with the Daghestanis and they did not augur well for the Muscovites. More important, the Russian activity was met with strong displeasure on the part of the Ottomans and the Ṣafavids (then ruling in Persia). Both powers were too strong for Moscow to compete with and for the following century and a half, though contacts with Georgia continued, Russia abstained from intervening on behalf of its co-religionists.

Russian offensive activity in the Caucasus was renewed by Peter the Great. This was part of his attempt to expand southward and open up a commercial route to India. Undeterred by the ill-fated expedition to Khīva in 1717,[3] Peter seized upon the Afghan invasion of Persia to make another attempt southward.[4] Immediately following the conclusion of the 'Northern War' with Sweden in 1721, the Russian emperor decided to lead a campaign in person in that direction. In 1722 a pretext for declaring war was found and the Russians seized Derbend, Targhū, Qubāh [Kuba] and Bāqū. By this time the Terek and Grebentsy Cossack 'armies' (*voiska*) had been fully integrated into the Russian state. During the 1722 campaign, Peter the Great settled Cossacks from the Don in the gap between the Terek Cossacks and the Grebensky. The newcomers were given the name Terskie-Semeinye (Terek family).

The Russians now controlled the littoral of the Caspian Sea as far as Astarābād, but did not penetrate the interior.[5] In one attempt to do so a detachment of cavalry trying to occupy Enderī [Andreevskii] was beaten by the Chechens. 'This was the first time that Russian regular troops had come in contact with that tribe in their native forests, and the result was ominous of what was to take place on numerous occasions during the ensuing 130 years.'[6]

With Peter's death in 1725 his ambitions were abandoned for nearly half a century. In 1735 a fort was established in Qidhlār [Kizliar], 'which up to 1763 was, so to speak, the Russian capital of the Caucasus'.[7] However, by that same year the Empress Anne had withdrawn all her forces to the northern bank of the Terek. It was Catherine the Great who renewed the southward expansion of the Russian Empire. She was also the first to combine the two above-mentioned channels of contact with the Caucasus.

In 1763, a year after Catherine's accession to power, the fortress of Muzlik [Mozdok] was established. This aggressive step led to a 14-year struggle with the Ghabarṭians (Kabardians) (1765–1779), during which the Caucasian Line was extended and a new Cossack regiment – the Mozdok Cossacks – was established and settled on the Ghabartians' land.

More importantly, this step contributed to the war with the Ottoman Empire (1768–1774), during which a Russian force, under Gottlieb Heinrich von Todtleben, was sent for the first time across the main range to Tiflis. Todtleben captured K'ut'aisi in 1770, but failed to storm P'ot'i and in 1772 the Russian force was recalled to the Line.[8]

The peace treaty of Küçük Kaynarca (1774) 'established the River Kuban as the boundary between Russia and Turkey', but the Russians failed to 'put an end to Turkish domination in Imeret'i and Georgia.' On the contrary, owing to a Russian mistake, the treaty in fact established Ottoman suzerainty over both Imeret'i and K'art'lo-Kakhet'i.'[9]

During the eight following years Russia's main preoccupation was to prepare for, and execute, the annexation of the Crimean Khanate – its main spoil of war.[10] But the newly annexed territories north-west of the Caucasus were not neglected. 'By the united efforts' of Jacobi [Iakobi] and the celebrated Suvorov, 'Russia's position on the Western portion of the border-line was very much strengthened, and a solid foundation laid for future success against the tribes inhabiting the country between the Terek and the Black Sea coast.'[11]

The Russians established the Lines along the Kuban and the Laba and erected the fortresses of Ekaterinograd, Georgievsk and Stavropol', which would later become the headquarters of the entire Line.

The process culminated in 1783 in Suvorov's 'merciless slaughter' of the Nogay nomads.[12] This left the area north of the Kuban open for colonisation by Russian state serfs,[13] the same as in the Crimea, 'whence the Crimean-Tatars, panic-stricken at Russian methods of government, fled to Turkey in such numbers that to this day [1907] the peninsula has never recovered its former population.'

All this time Georgia, though left alone for the time being, was not forgotten in St. Petersburg. The empress, it seems, waited for an opportunity to intervene there, and such a pretext came her way in 1783. When ʿAlī Murād Shāh demanded subjugation, Erekle II, king of K'art'lo-Kakhet'i, appealed for help to Russia. Catherine's reaction was swift: on 5 August a treaty was signed at Georgievsk under the terms of which a Russian protectorate was established over K'art'lo-Kakhet'i,[14] and on 15 November two Russian battalions with four guns, commanded by Pavel Potemkin,[15] entered Tiflis.

On his way to Tiflis, Potemkin established the fortress of Vladikavkaz at Burav, linking it to Muzlik by a chain of forts. He also converted the bridle path across the main chain through the Daryal pass into 'something in the nature of a road'.[16] This would later be expanded and improved into what would become known as the Georgian-Military-Highway – Russia's lifeline to its possessions in Transcaucasia.

But this was all still in the future. The Russian troops were soon – in February 1784 – withdrawn from Tiflis, and in 1788 abandoned Vladikavkaz. 'In the absence of military protection the Empress's interference proved worse than useless; it helped to exasperate Persia and contributed thereby to the invasion of Āghā Muḥammad Khān.'[17]

The founder of the Qājār dynasty had demanded Erekle's submission in progressively menacing terms since the early 1780s. In the spring of 1795 Āghā Muḥammad Khān laid siege to Shūsha. On 23 May he suddenly appeared in front of Tiflis. On the following day he defeated Erekle's small forces and entered the city. Deciding to make an example of Tiflis, the Qājār leader let his warriors engage in 'barbarous and horrid excesses' of 'carnage and rapine'.[18]

Upon receiving the news of the 'monstrous' sack of Tiflis, Catherine declared war. The Russian forces conquered Derbend for the third time[19] and Qubāh and Bāqū for the second. However, after Catherine's death that same year (1796), her successor Paul [Pavel], 'who bore no goodwill to his mother or her policy, made haste to relinquish Catherine's Persian conquests as completely as Anne had relinquished those of Peter.'[20]

However, as in many similar cases throughout history, Paul's attempt at disengagement from the Caucasus and Georgia ended with a far greater involvement. In 1799, Fatḥ ʿAlī Shāh, Āghā Muḥammad's successor, demanded that Giorgi XII, Erekle's successor,[21] send his son to Tehrān as hostage.[22] Paul concentrated an expeditionary force on the 'Line' to counteract any attempt by Fatḥ ʿAlī Shāh on Georgia and informed Giorgi of his (Paul's) determination to protect him.[23] Indeed, the Russian force deterred the *shāh* from attacking Kakhet'i and beat off an invasion by ʿUma[r] Khān of Avāristān.[24]

Soon afterwards Giorgi XII, on his deathbed, appealed to the Russian emperor to accept direct authority over K'art'lo-Kakhet'i. On 30 December 1800 – just ten days before the king's death – Paul signed a manifesto in which he accepted Giorgi's offer.[25] Alexander I, his successor, confirmed this manifesto after long hesitation and deliberations on 24 September 1801.[26]

These two events were a watershed in the Russian involvement in the Caucasus. There is room for argument whether Paul was aware of the implications of his decision or not, but none with regard to Alexander. He moved on purpose from intervention to annexation and thus to aggression against the Muslim powers to the south of Georgia and the tribes to the north. This was inevitable, since K'art'li and Kakhet'i as well as the road from Vladikavkaz to Tiflis (rebuilt in 1799) were regarded as indefensible without further conquests and annexations. Thus began a process which would, after six and a half decades of war and struggle, put Russia in full control and possession of the Caucasus.

But at the moment the future of Russian rule in Georgia was uncertain. There had been opposition to the Russian protectorate before Paul's manifesto. Giorgi's brother Alexander, for example, had had pro-Qājār tendencies. In 1800 he fled to Tehrān, from where he continued to stir up his countrymen. The widow and sons of Giorgi, as well as others of the royal blood, were opposed to the protectorate and tried to undo it.

In addition, Paul chose to incorporate K'art'lo-Kakhet'i into the Russian Empire without leaving any role for the local dynasty, as Giorgi XII had originally requested. Alexander chose to adhere to his father's decision against the advice of some of his confidants and the expressed wishes of the Georgian negotiators.[27] This alienated many more among Georgia's nobility.

And as if that were not enough, the Russians had very soon become extremely unpopular in K'art'li and Kakhet'i because of the misconduct of their officials and officers headed by Karl Knorring, the commander of the forces in the Caucasus, and Petr Ivanovich Kovalenskii, the loathed ex-ambassador to Tiflis.[28]

The result was that Russia's hold over Georgia remained insecure for decades to come. As late as 1832 a conspiracy was plotted against Russian rule.[29] In 1839–40 the population – Muslim and Christian alike – awaited the arrival of Ibrāhīm Pāshā (the son of Muḥammad ʿAlī Pāshā of Egypt) as liberator,[30] and in 1841 a revolt broke out in Guria [Guriel].[31]

Alexander I, when deciding to confirm his father's manifesto, accepted also a suggested plan by Zubov 'to occupy the lands from the river Riani down the Kura (Mtkvari) and the Aras (Rakhs) to the Caspian Sea'.[32] In August 1802 the emperor recalled Knorring and Kovalenskii and nominated Prince Pavel Dmitrievich Tsitsianov (Tsitsishvili) as commander-in-chief of the Caucasian Line and chief administrator in Georgia, with vice-regal powers:

> Acquainting him with Count Zubov's plan . . . , the emperor instructed him to bring clarity and order into the confused affairs of the country and to try by gentle, just, but at the same time firm, conduct to obtain trust in the [Russian] government *not only in Georgia but in the different neighbouring principalities*.[33]

Alexander could not choose a man more eager for this. Tsitsianov 'enjoyed a deserved reputation as a valiant commander, and outstanding administrator, and on top of this he was a Georgian by origin'.[34] These qualities, and his 'extreme energy', were 'coupled with an aggressive over-bearing spirit' and 'a biting wit, freely expressed on all who roused his animosity or contempt'.[35] Acting 'with his usual promptitude and firmness',[36] he stabilised Russian rule in K'art'lo-Kakhet'i by exiling the late king's widow and sons to St. Petersburg.

He then turned immediately to execute the Zubov plan. Using the antagonism between Christians and Muslims,[37] he tried to convince the Christian-Georgian principalities to accept Russian suzerainty. In 1803 Mingrelia accepted a Russian protectorate. In 1804 Imeret'i and Guria followed suit. The Muslim neighbours were treated differently. In 1803 the Lesghian communities of Chārtalah and the *sulṭān* of Iliṣū [Elisu] were subdued. The following year Ganja was stormed (14 January 1804), its *khān* killed and the Khanate annexed to Russia and renamed Elizavetpol'. In 1805 the *khāns* of Qarābāgh, Shirvān and Shekī swore allegiance to Russia.

These were Tsitsianov's last achievements. On 20 February 1806 he was treacherously murdered under the walls of Bāqū by its *khān*, Ḥusayn Qūlī, who had pretended to submit to Russian rule. Tsitsianov's head was cut off and sent to Tehrān to Fatḥ ʿAlī Shāh.[38]

'During the three and a half years of his administration,' wrote a Russian author, 'Tsitsianov extended the borders of Russia's possessions from the Black to the Caspian Sea.'[39] But this rapid territorial expansion and aggressive policy led Russia into trouble: 'the two Great Muḥammadan Powers' – as well as Britain and France –

> could not fail to take alarm at the rapid progress of Russia: moreover, Ganja and others of the Khanates were still counted as vassal states by the *shāh*, however shadowy his sovereignty may have become and as Turkey in the west, so Persia in the east soon saw that war with Russia was inevitable.[40]

Indeed, by 1804 Russia was at war with the Qājārs and by 1807 with the Ottomans, in addition to its involvement in the Napoleonic Wars.

Thus, for the following eight years a succession of Russian governors in Georgia had to fight on two fronts simultaneously. They could rely only on their own resources and troops, whose dwindling number they had no hope to reinforce because 'the Napoleonic Wars imposed an immense strain on Russia's resources, and prevented the deployment of large forces in remote Caucasia'. Furthermore, they had to deal with uprisings by the local population – Christian and Muslim alike – 'resulting from the exactions of the [Russian] military commanders and the corrupt ways of tsarist officialdom'.[41]

In spite of such a desperate situation, Russia emerged victorious in both wars. The peace treaties of Bucharest with the Ottomans (1812)[42] and of Gulistān with the Qājārs (1813)[43] confirmed Russian possession of, and Ottoman and Qājār disclaimers to, K'art'lo-Kakhet'i, Imeret'i (annexed in 1810), Mingrelia, Abkhazet'i (accepted protectorate again in 1810), and the Khanates of Ganja [Elizavetpol'], Qarābāgh (1805), Shekī (1805), Derbend (1806), Qubāh (1806), Bāqū (1806) and part of Ṭalīsh (1812). The Qājārs also renounced any claim to Daghestan.[44]

These territorial gains were augmented in the second round of wars with the Qājārs (1826–28) and the Ottomans (1828–29).[45] The peace treaty of Turkumānchāy (1828)[46] added the rest of Ṭalīsh and the Khanates of Erivan and Nakhichevan (Nakhjivān) to Russia. In the peace treaty of Adrianople (1829),[47] Russia finally retained Anapa, Akhalk'alak'i and Akhaltsikhe, and the Ottomans renounced their sovereignty over the eastern coast of the Black Sea.[48]

In between these two rounds of wars, the Russians turned towards the mountains to secure their rear and communications. However, before describing this, the geography and the nature of the two rivals – the Russian army in the Caucasus and the mountaineers – have to be considered.

MAP 1: RUSSIAN ADVANCE IN THE CAUCASUS 1800–1830

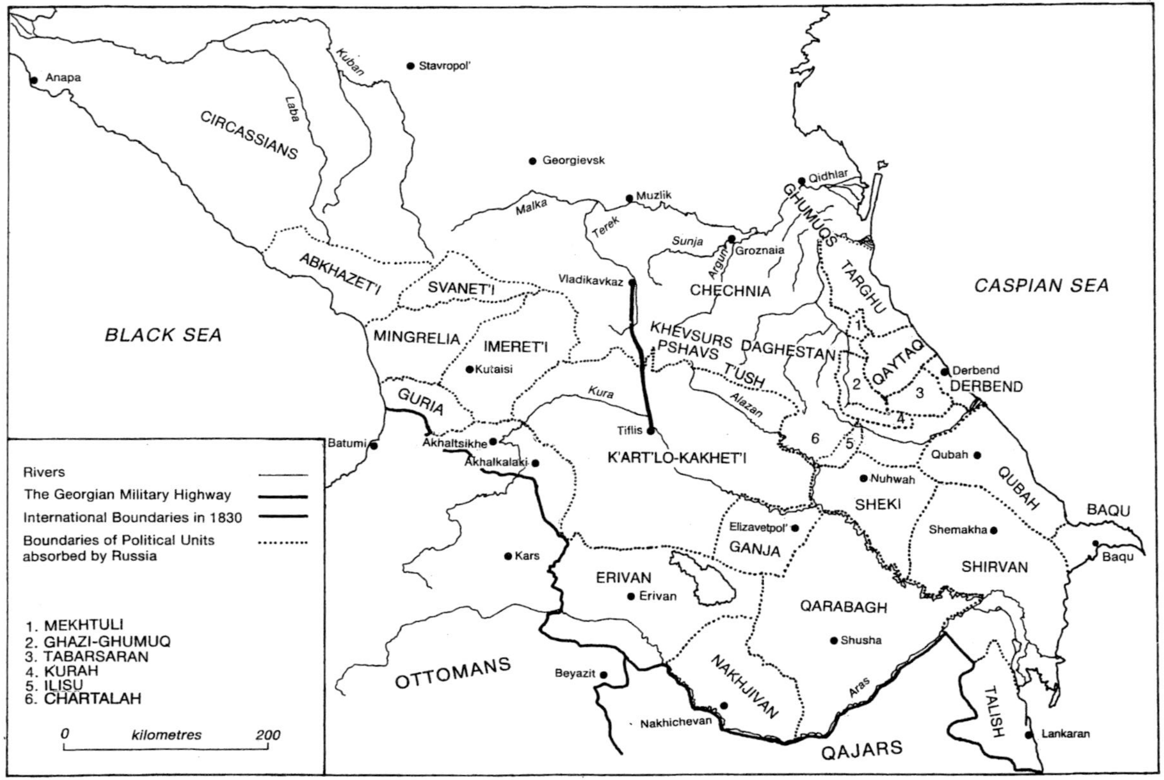

Part 1

The Setting

Chapter 1

The Theatre

> The Caucasus Mountains have often been compared with the Pyrenées because of their asymmetry and steep southern slopes, their lofty deeply trenched eastern mass, their central ice-capped barrier bristling with high peaks, and their western division which gradually narrows and loses height, but gets more and more rain as it goes towards the sea. As in the Pyrenées, difficulties of communication, and the consequent isolation due to the relief explains the fact that the Caucasus region forms a veritable human patchwork. This isolation has resulted in a long-dated insecurity which is reflected in the form of dwelling and has made its conquest so difficult. Lastly, like the Pyrenées it is an almost impassable barrier, which has forced most migrating nations to go round the ends, and yet it does not separate peoples, for nearly all those found on one slope are represented on the other.[1]

Usually regarded as the dividing line between Europe and Asia,[2] the Caucasus extends for over 1,100 kilometres between the Taman peninsula on the Black Sea in the northwest and the Apsheron peninsula on the Caspian Sea in the southeast.[3] Its width ranges between 32 and 180 kilometres, and the highest point is Mount Elbrus, an extinct volcano, with twin peaks reaching 5,629 and 5,593 metres.

The backbone of the mountain system consists along most of its length of two parallel ranges 10 to 15 kilometres apart. The main [glavnyi] or water divide range [vodo-razdel'nyi khrebet] has an average elevation of 3,600 metres. The front [peredovoi] or side [bokovoi] range to the north is in many places higher than the main range.[4] Both ranges tower above the permanent snow line, which rises from west (2,750 metres) to east (3,900 metres), 'due to the fact that the moisture comes from the west'.[5] Hence their nickname of 'snow' or 'ice' mountains in Russian sources.

To the north of the front range lie much lower and gradually decreasing ranges which do not reach the snow line. The two most notable are the rocky [skalistyi] range (average elevation over 3,300 metres) and the 'black mountains' [chernye gory] (average elevation 2,300 metres), called so because of the dense forests that covered them. North of the line of the Kuban and Terek rivers lie the Ciscaucasian steppes, which are the continuation of the Russian steppes. The Manych depression 'marks the northern boundary of Ciscaucasia mainly by its man-repellent poverty'.[6]

To the south of the main range there are fewer ranges, which fall steeply into the depression of the Kura. In the area of Daghestan, the southern slope of the main range 'rises like a wall above the alluvial plains of the Alazān and Kura valleys'.[7] The two main ranges, as well as the others, are connected to each other by cross ranges. 'These connections give rise to mountain basins, which have a relatively dry climate.'[8]

Chechnia and Daghestan form the northeastern part of the Caucasus. Chechnia – named after the people inhabiting the area – is a quadrangle between the Terek and Sunja rivers in the west and the north, the ʿAndī range in the east (which separates it from Daghestan) and the main range in the south. In Russian sources Chechnia is divided along the Argūn River into Lesser to the west of it and Greater to the east.[9]

Like other parts of the Caucasus, Chechnia is divided by parallel ranges, the northernmost of which are the Terek [Terekskii] and Sunja [Sundzhenskii], located in between the rivers after which they are named. The heartland of Chechnia – the lowland – lies between the Sunja range and river and the 'black mountains'. It is, in fact, the widest of the valleys situated in between the different ranges. It is crossed by the numerous tributaries of the Sunja, which cut through the mountain ranges in deep ravines and canyons. Their high water, as all over the Caucasus, occurs in the summer, when snow and ice melt in the higher altitudes.

Most of Chechnia is situated within the forest zone of the Caucasus. With the exception of the Terek and Sunja ranges – 'formed of rounded hills, bare of trees, though covered with luxuriant herbage to their summit' – and 'one or two spurs likewise denuded of trees', the country forms a 'vast succession of forest-clad hills rising wave behind wave to the mighty walls and bastions of the Jurasic limestone topped by the great mountains' of the two main ranges, 'affording in fine weather a glorious

MAP 2: THE CAUCASUS

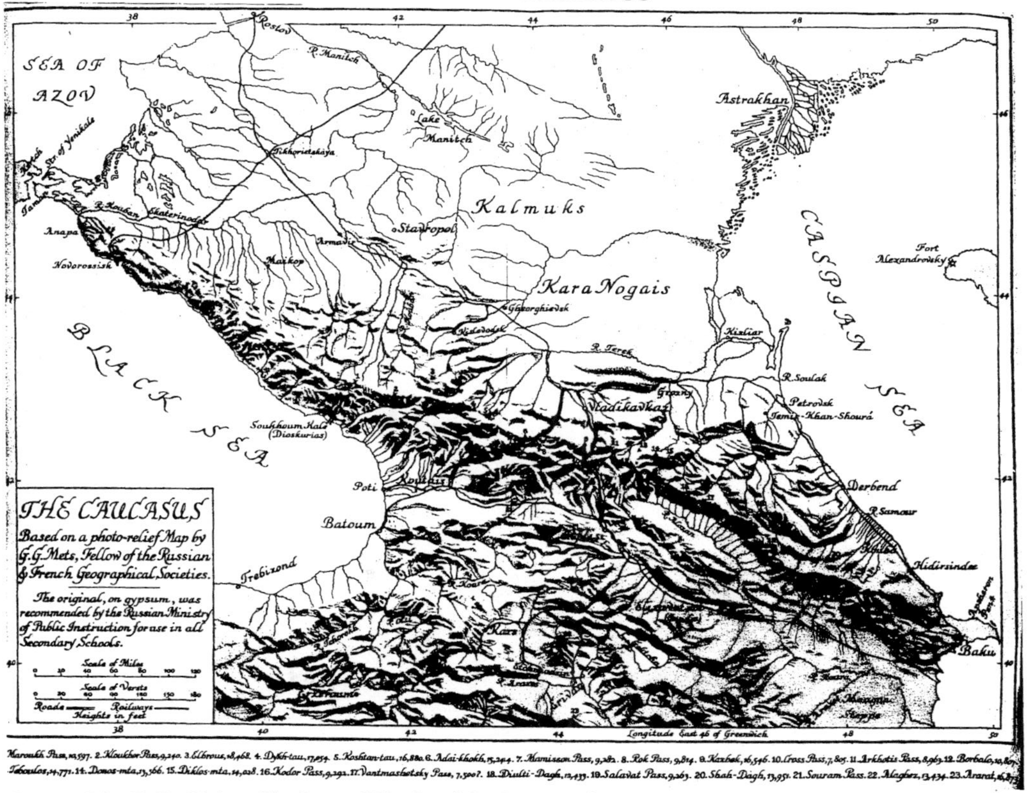

Source: John F. Baddeley, *The Rugged Flanks of the Caucasus* (London, 1940).

panorama of snowy peaks and rocky ridges rising from a sea of verdure'.[10]

Daghestan (literally 'mountainland')[11] forms a triangle bounded by the main range in the southwest, the 'Andī range in the northwest and the Caspian Sea in the east. The inner heartland – Upper Daghestan – is completely surrounded by ranges 2,000–3,000 metres high, 'the only outlet for the water of the area [being] the deep and narrow ravine of the Ṣūlāq'.[12] The area inside is composed of both 'asymmetric ranges with pointed crests and triangular cross sections' and 'high synclinal plateaus'.[13] These fall in many cases in 'sheer high precipices, in most cases inaccessible, which add a wild rocky character to the country'.[14]

In addition, these ranges and plateaus are cut in many places by the four Koyṣū rivers, which unite to form the Ṣūlāq, and by their numerous tributaries. These rivers form canyons hundreds of metres deep.[15]

> Usually, the river occupies the entire width of the bottom of such a canyon leaving no place for . . . a road. The headbreaking curly tracks either meander high above the river along the cornices of the slopes, or pass completely sideways from the river valleys, along the plateaus and the crests of the rivers . . . Here the valleys do not at all facilitate communications between the different parts of the country. Rather, they render [communications] more difficult by forcing the roads into numerous winding, steep descents and ascents.[16]

In Daghestan, remarked Marlinskii, 'the Minister of Ways and Communication must be the Devil himself'.[17]

Enclosed within such barriers, the interior of Upper Daghestan has a dry climate, which does not encourage the growth of forests. The sparse vegetation and the numerous rocky precipices create a desolate landscape. Inner Daghestan is thus

> a chaos of mountains, its most characteristic natural feature the water-worn chasm; to which it may be added that man's handiwork . . . , was chiefly evidenced by paths that looked fitter for wild goats than for human beings; by terraces cut out of the mountain sides with infinite labour for the purpose of cultivation: by a system of irrigation devised and executed with astonishing skill and patience; and by clusters of low, flat-roofed dwellings built of stone and piled up tier above tier against the faces of the rocks, high above some river or mountain torrent.[18]

MAP 3: CHECHNIA AND DAGHESTAN : THE THEATRE OF OPERATIONS

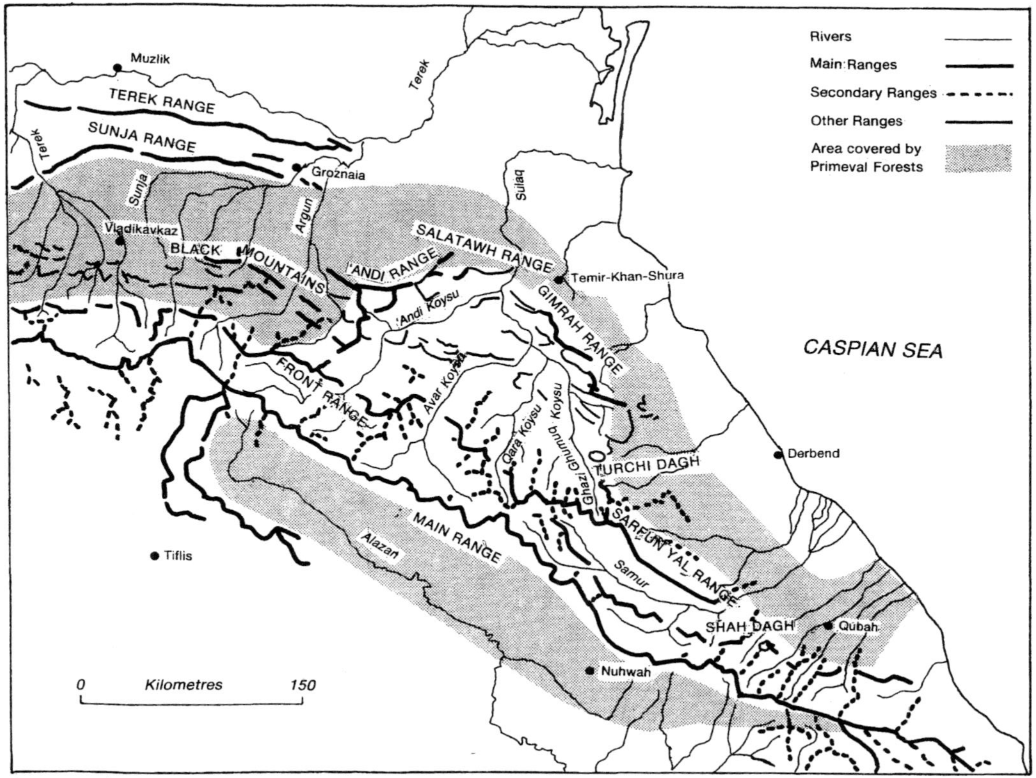

Source: John F. Baddeley, *The Rugged Flanks of the Caucasus* (London, 1940).

The outer slopes of the ranges surrounding Inner Daghestan from the north and east have a wide strip of forests. These are especially widespread in Qaytāq [Kaitag, Kaitakh] and Ṭabarsarān [Tabassaran], but nowhere reach the extent and density of the forests of Chechnia. From the forest zone these ranges descend gradually to the semi-arid Ghumuq (Qumiq) [Kumyk] plain in the north-east and the narrow strip of lowland along the Caspian shore. This strip is cut in a few places by the mountains reaching the sea. The most important of these is near Derbend – erroneously translated by many as 'the gate'[19] – which was the only city in Daghestan.

The areas to the south of Daghestan – Qubāh, on the northern side of the main range and Shirvān, Shekī and Chārtalah on its southern side – have had traditional ties with Daghestan.[20] They have similar landscapes to the outer slopes of Daghestan; the mountains descend through a strip of forests to a semi-arid steppe.

The Caucasus imposes two of the most difficult modes of war on an invading army: mountain and forest warfare. Although completely different types of warfare, both give enormous advantages to the defenders, making it very difficult to wage a pitched battle and use artillery efficiently and posing tremendous problems of logistics and communications[21] Before any battle the invaders have to overcome nature. The Russians had to cut (or fell) a way through the forests for the use of their artillery and supply convoys, and even then pack-horses often had to be led one by one and artillery pieces carried by soldiers. Even in peacetime, for example, three battalions with four guns needed ten hours to cross a 200-metre-long defile in Daghestan.[22]

Mountain warfare had to be waged in Daghestan and forest warfare in lower Chechnia. Only in upper Chechnia did the two converge. Chechnia and Daghestan thus formed separate theatres of war, necessitating completely different – sometimes even diametrically opposed – tactics.

Even the preferable season for operations was different. In Chechnia, the high water occurs in the spring and summer and in the autumn the rains turn the soil into mud, so that winter, when the ground is frozen and hard and the rivers at their lowest, even if not frozen, was the best time for campaigns. In addition, in the winter the trees and many bushes are bare of leaves, thus denying the Chechens cover.[23] In Daghestan, to the contrary, the mountain passes were impassable until the thaw of the snows and even then the Russians could not conduct operations before the appearance of fodder for their horses in about June. By October–November the first snowfalls rendered any campaign impossible.

Of the two, Chechnia was the more difficult theatre to fight in and it was here that the Russians suffered their greatest defeats and disasters. But Daghestan was the more alien, frightening and psychologically imposing:

> However savage the campaigns in [Chechnia], where sharpshooters lurked behind every tree, and Russian losses were terrible, the land itself was not hostile. There were trees, grass, streams; it was a world they knew. Dying there, the men still felt themselves among friends. Not so in Daghestan, where nothing lived; where an endless labyrinth of precipices and phantasmagoric peaks formed an accursed desolation – a hell, which they had reached before death.[24]

Chapter 2

The People

The Caucasus is probably the most varied area in the world with regard to the ethnic and linguistic composition of its population.[1] Daghestan takes the lion's share of this variety. No fewer than 30 ethno-linguistic groups inhabit this area, some being confined to the population of a single village. The four most important groups are the Avārs, the Darghīs, the Laks and the Lesghians.[2] All these groups speak languages belonging to the north-eastern group of the Caucasian, or 'Japhetite', linguistic family. Many of them also live south of the main range in present-day Ādhārbāyjān [Azerbaidzhan]. Some, like the Lesghians, are present there in greater numbers than in Daghestan, while some groups related to them live only in northern Ādhārbāyjān. The Ghumuq plain and most of the coastal strip are inhabited by the Ghumuqs. In the environs of Derbend the Ādhārī Turks (Azeris) prevail. Both speak Turkic languages. Speakers of Iranian languages are represented by the Tats and the Mountain Jews in the mountains south and west of Derbend.

Chechnia is mainly populated by the Chechens (Chehān), whose Russian name derives from the village of Great Chechān, where the Russians first encountered them. The western and south-western part of the country is inhabited by the Ingush. (The two groups are in fact so close to each other that according to some scholars they are separated 'only because of their different historical backgrounds. The Ingush did not participate either in the Shamil movement . . . or in the revolt of 1920–22.'[3] This statement is generally correct, though some of the Ingush did in certain instances take part in the Shamil movement.) In the south, on the lower slopes of the main range, live the Kists, who are regarded by some scholars as a separate group. Most sources, however, consider them to be a Chechen tribe. The upper slopes of the main range are inhabited by the Khevsurs, a Georgian Christian mountain tribe.

The great ethnic-linguistic divergence notwithstanding, all the

MAP 4: CHECHNIA AND DAGHESTAN : APPROXIMATE ETHNO-LINGUISTIC DIVISION c. 1830

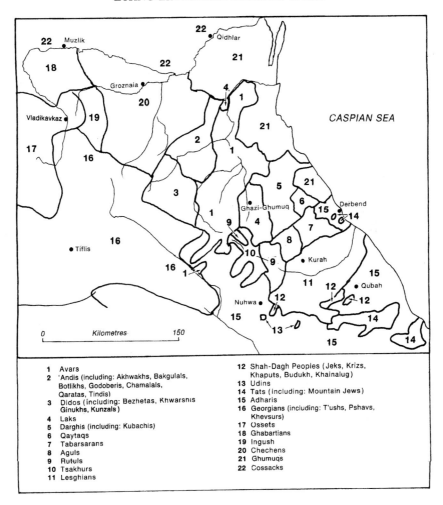

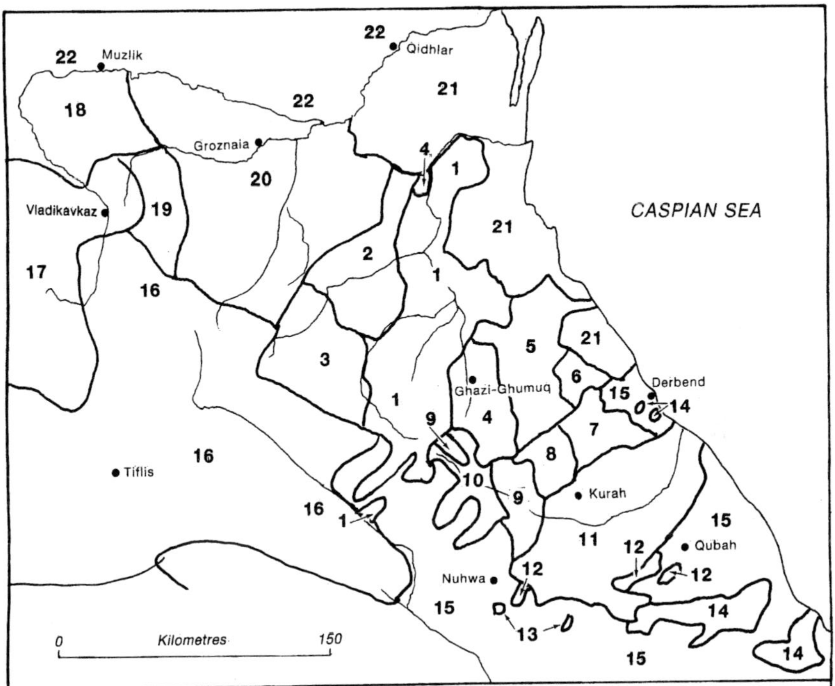

1 Avars
2 'Andis (including: Akhwakhs, Bakgulals, Botlikhs, Godoberis, Chamalals, Qaratas, Tindis)
3 Didos (including: Bezhetas, Khwarsnis Ginukhs, Kunzals)
4 Laks
5 Darghis (including: Kubachis)
6 Qaytaqs
7 Tabarsarans
8 Aguls
9 Rutuls
10 Tsakhurs
11 Lesghians
12 Shah-Dagh Peoples (Jeks, Krizs, Khaputs, Budukh, Khainalug)
13 Udins
14 Tats (including: Mountain Jews)
15 Adharis
16 Georgians (including: T'ushs, Pshavs, Khevsurs)
17 Ossets
18 Ghabartians
19 Ingush
20 Chechens
21 Ghumuqs
22 Cossacks

inhabitants of the Caucasus, or the mountaineers as they are usually called by Russian sources, shared the same way of life, traditions, customs and even costume.[4] Their common culture is classified by Luzbetac as belonging to the nomadic-patriarchal type,[5] even though the mountaineers were not nomads. The population was divided along patrilineal lines into extended families, clans and tribes. These served, with different emphases at the different levels, as foci of identification and mutual responsibility and were at the basis of the mountaineers' political, social and economic structure.[6] In some cases the boundaries of the clans and tribes (sometimes called by the Russians 'communities' [*obshchestva*]) corresponded to those of ethnic-linguistic groups. In Chechnia and great parts of Daghestan these communities were 'free', that is, independent of outside control. Many of these communities were headed by an elected *qāḍī*.[7] In all of them important decisions were taken by the elders and a general assembly of all the men. Because of this some Russian authors called these communities 'democracies' or 'republics'.

Sometimes several such communities formed a loose confederation. The strongest of these in Daghestan was Aqūsha (also called Darghī), which in 1744 defeated Nādir Shāh.[8] The eastern part of Daghestan was divided into a number of such confederations, or principalities. The rulers of some of them had special titles: the *Shāmkhāl* of Targhū; the *ʿUtsmī* of Qarāqaytāq; the *Maʿṣūm* of Ṭabarsarān. The ruler of Iliṣū had the title of *Sulṭān* and the others – Ghāzī-Ghumuq [Kazi-Kumukh], Kurāh [Kiurin],[9] Mekhtulī and Khunzakh (also known as Avāristān [Avaria] – had the title of *Khān*. The degree of autonomy of the different communities within these principalities always depended on the personality and power of the individual rulers.

Farming was the main occupation of the population. The mountaineers grew a great variety of cereals, fruit and vegetables. But the basis of economic life was livestock and people kept their wealth in herds of horses, cattle and especially sheep and goats. These were the targets of mutual raids. Such raids, especially on the lowlands, were in some areas of great importance to the local economy.

In Chechnia and some of the 'free communities' of Daghestan social structure was not stratified. Land was owned communally and all men belonging to the group were free – *uzdens*. Prisoners were enslaved or exchanged for ransom.

In the principalities and their satellite communities, as well as among the Ghumuqs, social structure was more complicated. A nobility (*beks*) existed which enjoyed some social, economic and political prerogatives, but in other respects were equal to the *uzdens*. Children of noble fathers and commoner mothers and their descendants, called *janka*, enjoyed some of the privileges and prestige of their fathers, and formed a separate group between the two. Land ownership was considerably more complicated and there were serfs as well as tenants.

In Chārtalah a confederation of five Daghestani communities and the sultanate of Iliṣū formed ruling élites over Georgian Muslim serfs (Ingilois) and free but unprivileged Turkic people – Mughals, now assimilated with the Ādhārīs.

The mountaineers were aware of their ethnic-linguistic divisions. Especially noticeable was the division between Chechens and Daghestanis – mainly Avārs and related groups – who were known to the Chechens as *Ṭawhlīs*.[10] Yet the ethnic-linguistic group was not a focus of identification above the tribal level. Rather, it was religion which served as such a focus. The Chechens and Daghestanis were *Sunnī* Muslims, at least nominally.[14] As such, they intermingled with the Ghumuqs, the Ghabarṭians and the Circassians [Cherkesy][12] and were opposed to the Shīʿī Ādhārīs and to the Christian (at least nominally) Georgian mountain tribes – the T'ush, Khevsurs and P'shavs. In the wider Islamic context they were aligned to the Ottoman *Sulṭān*, the head of *Sunnī* Islam. This identification as *Sunnī* Muslims would play an important role in the struggles against the Russians.

Three other characteristics of the mountaineers resulting from their cultural and social milieu must be singled out for the role they played in the struggle with the Russians. One was the extreme vigilance over their freedom and the strong rejection of any authority external to the tribe or clan.[13] Another was the blood feuds [*kanly*], which sometimes lasted for generations and caused the destruction of entire villages and communities.[14] The third was the mountaineers being in nineteenth-century terminology a 'martial race', raised from childhood to be warriors. Their bravery, accomplished horsemanship, superb mastery of dagger (*kinjāl*), sword (*shashka*) and musket, and their ability to find cover and to disguise themselves were admired by the Russians, who lagged far behind in these qualities.[15]

Many also admired the swiftness of the mountaineers' moves, whether on horseback or on foot. Unlike a regular army, they were not bogged down by supply trains. Being used to a frugal way of life, they had all they needed with them and once their supplies were exhausted, they could always live off the land – being supported either by friends or by raiding enemies.

But the main thing to be admired in the mountaineers was their adaptability. The Russian army, like all its Western counterparts, when facing non-Western forces, relied heavily on very specific tactics which were based on rigid discipline and superior fire-power to secure victory in a pitched battle. Indeed, in defence, the infantry carré proved impregnable and in attack the bayonet usually overpowered the enemy; in both cases artillery fire, and especially the use of grapeshot, was indispensable to secure success.[16]

The mountaineers were not used to pitched battles. Their warfare centred on swiftness of manoeuvre rather than on fire-power. It mainly took the form of raids and counter-raids aimed at catching cattle and prisoners. But they soon adjusted to the Russian tactics and learnt how to use to their advantage their adversary's weak points, while circumventing the strong ones. The Russians were, thus, confronting in the north-eastern Caucasus a population of about 200,000, 40–50,000 of whom were accomplished warriors ready to strike at any moment.

Chapter 3

The Russians

The Russians were the mountaineers' exact opposites in every conceivable way. They were heavy and slow; they depended on, and were hampered by, long trains of supplies (logistics, never the strong point of the Russian army, often collapsed in the extremely difficult terrain of the Caucasus);[1] they relied on infantry and firepower (artillery);[2] and rigid discipline and robot-like execution of orders worked against personal initiative.

The Russian forces in the Caucasus, later successively named 'the Caucasian Corps'[3] and 'the Caucasian Army', consisted of three elements:

1. Regular army units were the backbone of the Caucasian Corps and bore the main burden of the fighting. These consisted mainly of infantry (jägers and musketeers) and artillery units, though at a later stage a regiment of dragoons took part in the operations as well. The soldiers in these units were mainly peasants drafted for 25 years. They were brave, loyal, obedient and 'went to battle as if to church'.[4] During their long service these soldiers showed great ingenuity and initiative when left alone. They specialised in different crafts (tailoring, shoemaking, etc.);[5] they grew vegetables and fruit in gardens in and near their fortresses; they had herds of cattle, sheep and goats.[6] Thus, the Caucasian regular units were in many – though not all – respects self-sufficient. Most important, the soldiers specialised in the local mode of warfare and learned how to behave in encounters with the mountaineers.
2. The Battalions of the Line [*lineinye batal'iony*] were second-rate troops, many of them unfit for field service, who were used to garrison forts and fortresses. They were seldom used in the field and were usually looked upon with contempt by the Russian commanders.[7]
3. The Cossacks fought in the same way as the natives. But neither they nor their horses equalled the mountaineers.

Usually not even the local Cossacks could stand their ground against the Chechens without the help of artillery, which was an integral part of their units.[8] They were usually used as auxiliaries, and treated with contempt by the Russian officers,[9] a sentiment many of them felt towards the 'Russians'.

Another auxiliary element was the local militias. These were mistrusted by the Russians, and were usually useless in the battlefield. The Russians, however, used them for political reasons as part of a 'divide and rule' policy.

All in all the number of these forces grew steadily from about 30,000 during the 1820s and 1830s to around 200,000 in the 1850s. The overwhelming majority of them, 80–85 per cent, were regular infantry units.

The army of Nicholas I was plagued by many problems. Some of them were characteristic of Russian armies in every historical period. Others were created, or at least strengthened, by the personality, outlook and polices of the tsar. Three of these problems were interconnected: the low standard of the officers' corps coupled with lack of NCOs; the unusually – by European standards – wide gap between them and the men; and the extremely harsh discipline and concentration on parade appearance rather than fighting efficiency. Promotion in the Russian army, wrote Karl Marx, was limited 'to mere parade martinets, whose principal merit consists of stolid obedience and ready servility added to accuracy of eyesight in detecting a fault in the buttons and buttonholes of the uniform'.

'Such sticks', rather than 'men of real military ability and intellectual superiority', and 'years of dulled service' rather than 'youth, activity and the acquirement of military science', were preferred in promotion. 'Thus, the army is commanded on the average by old valetudinarians, or by ignorant corporals, who might manage a platoon, but have not brains and knowledge enough to direct the extensive and complicated movements of a campaign.'[10]

The Caucasian Corps was in many respects an exception in the Russian army. Engaged in constant fighting, it was less formal, less 'parade-ground-like', than other units. The discipline was not as tight; the relationship between officers and men was closer. Nevertheless, the same malaise manifested itself in the Caucasus, though, perhaps in a milder form.

In spite of the comradeship in arms, the gap between officers and men remained wide. The Russian officer, usually from the landed gentry, and the soldier, usually an ex-serf, could not erase this lord–serf relationship. Thus 'the Caucasian commander has, from the earliest days, entertained the notion that the soldier is a machine able to work anytime, and therefore should not be spared'.[11]

Furthermore, commanders used their soldiers as a workforce in their private enterprises, which was one part of the widespread general corruption. When Murav'ev, for example, arrived in the Caucasus in 1854, he 'was able to gather almost 16,000 men who although listed in the service lists, had, in fact, been used for private work'.[12]

The quality of the officers, though perhaps higher than in other parts of the empire, was still low. Few Russian officers chose the Caucasian Corps as their career. Most of the officers and NCOs were either exiled there – Nicholas I used the Caucasus as a 'warm Siberia' for his political opponents – or 'pheasants' (young officers coming for a season to be decorated and then go back to Russia).[13] Naturally, very few among those officers, and especially the large contingent of Poles filling the ranks of the Caucasian Corps after the revolt of 1831, were highly motivated.

Those who did possess ability and motivation were stifled by the strict discipline: any personal initiative, whether successful or not, was punished (unless, of course, the perpetrator was very well-connected in St. Petersburg), and all Russian officers soon discovered the truth in the maxim of Thomas à Kempis: 'It is much safer to be in a subordinate position than in one of authority.'[14] Thus an attitude of what might be called 'prudent inactivity' was widespread throughout the ranks.

Another general malaise in the Russian army which was felt in the Caucasus was 'the spirit of intrigue . . . that moral ulcer marring many an illustrious name in the upper echelons of the Caucasian Army'.[15]

With hindsight, however, the greatest Russian problem in conquering the Caucasus seems to have been a psychological one – their contempt for the mountaineers as 'Muslims', 'Asiatics' and 'Tartars' (with all the negative emotional charge of the latter name for Russians). This contempt, emanating from the very top, was reinforced by several factors: Russia's rejection by the West;[16] the general feeling of military might following the Napoleonic Wars (boosted by the wars with the Ottomans and Qājārs); the usual Russian fascination with numbers, which led them repeatedly to believe that the sheer numerical strength of their forces would discourage their opponents; and the complacency which Russian sources often claim to be characteristic of the Russians.

All these factors prevented Russian commanders from taking the mountaineers seriously, let alone studying and learning true lessons from their tactics, social structure and political divisions. Being ignorant of all these,[17] Russian commanders often repeated their predecessors' blunders and achieved results adverse to their aims.

> There's a price for too much arrogance, a price for too much greed.
> And in complacent ignorance we've sown the whirlwind seed![18]

These words by two modern bards are a good description of the Russians' behaviour in the Caucasus. They apply particularly well to the first Russian general to launch an overall offensive into Chechnia and Daghestan: Aleksei Petrovich Ermolov.

Part 2

The Background

Chapter 4

Ermolov

Although some mountain tribes had been subjugated during or immediately after the first round of wars with the Qājārs and the Ottomans,[1] the offensive into the mountains was connected with Ermolov, who was appointed in 1816 governor and chief administrator of Georgia and the Caucasus, commander-in-chief of the Separate Georgian Army Corps, and ambassador extraordinary to the court of Fatḥ ʿAlī Shāh.[2] Enjoying the full confidence and backing of Alexander I, Ermolov had, in fact, a free hand in the Caucasus and soon got the nickname of 'Proconsul of the Caucasus'.[3] Aleksei Petrovich Ermolov,

> only forty years of age at the time of his Caucasian appointment, had already made a brilliant military career for himself. He had been decorated on the field by Suvorov while still in his teens; at twenty he was Colonel. At the fall of Paris in 1814 he commanded both the Russian and Prussian Guards, and with the deaths of Kutuzov and Bagration he became the most illustrious and popular soldier of the Empire.[4]
>
> In person no less than in character, Ermolov impressed all who came near him as one born to command. Of gigantic stature and uncommon physical strength, with round head set on mighty shoulders and framed in shaggy locks, there was something leonine in his whole appearance, which, coupled with unsurpassed courage, was well calculated to excite the admiration of his own men and strike terror into his semi-barbarous foes. Incorruptibly honest, simple, even rude in his habits, and of Spartan hardihood, his sword was ever at his side, and in city as in camp he slept wrapped only in his military cloak, and rose with the sun.[5]

Ermolov's central idea was that the whole of the Caucasus must, and should become an integral part of the Russian Empire; that the existence of independent or semi-independent states or com-

> munities of any description, whether Christian, Musulman, or Pagan, in the mountains or in the plains, was incompatible with the dignity and honour of his master, the safety and welfare of his subjects.[6]

He therefore 'set himself the aim of destroying any non-Russian nationality in the country'.[7]

First, and most urgent, Ermolov had to carry out his mission to Tehrān, which consisted of evading a promise actually given by Alexander I to Fatḥ ʿAlī Shāh to restore to him part of the territories acquired by Russia in the treaty of Gulistān.[8] Ermolov succeeded in his mission by a combination of amazing vanity, 'the grossest flattery of the *shāh* and sheer bullying of his ministers'.[9] In the long run, however, this vanity and bullying and Ermolov's subsequent displays of high-handedness and contempt in his dealings with the Qājārs, and especially towards ʿAbbās Mīrzā the *valī ʿahd* (successor to the throne), played a great part in provoking the war of 1826–28.[10]

Upon his return, Ermolov immediately set about the conquest of the mountains. In November 1817 and again in May 1818,[11] he sent the emperor detailed plans. He suggested dealing first with the Chechens – 'a bold and dangerous people'.[12] He intended to establish a new line along the (lower) Sunja, and settle Cossacks between that river and the Terek. 'By this means we shall come nearer to Daghestan, and improve communications with the prosperous province of Qubāh and thence to Georgia.'[13]

When the line was ready, Ermolov wrote to the emperor,

> I shall offer the villains dwelling between the Terek and the Sunja, called peaceful [i.e. pacified], rules [to regulate their ways] of life and a few duties, which will make clear to them that they are subjects to Your Imperial Majesty, and not allies, as they have hitherto hoped. If they submit properly, I shall apportion them according to their numbers the necessary amount of land, dividing the rest among the cramped Cossacks and the Qarā-Nogays; if not, I shall propose to them to retire and join the other outlaws from whom they differ in name only, and in this case the whole of the land will be at our disposal.[14]

Thus, 'the Chechens will be constrained within their mountains', and by losing 'agricultural land and pastures, in which they shelter their flocks in winter from the severe cold in the mountains', would have no choice but to submit to Russian rule.[15]

Intending to complete this task by 1819, Ermolov suggested thereafter to move to Daghestan, continue the above line to the Ṣūlāq, station troops in the dominions of the *shāmkhāl* and take possession of 'the rich salt lakes, which supply [with salt] all the mountain people including the Chechens'.[16] This would give the Russians a lever to press the mountaineers into submission. Finishing with Daghestan in 1820, Ermolov proposed then to move to Ghabarṭa and the Right Flank.

This was the first exposition of what Russian authors would later erroneously call the 'Ermolov system'. Although practised by Ermolov, it was actually given its famous formulation in 1828 by Vel'iaminov (and wrongly attributed by many Russian writers to Ermolov):

> The Caucasus may be likened to a mighty fortress, marvellously strong by nature, artificially protected by military works, and defended by a numerous garrison. Only thoughtless men would attempt to storm such a stronghold. A wise commander would see the necessity of having recourse to military art; would lay his parallels; advance by sap and mine, and so master the place. The Caucasus, in my opinion, must be treated in the same way, and even if the method of proceeding is not drawn up beforehand, so that it may be continually referred to, the very nature of things will compel such action. But in this case success will be far slower owing to frequent deviations from the right path.[17]

Only a year younger than Ermolov, Vel'iaminov

> never achieved one-tenth of [Ermolov's] popularity or fame; yet his career was almost equally brilliant and his merits in some respect greater. The reason is not far to seek. A man of great parts, assiduously cultivated, a zealous student of military history, who brought the teaching of the past to bear on problems of the day yet with a mind ever ready to profit by the circumstances of the moment and adapt tactics and strategy to immediate requirements; prompt to conceive and quick to strike, of an iron will and invincible determination; an able organiser; absolutely fearless in battle and no less richly endowed with moral courage, he possessed in a superlative degree all the qualities that command the respect of soldiers, but few that excite enthusiasm, none that enlist their affection. Calm, cool, silent, impenetrable, he was inexorably severe to his own men, merciless to the foe, and he was feared, admired and hated by both.[18]

Vel'iaminov served with Ermolov in the Napoleonic Wars, and the two struck a close friendship. When nominated to the Caucasus, Ermolov obtained the nomination of Vel'iaminov as chief-of-staff of the Georgian Corps.[19] Here, in Tiflis, Vel'iaminov's analytical and organisational skills made a major contribution to Ermolov's successes. The siege strategy *vis-à-vis* the Caucasus and the reorganisation of the Caucasian Corps, associated usually with Ermolov, must have been worked out, if not originated, by Vel'iaminov.

It was at this time that the Caucasian Corps was given its structure for the following quarter of a century. *Inter alia*, the different regiments were given their permanent areas and headquarters, integrated into the parallels of the siege system and made into economically productive, and in some respects self-sufficient, units.

Immediately upon receiving the emperor's approval of his plans, Ermolov set out for Chechnia.[20] On 22 June 1819 the fortress of Groznaia ('menacing') was founded. The Chechens' attempt at resistance was crushed with cannon. The following year Ermolov erected a fortress opposite Enderī called Vnezapnaia ('sudden'), and in 1821 the line was completed by the erection of Burnaia ('stormy') near Targhū.

'The building of Groznaia, together with what was known of Ermolov's further intentions', alarmed not only the Chechens but their neighbours to the south and south-east. The rulers of Avāristān, Ghāzī-Ghumuq, Mekhtulī, Qarāqaytāq and Ṭabarsarān and the community of Aqūsha formed an alliance against the Russians.[21]

> Ermolov, informed of what was taking place, ordered Colonel Pestel [the commander of Daghestan] with two battalions and some native cavalry to occupy Qarāqaytāq . . . this being the first Russian campaign in Mountain Daghestan, as distinguished from the eastern declivities, and the narrow strip of flat land forming the Caspian coast.

> [Pestel] advanced to Bashlī, the chief town of Qarāqaytāq, was there surrounded by the allies in vast numbers, and attacked in the narrow streets, where artillery could not operate. It was thanks to the valour and ability of Colonel Mishchenko and others that, with a loss of 12 officers and 500 men, the Russians secured their retreat to Derbend. All Daghestan went wild with joy; and in

distant Tabrīz, ʿAbbās Mīrzā celebrated the victory with feasting and cannon-fire.[22]

Soon, however, Ermolov arrived in person in Mekhtulī with five battalions, 300 Cossacks and 14 guns. He stormed Pīrī Awul [Paraul] and Jengutay, the two main townships. At the same time Mishchenko, upon his orders, stormed and destroyed Bashlī.[23] Ḥasan Khān of Mekhtulī fled and the Khanate was abolished. Part of it was given to the *shāmkhāl* and part annexed to the empire. But the allies were not yet beaten. The following spring they attacked in two directions.

In the south they cut off communications with Derbend and threatened Kurāh and Qubāh. Madatov, Pestel's successor, was 'a *beau sabreur* . . . whose ideas of subordination were somewhat loose'.[24] On his own initiative he led a force of two battalions, 300 Cossacks and eight guns into Ṭabarsarān, and cowed it into submission.

In the north, Sulṭān Ahmad Khān of Avāristān, at the head of about 6,000 men, attacked in mid-September the Russian force engaged in building Vnezapnaia. He was routed, deposed, and the title of *khān* bestowed upon his *janka* son Surkhāy.[25]

In October Madatov marched again into Qarāqaytāq. Bashlī and Yanghī-kent, the residence of the *ʿutsmī*, were stormed. The *ʿutsmī* fled, his rule was abolished and Qarāqaytāq was annexed to the empire. At about the same time Chirkah [Chirkei] submitted and was pardoned.[26]

In mid-November, completing the construction of Vnezapnaia, Ermolov moved against Aqūsha with nine battalions and 'many guns'.[27] On 31 December he defeated the forces of Aqūsha near Lavashī.[28] Ermolov's appointment of a new *qāḍī* who 'was in the full meaning of this word our friend, and 24 hostages from the most important families held in Derbend, were reliable guarantees of its calm'.[29]

In June 1820 Madatov conquered Ghāzī-Ghumuq. Surkhāy Khān fled and Aslān Khān of Kūrah was nominated in his stead.[30] 'The subjugation of Daghestan begun last year', reported Ermolov to the emperor, 'is now complete; and this country, proud, warlike, and hitherto unconquered, has fallen at the sacred feet of Your Imperial Majesty.'[31]

He was sure that the subjugation of the parts hitherto untouched by the Russians would follow suit without much effort and mainly by means of an economic blockade or 'siege'.[32] In this belief, however, he was mistaken, as many of his successors would be. 'He did not note,' wrote a Russian chronicler, 'that although the crater of the volcano had been cleansed, the internal fire was far from extinguished.'[33]

At the moment, however, everything seemed to be progressing well. Completing Burnaia in 1821, Ermolov turned his attention to the Centre and Right Flank of the Caucasian Line. In 1822 he moved the line forward in Ghabarṭa and in 1825 he started to do the same on the Right Flank.

'Nothing has any influence on Ermolov,' wrote the director of Nicholas's secret police, 'except his own vanity.'[34] In this vanity Ermolov stated: 'I desire that the terror of my name should guard our frontiers more potently than chains or fortresses, that my word should be for the natives a law more inevitable than death.'[35]

To achieve this state Ermolov acted with extreme cruelty. 'He was,' wrote a Russian author, 'at least as cruel as the natives themselves.'[36] In fact, he was considerably crueller, and his actions drew rebukes from both Alexander I and Nicholas I. 'Gentleness, in the eyes of Asiatics,' Ermolov replied, 'is a sign of weakness, and out of pure humanity I am inexorably severe. One execution saves hundreds of Russians from destruction and thousands of Muslims from treason.'[37]

However, the executions were not confined to single cases, nor to the guilty ones. On one occasion at least, the house of a suspect was blown up, with Ermolov's approval, killing all the family inside.[38] When he decided to push the Chechens south of the Sunja, he attacked a village and slaughtered all its inhabitants, men, women and children.[39] On other occasions captured women were sold as slaves[40] or distributed to Russian officers so that in winter quarters 'for the officers, at least, the Commander-in-Chief setting the example, the time passed pleasantly enough in the company of native wives'.[41]

Baddeley wondered why 'Russian writers, so far, fail to see any connection between the vaunted "Ermolov system" and the Murīd war'.[42] One answer might be found in the fact that, as an Austrian diplomat remarked, 'the whole art of the Russian government is in the use of violence'.[43] This was true in Russia proper, and even more so in the Caucasus. The great majority, the 'Suvorov school' as Baddeley called them, held firmly to the view that 'Asiatics' could understand only force, and the very few who tried to promote another view, that 'it is impossible to achieve by coercion and brute force what can be obtained through the love and trust of the people',[44] were treated 'with scorn', condemned 'in no measured terms' and 'stigmatised as both weak and incapable'.[45]

From the very beginning Russian rule in the Caucasus was built on the premise that 'fear and greed are the two mainsprings of everything that takes place here' and that 'these people's [i.e. the natives'] only policy is force'.[46] In this respect Ermolov was well within the existing consensus. If he exceeded it, he did so only in the severity of his measures, in the amount of force he used, and in his brutality and cruelty. Indeed, in the very few instances when Ermolov was criticised by Russian pre-revolutionary authors,[47] it was for such excesses or for very specific actions of his, which were regarded as mistaken.

The main flaw in relying solely on the use of force is that, to paraphrase Abraham Lincoln, 'one can terrorise all the people some of the time, or some of the people all the time, but one cannot terrorise all the people all the time.' Ermolov did not succeed in either, though his name remained for generations in the mountaineers' memory.[48] He cowed part of Daghestan for a while mainly by the extensive use of artillery, then seen for the first time in the mountains.[49] But the Chechens were a different story. Ermolov found it beyond his power and ability to subdue them.

All he could do was to carry out devastating 'punitive expeditions', in which he destroyed gardens, fields and whole villages. Unlike the mountain *awuls*, which were built of stone, resembled fortresses and presented very great difficulties for the attacker, the villages of the lowlands of Chechnia were built of wood. They were much easier to destroy, but also to rebuild. Therefore, they were also easier to conquer because the Chechens did not usually defend them, if they had had time enough to escape with their families and livestock. These expeditions did not achieve much more than occasional booty for the soldiers. But they definitely served to increase the Chechens' exasperation.[50] This was not, however, Ermolov's view, and he instructed the commander of the new Sunja line to continue such expeditions.

Nikolai Vasil'evich Grekov[51] surpassed his superior in vanity, brutality and cruelty. He 'looked at [the Chechens] from a very mean point of view, and in speech as well as in official papers had no other name for them than rascals, and [called] any of their representatives – either robber or cheat'.[52] Grekov 'devoted himself heart and soul to the carrying out of Ermolov's policy and instructions', that is to destroy *awuls*, hang hostages, and slaughter women and children'.[53]

'Whatever the faults of the Chechens,' wrote Baddeley, 'no impartial reader of the Russian accounts of this period – and we have no other – can doubt that they were cruelly oppressed'.[54] The exasperation of the Chechens soon acquired a religious dimension, especially following the arrival of Mūlā Muḥammad[55] from Daghestan to Mayurtūp in 1824. He soon proclaimed a certain Avkō from Germenchuk[56] to be the long awaited *imām* chosen by God to lead their *jihād* against the Russians.[57] The military commander, however, was Beybulat Taymāzoghlū [Taimazov], a very influential person in Greater Chechnia and a renowned war leader, who, holding a personal grudge against Grekov,[58] had been a thorn in the Russian's flesh for five years.

The revolt soon spread all over Chechnia, and the Ingush, the Ghabarṭians and the Aqsay Ghumuqs, as well as some Ossets and a few hundred Daghestanis, joined in.[59] Grekov, who ignored the revolt in its first stages, was soon compelled to act. He 'resorted to all his usual methods, but in vain. One of the popular leaders was publicly flogged to death, others to within an inch of their lives. But no punishment he was able to inflict made any serious impression on the enemy; or rather, his cruelty served only to exasperate him.' In a foretaste of what in 15 years would become a common occurrence, 'Grekov marched hither and thither, but the Chechens evaded him or suffered only minor defeats'.[60]

On the night of 20 July 1825 the mountaineers, led by Avkō and Mūlā Muḥammad, stormed and destroyed the Russian fort at Amīr-Hājjī-Yūrt. Of its 181 defenders, 98 were killed and 13 taken prisoner. Among the rich booty the Chechens captured one gun. On that day they laid siege to the fort of Gurzul [Gerzel Aul], which continued for seven days. On 27 July Grekov and his immediate superior Lisanovich relieved the fort. The following day the Russian generals invited 300 men from Aqsay into the fort, intending to arrest them. Lisanovich strongly abused and insulted them in their own language, and then, threatening to punish them for treachery, ordered them to give up their *kinjāls* (daggers). A certain Ḥājj Uchar Yaʿqūb refused to do so. Grekov lost his temper and struck Uchar in the face. Within seconds the *ḥājj* killed Grekov and two other officers and mortally wounded Lisanovich. Before dying, however, the Russian general ordered his soldiers to kill all 300 mountaineers.

Ermolov, upon receiving this news, set out immediately to Vladikavkaz. Here he spent the rest of the year relocating the Line, destroying some forts and building others. Meanwhile, the rebellion spread and different Russian forts and *stanitsas* were attacked and some of them taken. Finally, in January 1826 Ermolov started his campaign. During January and February, and again in April and May, he criss-crossed the country and 'punished the rebellious Chechens, burning their villages, destroying their forests, beating them in skirmishes that never developed into battles, and, occasionally even seeking to win them over by an unwonted display of clemency'.[61]

A close examination of the events shows clearly that Ermolov's movements had, in fact, a very minimal effect. Rather, the revolt collapsed from within, mainly owing to poor leadership. This is best illustrated by the fact that its leaders continued to live peacefully in their communities unmolested by the Russians. This fact, however, was not visible at the time. And since 'to outward appearance his success was complete',[62] Ermolov returned to Tiflis. This was, however, his last triumph. Soon his career came to an abrupt end.

On 31 July 1826 ʿAbbās Mīrzā invaded the Caucasus. Ermolov, in spite of his frequent warnings of a possibility of war with the Qājārs, was caught completely unprepared and reacted with unexplained passivity.[63] Nicholas I, ill-disposed towards Ermolov for a long time, sent Count (later Prince) Paskiewicz [Paskevich][64] to take command of the forces on the front. Not surprisingly, this appointment resulted in six months of mutual intrigues and accusations. Finally, the emperor sent Count Diebitsch, ostensibly to investigate the relationship between the two but in fact to depose Ermolov.[65]

On 9 April 1827 Ermolov left the Caucasus and was succeeded by Paskiewicz, but his gigantic figure continued to cast its shadow on the Caucasus, and all his successors had to compete with it. One of his legacies in particular, to which all Russian sources remained blind, proved to be very detrimental to his successors in their dealings with the mountaineers: his extreme brutality achieved results opposite to his intentions and made the natives immune to terror. Experiencing the worst, they were afraid of the Russians no more.

The wars with the Qājārs and the Ottomans kept the Russians

busy until 1829. When, in 1830, they turned their full attention back to the mountaineers, they soon found that the scene had changed and that a new factor had entered the equation.

Chapter 5

The Naqshbandiyya-Khālidiyya

The Naqshbandiyya is one of the major *ṣūfī ṭarīqas* and *ṭā'ifas*.[1] Originally called *ṭarīqat al-khawājagān*[2] and founded by Abū Ya'qūb al-Hamadānī (d. 1140), it is named after Muḥammad Bahā' al-Dīn al-Naqshbandī (1318–89), who gave it its final structure.[3] The Naqshbandiyya was from its beginning 'strictly' orthodox[4] and was 'especially important in ensuring the attachment of the Turkic peoples to the Sunnī tradition'.[5]

From its area of origin – Central Asia – the Naqshbandiyya spread to other parts of the Muslim world. In India al-Shaykh Aḥmad Fārūqī Sirhindī (1564–1624) transformed it into 'the vanguard of renascent Islamic orthodoxy'.[6] From India 'the militant revivalism'[7] of the Naqshbandiyya-Mujaddidiyya, as it became known after Sirhindī's title *mujaddid-i alf-i thānī*[8] – spread to the Middle East and from there into the Caucasus.

According to local traditions,[9] the first Naqshbandī leader in the Caucasus was al-Shaykh Manṣūr, who was in many respects the precursor of the movement in the nineteenth century.[10] He was 'the first to preach and lead the . . . Holy War against the infidel Russians in the Caucasus', and although he failed 'in his endeavour to unite . . . the fierce tribes of the mountain and the forest, he it was who first taught them that in religious reform lay the one chance of preserving their cherished liberty and independence'.[11]

If indeed a Naqshbandī, Shaykh Manṣūr did not establish the order in the Caucasus. This was done, in fact, by the Naqshbandiyya-Khālidiyya, a branch of the order named after al-Shaykh Ḍiyā al-Dīn Khālid al-Shahrazūrī (1776–1827).[12] One of his disciples, al-Shaykh Ismā'īl al-Kūrdumīrī, was active for a few years in Shirvān as Shaykh Khalīd's *khalīfa* (deputy) in the late 1810s.[13] Following the annexation of the Khanate in 1820, the Russian authorities started to persecute the movement. Two of Shaykh Ismā'īl's *khalīfas* were exiled to Siberia and he himself followed a 'gentle hint' from the Russian governor and left for the Ottoman Empire.

With his departure the spread of the movement in Shirvān was temporarily arrested. But the seed sown by Shaykh Ismāʿīl found a fertile ground in Daghestan, where it was transferred by another of his disciples, al-Shaykh Khāṣ Muḥammad al-Shirvānī. He ordained al-Shaykh Muḥammad al-Yarāghī, who in turn ordained al-Shaykh al-Sayyid Jamāl al-Dīn al-Ghāzī-Ghumuqī.[14]

Russian[15] and later Soviet[16] sources call the Naqshbandiyya-Khālidiyya in the Caucasus *Miuridizm*.[17] With very few exceptions[18] they describe 'Muridism' as a separate movement, completely different from, and even opposed to, its parent movement, 'Sufism'.[19] Accordingly, Muḥammad al-Yarāghī was considered

> as the founder of the politico-religious movement which, under the name of Muridism, united for a time in the great struggle for freedom a majority of the Muslim inhabitants of Daghestan and Chechnia, but he never took upon himself the actual leadership, and is wrongly counted by some as the first *imām*.'[20]

The area in which the movement began to flourish, the Daghestan of the late 1810s and early 1820s, was in turmoil. Russian rule undermined the traditional way of life and the political, economic and social structure not only of the country under their control, but of many communities which had not yet come under Russian domination. The economy of the still independent, or 'unpacified',[21] communities was strongly affected by the Russian economic warfare.[22] Boycotts against specific communities and the prevention of others from using fields and winter pasture in the lowlands disrupted traditional patterns of commerce and food production upon which the mountaineers were dependent, since they were not self-sufficient.

The Russian 'punitive expeditions', destroying everything in their path, further disrupted the economic life of these communities, while the Russian-imposed constraints on raiding – a traditional way to supplement income – played its part as well. A strong blow was dealt to the traditional economy of Chārtalah when the Russians stopped the slave trade of these communities with the Ottoman Empire, the slaves usually being Georgians and Armenians captured in raids.

The submitted, or 'pacified',[23] parts of Daghestan had other burdens, apart from the damage incurred by the disruption of commerce. In addition to the taxes to their rulers, which in many cases were raised, the inhabitants had now to supply the Russian forces with food, firewood, pack-horses and two-wheeled carts (*ʿarabas*) on demand and for negligible prices at best. The owners were not compensated if their horses died or their carts were broken. Furthermore, *corvée* was imposed on them, mainly in constructing and maintaining roads. 'All the economic burden,' wrote a Russian general in 1841, 'of maintaining and spreading our conquests in Daghestan, lies on the small, pacified part, which has, in addition, to supply [us with] militia.'[24]

In Chechnia the situation was worse. In addition to the economic warfare and the 'punitive expeditions', the Russians pushed south the population between the Terek and the Sunja and settled Cossacks in their stead, depriving the Chechens of a great deal of fertile land. The impact of this push was much stronger because of the long – at least a century-long – process of Chechen migration north and north-eastward.[25] Thus, the human counter-wave fleeing south, being contrary to the long-standing pattern of migration, created havoc among the Chechens.[26]

The contact with Russia created other changes as well, which undermined local traditions and the very fabric of society. One of the most important was the introduction – planned or accidental – on a massive scale of alcoholic drinks.[27] This had rapid results. In 1819, for example, the people of Aqūsha were praised by Ermolov 'for their morality, good nature and industry . . . "But dissoluteness has already made its appearance in the wake of strong drink" for which of course they had to thank Russian "civilisation".'[28]

In addition, the Russian anti-Islamic policy – and despite all their declarations to the contrary, it *was* anti-Islamic[29] – threatened the people with loss of their identity. In the political sphere,

> what all the rulers found, even when they were initially well disposed toward Russia, was that Russian sovereignty was much more restrictive than the traditional patterns of dominance in the region. Rulers who openly opposed the Russians were ousted, but even those who agreed to Russian terms lost most of their power and their territories were eventually annexed.[30]

In these circumstances an atmosphere of *après moi le déluge* prevailed. The different rulers, whether out of weakness of character, despair or other reasons became engrossed in drinking, gambling and in some cases, debauchery.[31] To finance these activities and/or to fill their coffers before being ousted by the Russians, they squeezed their subjects. And since their authority had already been undermined they used brutal force against their subjects.

One such ruler, much trusted and respected by the Russians, was Āghālār Bek, the ruler *de facto* of Ghāzī-Ghumuq in the 1840s and 1850s. He was described as passing his time in endless drinking sessions. Any servant who was not quick enough to serve him a bottle would be pricked by a fork, a knife or any other instrument in the *Bek*'s hand. By indiscriminate beating and flogging he 'severely inculcated reverence towards the Russians upon his people'. 'The entire Khanate trembled before him.'[32]

To their subjects such rulers appeared increasingly illegitimate and unjust. The mere fact that they were appointed by the Russians in disregard of local customs and traditions sufficed to deprive them of any legitimacy. Furthermore, their behaviour, being contrary to both the *ʿādat* and the *sharīʿa*, was therefore sheer *ẓulm* and further discredited their rule.

Thus, the people felt that they were abandoned by their leaders just when they needed them most – when their physical and spiritual world was crumbling. It was at this precise moment that the Naqshbandiyya-Khālidiyya arrived on the scene with what seemed to be the right answers.[33] The Naqshbandīs, and among them Shaykh Khālid, believed that the *umma* had gone astray. They regarded it as their duty to restore it to the right path, which was to imitate the ideal period of the Prophet and his companions. Naqshbandī adherents, therefore, were instructed to lead their life according to the *sunna* of the Prophet, to fulfil exactly the commandments of the *sharīʿa* and to avoid *bidʿa*.

But adherence to the *sharīʿa* was not only the duty of each individual. The *sharīʿa* was meant to guide public life and the duty of the rulers was to rule according to it. And it had been the failure of the rulers to do so in the first place that had led the *umma* astray. It was, therefore, the duty of the Naqshbandiyya to guide the rulers back to the right path. Otherwise, there was an implicit threat: the duty of the people to obey their rulers was valid only as long as their orders did not contradict the *sharīʿa*.[34]

Also, Shaykh Khālid was extremely hostile to all those who did not belong to the *ahl al-sunna*, and he ordered his followers to 'pray for the survival of the exalted Ottoman state upon which depends Islam for its victory over the enemies of religion, the cursed Christians and the despicable Persians'.[35]

Propagating such views, the Naqshbandiyya-Khālidiyya, not surprisingly, had a spectacular success in Daghestan and Chechnia:

> While the glittering circle of Russian bayonets closed in on every side, Mūlā Muḥammad [al-Yarāghī]'s influence had been growing steadily year by year. Intangible, immaterial, it passed surely and silently through the hedge of bristling steel as a miraged ship through opposing cliffs, or as a moss-bog fire creeps up against the wind. The two forces, material and moral, moving in concentric rings of opposite direction, kept equal pace, and just when to outward seeming the last spark of liberty was trampled under foot in Central Daghestan by the soldiers of the *tsar*, the sacred flame was ready to burst forth and illuminate the land on every side, even to its outermost borders.[36]

The Russian sources claim unanimously that Muḥammad al-Yarāghī and his disciples preached *jihād* against the Russians from the very beginning. This would not be surprising. After all, the Russians were the aggressors in this case, and the *sharīʿa* obliges all Muslims to conduct a *jihād* in defence of Muslim lands.[37] In 1819, for example, it was an important *ʿālim* and later an opponent of the Naqshbandīs – Saʿīd Efendī al-Harakānī – who declared *jihād* on the Russians and called upon all the people and rulers of Daghestan to join it. Furthermore, the role of *ṣūfī ṭāʾifas*, and especially of the Naqshbandiyya, in *jihād* movements all over the Muslim world has been emphasised.[38] The Russian sources also attribute some disturbances in Daghestan in 1829[39] and the great revolt of 1825–26 in Chechnia and Ghabarṭa[40] to the influence of Muḥammad al-Yarāghī's preaching.

However, a close examination of the sources shows clearly that any emphasis on the duty of *jihād* was in principle only. In practice, *jihād* was relegated to a secondary place and an unspecified future. The first concern of Muḥammad al-Yarāghī and his disciples was to establish and enforce the *sharīʿa* and eradicate the *ʿādat*. 'O people,' the Shaykh rebuked the mountaineers,

> you are neither Muslims nor Christians, nor pagans . . . The Prophet said: 'He is a true Muslim . . . who obeys the *qurʾān* and spreads my *sharīʿa*. He who acts according to my commandments, will stand in Heaven higher than all the saints who preceded

> me' . . . Vow, o people, to stop all your vices and henceforth to stay away from sin. Spend [your] days and nights in the mosque. Pray to God with zeal. Weep and ask him for forgiveness.[41]

Only when the *sharīʿa* was established and the Muslims returned to the right path would they become virtuous and strong again, able to wage a *jihād* and liberate themselves. Meanwhile, until 'the right time to take up arms against the unbelievers'[42] arrived, or until 'one of the powerful rulers of the East subdues the Russians to the glory of the *qur'ān*' the mountaineers 'are allowed to submit to the Russians' and even to 'give them hostages'.[43]

Thus, far from being the blind fanatics of the Russian sources, the leaders of the Naqshbandiyya-Khālidiyya in the Caucasus displayed from the very beginning remarkable pragmatism. If approached, they might even – though not necessarily would actually – have come to an accommodation with the Russians. But the Russians persecuted the movement from the very beginning[44] and if this persecution was intermittent, this was only because, on the one hand, the Russians were preoccupied with other problems, and because of the remoteness and inaccessibility of many parts of Daghestan, on the other.

This attitude towards 'Muridism' stems from the traditional Russian attitude towards Islam, in fact towards any religious movement other than the state-run Orthodox Church.[45] The numerous Russian manifestos to the natives notwithstanding, the Russian policy was indeed anti-Muslim. The repeated efforts to spread (Orthodox) Christianity among the mountaineers would alone suffice to demonstrate this face of Russian policy.[46] These were reinforced by measures restricting Muslim religious practice, the one to cause the greatest uproar being the prohibition to perform the *ḥajj* – the pilgrimage to Mecca and Medina.[47] But, there is more direct evidence. A Russian document stated with rare and unusual candour:

> A complete rapprochement between them and us can be expected only when the Cross is set up on the mountains and in the valleys and when temples for Christ the Saviour replaced the mosques. Until then force of arms is the sole true bastion of our rule in the Caucasus.[48]

This xenophobia, coupled with the usual Russian suspicion and intolerance of any movement or activity independent of the authorities,[49] resulted in 'Muridism' being defined from the very beginning as a 'fanatic' movement – fanatic meaning anti-Russian. Equally, the call to implement the *sharīʿa* became synonymous with a call for *jihād* in the Russians' eyes, even when it came from their native allies.[50]

During the wars of 1826–29 both Daghestan and, to a lesser degree, Chechnia remained fairly quiet. The little trouble given to the Russians was instigated by Ottoman and Qājār agents:[51]

> Persians and Turks in turn sent emissaries to stir up the mountaineers against the Russians in the hope of diverting part of the army of the Caucasus from the scene of conflict. The Persians furnished their agents with money, and sought to achieve their end by an appeal to their cupidity. The Turks, better inspired, or more sagacious, were content to work upon their religious feelings, and to the honour of the Daghestanis, be it said, they proved far more susceptible to moral than material inducements.[52]

A partial reason for this relative calm was the fact that the Naqshbandī leadership refrained from declaring a *jihād* in favour of the Ottomans. (Their anti-*shīʿī* bias precluded a *jihād* in favour of the Qājārs anyway.) Whatever their reasons for doing so – out of realistic appreciation of the balance of power, or because they hoped the Ottomans would win and oust the Russians from Daghestan – they now had to face two consequences of the Russian victory:

1. The Russians were now intent on the final pacification of all the mountain areas which had escaped their rule so far. Paskiewicz chose to deal his first blow to the Daghestani communities in Chārtalah, which he carried out between 8 and 15 March 1830.[53] The mountaineers realised the Russian intention fully not only by witnessing their military activities and preparations,[54] but also because the Russians did not try to keep their intentions secret.[55]
2. The Ottoman defeat had a shattering psychological effect on the population and despair considerably crippled resolve to resist the Russian offensive into the mountains. Many said openly that if 'the Russians have beaten the *sulṭān* and the *shāh*, how could we fight them? God help us, if they come here. It will be the end of this world.'[56]

Some Naqshbandī activists felt strongly that the situation was critical. 'We have not paid [proper] attention to our strong infidel enemy and his preparations,' declared one of them, while the Russians had 'conquered Aqūsha, Targhū, Mekhtulī and Khunzakh and defeated the Qājārs and the Ottomans. Now we hear that he [the enemy] has arrived in Chārtalah. In all of Daghestan only Hindāl, Kunbūt . . . , Avāristān . . . and the people of Gartolu [?] are still free,' and even here, 'the rulers of Avāristān . . . intend to make peace with the Russians.'[57]

They felt that urgent action was needed to unite the mountaineers and resist the Russian advance and they acted accordingly. In late 1829 a gathering proclaimed the most prominent among them the *imām* of Daghestan.

Part 3

The First Two *Imāms*

Chapter 6

The First *Imām*

Ghāzī Muḥammad ibn Ismāʿīl al-Gimrāwī al-Dāghistānī [Kazi Mulla of the Russian sources] was born in the early 1790s[1] in the village of Gimrāh, the second largest in the community of Hindāl (known otherwise as Koyṣūbū [Koisubu]). From a very early age Ghāzī Muḥammad had shown an inclination to religious studies. Receiving instruction from the greatest '*ulamā*' in Daghestan, he was finally taught by Saʿīd al-Harakānī, the *qāḍī* of that village and community, and probably the most prominent of them all.

Completing his studies under Saʿīd in the mid-1820s, Ghāzī Muḥammad went to Shaykh al-Sayyid Jamāl al-Dīn al-Ghāzī-Ghumuqi, who initiated him into the Naqshbandiyya-Khālidiyya. Jamāl al-Dīn then took Ghāzī Muḥammad to his *murshid*, Shaykh Muḥammad al-Yarāghī, 'to complete his instruction in the *sharīʿa*. Transmitting to [him] all his knowledge of the *ṭarīqa*, Muḥammad Efendī allowed [him] to spread it in Daghestan and gave Ghāzī Muḥammad his [own] daughter in marriage.'[2]

Ghāzī Muḥammad, thus, became one of Jamāl al-Dīn's *khalīfas* and acted very energetically and successfully. 'He combined in a rare degree the silver and gold of speech and silence. Shamil said of him that he was "silent as a stove", others that "men's hearts were glued to his lips; with a breath he raised a storm in their souls".'[3] By 1827 Ghāzī Muḥammad's fame was so great that the *shāmkhāl* Mahdī Khān invited him to 'come and teach me and my people the *sharīʿa*', which Ghāzī Muḥammad did in 1829 after additional requests from the *shāmkhāl*.[4] By that time he had his own deputies, some of whom practised *rābiṭa* with him.[5]

By the end of 1829, 'almost all the subjects of the *shāmkhāl*, and a significant part of the Avārs, the people of Kunbūt [Gumbet], Salaṭawh and the Ghumuqs' followed Ghāzī Muḥammad. He 'had the clergy of Hindāl at his disposal and enjoyed the fullest devotion from the people of Chirkah'.[6] It was then – in late 1829 – that Ghāzī Muḥammad realised that time was pressing. Until then he had been preaching what could be called 'passive resistance' to the Russians. Now with the Russian onslaught imminent, he decided that force had to be used to implement the *sharīʿa* and by that means to unite the mountaineers in order to resist the Russian encroachment.

Being the most prominent among the like-minded Naqshbandī activists, he was proclaimed *imām*[7] of Daghestan late in 1829, and again, at the beginning of 1830 by a larger gathering of '*ulamā*' and dignitaries. Following that, Ghāzī Muḥammad sent proclamations calling on the rulers and people of Daghestan to implement the *sharīʿa*, threatening to use force against those who failed to do so.[8] Soon afterwards he proclaimed *jihād* against the Russians.

Part of Naqshbandī leadership, however, opposed these activities. First and foremost among them was al-Sayyid Jamāl al-Dīn. To overcome his *murshid*'s opposition the *imām* had to appeal over his head, directly to Muḥammad al-Yarāghī.[9]

With Muḥammad al-Yarāghī's blessing, Ghāzī Muḥammad gathered his followers and started to 'go around the villages in order to return [forcibly] sinners to the right path, to straighten up the crooked and to crush the criminal leadership of the villages'.[10] Among the first villages the *imām* entered was Harakān, where he destroyed the house of his teacher, Saʿīd, and caused the wine stored there and in the village to be poured on the ground.[11]

By mid-February 1830 Ghāzī Muḥammad was in 'Andī, where he entered into communications with Pakhu Bike, the regent of Avāristān for her minor son.[12] He appealed to her to join his forces and to break her relations with the Russians. Having received no satisfactory answer, he entered Avāristān and laid siege to Khunzakh, but on 24 February suffered a defeat.[13] Russian sources rightly attributed this defeat to the fact that Ghāzī Muḥammad acted prematurely because of the Russian threat to Chārtalah.[14]

This, however, proved to be only a temporary setback to the *imām*'s plans. The Russian conquest of Chārtalah (in March 1830)[15] created a strong backlash in Daghestan, which proved very helpful to him. The appeals for help from the communities of Chārtalah were readily answered by their brethren in Daghestan and between May and December 1830 several large forces of mountaineers, led by deputies of Ghāzī Muḥammad, descended into the Alazān valley and clashed with the Russians.[16]

Inside Daghestan, there was now a general movement towards a united stand against the Russians.[17] No less important, Shaykh Muḥammad al-Yarāghī moved now from tacit to open support of Ghāzī Muḥammad and in September 1830 declared *jihād* against the Russians.[18]

Ghāzī Muḥammad's influence was widespread. Already by April 1830 it could be well felt among the Chechens and the Ghumuqs.[19] In Chechnia he enjoyed from the beginning the co-operation of the leaders of the 1825–26 rebellion – Avkō, Muḥammad al-Mayurtupī and Beybulāt.[20] In May 1830 the *imām* sent one of his deputies, Shaykh ʿAbdallah al-ʿAshilṭī, to Chechnia. This proved to be an excellent choice, 'Abdallah being exceptionally efficient in mobilising and leading men.[21] Finally, the *imām* consolidated his influence in Chechnia by personally making a tour in September-October 1830.[22]

As for Daghestan, according to a Russian writer,

> 1830 witnessed the Daghestanī communities joining Miuridism, raids by the mountaineers on villages [which had] submitted to us, and their success in drawing inhabitants of the lowlands to their side. Meanwhile our small columns dashed hither and thither, exchanged fire with the mountaineers, drove them out of one village in order to drive them out of another the following day . . . Proclamations were issued, influencing no one, agreements were concluded, kept by no one, and most important reports and instructions were written extensively.[23]

This description, extremely critical and caricatural as it is, is in essence true. The Russian reaction helped Ghāzī Muḥammad and augmented his movement.[24] At first, as in so many similar cases in history, the Russians did not take the *imām*'s activity seriously. By the time Paskiewicz, busy with his plans for a general onslaught on the mountaineers,[25] became interested in the subject, he received contradictory intelligence from the different local commanders, who had also pursued different policies.

To rectify this situation, Paskiewicz sent one of his protégés, Major Ivan Korganov, with full powers to assess the true situation and decide on a unified policy.[26] Korganov – since then known as 'Van'ka Kain' – however, misused his powers for personal gain, became involved in the web of intrigues centring in, and on, the Avār ruling house,[27] and generally further confused and complicated matters.[28] In fact, he brought the local population to the brink of revolt by arresting Abū Muslim, the *shāmkhāl*'s popular brother. Only the outbreak of an epidemic of cholera prevented an open uprising.

The result was that the Russians tried all possible measures – from negotiations with Ghāzī Muḥammad,[29] through the use of force and economic pressure,[30] to attempts to arrest the two *murshids*[31] and to capture the *imām* dead or alive and even to assassinate him. All these attempts had adverse results because none of them was pursued thoroughly. Rather, they were pursued simultaneously or in quick succession, neutralising the effects of each other and creating confusion. For example, attempts to negotiate with the *imām* were made at the same time as another commander tried to arrange for his assassination.[32] By the end of 1830 Paskiewicz sent a present of a dress and 50 Dutch guilders to Ghāzī-Muḥammad. But a local commander decided not to forward them to the *imām* and they were given to one of the local rulers.[33]

By the end of May 1830 the Russians sent a column of about 6,000 men, 23 cannon and six mortars against Gimrāh. But its commanding officer, Major-General Rosen,[34] stopped short of storming the village because he considered his force too weak. Instead he seized the herds of the villages of Hindāl, then still at their winter pastures in the lowlands, trying thus to achieve the area's submission and the surrender or expulsion of the *imām*. This scheme backfired and created great bitterness against the Russians, not least because a large number of the captured animals were 'lost'.[35]

Although the mountaineers realised that Rosen's campaign had been unsuccessful, the loss of their herds was a bitter blow. It 'forced Ghāzī Muḥammad to take up position in Aghach Qalʿa' (Chumkeskent) in the beginning of March 1831.[36] From here he could defend Hindāl and at the same time challenge the Russians in the lowland.

The Russian reactions were even more confused and incompetent than in the previous years:[37] Bekovich-Cherkasskii, the commander of Daghestan, tried unsuccessfully to storm the position on 19 April. He then retired to Derbend, leaving the force under the local commander, Colonel Mishchenko. The latter attempted again to storm the position on 1 May, with similar results.

On 16 May the *imām* shifted his position to Altī Buyūn. On 20 May the commander of the Left Flank, Taube, tried to storm the new position, again unsuccessfully. Eight days later, Taube retired hastily, 'leaving Daghestan in a worse position than he had found it'.[38] These events taught the *imām* and his followers a valuable lesson, which they would continue to act upon: that fighting from a well-fortified position, they had a good chance to repel Russian attacks, Russian artillery notwithstanding.

The situation was exacerbated from the Russian point of view by the 1831 rebellion which broke out in the kingdom of Poland and in the neighbouring provinces which had been part of it before the partitions. The emperor ordered some units from the Caucasus to be sent to the front. More importantly, he nominated Paskiewicz to command the operations there. On 10 May, Paskiewicz left Tiflis. He divided his command between Generals Emmanuel on the Caucasian Line and Pankrat'ev in Transcaucasia, and ordered both to refrain from offensive operations.

Ghāzī Muḥammad noticed these events and took advantage of them. Realising how cumbersome the Russians were compared to the swiftness of the mountaineers, he now kept them constantly on the run, initiating a series of surprise attacks, in some of which he defeated Russian detachments and gained great prestige.[39]

At the beginning of June, the *imām* lured Kakhanov into futile chases to Altī Buyūn, Pīrī Awul and Aghach Qalʿa. Meanwhile he captured Targhū and laid siege to Burnaia and Nizovoe. With Kakhanov's arrival there, the mountaineers retreated. But the *imām* did not disperse his force. Rather, he continued to harass the Russians, whose commander 'was disinclined to test his luck any more' in offensive operations.[40]

On 26 June Ghāzī Muḥammad left for another front and large-scale fighting stopped. The mountaineers, however, constantly raided the area. So extensive were these raids that the garrison of Burnaia 'could not show themselves outside the walls of the fortress'.[41]

ʿAbdallah al-ʿAshilṭī, meanwhile, had had tremendous success in mobilising the Chechens and the Ghumuqs for the *imām*'s cause. One reason for his success was Vel'iaminov's winter campaigns, in which he destroyed between 30 and 35 villages.[42] This pushed the outraged and vengeful Chechens into the *imām*'s arms. Starting his activity in mid-May 1831, ʿAbdallah appeared with a formidable force in the vicinity of Vnezapnaia on 7 June. By 17 June all the roads to that fortress were cut off and the Ghumuqs and even the Qarā Nogays joined him. On 26 June 'Abdallah started to besiege the fortress. Three days later the *imām* arrived, tightened the siege, and sent a small detachment to raid Qidhlār.[43]

The Russian reaction was again slow and confused. Emmanuel, the commander of the Caucasian Line, 'was amazed by the inactivity of Kovalev, indignant at the imperturbability of Sorochan . . . and all that time did not himself move from his place'.[44] Only on 10 July, having concentrated a sufficient force, did the Russians move to relieve Vnezapnaia. On the following day Ghāzī Muḥammad retreated. Emmanuel now decided to follow the *imām* and defeat his force. On 13 July, near Aghdash ʿAwkh [Aktash Aukh], the Russians were attacked in a thick forest and beaten. They lost almost 400 men killed and wounded (out of 2,500) and one of their cannons (out of ten) was captured by the Chechens.[45]

This victory gave great momentum to the *imām*'s cause, and during the following two months his emissaries were very successful among the Qarābulāqs, the 'semi-Pagan Ingush, who had nothing in common with the *sharīʿa*',[46] and the Ghabarṭians. The Ingush even formed a band of 500 men and interrupted Russian communications along the Georgian Military Highway.[47]

Ghāzī Muḥammad left Chechnia in the second half of July, but he did not remain quiet for long. His followers had been active for quite a while in Qaytāq and Tabarsarān, and already at the end of June a strong force occupied Velikent and stopped for four days a Russian force on its way to reinforce Kakhanov, then bogged down at Burnaia.[48]

In mid-August the *imām* arrived in Irpilī [Erpeli] and in Gubden. On 24 August he was in Bashlī. Four days later his scouts were in the vicinity of Derbend.[49] On 29 August Ghāzī Muḥammad sent two declarations into the city. One called upon the Russian commander to surrender and accept Islam with all his troops. The other called upon the inhabitants to join him, promising that 'we shall harm no Muslim – be he a *shīʿī* or a member of any other sect, as long as he obeys the commandments of the *sharīʿa*'.[50] On 31 August Derbend was cut off and the following morning the eight-day siege started.

On 8 September, as Khakanov was approaching the town, the *imām* withdrew into the mountains. He remained in Qaytāq and Tabarsarān for ten days, arranging their defences and leaving instructions. From there he went to Targhū and Gimrāh, doing the same. Then he went to Salaṭawh, which seemed to be the target of a Russian counteroffensive.[51]

MAP 5: THE CAMPAIGNS OF GHĀZĪ-MUHAMMAD

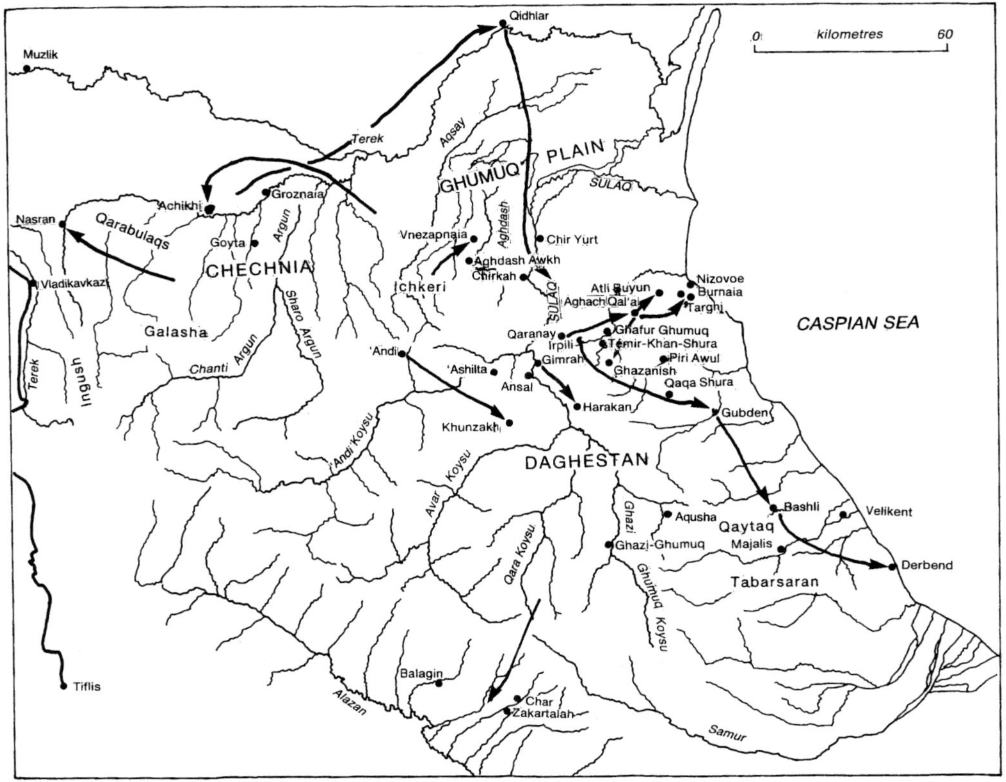

Pankrat'ev, from whose considerations 'offensive operations were completely excluded',[52] arrived on 16 September in Shemākha and spent the following month issuing manifestos to the mountaineers. Finally, on 15 October he moved into the mountains,[53] fought two battles in the second of which 'the enemy showed such determination and energy, that during all the intense battle from 6 a.m. to 11 p.m. our small force could by no means get the upper hand, and the end of the battle was due to the late hour rather than to [our] success'.[54] Following, however, the destruction of about 20 villages, both Qaytāq and Tabarsarān submitted, on 23 October, but without relinquishing the *sharīʿa* as the Russians had demanded.[55]

At this stage both Pankrat'ev and Vel'iaminov, who replaced Emmanuel in September, 'accidentally guessed each other's plans'[56] and engaged in simultaneous concentric attacks on Salaṭawh.[57] Taking advantage of the Russians' preoccupation there, the *imām* crossed the Sunja and operated in the area between that river and the Terek, threatening Groznaia.[58] Vel'iaminov hastened now to counter Ghāzī Muḥammad's activity. Having achieved his first aim, the *imām* disappeared with all his horsemen on 12 November, leaving his infantry at Achikhī. The following day, while Vel'iaminov engaged the force at Achikhī, Ghāzī Muḥammad carried out a devastating raid on Qidhlār.

This 'terrible catastrophe'[59] totally upset the plans of Vel'iaminov who had 'hoped for great results from his success' in Salaṭawh.[60] In all 134 people (126 of them civilians) were killed, and 45 wounded (38 of them civilians). Thirty houses and three churches were completely burnt. The damage was valued at 200,000 rubles. And most important, 168 people, most of them women, were captured, whose ransom 'supplied Ghāzī Muḥammad and his followers with a solid sum of money'.[61] The *imām*'s prestige soared all over the Caucasus, and the raids on the Russian lines multiplied.

In the beginning of December 1831 the *imām* took position in Aghach Qalʿa with a force of about 600 men.[62] Implementing the lessons of his previous stay there, he intended to lure the Russians to attack him. Indeed, the Russians tried unsuccessfully to storm his position on 6 December. But a second attack on 13 December was successful. Most of the defenders were killed as no quarter was asked or given, though the *imām* and a few others managed to escape. But this 'success' cost the Russians huge losses – 96 killed[63] and 296 wounded. Pankrat'ev now 'arrived at the conclusion . . . that Ghāzī Muḥammad had been rendered powerless forever' and on 22 December sent the troops to their winter quarters.

> But in a few days it became clear that Pankrat'ev's beliefs and conclusions were only . . . a pleasant illusion . . . Not only Ghāzī Muḥammad's followers . . . but even those who had deserted him . . . gave the battle of Aghach Qalʿa a completely different interpretation . . . They . . . regarded the slaughter of Aghach Qalʿa as a new glory for the *imām*, and our terrible losses . . . as a failure.[64]

The rest of the winter passed in relative calm in Daghestan, i.e. in small-scale raids and clashes. The Russians' main preoccupation was to arrange for the *imām*'s assassination.[65] In Chechnia, Vel'iaminov conducted two 'punitive' expeditions into 'Awkh and Salaṭawh and a third along the left bank of the Sunja, destroying about 15 villages.[66]

On 20 October 1831 a new commander-in-chief of the Separate Caucasian Corps and chief administrator of Georgia and the Caucasus arrived in Tiflis: Baron Grigorii Vladimirovich Rosen, who had started his service in 1789 and served for quite a long time under Paskiewicz.[67] The new commander, being unacquainted with the Caucasus and its problems, initiated a long process of rethinking and reformulation of the Russian – mainly his predecessor's – policy and plans and the assumptions they were based on.[68]

With regard to Ghāzī Muḥammad, Rosen soon came to the conclusion that 'our actions, not being followed up or having been failures, enhanced his false prophethood'.[69] He therefore decided first of all 'to re-establish peace as soon as possible and to calm down the general irritation of the mountaineers'.[70] Soon, a major campaign was contemplated to defeat the *imām* once and for all.[71]

But Ghāzī Muḥammad preferred to take the initiative. At the end of March 1832 he appeared suddenly in the area of Vladikavkaz and tried to attack Naṣrān [Nazran].[72] Unable to secure the co-operation of all the Ingush and Ossets, and especially failing to make arrangements to cut the Georgian Military Highway, he retreated as suddenly as he had appeared.[73] On 8 April, on his way back, the *imām* arrived in the vicinity of Groznaia.[74] As a Russian writer remarked shrewdly,

> it caused him no harm to stay near Groznaia, to cause panic in the nearby *awuls*, and along the Line, and to see again the Russian forces shutting themselves in the fortress because of him. In addition, such manoeuvres trained the Chechens to obedience, to concentrations and marches, increased their ties to the *imām*, and gave him plentiful material for thought for the future without taking any risk at all.[75]

On the eve of the Russian major campaign, the *imām* acted again. Chārtalah had remained relatively quiet during 1831,[76] which enabled the Russians to plan and start the construction of the 'Lesghian Line'.[77] Now Ghāzī Muḥammad sent there one of his lieutenants, Ḥamza Bek, who operated there between 20 July and 12 August. His retreat should be attributed to the gathering storm in the north rather than to the skirmish on 12 August as the Russian sources state.[78]

On 1 July the *imām* himself took up a fortified position at Yol-Sus-Ṭawh, near Irpilī.[79] He had already made a similar move on 27 May, when he took up position at Kalanchar in the same vicinity. The local Russian commander had found this position unassailable but Ghāzī Muḥammad had eventually left. This time, however, the new commander, Colonel Klüge-von-Klugenau, followed his instructions literally[80] and stormed the position in a two-day battle (2–3 July). In the following three months the area remained relatively calm.[81]

Meanwhile, Rosen was leading a force along the Georgian Military Highway and subduing the neighbouring tribes. Ending that, he campaigned against the Galgay (an Ingush tribe) between 24 July and 5 August. At the same time, between 25 July and 9 August, Vel'iaminov campaigned against the Qarābulāqs and the Galashas. Between them the two generals destroyed 25 villages.[82]

On 15 August the two forces united and two days later Rosen led a force of 15,000–20,000 men into Lesser Chechnia.[83] Between that day and 6 October the Russians crisscrossed Lesser and Greater Chechnia and Ichkerī, systematically pillaging and destroying gardens, fields and villages.[84] They encountered strong resistance. Particularly fierce were two battles in the forests near Goyta (27 and 30 August), and the conquest of Germenchuk (4 September). The *imām* came in person to the Chechens' help. On 22 August he made a demonstration against Vnezapnaia, and on the 31st he ambushed a 500-strong Cossack force, causing 155 casualties and capturing two cannons.[85] However, realising that he could not stop the Russian advance, Ghāzī Muḥammad returned on 10 September to Gimrāh.

In the face of the massive Russian campaign, the *imām* changed his strategy. Whereas the previous year he had been pursuing what might be called the strategy of Shaykh Manṣūr – the unification of all the Muslim mountaineers in order to expel the Russians, or at least to put a stop to their advance – now, having demonstrated his nuisance value, the *imām* tried to come to an accommodation with them. Already in July 1832, that is before his departure to Chechnia, Ghāzī Muḥammad had tried to enter into negotiations with the Russians. When Klugenau called upon Anṣāl to submit, their *qāḍī*, Sha'bān, offered to mediate between the Russians, the *shāmkhāl*, the Avār *khān* and the *imām*.[86]

Now, at the end of September, Ghāzī Muḥammad used one of his Russian prisoners to write a letter to Klugenau in which he offered a truce 'if you do not oppress our law by your taxes' and proposed to Klugenau to send negotiators.[87] Klugenau's answer was unequivocal: 'Tell Ghāzī Muḥammad . . . to come personally with all the *abreks* to the commander-in-chief [Rosen] and surrender to the great clemency of our sovereign . . . [He] is very gracious and magnanimous, and he may allow Ghāzī Muḥammad to go to Mecca'.[88] A second letter was answered in similar terms,[89] leaving the *imām* no choice but fight to the last. He thus hastened his fortification works, which he had started while still corresponding with the Russian general.[90]

Meanwhile, Rosen continued his campaign. On 10 October he received the submission of Salaṭawh. On 29 October his force arrived at Temir-Khān-Shūra and the Russians started to plan their final assault on Gimrāh, where the *imām* had been preparing to make a stand.[91] On 29 October the Russians stormed Ghāzī Muḥammad's fortified position which protected the approach to Gimrāh. The wall across the pass was taken and the *imām* with about 50 followers was surrounded in a house nearby. All but two[92] were killed. On the following day the Russians entered Gimrāh unresisted.

The Russians were sure that the death of the *imām* would put an end to their trouble and that the movement he had founded would collapse. They were to be disappointed. Within a few days a new *imām* of Daghestan was proclaimed.

Chapter 7

The Second *Imām*

Ḥamza Bek ibn ʿAlī Iskandar Bek al-Hutsālī [Gamzat Bek] was born in 1789 in Hutsāl, one of the biggest villages of Avāristān, into a *janka* line.[1] His father – a confidant of ʿAlī Sulṭān Aḥmad Khān – 'was respected by the Avārs for his gallantry and administrative ability.'[2] In his teens Ḥamza lived for a few years at the *khān*'s residence, where Pakhu Bike, ʿAlī Sulṭān Aḥmad's widow, arranged for his education. As a young man he indulged in drinking, but a meeting with Ghāzī Muḥammad reformed him.[3] Ḥamza became a devout Muslim, turned into one of Ghāzī Muḥammad's disciples and joined the Naqshbandiyya. He followed and supported Ghāzī Muḥammad when he became *imām* and proclaimed *jihād* on the Russians. In fact, being involved already in 1826 in anti-Russian activities,[4] he might have been one of those who encouraged Ghāzī Muḥammad to do so.

Under Ghāzī Muḥammad, Ḥamza held a prominent position and led one of the counterattacks on the Russians in Chārtalah, in 1830.[5] Together with al-Shaykh Shaʿbān al-Buhnudī, the leader of another force, he went to the Russian camp to negotiate and was arrested and kept in Tiflis for several months.[6] Upon his release – the Russians hoped to use him against Ghāzī Muḥammad – he rejoined his *imām* and became his deputy. In the beginning of 1831 he co-signed at least one document with Ghāzī Muḥammad.[7]

Ḥamza Bek was wounded in the battle of Yol-Sus-Ṭawh (2–3 July 1832).[8] This, however, did not stop him from leading the campaign in Chārtalah in July – August that year.[9] When the Russians assaulted Gimrāh, Ḥamza was in Hutsāl. He hastened with reinforcements but could only witness helplessly from afar the Russian assault and Ghāzī Muḥammad's last stand.[10]

After the *imām*'s death "the '*ulamā*' and dignitaries appointed Ḥamza Bek in his place".[11] This gathering and the appointment of the new *imām* were the initiative of Shaykh Muḥammad al-Yarāghī. His was also the choice of Ghāzī Muḥammad's successor. By this prompt action the *murshid* saved the first *imām*'s unfinished project from collapsing at its most vulnerable stage, when the death of the *imām* could lead to despair and disillusion. Muḥammad al-Yarāghī, understanding well that the negative effects of Ghāzī Muḥammad's death would become stronger with the passage of time, prevented them at the very beginning by the swift appointment of a new *imām*.

'At the beginning his [the new *imām*'s] authority was acknowledged only by Hutsāl ʿAshilṭa, Gimrāh, Ṭiliq and Mohokh . . . He employed all possible efforts to convince people [of other places] to accept his authority and to establish a proper administration. But they did not recognise his rule and declared war on him.'[12] Ḥamza Bek turned now to the sword, and subdued the different villages and communities one by one.[13] By the autumn of 1833 the *imām* had become powerful enough to cause worry to the Russians.[14]

Among the first actions of the new *imām* was an attempt to reach an accommodation with the Russians.[15] He informed the Russians of this through negotiators from Gimrāh. Kakhanov 'suggested to Ḥamza Bek to come [personally] to Temir-Khān-Shūra for face to face talks . . . but the cautious and distrustful' *imām* – how could he be blamed after his experience in 1830? – 'sent letters instead'.[16] Of these two letters one was couched in very general terms.[17] The other informed the Russians that 'we agree to a reconciliation with you on condition that it causes no harm to our *sharīʿa*.'[18] Furthermore, Ḥamza Bek stated explicitly that he was engaged in enforcing the *sharīʿa*, and expected the Russians not to object to it.

Not receiving an answer Ḥamza Bek approached the *shāmkhāl* to mediate between him and the Russians. He was obviously unaware of the fact that the *shāmkhāl* had been prompting the Russians to use force against the *imām*. The Russians did not believe in Ḥamza Bek's sincerity. Still, Rosen instructed the *shāmkhāl* to inform the *imām* that 'if he is indeed interested in reconciliation and [is willing] to go to Mecca, let him send his son as hostage'.[19] The *imām* agreed on condition that one of the *shāmkhāl*'s sons be given to him as hostage. To this Rosen replied sharply that 'the word of a Russian commander should be enough for him'.[20] On this note negotiations were abandoned, never to be renewed during Ḥamza's reign.[21]

Now with no chance to lead the *imām* into submission – and that was the Russian aim in any negotiation – Rosen pressed the

Avār ruling house to arrest and extradite him to the Russians. After all, he claimed, Ḥamza's place of residence, Hutsāl, was within the Avār Khanate. This, however, the *khān* neither could nor would do, the *imām* being too strong, too prestigious, and anyway closely tied to the ruling house.[22]

Unsuccessful, the Russians proceeded to try to unite all the local rulers – the Avār *khān* included – against Ḥamza Bek. In October 1833, when the *imām* threatened Girgil [Gergebil], its people were assisted by the *shāmkhāl*, the *khān* of Mekhtulī and the confederation of Aqūsha. However, the allies were beaten and Girgil submitted to Ḥamza's authority.[23]

Now the *imām*'s territory surrounded Avāristān from three sides, and it was obvious that Khunzakh would be his next target. It was not surprising, therefore, in these circumstances that a rivalry developed between the two, especially as the Russians did all in their power – including a stop to subsidies – to force the *khān* and his mother to resist the *imām*.[24] The rivalry became so intense that in March 1834 Pakhu Bike tried secretly to arrange for the assassination of Ḥamza Bek.[25]

Finally, at the beginning of August, the *imām* attacked Avāristān and laid siege to Khunzakh. After a fortnight an agreement was reached and Pakhu Bike gave two of her sons as hostages until its fulfilment. On 25 August the third brother arrived for negotiations. There was a shoot-out in which the two elder brothers, Nūsāl Khān and ʿUmma (ʿUmar) Khān and all their companions, as well as the *imām*'s brother and a few of his followers, were killed. (The younger son of Pakhu Bike, Būlach Khān, then a little boy, was held in Hutsāl.) On the same day Ḥamza ordered the murder of Pakhu Bike and all the other womenfolk of the Avār ruling house. Only one of Nūsāl Khān's wives was spared because of her pregnancy.[26]

Later, Russian sources unanimously claimed that the killings were premeditated and that Ḥamza Bek did it upon the instigation of Aslān Khān, the ruler of Ghāzī-Ghumuq and Kurāh, who had a grudge against Pakhu Bike for refusing him her daughter's hand. This was used very successfully as propaganda against both Ḥamza Bek and his successor. In fact, the Russians were so successful that a great number among the mountaineers accepted this version.[27] The first Russian reports, however, tell a completely different story. According to them it all started from a row between two junior members of the parties of both sides. Someone drew a dagger, someone else a pistol, and in an instant the entire place became a slaughterhouse.[28]

The annihilation of the Avār ruling house – whether intentional or not – was the single most important event during Ḥamza Bek's rule and maybe even in the history of the movement, because it changed permanently and irrevocably the strategic balance in Daghestan: it eliminated the only local force which was strong enough to resist the *imām* and which was located so as to prevent the spread of his rule over all of inner Daghestan; it deprived the Russians of important local allies in inner Daghestan; it prevented any possibility of a buffer between the Russians and the *imām* and thus made a direct confrontation inevitable; finally, it hastened such a confrontation because of the power vacuum it created, and the emotional reaction of the Russians to the event.

Immediately after the conquest of Khunzakh, Ḥamza Bek dispersed his force to their homes, the men being exhausted and out of supplies.[29] However, at the beginning of September, he gathered them again and marched against Tsudaqār [Tsudakhar], where he was checked by the forces of Aqūsha (Tsudaqār being a member of this confederation).[30]

In spite of this setback, the Russians regarded the *imām* as a growing threat, especially after Ḥājj Tāshō – a Ghumuq from Indirī who had become an important war leader among the Chechens – accepted Ḥamza's authority.[31] They started, therefore, to plan and to make preparations for a campaign against the *imām*.[32] This expedition, however, was never necessary. On 19 September Ḥamza was assassinated while entering the mosque of Khunzakh to lead the Friday noon prayers.[33] The assassins had personal rather than political reasons – they were led by a 'milk brother' of the *khān* and their motive was to avenge his killing.

It is difficult to overstate the importance of the first two *imāms*. Ghāzī Muḥammad, as the first *imām*, established many, if not all, of the policies, practices, strategies and tactics which were followed by his successors. He was, for example, the first to use against the Russians the twin strategies of total struggle of all the mountaineers, on the one hand, and an accommodation from a position of 'nuisance value', on the other. He was also the first to grasp, and to point to, the Russians' weak points and to show how to exploit them by swift movements and surprise attacks, as well as by defending fortified positions. Most important, he taught his successors the importance of taking the initiative.

But his importance reached further. Ghāzī Muḥammad consciously prepared the mountaineers for a long struggle, trying 'to mould together this scattered raw material . . . to train [them] to singleminded actions'.[34] In his campaigns he endeavoured to accustom them to long manoeuvres beyond their immediate areas. The *imām* even shrewdly devised a way of disinforming the Russians by keeping his intentions secret, while spreading false rumours.[35]

In addition it was Ghāzī Muḥammad who advised the Chechens to live in the forests and to cultivate maize instead of wheat.[36]

> This advice had an extraordinary importance . . . Henceforward the Chechens would live in the midst of inaccessible forests . . . They would lose nothing when their huts were destroyed, and would be able to rebuild them promptly . . . The forests would provide shelter for their families, livestock and the little property they had . . . The change from wheat to maize was calculated to preserve the inaccessibility of the country by limiting the cultivated area. The rich crops of maize . . . could easily feed the population and replace the loss of bread.

All these measures, the Russian commentator concluded, were intended to make the Chechens 'vigilant, always ready to fight or run, and little sensitive to destruction . . . A well-conceived system of popular war was being organised against us, which could not be better suited to the local conditions and the primeval way of life of the Chechen tribes.'[37]

Even if, as has been argued, not all of these measures originated with Ghāzī Muḥammad or even if their outcomes were not all foreseen by him,[38] the first *imām* still cuts an impressive figure. In fewer than three years he accomplished a great part of his original aims. He laid down the rules of the game to be played by his successors, rules that would subsequently be changed very little.

Still, Ghāzī Muḥammad's work was far from completed by the time he died. Everything he had built was still fragile, and a great deal depended on him personally, the *imām* being the central axis around which everything rotated. His death, therefore, could have undone all his work. It did not do so for two reasons: the prompt action by Shaykh Muḥammad al-Yarāghī in proclaiming Ḥamza Bek *imām*; and the guilt now felt by the people of Gimrāh (and other villages of Hindāl), who had not stayed by the first *imām* in his last battle. Like the people of Kūfa and Baṣra after ʿAlī's and Ḥusayn's deaths, the people of Gimrāh now became firm supporters of the new *imām*.

Unlike his predecessor, Ḥamza Bek has not been duly appreciated in either Russian or Daghestanī sources, and this in spite of the fact that he was 'learned and wise, and no one in Daghestan could rival his gallantry'.[39] His short rule was overshadowed by those of both his predecessor and successor. Furthermore, the annihilation of the Avār ruling house marred all of Ḥamza's rule and, made yet worse by the Russian propaganda version of that event, succeeded in reducing his image to that of simply a slaughterer.

The consequences both of this deed and of the mere fact that Ḥamza Bek immediately succeeded Ghāzī Muḥammad, however obvious, must be mentioned and emphasised. But the second *imām* was not a passive figure. Neither was his contribution negligible. It is difficult to assess Ḥamza Bek's influence on Ghāzī Muḥammad's actions, though it might safely be assumed that it existed. As *imām*, Ḥamza Bek continued and further developed his predecessor's work. Although it cannot be proved positively, there are more than hints in the sources to the effect that it was the second *imām* who began the creation of the administrative structure of the emerging state, in his time still in embyronic form.

The activities of Ḥamza Bek, thus, created a firmer and wider base from which his successor could start his activities. And, indeed, such a successor was in power a few days after the second *imām*'s assassination.

Part 4

Beginnings

Chapter 8

The Third *Imām*

The third *imām* was born in the year 1212 AH (AD 1796/7). His father, Dengaw Muḥammad, was an *uzden* while his mother belonged to a side branch of the ruling family of Ghāzī-Ghumuq, living in ʿAshilṭa.[1] At his birth the future *imām* was given the name ʿAlī. But as he was sickly, his name was changed to Shamū-yil[2] (pronounced Shamīl in the Caucasus[3]) in accordance with the widespread belief that a change of name is followed by a turn in a person's luck.

Shamil grew out of his illnesses to become an exceptionally tall (well over six feet), strong and athletic young man. Stronger, faster and tougher than most of his contemporaries, he also became, through endless exercise, an almost unrivalled horseman and could outdo almost everyone in his mastery of musket, sword and dagger. Stories and legends about his exceptional strength, endurance, luck and exploits undoubtedly contributed to his prestige and helped to create an aura of leadership around him. But that was not all. Shamil seems to have possessed the natural ability to lead men, coupled with intelligence, iron will, self-discipline, self-control and tenacity.

From his early childhood Shamil fostered a friendship with Ghāzī Muḥammad, only four or five years his senior and a distant relative by marriage.[4] This friendship continued until the first *imām*'s death. It was Ghāzī Muḥammad who first introduced Shamil to religious instruction. Later, Shamil followed his elder friend to study under Saʿīd al-Harakānī, to be initiated into the Naqshbandiyya by Shaykh al-Sayyid Jamāl al-Dīn and to be ordained as a *khalīfa* by Shaykh Muḥammad al-Yarāghī.[5]

When Ghāzī Muḥammad started his political activity and became the first *imām* of Daghestan, Shamil followed initially his *murshid*, Jamāl al-Dīn. Soon, however, he joined the *imām* and became one of his lieutenants.[6] Shamil took part in Ghāzī Muḥammad's last stand at Gimrāh in 1832, and was one of the only two survivors. His miraculous escape, and recovery from a

Shamil, his sons and some of his lieutenants

deadly wound,[7] being neither the first nor the last one,[8] could not but contribute to his image of being under special heavenly care.[9]

After his recovery Shamil served in the same capacity under the second *imām*, and with the exception of a short period of misunderstanding, enjoyed Ḥamza Bek's full confidence. His official chronicler even states that Ḥamza nominated Shamil as his successor.[10] This claim, however, should be taken with more than a grain of salt, as other evidence suggests that Shamil was on an equal footing with others, like Saʿīd al-Ihalī, Ghāziyō al-Karāṭī, Qibid Muḥammad al-Ṭiliqī and ʿAbd al-Raḥman al-Qarākhī.[11] All of them appear to have been *nāʾibs* – although this term was not yet in use – in their native areas, Shamil being responsible for Hindāl.[12]

The news of Ḥamza's assassination reached Shamil in Gimrāh. He immediately collected a force and went to Hutsāl. There he 'seized on the treasury, and [forced] Ḥamza's uncle to surrender the boy-prince Būlach Khān' (the remaining member of the Avār ruling family).[13] Shamil then hurriedly summoned a meeting of '*ulamā*' and other dignitaries near ʿAshilṭa (i.e. in his own territory) to choose a new *imām*. By then, as he recalled 25 years later, 'the people had for a long time been prepared to [choose him due to] his [Shamil's] previous exploits and through acquaintance with his personality . . . [All] Shamil had [to do was] only to *remind* [them] of his existence in order to be elected, and he [indeed] reminded [them] . . .[14]

Indeed, the participants unanimously chose Shamil. But he declined, suggesting a few other, better qualified, candidates; these, however, refused, insisting that Shamil was the only qualified person for this position. In this they were influenced by the strong support given to Shamil's nomination by Sayyid Jamāl al-Dīn – the only *murshid* in Daghestan after the death of Muḥammad al-Yarāghī – no less than by Shamil's strong personality and by the circumstances of the election.[15] Years later, Shamil recalled that the people asking him to accept the nomination and he himself, refusing, were so moved that they all started to weep.[16] Finally, after a 'stubborn resistance' which '*almost* convinced them',[17] Shamil accepted the nomination. The people then cheered and swore allegiance (*bay'a*).[18]

Shamil's first action as the new *imām* was to have Būlach Khān killed. He then started to march toward Khunzakh. Both actions were ostensibly to avenge Ḥamza's assassination. Nevertheless, both were also aimed at immediately re-establishing control in Avāristān and eliminating the only survivor of the ruling house who could endanger this control.[19] On his way news reached Shamil that the Russians were attacking Gimrāh.

According to Russian sources the village was stormed and taken on 26 September by a force under the command of Major-General Lanskoi, the new commander of Northern Daghestan.[20] The next day the Russians completely destroyed the village and its fields and vineyards; thus, Shamil, who immediately returned to Gimrāh, found it a mess of ruins. Discovering that one of the

Gimrāh

villagers had served as an informer for the Russian force, he executed him as an example to 'all traitors'.[21] Daghestani sources, which seem to be more accurate, stated that the *imām* attacked the Russians from both flanks, 'killed a senior officer'[22] and 'retook Gimrāh by storm, putting Lanskoi to flight'.[23]

Not two weeks later the long-planned expedition to Khunzakh set out from Temir-Khān-Shūra, headed by Colonel Klüge-von-Klugenau, commander of the Apsheron infantry regiment and of Temir-Khān-Shūra.[25] Its aim was to 'extinguish any encroachment' by the new *imām*[25] and more particularly 'to disperse the *murīds*, compel the Avārs to acknowledge our nominee [i.e. Aslān Khān of Ghāzī-Ghumuq] as their ruler, and to keep in peace Avāristān as well as other mountain communities'.[26]

All these aims were achieved, and quite easily, it seemed. Leaving Temir-Khān-Shūra on 14 October, Klugenau received the submission of Aqūsha on the 17th and entered Girgil unopposed on the 23rd. Leaving the village on 27 October with a 3,500-strong force, he dispersed a 1,000-strong force led by Shamil near Mohokh.

On 30 October Klugenau stormed Hutsāl and there on 1 and 2 November he received 'the elders of Khunzakh and all those involved in the assassination of Ḥamza Bek'. The delegates 'ask[ed] him in the name of all the people' to nominate Aslān Khān of Ghāzi-Ghumuq and Kurāh to rule them until the new-born son of Nūsāl Khān came of age. Aslān Khān was accordingly invested as interim ruler of Avāristān and the delegates swore allegiance to the Russian emperor and to him. Klugenau then returned to Temir-Khān-Shūra, destroying Hutsāl and Jalda on his way.[27]

Satisfied with completing this mission, the Russians did not return to this area for well over a year and a half, leaving Shamil to establish and increase his power unmolested. Drozdov – the only Russian author to study the early years of Shamil's rule – tried to explain this inactivity by three reasons. Shamil's weakness and passivity during 1835 was one of them. Another was the chronic Russian shortage of manpower, which left Klugenau with 2,500 men (instead of 4,000) at his disposal, of whom 400 were in hospital. Taking into account the men needed for the construction works on the forts of Temir-Khān-Shūra and Nizovoe and for other duties, Klugenau could put into the battlefield no more than 1,500 bayonets. The third, and most important, reason was the fact that the Russians chose to concentrate their efforts on the Western Caucasus. This decision was not surprising, taking into account contemporary circumstances and considerations.[28]

Russia's claim to sovereignty over this area was equivocal at best,[29] and the other Great Powers – most significantly Britain and France – refused to recognise it. Therefore, the task of establishing control over the 'Right Flank' was a matter of extreme urgency for St. Petersburg. Daghestan and Chechnia did not pose such problems. Being completely surrounded by Russian territory and ceded officially to Russia by the Qājār Empire in the treaties of Gulistān and Turkumānchāy, their 'pacification' did not pose any international problem and could be regarded and presented as an internal matter.

Furthermore, while Daghestan was more or less calm, and seemed to be well on its way towards submission to the emperor, the situation on the Right Flank seemed to be completely different. The tribes inhabiting this area seemed to be much more numerous, powerful and fierce, and their geographical position – especially the long shore along the Black Sea – enabled them to maintain extensive contacts with the Ottoman Empire and other foreigners, most notably Britons.[30] These contacts strengthened the Circassians both militarily and morally and stiffened their resistance to Russian penetration.

With the Caucasian Corps unable to launch more than one strategic initiative, the decision to concentrate on the Right Flank meant the cancellation of all the modest activities planned originally in Daghestan.[31] Klugenau was, therefore, 'compelled to turn a blind eye to Shamil's activities and even thanked him in his heart for leaving our frontiers in peace'.[32]

But Klugenau did not confine himself to that. Born into a noble family in Bohemia, Franz Klüge-von-Klugenau [Frants Karlovich Kliuki-fon-Klugenau] joined the Austrian army but left it in 1818 as a young lieutenant. Entering Russian service that year, he was transferred to the Caucasus in 1820. There he continued to serve until his retirement.[33] Thus, when in 1833 he was promoted to major-general appointed to command the Apsheron Regiment and charged with constructing its new fortified regional headquarters in Temir-Khān-Shūra, Klugenau was not a novice to the Caucasus or to Daghestan. Well-known in the Caucasian Corps for his quick temper, honesty and legendary courage and gallantry, he was regarded as an excellent fighter and leader of men.[34] But he had not had much political experience, having served mostly as a field commander. In the expressed opinion of some of his superiors, and of some commentators in later years,[35] his strategic, political and administrative abilities were questionable.

Such opinions, however, seem to have been partly influenced by political differences. Klugenau, it seems, belonged to the minority of Russian officers and officials who preferred to subdue the Caucasus by peaceful means. But he went a step further: unlike his Russian-educated colleagues, he did not automatically refuse to consider the possibility of an accommodation with Shamil.

In his view, there were only two viable ways to pacify Daghestan: 'Either to convince Shamil to live in peace, or to deal the mountaineers a decisive blow'.[36] He personally preferred and recommended the former approach, not only because of the lack of any means to use force, but because, according to him, 'the *sharīʿa* was harmless'[37] and Shamil 'and the *murīds* cause us less trouble than many of the pacified mountaineers, especially the people of Anṣāl'.[38]

It is not surprising, therefore, that some kind of understanding was soon reached between the *imām* and the general. Through the mediation of two local headmen,[39] an agreement was reached at the end of 1834 or the beginning of 1835 between Shamil and the *shāmkhāl* Sulaymān Khān. To guarantee its implementation the *imām* gave the *shāmkhāl* his cousin as hostage.[40] Officially, Klugenau was probably not a party to the agreement. Therefore he could deny it in full honesty when accused later of reaching an accord with Shamil.[41] However, there can be little doubt of his deep involvement in it, as there can be little doubt of Klugenau's superior's knowledge of it.[42]

What can be doubted is whether either was fully acquainted with its details or completely understood their far-reaching implications.[43] And far-reaching they were. Although the undertakings must have been mutual, the available sources mention only those of Shamil. These were three:

1. Shamil formally accepted Russian suzerainty, though this might have been less unequivocal than Russian reports and translations of his letters lead one to believe.
2. Shamil undertook not to raid the lowlands and to prevent others from doing so.
3. In the mountains, the *imām* pledged 'to have to do with no

one [*ni skem ne imet' dela*]',[44] meaning that he would not initiate war with others. But this undertaking was conditioned on the 'implementation [*tanfīdh*] of the *sharīa*'.[45]

Clearly the beneficiary of this agreement was Shamil. To start with, it removed the threat of immediate military action by the Russians and their local vassals and granted him essential time to consolidate and spread his power in Daghestan. Furthermore, the knowledge that Shamil had such an agreement with the Russians – and he himself always believed it to be so – and therefore might enjoy their backing increased the new *imām*'s power and prestige, outweighing any possible loss of legitimacy.[46] Second, the agreement was tantamount to an implicit recognition of Shamil's rule and acceptance of him as a legitimate and equal party. Furthermore, by accepting Shamil's condition of implementing the *sharīʿa*, his legitimisation was accepted as well. Third, by referring to the lowlands as belonging to the Russians, Shamil's claim that the mountains were his domain was implicitly recognised. Finally, acceptance of Shamil's demand to implement the *sharīʿa* within the mountains gave him, in fact, an almost free hand to establish and consolidate his rule there.

The price to be paid for these benefits was quite low from Shamil's point of view. His acknowledgement of Russian suzerainty was only a gesture, not entailing any substantive consequences. Therefore, it could easily be – and successfully was – kept a secret from his followers. As for the *imām*'s undertaking 'to have to do with no-one', it was vague enough, and accompanied by the undertaking to implement the *sharīʿa*, could be easily circumvented.

The most important aspect of the agreement was that for Shamil it could not have come at a more opportune moment. Shamil was chosen, or rather confirmed as *imām* by most, but not all, the members of his movement. Among his peers – that is, the other lieutenants of the previous *imāms* – his authority was non-existent. At least one of them, Hājj Tāshō al-Indirī, openly challenged the new *imām*'s title and authority.[47] Others, like Qibid Muḥammad al-Ṭiliqī, Saʿīd al-Ihalī, Ghāziyō al-Karaṭī and 'Abd al-Raḥman al-Qarākhī, simply disregarded Shamil and took care of their specific local concerns.[48] In several cases, when he was attacked by enemies, Shamil could only deploy a dozen or two of his followers.[49]

The first to attack Shamil were the people of Anṣāl, who had a long-standing feud with Gimrāh. On this occasion, the *shāmkhāl* – no doubt with the knowledge, if not the encouragement, of Klugenau – intervened, stopped the fighting and mediated a settlement.[50] This, however, did not last for long, and soom Shamil was attacked again by Anṣāl and other communities. During 1835 Shamil had to leave Gimrāh and settle in ʿAshilṭa, his mother's native village. For a while even that place did not prove safe enough, and the *imām* had to stay in the village of ʿIsh.[51]

In this context, the agreement and Klugenau's subsequent assistance in warning the *imām*'s opponents not to use arms against him, were invaluable,[52] and Shamil took full advantage of it by being neither slow nor hesitant in spreading this piece of information.[53] Here Shamil demonstrated for the first, but not the last, time his remarkable ability to use adverse circumstances in his favour and to turn weakness into strength, losses into victories. Not being strong enough to force others into obedience, he preferred to lead an ascetic's life. In fact, 'during the entire year of 1835', the *imām*, by 'absorbing himself in reading and interpreting the *qur'ān*, preaching and sending sermons to the Daghestani communities, played the pious and modest *imām* devoted to fasting and praying for the sinners who deviated from the rulers of the *sharīʿa*'.[54]

By acting thus, Shamil enjoyed several advantages. First, among the mountaineers his image as a pious and devoted Muslim was strengthened; second, both Klugenau and many local communities were now convinced of his peaceful intentions and the lack of expansionist designs on his part; third, his opponents were presented as aggressors and he as their victim, and Shamil was not slow in complaining of these aggressions to Klugenau and Réoute.[55] Thus, the *imām* was able to ask for – and obtain – Klugenau's intervention. When the *imām*'s power grew, this would enable him to fight his opponents and openly spread his authority without seeming to break a promise 'to have to do with no one'.

The situation changed at the beginning of 1836. In what could be understood as a challenge to Shamil, Ḥājj Tāshō sent an appeal to Shamil, Qibid Muḥammad and the various communities of Daghestan, remonstrating with them for their failure to spread the *sharīʿa* and conduct the *jihād* against the Russians. Reminding them that he had a strong force under his command, he threatened to destroy them.[56]

Shamil praying before battle (*a modern photomontage*)

A Ghumuq from the village of Indirī, Ḥājj Tāshō was among the first followers of Shaykh ʿAbdallah al-ʿAshilṭī in Chechnia. Through his courage and martial abilities he soon became a renowned war leader in Chechnia. Ḥājj Tāshō was regarded by himself and by others as a candidate to the title of *imām*; when Shamil was proclaimed *imām*, Ḥājj Tāshō did not accept his authority.[57] In the beginning of 1835, he erected a fort on the Michik near Zandaq, from where he controlled a considerable part of Chechnia.[58]

In challenging Shamil and his broader base of legitimisation, Ḥājj Tāshō could concentrate only on his qualities as a war leader, and on his tenacity in enforcing the *sharīʿa* and conducting the *jihād*. Unable to sway the Ghumuqs – they had not forgotten the main lesson of their joining the first *imām*, namely that their flat country lacked natural shelters from Russian retaliation, unlike the forests of Chechnia or the mountains of Daghestan – Ḥājj Tāshō turned to harassing the Russian Line by frequent raids.

Shamil was quick to respond to Ḥājj Tāshō challenge. A few days later he summoned all his followers as well as Ḥājj Tāshō and Qibid Muḥammad to Chirqaṭa. This proved to be the first step in establishing the new *imām*'s authority over his peers as well as over the country. In Chirqaṭa Shamil managed to reconcile Ḥājj Tāshō and Qibid Muḥammad, and the three agreed henceforth to work together.[59] Thus started the process which would culminate in Shamil's peers becoming his lieutenants.[60]

From Chirqaṭa the united force, numbering only 150 men subdued Ihalī and Oroṭa.[61] Then, the *imām* returned to 'Ashilṭa and stayed there until July 1836. During these months his authority spread rapidly, mainly by peaceful means. The few instances in which force was used were always in response to requests for help addressed to the *imām*. Even the Russian sources, their talk of 'terror'[62] notwithstanding, had to admit that 'almost all the Daghestani and several Chechen communities submitted voluntarily to the new *imām*'.[63]

By that time, mid-1836, Shamil was surrounded by devoted *nā'ibs* who were his own men, like Surkhāy al-Kulāwī, ʿAlī Bek al-Khunzakhī and Akhbirdi Muḥammad al-Khunzakhī, who were ready to enforce his commands and to punish any disobedience. He also had a growing number of troops at his disposal to carry out this policy. This ability, and readiness, to enforce his will coupled with his title, legitimacy and the support of the spiritual head, Sayyid Jamāl al-Dīn, made any opposition futile.

Having established his control over large parts of Daghestan and Chechnia, Shamil now started to organise his realm. The old division into communities remained. Shamil only nominated a *nā'ib* over each. Usually, but not always, these *nā'ibs* belonged to the local big families. Taxation was organised, and started to flow to the *imām* and his *nā'ibs*. A steadily growing standing army was organised, always at the disposal of Shamil and his lieutenants. It was organised in hundreds (*mi'āt*) of infantry and cavalry.[64] The problem of its upkeep was solved by ordering every tenth household to furnish a *murtāziq*[64] – a Cavalry fighter always ready to be called to war, and relieved from any other occupation.[65] The foundations of a state had begun to emerge.

Chapter 9

Ṭiliq

By the summer of 1836 Rosen, preoccupied with the affairs of Circassia, had to turn his attention to Chechnia and Daghestan. Although he believed in peaceful penetration, Rosen 'did not share Klugenau's optimism';[1] that is, he would not hear of an agreement with Shamil. He demanded the *imām*'s unconditional submission.[2] Shamil's quick rise to power and his widening control must have seemed to him an alarming development. The acuteness of the situation was further underlined by the power vacuum following the death and succession of both the *shāmkhāl*[3] and the *khān* of Ghāzī-Ghumuq.[4] By the summer the problem became urgent when Shamil seemed on the brink of taking control of Avāristān.

In Chechnia also the situation was coming quickly to a boil. Ḥājj Tāshō's frequent raids on the Caucasian Line reached such a proportion that

> the daily alarms caused by small raiding parties penetrating through the cordon along the Terek kept the troops constituting the cordon constantly with muskets in hand and mounted. The position of the dwellers of the *stanitsy* was even worse, because they, awaiting a raid every minute, could not engage in their agricultural work.[5]

The Russian response was completely inadequate:

> In order to contain the Chechens our troops used to carry out raids within the foe's territory. We used to burn his [the foe's] villages, seize goats, sometimes to capture a number of men and women as prisoners, to bring into submission the frightened savages, to take hostages from them in order to keep them in submission, and accomplishing, in fact, nothing, to return to the Sunja with a train of killed and wounded officers and lower ranks. The [destroyed] villages would then be re-established and Ḥājj Tāshō would reappear in our wake among the[ir] devastated dwellers.[6]

Thus, in the summer of 1836 Rosen decided once and for all

to eliminate Shamil, Tāshō and 'Muridism' in general. At first an attempt was made to undermine Shamil's authority by dispatching an *ʿālim* loyal to the Russian government to convince the mountaineers to come to terms with the Russians. Tāz al-Dīn ibn Muṣṭafā Efendī [Tazadin Mustafin] from Qazān was approached and agreed to accept this mission. However, all the communities under Shamil's rule denied him entry, some even under the threat of death.[7]

In view of this failure, and in order to stop any further development of 'Muridism' Rosen 'found it necessary to carry out an offensive into Chechnia and Daghestan and by force of arms to teach sense to the credulous mountaineers'.[8] A two-pronged attack was planned. Pullo was to rout Ḥājj Tāshō from Zandaq, while at the same time Réoute was to advance into Daghestan, capture Irghin [Irguany] and by that to deal a blow to Shamil's authority.[9]

Pullo set out from Groznaia on 2 September 1836 and captured Zandaq two days later. The stubborn resistance of the villagers – including women and children – ended in a 'terrible massacre'. Following that Pullo accepted the submission of neighbouring villages, 'both he and the submitting [persons] knowing . . . that as soon as our troops moved out Shamil's rule would be re-established'.[10]

Réoute, who had led a 'reconnaissance patrol' to Irghin from 2–6 August, to deter Shamil from attacking Avāristān,[11] decided instead to go to Avāristān. Réoute reached his destination unresisted – Shamil concentrated a force of 3,000 men, but dispersed it and went back to ʿAshilṭa – nominated Aḥmad the *khān* of Mekhtulī instead of Muḥammad Mīrzā Khān of Ghāzī-Ghumuq as temporary ruler of Avāristān and returned to Temir-Khān-Shūra.[12]

From the Russian point of view the activities of 1836 achieved 'adverse results' and instead of 'discrediting Shamil's authority' he 'was held by the mountaineers in higher esteem' than before.[13] To Shamil, these expeditions into Daghestan were clear violations of his agreement with the Russians, and he promptly protested to both Klugenau and Réoute.[14] If Shamil regarded the agreement as a tactical means to keep the Russians out of the mountains until he was strong enough to confront them, then these were the first Russian acts of 'treachery' to be used as a justification for refusing to negotiate with them. If, to the contrary, he concluded the agreement in good faith, then these events must have caused the first cracks in his belief in the possibility of accommodation with the Russians. In any case, while only several months earlier he had been telling the mountaineers that he was in agreement with the Russians,[15] now he was calling upon them to join the struggle against the infidels.[16]

Still, Shamil tried to maintain contact with the Russians. At the beginning of November 1836, he wrote letters to Réoute, Klugenau and other Russian commanders, urging them to conduct negotiations with him as the ruler and representative of all the mountain communties, and pledging to keep his agreement with them.[17] By that time, however, local commanders had received orders not to communicate independently with Shamil,[18] and his letters were sent to Rosen. The commander-in-chief was unequivocal; prohibiting any contact with the *imām* Rosen suggested that,

> if he [Shamil] really wants to remain peaceful [*pokoinyi*] and gives his word not to spread his *sharīʿa*, then he may address a petition to the commander of the corps, directly or through General Réoute, to be granted this grace [*milost'*] and to send his son as hostage to Tiflis.'[19]

In April 1837, Shamil tried again, sending messengers to Rosen.[20] The results of this initiative were the same – naught. The Russians left no room for compromise. Shamil was bluntly given the choice of complete surrender, willingly or by force.

Rosen's plans for 1837 as approved by St. Petersburg concentrated, as in previous years, on the Western Caucasus. Only defensive measures were prescribed for Daghestan and Chechnia.[21] However, some of Rosen's subordinates were more than ready to take advantage of events and turn the defensive into a full-scale offensive against Shamil.

First and foremost among they was Faesy. A Swiss by birth, Karl Faesy [Karl Karlovich Fezi] left the Swiss army and entered Russian service in November 1816. Serving under Rosen, Faesy moved with him to the Caucasus. In 1837 he was nominated acting commander of the 20th Infantry Division and of the Left Flank of the Caucasian Line.[22] 'A great master of the pen',[23] Major-General Faesy belonged 'to that sort of people of whom it is said that they will use the same pair of soles to serve seven kings'.[24]

Soon after his arrival in Groznaia in January 1837, Faesy conducted two expeditions into Lesser (4–12 February)[25] and Greater

Chechnia (16 February–11 April).[26] The detailed study of these otherwise insignificant expeditions shows a pattern of behaviour which would be repeated in all of Faesy's future and more important campaigns. Starting forcefully, Faesy lacked the stamina to carry on if no quick results were achieved. At this stage he would gladly come to any agreement his adversary proposed, as long as it enabled him both to retreat without loss of face and to report to his superiors that his opponent had submitted to Russia. In this campaign Faesy accused his lack of results on Klugenau.[27]

'The unplanned expedition into Chechnia had not ended yet,' wrote a Russian source, 'when the circumstances demanded no less an unexpected movement by our armies into upper Daghestan. The reason for this was the danger threatening the Avār Khanate.'[28] Baddeley more correctly stated that the 'Avār expedition of 1837 was a result of an intrigue on the part of Aḥmad Khān of Mekhtulī, the temporary ruler of Avāristan and, reading authorised accounts, it is difficult to acquit the Russians of deliberate treachery'.[29] Indeed, it is impossible to acquit Faesy of complicity in Aḥmad Khān's intrigue and Rosen of exploiting it.

The Khān, who 'according to the will of the people' had replaced the 'unpopular' Muḥammad Mīrzā Khān as temporary ruler of Avāristān in 1836,[30] secretly approached Faesy requesting a Russian garrison in Khunzakh. Faesy replied that if the people consented to the Russian presence, he would immediately start with a column to Khunzakh. Simultaneously, he sent a public proclamation offering help to the Avārs. Aḥmad Khān then gathered a meeting of all the village elders and stage-managed a request for Russian troops while pretending to hold the opposite opinion.[31]

Rosen received word of what had happened together with an official request for a Russian garrison in Khunzakh on 6 February 1837. Even though the commander of the corps 'considered Aḥmad Khān's fears exaggerated and premature', he decided 'to take advantage of the favourable occasion and plant a firm foot in Avāristān'.[32] Less than a fortnight later instructions were sent to Temir-Khān-Shūra to start preparations for an expedition with a twofold aim: 1. 'To annihilate Shamil's influence', which 'was a necessary prerequisite for the maintenance of peace amongst both the pacified and semi-pacified tribes. . . . The best means to achieve this end Baron Rosen considered the destruction of ʿAshilṭa, the headquarters of the *murīds*'; 2. 'To establish ourselves in Avāristān.' While making the achievement of the first

Khunzakh

aim conditional on favourable circumstances, Rosen clearly stated that 'the expedition into Avāristān was to be carried out by hook or by crook'[33]

Faesy was nominated to head the expedition.[34] Arriving in Temir-Khān-Shūra on 13 May, Faesy left on the 19th with 4,899 infantrymen, 343 Cossacks, 18 guns and 4 mortars. 'Marching on a roundabout route under the greatest difficulties by a road that for the most part had to be made for it', the force entered Khunzakh on 10 June.[35] Here the Russians stayed for six days, converting the old palace of the *khāns* into a 'citadel'.[36]

In Khunzakh, Faesy received information that Shamil, Qibid Muḥammad and Ḥājj Tāshō were in Ṭiliq, confronted by Aḥmad Khān and Muḥammad Mīrzā Khān. He immediately sent a battalion and some Cossacks with three mountain guns to reinforce them while he himself, on 17 June, marched out toward ʿAshilṭa. On the 18th he entered Anṣāl and his advance guard reached the plateau of Betl overlooking ʿAshilṭa.

On 21 June[37] the Russian force, depleted now to 3,000 men, advanced on ʿAshilṭa. It was met by the levies of Hindāl and Kunbūt about four kilometres from the village. A long and terrible battle ensued from terrace to terrace and from house to house.[38] Like in so many battles of Faesy (and other Russian generals) 'no prisoners were taken, which is explained by the obstinate nature of the defence and the exasperation of our troops.'[39] Next Faesy moved to Akhulgoḥ, and stormed it on 24 June.[40]

On 27 June, on his way back, Faesy was attacked by a newly gathered force under the command of ʿAlī Bek al-Khunzhakhī and Surkhāy al-Kulawi. In a 24-hour-long battle the Russian force was saved from defeat only by the arrival of three fresh companies recalled in haste from their way to Gimrāh.[41] Faesy was now forced to retreat to Anṣāl to replenish his force. On 1 July he returned to the plateau of Betl, whence he turned on 5 July to Ṭiliq, where the *imām* had been besieged for a month now.

Faesy arrived in Ṭiliq on 8 July, just in time to deter the levies of Qarākh and Antsukh from an attempt to relieve their *imām*. On 9 July the artillery arrived from Khunzakh and started to bombard the village. During the following days the Russians managed to capture a few buildings on the outskirts of the village. On 17 July, Faesy carried out a general attack. In a bitter day-

MAP 6: CENTRAL AND NORTHERN DAGHESTAN

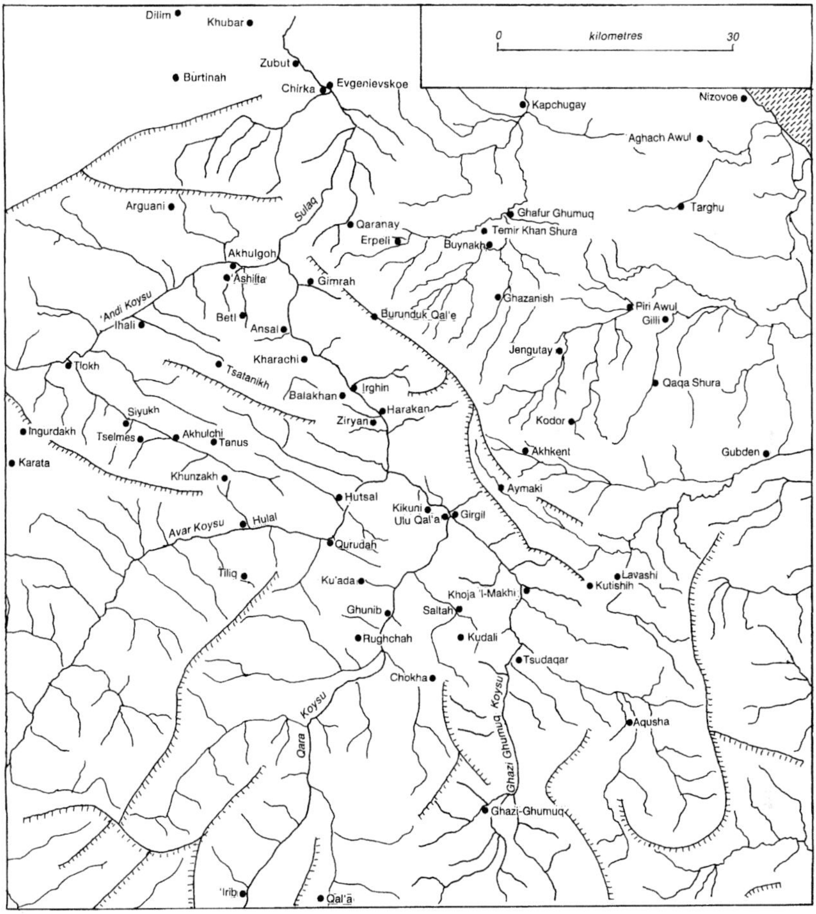

long battle the Russians succeeded in occupying the upper half of the village.

At that moment Shamil sent an envoy to negotiate a truce. On 18 July Faesy withdrew his troops from the village and concentrated them on the heights above it. The negotiations continued all that day and were concluded in the evening. According to a Russian source,

> Shamil [and the others] offered their submission and swore on it in the presence of delegates named by Faesy, signed a separate piece of paper [i.e. some kind of document] and gave them hostages, including Shamil's nephew. In addition, the *imām* sent the general a special letter. The terms in which this letter was couched were so strongly disagreeable to Faesy that he, already on the retreat from Ṭiliq, sent Muḥammad Mīrzā Khān, who had conducted the negotiations with Shamil on behalf of the general, to replace it with another [letter], *the tone of which would be more suitable to the relations between a Russian general and a leader of a crowd of savages*. When our column was already on its way back the commander of the column received a second, *corrected message* from the *imām* which, by the way, *differed little from the first document* . . .
>
> On 19 July in consequence of an intimation by Muḥammad Mīrzā Khān that the *murīds* could not make up their minds to leave Ṭiliq, as it were, under the muzzles of our guns, the column returned to Khunzakh by [the roundabout] way of the Kū'āda defile and the Qurūda bridge.[42]

On 24 July Faesy reported the completion of the campaign and the attainment of all its aims.[43] The truce with Shamil, or his 'submission', as Faesy called it, was presented in somewhat contradictory terms both as a big victory and as a temporary expedient to enable Faesy to construct the road from Temir-Khān-Shūra to Khunzakh and to stock in the latter all the needed supplies.[44]

The truth was somewhat different. 'As a matter of fact,' admitted a Russian source:

> [Faesy] was compelled to retreat by the total material disorganisation of the expeditionary corps, the enormous loss in personnel, and the want of ammunition. From the beginning of the campaign the force had lost in killed, wounded, sick and dead of diseases 4 senior and 26 other officers (including 14 company commanders)

and about 1,000 other ranks. The loss in horses had also been considerable and half of those remaining could hardly drag one leg after another. Of 10 mountain guns, 5 were rendered useless. Wagons, and even *ʿarabas* obtained from the natives for use in the mountains, were almost nonexistent. The troops had worn out their clothes and boots and went in rags.[45]

How desperate Faesy's situation must have been and how eager he had been to conclude a face-saving agreement can be clearly seen from the texts of his agreement with Shamil. The document signed by the *imām* has never been published, and has probably not survived. Its contents, therefore, can only be deduced from Faesy's report, according to which the *imām* again undertook 'to have to do with no one [*ni skem nichego ne imet*]'.[46] As for the letters addressed to him by Shamil the text of the first which Faesy did not like, is as follows:

> From Shamil, Ḥājj Tāshō, Qibid Muḥammad, ʿAbd al-Raḥman al-Qarākhī, Muḥammad ʿUmar-Oghlū and other honourable and learned men of Daghestan. Giving hostages to Muḥammad Mīrzā Khān, we concluded a peace [*mir*] with the Russian emperor which none of us will break, on condition, however, that neither side should do the slightest wrong to the other. If either side breaks its promises it will be considered as treacherous, and traitors are held accursed before God and the people. This letter of ours will explain the complete exactitude and fairness of our intentions.[57]

The second, 'corrected' letter stated the following:

> This letter explains the conclusion of peace [*mir*] between the Russian ruler and Shamil. This peace is marked by the delivery of hostages to Muḥammad Mīrzā Khān – on behalf of Shamil of his cousin, pending the arrival of his nephew; on behalf of Qibid Muḥammad of his cousin; and on behalf of ʿAbd al-Raḥman al-Qarākhī, of his son – so that this peace may be lasting, on condition that neither side does any wrong or treachery to the other; for traitors are held accursed before God and the people.[48]

The similarity between these conditions and those of the understanding of two years earlier is clear, and needs no elaboration. The only difference lies in the fact that this agreement was concluded openly and officially between the *imām* and a Russian general, which was tantamount to Russian recognition.[49] For Shamil, the lesson must have been clear: the stronger he was and the fiercer his resistance, the readier would the Russians be to come to an accommodation with him.

After Faesy's retreat Shamil sent the following proclamation to all the communities under his rule:

> Ye warriors of Daghestan! When the leader of the Russians sent forth his call to you in the month of Shawwāl [January-February] to seduce you from your faith in the truth of my mission, there arose doubt and murmuring among you; and many of you became unfaithful and forsook me . . . But with the few, they who remained faithful, I went forth against the unbelievers, slew their leader, and drove them away in flight . . . Ye have seen how small was the number of the warriors in comparison with the hosts of the enemy, and yet they gave way to us, for strength is with the believers. The Russians have taken Akhulgoḥ and have raised its walls. Allah permitted this to chastise you for your unbelief: for He knows all your projects and all your thoughts. But I mocked at the power of your enemies, and drove them from ʿAshilṭa, and smote them at Ṭiliq, and turned their deeds to shame. When afterwards the *pāshā* [General Faesy] with his great army drew near Ṭiliq to avenge the slain, and when in spite of our brave resistance, he succeeded in taking possession of one half of the *awul*, so that day after day we looked for the last decisive struggle, then suddenly Allah lamed his arm and darkened his sight so that he could not use his advantages, but hastened away whence he came . . . Verily God is with those who do His will! Ye have seen that though great the numbers of the unbelievers, they must ever fail. When they sent to Ḥamza Bek and summoned him to surrender, they said 'Lay down your arms; all opposition is in vain; the armies which we send against you are like the sands on the seashore innumerable'. But I answered them in his name and said: 'Our hosts are like the waves of the sea which wash the sands and devour them!'[50] Ye have seen that my words came to pass. But the looks of the Russians are falsehood, and their words are lies. We must destroy the works of their hands, and slay them wherever we find them, in the house or in the field, by force or by cunning so that their swarms shall vanish from the face of the earth. For they multiply like lice, and are as poisonous as the snakes that crawl in the desert of Muhān . . . Therefore lay to heart that which I have declared unto you, and be strong and hold fast together like the tops of the mountains above your heads . . .[51]

This oratorical masterpiece which plays so skilfully upon all the strings of the listeners, reveals how Faesy's expedition was perceived in the mountains; the capture and destruction of ʿAshilṭa and Akhulgoḥ – obvious reverses – were overbalanced by what were rightly seen as the victorious battles of the ʿAshilṭa Bridge (14 March), the Betl Plateau (27 June) and Ṭiliq (19–20 June). Faesy's retreat from Ṭiliq after having had the upper hand was regarded as divine intervention, another in a long series which proved God's special care for His chosen leader of His people.[52]

More important, this declaration and the two letters addressed to Faesy clearly show the *imām*'s suspicion that the Russians would violate the agreement. Faesy himself soon confirmed all Shamil's suspicions. All of August and part of September he was occupied in paving the road from Temir-Khān-Shūra to Khunzakh, in stockpiling supplies, and subduing some Avār villages which had not accepted the authority of Aḥmad Khān. Now, having finished his assignments, he wrote to Rosen:

> Even if Shamil had remained completely quiet, my opinion would still be that we should now, under any pretext, return to him his hostage in order to prove to him that we neither believe him nor [do we] need his submission, because as long as even one Muḥammadan tiny village [*derevushka*], in the Caucasus or in Trans-caucasia, remains unsubmitted he will not stop his efforts to propagate secretly or openly his *sharīʿa*.[53]

On 5 September, Faesy sent a proclamation to the different communities belatedly denying that Shamil had been recognised as their ruler and that the hostages had been given for them all. Faesy demanded that each community make its submission separately and send its own hostages.[54] On 9 September Faesy sent Shamil a copy of this proclamation and warned the *imām* that 'if he did not stop dissuading' communities from submitting to Russia, his nephew would be treated accordingly. Not waiting for the *imām*'s reply, two days later he approached Muḥammad Mīrzā Khān and demanded that he 'send to me Shamil's hostage. However', he assured his superior, 'I have not done it with an intention to punish him, only to scare Shamil and prove to him that we are determined'.[55] The lesson Shamil drew from this episode is obvious.

Rosen's report 'of the conquest of the fortified settlement of Ṭiliq, after which the Daghestani fanatic Shamil surrendered, taking an oath of allegiance to Russia and giving hostages'[56] created a great impression in St. Petersburg. The emperor expressed his wish that Shamil and his main collaborators – Ḥājj Tāshō, Qibid Muḥammad and ʿAbd al-Raḥman al-Qarākhī – 'be convinced to use the arrival of His Imperial Majesty to the Caucasus to ask for the favour of an audience with the Emperor, in order to personally implore his most gracious pardon, and offering with utmost sincerity [their] repentance for past deeds, to express [their] feelings of devotion as loyal subjects'.

Rosen, or Faesy, should in no way approach Shamil in the name of the emperor; rather the offer should be made in the name of either of them. The meeting should take place at any point, though preferably in Tiflis. In case of failure, a demand should be made to Shamil 'to agree to be sent to His Imperial Majesty as a proof of [his] sincerity and as evidence of his openheartedness in the oath he had taken.'[57]

Rosen transmitted the order to Faesy[58] who passed it to Klugenau.[59] The latter geared into action even before receiving Faesy's written instructions on 26 September 1837. On the 25th he sent a letter to Shamil. Reminding the *imām* that 'I always gave you good advice both for you personally and the mountaineers', Klugenau stated that 'now I would like to consolidate forever your prosperity; but how to attain it, that I can only tell you personally'. He offered Shamil to meet near Chirqaṭa on 29 September, reassuring him that 'you know that I have never betrayed my word, and therefore you may rest assured about your [personal] safety'.[60]

Since the matter concerned also Ḥājj Tāshō, Qibid Muḥammad and ʿAbd al-Raḥman al-Qarākhī, Klugenau asked Shamil to notify them, attaching a free pass for the messengers through Avāristān. Shamil accepted the invitation but postponed the proposed meeting by a day, to which Klugenau hastened to agree.[61]

In the meeting, Klugenau spoke 'long and earnestly', 'exerting all his powers of persuasion, meeting all his adversaries weightiest arguments by others he deemed more weighty still, until at last it seemed that his eloquence was to have the desired effect'. Shamil 'clearly moved', told the general that he 'fully realises the truth and soundness of his words', but he could not 'give now an affirmative answer only because between him, Ḥājj Tāshō, Qibid Muḥammad and 'Abd al-Raḥman al-Qarākhī there is an agreement fastened by an oath to undertake nothing of importance without a unanimous approval'.[62]

Despite an incident at the end of the meeting which almost

caused bloodshed,[63] Klugenau 'did not lose hope for success, because during the negotiations Shamil's face had shown clearly [his] willingness to take advantage of the Russian suggestion'.[64]

Nevertheless, pressed by the approaching visit of the emperor, Klugenau sent Shamil another letter on 1 October. In it he expressed his certainty that the *imām* 'would wholeheartedly like to take advantage of the good luck which [Rosen] so graciously offers you'. He urged Shamil not to listen to contrary advice, and 'if the others are not convinced by your persuasion . . . come to me alone. If you cannot do it openly, do it secretly.'[65]

Klugenau received Shamil's answer on 6 October. In it the *imām* assured the general that he had consulted 'all the *ʿulamāʾ* and elders of my realm' trying hard to convince them 'how beneficial it would be for me to go to Tiflis'. However, 'they disagreed, expressed their displeasure, and finally, took an oath that if I really intended to go to Tiflis, they would kill me.' Therefore, he informed Klugenau, he was unable to come openly or secretly. However, 'with the exception of this matter, I shall carry out any command of yours, in accordance with our mutual trust'. Shamil implored the general not to blame him for his inability to oblige him on this matter and 'to postpone it, and order [me] to do anything else having to do with my welfare'.[66]

The messengers who brought this letter confirmed that Shamil had done everything possible to persuade his colleagues, but in vain. At that time, while the dispute was taking place, Shamil received a surprise letter from Pullo 'demanding, in case the *imām* was unable to come in person, to send to Groznaia two representatives to be presented to the Emperor'.[67]

This new development, according to the messengers, had both supplied ammunition to Shamil's advisers and served to arouse the *imām*'s suspicions. However, it seemed to have supplied Shamil with a solution, and the messengers were quite confident that he would send representatives to Groznaia rather than venture to go himself.

Klugenau, now hard-pressed – for the emperor had started his visit on 4 October, and after a short detour to the Crimea, was due back to the Caucasus on 10 October[68] – made another desperate effort. He sent Shamil a letter, 'written in the same spirit as the previous ones and instructed [the messengers] to tell him orally not to pay attention to the threats of insignificant people, but rather hasten to oblige [Rosen's] will, because his [i.e. Shamil's] disobedience will evoke the displeasure of the authorities and then all his followers will not save him from a severe punishment.'[69]

The answer to this was not delayed. On 10 October Shamil sent the following letter:

> From the poor writer of this letter who leaves all his affairs to the will of God, Shamil . . . This is to inform you that I have finally decided not to go to Tiflis, even though I were cut into pieces [for this], for I have oftimes experienced treachery on your [i.e. the Russians'] part, which is known to everyone.[70]

This episode demonstrates clearly Shamil's political and diplomatic skills and how superior they were to those of Klugenau. That Shamil had enough reasons not to go to Tiflis is quite obvious. First, he had enough examples of treachery by Russian generals, the most recent one being Faesy's arrest of his nephew.[71] Second he was offered far less than his minimal demand. Nowhere in the written letters is there an intimation that Shamil was offered more than a personal pardon. On the contrary, Klugenau's words 'having been given a most gracious pardon from our Emperor you will live anywhere you like' without the need 'to move around to look for haven among people unsubdued by our Government',[72] clearly show that the pardon was meant to be given to Shamil the person, not to the *imām*. Third, even if he was offered a pardon and recognition as a ruler, he could not accept it. It was relatively easy to recognise the tsar's suzerainty in secret undertakings and sealed and private letters; it was a different matter to do it publicly. Such a move would delegitimise the *imām*'s rule in the eyes of his own people and render him personally a traitor. Neither could a secret meeting with the Russian emperor do; it would not remain a secret for long.

Although unable to accept the Russian offer, Shamil could not afford to reject it either. He chose the obvious solution, favoured by so many past and present politicians. Pretending to regard favourably the suggestion, he said he had to consult his colleagues. Then, seeing to it that his colleagues unanimously opposed the proposal, he apologised for being helplessly unable to accept it, very much against his own will and inclination.

That Klugenau reported that Shamil's face reflected his willingness to accept the offer, only shows how good a negotiator (and an actor) Shamil was. That Klugenau regarded Pullo's intervention as the cause for his failure is natural. That Klugenau's superiors, like Iurov 47 years later, accepted his version only shows how grossly the Russians misjudged and misunderstood the Caucasian situation.

In fact, Pullo's letter might have rendered Klugenau's mission successful by supplying Shamil with a solution for his dilemma. It was Klugenau's last letter, or rather the explicit threat accompanying it, which seems to have triggered Shamil's final and angry refusal to come and meet the tsar.

Meanwhile, the emperor spent almost the entire month of October on his inspection tour of the Caucasus. The two results of this tour most affecting Shamil were, first, the dismissal of Rosen and the appointment on 12 December of Golovin as the new commander of the Caucasus, and second, the higher priority and urgency now given to the pacification of Daghestan and Chechnia. Offended by the *imām*'s 'betrayal' and refusal to meet him, the tsar decided to crush him with a mighty blow.

Chapter 10

Akhulgoḥ

Evgenii Aleksandrovich Golovin, a graduate of the University of Moscow, had had varied experience in both fighting and administrative capacities since entering the service in 1797. Past his prime physically and intellectually, but in general possession of his faculties, Golovin spent more than three months in the Archives in St. Petersburg to study all the files on the Caucasus.[1] Arriving in Tiflis on 31 March 1838, he soon found out that in the entire country 'the internal security was undisturbed only in the Christian parts'.[2] Among the main problems in the eastern Caucasus were the continuing state of warfare in Southern Daghestan, following the revolt in Qubāh in 1837;[3] the ongoing tension following an outbreak in 1836 of hostilities between Muslim Ossets and their neighbours who had converted to Orthodox Christianity;[4] and the consequences of the *shīʿī* uprising in 1837 led by a certain Muḥammad Ṣādiq [Mamed Sadyk], who had claimed to be the *wālī* of the hidden *imām*, and proclaimed *jihād* on the Russians.[5]

Daghestan and Chechnia, on the contrary, were relatively calm, which the Russians attributed to the success of Faesy's expedition.[6] Priority was, therefore, given in their planning to operations in the south. Only pending a successful conclusion of those operations were the Russians to undertake an attack on Shamil.[7]

Southern Daghestan, however, occupied the Russians' attention for the entire year. Faesy's expedition to the Samur valley in June followed the pattern of his campaigns in Chechnia and central Daghestan.[8] He was so 'successful' in 'subduing' the local tribes that in September he was recalled to quell there a new rebellion, this time engulfing Nukhwa as well.[9]

Thus with the exception of a single confrontation with Faesy near Karaṭa[10] and a minor Russian expedition in Chechnia,[11] Shamil was left to engage quietly 'in a double work of construction, moral and material, that absorbed every faculty, engrossed all attention, claimed every waking hour.[12]

The events of 1837 – the siege of Ṭiliq, the destruction of ʿAshilṭa and, most important, the placement of a Russian garrison in Khunzakh – had had a tremendous impact on Shamil and his colleagues. These and the subsequent threat of a renewed offensive by Faesy and the negotiations with Klugenau (and their outcome) convinced the mountaineers that a further Russian campaign was inevitable. Under this impression, many of Shamil's lieutenants suggested a migration (*hijra*) to Chechnia, from where they could operate more freely. The idea must have crossed Shamil's mind as well, but at a meeting of the *nāʾibs* and *ʿulamā*ʾ, he strongly opposed it. The decision therefore, was to stay in Daghestan and to fortify Akhulgoḥ.[13]

The choice of Akhulgoḥ was made for many reasons. It was an ideal place for a fort, and had been traditionally used as a shelter by the people of Hindāl. It was more or less equidistant 'to the possessions of *shāmkhāl* and the *khān* of Mekhtulī, to Khunzakh and to the Ghumuq plain. In one word, Akhulgoḥ could become a base of operations in any direction.' Finally, it 'was located at the very heart of Hindāl, the population of which had started to give in to the enemy.'[14]

In fortifying Akhulgoḥ, as in all his other preparations, Shamil implemented all the lessons of the previous campaigns. (How well he had learnt these lessons would be demonstrated in the campaign of 1839.) The fortifications destroyed by Faesy were now reinstated and extended. To the original fort of 'old' Akhulgoḥ the higher peak of 'new' Akhulgoḥ was added. Instead of the high towers which crumbled so quickly under Russian artillery fire, low, sheltered positions were built, camouflaged and protected by masses of rock. Ammunition and food were stored in Akhulgoḥ and nearby villages in readiness for a prolonged siege.

Other places were fortified as well, notably Irghin, which commanded the approach to Akhulgoḥ from the direction of Groznaia and Temir-khān-Shūra. The roads leading into the country were systematically rendered impassable. Finally, great stress was laid on increasing the forces at the *imām*'s disposal.

Outside his domains, Shamil was engaged in a major propaganda effort. This had the double purpose of increasing his authority and expanding his dominions and power, and arousing communities which for various reasons could not at that moment be incorporated into his area of control so as to keep the Russians busy and gain more time to complete his preparations.

Thus, at the end of 1837 he sent a letter to the elders of the upper *maḥāl*s of Qubāh calling them to 'take up arms and rise up against the enemy of our faith and traditions'.[15] In 1838 he bestowed the (honorary) title of *nā'ib* on ʿAli Bek al-Rutulī, the most prominent leader in the upper Samur valley.[16] In a declaration intended for internal consumption, Shamil boasted that after 'destroying' the Russian forces near ʿAshilṭa and Ṭiliq and forcing them 'to concentrate all their troops against me . . . I stirred all the Daghestani peoples, even those living beyond the Sambur [*sic!*] and further up to the sea.'[17] His influence on the events of 1837 and 1838 in Southern Daghestan, however, seems to have been marginal.

Shamil also tried to enlist the help of Muslim potentates. To this period date his first attempts to solicit help from Mahmud II, the Ottoman *sulṭān*, and from Muḥammad ʿAlī (Mehmet Ali) the *pāshā* of Egypt.[18]

The Russian authorities in the Caucasus were not blind to Shamil's preparations and his steadily growing power. Alarmed by his 'growing might' they concluded that 'it was necessary at last to take the most effective measures against him'.[19] Frustrated by the inability to act against the *imām* in other ways, Golovin instructed Pullo to try to find 'valiant men who for an appropriate financial reward will take it upon themselves to deliver to us the head of the rebel'.[20]

In the planning for 1839 priority was given for the first time to the Left Flank – two expeditions were planned in Daghestan, with only one effort on the Right Flank. Golovin himself was to lead an expedition into the Samur valley in order to 'finally subdue' its population, 'to erect a line of forts and by so doing to put once and for all a barrier to the spread of disorders from Daghestan into our Muslim provinces, and to open the possibility to freely operate in Daghestan'.[21]

The other, bigger, expedition was aimed at 'paralysing the rule and influence of Shamil in Northern Daghestan' by 'inflicting a heavy blow on his hordes on the battlefield, [by] destroying his formidable stronghold – Akhulgoḥ – and by fortifying at least one point along the ʿAndī Koyṣū in order to . . . hold in terror Kunbut and ʿAndī'.[22]

This expedition was entrusted to the new commander of the Caucasian and the Black Sea lines, Lieutenant-General Baron

Paul (Pavel Khristiforovich) Grabbe. Having spent most of his service in St. Petersburg,[23] Grabbe was inexperienced in Caucasian affairs and warfare. But he was extremely well connected in the capital and, more important, enjoyed the confidence of the emperor.

In Grabbe's interpretation of his instructions, the capture of Akhulgoḥ should be only the *coup de grâce* to Shamil's rule. It should be preceded by 'defeating the mountaineers wherever and whenever their hordes were met', no matter 'how dearly our troops had to pay for it'. Only by such successes would it be possible 'to impress the mountaineers' minds, to shake their trust in Shamil's might and invincibility and to destroy the foundations of his power in the mountains'. Therefore, he decided 'to seek encounters with the mountaineers'.[24]

The force was ready to move on 13 May 1839. In the meantime the Russian authorities tried to 'deflect the miseries of war'. Several 'devoted natives' were sent to 'persuade Shamil to humble [*smiritsia*]', i.e. to surrender. No wonder that the *imām*, after arresting the messengers, released them with the warning that in the future he 'would hang anyone who dared to undertake such a mission'.[25] Shamil was, thus, given due warning.

Even without the above attempt, Shamil was well aware of the impending campaign and took countermeasures. He 'trumpeted that the Russians' entry into the valley of the ʿAndī Koyṣū would become their certain destruction, that the column would be surrounded, cut off and deprived of all the means of supplies'.[26]

His actions indicated that this was not mere propaganda. First he intended to pursue tactics of 'scorched earth'. All the villages on the Russians' route of advance would be found empty of population and bare of food.[27] Ḥājj Tāshō, operating in Chechnia, was reinforced and given the task of engaging the Russian column from its flank and rear, cutting it off from its base and at the same time of invading the Ghumuq plains.[28] Thus, the Russian troops would be completely dependent for their supplies on their bases, and these would be cut off, or at least heavily harassed.

In view of this threat, Grabbe had to change his plans and move now against Ḥājj Tāshō first. His week-long (21–27 May) 'search for Ḥājj Tāshō'[29] achieved, in fact, nothing, and on 2 June Grabbe started his campaign against Shamil,[30] with no information at all about the force facing him.[31]

On 5 June, near Burtinah [Burtunai], the Russians observed

Shamil with his force 'in a flanking position from which he could threaten the rear of the Russian force if it advanced. Disregarding the strength of the position . . . General Grabbe without hesitating, decided upon an immediate frontal attack on the enemy: to leave him unattacked – would have meant to disclose at the very first encounter a weakness in the mountaineers' eyes, to encourage them, and to leave Burtinah unpunished'.[32] The Russians stormed the position and found Burtinah empty and burnt.

During the following six days the force advanced slowly, having literally to cut or blast a road out of solid rock. A fort was built to serve as base of operations and called Udachnoe (Successful). On 11 June the Russians arrived at Irghin, where Shamil now awaited them with a large force.[33]

The Russians 'had to take possession of the *awul* at any cost, because any retreat across the mountains whose peaks were occupied by crowds of mountaineers, had become impossible'.[34] Grabbe tried to storm the village immediately upon his arrival there, i.e. on 11 June in the afternoon, but was repulsed. 'In [his] report, this attack was named a mere reconnaissance patrol'[35] – a euphemism quite commonly used by generals. The fighting continued almost uninterrupted for two more days, until the village was finally conquered. It was heavy and bitter and caused considerable losses on both sides.[36]

Thus, the preliminary stage of the expedition was over. Grabbe overcame Shamil's defences and the way to Akhulgoḥ – to where the *imām* now retreated, though not without leaving a few *nā'ibs* outside – lay open. However, this success proved soon enough to be (as the entire expedition would) a Pyrrhic victory. The Russians now found themselves cut off from both Vnezapnaia and Udachnoe and unable to meet the force escorting the provisions from Temir-khān-Shūra. For the next ten days the force had to literally cut its way through to the ʿAndī Koyṣū and then to bridge it. When communications were finally established and provisions arrived, the troops were on 'the last biscuit'.[37]

On 24 June the force crossed the ʿAndī Koyṣū and the 80-day siege of Akhulgoḥ began. 'Soon, however [Grabbe] became convinced of the difficulty to take possession of Shamil's last shelter, the more so because his force had already suffered in the previous actions a considerable loss of men; yet to withdraw without taking possession of [Akhulgoḥ] would have meant to lose the fruits of hard won successes'.[38]

In fact, both sides were now under partial siege; on the one

MAP 7: GRABBE'S CAMPAIGN, 1839

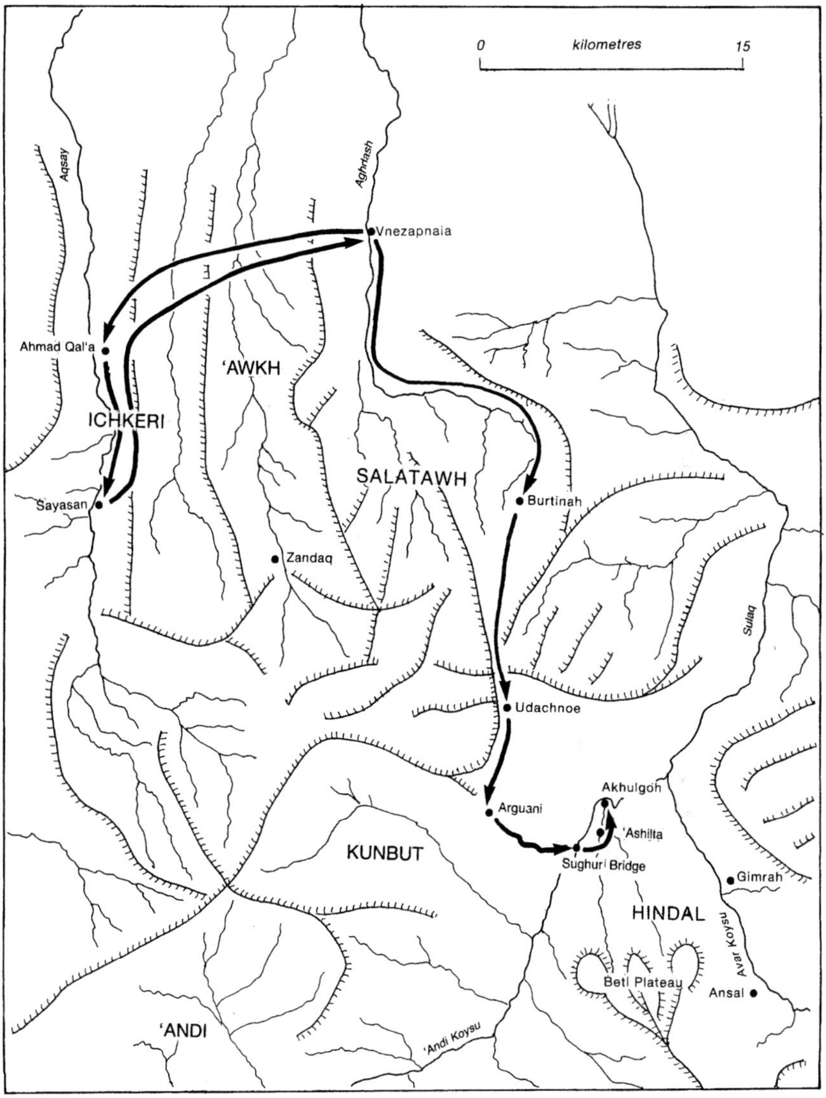

hand Grabbe had not enough manpower to lay a full siege and had to withdraw his force from the left (western) bank of the ʿAndī Koyṣū, which enabled Shamil to bridge the river with a few planks and maintain uninterrupted communications with his *nāʾibs* outside. On the other hand, the Russians' only supply route, from Temir-Khān-Shūra, had both to be cut through and constantly guarded against frequent raids. Soon a shortage in supplies began to be felt in Grabbe's camp. Especially acute was the shortage in artillery shells and bombs, because the outstanding quality of the fortifications of Akhulgoḥ forced the Russians into massive bombardments in order to achieve any effect at all.

In the meantime Shamil did not remain passive. After the fall of Irghin he had despatched three *nāʾibs* to raise forces. The newly gathered force – 1,560-strong – was placed under the command of Akhbirdi Muḥammad. In co-ordination with the *imām*,[39] this *nāʾib* raided the Russian camp on the night of 30 June – 1 July. He moved 'almost under the eyes' of the *shāmkhāl*, and entrenched himself in ʿAshilṭa. The *nāʾib* thus 'suddenly appeared at the rear of the besieging force from the very same side which had been thought to be secure'.[40]

Had Akhbirdi Muḥammad attacked immediately, 'it is possible that he might have inflicted a serious if not fatal reverse on the Russians', because they 'were occupied in making a reconnaissance in force of Shamil's stronghold, and the headquarters staff remained for the moment almost unprotected'.[41] As it happened, he attacked in the morning and was repelled towards the bridge of Sughūr.

Here he posed a constant threat to the Russians and Grabbe had to take almost half his troops off the siege on 4 July and push Akhbirdi Muḥammad to the other bank of the ʿAndī Koyṣū On that very night, before Grabbe's return, Shamil carried out a sortie against the besieging force and destroyed some of the works.

The rock formation of Akhulgoḥ resembles a square, surrounded on three sides by the ʿAndī Koyṣū. It is divided by the river ʿAshilṭa into the small Old Akhulgoḥ and the bigger New Akhulgoḥ, which overlooks the former. Old Akhulgoḥ could only be reached from the village of ʿAshilṭa by a 'razor edged path', while access to the other part 'is barred, and the whole promontory completely dominated'[42] by Shulatl ul-Guḥ, called Surkhāy's Tower in Russian sources. It was defended by 100 of Shamil's best fighters commanded by ʿAlī Bek al-Khunzakhī.

Having failed to storm Old Akhulgoḥ, Grabbe now directed all his efforts at Shulatl ul-Guḥ. The first attack on 11 July was repulsed with heavy lossses to the Russians, but the second assault, on the 16th, succeeded after bitter fighting and with many losses. Now, Grabbe could tighten the siege, though he still could not occupy the left bank of the ʿAndī Koyṣū. Shamil was thus left free to communicate with his lieutenants, evacuate his wounded and receive reinforcements and supplies. These enabled him to carry out nightly sorties against the besieging troops, while his *nā'ibs* harassed the Russian supply routes.

On 24 July three battalions sent by Golovin arrived. This brought the total of the troops at Grabbe's disposal to 10,092 men, not including the militias.[43] 'Grabbe, instead of taking possession of the left bank' of the ʿAndī Koyṣū and by that action 'deny the enemy any contact with that side, as he himself had proposed earlier, used the new troops to storm, on 28 July, the plumb rock . . . . This enterprise, being based solely on the hope of somehow having success by sheer luck, turned into a total celebration for the enemy . . . .'[44]

A few days after the attack, when his own disposition 'calmed down' and the troops had 'forgotten the failure',[45] Grabbe finally decided to complete the encirclement of Akhulgoḥ. On 15 August the ʿAndī Koyṣū was bridged and the following day a Russian force took position opposite Akhulgoḥ. 'From that moment there was almost no place in Akhulgoḥ hidden from the fire of our batteries: there was no secure shelter for the women and children. Even the descent to the river for water was now under [our] fire.'[46] As the siege continued, the situation in Akhulgoḥ became more difficult, the exceptionally hot weather taking its toll. The Russians' lot was not much better. The force was weakened by diseases and food shortages to such an extent that the Cossacks and the native militiamen had to be sent back home.[47]

The full encirclement of Akhulgoḥ marked the beginning of the last stage of the siege, in which negotiations intermingled with fighting. Shamil had made his first attempt to negotiate on 9 July, a few days after Akhbirdi Muḥammad's and his own attacks on the Russian camp. Grabbe disregarded this overture.[48] The *imām* tried again on 5 August, after the failure of the Russian general assault.[49] This time Grabbe replied, offering the following terms of submission:

MAP 8: AKHULGOH

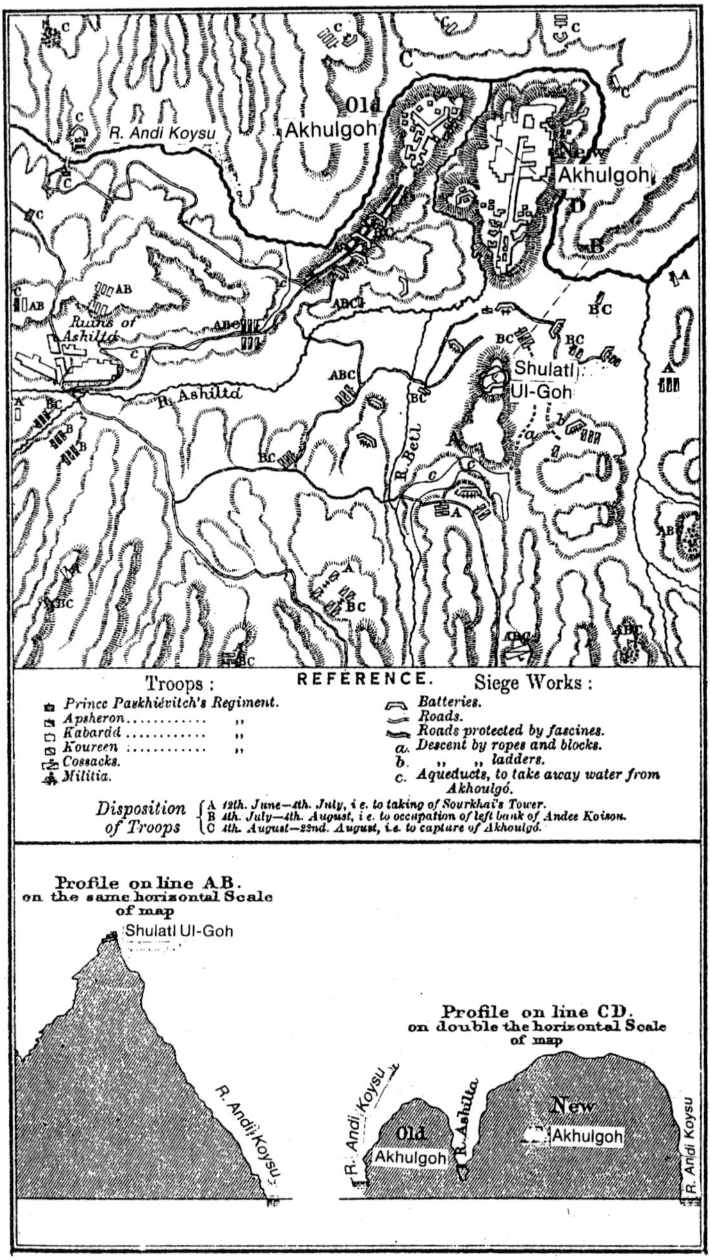

Source: John F. Baddeley, *The Russian Conquest of the Caucasus* (London, 1908).

1. Shamil shall without fail submit his son as a hostage.
2. Shamil and all the *murīds* now present in Akhulgoḥ will surrender to the Russian government; their life, property and families will remain inviolable; the government will assign their place of residence and [their] upkeep; anything else will be left to the magnanimity of the Russian emperor.
3. All weapons now in Akhulgoḥ will be delivered to the Russian command.
4. Both [parts of] Akhulgoḥ will be forever considered as the Russian emperor's land and the mountaineers shall not settle on it without permission.[50]

On 8 August Shamil's envoy returned with the *imām*'s answers, but was 'kicked out'[51] by Grabbe because 'he spoke in a manner which was indecent for a Russian general to hear'.[52] As for Grabbe's conditions, Shamil had counter-proposals. He would send as hostage one of his relations, but not his son. He was ready to send two more hostages, one hostage for each group of people from ʿAshilṭa and Chirkah present in Akhulgoḥ. And, most important, he demanded free passage out of Akhulgoḥ for everyone there.[53] Shamil's envoy returned on the following day, but was not received by Grabbe. The general demanded 'the surrender without fail, as a hostage, of his [Shamil's] son as a pledge of submission'.[54] The negotiations thus broke down.

On 19 August, three weeks after the failure of the first general storming, Shamil made another overture. Grabbe answered by demanding the *imām*'s surrender as a 'prisoner of war'.[55] This time, however, the negotiations continued. The following few days witnessed a series of cease-fires and negotiations between periods of fighting, with both sides taking advantage of the cease-fires to improve their positions. But neither side was ready for a compromise. The bone of contention was Shamil's refusal 'to surrender himself as a prisoner of war' and to order the garrison 'to lay down its arms'.[56] Finally, seeing that 'the negotiations were conducted in an Asiatic manner – leading nowhere',[57] Grabbe decided to break the impasse. On 28 August he gave Shamil an ultimatum: if by dusk his son did not arrive in the Russian camp, Akhulgoḥ would be stormed the following morning.[58]

On the morning of 29 August the Russians started their second general assault on Akhulgoḥ. After a few hours of fighting Shamil asked for a cease-fire. Grabbe, 'taking into account that the main storming column . . . was exhausted and . . . could not be replaced by fresh units, that there were still extreme difficulties ahead . . . and, finally, that the continuation of the attack . . . would cost us enormous losses',[59] agreed.

Shamil sent his eldest son, Jamāl al-Dīn, as a hostage and the negotiations were resumed. On 30 August Shamil met Pullo. An officer who was present at the meeting reported 11 years later:

> General Pullo offered to Shamil to temporarily live either in Russia, in Stravopol, or finally, in [one out of four villages] whose elders were famous for their loyalty to us. But Shamil resolutely disagreed, asking to be permitted to reside either in ʿAshilṭa . . . Gimrāh . . . or Avtiri . . . Of course, such conditions could not be agreed to, because this would not be the end of the rebellion, but a repetition of the mistake committed by General Klugenau in 1836 [*sic!*].[60]
>
> Afterwards, Shamil started a long argumentation, remarkable in its common sense, about the means which the mountaineers possessed to continue the struggle, about the difficulties ahead of us – our successes notwithstanding – about the services he could render us in order to pacify the country, and how convenient it would be for us to have to deal with a single person, and not with an embridled crowd. But, he had no intention at all to surrender into our hands.[61]

Shamil refused to go to the Russian camp to surrender there officially to the Russian general. As for his son, he insisted that Jamāl al-Dīn be kept in the custody of Jamāl, the headman of Chirkah. These issues and the question of Shamil's future place of residence, remained the bones of contention during the following two days.

On 31 August, the *imām* sent two letters to the Russian general.[62] In one of them he asked Grabbe 'not to demand of me' to come to surrender at that moment, and thus to spare the *imām* the humiliation of doing it in front of the Muslims surrounding Grabbe 'who have a fierce enmity towards me'. He promised to do it 'as soon as we start to disperse'. In the second letter, he asked to be allowed to live with his family in Gimrāh, where 'I shall be a simple resident, equal to all the others'. He also asked for a month's grace before leaving Akhulgoḥ.

Grabbe was not moved. To Shamil's 'Asiatic' letters he replied by demanding his surrender within three days, and suggested that the *imām* would be kept in Groznaia. 'We have not been amusing ourself in children's games with him, in order to end with almost no results', he wrote in his diary.[63]

In a last effort the general summoned Yūnus, the *nā'ib* who had come with Jamāl al-Dīn, and suggested to him to convince Shamil to surrender.[64] When the latter did not yield either, Grabbe, 'worried by the forthcoming cold rainy autumn, decided to waste no more precious time and to do away with Akhulgoḥ at any price'.[65]

Taking advantage of the cease-fire to reorganise and relocate his troops, he ordered to prepare for another assault. On 2 September the Russians stormed Akhulgoḥ for the third and last time, and in two days of desperate fighting conquered it.

The campaign of 1839 bears witness to the extent to which Shamil learnt the lesson of previous campaigns. At the same time it is a prototype of following campaigns, especially that of 1845 and the great sieges of 1847–49. Until the very final stage Shamil kept the initiative. Already at the beginning he compelled his opponent to change his plans and to attack Ḥājj Tāshō first. All the following engagements took place where and when the *imām* chose. Carefully preparing the ground beforehand, Shamil in fact dictated to Grabbe the route of advance in a manner calculated to cause the greatest difficulties and losses to the advancing army. The defence of Irghin, while not stopping Grabbe's advance, compelled him to pay a high price for its conquest and delayed his forward movement. During the further offensive the Russian army faced a real danger of starvation: indeed throughout most of the siege of Akhulgoḥ the Russians were no less besieged than besiegers.

In Shamil's strategy, diplomacy had an important place. Negotiations could lead to an agreement along the lines of those concluded in previous years. Alternatively, if the Russian force had not yet been weakened enough, negotiations could gain more time – something to be gained whenever possible. The longer the Russians stayed in the mountains, the higher the price they would have to pay, and if the campaign had been long enough, until the autumn, Grabbe would have had to retreat with no achievement at all. Accordingly, Shamil tried several times to start negotiations, the obvious claim by Daghestani sources that it was Grabbe who initiated the negotiations notwithstanding.[66] Characteristically, each of the *imām*'s overtures was made after a Russian reversal.

Shamil failed because of four factors. First, he stayed inside the besieged place. This lesson would be learnt and acted upon in the future. Second, the extraordinarily hot summer rendered the suffering of the besieged unbearable. Third, the Russians had learnt that anything short of the *imām*'s complete surrender would be, as in the past, a victory for him and a springboard for further expansion and strengthening. Fourth, Grabbe's strong will, determination and stubbornness, his readiness to pay any price without any sensitivity to the lives of his own troops and his inexperience in Caucasian warfare rendered him, at least partially, blind to dangers and threats. Like a bulldog clinging with his teeth to his prey and not letting go, Grabbe would not allow any thought of retreat from Akhulgoḥ.[67]

It is irrelevant whether Daghestani sources are right when they allege that the Russian general conducted the negotiations in bad faith, introducing his demands gradually and making them progressively harsher.[68] Shamil knew what the Russians were after. It had been repeated to him since the end of 1836. It was because he knew their demands and the fate of his nephew that the *imām* refused for so long to send his son as a hostage. Finally, unable to resist any longer the pressure of his confidants, he gave in and sent Jamāl al-Dīn to the Russian camp.

At that moment, when Shamil seems to have been overcome by shock and despair, and to have seriously considered giving up his leadership, the Russians were closer than ever before – and for many years to come – to a complete victory. But the same stubbornness which helped Grabbe to win, together with his vanity, stood in the way of such a victory. A display of tact and small, meaningless concessions might have brought Shamil to surrender. In the event, Grabbe's stubbornness served to stimulate Shamil's determination to go on.

After the conquest the Russians had to fight for eight more days in the caves, where many natives had found refuge. On 11 September, when all fighting ceased and all the bodies had been accounted for,[69] it became apparent that Shamil had escaped. Accompanied by his family and a few confidants he crossed the river on the night of 2–3 September, i.e. while the final attack was taking place, and made his way to Ichkerī.[70]

In spite of this the Russians were in a triumphant, self-congratulatory mood. Grabbe considered the matter 'finished':

> Even if the rebel, against all odds, succeeded in escaping, he enjoys no more trust in the mountains, no more haven . . . : nowhere can

> he find a place more inaccessible as his previous nest, Akhulgoḥ, or followers braver than those who have sacrificed their lives for him. His party is finally destroyed; his *murīds*, abandoned by their leader perished.[71]

The enormous number of casualties[72] was disregarded. So was the fact that Grabbe was unable to carry out the original plan to establish a fort on the ʿAndī Koyṣū.[73] No one paid attention to the fact that a Russian force was attacked in Chirkah and that Grabbe, 'unable to continue operations, because of the complete material disorganisation of the force', could only 'impose on the residents of Chirkah a fine which, by the way, they never paid' and 'dismissed the troops to their winter quarters'.[74]

With the influx of tribes submitting to Grabbe, 'the higher echelons of the local administration', were already discussing 'the correct division of these tribes, the appointment of Russian governors everywhere, and the introduction of an annual tax to be paid in weapons, with the aim to gradually disarm the population'.[75] These discussions and congratulations, however, soon proved premature.

Part 5

'The Rise of the Phoenix'

Chapter 11

Chechnia

By the end of 1839 Shamil was 'like a dropped rag; no one looked at him and no one approached him'.[1] By the end of 1840, 'all tribes between the Sunja and the Avār Koyṣū submitted to the iron will of Shamil, acknowledging him as an absolute ruler, and at a single gesture by him rushed in any direction [he pointed to]'.[2] Several circumstances, masterfully taken advantage of by Shamil, assisted this phoenix-like rise to power, not the least being misdeeds by the Russians: 'We ourselves co-operated with Shamil as only true friends could,' wrote Iurov in bitter irony.[3]

In 1839 the Russians considered the spirit of the natives finally broken. The execution of the plans for 1840, wrote Grabbe, 'will meet no resistance . . . No serious unrest, nor a general uprising, need be anticipated'.[4] The time thus seemed ripe to introduce direct rule into Chechnia. 'Inspectors' [*pristavy*], many of them natives who had served the Russians, were appointed to the different communities.[5] They settled in the midst of these communities and 'strictly watched the conduct of the villages under their supervision'.[6]

Soon enough the Chechens became acquainted with the 'benefits' of Russian rule:

> Under the pretext of collecting taxes and fines their best [belongings] were taken; it happened that completely innocent people were arrested because of a denunciation by simple and often ill-meaning translators; detainees and even hostages were treated inhumanly. . . during [military] expeditions forced collections [of food and livestock] were permitted.[7]

These acts of corruption, probably not greatly exceeding the usual norm elsewhere in the empire, were unbearable to the freedom-loving Chechens, who had not been used to any rule at all. However, a bigger Russian mistake followed when they started to confiscate firearms. Twenty-two years later, Shamil recollected that he had followed, 'not without satisfaction',

Pullo's attempt to disarm the Chechens and had awaited 'at any moment the secession of Chechnia which he had very well foreseen'.[8]

As noted above, weapons for the mountaineers were more than a practical necessity; they were their pride and signified their manhood and freedom. Weapons were handed down through generations from father to son, and were regarded as among a man's most precious possessions. Disarmament was, therefore, a terrible humiliation.[9] Naturally, the Chechens expected more and greater humiliations to follow. Soon the country was swarming with rumours about Russian intentions to press the disarmed population into serfdom, to conscript the men into the military and to force the women into domestic service.[10] A few 'careless words' attributed to Pullo had a particularly strong effect: 'Now that we have taken away their arms, we have only to take away their women's trousers.'[11]

Not surprisingly, villages in the mountains of Upper Chechnia which could not be easily reached by the army refused to submit and accept *pristavs*. In order to subdue them, the pacified villages were forbidden to have any contact with them. More specifically, they were forbidden to sell them grain and let them use the pastures, this being considered an especially effective measure because the crops that year were bad all over the Caucasus.[12]

The Russians afterwards blamed the 'extremely cruel, unscrupulous and often unjust' Pullo and his 'draconian rule' for the deteriorating situation.[13] Pullo was, however, clearly used by Grabbe as a scapegoat. Born in Odessa to a gentry family of Greek origin, Pullo entered service in 1805 and in 1834 was nominated to command the Sunja Line. He was convinced that 'it would be impossible' to subdue the Chechens 'by peaceful means and that the use of the force of arms should be the necessary and main way to pacify them'.[14] In this, however, he did not differ from his superiors. Furthermore, in all his actions he followed plans and instructions from them, especially from Grabbe, though one should not forget that he followed those instructions with extreme eagerness. Pullo's guilt consisted of his inferior rank, and his much humbler social origins than Grabbe, as well as his lack of connections in St. Petersburg.

'By March 1840 [there were] more than enough explosives amassed in Chechnia – only a spark was needed to cause a total explosion.'[15] This was supplied by two external series of events. The first was connected with the 'Eastern Crisis' of 1839–41, which involved the Ottoman *sulṭān*, Mahmud II, and the *pāshā* of Egypt, Muḥammad ʿAlī. In April 1839 the *sulṭān* ordered his army to cross the border into the domain of his nominal, but disobedient, vassal in an attempt to recover Syria and to avenge his humiliating defeat in 1831.[16] On 24 June the Ottoman army was overwhelmingly defeated by Ibrāhīm Pāshā, Muḥammad ʿAlī's son. On 30 June Mahmud II died. A week later the commander of the Ottoman navy sailed with the bulk of his fleet into Alexandria and joined Muḥammad ʿAlī. İstanbul, without an army or a fleet and with a 16-year-old boy as the new *sulṭān*, lay completely open to Ibrāhīm. The new crisis, involving, again, all the major European powers, was resolved only by June, 1841.[17]

The news of these events, often grossly exaggerated, did not fail to reach the Caucasus and impress its inhabitants. For the Caucasian Muslims, as for all their co-religionists all over the Middle East who had not lived under his rule, Muḥammad ʿAlī had become by then a popular and legendary hero and his figure had acquired semi-messianic proportions.[18] Among the Muslims of the Caucasus a strong belief was spreading that 'the victory of the crescent over the cross' was imminent,[19] and the Russian authorities were worried by the fact that 'our Muslim provinces bordering on Turkey' like 'all of Asiatic Turkey' were ready for a general uprising in favour of the Egyptian *pāshā* at the first movement of his son Ibrāhīm'.[20]

Soon, emissaries – real or self appointed – of Muḥammad ʿAlī appeared in the Caucasus carrying written and oral messages.[21] Two such letters were published in Russian translation. One, from Muḥammad ʿAlī to 'all the ʿulamāʾ and influential persons in Daghestan', ran as follows:

> I have by now waged war on seven sovereigns – the English, the German [obviously Austrian = *Namsawī*], the Greek, the French, the *sulṭān* [ʿAbd al] Majīd [Abdül Mecid] and others, who, by the grace of God, have completely submitted to me. Now I am turning my arms against Russia, wherefore, appointing Shamil Efendī as your *shāh* [*sic!*] and sending him two seals. I order you to yield him full obedience and to help me in my undertaking. At the same time I promise to send you soon part of my forces. Those who fail to carry out my orders will have their heads cut off, together with the heads of the unbelievers.[22]

The other letter, from Ibrāhīm to 'all the Chechen and Daghestani *ʿulamāʾ* and elders', stated:

> Since the lands which you inhabit belong to me by right of inheritance, I, believing in the one and only God, am stepping forth to assert my rights. I have under my command innumerable troops, and when I lead them at the end of the winter and the beginning of spring into the boundaries of Georgia, you are to assemble on the upper Terek. We shall endeavour together, conquer the provinces of Daghestan, take Astrakhān, Derbend and Anapa and shall drive the unbelievers out of the lands of Islam.[23]

Whether these and other such letters were faked or not, and whether the *pāshā* of Egypt intended indeed to invade the Caucasus – a controversial question to Russian officials and historians – are not important within the context of this book. What is important is that Muḥammad ʿAlī had the motivation,[24] the ability and the opportunity to stir up the Caucasus; that he used this ability to bargain with the Sublime Porte and the European powers:[25] that the Russian authorities, at least in Tiflis, were alarmed by this possibility; and, most important, that the letters made an enormous impression on both the Circassians and the Chechens, and thus contributed their share to the events in the Caucasus.

The second series of events that supplied a spark to the Chechen explosives took place in the Western Caucasus. The Circassians exasperated by the steady Russian advance into their territory, and suffering from hunger because of the bad crops and the Russian economic blockade, were driven to the verge of raiding *en masse* the Russian lines. Foreign agents were not slow in exploiting the explosive situation.

In Britain, which had never recognised the right of Russia to annex the eastern coast of the Black Sea, the attempts at the pacification of Circassia 'gave great opportunities to anti-Russian propagandists'. The Russian Empire 'seemed once more, as in Poland, to be crushing a people struggling to be free. In the process it appeared to be strengthening dangerously its position in the Caucasus and thus its ability to move against the Ottoman Empire, Persia or even India.'[26]

In 1834 David Urquhart, then secretary of the British Embassy in İstanbul,[27] visited Circassia and henceforth became active in enlisting British and European support for the Circassians and trying to initiate British intervention in the Caucasus. He and his agents, most notably Bell, Longworth and Spencer,[28] encouraged the Circassians to resist Russian penetration, promised them

British intervention and supplied them with smuggled weapons and ammunition.[29]

By the end of 1839 British agents were joined by those of Muḥammad ʿAlī in propagating news of the latter's imminent campaign against Russia and in calling the Circassian tribes to a common uprising.[30] These activities contributed to – though by no means could they be regarded as the main cause of – the following events.

On 19 February 1840 Circassian tribesmen stormed and destroyed the Russian Fort Lazarev on the shores of the Black Sea. Following this success other forts were stormed. The Russians, after a short period of complete surprise and confusion, reacted forcefully; reinforcements were sent to the Black Sea Line from the Crimea and by the end of November 1840 all the forts were re-established and fortified even more strongly than before.[31]

Still, these successful attacks caused immense damage to Russian efforts to subdue the Caucasus, and their consequences were felt for years to come. The news of the fall of Fort Lazarev and following events electrified Chechnia. It supplied the needed spark to set the country ablaze. All the Chechens needed was a leader – and such a person had been living among them for half a year.

Arriving in Ichkerī with only seven followers, Shamil settled in Gharashkitī in the community of Shubūt. Immediately following the storming of Akhulgoḥ and the *imām*'s escape, several *nā'ibs* displayed willingness to succeed him.[34] Three of these – Shuʿayb al-Tsunuturī, Ḥājj Tāshō and Jawād Khān al-Darghī – backed down as soon as it became clear that Shamil had no intention of giving up his title and remained loyal to him.[33] With their support he started

> to tame the residents of Gharashkitī. The *imām*'s modest work was crowned by unexpected results . . .: Rumours about his sagacity, his wise and just resolution of various quarrels and lawsuits spread in the entire area. The residents of Shubūt started to flock to Shamil asking [him] to teach them how to live according to [the Commandments of] religion and truth. The fame of the *imām* grew and spread rapidly [and] the Chechens who were under the administration of Russian *pristavs* could not but involuntarily compare Shamil's conduct with the activities of our administration, and once such a comparison had been made it, of course, proved

> to be far from favourable toward the latter. Then, the Chechens, led to extremities by our incompetence and abuses, decided to offer the *imām* . . . to head their armed rebellion.[34]

Approached by successive delegations from Lower Chechnia, Shamil initially declined to lead them, but at the end 'reluctantly' agreed. While agreeing, however, Shamil did not forget to take a solemn oath of absolute obedience from the Chechens and hostages from the most influential families.[35]

But, before being able to lead the Chechens, Shamil had to deal with another contender. Ḥājj Muḥammad Efendī belonged to an influential family in Aqsay and was the son of the famous Ḥājj Uchar Yaʿqūb, who had killed Generals Lisanovich and Grekov.[36] Reinforced by the title *ḥājj* (he had returned from Mecca in 1837/8) and by letters from Urquhart and Ibrāhīm Pāshā,[37] he now tried to establish his authority and to oust Shamil from the Argūn defile.[38] However, inferior to Shamil in personality, legitimacy, influence and power, Ḥājj Muḥammad had to come to an accommodation with the *imām*. This entailed, if a Russian translation of one letter can be trusted, Ḥājj Muḥammad being given the title of second or secondary *imām*.[39] Soon, however, Ḥājj Muḥammad disappeared from the scene. The last information about him mentioned his intention to go back to İstanbul.[40]

Accompanied by a strong party from the community of Shubūt, Shamil advanced from village to village in Lower Chechnia and was welcomed everywhere with delight.[41] Pullo marched out twice from Groznaia to 'keep the Chechens in obedience',[42] but his reported victories 'had no favourable results'.[43]

Soon Shamil and his lieutenants demonstrated that they, unlike their adversary had fully absorbed and implemented the lessons of previous years. Abandoning any attempt to make a stand at a fortified location, they now operated in classic guerrilla tactics:

> He threatened the enemy north, east, [west] and south, kept them continually on the move, dispersed his commandos to their homes, gathered them again as if by magic, and aided by the extraordinary mobility of mounted troops who required no baggage, nor any equipment or supplies but what each individual carried with him, swooped down on the Russians continually where least expected.[44]

These bands,

> establishing a new mode of operations to be consistently followed

> in the future, almost always successfully avoided pitched battle with our forces, thanks to their amazing speed. Our columns were [only] brought to extreme exhaustion by [trying] to chase them.[45]

With regard to strategy, the *imām* and his *nā'ibs* continued to operate in a manner traditional to mountain dwellers throughout history – what Ber called the 'Defensive-Offensive Strategy'.[46] This involved a tendency by the mountaineers to contain an offensive by their enemy in the terrain so favourable to them before counter-attacking the exhausted foe. Thus, the period under discussion can characteristically be divided into interchanging phases of containment and offensive, or to extrapolate Shamil's imagery,[47] into the workings of high and low tide. These phases, or rounds, quite short at the beginning, continuously grew both in time and space. The period of March–November 1840 can be divided into 13 such rounds. The detailed description of these rounds is, however, beyond the scope of this book.

At the beginning of April, Shamil divided Chechnia between four *nā'ibs* – Akhbirdi Muḥammad, Jawād Khān, Shuʿayb and Ḥājj Tāshō – and sent them to operate in different directions. Thus, for example, on 17 April Akhbirdi Muḥammad and Shuʿayb fought battles in areas as far apart as Naṣrān and Gurzul. By 26 April Shamil was in ʿAwkh, while Akhbirdi Muḥammad threatened Groznaia and Ḥājj Tāshō Vnezapnaia.[48]

Not alarmed by Pullo's reports, Grabbe's only step was to advance the departure to Groznaia of Lieutenant-General Galafeev,[49] the intended commander of operations on the Left Flank, instructing him to start earlier than planned the construction of the fort at Gurzul.[50] Galafeev arrived in Groznaia on 22 April, and during the following six months he divided his time between an attempt to construct the fort, and five expeditions in which 'he marched throughout Chechnia, sustained heavy losses, and achieved no results at all'.[51] One of his battles on the river Valerik, in which he lost 346 men, was immortalised in a poem by Lermontov.[52]

Writing several years later, Golovin accused Galafeev – and his superior, Grabbe – of choosing to concentrate on the construction of the fort in Gurzul at a time when 'immediate and most energetic measures were needed to quell the unrest in Chechnia'. This inactivity, he claimed, gave Shamil much-needed time to consolidate his power, so that when finally Galafeev took the initiative it was too late.[53] While it is true that Galafeev had shown extreme incompetence in some circumstances,[54] his inactivity was not necessarily to the Russians' disadvantage. Taking into account the fact that the Russians were ill-equipped, both physically and conceptually, to counter Shamil's new method of warfare, more energetic activity on their part, even had it been possible physically, might have caused them many more and bigger disasters.

While luring Galafeev into aimless marches in which all he did was 'burn simple huts and stamp fields',[55] Shamil hit in all directions. On 6 June Akhbirdi Muḥammad and Jawād Khān defeated a Russian force near Naṣrān. This resulted in 'the complete secession of the Galashas and the Qarābulāqs . . . , and the beginning of unrest among the Ingush'.[56] However, an assassination attempt against the *imām*, which confined him for 20 days to bed, prevented him from taking full advantage of this situation.[57]

In July Shamil turned his attention to Northern Daghestan. On 22 and 23 July the *imām* overwhelmed Klugenau near Ishkartī and Irpilī. Then, until the end of September, he played a cat-and-mouse game with the general.[58]

On 11 October Akhbirdi Muḥammad raided Muzlik, killed 22 soldiers and 6 civilians, wounded 19 soldiers and 9 civilians and carried away 11 women and children.[59] 'The news of [this] raid . . . painfully affected General-Adjutant Grabbe's heart.'[60] He now, finally, arrived at the Left Flank and took personal command. From 8 November to the end of that month he led two expeditions into Lesser and Greater Chechnia, with 'the same failure as before'. All Grabbe could do was 'to destroy those hamlets which had not been burnt by Galafeev', and to 'lose many people'.[61] On 30 November Grabbe reached Gurzul and dispersed the troops to their winter quarters. The late season and the total exhaustion of the men following eight months of continuous marching made it impossible to think of any further offensive.

Shamil's dramatically changed situation during 1840 is reflected in the following two facts. In September 1839 he had approached Grabbe and offered his submission together with that of Ḥājj Tāshō, Shuʿayb and 'the people of Ichkerī'. Grabbe offered him the same terms as in Akhulgoḥ and the negotiations were discontinued.[62] In October 1840 it was Golovin who intiated negotiations. He sent one of his aides, Lieutenant-Colonel Melik-Begliarov, to Temir-Khān-Shurā to enter into secret negotiations with Shamil. The essence of the offer given to the *imām* was the same as on previous occasions; Golovin hoped 'to convince him not only to [make] peace, but even to co-operate with the projects of the government'.[63]

Shamil's answer was given in no uncertain terms: 'If there is truth in the words of the Russians . . . , let them destroy the forts in Avāristān, Ziryān [Zyriany] and Miyartuḥ [Miatly] . . . and then we shall start to talk to them about peace.' Until then, he added, everyone who dared to bring similar Russian proposals would be punished by having his nose cut off.[64]

This was the last time Golovin tried to negotiate with Shamil. By mid–1841 he arrived at the conclusion that

> as long as Shamil is alive we have no hope for a voluntary submission [to Russia] of the tribes enslaved by him, the resistance will continue to the utmost extremes . . . We have never had in the Caucasus an enemy so savage and dangerous as Shamil. Owing to a combination of circumstances his rule has acquired a religious-military character, the same by which at the beginning of Islamism Muḥammad's sword shook three quarters of the Universe. Shamil has surrounded himself with blind executors of his will, and inevitable death awaits everyone who draws down on himself the slightest suspicion of a desire to overthrow his rule. Hostages, in the event of betrayal by the families they are taken from, are executed without mercy; and the rulers he has put over the different tribes of the Caucasus are his unswervingly loyal slaves and [are] induced with power of life and death. The suppression of this terrible rule must be our first care.[65]

Chapter 12

Daghestan

The retirement of the Russian troops to their winter quarters left the field to Shamil, and he did not fail to take advantage of this fact. 'During the entire . . . winter [of 1840–41] bands from Chirkah and Chechnia broke through across the Ṣūlāq and penetrated as far as Targhū; [they] drove away sheep and carried out robberies in the vicinity of Temir-Khān-Shūra; the communications of the latter with the Line were possible only under a heavy convoy.'[1]

Meanwhile much more significant events were taking place in Daghestan which considerably changed the situation. Foremost among them was the defection of Ḥajimurād al-Khunzakhī. A nobleman and a foster brother to the Avār *khāns*[2] who were killed by Ḥamza Bek, Ḥajimurād was among the assassins of the second *imām*. On that occasion his brother, 'Uthmān, was killed, giving additional force to his blood feud with the *murīds*.

An accomplished fighter and horseman, courageous and gallant, but quick-tempered, Ḥajimurād was a renowned war-leader whose tactical ingenuity was rivalled only by that of Akhbirdi Muḥammad, and a (if not the) most influential leader in the Avār Khanate. He played a crucial role in keeping Avāristān within the Russian fold and in defending it from Shamil's encroachments. Twice he ruled the country for a short while and twice he had to step down and transfer command to a Russian nominee – to Muḥammad Mīrzā Khān in 1834 and to Aḥmad Khān in 1836. Ambitious as he was, Ḥajimurād swallowed his humiliation and disappointment and remained loyal to the Russians, probably because his blood feud with the Naqshbandīs seemed to have left him no choice. However, things changed in November 1840.

Since the installation of Aḥmad Khān as temporary ruler of Avāristān, a personal rivalry had existed between him and Ḥajimurād, which had deteriorated into a feud. On 13 November 1840, Aḥmad Khān convinced the Russian commander of Khunzakh to arrest Ḥajimurād on suspicion of maintaining secret contacts with Shamil. Klugenau, upon receiving the reports, ordered Ḥajimurād to be brought to Temir-Khān-Shūra for interrogation. On 22 November under the very eyes of 40 soldiers and four officers, the Avar leader made good his escape and went to his village, Tselmes. There he found his house destroyed and his property and livestock plundered on the instructions of the Russian commander in Khunzakh.[3]

'For six years,' Ḥajimurād wrote to Klugenau, 'I had served the [Russian] government with zeal. Furthermore, I led you [the Russians] into Khunzakh. But you, forgetting my services, have done on the whole whatever you wanted.'[4] These lines reflected a widespread feeling among the local collaborators with the Russians.[5]

The Russians, like authorities in innumerable similar situations throughout history, were eager to lure the opposition. They were therefore showering them with gifts, pardons and titles. At the same time, those loyal to the government were felt to be 'in the pocket' and therefore too often neglected. They were furthermore asked to contribute to the cost and efforts of the occupation and administration of the country. Often these contributions were beyond their abilities. For all that, they could rarely rely upon the Russians even to protect them. Thus all the natives – pacified and unpacified alike – were clearly shown that resistance to the Russians was rewarded while loyalty to them was punished.

In the case of Ḥajimurād, he was 'rewarded' by his arrest, and – what was even worse – by 'humiliation inflicted upon me by an infidel on the staff of the commander of the citadel in Khunzakh' who 'dealt me strong blows and, in addition, spat at me'.[6] In these circumstances it was natural for Ḥajimurād to come to the conclusion that the Russians were after his head. The actions of the commander of Khunzakh pointed to it. Thus his bitter remark to Klugenau: 'I do not trust you [the Russians] at all, because I know positively that you dislike a brave man.'[7]

If Ḥajimurād's arrest could be explained as a mistake or misunderstanding, the following events were a succession of follies, which demonstrated that the Russians had learnt nothing in their dealings with the mountaineers. 'Extremely worried by Ḥajimurād's act of treason',[8] Klugenau tried to lure him back into the Russian camp, and engaged in correspondence with him.[9] It was, however, too late. No verbal promises would do, and deeds to rectify the wrong were not forthcoming. Furthermore, Klugenau's letters included too many threats of punishment if Ḥajimurād did not come to Temir-Khān-Shūra, which, as in the case of Shamil,[10] served only to irritate the recipient.

At this juncture Shamil dealt the Russians a master-blow. He sent to Ḥajimurād suggesting that they forgive and forget the past and join hands against the Russians and Aḥmad Khān. To the Avār leader, in his desperate situation, this suggestion must have been the only ray of hope. He went to Chechnia, pledged allegiance to the *imām*, was installed as *nā'ib* of Avāristān and in January 1841 returned to Tselmes to stir up that Khanate.[11]

Golovin, learning of the events, decided 'without fail to capture Ḥajimurād or [at least] drive him out of Avāristān'.[12] The command over this attempt was taken over by Major-General Bakunin, commander of the Imperial Artillery Corps in St. Petersburg, who was on a tour of inspection in the Caucasus. 'Assuming that my experience would not be without benefit,' he reported, 'I decided to lead personally the force storming Tselmes on 17 February.'[13] The attackers 'encountered strong resistance and suffered considerable loss'[14] 'with no substantive benefits'.[15] Following a successful storm of Tselmes on 9 April, Ḥajimurād moved to Tlokh and continued his activity with such vigour that later that month Golovin had to augment the force in Daghestan by four battalions.

Now, Golovin instructed both Klugenau and Schwartz – the commander of the Lesghian Line – to start negotiations with Ḥajimurād. Coming so soon after Tselmes, this was tantamount to an admission of failure and weakness and could not but result in loss of face and additional failure. The *nā'ib* answered Schwartz in a noncommital letter.[16] Klugenau's letter, on the other hand, was handed to Shamil by its bearer. This, and the fact that Aḥmad Khān killed three of Ḥajimurād's relatives who had been held by the Russians as hostages in Khunzakh, convinced Ḥajimurād that the Russians were determined to destroy him and, naturally, fed the fire of revenge in his heart. At the same time, this matter eliminated the only reason for him to engage in negotiations with the Russians. 'There is nothing left now to lure Ḥajimurād to return [to the Russian camp], but the open danger of losing his life,' he told Klugenau's messenger.[17]

The results of Ḥajimurād's defection were soon felt: 'By April 1841 Shamil ruled an area three times as large as in the beginning of 1840.'[18] In Daghestan, 'all the tribes, with the only exception of Koyṣūbū (Hindāl) and the Avār Khanate, were hostile to us'.[19] On the Left Flank, 'with the exception of villages situated under the barrels of the guns of our forts, only the Ghumuqs and a couple of Chechen villages remained in submission to us'.[20]

But worse still was in store for the Russians. Ḥajimurād was soon followed by al-Ḥājj Yaḥyā, the nephew of Aslān Khān of Ghāzī-Ghumuq and Kurāh and the son of Ṭāhir Bek. He had co-operated with Ḥajimurād in the past, and served twice as the regent of Avāristān for Aslān Khān and for Muḥammad Mīrzā Khān. Ḥājj Yaḥyā's importance lay in the fact that he belonged to the ruling house of Ghāzī-Ghumuq and that his two brothers, Hārūn Bek and Maḥmūd Bek, were the regents in Kurāh and Ghāzī-Ghumuq respectively in the name of Muḥammad Mīrzā Khān's widow, Umm Kulthūm [Umi Giulsum] Bike. Thus, Shamil could use Ḥājj Yaḥyā either to communicate with his brothers or as a claimant to the throne of the two Khanates. He was, thus, appointed *nā'ib* and, being a good war-leader, soon distinguished himself on the battlefield.

These two *nā'ibs* were soon joined by Qibid Muḥammad. Belonging to one of the two big houses in Ṭiliq, Qibid Muḥammad organised the slaughter of the rival family, a fact used by some Soviet historians to prove that the '*Murīd* Movement' was a 'class struggle'. Having joined Ghāzī Muḥammad, Qibid Muḥammad was one of Ḥamza Bek's lieutenants. He acknowledged Shamil as *imām*, but his obedience to the third *imām* left much to be desired. Now, having renewed his support for Shamil in the summer of 1840, Qibid Muḥammad started to act openly on the *imām*'s behalf. Soon he drew Golovin's attention. In July 1841 the Russian commander initiated an attempt to pull the *nā'ib* into the Russian fold, but it failed.[21]

In view of these developments, Golovin had to change his plans.[22] He had already secured in the winter the reinforcement of the Caucasian Corps by the 14th infantry division (16 battalions).[23] Now, by the end of May, he concentrated all the forces intended to operate in Chechnia and Northern Daghestan – 25,000–30,000 men and 70 guns – and advanced to Chirkah.[24]

Here, on the opposite (right) bank of the river he erected a fort during the entire summer. On 10 October the fort was christened in accordance with the tsar's orders, Evgenievskoe, after Golovin.[25] Meanwhile, Grabbe, after parting with Golovin, erected two forts at Kazākh Kichu and Zakān Yūrt, on the Sunja. Then, between 27 October and 13 November, he 'marched again through Chechnia with great losses and no results'.[26]

Concentrating all summer on the erection of Evgenievskoe,

Golovin completely neglected Daghestan.[27] Shamil's *nā'ibs* there did not fail to take advantage of this fact. While the Avār Khanate was repeatedly raided by Ḥajimurād,[28] the communities along the Lesghian Line acknowledged Shamil's rule and raided T'ushet'i and Khevsuret'i.[29] But most important, Qibid Muḥammad subdued most of the strategic community of ʿAndāl.[30] He achieved this by political means only, exploiting Russian blunders. This meant that Avāristān was now surrounded on three sides by the *imām*'s dominions and the stage was ready for his next enterprise.

On 8 October Shamil convened a meeting of his *nā'ibs* in Darghiyya [Dargo] in which his plans were finalised. At the end of October Qibid Muḥammad and Jawād Khān started a roundabout movement through the communities of ʿAndāl and Qarākh. Crossing the Qurūdah bridge over the Avār Koyṣū, they entered Avāristān from the east. Ḥajimurād, in the second prong of a pincer attack, entered Avāristān from the west. Klugenau, whose force had been reduced by sickness and death to 1,500 men only, 'was chained' to Temir-Khān-Shūra by the activities of Ullūbey and Abū Bakr [Abuker]. These activities 'cannot be regarded but as a diversion'.

> They give us a clear understanding of Shamil's plan first, and second, shed the most favourable light on his military talents as well as on the capabilities of those to whom he entrusted to carry it out. The diversion achieved a few targets at the same time. It diverted our forces' attention and Klugenau himself away from the main theatre of operations; [it] turned over our machinations to keep in peace Salaṭawh which we had conquered only a short while before; and most important, – together with the activities of Qibid Muḥammad and Ḥajimurād, [it] forced [us] to stop our military operations in Chechnia.[31]

Although 'our situation . . . could not be worse',[32] the threat to Avāristān was not carried out and both *nā'ibs* turned back. Sure that the danger was over, the Russians retired to their winter quarters.[33] But Shamil had other plans.

Towards the end of November the *imām* arrived in Daghestan. On 23 November Shuʿayb raided Qidhlār. 'On this raid the mountaineers, in addition to a huge booty, took away from us a cannon and, on their way back had the upper hand over Major-General Olszewski [Ol'shevskii] who wanted to cut off their [way of] retreat.'[34] Six days later another attack on Avāristān began.

A Russian force crossing the bridge of the Qarā-Koyṣū near Salṭū (*drawing by a contemporary artist*)

This time it was a three-pronged attack with Qibid Muḥammad advancing again from the east, Ḥajimurād and Jawād Khān from the west and Abū Bakr al-Irghinī, Ghāziyō al-ʿAndī and Tontil al-Karaṭī from the north.[35] The Russians' surprise was complete.

'We knew nothing of what had been happening around us until the very minute when the storm burst out.'

Like a goalkeeper in soccer facing a penalty kick, Klugenau realised that 'all he could do was to – march quickly forward . . . and counting on one's luck to guess the right direction and moment for an attack'.[36] Leaving Temir-Khān-Shūra on 4 December, Klugenau encountered extreme difficulties:

> The ice-crusted ground extremely exhausted the force and halted the march; the men hardly moved, the horses were injured; the axles under the ammunition wagons broke down, the cannons and wagons had to be dragged up by hand.[37]

Only on 7 December did he arrive in Moksokh to find that the storm had passed. Positioning the troops in a new order, Klugenau returned to his headquarters without seeming results. 'Avāristān and Hindāl remained exactly in the same situation as before his expedition,'[38] wrote Golovin. The Russians attempted to explain Shamil's retreat in both campaigns by enumerating different reasons – Grabbe's campaign in Chechnia; the fast of *Ramaḍān*; the exceptionally strong frost in December; and Shamil's serious illness. None of these reasons, however, is convincing.

As it seems, both offensives were more harassments than general onslaughts. The number of troops employed by the *imām*, especially compared with the numbers in 1843, indicates this clearly. Shamil must have felt that the time was not yet ripe to conquer Avāristān, because his forces were not strong enough for a decisive contest with the Russians in that Khanate. Accordingly, he intended to keep his adversary fully occupied and thus bide his time.

During the winter of 1841–42 his lieutenants kept up the pressure in all directions.[39] Daghestan, in particular, was in a 'persistent blockade'.[40] Communications between Khunzakh and Temir-Khān-Shūra and between the latter and Qidhlār were 'extremely dangerous', and could be maintained only 'with considerable convoys'. The movement of small forces was impossible.[41] 'This disorderly state of the country and the continuous alarms and attacks were far worse for us than a general battle, because it held us in constant tension and danger, in which we could not vouch for the safety of any enterprise.'[42]

On the last day of 1841 (Old Style), Klugenau reported that 'all I can do is to keep the mountains under physical control, when morally they are already lost to us'.[43]

With all my willingness to keep under control the country entrusted to me, I cannot vouch for my success, especially in early spring, before the troops destined for the campaign arrive, when the rebels will take advantage of the situation to cause us the greatest harm possible . . . I am not in a position to take responsibility for all the adverse results, which could happen to us in the future.[44]

Chapter 13

Ghāzī-Ghumuq and Ichkerī

'The results of the campaign of 1841,' wrote Golovin, 'were incomparably more favourable than the consequences of the expedition of the previous, 1840th year.'[1] How 'favourable' these results were could be seen from the mutual recriminations between Golovin and Grabbe, which started in the summer of 1841 – that is, in the midst of the campaign.[2] As the situation deteriorated during the winter of 1841–42, the tension between the two developed into a bitter quarrel. In St. Petersburg, the emperor did not see the desired 'results corresponding to the extraordinary means granted to the Caucasian Corps'.[3] Impatient for quick results, he rejected Golovin's plan of campaign.[4] He wanted an expedition to be mounted against Darghiyya – the residence of Shamil – and a fortress built in the defile of the ʿAndi Koyṣū.[5]

In the beginning of 1842 Grabbe visited St. Petersburg and agreed to lead this expedition. He was given an independent command to include all the forces of the Caucasian Line and Northern Daghestan. But in return he had to accept the direct supervision of the expedition by the minister of war, Prince Chernyshev.[6]

While Grabbe was away, Golovin removed Klugenau and appointed Faesy commander of Northern Daghestan. Although Golovin denied that he had appointed Faesy in order to allow him an opportunity to gain fame before leaving the Caucasus,[7] this was exactly how everyone, including Faesy, interpreted his nomination. On his return Grabbe immediately reinstated Klugenau.

Taking over on 18 February, Faesy spent the following two months marching to and fro through Avāristān. He captured a few villages, some of which were immediately afterwards recaptured by Shamil. It is obvious that Faesy was avoiding a serious encounter with the *imām*. Such an encounter would be too risky and might not reflect as impressively on his record as the easy seizure of a few central villages did.[8]

Meanwhile, Shamil attacked Ghāzī-Ghumuq, took the township on 2 April and the *khān*'s palace the following day. A rare document gives Shamil's official version of the event, as promulgated at that time:

> With trust in God, [His] slave Shamil to the valiant Chechen people, peace and God's blessing be upon you, Amen!
>
> I congratulate you with an event which Providence has allowed me to accomplish in Ghāzī-Ghumuq.
>
> With God's help I took with no difficulty at all the town of Ghāzī-Ghumuq – the mother of all settlements [*umm al-qurā*]. Five hundred prisoners, both infidels and [Muslim] renegades, the *khān*'s treasure, and the most precious local treasures are the trophies of my victory.
>
> The entire Khanate [*wilāya*] of Ghāzī-Ghumuq and the neighbouring communities up to Derbend itself submitted to my rule without resistance.
>
> The people of Aqūsha have entered an agreement with me and sent their *qāḍī* and honourable elders with bowed and guilty heads to negotiate. In one word, this campaign is overfilled with such miraculous events that the believers have a reason to rejoice while the infidels – to torment themselves in annoyance.
>
> I have taken 35 hostages from the rulers of Ghāzī-Ghumuq.
>
> Everything told here is as true as the language you speak.[9]

The attack on Ghāzī-Ghumuq seems not to have been a planned campaign, but rather a response by Shamil to internal developments in the Khanate. Again, a combination of local intrigues and Russian mistakes caused defections to the *imām*'s camp. Rumours to the effect that the *khānum* intended to depose Maḥmūd Bek, the regent of Ghāzī-Ghumuq, in favour of his cousin, and that the Russians intended to erect a fort in Ghāzī-Ghumuq, caused Maḥmūd Bek, his brother Hārūn and their followers to appeal to Shamil for help. The appeal was made through both Ḥājj Yaḥyā, their brother, and Shaykh Jamāl al-Dīn, with whom they had maintained contact through his nephew.[10]

Unable to refuse these appeals, Shamil invaded the Khanate, took control of it with no opposition and nominated Ḥājj Yaḥyā as *nā'ib*. A few days later Shamil headed back towards Avāristān where his main interest lay and where Faesy's force, still present, threatened his rear. The claim by Russian sources that Shamil's 'unexpected invasion of the Khanate of Ghāzī-Ghumuq . . .

exposed to a great danger not only Central and Southern Daghestan, but could shake the very peace of the Caspian province',[11] was therefore grossly exaggerated.

At the time, however, things looked different. All the Russians could spare at that moment were 800 men and two cannons. On 8 April, these, under the temporary commander of Southern Daghestan, Colonel Zalivkin, took position at the southern border of the Khanate of Kurāh. Encouraged by the fact that he was facing a completely passive adversary, and reinforced by 700 men and two more guns, Zalivkin entered the Khanate on 24 April. On 28 April he reached the capital, Kurāh, where he stayed put for another couple of weeks. When he tried to advance towards the border of Ghāzī-Ghumuq, however, he was checked near Richa by ʿAbd al-Raḥman al-Qarākhī, Qibid Muḥammad and Ḥajimurād, who had come to the assistance of Ḥājj Yaḥyā.[12]

Only on 22 May, seven weeks after Shamil had seized Ghāzī-Ghumuq, did the Russians concentrate a sufficient force – 2,500 men and 8 guns – to start their counterattack.[13] It was headed by the 'cunning, shifty, uneducated' Armenian colonel, Prince Moisei Zakhar'evich Argutinskii-Dolgorukii.[14] Spotted by Ermolov and sent to St. Petersburg for military studies in 1818, he returned to the Caucasus in 1827. In 1840 he was appointed commander *de facto* of the Samur Line.

Argutinskii entered the Khanate, and after a skirmish at Shawūkrah [Shovkra] on 24 May, entered Ghāzī-Ghumuq on the following day.[15] A few days later, however, Akhbirdi Muḥammad and Ḥajimurād arrived with reinforcements. They were followed by the *imām* himself with another force early in June.

Argutinskii was now put in a very difficult position. His communications with Qubāh and Derbend cut, he was squeezed between Shamil to his front and Akhbirdi Muḥammad to his rear.[16] On 13 and 14 June, Argutinskii had two inconclusive battles – his boastful reports notwithstanding – with Akhbirdi Muḥammad and Shamil respectively. That night

> Shamil, taking advantage of the darkness, fled in the direction of the township of [Ghāzī-] Ghumuq, in the citadel of which one company and all the load of the force had been left . . . Shamil's flight was in such a rush that by 7 o'clock in the morning he appeared in front of [Ghāzī-] Ghumuq and suddenly attacked it.[17]

On 15 June Shamil left the territory of the Khanate on his way north. Far from being a great victory for Russian arms as some

MAP 9: SOUTHERN DAGHESTAN

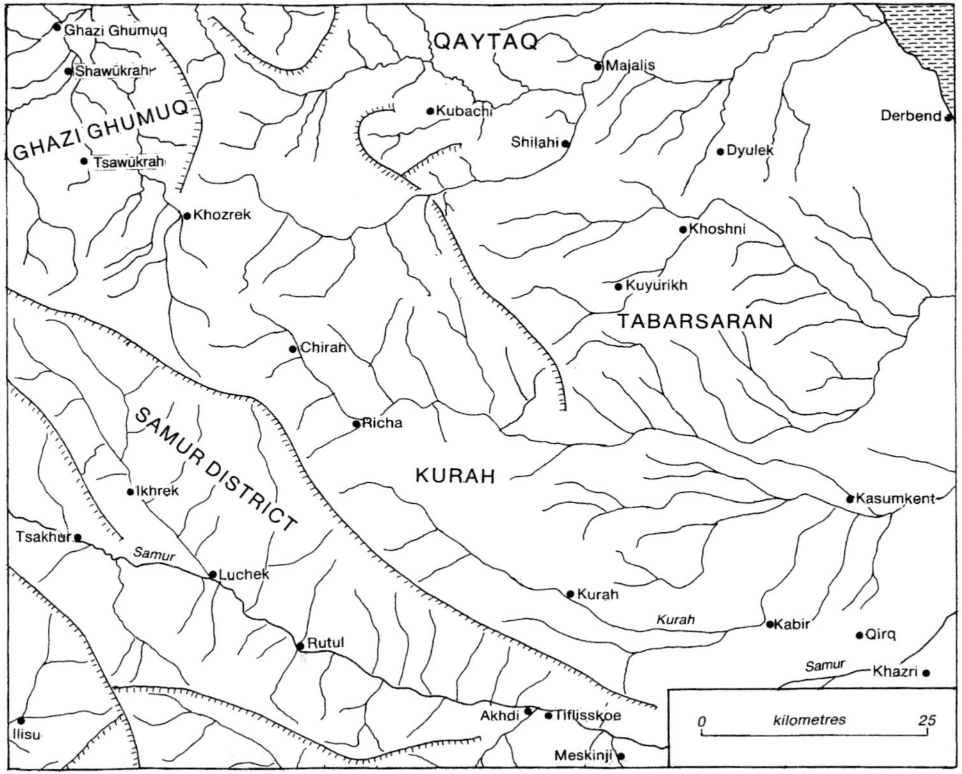

Source: John F. Baddeley, *The Russian Conquest of the Caucasus* (London, 1908).

Russian sources describe it,[18] Shamil's 'flight' was in fact in response to Grabbe's campaign in Chechnia.[19] Nevertheless, Argutinskii's position continued to be dangerous, especially in view of the adverse results of Grabbe's campaign.[20]

The affair of Ghāzī-Ghumuq was for Shamil a side issue, and his activities show clearly that he regarded it as a distraction from the main theatres of operations. The Russian estimates of the dangers of the situation in their later reports were grossly exaggerated, because Shamil could not afford to stay away in a side theatre as long as the Russians were in possession of Avāristān and threatened to cut him off from the centre of his domains. The affair, however, demonstrated again some of the weaknesses of the Russian army – slow reaction, passivity, lack of initiative and personal rivalries hindering operations. It also demonstrated the fact that there were quite a few 'soft underbellies' to the Russian defences in Daghestan. These facts would be thrown into sharper relief in 1843.

While Shamil was busy in Ghāzī-Ghumuq, Grabbe started his planned expedition to Darghiyya. Golovin described it in the following words:

> Grabbe . . . marched from Gurzul on 11 June up the defile of the Aqsay on the left bank of that river, towards the villages of Shūwan [Shuani] and Darghiyya, having under his command over 10,000 men and 24 guns . . .
>
> His intention was to reach Darghiyya quickly, destroy that village, then cross the range dividing Chechnia from northern Daghestan and subdue Kunbut and ʿAndī. It must be noted that he undertook this movement at a time when he knew already that all Shamil's forces had been directed against Ghāzī-Ghumuq, and when he might clearly see that by leaving Daghestan unprotected and abandoning Prince Argutinskii's small division to its own resources, he exposed the whole of that country to the greatest danger.[21]
>
> At the same time the very magnitude of the force he collected for this movement served to impair efficiency. He had with him, to carry his military stores and provisions, a large number of carts and some 3,000 horses. On the march this baggage train, owing to the difficult nature of the roads, covered a distance several *versts* and to protect it even by a thin line of soldiers took nearly half the column. With a couple of battalions told off for the advance guard and as many for the rear, and the rest broken up to form

the protecting lines on each side or help the train along, the whole force became extremely weak, having no man free to support the various units; besides which, it had to overcome very great difficulties, presented not only by Nature but by the efforts of the mountaineers, who quite understood that the march through the deep forests of Ichkerī gave them their only chance of success, and that once the column emerged from the difficult defile they would be unable to do it any harm.

On 11 June the column made only 7 *versts*, though no enemy was met. All that night rain fell heavily, making the roads still worse, and delaying progress to such an extent that up to the evening of the 12th after 15 hours' march, fighting all the time, the column had only made 12 *versts* more, and was forced to bivouac for the night on a waterless plain.

Next day the number of the enemy had increased, though according to trustworthy accounts it reached less than 2,000, owing to their main forces being with Shamil in Ghāzī-Ghumuq; the road was yet more difficult, barricades more frequent, and for the second day the troops were without water. There were already several hundred wounded, and the general confusion increased hourly.

In this way the column made only 25 *versts* in three days, and General Grabbe saw that it was already impossible to continue the advance. On the night of 12–13 June, abandoning his enterprise, he gave orders to retreat by the same road.

If the advance was unfortunate, the retirement was infinitely more so.

The troops lost . . . spirit; the confusion and want of control became extreme; no one made the proper dispositions, and no one troubled about keeping the column together. The retreat, which necessitated the abandonment or, when time allowed, the destruction of everything that could impede movement, if only to save the wounded, the guns, and perhaps some portion of the impedimenta, assumed the appearance of a complete rout; there were battalions that took flight at the mere barking of dogs. In these conditions the losses were bound to be excessive.

This picture, however sad, presented unfortunately the simple truth, without any exaggeration whatever . . .

At last, on 16 June, the Chechen column got back to Gurzul, having lost in killed, wounded and missing 66 officers and more than 1,700 lower ranks besides one field-gun and nearly all the provisions and stores.[22]

The impact of Grabbe's defeat was even greater because he faced only the local levies of two *nā'ibs* – Shuʿayb and Ullūbey.[23]

By the end of June Grabbe decided to launch 'a small campaign to show that the events in Chechnia have not deterred us'.[24] He marched on Ihalī,

> in an attempt to seize it, build a fortified ford and thus to secure our control over both banks of the 'Andi Koyṣū. The village of Ihalī, having been burnt by the residents, was taken on 8 July without any resistance; but staying there for four days and realising the impossibility to seize the ford . . . from one bank only . . . Grabbe, on the night of 10–11 July, set out on his return and reached Tsatanikh with a loss, in this fruitless attempt, that from its inception did not promise success of 11 officers and 275 lower ranks. The night retreat from Ihalī was accompanied by the same disorders as in the campaign in the forests of Ichkerī, while the enemy on this occasion, according to Aḥmad Khān of Mekhtulī, did not exceed 300 men.[25]

Soon afterwards Grabbe was released from his command according to his own request, and Golovin's authority was restored over Northern Daghestan as well as the Caucasian Line.[26] But not for long: on 7 December 1842 Golovin was replaced.[27] This signified among other things a change of policy.

Part 6

To the Peak

Chapter 14

Avāristān

On his tour of inspection in the Caucasus, Chernyshev discovered that 'there was no unity of command in the Caucasus and consequently no unity of action'.[1] While Grabbe obtained his independence from Golovin, Raevskii, the commander of the Black Sea Line, 'liberated himself from direct subordination to both', and so did many other local commanders. Accordingly,

> each commander had his own policy and conducted his own war. The minister of war, Prince Chernyshev [or rather, the emperor] was, of course, sure that he was holding all the threads of Caucasian affairs in his hands and directing them towards a definite aim; but who does not know what it is like to direct military operations from a distance of 5,000 *versts*?

Furthermore, 'the system of dividing authority did not stop here. Each local commander, if he enjoyed the trust of his superior, could conduct the war according to his own views.' The result was that many an officer 'let his instincts loose and turned the war with the mountaineers into a special kind of sport, aimless and with no relevance to the overall situation'.[2]

This 'sport,' – raids into the mountains – it was noted, 'turned in the final account to our disfavour' because they 'exhaust the troops by forced marches in the winter, and provoke the enemy by the cruelties and robberies' which 'unavoidably accompany' them.[3]

Grabbe's defeat in Chechnia, to which Chernyshev was witness,[4] dealt a shattering, though not final – at least not in the emperor's mind – blow to the concept of a victory by one effort:

> The operations against the mountaineers with large masses of troops do not achieve the government's aim of pacifying the mountaineers; on the contrary, the almost uninterrupted [chain of] failures boost the mountaineers' morale, while our troops get disorganised, exhausted and dispirited.[5]

Moreover, these annual campaigns were 'the main reason for that dangerous unanimity and unity of action, so uncharacteristic of the mountaineers.'[6] Therefore, second thoughts about the policy in the Caucasus appeared. As Chernyshev stated,

> the system of our activity, being based exclusively on the use of force of arms, has left political means completely untried. The English have been able to consolidate their power in India by political means. They, thus, preserved their forces and gained time in subduing that country. Should we not try this system as well?[7]

What Chernyshev meant by 'political means' was 'secret relations conducted adroitly and cautiously, and supported by money', with the different communities under Shamil's rule, and especially with some of his lieutenants.[8]

The emperor, who had himself been considering non-military methods of warfare earlier that year,[9] shared Cherynshev's view of 'the necessity to sow disunity' among the mountaineers 'by all the means at our disposal'. Political means were, therefore, regarded as a very important tool in achieving that aim, and their application could 'considerably facilitate the success of all our forthcoming enterprises'.[10]

To implement the new policy the emperor chose Aleksandr Ivanovich Neidhardt [Neidgardt], the temporary military governor of Moscow. Starting his military service in 1798, Neidhardt had had experience in military and administrative matters. More important, he was acquainted with ways of 'handling natives', being at one stage in his career the commander of the Separate Army Corps in Orenburg.[11]

Before leaving for Tiflis, Neidhardt was briefed personally by the emperor. In these detailed discussions he was told 'not to spare money' in order to 'draw to us some of Shamil's brothers in arms', to 'sow discord and contention among the others' and to 'reassure and encourage [both] the pacified and oscillating tribes'.[12]

To facilitate the new policy and to prevent any further disaster like Grabbe's, a two-year ban on campaigns and raids was imposed. Local commanders were told that in no circumstances were they allowed to take the initiative without previous and special permission from Tiflis and St. Petersburg.[13] The Russians intended to take advantage of this cease-fire to execute a large-scale reorganisation and relocation of their forces. This included rebuilding and improving many of the forts, erecting new ones and cutting through roads.[14]

In the political sphere, several attempts were made to contact Shaykh Jamāl al-Dīn and some of Shamil's *nā'ibs*, such as Ḥajimurād and Qibid Muḥammad.[15] But what seemed the most promising development was a new contact with Shamil himself. By the end of 1842 or beginning of 1843, that is, after both Grabbe and Golovin had left the Caucasus, Shamil approached Klugenau demanding the return of his son, Jamāl al-Dīn, given as hostage to Grabbe in 1839. Klugenau's answer was that such a demand could not be fulfilled. Shamil then approached Neidhardt. The latter reported the matter to St. Petersburg and was instructed to tell Shamil that his son was under the emperor's personal patronage and that the *imām* was welcome to send someone to St. Petersburg to see the boy.

In both Tiflis and St. Petersburg this contact raised high hopes as a possibility 'to persuade Shamil into voluntary submission'.[16] Since however, the Russians had nothing to offer to him personally (such as the return of his son) or politically (such as recognition of his authority in Daghestan and Chechnia), the *imām* discontinued these contacts.

The cease-fire, however, was more than welcome to him, since he was busy reorganising his forces. Without a threat of Russian expeditions he could concentrate on rebuilding his regular army, the *murtāziqs* and especially on establishing an artillery corps.

Absorbed in this task, Shamil kept quiet as well, with the exception of a few raids by the *nā'ibs*. The most notable of these was the attack on 24 June on Shatil, the main settlement of the Khevsurs, in which Akhbirdi Muḥammad was mortally wounded.[17] Akhbirdi Muḥammad's death was a great loss to Shamil, as further events would show. The period between August 1842 and August 1843 was, thus, one of almost complete calm in Chechnia and Daghestan. This calm, however, was not devoid of tension, since Shamil kept alarming the Russians by frequent large-scale mobilisations of his forces, accompanied by widespread and contradictory rumours about his intentions.[18]

By the end of August Shamil was ready to move. His preparations were completed and his forces ready while the Russian forces in Daghestan 'were broken up into small bodies, holding numerous poorly-fortified places, scattered over a vast extent of extremely difficult country seething with discontent'.[19] This dislocation of the Russian forces was partly a result of the constant raids carried out by Shamil and his lieutenants between 1840 and 1842. Whether he had intended to cause this dispersion of Russian forces or not, by 1843 he undoubtedly had grasped its significance. Also in Shamil's favour was the fact that, accustomed to his frequent mobilisations and false rumours, the Russians were now less attentive to his moves.

At the beginning of September Shamil concentrated his main force in Dilim, spreading rumours that he intended to attack the Ghumuq lowlands. At the same time Ḥajimurād and Qibid Muḥammad concentrated forces at Karaṭa and Ṭiliq respectively. On 8 September, after crossing more than 70 kilometres in less than a day, Shamil suddenly attacked Anṣāl. On that day, Ḥajimurād and Qibid Muḥammad arrived there as well. The village, which in March 1842 had betrayed the *imām* and handed over 79 of his men to the Russians,[20] offered stubborn resistance, since it could not hope for mercy.[21] But the odds were overwhelming. Shamil had at his disposal 1,040 infantry, 1,500 cavalry, 1,025 levies and three cannons (two of them captured from the Russians during the fighting). By 12 September Shamil was in possession of both the village and the nearby Russian fort.[22]

On 10 September, while fighting for the village, the mountaineers completely routed a hastily gathered force which tried to rescue Anṣāl. Out of 489 men only one soldier escaped to tell Klugenau the story.[23] On 13 September, receiving the news of the fall of Anṣāl, Major Kosovich, the commander of Kharachi, retreated to Balakin, contrary to instructions received only two days earlier to hold that fort until the last man. The village was immediately taken by the mountaineers and a Russian attempt to recapture it on 13 September ended in failure with 191 losses out of 600.[24]

Meanwhile, on 11 September, Klugenau arrived in Tsaṭanikh and concentrated there about 1,100 men. Now, after the fall of Kharachi, his communications with Temir-Khān-Shūra were threatened. Having to choose between retreat or advance into Avāristān, the general chose the latter option, hoping that by holding Khunzakh until the arrival of a relief force, Russian rule there could be preserved. On 14 September he left Tsaṭanikh and arrived in Khunzakh on the following day. Here he was under siege until 26 September, while Shamil conquered and destroyed all the Russian forts in Avāristān.[25]

In Klugenau's absence, Lieutenant-General Renenkampf, who happened to be in Temir-Khān-Shūra, took over command there.[26] But neither he, Hurko nor Freytag could do much to rescue Klugenau.[27] The only hope lay in Argutinskii. He, however, tried to avoid doing it and engaged in 'attempts to distract Shamil'. Only after receiving an explicit order from Neidhardt did Argutinskii move to Klugenau's rescue. On 26 September he reached Khunzakh after a battle with Ḥajimurād in Hutsāl.[28]

The combined force – 4,008 infantry, 2,066 cavalry and 17 cannons – now under the command of Klugenau, advanced towards Ṭānūs where Shamil's main force – 1,500 infantry, 1,900 cavalry and five cannon – occupied a strong position. Due to arguments between Klugenau and Argutinskii, the Russians limited their activity to an artillery duel, in which Shamil's guns, thanks to their better position, had the upper hand. At last, on 29 September Klugenau returned to Khunzakh.[29] Between 1 and 3 October Shamil evacuated the population, burnt the villages and then left Avāristān.[30] On the night of 11–12 October he raided Enderī and the nearby fortress of Vnezapnaia. Afterwards he dispersed his forces, telling them to be ready for another possible campaign by 1 November.[31]

Thus ended this round. Within 24 days Shamil had taken and destroyed all the Russian forts in Avāristān, with the exception of Khunzakh. The Russians had lost in killed, wounded and prisoners, 2,064 men, 65 of them officers, and 14 guns.[32] On 10 October Klugenau returned to Temir-Khān-Shūra and 15 days later Argutinskii retired to Ghāzī-Ghumuq.

The Russians had to decide now what to do with Avāristān, which had been left by Shamil scorched like a desert. Hurko, Grabbe's successor as commander of the Caucasian Line, thought that leaving a garrison in that Khanate as it was, empty of people, food and shelter, would put too big a strain on the troops and resources of Northern Daghestan. 'Educated, talented and personally far from being a coward', Vladimir Osipovich Hurko [Gurko] 'dreaded responsibility'.[33] Klugenau, under the influence of Lieutenant-Colonel Passek, his chief-of-staff, stated to the contrary that it was possible to hold to Khunzakh. If it was held to successfully until the spring, when reinforcements were due and offensive operations planned, Russian rule in Avāristān could be easily restored.[34]

Neidhardt tended to accept the view of Hurko, but St. Petersburg supported Klugenau's stand.[35] He thus reinforced Klugenau with 3,600 troops to complete his own units, and an additional six battalions, 300 Cossacks and six cannons. These forces were distributed among the different posts, and supplied with all their needs for the winter in a rushed operation during October.[36] 'Thus, apparently everything needed for the defence of Daghestan was done; unfortunately, the due attention was not paid to Girgil and Burunduk Qalʿe had been completely forgotten.'[37]

The Russians had many indications that Shamil planned a new offensive. Not the least of them was a series of ultimatums from various communities, some of which had until then been pacified. These demanded that the Russians evacuate Daghestan.[38] The Russians did not know, however, where he intended to deal his blow. Here again Shamil displayed his ability for deception. Concentrating his force at Dilim, as before, the *imām* again convinced the Russian command that he intended to invade the Ghumuq plain and on 3 Novemeber, Hurko left Temir-Khān-Shūra to the Left Flank. A raid by Shuʿayb on the night of 6–7 November caused both him and Freytag to rush to Vnezapnaia.[39]

On the very day when Hurko arrived in Vnezapnaia – 9 November – Shamil arrived in Girgil and invested the nearby Russian fort. Hurko now rushed back to Temir-Khān-Shūra, whence he and Klugenau hurried to relieve the garrison of the besieged fort.

On 16 November Hurko arrived at the range overlooking Girgil. He, however, hesitated to descend the difficult slope against a stronger enemy because that 'would be tantamount to dooming the force to certain destruction, without any benefit to the fort'.[40] Hurko thus convened a council of his senior officers – a clever device to avoid responsibility – which decided not to attempt a rescue, but rather wait until the arrival of Argutinskii and possibly Passek.[41]

Thus, for the following couple of days there was a stalemate: 'We did not disturb him [Shamil] from smashing the fort, and he did not disturb us from taking delight in his successes.'[42] On 17 November, Hurko received word from Argutinskii that he was unable to come. On that day the mountaineers finally overran the fort.[43] That night Hurko decided to retreat to Temir-Khān-Shūra. The troops were completely demoralised, and in the dark they soon became a panic-stricken mob.[44]

The fall of Girgil was like the breaking of a dam. The population of the lowlands, which had been in a state of unrest since Shamil's previous successes in Avāristān in September, now revolted openly and joined the *imām*'s forces.[45] On 20 November an advanced force of Shamil reached Targhū and three days later the *imām* entered the *shāmkhāl*'s palace in Ghazānish where he

MAP 10: SHAMIL'S CAMPAIGNS IN DAGHESTAN, 1843

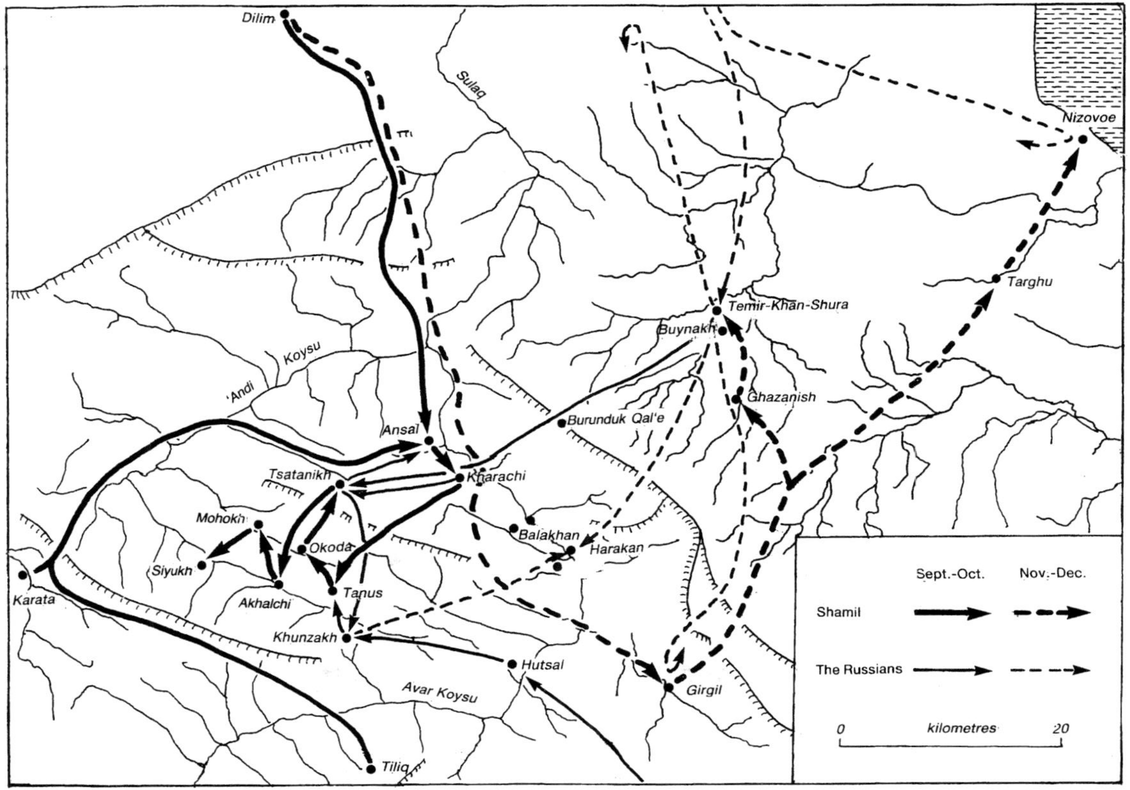

stayed for the following 23 days. On that day, 23 November, 'every Russian in arms in Northern Daghestan was shut up within the entrenchments at one or other of these four places' – Temir-Khān-Shūra, Nizovoe, Evgenievskoe or Khunzakh – and 'without outside help further disasters were inevitable, involving the loss of all Northern Daghestan'.[46]

Such outside help could come only from either Argutinskii, Freytag or both. Argutinskii was evasive as usual and arrived too late to influence the events. Freytag, for his part, could not leave the line because of the activity of Shuʿayb. However, as soon as Shuʿayb was recalled by Shamil to Ghazānish,[47] Freytag moved to Sulṭān-Yanghī-Yūrt and made, on 1–2 December, a quick dash to rescue the garrison of Nizovoe.[48]

Karl Robertovich Freytag [Freitag], one of the most brilliant generals in the Caucasus, entered service in 1820. Transferred to the Caucasus in 1838, he supervised the construction of the Lesghian Line, was given command over the Kiurin Regiment (1840) and over the Left Flank (1842).[49] He now waited for reinforcements. As soon as these arrived, on 19 December, he left Sulṭān-Yanghī-Yūrt and relieved Temir-Khān-Shūra on the 26th.[50] This was only the first in a series of moves in which Freytag saved Russia from great disasters.

On 28 December the combined Russian force, under the command of Hurko, left Temir-Khān-Shūra, relieved Passek, and all the forces returned to Temir-Khān-Shūra on the last day of the year.[51] Both rescues encountered weak opposition, because by then Shamil, his force 'fatigued by the long stay in one place',[52] evacuated the population into the mountains and burnt the villages.

The campaign was over. In fewer than four months the Russians had lost 2,620 men killed, wounded and prisoners (92 of them officers), 27 guns, 2,152 rifles, 13,816 shells (6,000 of which fell into the hands of Shamil), 35,000 bullets, 819 kilograms of gunpowder, 368 armouries, hundreds of horses, different tools belonging to artillery, engineers and commissariat, 12 (according to another count, 15) fortified places, which had been completely destroyed and, most important, most of the territory they had controlled in Northern Daghestan.[53]

The two campaigns of the autumn of 1843 – Shamil's most successful offensive operations – show the *imām* at his best as a military leader: a master of deception; in full control of his forces during the most complicated manoeuvres; realistically appreciating the balance of power and the advantages and disadvantages of both his and his enemy's forces; determined and confident in his moves, yet flexible in both preparing and carrying out his plans and quick to take advantage of his foe's mistakes.

Meticulously preparing his campaigns, he did all in his ability to ensure success before staging them. Shamil, thus, succeeded in surprising the Russians on several counts. First, the location of his first blow: twice he convinced the Russians that he was intending to invade the Ghumuq plains, only to attack in Daghestan. Second, the swiftness of his moves both towards the targets of his first attack and afterwards. Third, the large force which he concentrated in both his attacks. Using the strategic principle of 'moving separately and fighting together', his force was concentrated in different locations (thus adding to the Russians' confusion as to his aims) and moved simultaneously towards the same target. Fourth, the discipline and tactical skill displayed by his forces, due no doubt to previous training and preparations. Thus, for example, according to a Russian source, the mountaineers used 'almost correct' siege tactics at Girgil.[54] Fifth, the use of artillery by Shamil, for which the Russians were completely unprepared.

The Russians' surprise was the result of an intelligence failure on their part. As in so many similar cases throughout history, this was essentially a failure of analysis. The facts were known to the Russians – the numbers of Shamil's forces, their structure, the fact that Shamil was building an artillery corps and was even trying to cast his own guns – but their established view of Shamil and the mountaineers prevented them from deducing the right conclusions.[55] Thus the Russians' failure was not merely strategic or tactical, it was conceptual. They were completely unprepared for the kind of war Shamil was fighting.

All these, and especially the first appearance of artillery among the mountaineers, had a tremendous psychological effect on both Russian troops and command, causing demoralisation, confusion and paralysis. The loss of the monopoly the Russians had had in the use of artillery – the main factor ensuring the Russian supremacy in the battlefield – was especially important since it caused the loss of the sense of self-confidence. Thus, overwhelmed by the mountaineers' numbers, successes, surprising tactics and moves, and their use of artillery, Russian generals – Klugenau at Tānūs, Hurko at Girgil – dared not attack.

Fully appreciating the psychological value of a victorious first engagement, Shamil showed determination and stamina in the siege of Anṣāl and Girgil and disregarded the costs of their conquest. In general, however, he showed great flexibility in both planning and carrying out his designs. It is reasonable to assume that had the Russians not been deceived into believing that he had intended to invade the Ghumuq plain, Shamil would have done exactly that, or dispersed his men, as he had done on so many previous occasions.

Once in possession of the first victory, the *imām* took full advantage of it and of the Russians' mistakes. Not letting his foe recover, he moved swiftly in unexpected directions, fully exploiting his momentum until it died out. By the time the Russians gathered reinforcements and moved to the rescue of their beleaguered forces, Shamil had achieved his aims, completed the evacuation of the population and left 'scorched earth' behind him.

Shamil's retreat did not automatically re-establish Russian authority in the territories of the *shāmkhāl* and the *khān* of Mekhtulī. In fact, the Russian forces were locked in Temir-Khān-Shūra and a few other forts in a state of semi-siege. Communications with Derbend, Vnezapnaia and other forts had to be done under strong protection. The soldiers were allowed even into the village of Temir-Khān-Shūra only in groups.[56] In January Renenkampf led a column out of Derbend in a vain attempt to pacify the area.[57] A complete pacification of these areas was a matter of years, not weeks.

Chapter 15

Darghiyya

Back in St. Petersburg, the emperor was exasperated with the events in Daghestan. He lacked patience and failed to recognise the need for restraint and for the use of slow, long-term means to victory in the Caucasus. Now Shamil's successful offensive, ending the hopes to lure him into submission by 'political means', brought Nicholas's patience to its limit. Already after Shamil's first campaign, in September, the emperor decided to deal a decisive blow to the *imām*. For this purpose the Caucasian Corps was to fill its ranks with 22,000 veterans and well-drilled recruits. In addition, the Fifth Infantry Corps was to move to the Caucasus from its area of deployment in 'New Russia'.[1]

Shamil's second campaign increased the tsar's determination to make 1844 'a year of requital to the enemy for the Avār catastrophe'. It was necessary, Nicholas felt, 'to deal Shamil a few strong blows' in order to both 'satisfy the honour of our arms' and 'undermine his importance and influence in the mountains'.[2]

The emperor, therefore, instructed Neidhardt in no uncertain terms to 'enter the midst of the mountains', to 'defeat and scatter all Shamil's hordes, destroy all his military institutions, take possession of all the most important points in the mountains, and fortify those the retention of which may seem necessary'.[3]

This reverse to the 'one blow solution', however, did not discredit the use of 'political means' alongside the military moves, and the emperor called Neidhardt's attention to the need 'to attract to our side some of Shamil's supporters, *regardless of expense*'.[4] For this purpose a special budget of 45,000 *rubles* was set aside, to be used at Neidhardt's discretion.[5]

'The minister of war,' wrote the tsar to his general,

> will give you all the details of the operations you are charged with. Completely not constraining you, they will reveal to you my view of the situation and the means assigned by me to attain the desired end. It will be up to you to accept these considerations wholly or

> in part, but in any case do keep in mind (1) that from such gigantic means I must expect corresponding results; (2) that the operations must be decisive and conducted straight to the point, by no means getting diverted by side causes; and (3) that in no case have I any intention of leaving in the Caucasus the troops assigned to reinforce the Corps entrusted to you beyond the forthcoming December of 1844.[6]

In spite of this, the drawing and execution of the plans for 1844 were supervised very tightly by St. Petersburg.[7] Neidhardt, who objected to the 'one blow' approach,[8] had no choice but to obey.

The plans envisaged two periods of activity. In the first phase a complicated co-ordinated offensive was to be conducted by three columns – from Chechnia, Northern and Southern Daghestan – which would be assisted by two auxiliary forces – from Naṣrān and the Lesghian Line. These were to be commanded by Hurko, Lüders (the commander of the Fifth Infantry Corps), Argutinskii, Nesterov and Schwartz respectively. The aim of this offensive was to conquer ʿAndī and to establish there a fort. In the second phase, the forces were to construct 'forts and fortresses wherever necessary for the safeguarding both of the territories already in Russian power and those new acquisitions to which the Emperor so confidently looked forward'.[9]

The emperor was sure that 'the appearance in Chechnia and Daghestan of armies more numerous than ever before', should 'transfer [the mountaineers] from the world of dreams and fantasies to the bitter truth'. To reinforce this impact, he ordered the distribution of proclamations which stated that the forces concentrated in the Caucasus were but a small part of the tsar's armies, that nothing was intended against the religion, customs and property of the mountaineers, and that the Russians intended 'only to punish Shamil and the supporters of that deceiver, who out of personal interests, greed and desire for power, stirred the mountain communities, subjected them to all the miseries of war and burdened them with heavy taxes'. The proclamations went on to call on the mountaineers to chose between sharing 'an exemplary punishment' with Shamil or submission, which would bring them 'the emperor's pardon and mercy'.[10]

The difficulties in concentrating such a huge force and the supplies it needed were exacerbated by Shamil's transfers of population and 'scorched earth' policy.[11] The Russians were, therefore, forced to start their offensive more than a month later than planned. In the meantime, they carried out a few raids 'to keep the troops occupied'.[12]

Shamil, for his part, did not stay idle either.[13] On 18 March he convened a meeting of *nā'ibs* in Daghestan and stated his intention to pre-empt the Russian campaign by an offensive in Ghāzī-Ghumuq.[14] Although Shamil himself was unable to march in that direction, because of the murder of Shuʿayb,[15] his *nā'ibs* kept Argutinskii fully occupied.[16]

All preparations completed, the 'Chechen' force, under the command of Niedhardt, started from Vnezapnaia on 18 June. On 25 June it reached the heights of Khubar. Shamil who had held there a strong position, retreated and the Russians took it on the following day. On 27 June the force reached Gertme where it was joined by the 'Daghestani' force, led by Lüders.[17] On 28 June the unified force stormed Shamil's position near Gertme only to find that the *imām* had retreated again.[18]

Shamil did not intend to give battle at all. 'The Russians,' he said to his *nā'ibs*, 'have supplies for three weeks only. Here they will find nothing but grass. Thus, they will not be able to stay for longer than that period of time, after which everything will return to the *status quo ante*.'[19]

Indeed, a shortage in supplies[20] had brought Neidhardt to the conclusion that the target, ʿAndī, was unattainable. He therefore changed his plans. With the approval of St. Petersburg he now intended to advance from two sides on Khunzakh.[21]

Accordingly, the forces of Lüders and Argutinskii met in Aqūsha on 12 June, and immediately stormed Shamil's position nearby. The *imām* retreated again without giving battle.[22] 'Our forces, instead of pursuing the defeated Shamil,[23] stopped to rest . . . and when after a three-day camp [they] moved forwards, they found the bridges over the Koyṣū so strongly fortified by the enemy that all they could do was to stop and rest again.'[24] Thus the plan was finally abandoned. The first phase was brought to its end, and Hurko – the second prong in the pincer attack on Khunzakh – was recalled.[25]

Hence with the exception of Argutinskii and Schwartz, who conducted aimless campaigns,[26] most of the forces in Chechnia and northern Daghestan were engaged in fortification works. In the long term the most important Russian action in 1844 was the erection of Fort Vozdvizhenskoe (Elevated) in Chakh Kirī. This was done between 3 September and 1 December by Freytag and Nesterov, the commander of Vladikavkaz, against strong resistance by the Chechens.[27]

The lack of results of the campaign of 1844 was very disappointing to St. Petersburg. Unable to understand the difficulties in the Caucasus, officials in the capital and inexperienced observers tended to accuse the generals there of hesitancy and passivity.

> Neidhardt, Lüders and Hurko stand in front of the Caucasus like children in front of an entrance to a dark room, arguing who should be the first to enter the door and telling each other: 'You step ahead and I'll be right behind you.' But Shamil stands behind the door with a cracker, and knocks on the nose the one who dares [to enter]; in fright he jumps back, pulling down the others.[28]

Neidhardt, it seems, could not make the emperor understand that the goals he had set were unattainable, that victory could be won only through a prolonged war of attrition and not by one blow and that most of the local generals in the Caucasus (as opposed to those belonging to the Fifth Infantry Corps) shared this view.[29] The fact that both Lüders and Hurko tried to shed responsibility for the failure by blaming Neidhardt made his task next to impossible.[30]

In these circumstances, and unwilling to change the aim he had set in 1844,[31] the emperor came to, and acted upon, two conclusions: first, that the campaign could not be conducted from St. Petersburg and therefore more authority had to be delegated to the commander-in-chief in the Caucasus; second, that Neidhardt was unable to conduct such a campaign both because he preferred a different policy and because his character was too 'soft' to keep his authority among his subordinates.

Thus, on 8 January 1845 Nicholas replaced Neidhardt by Vorontsov, giving him the title of 'viceroy [*namestnik*] of the Caucasus and commander-in-chief of all the forces in the Caucasus'. Count Mikhail Semenovich Vorontsov,

> being the son of the Russian ambassador, had been educated in England and possessed a European education quite exceptional among the higher Russian officials of his day. He was ambitious, gentle and kind in his manner with inferiors and a finished courtier with superiors. He did not understand life without power and submission. He had obtained all the highest ranks and decorations

> and was looked upon as a clever commander, and even as a conqueror of Napoleon at Krasnoe.[32]

His greatest fame, though, was as an administrator. As such Vorontsov was the one who developed 'New Russia' (Southern Ukraine) economically and culturally. He made it into one of the most important areas of the empire and transformed Odessa into 'a third capital, in which, in many aspects, it was much more pleasant to live than in the former two [St. Petersburg and Moscow]'.[33]

However, Vorontsov had not held military command since the Napoleonic Wars and had no experience or knowledge of Caucasian affairs whatsoever. He thus took upon himself a heavy responsibility, much heavier than he had expected.

Vorontsov arrived in Tiflis on 6 April. Here he decided to reject the plans of the campaign prepared by Neidhardt, and to move in a single column.[34] On 8 May he left for a tour of inspection of the Left Flank and Northern Daghestan before embarking on the campaign.[35]

Meanwhile, Shamil had his hands full. The erection of Vozdvizhenskoe prevented the neighbouring Chechens from using their fields. In addition, its commander, Major-General Patton, conducted an active policy and raided the neighbouring communities. As a result, about 400 families went over to the Russians and were settled in 'peaceful' villages. The neighbouring communities entered into negotiations with Patton, and even some of the *nā'ibs* started to talk of the need to reach an accommodation with the Russians. Only by April did the situation in Chechnia stabilise.[36]

On 15 June Vorontsov started his campaign from Gertme with 21,000 men, 42 pieces of artillery and a battery of rockets.[37] On that day the force occupied the fortified position of Terengul, which had been abandoned by Shamil. The *imām* retreated to Michikal, where he blocked the road to Kunbūt. However, Vorontsov chose to advance through the much more difficult pass of Qirq [Kyrk], which had been left weakly guarded because the mountaineers had deemed it impassable for the Russian army. On 17 June, the advanced guard under Passek took possession of the pass and of Anchimʿer.[38]

On 18 June, Passek, without explicit orders from Vorontsov,[39] took position on Zunumʿer, about 15 kilometres from the camp of the main force. For the following five days, he was cut off by snowstorms from the main force, the soldiers without food, shelter, or proper clothing. By the time the force was relieved, 12 people had frozen to death and about 400 suffered from frozen limbs.

On 16 June, Vorontsov resumed his advance, with a force depleted by some 4,000 soldiers and 10 cannon.[40] The pass of Butsrah, otherwise known as the 'Gates of ʿAndī', was found abandoned. Contrary to intelligence, which had assured that he had intended to make a stand there, Shamil had withdrawn, evacuating all the population and burning the villages. Vorontsov's advanced guard, commanded by Klugenau, entered on that day the ruins of ʿAndī.

Vorontsov remained for three weeks in 'Andī, almost completely passive. This was something none of the Russian analysts could explain. During this stay the force experienced shortages of supply. The reasons for this were bad roads; the severe weather; the resulting death of more than half of the pack horses;[41] the desertion of many of the native horse drivers;[42] and, most important, the logistical incompetence of Vorontsov's headquarters.

Finally, on 17 July Vorontsov left ʿAndī a few days before the expected arrival of a large supplies transport, a fact that drew criticism afterwards. On 18 July he led a force of 11,500 men[43] and 16 guns into the smouldering ruins of Darghiyya. To do this, however, he had to overcome strong resistance in a forest a few kilometres from Darghiyya, in which the Russians lost 35 killed and 171 wounded.

> Thus, the main target set by the armchair strategists in the capital was apparently achieved. Shamil's so-called capital was occupied. But after the experience of that day many were forced to ask the same question: 'What is going to happen now?' Shamil [for his part] did not delay showing how much his spirits had been shattered by the occupation of his capital. As soon as the [Russian] camp had been pitched, enemy shells started to fall in it one after the other and forced [us] to change its location.[44]

On 20 July Labynstev, in order to stop this shelling, stormed the mountain across the river on which Shamil had taken position. The mountaineers dispersed, but attacked the Russians from all sides when they started their retreat through the broken wooded ground and fields of maize.

> The moment when the force, which had so gloriously driven off the horde of mountaineers, began to retire was, as it were, the turning point of our campaign. We felt this instinctively, and an inexplicable depression pervaded the army.
>
> One had to see how faces, that a few minutes before had been cheerful, became suddenly serious and sad.
>
> It was not the sight of 200 people killed and wounded which caused this depression – we were more or less used to that kind of spectacle – but undoubtedly the conviction of the uselessness of this loss.[45]

On 21 July a transport of supplies arrived at the other side of the forest through which the Russians had fought their way to Darghiyya.[46] Vorontsov decided that each unit would send half its men to bring in the supplies – another point to be criticised later. Commanded by Klugenau, the force started on 22 July, and had to fight its way through. In the forest, the mountaineers attacked the Russians from all sides, taking a heavy toll of killed and wounded. On 23 July, the scene was repeated when the force fought its way back.

The 'biscuit expedition', as this affair has been dubbed ever since, did not succeed in bringing any provisions at all. Instead it lost 556 killed (including two generals), 858 wounded and three cannon. Vorontsov's position was now critical. He was encumbered by 1,362 wounded; the morale of the troops was lower than ever before, and the mountaineers boasted that the infidels had no way out and all would perish.[47] Vorontsov had no choice but to move through the forest of Ichkerī towards Gurzul.

On 25 July, the Russians left Darghiyya, after destroying all but the most essential luggage. They had to fight their way through forests where the scenes of the 'biscuit expedition' (and of Grabbe's ill-fated campaign) were repeated again and again, each time with more catastrophic results. On that day the force made about 5 kilometres, losing 6 killed and 72 wounded; on 26 July it marched 8 kilometres, suffering 71 killed, 215 wounded and 8 missing; on the 27th it advanced 4 kilometres only, having 15 killed, 66 wounded and 2 missing; on the following day it made 5 kilometres, sustaining 109 killed, 365 wounded and 15 missing. That evening the force reached Shāmkhāl Birdī, about 15 kilometres from Gurzul, 'resembling a mare badly wounded by wolves'.[48]

Unable to advance any more, Vorontsov stopped, hoping that Freytag would come to his rescue.[49] Here the force remained with almost no food or ammunition and under constant fire. This was the state of the force when Freytag arrived on the opposite range, on 30 July before dusk. On the following day Vorontsov joined Freytag, but not without losing further 94 killed, 216 wounded and 23 missing. On 1 August the force reached Gurzul, and two days later the units – or rather their remnants – were sent to their winter quarters.

In this campaign Vorontsov's force lost 984 killed (including three generals), 2,753 wounded, 179 missing, 3 guns, a great sum of money in coins it carried, and all its baggage. The forces manning the positions on the route of supplies between Evgenievskoe and 'Andī retreated to that fort. The operations of Argutinskii and Schwartz which had been planned as diversions 'have been insignificant though inflated accounts have endeavoured to give them importance'.[50] With this hostilities ceased. The second half of 1845 passed in almost complete calm, with only a few small and insignificant raids in Chechnia and in Southern Daghestan.[51]

Severe criticism of the way Vorontsov led the campaign was voiced in Russian sources, especially after his death. Some of the points have been enumerated above. Other points included the fact that Vorontsov displayed complete ignorance of Caucasian warfare and was unwilling to accept criticism or even advice.[52] This resulted not only in the exclusion of many experienced generals from the campaign, but in the misuse of those who did participate in it.[53] If Vorontsov did accept advice it was from his inexperienced aides whom he had brought along with him, rather than from old Caucasian hands. Moreover, he was too 'soft' on discipline, allowing too many cases of disobedience by senior officers.[54]

Vorontsov brought with him a large entourage. Among these were many young men of good families from St. Petersburg and Moscow, who had come to participate in the final conquest of the Caucasus and win decorations.[55] These, with their numerous servants and enormous luggage of luxurious objects, both swelled the force with non-effectives, who in battle panicked and helped to create disorder, and burdened to extremes the logistical means, overstrained already as they were. Hence their nickname: 'l'armée de Xerxès'.[56] Furthermore, an antagonism soon developed between these newcomers and the Caucasian troops, which contributed to the lapse in discipline.

MAP 11: VORONTSOV'S CAMPAIGN, 1845

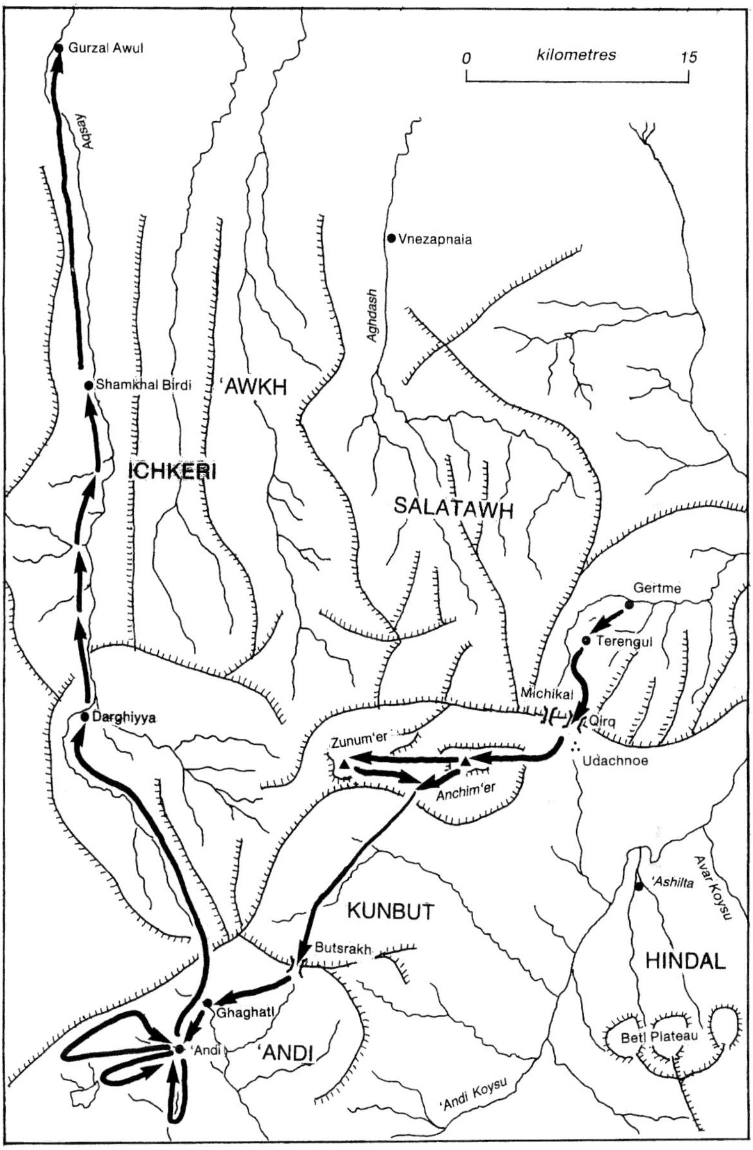

The great majority among Vorontsov's critics were ignorant of the fact that the military plane was but one facet of the expedition and that the campaign had another, more important, dimension.[57] As stated above, 'political means' were not dropped when the emperor returned to the notion of a solution by one blow. Rather, they were intended to be the very heart of such a blow. According to a document in the summer of 1844,

> the main aim of the general offensive is to assist all the tribes nearest to us, who according to our information *have already given their consent to rise against Shamil*, and to restore the communities which have been transported into the mountains, back to submission and to their previous places of residence, [all this] in order to weaken the volume of the general insurrection.[58]

Since 1840, when they had enthusiastically welcomed Shamil, many of the Chechens had become discontented with his rule. This was presented to the Russian authorities in an exaggerated manner by their native collaborators. Among those discontented with Shamil's rule, the community of ʿAndī occupied a prime place:

> It was a known fact that the residents desired our arrival and even demanded it. We, for our part, indulged in the hope that the secession of the people of ʿAndī would lead to the secession from Shamil of other peoples of Daghestan, who had been in the habit of following the example of ʿAndī.[59]

This is the reason behind the emperor's insistence both in 1844 and in 1845 on advancing to ʿAndī and on establishing Russian rule there. To the tsar (and his confidants), the proposed campaign appeared a possible short cut to the pacification of the Caucasus, which suited more his temperament. To attempt it, even if it failed, he felt, could do no serious harm; and if it failed, the slow method would always be there to fall back on. Vorontsov shared these views.[60] This is why he took it upon himself to carry out this *coup*.

On his stay in Vnezapnaia, during his tour of inspection, Vorontsov was approached by some Chechen leaders, including the *qāḍī* of Urus Martan. They expressed willingness to accept Russian rule if a force were sent to protect them. To verify their intentions Lüders was sent with a small force, but met resistance.[61] The reason for that, probably unknown to the Russians at the time, was that one of the persons involved warned Shamil of the plot, enabling the *imām* to take countermeasures.[62]

Neither this event, however, nor the warnings of local generals, first and foremost of Freytag, seem to have diminished Vorontsov's self-confidence. Nor did they significantly undermine his belief that such an attempt was worthwhile trying and could cause no harm.[63]

Shamil was aware of the Russian plan – though probably not of the full extent of their contacts – and warned the community of ʿAndī of it.[64] In preparing his defence, the *imām* drew upon the lessons of Akhulgoḥ, as well as of those of 1842 and 1844. He occupied a strong position in Michikal, counting on one of three possibilities: to deter the Russians, as he had done in 1844; to repel their attack; or to delay them. Once they outflanked him through Qirq, he withdrew quickly to ʿAndī.

At first he probably intended to make a stand at the Butsrah pass with the same aims in mind. But either reconsideration, or the discovery of the extent of the contacts of the people of ʿAndī with the Russians made him change his mind.[65] He now decided to abandon ʿAndī to the Russians, but not before burning all the villages and evacuating the people and supplies. By that he would kill two birds with one stone: the Russians would reach their target but win a hollow victory, and their line of communications would become vulnerable; and the people of ʿAndī would be punished for their treachery.[66]

Thus, when the Russians entered 'Andī, instead of a friendly country they 'found themselves behind bare cliffs covered by the smoking ruins of the peoples' houses'.[67] 'ʿAndī slipped away from us', wrote a participant with the benefit of hindsight, but 'only the natives and two Russians . . . understood the significance of this event . . . The majority saw nothing or preferred to see nothing.'[68]

It was probably at this stage that Shamil tried to negotiate with Vorontsov, but was rejected.[69] First, to Vorontsov and the Russian authorities the destruction by one way or another of Shamil was by now an axiom and they had ruled out negotiations with him. Second, Vorontsov and his staff had not lost hope yet of attaining their goal. Not only did some natives, who had escaped Shamil's evacuation, come to Vorontsov,[70] but a string of 'native emissaries resorted to his camp with assurances from day to day that the people would come forward from various quarters'.[71] Among these emissaries were several from some *nā'ibs* in Chechnia.[72]

While Vorontsov stayed in ʿAndī, Shamil went to Chechnia and obtained an oath on the *qur'ān* from the *nā'ibs* and their levies not to engage in separate contacts with the Russians.[73] Upon his return, he ordered Ramaḍān, the *nā'ib* of ʿAndī, to stop all (unauthorised) contacts between the scattered people of ʿAndī and Vorontsov. Ramaḍān caught three people who had visited the Russian camp, cut their heads off and displayed them with a notice warning anyone collaborating with the Russians of a similar fate.[74]

The heads were found on 13 July,[75] but no one at Vorontsov's headquarters paid attention to this. There, the hopes were still high to bring about the submission of some tribes.[76] Only Benckendorff, in hindsight, observed that 13 July was a turning point. Since then, he wrote, 'we have lost not only our sympathisers but our spies as well'.[77]

This action stopped all contacts between the mountaineers and Vorontsov, leaving the field open for Shamil to overturn the viceroy's table on him in this game of intrigue and espionage. Thus, emissaries supposedly from the *nā'ibs* of Chechnia continued to arrive in the Russian camp. They offered 'to tender their submission, provided only the [Russian] army would advance', and asserted that,

> its apparition in Darghiyya would be a signal for a general rising against Shamil; and the semblance of a regard for the sacred character of the *imām* went some way in adding credit to their professions; for they appeared earnestly to stipulate for his life and liberty, and they returned more than once to discuss the precise means by which he was to be enabled in safety to withdraw into Egypt.[78]

These negotiations were a major cause of Vorontsov's decision to go to Darghiyya. There he still waited for messengers to arrive.[79] It was only during and after the 'biscuit expedition' that Vorontsov and his staff realised that they had been outmanoeuvred. But then it was too late. Shamil had the Russians exactly where he wanted them to be.

That Vorontsov's force escaped complete destruction is a matter of luck only, the overall balance of power notwithstanding; had the commanding officer of the Left Flank been someone else, or had Freytag been a less resourceful general, the campaign would have ended in complete disaster. Even with Freytag's rescue, the campaign proved to be an unprecedented defeat. Thus, by the end of 1845 Shamil was at the peak of his prestige and power while the Russians were at their nadir. Furthermore, by the spring of 1846 their forces were to be weakened even further by the return of the Fifth Corps to Russia.[80] It was exactly at that moment that the *imām* chose to carry out his most daring enterprise ever.

Chapter 16

Ghabarṭa

The winter of 1846 did not pass quietly. In Daghestan Shamil's *nā'ibs* threatened the Alazān valley and the confederation of Aqūsha. In Chechnia the *nā'ibs* continually raided the Ghumuq plain and the Line. The Russians had not planned any offensive operations for 1846. Thus, their activity came mainly in response to the mountaineers' initiatives.[1]

Keeping the Russians occupied in this way, Shamil made preparations for a big operation. In the second half of April, upon his orders, large numbers of mountaineers concentrated in Shalī and Shubūt.[2] The Russians were aware of this, but had no knowledge in which direction the *imām* intended to strike. Argutinskii and Vorontsov were convinced that Shamil's

> chief aim was Aqūsha in central Daghestan, and so satisfied was the Russian commander-in-chief on this head that, remaining himself at Shemākha in the south, he sent orders to Freytag expressly forbidding him to delay the homeward march of the 5th Army Corps battalions.[3]

Thus Shamil succeeded in almost completely surprising the Russians when he marched westward into Ghabarṭa.

Mutual contacts and influence had always existed between the two flanks of the Caucasus. Thus, while the successes of the Circassians encouraged the Chechens to rise against the Russians in 1840, the former in their turn were encouraged to attack the Russian forts by rumours that Shamil had recaptured Akhulgoḥ and was calling upon the Circassians to rise.[4] The successes of their neighbours to both east and west stirred the Ghabarṭians and the Ossets, and the Russians had some trouble with the latter in 1840 and 1841.[5]

By the end of 1840, 'Greater Ghabarṭa remained peaceful, but . . . if the *imām* with his hordes appeared on the Georgian Military Highway, he would succeed with little difficulty to rally the Ghabarṭians to him'.[6] The raid by Akhbirdi Muḥammad on

Muzlik on 11 October 1840 was greatly assisted by the Ghabarṭians, as a subsequent Russian enquiry revealed.[7]

It was at that period that Shamil started thinking in terms which were a revival of the erstwhile strategy of Ghāzī Muḥammad and of Shaykh Manṣūr before him, i.e. the unification of all the mountain tribes of the Caucasus against the Russians. Following Grabbe's defeat in 1842, the *imām* sent Akhbirdi Muḥammad to the Ghabarṭians, and Ḥājj Muḥammad to the Circassians. Their aim was twofold: first, to mobilise as many warriors as possible to join Shamil; and second, to prepare them for a combined venture in which they would revolt and simultaneously the *imām* with his army would join them. With their forces combined, the mountaineers could overpower the Russian Line and cut Georgia off from Russia.[8] By 1843 these intentions of Shamil were known to the Russians as well as to the French consul in Tiflis.[9]

Both Akhbirdi Muḥammad and Ḥājj Muḥammad were unsuccessful; the former because of his attempt to raise a tax, the latter because he was killed shortly after his arrival.[10] However, some individuals joined Shamil – like the Ghabarṭian prince Aslān Bek Misistov,[11] and the Circassian Ḥājj Ismā'īl, who was killed in November 1844 on his way back carrying Shamil's messages.[12]

Shamil kept contact with the tribes of the Right Flank and the Centre throughout 1843 and 1844, and even intensified it in 1845 when he sent new messengers to the Circassians, headed by Sulaymān Efendī who, however, returned soon to the *imām* unsuccessful.[13]

After Vorontsov's campaign some of the leading princes of Ghabarṭa – among them Christians – contacted Shamil and requested his presence. The *imām*, having come to an understanding with them, decided to carry out this bold move in the spring, during or immediately after the withdrawal of the Fifth Corps.

Telling only a few trusted *nā'ibs* of his plans, Shamil marched out of Shalī on 25 April. According to Russian sources he headed a force of about 14,000 men, only 1,000 of them infantry, and eight guns.[14] The bulk of the infantry, about 8,000 men, were sent on a separate mission under Nūr 'Alī. On that afternoon the *imām* crossed the Argūn, covering the trails of his guns by letting the bulk of his cavalry stamp over them. On 26 April he crossed the Fortanga and on the 27th, after a diversion towards Kazakh Kichu, he crossed the Sunja near the Cossack *stanitsa*

Sundzhenskaia. On 28 April Shamil reached 'the heart of Lesser Ghabarṭa', the river Kupra, and spent the night there at Akhlov's *awul*. On 29 April the *imām* detailed three *nā'ibs*, Sa'īd Abdallah [Saibdulla], Duba and Atabay, to transfer the local population from their villages.

He himself crossed the Terek at the ford near the Minaret and took up a strong position nearby. This position, from where he 'could observe all the Ghabarṭa plain', had been his target, since by using it as 'the strategic base for his operations' Shamil 'could influence Ghabarṭa, the neighbouring Ossetia and have an effect on the communciations of the Northern Caucasus with Georgia'.[15] From this position the *imām* sent messengers to the Gharbarṭians and the Circassians to rise, but according to his own testimony, he was told that he had come 'too late'.[16]

The cause for this was the fact that Shamil succeeded in almost completely surprising the Russians. Unlike all the other generals, however, Freytag (with his partner Nesterov) was on the alert. In possession of an excellent intelligence network,[17] this brilliant general was on his feet as soon as he got wind of the gathering of Shamil's force. On 23 April he sent a message to Hasfort, Commander of the 15th Infantry Division (5th Corps),

> requesting him, despite the positive orders received from St. Petersburg, and confirmed so recently by Vorontsov, not only to stay the homeward march of the two battalions, part of the 5th Army Corps already at Muzlik, but to direct them to Nikolaevskaia, a cossack *stanitsa* on the Terek, 30 miles north-west of Vladikavkaz.
>
> It was no light thing to disregard, on little more than a mere surmise, the commands of such a ruler as Nicholas I, who had . . . issued positive orders for [the Fifth Corps'] return. Prince Vorontsov dared not incur so grave a responsibility, and from this we may measure the moral courage of his subordinate.[18]

On 24 April, upon receiving word that Shamil himself was in Shalī, Freytag reiterated his request to Hasfort. In addition he detained another battalion of Hasfort's at Qidhlār, and alerted his own and Nesterov's forces. On 26 April, hearing that Shamil had crossed the Argūn on the previous day, Freytag set out to Zakān Yūrt. On 27 April he marched to Kazākh Kichu.

Hence the general kept constantly on the *imām*'s heels, in spite of the latter's attempts at disinformation. On 28 April he moved through Nikolaevskaia to Achaluk, where he learned that Shamil had passed fort Konstantinovskoe three hours earlier. On 29

April Freytag reached the Kupra, where Shamil had bivouacked the previous night. The following day Freytag hurried to the Terek, and came upon the three *nāʾibs*, detailed to transfer the local population, about six kilometres from the ford. The *nāʾibs* abandoned the convoy and hurried across the river to join Shamil. The general, thus, caught up with the *imām*.

Freytag's arrival was a decisive factor in the failure of Shamil's plans:

> The bargain between the Ghabarṭians and the *imām* was that he on his part would sweep away every Russian fort and settlement on the banks of the Terek and its effluents, provided that they joined forces with him; but seeing the Russians already at Shamil's heels, and led by a commander whose prowess they knew and feared, they hesitated to take up arms, though in fact they had thrown off their allegiance (to Russia). What each party to the contract now said was, 'you do your part and we will do ours,' with the natural result that neither did anything at all.[19]

Still, Shamil did not give up. In an attempt to 'shake off' Freytag, he left his camp on the night of 30 April–1 May undetected. Moving up the Urukh, he sent messengers to rouse the Ghabarṭians, Balkars and Circassians. On that day the *imām* camped near Prince Kaziev's *awul*, where he stayed for the following three days.

'Ignorant of the topography of the neighbourhood, and with neither guides nor maps',[20] it took Freytag a day to find out Shamil's whereabouts. On 2 May Freytag moved to fort Cherekskoe. At that stage, 'we, in fact, ruled only the forts and *stanitsas* along the lower Georgian Military Highway; normal communications were cut off'. Freytag, therefore, decided to stay at Cherekskoe. Any further pursuit of Shamil 'would be useless and tiresome' since Shamil could always either 'avoid our forces' or 'distracting them in one direction, suddenly attack in the opposite direction'. Freytag was then 'left with one task – to preserve whatever was left of our possessions and restore communications'.[21]

> Freytag's position was no enviable one. The danger to the exposed Left Flank in case Shamil did double back was greater than ever. The Russian force, too, had arrived in light marching order; the want of both ammunition and food supplies was already felt; the Chief of the Central Line, Prince Golitsyn, proved himself utterly

> incompetent, and the store depots throughout his command were found to be depleted. The enemy was numerically by far the stronger, and the Ghabarṭians, a brave and warlike race, might yet be induced to fight.[22]

In such a case, 'the revolt in Ghabarṭa might spread into the Ghumuq plain' at a time when 'the Line was bare, and on the Left Flank there were no troops nor anyone in command'.[23]

Yet Freytag, in spite of all the difficulties and his anxieties, thought of one thing only – to trap Shamil and deal him a decisive blow. Thus, on 3 May he detailed about 2,300 infantry, 500 cavalry and six guns under Colonel Meller-Zakomelskii to the Minaret, with instructions to block Shamil's retreat. With the rest of his force – about 5,700 infantry, 500 cavalry and six guns – Freytag stayed at Cherekskoe and tried to obtain supplies from Golitsyn in Nal'chik.

On 5 May Shamil moved to the abandoned fort Urvanskoe, threatening Freytag's communications with Nal'chik. Freytag made a countermove in view of which the *imām* returned to his previous camp. On the following day Shamil decided to return to Chechnia. Not only were the Ghabarṭians still undecided and reinforcements were approaching from the north – (two battalions of the Fifth Corps) but further reinforcements (three battalions) were also approaching Vladikavkaz from Tiflis. The meaning of this movement, which threatened to cut off the *imām* from his domains, was that Nūr ʿAlī had failed.

Nūr ʿAlī at the head of the bulk of the infantry – 8,000 men – started his march from Shubūt on the same day as Shamil. His target was the Daryāl pass. On 27 April he entered the territory of the community of Aki, and reached Tsori. There he stayed for a few days, trying to arouse the Galgays and Kists. On 2 May Nūr ʿAlī finally moved towards the Jerākh gorge. But on the same day he changed his mind and moved to Tars, where he threatened to cut off the road at Balta. On 4 May Nūr ʿAlī abandoned his target and retreated to Chechnia.

As it seems, Nūr ʿAlī faced the same predicament as his chief faced in Ghabarṭa – he could not attack the Russian force without the help of the local population, but the people would not help him before he had given the Russians a beating. While another, more enterprising, leader would have tried other ways, Nūr ʿAlī waited passively and lost momentum. Finally, in view of the

MAP 12: SHAMIL'S CAMPAIGN IN GHABARṬA, 1846

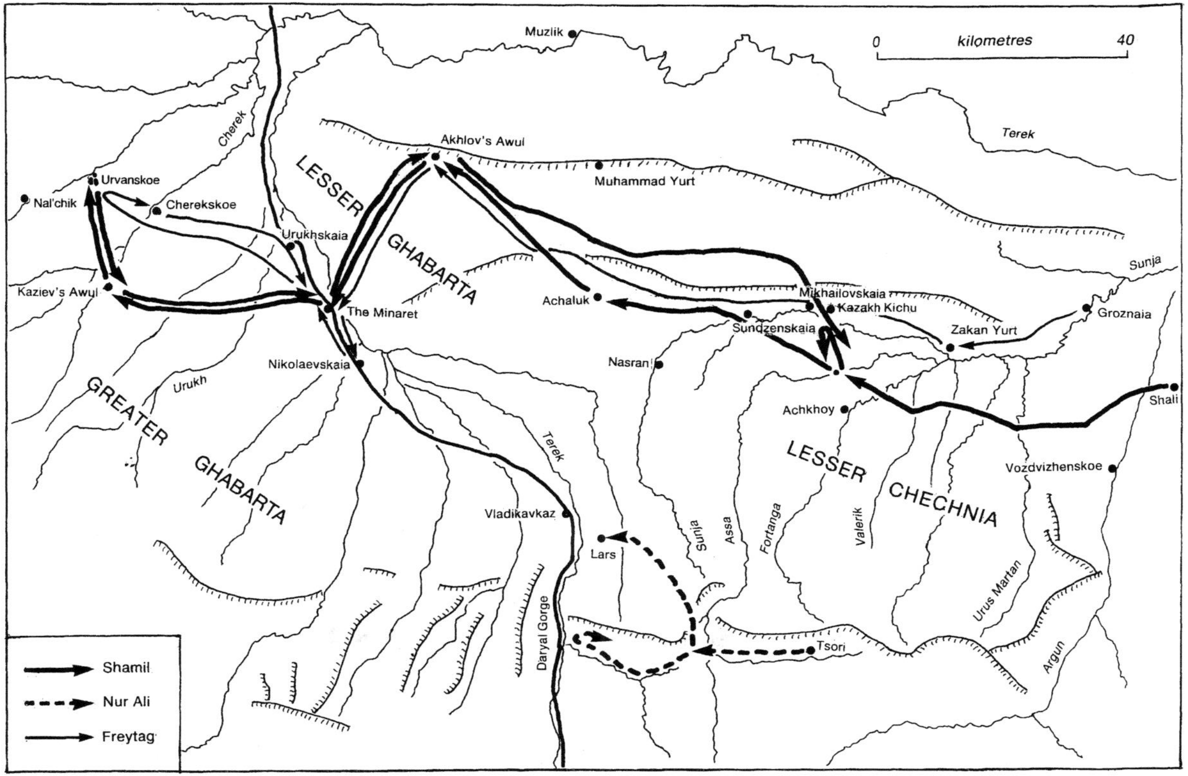

reinforcements from the south – the above mentioned three battalions – he had to retreat.

On 7 May, by dusk, Freytag observed that Shamil's camp had been suspiciously silent. He despatched a patrol which found it empty – Shamil had slipped away under the eyes of the Russians.[24] On 8 May in the morning the *imām* encountered Meller-Zakomelskii at the Minaret, and managed to lure him out of a strong position, which he himself had occupied on 29 and 30 April. The *imām* then seized the position himself and, 'ably seconded by Ḥajimurād, rapidly passed the whole of his forces to the right bank with insignificant loss from Meller-Zakomelskii's fire'.[25] Meller's report that he was pursuing Shamil 'on his heels, not letting him stop', was greeted with irony even by the Russian chronicler.[26]

Shamil, in a brilliant manoeuvre, frustrated any Russian thought of pursuit by crossing a 100-kilometre waterless plain. On 9 May he crossed the Sunja between Mikhailovskaia and Kazākh Kichu, 'drove back into the fort' a force of 400 men 'who had sallied out to intercept' him, 'and from that moment were safe from pursuit'.[27] Several Ghabarṭians joined Shamil. The most eminent among them were the clan of Anzāwr [Anzorov], whose head, Muḥammad Mīrzā, was nominated *nā'ib* of Gekhī.[28] Others, like 'Umar Sharatluk [Sharotlokov], were punished by the Russian authorities.[29]

Shamil's campaign was ably planned and masterfully executed, and were it not for Freytag, he would have caused much trouble and harm to Russia. As in his previous campaigns, so successful was Shamil in his deception and disinformation that even after he had entered Ghabarṭa, most Russian generals – including Vorontsov – believed this move to be a diversion. Major-General Nordenstam, the deputy chief-of-staff and the most senior commander left in Tiflis, realised 'the real situation'[30] only on 29 April, and Vorontsov even later, on 3 May.

Surprised and unprepared, the Russian generals, as in 1843, reacted passively. Golitsyn, in whose area the activity took place, 'let [headquarters] know of his existence by a couple of reports'.[31] Lieutenant-General Zavadovskii, the commander of the Caucasian and Black Sea Lines, remained all the time in Stavropol' and, 'seated in his office, moved troops, the location of which he did not know, reinforced garrisons of unthreatened places . . . and sent big transports to transfer nonexistent provisions'.[32] Hurko, the ex-chief-of-staff, now on his way to Russia, 'was not allowed to leave Vladikavkaz',[33] not to his dissatisfaction. His only contribution was the fact that his letters to Nordenstam and Vorontsov finally woke them up to reality.

All this brings into sharper relief Freytag's alertness, independence of mind, initiative, sense of duty and responsibility. And in order really to appreciate all this, one has to remember that he led a hurriedly assembled and heterogeneous force into an unknown country, and overcame quite a few attempts at disinformation by Shamil. Throughout the entire episode Freytag displayed only one personal shortcoming, when he was too timid in acknowledging Nesterov's share in his success.

Freytag's bold and immediate action was acknowledged by both the emperor and Vorontsov. But his real 'reward' came in 1848, when he was transferred to the Main Active Army, where Paskiewicz took care to make him quartermaster-general, 'a routine post where his ability was completely wasted'.[34] Clearly, the Russian army, even the Caucasian Corps, could not tolerate an independent general who preferred to take the initiative and win, rather than barricade himself behind his superior's orders.

Moreover, Freytag clearly rescued too many people too many times. Vorontsov, for one, neither forgot nor forgave that he had to acknowledge twice within ten months his indebtedness to Freytag. By rescuing him twice the general not only cast a shadow on the viceroy's prestige, but actually revealed the latter's mediocrity as a military commander.[35] This Vorontsov could not forgive, and this – rather than Freytag's German name, as Baddeley thought – is the main reason for the fact that by the end of the century he held a 'small place in the memory and affection of the Russians of today'.[36]

This campaign again demonstrated Shamil's qualities as a commander. But it demonstrated two other things. First, it showed what a great loss the deaths of Akhbirdi Muḥammad and Shuʿayb were to Shamil. Shamil now had to choose between a competent war leader, like Ḥajimurād, and someone of whose loyalty he could be sure, like Nūr ʿAlī, with the consequent shortcomings of each choice.

Second, and more important, it revealed Shamil's huge disadvantage in the overall balance of power with Russia, though no one at the time seems to have noticed it. So large was the disparity that he had no chance of winning a strategic victory. At the most, Shamil could gain only partial victories and then only if he succeeded in catching the Russians by surprise. Having attained this condition, he won his campaign in Daghestan. Once, however, he came across an alert general, his chances of winning were reduced to nil.

Another thing which contemporaries – with the possible exception of Shamil himself – could not notice, was the fact that the invasion of Ghabarṭa was Shamil's peak, and with it his power reached its furthestmost limits. For Shamil this campaign had a very special – one is tempted to use the word sacred – meaning and witnesses described that he was in a very festive, merry and affable disposition. The force marched in somewhat solemn order. The *imām* explicitly forbade plundering or using force against local people, saying: 'I shall coerce no one; they themselves will follow whatever is agreeable to God'.[37] Consequently, the failure was felt strongly by him, even if to his followers it did not look a failure, the blame for the lack of success having been laid on the hesitancy of the Ghabarṭians. Shamil must have felt that he would never undertake such a campaign again, even if he hoped to the contrary. Outwardly, however, he stated that he would repeat it,[38] and both the Russians and the natives expected another invasion of Ghabarṭa, especially during the summer and autumn of 1846.[39]

These expectations and rumours were taken advantage of by the *imām* to surprise the Russians, when he attacked in Daghestan. On 20 October Shamil seized Tsudaqār, Aqūsha and Khōjā al-Makhī. On the 25th he seized Aymakī. However, again, as in Ghabarṭa, the *imām* was told that he had come 'too late'.[40]

Bebutov, the commander of Northern Daghestan, marched out of Temir-Khān-Shūra immediately upon receiving the news of Shamil's offensive. Leaving Ḥajimurād to defend Aymakī against Bebutov, Shamil moved with the bulk of his force and one cannon to Kutishih, from where he could strike at Bebutov from the flank and rear if the latter attacked Aymakī. The general, however, was well informed of Shamil's location and plans. He, therefore, attacked Shamil at Kutishih on 27 October, and completely routed the mountaineers, capturing the cannon and even Shamil's personal *kinjāl* and *burka* (fur), all at the minimal cost of 28 killed and 77 wounded.

Bebutov's complete success was due to his being able to surprise the mountaineers on two accounts: first, his correct intelligence enabled him to attack them at a time and place they did not expect; second, for the first time in Daghestan, dragoons were used. The surprised mountaineers panicked and fled at the sight of cavalry charging in closed formation.[41] This defeat, however, was not as decisive or lasting as the Russians thought. By January 1847 Shamil was operating in Aqūsha again.

The year in general, before, between, and after these two great campaigns, was marked by great activity. The mountaineers raided Russian territory continually and held the Russians in constant alert. The Russians for their part were on the defence with the partial exception of Chechnia.[42]

On the night of 25–26 December, Ḥajimurād gave a dramatic ending to the year: 'With 500 men he entered Jengutay, the capital of Mekhtulī', and 'carried off under the noses of a strong Russian garrison the widow of his old enemy, Aḥmad Khān'.[43]

In view of all these events, Vorontsov, at the year's end, could only sigh with relief and write that 'we have finished our year tolerably well'.[44]

Part 7

'The System of the Axe'

Chapter 17

Lesser Chechnia

The narrow escape of 1845 convinced Vorontsov that 'now we have to follow a less offensive system, a more systematic war, which will in due time improve our situation here in a more certain, albeit less spectacular, fashion'.[1] In his correspondence and discussions with the emperor, whom he met in the Crimea during the second half of September 1845,[2] the viceroy succeeded in persuading the tsar to return fully to the siege strategy. Thus, the areas under Shamil's rule were to be encircled by steadily closing defensive lines.

Vorontsov' first priority was to complete the existing lines and roads, the construction of which had constantly been delayed by St. Petersburg's demands for expeditions in the early 1840s. To this end the rest of 1845 and 1846 were to be devoted. To enable him to execute this programme the Caucasian Corps was to be augmented, reorganised and relocated. The Fifth Infantry Corps, on its return to Russia, was to leave behind the second battalion of each of its regiments. These were to become the nuclei of four new regiments. Accordingly, the Caucasian Corps was to be reorganised into three infantry divisions.[3]

Two of the new formations – the Daghestan and the Samur regiments – were allocated to close gaps in the defences of Daghestan. They established their headquarters in Ishkartī (1846) and Jedaghor (1847) respectively.[4] To close the gap in the defence of the Ghumuq plane, a fort was erected in Chir Yūrt (1845) as the headquarters of the Nizhnii Novgorod Dragoon Regiment – transferred there from Georgia (1846).[5] In the west, the 'Upper Sunja Line' was established in 1845 and 1846 to protect the Georgian Military Highway and the areas of Vladikavkaz and Naṣrān. It consisted of five Cossack *stanitsas* which formed the First Sunja Cossack regiment.[6] In addition, a great effort was made to stengthen existing fortifications, to improve barracks and to maintain and construct roads. Among the latter, of primary strategic importance was the construction of the military highway from Georgia to Akhdī [Akhty] in the Samur district.[7]

In Chechnia a decidedly more offensive strategy was contemplated. Experienced Caucasian generals had for a long time held the view that Chechnia constituted both Shamil's strongest point and Achilles' heel. It provided Shamil's realm with a large proportion of its food and the *imām* with a great number of his best warriors. Furthermore it protected the 'soft underbelly' of Daghestan (though this point would not be fully comprehended by the Russians for another decade). To deprive the *imām* of these advantages would, therefore, bring him more than halfway to his downfall.

This seemed to be all the easier because the Chechens were less politically reliable, from Shamil's point of view, than the Daghestanis. And while fighting in the forests of Chechnia was much more difficult for the Russians, the forests, unlike the mountains, could be relatively easily neutralised by felling. Thus, 'the system of the axe replaced the system of the bayonet'.[8]

Vorontsov chose to concentrate his effort in Lesser Chechnia first, where he intended to 'consolidate the communications between Vozdvizhenskoe and the new colonies [*stanitsas*] as well as the old forts on the Sunja'. Then, in the spring of 1846, he planned to continue the construction of the 'Advanced Chechen Line' (started in 1844 by the establishment of Vozdvizhenskoe) by personally choosing the location and then erecting the planned fort near Achkhī [Achkhoy] 'which should be completed by the autumn. Then all Lesser Chechnia will be completely in our hands. One might hope that it will submit, but even if not, it will be in no position to harm us'.[9] In typical excessive self-confidence and optimism, Vorontsov planned to move operations to Greater Chechnia in 1847. By the spring of that year he expected to erect a fort at Mayurtup, 'whence it will be possible to quickly and easily . . . advance farther . . . to the centre of [Shamil's] realm'.[10]

The new strategy, thus, intended to 'supply many [people] in the mountains, who want it, with an opportunity to migrate quietly to our territory',[11] and to deprive the rest of the use of their fields and pastures in the lowlands, thus compelling them eventually to submit. The Russians were, thus, turning the 'scorched earth' strategy, which Shamil had used with such tremendous results, against the *imām*.

In modern terminology, Vorontsov's strategy included

elements of economic, demographic and psychological warfare.[12] It used military, economic and especially 'political' means. The experience of Darghiyya did not deter Vorontsov from entering into negotiations with some of Shamil's *nā'ibs*. These contacts culminated in October 1846 in the defection of Sulaymān Efendī, who following his return from Circassia had fallen out with Shamil.[13]

This defection gave a boost to the viceroy's ideological warfare against Shamil. For a while Vorontsov played with the idea of using the (Crimean?) *kaziasker* (*qādī ʿaskar*), al-Sayyid Khalīl Efendī, to attack Shamil on religious grounds.[14] Sulaymān Efendī's defection gave a better opportunity for such a move because he was a renowned *ʿālim*. Indeed, Sulaymān Efendī produced a list of seven deviations of Shamil from the *sharīʿa*.[15]

The list was given wide circulation in the territories under Russian control, among Muslims and non-Muslims alike. It was probably no accident that a few months later a Muslim chief loyal to the Russians accused Shamil of deviations from the *sharīʿa* and of following 'the ways of the *Khawārīj*'.[16]

This accusation is connected with another step of Vorontsov – that of reversing the neglect of the local Muslim leadership by his predecessors. The Muslims' 'way of thinking and disposition towards us', he wrote to the emperor, depended on 'our government's relations with them' no less than on 'the military events in Daghestan'.[17] Vorontsov therefore was intent on changing the disposition of the Muslim population, and especially of their élite. He asked and received the emperor's permission to restore some of the privileges of the *āghālār*, the *beks* and the *'ulamā'*, taken away from them in previous years.[18] He displayed attentiveness and kindness to Muslim collaborators, showering them with gifts, honours and titles.[19] His final aim seems to have been their co-optation into the imperial service nobility, as he had successfully done with the Georgian and Armenian élites.[20]

Following the new plan, Freytag cleared, in the winter of 1845–46, a passage along the 'Great Russian Highway' through the forests along the Goyta (16 December 1845–5 January 1846) and the Gekhī (27 January–22 February).[21] The clearing, as all the following ones would be, was made wide enough on both sides to prevent the Chechens from using cannon from the forest against troops moving on the road. Nesterov, who assisted Freytag in Gekhī, cleared for his part, a throughway to Achkhī. In the summer Vorontsov used this way to march and establish, on

30 June, a fort at that place. The fort was completed by Labyntsev on 22 October 1846.[22]

The following winter, between 20 January and 1 February 1847, Nesterov cleared the forest along the Assa river, cutting through roads to the Galasha community. His activity was preceded by a large-scale raid undertaken by Freytag between 26 December 1846 and 6 January 1847 in the vicinity of Aldī, and several smaller ones from the new fort of Achkhī.[23]

As a rule, the clearing operations were accompanied by the systematic destruction of hamlets, stocks and crops, the stamping of fields and the capture of livestock. This destruction was 'intended to force the Chechens to realise the necessity to migrate into our territory, where no one would disturb them any more from indulging in peaceful occupations; they had to be shown the uselessness of any further resistance'.[24]

Operating from fortified camps and in strong columns, with powerful artillery support, the Russians were impregnable. The most the Chechens could do was to harass the Russians by occasional sniping and artillery fire, and by diverting their water supplies. This fact was clearly reflected in the Russian losses; entire clearing expeditions returned to base with fewer casualties than in most of the raids.[25]

In the summer of 1847 the Russians planned to erect a tower on the Goyta, but an epidemic of cholera forced them to cancel the campaign.[26] The winter campaign, however, proceeded as planned. Freytag, with a force of about 7,500 infantrymen, 318 Cossacks, 200 dragoons, 16 guns and four mortars, first cleared the vegetation which had covered the road he had cut through the Goyta forest in 1845–46 (30 November–11 December). He then proceeded to clear the forests between the Goyta and the Urus Martan (15 December 1847–5 January 1848), between that river and the Roshna (22 January–7 February) and finally between the Shalasha and the Netkhī [Netkhoi] (14 February–2 March).[27] On 18 December Freytag raided and destroyed the hamlet of Saʿīd ʿAbdalla, the *mudīr* of Lesser Chechnia.

Completing his campaign with a loss of 62 killed and 548 wounded, Freytag returned to Groznaia. The Great Russian Highway was rendered secure and a road cut through to the designated place on the Urus Martan where Vorontsov planned to erect a fort in the summer campaign. Furthermore, as a direct result of the Russian operations since the winter of 1845–46, about 3,000 Chechen families defected to the Russians and settled in the vicinity of the new forts.[28]

As a prelude to the summer campaign, Vorontsov left Groznaia on 19 June 1848 with a force of about 2,500 men. Reaching Vozdvizhenskoe, he construced there a tower on the opposite bank of the Argūn to protect the bridge built in the previous winter.[29] On 13 August, Vorontsov left Vozdvizhenskoe with a force of about 6,600 infantry, 800 Cossacks, 200 dragoons, at least 16 cannons, rockets and engineers. The force reached on that same day the right bank of the Urus Martan, and on 16 August started the construction of the new fort. It was completed on 1 October.

Shamil, unable to leave Daghestan because of the Russian summer campaign there,[30] called upon the Chechens to put up stubborn resistance.[31] He nominated Abākār Dibīr, the *nā'ib* of Kunbūt, to command the operations in Lesser Chechnia, and released a large quantity of bombs from his store at New Darghiyya. Indeed, the Chechens tried desperately to stop the Russians from erecting their fort. They harassed the Russian camp with artillery and small-arms fire – and as in Daghestan, the Russian sources mention time and again the precision of the mountaineer's artillery; they ambushed Russian columns and attacked their communications; they spoilt all the fords in Lesser Chechnia; they even diverted the Urus Martan and the Roshna to deprive the Russians of water. But they could not stop the fort from being built.

The Russians, however, did not fully achieve their aim either. Neither the completion of the fort, which closed the gap between Vozdvizhenskoe and Achkhī, nor the systematic destruction of all the villages, hamlets, fields and gardens 'encourage[d] the greater part of Lesser Chechnia to submit'.[32] And if Vorontsov had believed that 'almost all the inhabitants want to do it',[33] he was disappointed: most of the population in the forests between the new line and the Sunja preferred to migrate south of the Russian line to, and beyond, the 'Black Mountains'.

In the campaign of winter 1848–49, Nesterov cleared roads between the Great Russian Highway and the Sunja 'without a single shot' being fired. This was mainly because most of the population had moved southwards. Part of the population, however, preferred to submit and surrendered a cannon to the Russians.[34] And although desultory warfare continued during the entire year, Vorontsov on his tour of inspection was able to 'cross

MAP 13: LESSER CHECHNIA

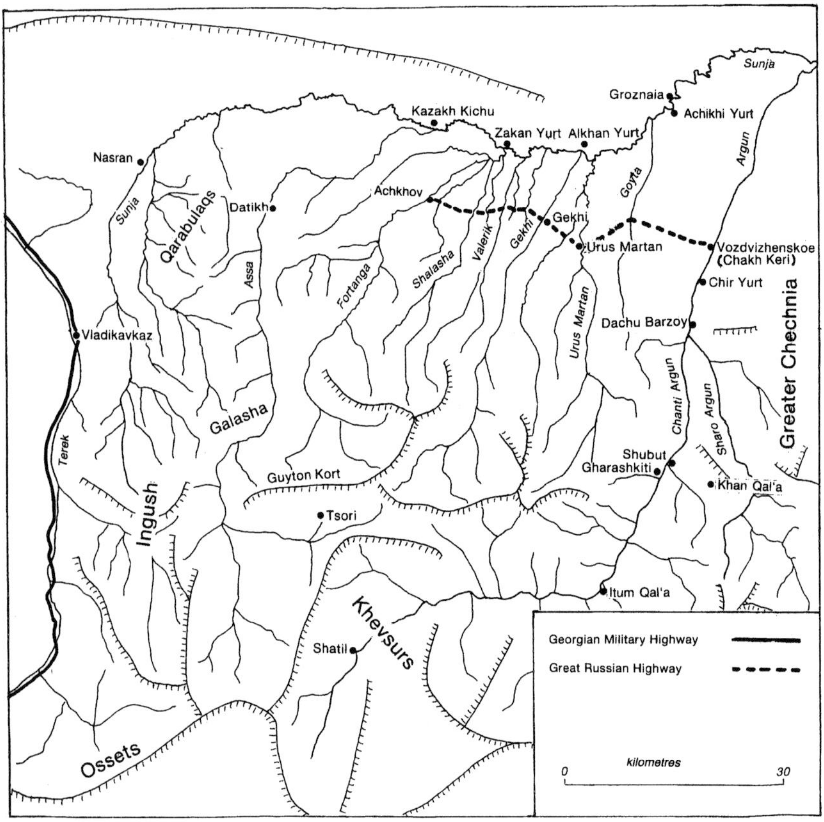

all of Lesser Chechnia, from Vozdvizhenskoe to Vladikavkaz, in the same manner as [if in] a peaceful country.[35]

In the summer of 1849 Nesterov built a tower on the Argūn, near the ruins of Greater Chechān. Commanding 'the best and almost only ford where strong parties with cannon can cross',[36] this tower contributed to the isolation of Lesser from Greater Chechnia and to its pacification.

Between 2 and 30 December 1849, Nesterov and a force of 5,000 infantry, 600 cavalry and eight cannons subdued the communities of Galasha and Qarābulāq.[37] The pacification of these communities, however, was far from complete. In late January and mid-February 1850, Sleptsov, the commander of the Upper Sunja Line, had to thwart two attempts – by Saʿīd ʿAbdalla[38] and Ḥajimurād[39] respectively – to restore Shamil's rule there.[40] 'The final pacification of the Galasha community took place only with the captivity of Shamil.'[41]

On the plain of Lesser Chechnia the situation was different. The Chechens continued to slip back into the area between the Sunja and the Great Russian Highway. The Russians on a few occasions mounted operations to chase the Chechens out.[42] On 13 October 1850 they finally rounded up the population and resettled it beyond the Terek.[43] The struggle for the lowland of Lesser Chechnia was won.

Shamil understood perfectly the significance of the new Russian strategy. Years later he said that by the winter of 1846 he had realised that the Russians by their clearing operations had 'moved out on to the proper road'.[44] On the tactical level the *imām* had no proper response to these operations. In due course he would try different means to stop the Russians, but his immediate reaction was to reinforce his prohibition to fell wood without his explicit permission,[45] and to increase the raids on the Line. Indeed, the raids increased enormously during 1847,[46] and by the summer of 1848, 'the Chechens did not cease to hold the Line in constant alert'.[47] These, however, were only momentary distractions, not real answers to the problem.

On the strategic level it was clear to Shamil, as before, that in the long run he could not withstand the Russians without the intervention from a foreign power, preferably the Ottoman Empire. In the intermediate future at least some time could be gained by trying to break through the Russian lines and expand his territory, or at least to stir up areas behind the Russian lines to keep them occupied. These might also divert the Russians' (and his own peoples') attention from Chechnia. In this he was once again helped by his adversary.

Chapter 18

Central Daghestan

Shamil's attack on Aqūsha and Tsudaqār in 1846[1] focused Vorontsov's attention on Central Daghestan. After an initial moment of euphoria and the feeling that 'the battle at Kutishih will for a long time take away from the enemy any desire to invade our borders again',[2] he realised that the area was completely open to any further invasion. The activities of Abākār Ḥājjī in January 1847 served to demonstrate this fact. Therefore, in his plans for 1847 – approved by the emperor – the viceroy decided to concentrate all the efforts on that area, and build a defence line along the Ghāzī-Ghumuq Koyṣū.

Over confident and underestimating the mountaineers, Vorontsov put forward the following aims, to be accomplished within three months (May–July 1847): to capture Girgil and build there a fort; to destroy Salṭah [Salty] and Sughūr; 'if necessary and possible' to destroy 'Irib. Furthermore Vorontsov proposed, if circumstances were favourable by the end of July, to 'undertake another offensive beyond the Qarā-Koyṣū'.[3]

The reason why Vorontsov chose the Ghāzī-Ghumuq Koyṣū was kept in complete secrecy: the lands on the right (eastern) bank of that river were considered the most fertile in the entire area. By taking possession of the right bank, therefore, Vorontsov intended to deny the mountaineers the use of these fields, and thus add to the general blockade of Shamil's realm.[4]

Another secret aim, which the viceroy did not keep to himself, was to find coal – there had been indications of its existence since 1843.[5] This would enable a force of two to three battalions (instead of two companies) to be kept in Ghāzī-Ghumuq during the winter, and to establish there the headquarters of the Samur regiment.

Although the Russians kept their plans in utmost secrecy,[6] Shamil, being 'very well served by his spies',[7] got wind of them. As a result, he gave orders to strengthen fortifications all over his dominions, and especially those of Girgil, Chōkha and Salṭah.

In mid-February 1847 the *imām* stated in public 'that this year he has no intention of initiating offensive activities in Daghestan proper, but that he will conduct a defensive war and shall defend himself with all his might, until exhaustion'.[8]

According to the original planning, it was Bebutov who was to storm Girgil.[9] But on 22 May, following a 'reconnaissance in force', he decided that 'it was too risky'.[10] He therefore asked Argutinskii to reinforce him, but the latter found enough excuses not to move to Bebutov's help.[11] Only when Vorontsov arrived in Khōjā al-Makhī on 6 June was Argutinskii prevailed upon to move to Girgil. On 13 June Vorontsov started to march towards the village, having under his command a force of 11,000–12,000 men.[12]

Shamil demonstrated again how well he had learnt the lessons of Akhulgoḥ. He concentrated, according to Russian sources, about 11,000 men – 700 inside Girgil, 1,000 in the gardens surrounding it, 2,000 in Salṭah, and 6,000 infantry and 1,000 mounted troops in different locations in the area. These were intended to harass the Russians' communications. The *imām* himself took up an impregnable position *outside* Girgil, across the river.[13] Soon, however, Shamil had to alter his plans, and even to disperse the force in the gardens, because of an epidemic of cholera.[14]

On the night following their arrival (13 June) the Russians positioned their batteries and on the 14th started to bombard the village. This bombardment was to continue day and night. On the following night Argutinskii's force took possession of the gardens around Girgil without any opposition.[15] On the evening of 15 June a breach had been made in the wall, and Vorontsov decided to storm the village on the following morning. Argutinskii was reportedly dismayed by this decision. 'On my honour I assure you, this is not the way to play a comedy',[16] he said to one of his staff officers, but he said nothing to Vorontsov.

After the attack the Russians realised that 'all the details of the fortifications . . . were known to us in advance, *viz.*, by the end of May, but unfortunately, we did not know the most important [fact] – that the houses had been transformed into traps'.[17] 'The flat roofs had been taken off the whole of the lower row of houses and replaced by layers of brushwood, thinly covered with earth.'[18] The thinning rows of the storming troops fell to their horror into this trap amid 'savage laughter' and abuse.[19]

The storming was 'a complete failure. Our defeat was total

and our losses – comparatively huge, entirely unexpected and unheard of'.[20] The two storming battalions lost 125 killed and 432 wounded – about half their strength – among them all their officers. 'For four days more a pretence was made of maintaining the siege, but beyond desultory artillery fire, nothing was done. Each night the enemy stole down the hills and harassed the Russians till they were well-nigh worn out.'[21] Finally, on 20 June Vorontsov made 'an offensive movement, or rather an offensive retreat, across the Ghāzī-Ghumuq Koyṣū'.[22] The retreating force was pursued by the mountaineers and lost another officer killed and 37 soldiers wounded.

As the main reason for the retreat Vorontsov gave the appearance of cholera among the troops – 'this accursed disease, which prevented us from doing away with Girgil'.[23] This was, however, clearly an excuse.[24] By then the Russians were out of almost all their shells and other supplies, and new ones could not be brought to the camp in under two or three weeks.[25] Vorontsov had no choice but to retreat.

Determined to have some success that year, Vorontsov decided to conquer Salṭah. One day after his retreat from Girgil, on 21 June, he ordered vast quantities of supplies and especially shells and other siege material to be ready by 13 July. For the following five weeks the forces of Bebutov and Argutinskii were separated and given time to recover and complete their supplies. Coal was discovered near Ulūchur and peat on Turchīdāgh, which sweetened for Vorontsov the bitter pill of Girgil.[26]

On 6 August the viceroy started his march on Salṭah with a force of about 10,000 men.[27] On the following day the Russians reached the village. On the night of 8–9 August they started their siege works, and the following day the bombardment of the village.[28]

'There is no doubt that Shamil somehow got knowledge of our intentions,' wrote a Russian chronicler, 'because simultaneously with the reconstruction of Girgil, intensive works were carried out in Salṭah, whereto fresh parties soon started to flock.'[29] All in all Shamil must have commanded at the vicinity of Salṭah a similar number of fighters to that at Girgil.

He positioned his forces on the heights above the village and the Russian camp, and constantly harassed the Russians with musket and artillery fire. The garrison – stronger than that of Girgil – also resisted fiercely. Both carried out nightly sallies against the Russian works and camp. To the Russians' surprise

MAP 14: GIRGIL

Source: Sbornik Opisanii Osad i Oboron Krepostei i Ukreplenii, Vol.I (St. Petersburg, 1869).

the garrison proved itself by no means 'powerless against our mining operations'. It 'was able and determined to wage an underground war', and counteracted all efforts to lay mines under the walls.[30]

The Russian command, divided by increasing rows between Kotzebue and Argutinskii,[31] deemed the force at its disposal 'not strong enough to surround the village from all sides'.[32] Thus, as in Akhulgoḥ in 1839, the Russians were besieged no less than besieging, since their lines of communications were constantly harassed. At the same time the garrison of Salṭah was able to evacuate its casualties and get supplies and reinforcements from Shamil's camp. Thus passed the first four weeks of the siege, with the Russians making some progress in their siege works, but with otherwise little results. As if to emphasize this,

> almost daily . . . at a fixed hour the enemy . . . sent into our position a dozen or two of shells and bombs; afterwards his musicians, from among our deserters, played our tattoo . . . This spectacle was enacted by the enemy at the moment when the commander-in-chief [Vorontsov] had finished his dinner.[33]

The situation changed only following the arrival of Burnod on 22 August. A Corsican by birth, Charles Burnod [Karl Ivanovich Biurno] joined the Russian service in 1820 as a young engineer lieutenant. He participated in all the wars and military expeditions of his time and accumulated much field experience. In 1844 he was transferred to the Caucasian Corps and promoted to major-general.[34]

Vorontsov had hoped that 'the first bombardment of the *awul* will infuse the mountaineers with the pious thought of humility and submission'.[35] But the 'proper' bombardment of the village on 27 and 28 August produced no such results. Now, Burnod suggested the obvious move – to seize the gardens surrounding the village in order to stop any communications between it and the camp of Shamil. On 3 September he led a force of up to 2,000 men and, after three days of hard battle, occupied the gardens and the two heights controlling them.[36]

This move proved to be the crucial step in the entire operation. In addition to making the siege a real one, it gave the Russians control of the stream which the besieged used. It was Burnod again who came up with the idea of, and was charged with, polluting the stream with excrement. He started doing this on 7

September, and on the following day the water became completely unusable.[37]

This was the most important factor in the final conquest of Salṭah,[38] since any other source of water was under direct Russian fire. The following two weeks, therefore, witnessed nightly attempts by the mountaineers to get food and water into the village, and to recapture the gardens, but in vain.

On 18 September, after new supplies of bombs with more cannons and mortars had arrived, the Russians started a massive bombardment of the village. This continued for three days. On the 21st the Russians stormed the village, and after a twelve-hour battle managed to occupy and hold on to a few houses on its southern edge. But the cost of this achievement was very high – 107 killed and 323 wounded – and the Russians needed another week to prepare for a new attack.[39]

On 26 September the Russians stormed again. In a hard day-long battle they captured about half of the village. Again the losses were huge – 246 killed and 943 wounded. That night, the garrison left the village and made its way to Shamil's camp. The following day the Russians entered the village and started to destroy it. On 7 October, completing the destruction of Salṭah and Kudalī, Vorontsov left the village.

Sometime during the summer campaign Vorontsov decided to unify Southern and Northern Daghestan under one command. Immediately after the campaign, he appointed Argutinskii to command the new area – renamed the Caspian Province – and nominated Bebutov chief civilian administrator of the Caucasus. Argutinskii was assigned the task of completing in 1848 Vorontsov's plan, i.e. 'to take and destroy' Girgil and 'erect there or nearby a fort', 'to complete our line along the Ghāzī-Ghumuq Koyṣū' (consisting of the proposed fort at Girgil and those under construction at Khōjā al-Makhī and Tsudaqār); to build a tower on the Ṣūlāq at the ford near Miyartuḥ; and 'in case of any encroachment by the enemy on our boundaries to undertake offensive actions whenever necessary'.[40]

The plans for the attack on Girgil were finalised during Vorontsov's tour of inspection in Temir-Khān-Shūra between 22 and 26 May.[41] Shamil, for his part, sent Ḥajimurād to improve the fortifications of Girgil and Chōkha. The *nā'ib* erected, in addition, a fort at Ulī [Uliab] – Ulū Qal'a – between Girgil and Kikuny.[42] With these works completed by mid-April, he attempted to disrupt the Russian preparations. Thus, 'the entire spring passed in continuous alarms taking place several times a week in different parts of Daghestan'.[43]

Argutinskii left Temir-Khān-Shūra on 17 June.[44] On 25 June he arrived at Girgil, followed two days later by the artillery. On that day Argutinskii had at his disposal a force of 11,000–12,000 men and 52 guns as well as rocket launchers of different calibre.[45] Occupying the same position as in the previous year, the Russians started their siege works on 28 June.[46]

Shamil positioned himself on the same peak as the year before, and his force – probably not more than half the number of the previous year, owing to Vorontsov's summer campaign in Chechnia – took up positions on the surrounding heights with a number of cannons. The village itself was defended by about 150 men and two cannon.

The mountaineers acted very energetically. The precision of their artillery was reported time and again in the Russian sources.[47] Occupying all the heights, it was indeed 'very easy for the mountaineers to hit their targets', because they could 'observe all the area occupied by us'. They fired an average of 30 shells and 30 bombs a day. Furthermore, they harassed the Russians with incessant small-arms fire 'from all sides'. In addition, 'considerable enemy forces' occupied 'all the environs with impunity, and used any opportunity to attack our communications'.[48]

On the opposite side, Argutinskii, who had criticised Vorontsov and Kotzebue the previous year for their eagerness to storm prematurely, now went to the other extreme. A Russian officer wrote in his diary:

> The plans are [kept] a secret even from us. We who have to carry them out seldom know the aim of any step and almost never see [in advance] the proposed operations for the following day. This waiting and secrecy . . . have involuntarily evoked displeasure . . . Our troops do not advance. What have we achieved during the last six days? – almost nothing.[49]

Only on 5 July did Argutinskii start the obvious move of taking possession of the gardens and heights surrounding the village. This was to be done in a pincer movement and cost 'very serious' losses.[50] 'The village was now surrounded, but the garrison continued to resist. At night . . . the mountaineers made their way across the Koyṣū into the village, bringing provisions and taking out the wounded.'[51]

During the following eleven days the Russians 'undertook neither military moves to defeat or disorganise the enemy, nor even the bombardment of the village'.[52] 'With the lesson of last year fresh in mind' Argutinskii 'used sparingly' his bombs.[53] He preferred 'to delay the [massive] bombardment of the village until the situation of the garrison became desperate'.[54] In actual fact, neither he nor anyone else had a 'clear idea' of 'how to finish this affair of Girgil'.[55]

The fate of the village was decided 'unexpectedly by accident'.[56] The Russians observed that the water reservoir of Girgil was in one of the towers along the wall. Argutinskii decided to destroy that tower amidst a massive bombardment of the village. On 18 July 25 cannon and mortars shot 5,000 bombs into the village during an 18 hour bombardment. The water reservoir was hit several times and collapsed.

On that night the garrison abandoned Girgil. On 19 July the Russians entered the village unopposed, and spent the following ten days in its destruction. On 26 July the force started its retreat, which was accompanied by heavy fighting with the mountaineers.

Argutinskii was 'unable to attack and take Chōkha and Tsughūr' in 1848 because of 'the need to fortify Aymakī'. Vorontsov expected him to do so in 1849.[57] The viceroy hoped that the conquest of Chōkha would be completed

> with no serious difficulty. There is no need for new garrisons either . . . The best people of Chōkha [who] are expatriates with us . . . will defend themselves. As for Tsughūr, they as a trading community will stay neutral (and then) . . . submit voluntarily.[58]

Argutinskii obviously did not share Vorontsov's hopes and designs. He set out from Temir-Khān-Shūra on 17 June with a force of about 9,500 infantry, 300 cavalry, 2,200 local levies and 38 cannon.[59] It took him 12 days to reach the slope of Turchīdāgh leading to Chōkha. Another 12 days were needed for the heavy guns to arrive. Finally, ten days later, and a month after leaving Temir-Khān-Shūra, Argutinskii started to descend towards Chōkha. The need to pave a road for the heavy artillery and to accumulate supplies as well as the Russians' complete lack of intelligence about the fortifications of Chōkha explain Argutinskii's slowness, but only partly: Argutinskii's lack of enthusiasm for this campaign must account for the rest.

Shamil did not hurry to Chōkha either. This was interpreted by the Russians as signifying the fact that he 'considered the fortifications of Chōkha and its garrison proper . . . strong enough and able to resist us on its own'. The *imām* himself arrived and camped across the river on 13 July, and parties continued to arrive for another month. By mid-August Shamil had, according to a Russian source, about 10,000 men in arms in and near Chōkha.[60]

The Russians' descent towards Chōkha on 17 July met with fierce resistance. The mountaineers 'retreated gradually . . . and, taking cover in the high grass and beyond the terraces, hit us with well-aimed fire, supported by shelling from the fort. We lost that day up to 70 men and barely saw the enemy.'[61]

During the following 36 days siege works were carried out. The description of this period reads like a copy of the siege of Girgil the previous year: 'Our camp, and our position in its entirety, were completely exposed to the enemy cannons, while the enemy's camp, being mainly behind the heights, could only be hit by projectiles.' The village could not be surrounded 'because Shamil had occupied the heights behind it'. His 'position was impregnable from all sides'.[62] And the mountaineers, as in the previous year, pursued active resistance, carrying out raids and sorties against the Russians.

'But the siege was necessary because, first, one could not retreat having done nothing, and second, only it [the siege] could show whether a storming was possible or not.'[63] Argutinskii, therefore, decided 'to turn Chōkha into ruins, to inflict a strong defeat by murderous artillery fire upon the garrison and Shamil's force, and in favourable circumstances take the fort by storm'.[64] From 23 August to 3 September, 22,000 shells and bombs were shot on the village, reducing it to practically a mass of ruins. But the resistance of the mountaineers was as strong as ever and Argutinskii decided not to storm the village:

> Taking into account that, on the one hand the main aim – the destruction of the fort – had been achieved, and on the other hand the capture of the surrounding heights would not give us any real advantage and would cost great losses in men and that, finally, Shamil's hordes had been punished by [suffering] huge losses – I abandoned the siege at Chōkha.[65]

On 4 September Argutinskii retreated to Turchīdāgh. His force was pursued by the mountaineers and lost 7 killed and 94 wounded.[66]

The retreat from Chōkha sealed with failure Vorontsov's plans

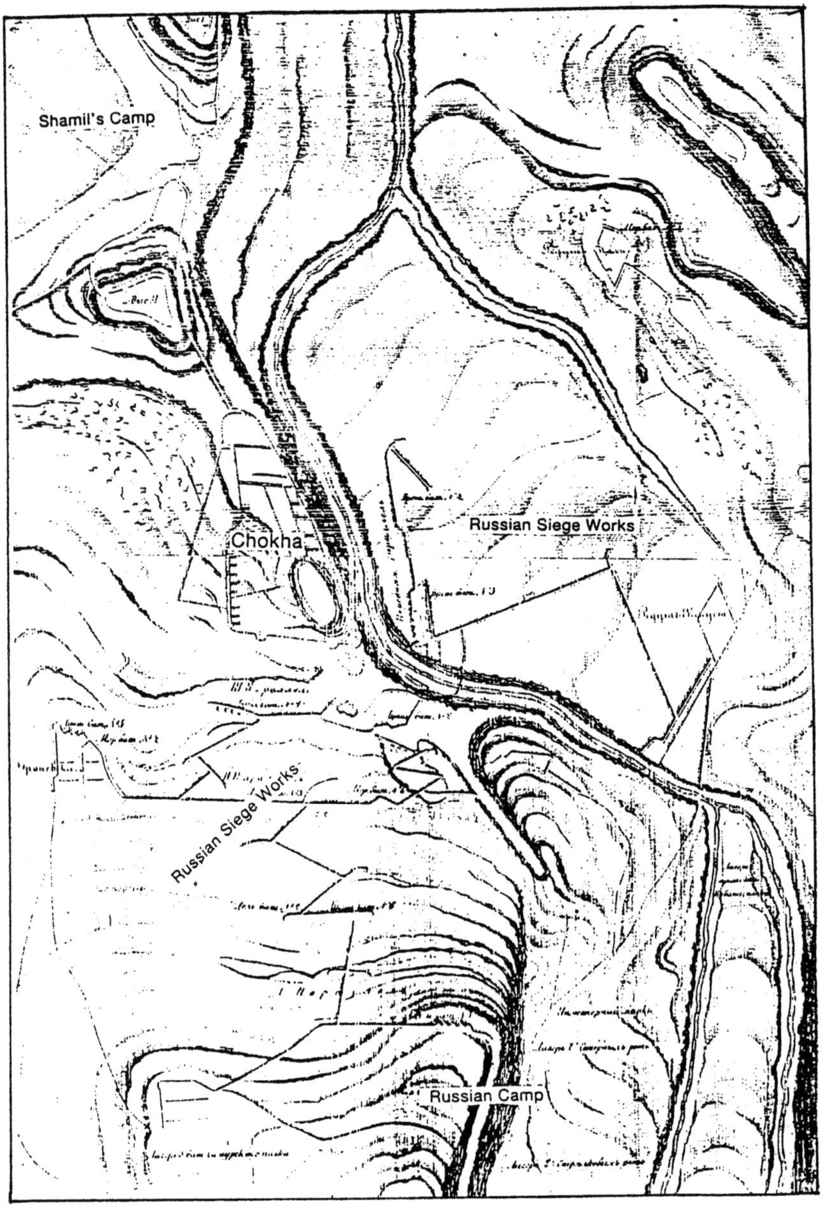

Source: Sbornik Opisanii Osad i Oboron Krepostei i Ukreplenii, Vol.I (St. Petersburg, 1869).

in Central Daghestan. As far as results were concerned, the siege of Chōkha itself was 'a repeat of the bombardment of Ṭiliq in 1844'.[67] But even the successful sieges of Salṭah and Girgil were, in fact, far from Russian victories. All these operations demonstrated how well Shamil had learned the lessons of Akhulgoḥ, how effective his fortifications were and how resolute the mountaineers were.

Vorontsov might have realised this after his failure at Girgil. This, the slow – much slower than expected – progress in Lesser Chechnia and Daniyāl's campaign in Chārtalah[68] might have convinced Vorontsov to try diplomacy. According to Mūsā Kundukh [Kundukhov], a native officer in the Russian service, he was instructed that year to negotiate a peace with Shamil. 'Negotiations were initially very successful . . . Shamil demanded independence of Russia for all the mountaineers then under his rule. The prince [Vorontsov] agreed to it, with the exception of Lesser Chechnia.' But then, probably following a veto on these conditions by St. Petersburg, an excuse was found to break negotiations off.[69]

The failure of the negotiations left the viceroy no alternative to the battlefield. Now, obvious questions of prestige made him insist on the repeated siege of Girgil. Originally, in 1847, Vorontsov wanted Shamil to 'pay with interest for the deplorable events of 1843, when he destroyed our garrison in Girgil in full view of our force'.[70] His failure increased his need to conquer that place. Even the 'destruction of [Salṭah] and its garrison in full view of Shamil', which was presented by him as 'a big blow to his [Shamil's] influence',[71] could not satisfy this need. Vorontsov's assertion, therefore, of Girgil's strategic importance[72] was sheer cover. Already during the siege of Girgil in 1847, it was decided to erect a fort at Aymakī.[73] Not only would the holding of Girgil necessitate a fort at Aymakī anyway, but it (Aymakī) was much better located to block the passage into Russian territory. Furthermore, it is clear that the erection of a fort at Aymakī did not necessitate the conquest of Girgil.

Thus, three years (instead of three months) of effort, 4,444 killed and wounded in the direct hostilities,[74] and a great amount of money, ammunition and supplies, would seem to be too high a price, even if Vorontsov's aims were achieved fully. But to invest all that only in order to destroy three villages, which soon after the Russian retreat were rebuilt and refortified, was simply a waste.[75] Furthermore, with the benefit of hindsight, one may add that it was doubly a waste because the effort and equipment could have been used for much better results, from the Russian point of view, in Chechnia.

In his reports and correspondence, Vorontsov emphasised the moral effect of these encounters, which 'with no exception end with either failure or shame for them'.[76] He pointed to the fact that the fall of Salṭah and Girgil caused quarrels between Shamil and Qibid Muḥammad and between the *imām* and Daniyāl.[77] The effect of Shamil's defeats, according to the viceroy, could be felt in tentative approaches by some of the mountaineers – like the villages of Gimrāh and Harakān[78] and Daniyāl[79] – to the Russians.

These contacts, however, had no results, and in the case of Daniyāl did not differ at all from previous attempts.[80] As for the moral influence of these campaigns, even before Chōkha, the mountaineers

> did not realise that they had suffered crushing defeats, and, of course, quite correctly so. To the contrary, they were sure that now they had proved themselves to be a fully worthy adversary to us, with whom any clash is very dangerous. [The campaigns] had no [negative] effect at all on Shamil's interests in the mountains. In the eyes of the Muslim population of the country his status rose higher and higher.[81]

Thus, from Shamil's point of view, even before Chōkha, these campaigns could not have come at a more opportune time. They were the perfect diversion for his people from their difficulties and from the Russian successes in Chechnia. Now, with the final results, his prestige and his peoples' morale soared even further. Once again the Russians 'co-operated with Shamil as only true friends could'.[82] Nevertheless, the *imām* did not fail to counter-attack the Russians.

Chapter 19

The South

In his counterattacks Shamil concentrated on Southern and Central Daghestan – the 'soft underbelly' of the Russian defences. During the winter of 1847 Shamil's *nā'ibs* were particularly active in Ghāzī-Ghumuq and Aqūsha.[1] These activities, especially coupled with the widespread rumours about Shamil's intentions, made life very difficult for the Russians.

> Not a single day passed without spies from among the unpacified mountaineers bringing us evidence that Shamil intended to invade [different areas]. All this evoked preventative measures on our side and forced us to move our battalions to and fro. To such an extent were the natives (and, I suppose, to a certain extent we as well) scared by the annual invasions of the mountaineers into our possessions[2]

However, the major attack that year was carried out in the south. By the beginning of 1847 the situation along the Lesghian Line and in Chārtalah resembled in many respects that of Chechnia in 1840. Until 1844 'three infantry battalions sufficed to guard the Cordonne [Line] as well as [to keep] peace and security inside the district'.[3] That year everything changed following the defection of Daniyāl, the *sulṭān* of Iliṣū.

The ruler since 1831[4] of a small principality astride the main Caucasian range,[5] Daniyāl enjoyed prestige and influence far beyond his real power. Following the policies of his father and elder brother, whom he succeeded, he displayed loyalty to the Russian authorities and fulfilled all their demands, on many occasions heading his militia in the Russians' service. Still, like all the other native rulers, he secretly kept in contact with Shamil, as an insurance policy.[6]

For his services Daniyāl was awarded the (honorary) rank of major-general. But in other respects he was like other natives loyal to the Russians, neglected and even wronged. In 1840 he was subjected to the (Russian) administrator of the Chārtalah district,[7] and his authority was severely curtailed. His appeals to reinstate it were not answered.[8]

With the appointment of Schwartz as administrator of Chārtalah, Daniyāl's position became more difficult. Grigorii Efimovich Schwartz [Shvarts] was a cavalry officer, one of those for whom the war in the Caucasus was a 'sport'. Entering service in 1803, he was transferred to the Caucasus in 1840 and replaced Freytag on the Lesghian Line in 1842. Soon Schwartz developed an antagonism to Daniyāl, which had both a political and a personal character.[9]

With the departure of Golovin, Daniyāl lost his only protector. Now the authorities in the Caucasus were clearly looking for a pretext to get rid of Daniyāl altogether and annex his realm.[10] In the summer of 1844, in 'a very gross instance of Russian injustice and folly',[11] an emissary was sent to Ilişū to provoke Daniyāl into an action which could be used as such a pretext.

This had its desired effect. On 16 June 1844 Daniyāl, according to Russian sources, publicly swore allegiance to Shamil at the mosque of his capital.[12] However, the contents of a letter which he sent to Neidhardt,[13] clearly contradicts this claim. In this letter Daniyāl enumerated his and his predecessors' services to the Russians and his complaints of ill-treatment, and notified the general that henceforth his services would be given only if his rights were restored.

However, Schwartz and Neidhardt had no intention of negotiating with Daniyāl now that they were given the pretext they had been looking for. On 17 June Schwartz called Daniyāl to Zakartalah to discuss the participation of Daniyāl's militia in the forthcoming campaign. His intention was to arrest the *sulṭān* as soon as he arrived.

But Daniyāl did not come. Instead, he sent a letter in which he stated that he had no intention of rendering services until his requests had been granted. Once this was done, Daniyāl wrote, 'I shall continue, as in previous years, to be truly devoted to the government. Until then, my realm remains calm'.[14]

On the following day, 18 June, Schwartz marched out of Zakartalah and on the 20th he entered Daniyāl's realm and had a skirmish with the local militia. Here Schwartz stopped for five days waiting for reinforcements. On 25 June he resumed his advance and defeated a 3,000-man force at Agatay. Here the Russians stopped again, for eight days.

On 3 July Schwartz marched on Ilişū and stormed it. Daniyāl, after a desperate resistance, had to escape to the mountains, where he became one of Shamil's *nā'ibs*. On 8 August the Russians established their administration in the village of Kākh. Ilişū was completely destroyed, the mosque being the only building to remain untouched. The small Sultanate thus became a regular part of the district of Chārtalah.

Daniyāl's defection was, perhaps, less damaging for the Russians than that of Ḥajimurād. Still, it was harmful to them and brought advantages to Shamil, not the least being the fact that it was yet another example of how the Russians 'rewarded' devoted collaborators. According to Shamil, Daniyāl was 'a bad fighter but a good adviser',[15] being by far the most experienced person in Shamil's camp in Russian and international politics. His advice was, therefore, taken seriously even though he himself soon came under suspicion because of his contacts with the Russians.[16] Perhaps Daniyāl's greatest contribution to Shamil was the fact that he 'secured to Shamil for many years to come the loyalty of whole districts of Southern Daghestan'.[17] The *sulṭān*'s connections with his ex-subjects proved an inexhaustible pool of spies and messengers for the *imām*.[18]

Since Daniyāl's defection 'our situation on the Lesghian Cordonne Line had become considerably more alarming and difficult'.[19] Three years of Schwartz's administration sufficed to exasperate the population of the district, while his raids into the mountains merely increased the hostility of the neighbouring mountain communities without bringing any benefit to the Russians.[20]

The widening discontent with Russian rule resulted in growing disorder in the district. Numerous 'gangs of brigands' composed of both mountaineers and runaway lowlanders operated in the area. They enjoyed active co-operation from at least part of the population and sheltered in the forests. By the end of 1846 they rendered 'the roads so insecure that the Russians could not pass on them otherwise than in at least 30- to 40-man detachments'.[21]

By January 1847 discontent reached such proportions that the population of Chār, Balagin and Ilişū sent deputations to Shamil to ask for his assistance. They promised to rise up as soon as his forces descended from the mountains.[22] In response Shamil charged Daniyāl to carry out an offensive in that direction.

By doing so, the *imām* had a few aims in mind: it would distract the Russians (and his own people) from Chechnia; it might disrupt the Russian plans and preparations for the summer

MAP 16: THE ABOLITION OF THE SULTANATE OF ILIṢU, 1844

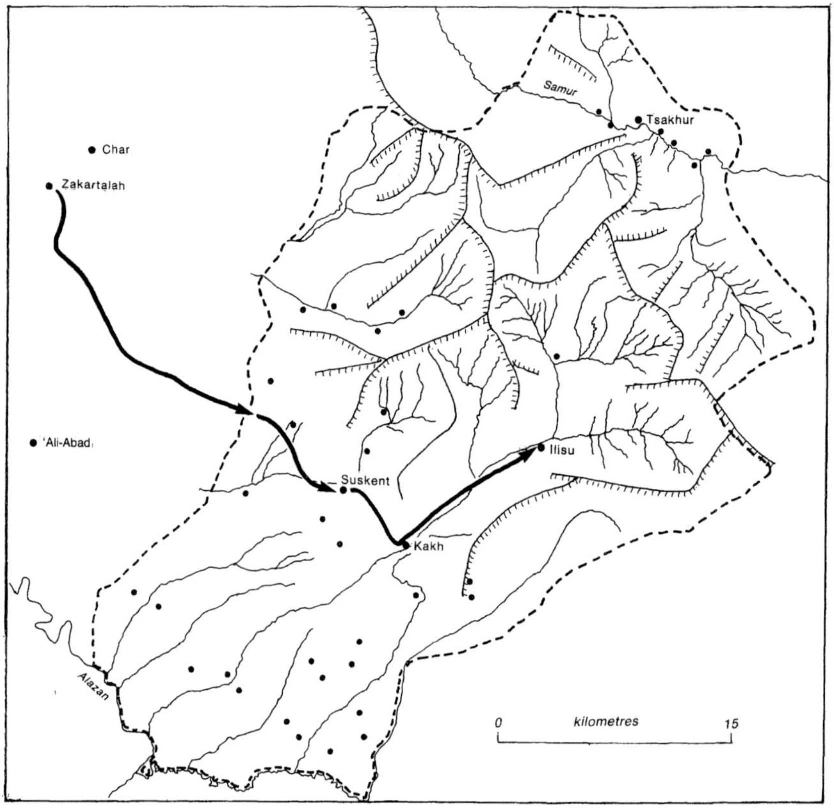

campaign in Daghestan; it would further enhance Shamil's influence among the Daghestani communities of the Alazān valley; and it would give satisfaction to Daniyāl, who had been most interested in retrieving his realm.

By 13 May three main forces were concentrated in front of the Lesghian Line, commanded by Daniyāl, ʿAddāl Maḥmūdshvili and Shaʿbān. On 16 May Daniyāl entered Iliṣū, ʿAddāl captured Balagin and Shaʿbān threatened the right flank of the line.[23] The mountaineers were welcomed and joined by the local population. The local militiamen either joined the mountaineers or dispersed. In spite of official secrecy, 'the residents of even the remotest villages knew what was happening, and were in an unusual state of alertness'.[24] The entire district as well as the province of Nūkhwa 'wavered in their devotion to us'.[25]

The Russians were caught completely off guard. Schwartz and Burnod, his deputy, had to concentrate their scattered forces quickly. Once they had done so, however, they found that the mountaineers were applying the same tactics as in the early 1840s in Chechnia. 'I have to be present everywhere simultaneously,' wrote Schwartz, 'but the continuous movements, battles and alertness extremely fatigue the troops and horses, while there are almost none to replace even part of them'.[26]

> I am absolutely unable to drive out the enemy from the district of Balagin. Wherever I move the force – the predators disappear; it is impossible to cut the mountain passes off; this would mean to completely split up the force [into small units] – without any benefit; the enemy will take cover in the forests and the population will not only feed him, but will also join him.[27]

The situation seemed to deteroriate further when Ḥajimurād was reported to be on his way to assist Daniyāl. Schwartz asked for help from Argutinskii.[28] The latter, however, did not (or pretended not to) believe that Daniyāl's attack was anything but a diversion from an intended attack on Ghāzī-Ghumuq. Finding additional reasons (or excuses) for his inability to march to Schwartz's aid, he moved only after Daniyāl's offensive had been stopped.[29]

On 9 June Daniyāl finally retreated behind the main range. Afterwards he stated that 'the aim of our movement into Georgia was not to fight the Russians but rather to snatch away the herds of sheep of our communities, in which we were fully successful'.[30]

MAP 17: THE ALAZAN VALLEY

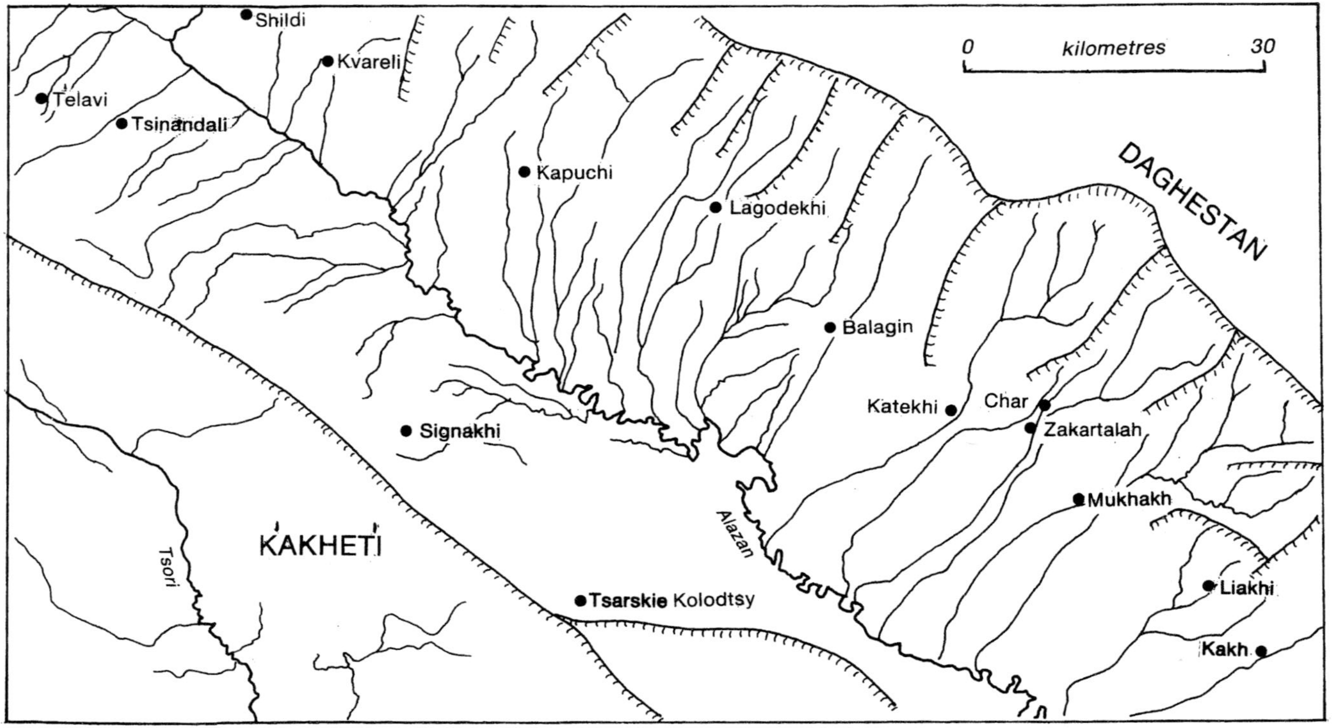

There is, however, little doubt that Daniyāl's aims were much more extensive.

That the events of 1840–41 in Chechnia were not repeated in the Alazān valley in 1847 was because the theatre of operations, the population and the circumstances were different. Furthermore, the military talents of Daniyāl, ʿAddāl and Shaʿbān were far from equal to those of Shamil, Akhbirdi Muḥammad and Shuʿayb. But most important, unlike Chechnia, Chārtalah remained a secondary theatre for Shamil (as well as for the Russians). This was underlined by the fact that the *imām* himself did not participate in the attack. As soon as he realised that the Russians were not diverted from their preparations in Daghestan, and that no quick gains could be made, he lost interest in this campaign and recalled Daniyāl.

The end of Daniyāl's offensive did not signal an end to hostilities. Desultory warfare continued until October, when the snow blocked the passes through the mountains. The mountaineers, in fact, carried out another three-pronged offensive between 26 September and 3 October.[31]

In November 1847, after the fall of Salṭah, Shamil intended to operate in Ghāzī-Ghumuq. He even sent a call to the residents to rise[32] and invaded Tsudaqār. But he had to leave for Chechnia due to the Russian winter campaign there.[33] After the fall of Girgil in 1848, Shamil had again decided to operate in the south. On 17 September, Daniyāl 'fell suddenly' on Qalʿa.[34] He was followed by three forces which advanced on Amṣār, Luchek and Ikhrek. All in all the mountaineers numbered, according to Russian sources, up to 12,000 men. 'We ourselves were unable to concentrate such huge forces at that moment in Daghestan, and Shamil, of course, knew it.'[35] On 18 September the mountaineers approached Kākh. 'Our [native] militia started to gradually disperse, abandoning the posts it was guarding.'[36] On 20 September Roth, the commander of the Samur district, tried to reconnoitre the Upper Samur, but was repulsed and shut himself up in the fort of Akhdī.

At about that time Daniyāl entered Rutul and reported to Shamil that the inhabitants of 'Akhdī and of other townships want to join us and invite us [into their villages], and many . . . have already joined us'. In general, he continued, 'the people would like you very much to come here'.[37]

The *imām*, indeed, arrived in Rutul on 24 September. The following day Daniyāl entered the village of Akhdī. On the

Shamil in Akhdī (*drawing by a contemporary artist*)

26th the fort near Akhdī was invested and the neighbouring fort Tiflisskoe stormed and its garrison put to the sword.[38] Thus 'the entirety of the Rutul and Dokuzparı *maḥāls* was in the hands of the *murīds*, who now approached the borders of the Khanate of Kurāh and the province of Qubāh'.[39]

Shamil's attack caught by complete surprise all the local commanders as well as Tiflis. 'No one could have guessed', claimed Vorontsov later, 'that Shamil would dare on a serious enterprise in this gap' in the Russian defences.[40] Neither had anyone believed that the *imām* was 'in a position to raise significant levies any more'.[41] Their reactions were the same as in similar cases in the past: Schwartz 'stalled',[42] 'spread rumours' about his intentions,[43] and finally 'decided to assist Argutinskii, when the latter did not need his assistance any more'.[44] Wrangel [Vrangel'], the governor of Shemākha, called for reinforcements, which arrived two days after the drama had ended.[45] Gagarin, the governor of Derbend, hearing that Ḥajimurād had arrived at Khazry, sent a battalion to Qirq, about ten kilometres from that village instructing them 'to fire a couple of cannon shots, and letting the garrison, the population of Khazry and the enemy thus know of the presence of our force, to return to Kurāh'.[46]

Argutinskii, whose responsibility Akhdī was, acted with 'incomprehensible slowness'.[47] Receiving news of Shamil's attack on 20 September, he waited for an official report from Roth (which arrived the following day) before moving out of Temir-Khān-Shūra on the 22nd. Not in too much of a hurry, he arrived with a force of about 7,000 infantry, 400 cavalry and ten guns at Kurāh on 29 September. It is difficult not to get the impression that everyone expected the fort of Akhdī to fall very soon and tried to be as far away as possible when it happened.

However, the fort though subjected to heavy fire, the garrison diminishing hourly,[48] its main gunpowder store blown up and its rations and water running out, resisted stubbornly. The spirit behind this heroic resistance was an officer who had volunteered to return to active service though he had not yet fully recovered from a severe wound and who now took over command from the wounded Roth[49] – Captain Novoselov.

On 30 September Argutinskii arrived on the range overlooking the fort, but found it impossible to proceed that way. He decided to retreat, well aware that such a step, reminiscent of Girgil in 1843, would deal a mortal blow to the garrison's morale, and lower the spirits and trust of his own troops. Yet, the garrison, with the power of despair, decided to resist until the last and then to blow up the fort.

Argutinskii, it seems, gave up hope of saving the fort. 'All I have laboured for for six years can be lost here,' he said to one of his officers, and added: 'from now on the column is our fatherland.'[50] Without hurry he concentrated his force between Kurāh and Akhdī and added about 4,000–5,000 local militiamen to his troops.[51]

Only on 2 October, having learnt the previous day that the fort was still resisting, did Argutinskii decide to act. He marched

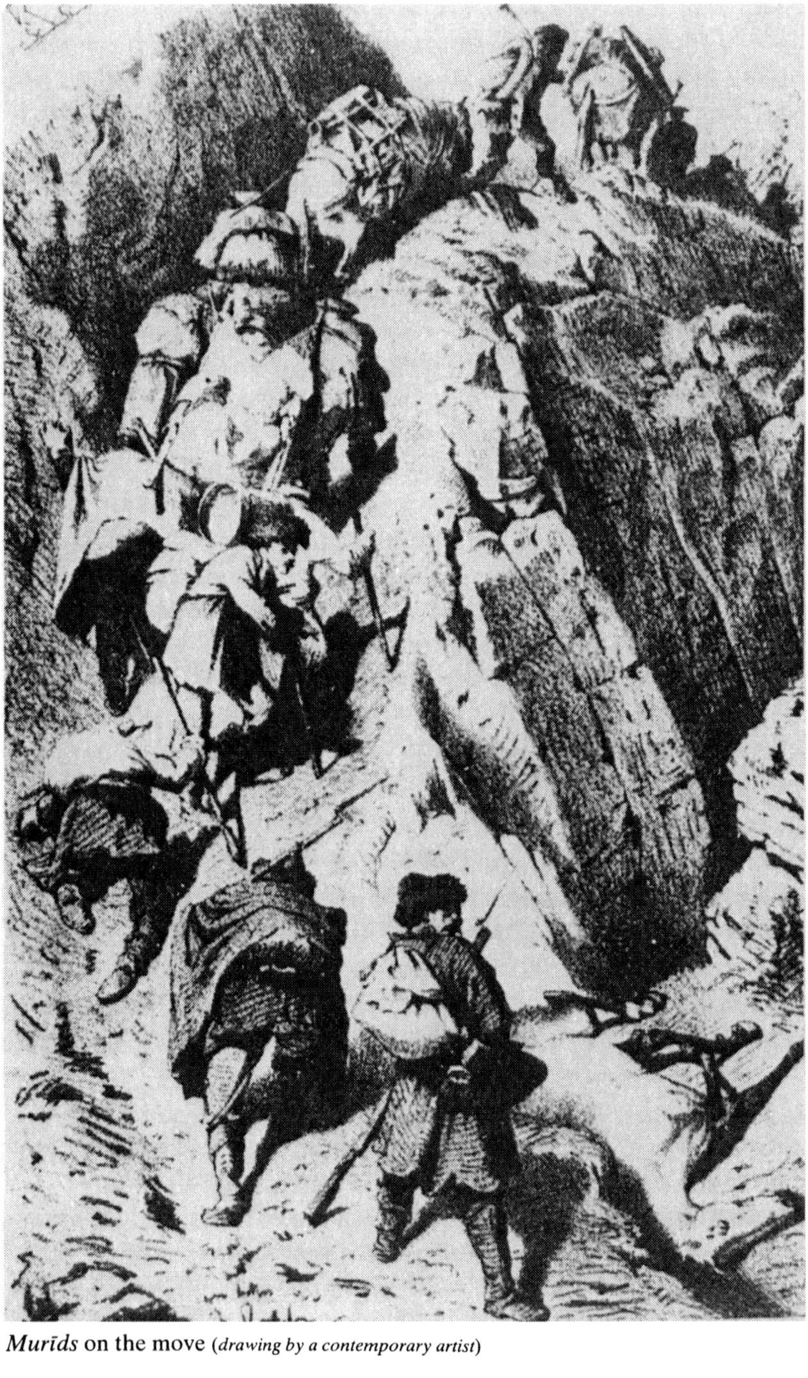

Murīds on the move (*drawing by a contemporary artist*)

MAP 18: AKHDĪ

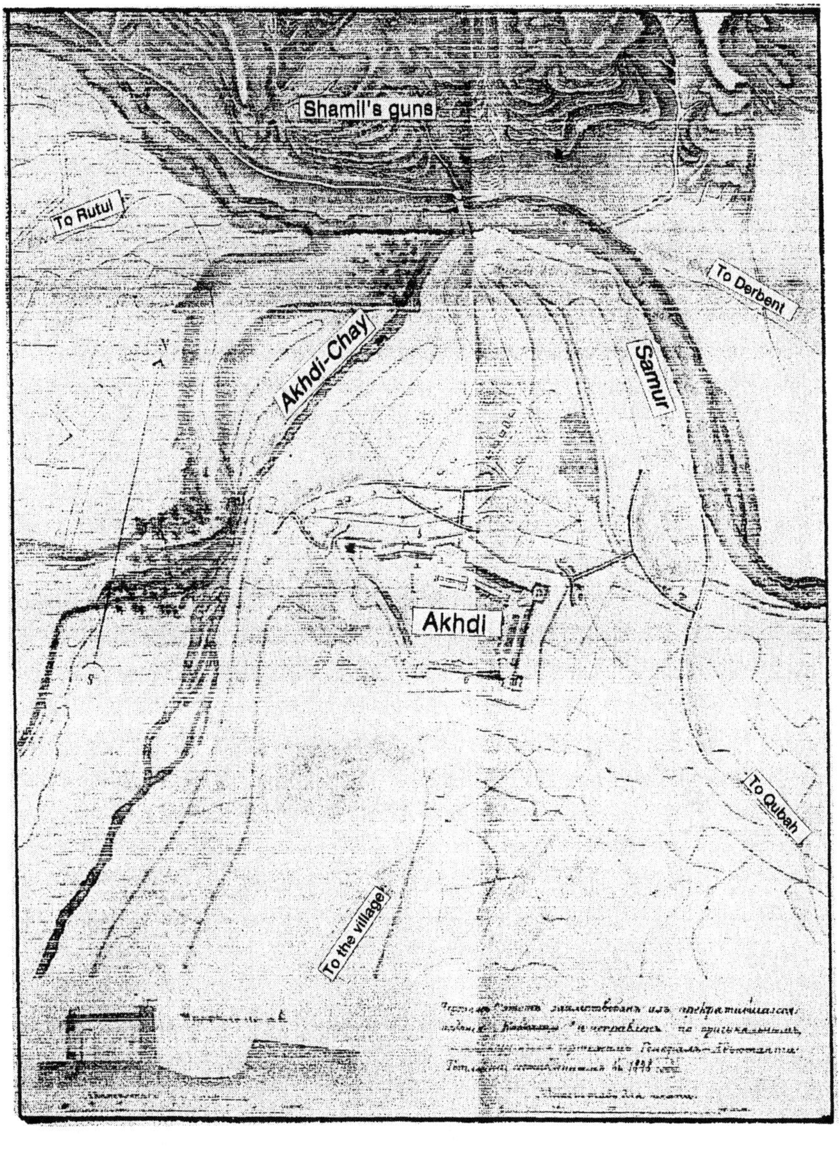

Source: Sbornik Opisanii Osad i Oboron Krepostei i Ukreplenii, Vol.I (St. Petersburg, 1869).

Shamil's storming of Akhdī, 1848 (*painting by a later artist*)

in a roundabout route, through Kabīr to Tall Sughūr, otherwise known as Tsuqūl [Zukhul or Tsukhul], which he reached on 3 October. On the following day he stormed the mountaineers' position at Meskīnjī, where Shamil had concentrated about 7,000 men under Qibid Muḥammad, Daniyāl and Ḥajimurād in order to stop the Russians from reaching Akhdī. Soon after the position had been stormed, Argutinskii reached the fort, and Shamil hastily retreated into the mountains.

Argutinskii now crisscrossed the Samur district with sword and fire. He ordered to shoot or bayonet on the spot people accused of joining Shamil and villages which had not hastened to resubmit were looted on his orders.[52]

According to Vorontsov,

> Shamil's main mistake (and not for the first time) has been his hope, that the population will not only rise against us but will strongly co-operate with him, both wherever he had already made his appearance and in the neighbouring communities. He gets invitations from people ill-disposed to us, but on the spot does not meet general co-operation. This happened to him in Ghabarṭa and then on the plain of [Ghāzī-] Ghumuq, twice in Aqūsha and finally now on the Samur.[53]

While essentially true, this appraisal tends, consciously or unconsciously, to disregard (or cover up) the fact that Shamil's 'hope' was very well anchored in reality. Argutinskii's savage reprisals prove not only to what extent the population co-operated with Shamil, but also how close the Russians (and Argutinskii personally) were to a disaster.[54]

As for the disposition of neighbouring communities, the population of Kurāh 'only awaited a small success on the part of the *murīds* to take their side'.[55] The local levies refused time and again to fight the mountaineers. The 1,500-man militia of Qubāh, for example, dispersed without a single shot in front of a few dozen horsemen, shouting 'Ḥajimurād!'[56]

Unlike at Ghabarṭa and Aqūsha, this time Shamil's plans were not checked by a resolute movement on the part of a Russian general.[57] Rather, it was the heroic stand of the small garrison of Akhdī which stopped the mountaineers. The wide publicity given to their deed was, therefore, well deserved. But in addition it served to cover up a state of affairs not at all complimentary to the Caucasian Corps.[58]

For the following five years Shamil did not undertake a major campaign in the south. But this did not mean that the Lesghian Line was quiet. During 1848 the mountaineers continually carried out small raids, causing 'grievous damage'[59] to the Georgian population and forcing Schwartz to be constantly on the move.[60]

By the end of that year Schwartz was relieved of his duties following a court martial.[61] His successor, Chiliaev [Chilishvili] was eager for action and would not be kept passive.

> By the end of 1848, soon after General Chiliaev took over command, it was discovered that even though the population had behaved well, it, being partly used not to be punished for its perfidy, and submitting to the influence of 'Muridism', did not give any right to count on its loyalty, especially in adverse circumstances. To keep it in submission, the most severe measures were needed – and, one must do justice to General Chiliaev, he did not fail to use them.[62]

The subsequent intensification in fighting[63] supplied Chiliaev with the 'necessity' for an offensive:

> Chiliaev undertook a raid on the community of Dido. The most important village of the Dido community, Khupro, abandoned by its residents, was taken and burnt after a few shots, made more to clear one's conscience than out of necessity. Covering himself thus with glory Chiliaev moved back. True to their custom, the mountaineers importunately pressed the retreating force, which lost more than a hundred men. Chiliaev sent the commander of the corps [Vorontsov] a report about this expedition in which he stated that Khupro was stormed and that the enemy lost up to 500 men. Nevertheless the truth came to be known and General Chiliaev was strongly compromised by his exaggerated report.[64]

Naturally, this raid did not stop the mountaineers, and during the rest of the year they continually raided the lowland.[65]

On 20 May 1850 Shaʿbān, one of Shamil's *nā'ibs* in the vicinity of the Lesghian Line, lured a force of 200 Georgian militiamen into an ambush and annihilated it.[66] Vorontsov strongly reprimanded Chiliaev for this incident. Chiliaev, who had not been responsible for it, left for medical treatment in Piatigorsk. He returned in early November only to die of exposure to the cold weather.[67]

Chiliaev's temporary successor, Bellegarde [Bel'gard], suggested a summer offensive into the mountains, which was approved by Vorontsov. He, it seems, even contemplated the conquest of 'Irib. During this campaign Bellegarde and his deputies Davydov and Melikov – all three protégés of Vorontsov – committed every possible mistake and folly.[68] The Russians were saved great disasters only because Shamil and his main lieutenants were busy elsewhere.[69]

Only in 1851 did the Lesghian Line become quieter. The main reason for this was that the new commander, Prince Grigorii (Grigol) Orbeliani,[70] was not looking for quick glory.

Chapter 20

Greater Chechnia

When he accepted the nomination to the Caucusus in 1845, Vorontsov did it not without hesitation. After all, he was then 63 years old and not in the best of health.[1] Vorontsov was also well aware that the emperor did not particularly trust and like him. He therefore did not expect to stay for more than a few years in this post, and hoped to subdue Daghestan and Chechnia before retiring.

This was one of the main reasons for his over-optimistic plans for operations in Lesser Chechnia in 1846 and in Daghestan in 1847. By June 1847, however, when Vorontsov had realised that the pacification of these areas would be a lengthy process, he was determined 'not [to] leave this country without having taken such measures, which will secure it and place it in a better state than before'.[2]

By April 1848 this more modest aim was within his sight. 'I dare think,' wrote Vorontsov, 'that some results of the three-year-old persistent system employed by me can already be seen. I hope that these results will be more discernible next year.'[3] He therefore decided to go to St. Petersburg in the summer of 1849 to report to the emperor in person. Vorontsov expected to be relieved from his post then, and was ready to retire gracefully. He was convinced that the situation had improved to such an extent that 'the change of chief will not cause such a change of outlook that could throw everything back into doubt'.[4]

Vorontsov arrived in St. Petersburg on 21 July and met the emperor on the same day. Two and a half weeks later he followed Nicholas to Warsaw, where he had three more meetings with the tsar and tsarevich Alexander, on 7, 9, and 14 August. The emperor 'agreed [with me] on everything and was very gracious'.[5]

On 6 November Vorontsov returned to Tiflis to continue his task. Abandoning almost all intentions to conduct offensives in Daghestan – though there were hints that Vorontsov still occasionally contemplated the capture of Chōkha and even of

ʿIrib[6] – the Russians concentrated now on Chechnia. This meant that the centre of operations was to move to Greater Chechnia, and so it did in January 1850.

Between 22 January and 7 March Nesterov, with a force of about 15,000, cleared an avenue through the forests near Shalī toward the heart of Greater Chechnia – Vedān or New Darghiyya, Shamil's place of residence since 1845. Shamil led in person a stubborn resistance and brought in levies from Daghestan. The Russians had three battles with the mountaineers, on 31 January, 1 and 18 February, and dozens of smaller skirmishes. How strong the resistance was can be measured from the level of the Russian casualties, which averaged 10–15 per day, not including losses in the three larger battles.[7] As soon as the Russians retired, Shamil blocked the new throughway by a 1,600-metre trench and clay wall, garrisoned by about 500 men with one cannon under Talgik.[8]

Any further initiative on the part of the Russians was rendered impossible, first by Nesterov's mental illness,[9] and later by the visit of the tsarevich Alexander.[10] The rest of the year passed, therefore, in intermittent warfare only, with one exception.

On his tour of inspection of the Left Flank between 30 June and 5 July 1850, Vorontsov instructed Kozlowski [Kozlovskii] – Nesterov's temporary replacement – to clear the forest between the Michik and the Kachkalyk range, a move which even the Russian narrator regarded as a mistake to be excused.[11] Kozlowski, without protesting, carried it out between 13 August and 16 September, but at a terribly high cost. His small force – 2,500 infantry, 800 cavalry and three cannon – 'melted away' and its situation 'became more difficult by the day'.[12]

Kozlowski appealed to his neighbours for reinforcements or diversions, but they were too busy in preparations for Alexander's visit to respond. The only exception was Sleptsov, who with a force of 700 of his Cossacks crossed all of Lesser Chechnia and on 3 September raided and destroyed Shamil's fortified trench in the forest of Shalī.[13]

This most daring and successful raid, which cost only 16 killed and 47 wounded, overshadowed any other event in Chechnia that year. It 'excited public opinion and all the press of the capital',[14] and Sleptsov was duly commended and promoted to major-general even though he carried out the raid on his personal initiative, hiding his intention from, and even misleading, his superiors. The mountaineers were greatly impressed as well, and on his way back through Lesser Chechnia, Sleptsov was greeted everywhere with congratulations by the population, pacified and unpacified alike.[15] But the raid had no other results. It came too late to draw pressure off Kozlowski, and Shamil re-established his fortifications, so that the following winter the Russians had to storm them again.

With Alexander's visit successfuly over, the Russians could concentrate again on the battlefield. Already in August 1850 Vorontsov and Nesterov made up plans for the winter campaign in Chechnia.[16] However, it was Kozlowski who had to carry it out, Nesterov having relapsed into insanity again.[17] Between 13 January and 12 March 1851, leading a force of 16,000 infantry, 1,600 cavalry and 24 cannons, he cleared the forests along the Argūn and near Shalī.[18] At the same time, between 30 December 1850 and 8 February 1851 Sleptsov was engaged in clearing operations at different places along the Upper Sunja.[19] Following that he started to pave a road from Alkhān Yūrt to Urus Martan, which he completed in May.[20]

Shamil resisted stubbornly. From early 1851 he concentrated a strong force at Shalī and strengthened the existing fortifications there. In addition to the usual harassment, the *imām* personally commanded a battle against Kozlowski on 4 February, after which he sent Ḥajimurād to try to attack either Kozlowski or Sleptsov from their flank.[21] However, the most important event, almost completely disregarded by the Russian sources,[22] took place one day before the conclusion of the winter campaign.

Unable to stop the Russians from clearing their way through, Shamil decided, according to his subsequent testimony, to use for the first and only time his *niẓām* [*jadīd*] – the regular infantry he had been building for a few years on the model of the Ottoman (and Muhammad ʿAlī's) *nizam-ı cedid*.[23] On 11 March he deployed this force, 5,000–6,000-strong, to block the Russian advance. But as in other cases of non-European units built on the European model but not commanded by European officers and NCOs, it failed, and Bariatinskii, with a force of 4,500 infantry, 1,600 cavalry and 24 guns, routed Shamil's *niẓām*. According to Russian reports, the mountaineers fled, leaving behind 276 corpses.[24]

No large-scale campaign took place in Chechnia (or anywhere else) during the rest of the year. However, intermittent fighting intensified enormously,[25] which resulted in the Left Flank 'occupying the first place in the number of casualties . . . in the [entire]

Caucasian Corps'.[26] This intensification was the result of two factors: Shamil's disavowal of any further attempt to fight the Russians in a pitched battle and his subsequent return to guerrilla tactics;[27] and Nesterov's disease and his subsequent final release from his duties.

Since 1848 there had been a constant increase in the number of raids initiated by the Russians. A new generation of colonels had come to command sections of the Line under Vorontsov, like Bariatinskii in Khasav Yūrt, Suslov on the Sunja and Terek Lines, and Sleptsov on the Upper Sunja Line. Young, ambitious, eager for action and glory, they took advantage of any excuse and opportunity to carry out 'searches in enemy territory', justifying them as 'necessary under the circumstances'.[28] Now that it was obvious to all that Kozlowski was only a temporary replacement, a race developed among the candidates for the command, first and foremost between Sleptsov and Bariatinskii.[29]

All these raids caused little damage to Shamil even when successful. When the *imām* realised that no further Russian large-scale offensives were forthcoming in Chechnia, he turned to Daghestan, where an opportunity had arisen to strike back at the Russians and make good his setback in the battle of 11 March. For some time Shamil had been repeatedly approached by the people of Qaytāq and Ṭabarsarān, who had asked him to lead their general uprising. On 29 June Shamil held a council with the *nā'ibs* of Daghestan in Rughchah [Rugdzha], where he acquainted them with his plans. The following day the *imām* occupied Turchīdāgh with his main force.[30] While he intended, thus, to divert the Russians' attention, ʿUmar, the *nā'ib* of Hutsāl, was to cross the Russian territory into Qaytāq and Ṭabarsarān.

The plan worked well. Argutinskii, upon receiving word of Shamil's move, left Temir-Khān-Shūra on 30 June. On 3 July he reached Turchīdāgh with a force of 4,000 infantry, 500 cavalry and eight pieces of artillery. On that day he stormed Turchīdāgh. That night, 3–4 July, ʿUmar and 300 horsemen left for Qaytāq and Ṭabarsarān, but had a skirmish with a Russian force and retreated. Shamil, appalled by ʿUmar's performance, dismissed him from his post, and instructed Ḥajimurād to carry out the plan.

The Avār *mudīr* undertook it reluctantly. On the night of 12–13 July he moved with 500 horsemen from Chōkha.[31] On 14 July at dawn he attacked Buynākh [Buinaki] on the highway to

MAP 19: GREATER CHECHNIA

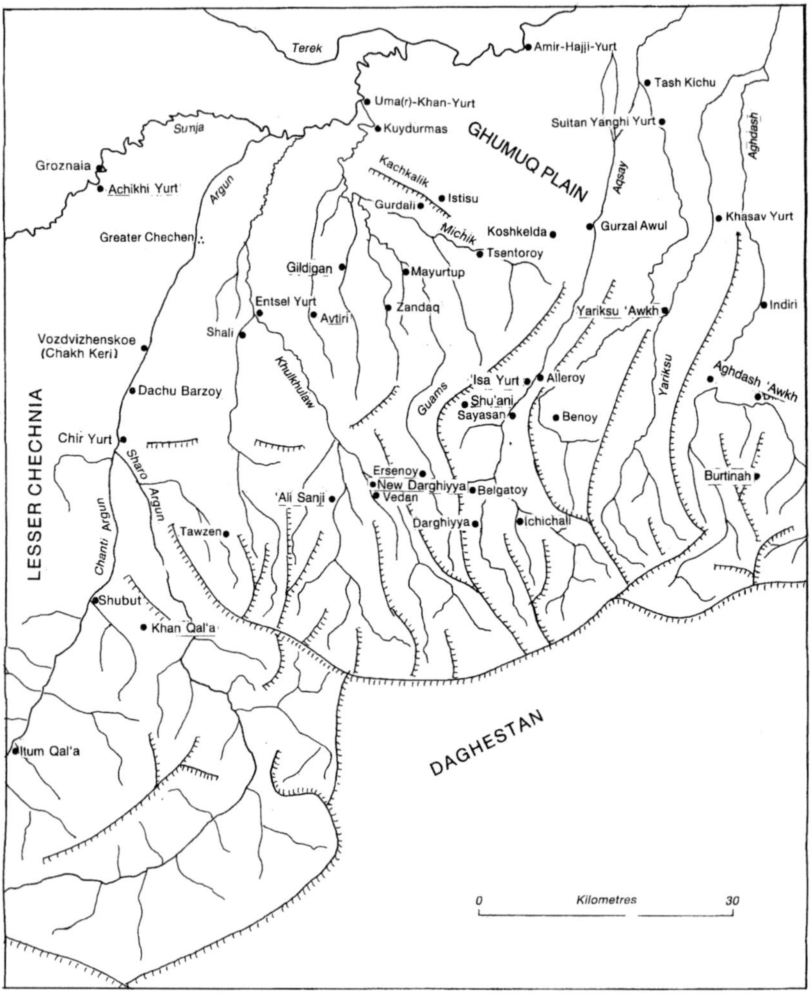

Derbend. The following day he passed through Qarāqaytāq and entered Ṭabarsarān. Thus, in 30 hours he crossed more than 150 kilometres over highly difficult terrain. As expected, the population of the areas he passed rose and joined him.

Argurtinskii comprehended what had happened only on 17 July. Concentrating a force of 4,500 infantry, 900 cavalry, ten pieces of artillery and rockets, he left Temir-Khān-Shūra on 19 July. On the 24th he reached the border of Ṭabarsarān to find that Ḥajimurād had disappeared behind a screen of contradictory rumours.

In full co-ordination with his *mudīr*, Shamil moved from Chōkha to Sughūr. On 23 July, when Argutinskii was already well on his way to Ṭabarsarān, Shamil made demonstrations towards Turchīdāgh, and then on the heights of Ghamashī, while Daniyāl made a demonstration towards Ghāzī-Ghumuq. These did not succeed in diverting Argutinskii from Ṭabarsarān, but by then his position would not allow him to leave that area anyway.

On 29 July the Russian force successfully waged battle against Ḥajimurād and his local levies near Kuiarykh. Arguinskii followed his success and entered Ṭabarsarān, only to find himself isolated in a hostile country. How precarious his position was could be seen when on 2 August Argutinskii sent back his train: the column had to fight its way through the same place where the winning battle had been waged four days previously.

Ḥajimurād himself attacked the Russian train further on its way. After a short skirmish the *mudīr* and his band galloped to the villages on the Russians' way, announcing everywhere that he had defeated the Russians; that the column due to arrive were the remnants of the Russian force; and that he, Ḥajimurād, presented the villagers with these remnants and their luggage if they only wanted to take them. The villagers raced to the column and attacked it. The Russians managed eventually to get through but not before losing 7 killed, 68 wounded and 40 pack-horses with their loads.

Yet Ḥajimurād's position was no less precarious. Not having brought a large enough force, he had to spare his fighters and to rely mainly on the local population. The locals, moreover, seeing a large Russian force in the midst of them, started to doubt the *mudīr*'s ability to defeat it. Furthermore, they increasingly felt that Ḥajimurād was ready to fight the war till the last of them but not the first of his own. When on 3 August Argutinskii advanced to and stormed Ghoshnī [Khoshni] in a hard battle, a popular assembly decided to send a delegation to negoiate with Argutinskii. On that night Ḥajimurād slipped away from his position and on 6 August reached Avāirstān.

Soon after Ḥajimurād's return, a delegation from Ṭabarsarān came to Shamil to complain of the *mudīr*'s conduct.[32] By then a rift had already opened and widened between the *imām* and his lieutenant. Ḥajimurād unwisely publicly expressed opposition on the question of Shamil's succession. Furthermore, he started to assume a higher profile and claimed that most of Shamil's successes and victories were achieved thanks to him, Ḥajimurād.

The *imām* therefore, seized the opportunity of these complaints to depose Ḥajimurād and replace him with Fatḥ ʿAlī, a distant relative of the Avār ruling house. Shamil also ordered the confiscation of Ḥajmurād's property. The *mudīr* turned over his part of the booty in the numerous raids he had led, but refused to part with his own property. For a few days it seemed as if an armed confrontation was unavoidable, but finally the two were persuaded to effect a reconciliation, which naturally was only temporary.

Always outspoken and tactless, Ḥajimurād threatened publicly to cause trouble to Shamil. The *imām* secretly convened a council in Avtiri and accused Ḥajimurād of treason. The council sentenced the ex-*mudīr* to death in secret. Warned, however, by friends, Ḥajimurād escaped to the Russians on 25 November 1851.

Any potential damage to Shamil by Ḥajimurād's defection was minimised first by the fact that he had left his family behind, and second, by the way the Russians treated him. Not knowing whether to trust Ḥajimurād and undecided as to what to do with him, Vorontsov played for time, keeping the Avār in a golden cage. Finally, Ḥajimurād lost his patience. On 7 May 1852 he tried to escape back to the mountains, but was intercepted and killed.[33]

The Russians, thus, played into Shamil's hands and set an example of what fate defectors might expect. This effect was not counterbalanced by the completely different treatment accorded to another ex-*nāʾib* – Batā. Adopted by Rosen's brother, Batā served as a Russian officer. In 1844 he defected to Shamil and was nominated by the *imām* as *nāʾib* of Michik. But Batā proved to be corrupt, and as the complaints against him by the population mounted, Shamil deposed him.

By the end of 1851 Batā defected back to the Russians, and

was welcomed by Bariatinskii,[34] who, unlike Vorontsov, showered Batā with favours and gifts. He became the young general's confidant and helped him by advice as well as by his influence in some parts of Greater Chechnia. But Batā's name and influence were too small to cause serious damage to Shamil, especially as he had been regarded unfavourably by many Chechens even before his defection.

Still, Ḥajimurād's and Batā's defections diminished Shamil's authority and prestige and no doubt affected his conduct of internal affairs. They also benefited the Russians, at least psychologically.

Ḥajimurād's failure did not deter Shamil from his intention to launch another assault in the autumn of 1851. This time he was dissuaded by his lieutenants.[35] But this was for a short while only. In January 1852, while Shamil was occupied in Chechnia, he sent Buq Muḥammad al-Ghāzī-Ghumuqī to Ṭabarsarān.

On the night of 11–12 January Buq Muḥammad left Ulū Qalʿa with 300 horsemen and reached Majālis on the following day.[36] To divert the Russians' attention from his attack, the mountaineers carried out a raid near Oghlū on 15 January. Argutinskii ordered Suslov[37] to march on Majālis. However, only on 26 January (i.e. two weeks later) did Suslov concentrate a sufficient force – 3,000 infantry, 600 cavalry, four guns and two mortars – and set off.

Two days later the Russians fought their way through the pass near Mishkeliu, and destroyed that village. On 30 January Suslov won a decisive battle against Buq Muḥammad near Shilahī [Sheliagi]. The village was destroyed and Buq Muḥammad himself taken prisoner. Shamil's plans in this area were thus checkmated.

This was the last offensive undertaken by Shamil in Daghestan in 1852, though between 17–24 March he stayed in Avāristān and made a demonstration towards Ghāzī-Ghumuq. The rest of the year passed in desultory warfare.[38] In July 1852 Daniyāl made a demonstration in the gap between the Lesghian and the Samur Lines. This gave Vorontsov the opportunity to transfer the semi-pacified population from the mountains to the plains, a move he had been contemplating since 1850.[39]

Meanwhile, in Chechnia, the contest between Bariatinskii and Sleptsov was settled by the end of 1851; the former was named commander of the Left Flank and the latter was killed in battle.[40] Bariatinskii's 'freshness' as commander and his youth 'explain many things, beginning with those military actions he undertook and finishing with [his] insufficient familiarity with Greater

Chechnia and pompous report[s]'.[41] Indeed, in 1852 the fighting in Chechnia was especially intensive, more so than in many previous years, which can be directly attributed to Bariatinskii's influence.

Bariatinskii started the winter campaign on 17 January.[42] He moved with a force of 10,000 infantry, 1,500 cavalry and 24 cannons from Vozdvizhenskoe to Shalī. His aim was 'to crush the enemy's hordes, to destroy all the means of the inhabitants and the enemy, and *then to act according to the circumstances*'.[43] Hearing that Shamil was away in Daghestan to deal with a local uprising, Bariatinskii captured Gildigān [Geldygen] and Avtiri on 18 January.

However, the *imām* returned surprisingly quickly and appeared from the least expected direction. The Russian general tried 'to retreat . . . but in such a way as to divert the enemy's attention'. Thus, he undertook what he called in his report 'a demonstration toward Vedān'. By this movement, however, he gave the Chechens enough time to fortify the hamlets along the way of his return. The ensuing battle, in which Shamil took part personally, sword in hand, was hard. 'The Russians had for a long time not met such a truly heroic resistance in Greater Chechnia.'[44]

While Bariatinskii was away with part of his force, the other part started to clear the forests in the area of Shalī. This continued with intervals until 29 January against fierce resistance. On the night of 29–30 January Bariatinskii, together with Vrevskii, carried out a double raid along the upper Goyta and Roshna in Lesser Chechnia, for which he was strongly criticised by all Russian sources.[45] The Chechens were warned in advance by one of Bariatinskii's native guides and were ready for the attack.[46] The Russians suffered 292 losses without, in fact, achieving anything.[47] After his return, Bariatinskii carried out a raid on Shamil's Daghestani reinforcements near Saʿīd Yūrt – 'a splendidly conceived but resultless excursion'.[48]

Between 1 and 12 February Bariatinskii cleared the forests in the vicinity of Mezoy. On 13 February he moved to Teplī on the Argūn, where his force cleared the forest until the 27th. His move was due to the activity of Shamil's artillery. At least that was how the Chechens interpreted it[49] and with raised spirits, they multiplied their efforts to resist the Russians.

On 29 February, two days after finishing in Teplī, Bariatinskii initiated 'the most outstanding event of the 1852 winter expedition, the catastrophe at the upper Goyta included'.[50] He intended to cross Greater Chechnia from the Argūn to fort Kurinskoe. In spite of the secrecy in which these intentions were kept. Shamil seems to have known or guessed them.[51] Gildigān was found empty. Rejecting Batā's advice to use the roundabout road, Bariatinskii chose to proceed directly to Mayurtūp through the Gildigān hazelnut forest.[52]

The result was a heavy four-hour battle in which the Russians lost 182 killed and 222 wounded. Unable to carry all the corpses and unwilling to cause demoralisation among the troops, Bariatinskii ordered their burial in a mass grave in Mayurtūp and lit fires over it in order to mask the grave from the Chechens.[53]

That night Bariatinskii sent a messenger to Baklanov in fort Kurinskoe, instructing him to move towards him.[54] Baklanov, the commander of Ghumuq plain, assembled 1,000 infantry, 1,000 cavalry, two cannons and two mortars and marched to meet Bariatinskii. The mountaineers did not attempt to hinder his movement. Bariatinskii's force, on the other hand, had to fight its way through to the meeting place. From there the united force had to do the same, arriving in Kurinskoe in the evening. That day, 1 March, the Russian official report listed 18 killed and 155 wounded.[55]

Bariatinskii returned to Groznaia on 5 March. Between 8 and 13 March he cleared the forests along the lower Argūn from the Michik to Kuydurmas [Gudermes] and a force from Urus Martan cleared the forests along the Goyta between 14 and 16 March. On 17 March 1852 the winter campaign was officially terminated and all the troops were sent to their quarters. All in all the campaign had meagre results, especially when the losses – at least 1,079 killed and wounded – were taken into consideration.

The rest of the year witnessed a series of raids and counter-raids.[56] 'The *imām* ordered his *nā'ibs* . . . to disturb [us] and not to leave us in peace' and they 'were glad to do their best. Hence, from the early spring . . . and until the midst of winter our cordons, were on constant alert.'[57]

The Russians for their part were similarly active. On 8 April Meller-Zakomel'skii, with a force of 3,000 men and six guns, raided the village of Talgik, the *mudīr* of Greater Chechnia, and captured the *mudīr*'s two guns. This was the most successful and impressive raid during the year, though the price – 17 killed and 156 wounded – was 'quite painful'.[58]

On 26 August Bariatinskii sent Vorontsov junior, the viceroy's son and commander of the Kurin Regiment, to raid the Argūn defile. But the Russians encountered a considerably stronger force than expected and were beaten back, losing 10 killed and 57 wounded. 'However much one tries to look for an intelligent and substantial side in this enterprise,' commented a Russian source, 'one cannot find one.'[59]

But, the greatest Russian catastrophe took place three days earlier, on 23 August. Shortly after the end of the winter campaign the inhabitants of two villages were persuaded by Batā to go over to the Russians. The newcomers were settled by the Russians in a new village, Istiṣū, and Batā was nominated their *nā'ib*. Eskī, Batā's successor as *nā'ib* of Michik, raided Istiṣū frequently. Apart from this, the *imām* established the village of Gurdalī across the Kachkalyk ridge, which he settled with volunteers who had taken upon themselves to harass their neighbours constantly. 'Since that moment the people of Istiṣū as well as we ourselves had become very uncomfortable.'[60]

Bariatinskii decided to get rid of this thorn in his flesh and ordered Baklanov to storm Gurdalī. Baklanov did it on 23 August with a force of 1,350 infantry, 800 Cossacks and seven cannon. The Russians were repulsed and chased back, losing 45 killed and 235 wounded, 30 of whom remained in the hands of the mountaineers. 'Such a battle,' wrote the Russian chronicler, 'had not been remembered for a very long time in the Caucasus.'[61]

In spite of such setbacks, however, the Russians in general continued to progress. Between 23 and 27 August Bariatinskii transferred a village to the lowland and destroyed several others with their fields. On 26 December he captured the village of Khān Qalʿa and transferred its population.[62] Even after the catastrophe of Gurdalī some 150 people crossed over to the Russians.[63]

The winter campaign of 1853 was again, as in 1851, conducted in both Greater and Lesser Chechnia.[64] In the latter, between 15 December 1852 and 27 April 1853, Vrevskii, with a force of 2,500 infantry, 1,100 cavalry and 12 cannons, systematically cleared the forests and paved roads. He destroyed a few villages and subdued the population along the upper Netkhoy. His crowning achievement was the taking on 13 April of the range of Karelam, 'the key to the extensive and fertile valley situated between the "Black Mountains" and the main Caucasian range'.[65]

In Greater Chechnia Bariatinskii chose to operate on the Michik. With a force of 8,500 infantry, 1,400 cavalry, 32 guns and some rocket-launchers, he cleared the forests, burned fields and destroyed villages from 16 January to 26 March 1853. On 1 March he stormed Shamil's fortified position on the ford across that river.

Although less systematic than Vrevskii, Bariatinskii's campaign resulted in the retreat of the population of the plain of Greater Chechnia to and beyond, the 'Black Mountains'. Vorontsov's hope that 'as in Lesser Chechnia, the entire lowland of Greater Chechnia will [soon] be in our hands'[66] was thus fulfilled.

Yet this was the last Russian achievement for several years to come. The plans for an extensive summer campaign[67] had to be abandoned in view of the mounting tension with the Ottoman Empire which culminated in the outbreak of the Crimean War. The spring and summer, therefore, passed relatively quietly in intermittent fighting.[68]

Part 8

'The State of God'

Chapter 21

Shamil's State

As far as can be established from the existing evidence, the first *imām* did not envisage himself as a ruler. Rather, he regarded himself as a guide to the various rulers and communities. He intended to act within, and through, the existing political structure. When the local rulers failed to join him, Ghāzī-Muḥammad tried to replace them by relatives who were his followers.[1] The transformation of the *imām* into a ruler, the formation of a state and the development of a state machinery grew out of the circumstances, events and needs of the struggle started by Ghāzī-Muḥammad.

The first steps towards the creation of a state were thus taken by the first *imām*. More deliberate ones were taken by Ḥamza Bek. Unlike his predecessor, who had appointed deputies on an *ad hoc* footing, the second *imām* had regular deputies, each responsible for a specific region.[2] After the elimination of the Avār ruling family,[3] Ḥamza Bek started to adopt some attributes of a ruler as well.

It was, however, under Shamil that this lengthy process reached its completion. By the mid-1850s the third *imām* was a sovereign ruling through a complex machinery. It seems best to describe this machinery as it was at its most developed in these years.[4]

The Administrative Structure

At the head of the pyramid was the *imām*, Shamil. He was the supreme temporal and religious authority, and the title used by him in his correspondence – *amīr al-muʾminīn* (the Commander of the Believers) – implied his claim to full sovereignty. In principle his authority was limited only by the rules of the *sharīʿa*, of which he was chief interpreter.[5]

The *imām* was also the chief justice. Two days a week (Satur day and Sunday) were devoted by him for hearing anyone with a complaint or grievance.[6] Justice was usually dispensed on the spot. Whenever it was needed, Shamil wrote a letter to the appropriate functionary or community instructing them to execute his decision. In case of a justified complaint against a functionary he would reprimand the offender and instruct him to redress the grievance of the complaining party.[7]

To help the *imām* in his political, administrative, religious and judicial duties a *diwān* (privy council) was established in 1842, though a similar informal institution is already mentioned in 1837.[8] The *diwān* consisted of a few of the closest confidants of Shamil. It served as a forum for consultation and for high-level decision-making, on the one hand, and as a body relieving the *imām* of the burden of daily routine decisions, on the other.

The *nā'ibs* (deputies) were the backbone of the administrative-military machinery. They were nominated by the *imām* to specific territories, usually one community only but on some occasions more.[9] Each community was notified by Shamil of the nomination of a *nā'ib* over them.[10] The number of *nā'ibs* varied at different times from four in 1840[11] to 33 in 1856.[12]

The powers granted to the *nā'ibs* and the areas under their command differed from one case to another.[13] In general a *nā'ib* administered the area under his command. He was responsible for law and order. More particularly the *nā'ib* had to collect taxes, to execute the sentences of the *sharʿī* judges and to judge his subordinates according to Shamil's military-administrative regulations. Most important, he was the military commander of his area, led its people on to the battlefield and was, therefore, responsible for their preparedness for war.

Under the *nā'ib*'s command were the *dibīrs*, or *maʿzūms*, who administered sub-districts. Under them were the village elders. Usually the *maʿzūms* also commanded a 'hundred' each, while the *nā'ibs* commanded several, usually five 'hundreds'.

As the administration became more complex and difficult to control, Shamil experimented with grading the *nā'ibs* into different ranks, until finally in the late 1840s the rank of *mudīr* was introduced. The *mudīr* supervised the different activities of several *nā'ibs*, and led them and their men in battle. In addition the *mudīr* fulfilled all the functions of a *nā'ib* in his community of residence, the same as the *imām* in the area around his own place of residence.

To exercise control over the *nā'ibs* and *mudīrs* and collect information independent of their reports, the *imām* had *muḥtāsibs*,[14] who travelled around incognito and reported to Shamil on the activities of his deputies. Sometimes, an open inspection of the activities of certain *nā'ibs* was undertaken, and the *imām* notified them of it in advance.[15]

The communications between the *imām* and all these functionaries were conducted by a special swift post service. Messengers to and from the *imām* had a special blank order which entitled them everywhere to fresh horses, food and sleeping facilities. Any report or order, thus, could reach the furthermost destinations within two or three days.[16]

The *nā'ibs* were forbidden to pass sentence according to the *sharīʿa*[17] For these affairs each *nā'ib* had a *muftī* and *qāḍīs*. Each *qāḍī* was responsible for a mosque and its community. He had to judge according to the *sharīʿa*, lead the prayer, deliver the *khuṭba*[18] and generally ensure that the people in his community behaved according to the *sharīʿa*.[19]

Each *muftī* was responsible for the same area as the parallel *nā'ib*. He had to nominate the *qāḍīs*, supervise their activities and decisions, resolve their queries and pass sentence in any case when people came to be judged by him. It was also his duty to correct any deviation from the *sharīʿa*, either himself or by informing the *nā'ib* of it.[20]

In their activities the *muftīs* and *qāḍīs* were bound by Shamil's instructions and interpretations of the *sharīʿa*.[21] The status of the *muftī vis-à-vis* the *nā'ib* is not completely clear.[22] However, it seems that they enjoyed at least partial independence, which allowed them on occasions to oppose their *nā'ib*[23] and left the *imām* another tool to supervise the activities of both.

The Military Forces

There were few categories of people exempt from military service. Because they performed important economic duties, merchants, the residents of two villages in the community of Karaṭa which produced salt, and those of two villages in Hindāl and three in ʿAndāl, which produced saltpetre, were excused from fighting.[24]

Virtually all the remaining male population consisted of warriors trained and ready to fight, so the *imām*s had from the very beginning a ready, highly mobile force at their disposal. Shamil tried to improve their discipline and standardise their equipment and provisions. According to his regulations the *nā'ibs* and the different commanders had to make sure that all the men between the ages of 15 and 50 had a specified amount of ammunition and provisions, and adequate equipment and clothing. Those who could afford a horse were expected to fight mounted. The *nā'ibs* were to ensure that these horses were kept in good health.

This pool of warriors constituted the bulk of Shamil's forces. In the immediate area of a particular campaign all the men were mobilised. From other areas they were mobilised according to quotas, fixed in each instance by the *imām*. These quotas were for men per household.

Such a force had its obvious shortcomings – lack of proper discipline and steadfastness in battle; weak motivation of the men to fight far away from their homes; their unavailability during the seasons of agricultural work; and, most important, the fact that the main focus of their loyalty was their tribe rather than the *imām* or the common cause. The need for a standing force was felt, therefore, from an early period.

The first two *imāms* had a permanent core, in the form of a few dozen, or even a few hundred, devotees who followed them everywhere. These were organised by Shamil and called *nā'ibī murīds* (to distinguish them from the usual *ṣūfī murīds* of the *ṭarīqa*).[25] These *murīds* numbered, according to the testimony of Shamil's son, about 400.[26] Of these, 120, with 12 commanders of 10, constituted the *imām*'s bodyguard. The others were distributed among the *nā'ibs* and the *mudīrs*. To all these the *murīds* were both bodyguards and trusted servants to be sent on special missions.

The *nā'ibi murīds* were renowned for their fearlessness, their absolute loyalty and their complete obedience to their *imām* and/or *nā'ibs* – even to the point of sacrificing their own lives. No wonder that the *murīds* 'even if they did not enjoy a special respect, [always] inspired fear'.[27] Their entire upkeep, including arms, horses, clothing and the maintenance of their families, was met by the *imām* and the *mudīrs* and *nā'ibs*.

The *murīds*, however fearsome and awe-inspiring, were but a small élite force. Already in the late 1830s Shamil had started to lay the foundations for a larger regular force. In the early 1840s every ten houses were obliged to contribute one armed horseman.[28] These horsemen, called *murtāziqs*, were freed from any other work – their own and their families' upkeep, their fields, herds, etc. were the responsibility of the other nine families – and had to dedicate themselves to military service (including guard duties, patrols, ambushes, etc. in the vicinity of their villages). The *murtāziqs* were organised in separate units and fought separately from the levies of their area.

The institution of the *murtāziqs* supplied a clever answer to several problems: It supplied a large and always ready force to fight the Russians or internal rebels with no cost to the treasury. At the same time it created a large group profiting from, and therefore interested in, the continuation of the *imām*'s rule, which could be trusted to control its fellow-villagers.

In addition to this cavalry Shamil established a regular infantry unit, probably in the mid-1840s.[29] Not much can be surmised from the sources about this infantry. Its name – the *niẓām* – indicates clearly its inspiration: the *nizam-ı cedid* (*al-niẓām al-jadīd*) of the Ottoman Empire and of Muḥammad ʿAlī. It seems that the *niẓām* was concentrated in Shamil's place of residence and was under his exclusive command, unlike the *murtāziqs*, who were under the *nāʾibs*' command. The only time the *niẓām* was put into action against the Russians, in 1851, it was routed.[30] In spite of this, and of Russian ridicule,[31] the *niẓām* must have been an important tool – at least as a deterrent – in enforcing the *imām*'s will in his domain.

The mountaineers of Daghestan traditionally produced gunpowder. Shamil, to supply his needs, established three factories for the production of gunpowder, one of them using water power.[32] The mountaineers even managed to produce some gunshells and bombs, but these were of very poor quality, mainly due to the lack of lead in the mountains. Most of the shells used, therefore, were those captured from the Russians.[33] Later on, Shamil started to produce and use rockets as well.[34]

In 1842 Shamil started to build his artillery, which he used with such devastating results in 1843. At first the artillery consisted exclusively of captured Russian pieces.[35] Later he started to cast his own cannon under the direction of Jaʿfar and Jabrāʾīl,[36] which were, however, of poor quality.[37] In both ways the *imām* accumulated a few dozen pieces of artillery.

Deserters from the Russian army played a major, if not an exclusive, role in the operation and maintenance of Shamil's artillery.[38] The *imām* did everything to facilitate his use of artillery, including the paving of special roads for the rapid movement of guns within his realm.[39]

The mountaineers received very high marks from the Russians for the way they used their artillery, for accuracy and especially for swiftness of manoeuvre. The Russians' intensive efforts to catch the *imām*'s guns in battle usually ended in failure. The mountaineers, however, did not use artillery as often as one might expect. One of the major reasons for this was the fact that Shamil, out of obvious considerations, kept an almost complete monopoly over this powerful weapon. Only a few of his lieutenants, usually *mudīrs*, received a piece or two of artillery.[40] The rest of the few dozen guns was kept near the *imām*'s place of residence.

Shamil also had a few engineers, who constructed fortifications, paved and destroyed roads, and, to the Russians' great surprise, counteracted the Russian mining efforts at the big siege operations of 1847–49.

From that period dates also the first appearance of military hospitals among the mountaineers.[41] For the first time, special places were allocated for the treatment of wounded. The treatment itself was according to traditional methods, which according to Russian testimonies were much more efficient than contemporary European medicine.

For the sake of more uniformity and discipline Shamil introduced specific colours of clothing for the regular units as well as for all the commanders and functionaries. Standard marks of distinction for commanders as well as for anyone who displayed courage on the battlefield were introduced in the early 1840s.[42] Conversely there were 'marks of shame' for cowards and standard punishments for those who transgressed discipline and military regulations.[43]

Financial Affairs

The treasury – *bayt al-māl* – was not Shamil's creation; he inherited it when he became *imām*.[44] But under him financial affairs became organised. The income derived from several sources:

1. Taxation. The two main taxes were the *sharʿī kharāj* (land tax) and *zakāt* (alms). The former was imposed only on a few villages which had been paying it to the Avār *khāns* and on some pasture lands. It was paid in money. The *zakāt* was paid

both in money (2–5 per cent) and kind – sheep (1–2 per cent) and cereals (12 per cent).[45] According to Shamil's treasurer,[46] the lowest annual income from the *kharāj* was 4,500 silver rubles and from the *zakāt* 3,200 silver rubles, 3,200 sheep and 523,102 measures of cereals. Usually, however, the numbers were higher, even double. The seven villages exempted from military service provided specific quotas of salt and saltpetre to the treasury and were obliged to sell all the surpluses to the *imām* at fixed prices.[47]

Occasionally, the *imām* levied an extraorinary tax in kind, to collect food for a specific campaign. These occasional taxes, justified by what in modern terminology would be called 'a state of emergency', became more frequent in the late 1840s and early 1850s and caused a great deal of resentment.[48]

2. The *khums* – one fifth of captured booty belonging to the ruler according to the *sharīʿa* – was probably the major source of income. This fifth included everything: goods, money, animals, captives[49] and their ransom money. In 1852, for example, the *khums* provided the treasury with 15,230 silver rubles.[50]
3. All the fines paid by people went to the treasury. Thus the fines became popularly known in Shamil's domains as *bayt al-māl*. The property of people who died without heirs went also to the treasury.
4. All the income of land belonging to mosques (*awqāf*), which had been used for the upkeep of the mosques and their clergy, now went to the treasury.[51]
5. A special source of income, which according to Shamil was used by him exclusively for his personal expenses, was the payment of three silver rubles per household per annum by the T'ush, to avoid raids by the mountaineers.[52]

In his expenses the *imām* tried to follow the *sharīʿa*. Although deviations were unavoidable, as Shamil himself admitted,[53] an attempt was made to keep the expenditure from each source of income generally within the area destined for it by the *sharīʿa*.[54] For this purpose it seems that each source of income was handled as a separate account.[55]

Thus, the income from administrative measures – fines, inheritance, confiscations, etc. – or part of it, went to the upkeep of the mosques and the *ʿulamāʾ*.[56] Part of the income from taxation, both in kind and in money, remained at the *nāʾibs*' disposal for their and their *murīds*' upkeep. What part of the income would remain at the *nā'ibs*' disposal was decided by the *imām*, though the *nā'ibs* had many opportunities to enrich themselves. The fifth of the *khums* destined for *sayyids* was meticulously divided among the 72 males claiming descent from the Prophet.[57] Changes were introduced in the expenditure of the other four-fifths,[58] though an effort was made to keep its charitable and military character. A major expense from the *khums* was the upkeep of the deserters from the Russian army.[59]

Contrary to Shamil's testimony that the *zakāt* was completely in the hands of the *'ulamā'* to dispose of as they saw fit,[60] the *imām* was actively involved in this.[61] Although some of the *sharʿī* destinations of the income from the *zakāt*, like the upkeep of *'ulamā'* and mosques, were covered by other sources, attempts were made to preserve its charitable nature. A central item in the expenditure of the *zakāt* money was the upkeep of, and assistance to, the *muhājirūn* – the Muslims who fled Russian rule and settled in Shamil's territory.[62]

Sharīʿa and *Niẓām*

As already stated, the implementation and enforcement of the *sharīʿa* was the first aim of the Naqshbandiyya-Khālidiyya and Shamil showed great energy in moving towards the fulfilment of this aim. To understand properly Shamil's *sharʿī* policy, one must not forget several facts: that the *sharīʿa* he enforced was of the fundamentalist interpretation adopted by the Naqshbandiyya; that it was enforced in opposition to, and in order to uproot, both the local *ʿādat* and some *bidʿas* resulting from contact with the Russians; that sometimes the word *sharīʿa* was understood as the Muslim way of life in its entirety.

Thus, for example, smoking and drinking were prohibited.[63] Women were obliged to dress modestly. They were specifically instructed to wear long trousers under their dress and to cover their heads and faces. Dances and music were limited to weddings and circumcisions.[64] Great efforts were made to solve all blood feuds according to the *sharīʿa* and suppress the customary laws pertaining to them.[65] In general, religious and administrative functionaries were instructed repeatedly to enforce the observance in public of the *sharīʿa*. The participation of all men in the Friday noon prayers and the observance of the fast of *Ramaḍān* were examples of this requirement.[66]

But the *imām* did not limit himself to enforcement. Traditional schools were established at the mosques, where children and adults were taught to be good Muslims. Shamil instructed his lieutenants repeatedly to give the population religious education, to teach them the prayers, the *qur'ān*'s correct pronounciation, etc.[67]

The *sharīʿa*, as the *imām* readily admitted,[68] had its lacunae and obscure or disputed passages which needed interpolation, interpretation and a choice between conflicting views respectively. Being himself an *ʿālim* and a *ṣūfī shaykh*, and having many others among his lieutenants, Shamil did not shrink from such activity. His instructions and regulations on such and on other matters known as *niẓām* were tantamount to legislation and can be compared to the Ottoman *kânûn*.[69]

Until the late 1940s only one copy of such regulations was known,[70] which led Russian and Soviet historians to lay special importance on 1847 in the development of the *niẓām*.[71] The publication, since then, of new documents – among them other copies of the *niẓām*[72] – have clearly proved the existence of the *niẓām* as early as 1842.[73]

The different regulations included in the *niẓām* can be divided according to the following categories.

The largest in volume were the instructions regulating administrative and military issues. This category appeared first chronologically – already in 1842 the *nā'ibs* were judging on military offences in accordance with 'a special code of laws issued by Shamil'[74] – and probably the name *niẓām* itself was originally limited to this category only. The regulations of this category defined the authority and responsibilities of the different functionaries and commanders; regulated their relationship to each other; dealt with various questions of military discipline, conduct and tactics; and enumerated the different punishments – usually corporal and fiscal, but occasionally involving demotion – for transgression of these regulations.

Another category involved regulations of a general non-religious character. Such were the prohibition to clear wood without special permission;[75] the prohibition on contacts with the Russians;[76] the obligation to accept small Russian coins minted in Tiflis, which the mountaineers had refused to use;[77] and the prohibition, under the threat of heavy punishment, to falsify Russian coins.[78]

These two categories had little to do with religious law. Still, the *imām* tried as far as possible to connect them with, and base them on, the *sharīʿa*. The other categories concerned the *sharīʿa* directly.

The third one involved regulations which repeated the stipulations of the *sharīʿa* or gave force to a certain interpretation of it. Such were, for example, the instructions to spare the lives of the garrisons which had submitted, and kill all those which had not,[79] or the different regulations dealing with marriage, divorce, bride-money, inheritance, etc.,[80] which replaced local customs in favour of the *sharīʿa*. To this category belonged also regulations settling problems arising from a conflict between two principles of the *sharīʿa*, as, for example, in the case of a man killed in a fight which he had initiated in the killer's house.[81]

The fourth category involved reinterpretations of, or in other words changes in, the *sharīʿa*. This involved mainly the *ḥudūd* (punishments). Thus, for example, the punishment for theft (cutting off the right hand) was now fixed at three months' imprisonment for the first two offences and death for the third.[82] For drunkenness, on the other hand, the number of beatings was increased above the 40 prescribed by Muslim law, and repeated offences led to a sentence of death.[83]

In general, Shamil seems to have preferred deterrent punishments, fines, or both, to bodily mutilation. Accordingly, the most common punishments were beatings, fines, imprisonments and public humiliations. A good example of the latter are the punishment for smoking and dancing. Both kinds of offenders, before being imprisoned, were paraded riding a donkey, their face to its tail, one with the smoking-pipe put through his nose, the other with his face smeared with pitch.[84]

Imprisonment was a very effective punishment and widely used. The prisoner was placed in a small pit under a hut, compared by both the *imām*[85] and those who experienced it,[86] to a grave. In addition, the prisoner had to pay for his food and for the guards. A few days in such a 'grave' could break the most stubborn man, and this punishment was highly effective as a deterrent.

Finally, the fifth category consisted of regulations which, though not *sharʿī*, extended the *sharīʿa* according to the principle of *a minori ad majus*. These usually aimed at strengthening and enforcing the Islamic way of life. Thus, for example, in addition to the prohibition on music, all instruments, with the exception of a small drum, were forbidden.[87] In addition to banning wine, the *imām* forbade the selling of grapes to people who knew how to make wine.[88]

To this category belong also some regulations concerning marriage.[89] In view of the high bride-money among the Chechens, which resulted in a growing number of unmarried men and women, Shamil imposed a maximum bride-price of 20 silver rubles for a virgin and 10 for a widow or divorcée. Not satisfied with this, the *imām* repeatedly instructed the *nā'ibs* to arrange the marriages of girls who had reached the proper age and of widows.[90] Contrary to Russian interpretations,[91] the *imām*'s main aim was to uphold the morals of the young[92] rather than demographic increase, though the latter also weighed with him.

All these measures to enforce the *sharīʿa* seem to have had a great effect. As early as 1842–43 Russian sources stated that great 'improvements' had taken place in the behaviour and morals of the mountaineers, particularly the Chechens.[93]

Chapter 22

The Ruler and the Ruled

At a very early stage of his rule Shamil made a comparison between his position in Daghestan and that of the Ottoman *sulṭān* in his domain.[1] As mentioned above, this claim to authority and sovereignty did not remain unchallenged. Both in 1834–37 and again in 1840 there were other claimants to the leadership and challenges to the *imām*'s authority.[2] However, eventually Shamil succeeded in pushing his rivals aside. The last to leave the scene was Ḥājj Tāshō, whose name disappears from the sources in 1843.[3]

By the mid-1840s Shamil had become a sovereign ruler with all the symbols and attributes of a Muslim sovereign – the title *amīr al-mu'minīn*, the executioner following him everywhere, the *khuṭba* delivered in his name. Only one attribute was lacking – the minting of coins in his name. Shamil abstained from doing so in order not to hamper trade with the areas under Russian control, because he realised that the Russians would not accept his coinage.[4] With the public proclamation of his son, Ghāzī Muḥammad, as his successor,[5] Shamil also became a potential founder of a dynasty.

All this, however, did not mean that Shamil had unlimited power. In principle and in practice the *imām*'s authority was always limited and therefore his rule was not despotic, as some Russian sources (for obvious reasons) described it. Among the factors checking the *imām*'s power were the *sharīʿa*, his position as a *ṣūfī* bound to follow his *murshid*, the internal balance of power between Shamil, his *nā'ibs* and other powerful persons and the population's acceptance or rejection of his commands.

The *Imām* and the *Sharīʿa*

According to *sunnī* political theory, it is the obligation of any Muslim ruler to uphold, implement and enforce the *sharīʿa*. Only as long as he keeps this obligation is his rule legitimate and are his subjects bound to obey him. The *sunnī* quietist approach notwithstanding, this check on the ruler's freedom of manoeuvre is stronger than it looks and a Muslim ruler could not afford a *great* deviation of the *sharīʿa* or a *deep* conflict with its interpreters – (the *ʿulamāʾ*), despite their usual dependence on the state.

In Shamil's case this obligation was greater. As an *ʿālim* and a Naqshbandī he was committed to follow and implement the *sharīʿa* in his private life as well as in the community. Furthermore, he was the leader of a movement which raised the banners of Islam and committed itself to enforce the *sharīʿa* in Daghestan and Chechnia. Such a strong commitment meant that any failure to follow the *sharīʿa* could be extremely harmful to Shamil and expose him to attacks on this ground.

On two occasions the Russians tried to portray Shamil as deviating from the *sharīʿa*.[6] These attempts might have proved effective had not the Russians, in their traditional mistrust of anyone independent, used such obvious stooges. As it was, the field was left wide open for the *imām* to use it to his advantage, and turn, as in so many other cases, a limitation into an advantage.

Shamil made sure that his personal meticulous observance of the *sharīʿa* and of his own *niẓām* was seen and known. One example out of many of this is his marriage to Zaynab, the daughter of ʿAbdallah al-Ghāzī-Ghumuqī. Being under pressure to marry a Chechen girl for political reasons, Shamil married Zaynab, paying 20 silver rubles bride-money. He divorced her on the same day, making sure that he had not stayed with her alone without witnesses for a moment, and returned the full sum of the bride-money, since the marriage had not been consumated.[7]

Further public demonstration of the *imām*'s adherence to the *sharīʿa* and his *niẓām* was given every time he sat to judge his people. His efforts to make the *niẓām*, even in those parts remotest from religion, conform to the *sharīʿa* were mentioned above. So were his efforts to educate the people in the spirit of Islam and the *sharīʿa* as well as to enforce it,[8] which were given their due publicity. Finally, Shamil publicly distanced himself from non-, or even anti-*sharʿī* practices of his *nāʾibs*.[9]

All this does not mean that Shamil used the *sharīʿa* cynically for political purposes, as some Russian sources claimed. He was a pious Muslim with a total commitment to the Muslim law and way of life. All his deeds were done out of his beliefs and sense of duty. But as a good politician, Shamil could not fail to notice the benefits to him of these deeds and take advantage of them, especially as they did not demand any special efforts.

A central part in Shamil's *sharʿī* legitimacy was the support given to him by the *ʿulamāʾ*. This support was manifest in each of their deeds, from reading the *khuṭba* in his name to judging in accordance with his interpretations of the *sharīʿa*. One explanation for this support is the *imām*'s control over the *ʿulamāʾ*: after all, he controlled their position (he could nominate and dismiss them) and income (he controlled the *awqāf* money), not to speak of his ability to coerce.

Yet, this is not a sufficient explanation. Such a continuing and wholehearted support by the *ʿulamāʾ* (with the one exception of Sulaymān Efendī[10]) could only have been the result of their full identification with the *imām*'s views and their trust and belief in him. Such feelings cannot result from coercion. Rather, they were due to Shamil's observance of the *sharīʿa*, his spotless way of life and the fact that he himself was an *ʿālim* and a *ṣūfī shaykh*. Most important, Shamil treated the *ʿulamāʾ* with respect[11] and succeeded in impressing upon his leading adherents that they had a real share in the decision-making process. Not only were the *ʿūlamāʾ* consulted on *sharʿī* matters, but they took part in gatherings which debated and decided issues of policy and strategy.

Shamil and the *Ṭāʾifa*

As mentioned above, Shamil was a *khalīfa* in the Naqshbandī-Khālidī order. His position as *imām*, though, did not leave him time to act as a *ṣūfī shaykh*. Yet no matter how high his rank, he was, as a *murīd*, bound to complete obedience to his *murshid*, Jamāl al-Dīn al-Ghāzī-Ghumuqī.

Indeed, during his entire reign, Shamil treated Jamāl al-Dīn with respect and veneration as his *murshid* and as a *sayyid*.[12] Jamāl al-Dīn was the only person who could openly and publicly criticise the *imām* with full impunity.[13] The *imām* treated each wish of his *murshid* as a command. In 1842, for example, he invaded Ghāzī-Ghumuq because he thought it was Jamāl al-Dīn's wish.[14] A year earlier, the *imām* established the *diwān* officially because Jamāl al-Dīn had suggested it.[15] Even on the question of whether to release Russian prisoners or not, Shamil followed the advice of his *murshid*.[16]

However, the *murshid* was far from an obstacle to the *imām*. On the contrary, his advice usually proved wise and benefited Shamil. Furthermore, Jamāl al-Dīn put all his weight and prestige behind Shamil's election as *imām*.[17] He repeatedly called upon the people to obey and follow the *imām*, both in his speeches[18] and letters;[19] used his connections in the local ruling houses in Shamil's favour;[20] and joined the *imām* in soliciting Ottoman help and support.[21]

Jamāl al-Dīn demonstrated his support for Shamil also by giving his daughter Zāhida in marriage to the *imām*, and taking Shamil's two daughters for his sons, ʿAbd al-Raḥman and ʿAbd al-Raḥīm. (Ironically, these marriages damaged Shamil in his last years, when his wife and her two brothers formed yet another of the many rival cliques surrounding the *imām*.[22])

Jamāl al-Dīn's support contributed greatly to Shamil's prestige and authority, and he made full use of it. But Shamil also had another source of prestige and authority at his disposal – the fact that he was a *ṣūfī shaykh* in his own right and second only to his master. Only he and his *murshid* mastered completely the *zulma* and *ʿishqallah*[23] and could conduct the *jazm*.[24] Shamil's ability to use the *zulma* both to see and hear people by what in modern terms would be called telepathy, and especially his ability to predict someone's imminent arrival and his reason for coming left, no doubt, a strong impression on the mountaineers, as it did even on sceptical Russians.[25]

Shamil's mastery of the *ʿishqallah* had a considerably stronger effect because he used it in public and in a very dramatic way. Usually, before important decisions, the *imām* would go into a *khalwa*. After several days of fasting, prayer and (silent) *dhikr* he would pass out. Afterwards, he would emerge and announce that the Prophet had appeared to him when he was unconscious and had given him certain instructions.[26] The story of one such *khalwa* which has been widely repeated in the literature, is an excellent demonstration of Shamil's ability to use the *ʿishqallah* to create the desired effect on the mountaineers.

In 1843 a Chechen delegation importuned Shamil, through his mother, to allow them to submit temporarily to the Russians. The *imām* when approached, went into a three-day *khalwa* after which he announced to the crowd outside that the Prophet had told him that the person who had first approached Shamil in this affair – his mother – must receive 100 strokes. The sentence was carried out immediately. But when after five strokes his mother lost consciousness, the *imām* kneeled in prayer in front of her. After a while he joyfully thanked the Prophet and all the saints and announced that Muḥammad allowed him to receive the rest of the flogging himself. Shamil immediately received 95 strokes and afterwards called the terrified delegation and told them in front of the crowd to go back and tell their people all that they had witnessed.[27]

On the night of 9 April 1847 a large comet was observed in New Darghiyya. On the same night a fire consumed the settlement of the Russian deserters nearby. Shamil immediately went into a *khalwa* from which he emerged saying that the Prophet had told him that these were omens sent by God to demonstrate the final victory of the Muslims and the fate awaiting the unbelievers both in this and the other world.[28]

Here is the place to remark that in these and all similar episodes Shamil did not necessarily cynically deceive the people as some Russian sources claimed. It seems he genuinely believed in these visions, though being a born actor he did not refrain from adding a dramatic effect to them. Another erroneous claim in Russian sources, which has also passed into contemporary Western literature,[29] was that Shamil called himself a prophet. Such a suggestion would be abhorrent to any good Muslim, and of course to Shamil himself. All he ever claimed was that the Prophet – not God or any angel! – talked to him in his visions, which was a legitimate *ṣūfī* assertion.

Obviously Shamil, in the role of a *ṣūfī shaykh* had a strong hold over a great part of the population. When, for example, he proclaimed in October 1842 that on a certain night the heavens would open up and all the truly pious men would be taken up directly into paradise, the people spent all that night in vigil.[30]

The Ruler and His Lieutenants

In principle, the *nā'ibs* and *mudīrs* owed complete loyalty and obedience to the *imām*. In practice, Shamil faced some obstacles in controlling his lieutenants. Even among his own men only two showed themselves fully loyal, trusthworthy and at the same time competent leaders, warriors and administrators – Shuʿayb al-Tsanaturī[31] and Akhbirdi Muḥammad al-Khunzakhī.

But many of the *nāʾibs* and *mudīrs* were not dependent upon Shamil for their powers, authority, prestige and legitimacy. One such group was composed of people belonging to the local great houses. Shamil, given the existing tribal structure of the country, had no choice but to appoint them *nāʾibs*. Another group consisted of people who had acquired power bases on their personality, leadership and military and other abilities. There were also those who considered themselves, and were considered by others, as Shamil's equals. These were either his peers in the movement, or important renegades from the Russian camp.

Such people could limit the actual power of the *imām* and his freedom of choice. Furthermore, they could, and on many occasions did, act independently of Shamil. The sources contain cases of disobedience to, and even open revolt against, the *imām* by *nāʾibs*;[32] of insubordination to him by refusing to obey colleagues nominated to head a certain campaign;[33] and of open rivalry and intrigues among them.[34] Many *nāʾibs* maintained contacts with the Russians without the *imām*'s approval or knowledge;[35] some were in the Russians' pay;[36] and others did not refrain from occasionally betraying the details of a raid planned by a colleague.[37]

Despite this, and Shamil's repeated complaints about his lieutenants' behaviour,[38] such cases clearly involved only a minority. Most of the time Shamil exercised his authority smoothly and the *nāʾibs* remained loyal and obedient. This can be attributed to several factors.

To start with, the *imām* was in an extremely powerful position *vis-à-vis* his lieutenants. He had an entire range of means to put pressure on each of them, whatever their local power. The local religious functionaries, other local (usually rival) leading families and persons, neighbouring *nāʾibs*, all could be used by the *imām* for his purposes. Furthermore, he could use his enormous prestige to appeal to the people over the head of their *nāʾib*. Finally, if these advantages were not sufficient, the *imām* could always use his overpowering military advantage – the regular units and the artillery.

Yet Shamil was sparing in the use of his power. When used, deposition of *nāʾibs* was the commonest outcome. This had a deterrent effect of its own, the *nāʾibs* having usually much to lose by deposition. As far as can be established, two reasons usually brought about the demotion of a *nā'ib* – incompetence, usually on the battlefield, and strong complaints from the population about his corruption.[39] Intrigues against the *imām* and maintaining contact with a foreign power (not necessarily with the Russians) without his knowledge and approval usually incurred exile to one of the villages inside the *imām*'s domain used by him for such a purpose.[40] Only open insubordination and spying for the Russians resulted in capital punishment.[41] Sanctions, as might be expected, were dependent on the power of the *nā'ib* in question.

As in other cases, Shamil extended to his *nā'ibs* incentives as well as deterrents. There were rewards and decorations for the deserving, and loyal lieutenants enjoyed the full public and private backing of the *imām*. Shamil, observed a Russian source, 'was a man of great tact and a subtle politician. Not only did he not adopt a suspicious attitude, like many rulers do, towards the popularity of his confidants, but, to the contrary, he tried to befriend them and thus to flatter the popular feelings'.[42]

Nā'ib loyalty was also reinforced by what seemed to be their participation in the decision-making process. Shamil held many gatherings of *nā'ibs*, regional and general, to discuss important issues, policies, strategies etc. For exceptionally important matters greater gatherings of *nā'ibs*, '*ulamā*' and other dignitaries were held.

Such meetings were occasions to voice and hear opinions, but their major aim was to approve decisions already taken by the *imām* and his confidants in the *diwān*. Usually, Shamil would prepare the meeting in such a way that someone else proposed the resolutions. But there were occasions on which the *nā'ibs* were told bluntly that if they felt they could not support and carry out the resolutions, they should resign.[43] The *nā'ibs* were aware of their role in these meetings, and on one occasion at least when Shamil posed a problem and asked for suggestions one of the participants said, 'whatever you decide we shall carry out'.[44]

There was one category of dignitary who limited Shamil's power more than the others, however. These were people who were both the *imām*'s equals and enjoyed a strong power base of their own, like Ḥājj Tāshō, Qibid Muḥammad, Ḥajimurād and Daniyāl.[45] This is clearly demonstrated by the fact that both Qibid Muḥammad (and his brother Murtaḍā ʿAlī)[46] and Daniyāl[47] were deposed on several occasions only to be reinstated and even promoted. Also, Ḥājj Tāshō was reinstated at least once.[48]

Shamil's relationship with his peers and equals had never been comfortable or tension-free. There was, however, a marked difference between those who challenged Shamil's authority and those who did not. Those belonging to the first group were undermined by Shamil by all the means at his disposal until they were completely pushed out. A challenger, even if he repented, was always considered a threat by the *imām*. Such a person would never be allowed a position if Shamil could enforce his will. Thus Ḥājj Tāshō disappeared and Ḥājj Muḥammad Efendī was forced to return to İstanbul.[49]

Others, like Qibid Muḥammad and ʿAbd al-Raḥman al-Qarākhī, were allowed greater – and real – share in power and decision-making. With the development of the administration they became *mudīrs*. Daniyāl's daughter, Karīma, was even given in marriage to Shamil's son, Muḥammad Shāfīʿ.[50]

This does not mean that the *imām* did not regard them as potential threats to his power. Rather, it should be understood that they were too powerful to fight with as long as they posed no direct challenge to his authority or power. Ḥajimurād is an outstanding example of this rule. He belonged to this privileged group until he became a challenger, though not to the *imām* directly.

In late March 1848 the *imām*'s eldest son present, Ghāzī Muḥammad,[51] was publicly proclaimed the successor of his father as *imām*.[52] Soon he was nominated *nāʾib* of Karaṭa and later he became a *mudīr*. Ḥajimurād refused to accept this proclamation and publicly announced that he might claim the title of *imām* for himself after Shamil's death. Like King Saul in the Bible, Shamil engineered a confrontation with his lieutenant in order to secure his son's succession. He used a pretext to depose the *mudīr*. This triggered the chain of events that led to Ḥajimurād's defection, escape and death.[53]

Ironically, a few years later, in 1857–58, Ghāzī Muḥammad could have become a threat and challenge to his father. Shamil's son was approached by some unidentified people who wanted to depose Shamil and proclaim Ghāzī Muḥammad *imām*. The successor declined on the spot.[54] By that time Shamil had lost much of his power and authority both because of the concentrated Russian attack from without and his growing isolation from the people through the growing activities and intrigues of rival cliques around him from within.

The Leader and His People

The ultimate test of any leader is the acceptance by the people of his authority and instructions. The mountaineers were not renowned for their acceptance of external authority. In fact, Shamil, in his captivity, complained that the mountaineers, and especially the Chechens, were extremely disobedient.[55] Russian sources also claimed that Shamil could not rely on the Chechens.[56] As early as a few months after the revolt of 1840 they started to report dissatisfaction with Shamil among the Chechens.[57] Even in Daghestan revolts occasionally occurred.[58]

According to Shamil, the major problem with the Chechens, which did not exist in Daghestan, was their insistence on being given a *nāʾib* of their own choice. Otherwise, though admittedly on rare occasions, entire communities would defect to the Russians.[59] Here Shamil seems to have referred to a specific case: the community of Chantī went over to the Russians during Evdokimov's campaign of winter 1858 following the nomination of the Daghestanī Ḥamza as *nāʾib* over them. By so doing, Shamil acted against the expressed wishes of the community, which wanted Mazha, the son of the late *nāʾib*, to succeed him.[60]

Chechen dissatisfaction with *nāʾibs* started at a very early stage. Already by the end of 1840 the people openly criticised and disobeyed Jawād Khān. Even Akhbirdi Muḥammad found it difficult to enforce his command.[61] In very rare cases, such disaffection could lead to the most extreme acts. In December 1840 Bulāt Mīrzā, Ḥājj Tāshō's successor, was assassinated. The neighbouring Russian commander gave shelter to the assassins.[62]

On 18 January 1844, Shuʿayb was assassinated in Tsanatur. Shamil's reaction, according to Russian sources, was swift and drastic. All the villagers of Tsanatur were punished for not preventing the assassination, as well as the inhabitants of the neighbouring hamlets for not arresting the assassins on their escape.[63] The deterrent effect of this particular response was tremendous. As late as 1857, the community of Shubūt dared not disobey its hated *nāʾib*, with whom many had blood feuds.[64]

However, as noted above, acts of communal disobedience[65] were very rare, perhaps because, *inter alia*, Shamil was more efficient than the Russians in taking the right hostages.[66] Much more common were acts of individual disobedience of different kinds which necessitated extensive use of punishment. Some of these, like incarceration, fines, exile and even 'the decapitation of many people' were mentioned above. Another, very common punishment was similar to the Russian *ekzekutsiia*. Drafted men were housed in the disobedient person's household, 'settled as if they were in their own home and brought the owners very quickly into obedience.'[67]

The drafted men used for these 'executions' were always Daghestanīs. This fact was damaging to the *imām*'s cause in the long run because it generated a great deal of bad feelings among the Chechens towards the *Ṭawhlīs*. On many occasions, this tension erupted in clashes between the two groups. On some other occasions, the Chechens intentionally stayed away and let the Russians beat the Daghestanīs who had come to reinforce them.[68]

However, a more detailed look at the facts shows this picture to be painted in too black colours. Indeed, both Shamil, in his post-1859 bitterness, and the Russians had their reasons to exaggerate in that direction. Actually the majority of the mountaineers, and especially the Chechens, who suffered most, stayed with their *imām* to the last, despite great deprivations and suffering. By doing so they often had to abandon their homes and fields and go back into the mountains. Only when driven to extremes did they go over to the Russians.

Such behaviour could not be explained simply by Shamil's power and coercion, or by his excellent system of control over the population. Neither would the hatred of the Russians suffice. Strong as it was, it was not universal. The inner Chechen communities, for example, who had not come into intensive contact with the Russians, received them in quite a friendly way in 1858.[69] Credit had to be given to Shamil's charisma as leader and his ability to use the entire range of means at his disposal to generate loyalty and obedience among the mountaineers. Among these an important role was given to justice.

Shamil was a stern and forceful ruler. But he was just and did everything in his power to see that justice was done and seen to be done both to individuals and to communities.[70] Anyone could complain against even the strongest official, and if the complaint was found to be justified he was given redress and the official was punished. Both the *imām* and some of his confidants, most notably Shaykh Jamāl al-Dīn toured the country and were always accessible for complaints. Furthermore, Shamil used occasions when people were gathered for campaigns – and such gatherings did not always end in a campaign – to ask for and receive complaints.[71]

Much has been written about the populism and egalitarianism of Shamil and the movement he led. Some pre-revolutionary Russian[72] (not to say Soviet) sources went to the extreme of describing the movement as essentially social in its character, the struggle as mainly a class struggle against the local nobility, and Shamil – as a champion of the poor.

The reality was somewhat different. Shamil, indeed, was hostile to the local rulers and sometimes even expressed himself in extreme terms about them.[73] But this attitude was mainly due to their refusal to observe the *sharīʿa* and to join the *jihād* against the Russians.[74] Rulers or members of their families who joined Shamil were received with all due honours and given positions of importance, like Daniyāl, Ḥajimurād, Ḥājj Yaḥyā (of the ruling family of Ghāzī-Ghumuq) and Muḥammad Bek, the brother of the *shāmkhāl*. Furthermore, this hostility did not prevent the *imām* from maintaining contact with virtually all the local rulers.[75]

Shamil abolished the status of serfs of the population of four villages belonging to the extinct family of the *khāns* of Avāriastān (and also of Russian prisoners who converted to Islam).[76] He also protected serfs from Russian territory who ran away into his domains and refused to return them to their Muslim masters. But the liberation of serfs was not general;[77] the fiscal obligations of the above-mentioned four villages remained as before,[78] the only difference being that their taxes went now to the *bayt al-māl*, instead of the treasury of the *khān* of Avāristān.

Nevertheless, there were elements of egalitarianism in Shamil's system – those existent in Islam in general – and his leadership did not lack signs of populism. In principle nothing barred a man of the humblest origin from reaching the highest position, provided he had the ability, loyalty, stamina and ambition.[79] Even if in practice only one *nāʾib* is particularly reported to have come from a very poor family,[80] the principle still had, from Shamil's point of view, its positive impact.

Also, the *imām* tried to keep in touch with the people on important matters. He sent letters and manifestos to be read in public, in which he would tell of victories, describe forthcoming difficulties, encourage and implore them to steadfastness.[81] On critical occasions Shamil met representatives of the people and discussed problems with them.[82] Usually the *imām* made sure in advance that such a meeting would adopt the desired resolution. Nevertheless, what mattered was the appearance of consultation and popular approval and support. Even in his last years in power, when according to even his closest confidants, Shamil had lost touch with the people and their concerns, he continued to convene such meetings.

Chapter 23

The *Imām* and His Neighbours

The Caucasian Tribes

As described above, during his first few years in power Shamil had closed a circle started by Ghāzī Muḥammad. The first *imām* began his struggle aiming at the grand strategy, associated with Shaykh Manṣūr, of expelling the Russians through the unification of all the Muslims of the Caucasus,[1] and with the assistance of neighbouring Muslim powers, mainly the Ottomans. In his final year, Ghāzī Muḥammad changed to a strategy of accommodation with the Russians. The third *imām* started from this latter strategy, which he had inherited from both his predecessors, and ended with the first strategy of all-out resistance.

This turn started already in 1837 and was marked by Shamil's rather minimal involvement in the revolts in Qubāh in that and the following year.[2] Starting in 1840, however, Shamil's commitment to this strategy expanded massively. Building on the activities of Ghāzī Muḥammad, Shamil sent messengers to every area of the Caucasus with a *sunnī* Muslim population to foment anti-Russian activity. His activities among the Ghumuqs, in Aqūsha and other parts of the north-eastern Caucasus have been dealt with above.[3]

So have his activities in, and contacts with, Qaytāq and Ṭabarsarān, which were of particular importance.[4] These two provinces had not been fully pacified and anti-Russian activity continued there until well after Shamil's surrender. Some activity in Shamil's name, sometimes spontaneous rather than conducted by him, was from time to time registered among the Ossets, part of whom were Muslim.[5] Even in the province of Elizavetpol' (Ganja) some activity in the *imām*'s favour was reported.[6]

Of central importance in this strategy were Shamil's relations with, and activities among, the Circassians and Ghabarṭians. The *imām* had started his contacts with the different tribes of the Centre and Right Flank already in 1840,[7] striving at a co-ordinated and concentrated attack which would join the two sides, cut the Georgian Military Highway and perhaps create the right conditions to push the Russians back along the Caucasian Line.

Already in 1842 Shamil had suggested such a plan to the Ubykhs and Shapsugs,[8] but he found that much more groundwork had to be done before such an enterprise could be attempted. This started a period of intense contacts with, and activity among, the Ghabarṭians.[9] To the Circassians the *imām* sent in 1843 one of his lieutenants, Ḥājj Muḥammad. This *nā'ib* was active for a few months only, before he was killed in battle, in May 1844.[10] Whether because his activity impressed the Circassians, because of Shamil's growing fame, or both, they sent a delegation to Shamil to ask him to send them another *nā'ib*.[11]

After some deliberations, Shamil sent Sulaymān Efendī. This *nā'ib* also acted for a few months. He assembled a force in May 1845 intending to cross Ghabarṭa and join Shamil. The Russians, forewarned by their spies, blocked the road. The Circassians dispersed and Sulaymān Efendī returned to Shamil.[12]

How the contact with Shamil and his lieutenants and probably more important the *imām*'s growing fame and power had changed the attitude of some Circassians can be seen from two documents. In 1844, the Circassians replied to a manifesto by Neidhardt with the words: 'Shamil, about whom you write, does not belong to us. [He is] not on our lands and our people are not with him. We have nothing in common with him.'[13] In 1847, a Circassian wrote to a Russian general: 'The rule over us . . . is entrusted to Shaykh Shamil, the ruler of the entire area from Temir Kapı [the iron gate of Derbend] to Anapa.'[14]

Between the dates of these two letters Shamil invaded Ghabarṭa unsuccessfully in 1846.[15] At that time the *imām* had no *nā'ib* among the Circassians who would lead them in a co-ordinated effort. Thus, although forewarned by Shamil about his campaign,[16] the Circassians did nothing at all to help him.

This failure, however, did not stop the *imām*'s efforts in that direction. The contacts with the Ghabarṭians continued.[17] In 1848, at the Circassians' request,[18] he nominated as *nā'ib* over them, Muḥammad Amīn (Mehmet Emin).[19] The new *nā'ib* proved to be a competent leader,[20] and operated successfully, mainly among the Abadzekh, for over a decade. Several times before and during the Crimean War the *imām* and his *nā'ib* intended to join their forces in a concerted attack, but none of these plans were carried out.[21] Muḥammad Amīn finally submitted to the

Russians after Shamil had written to him from his place of exile suggesting – not ordering – that he do so.[22]

Shamil did not limit himself to the *sunnī* Muslims in his search for allies against the Russians, although, as far as can be established, he had no contacts with the *shīʿī* population of Russian Ādhārbāyjān. Traditional *shīʿī* suspicion and hostility and the geographical and mental distance between the two communities, reinforced by traditional Khālidī hostility to the *shīʿa* and Ghāzī Muḥammad's failure to approach them, prevented any meaningful attempt at co-operation.[23]

The Christian (at least nominally) Georgian mountain tribes, on the other hand, were much closer both geographically and mentally to the Daghestanīs. Shamil, who had a relationship with some of them – they had been paying him money not to be attacked[24] – attempted unsuccessfully to bring them into his fold and enlist them in an anti-Russian alliance.[25] According to one Russian source, Shamil, in order to facilitate such efforts, spread rumours to the effect that he was an (illegitimate) son of Alexander, the crown prince of K'art'lo-Kakhet'i.[26] This information should, however, be taken with more than a grain of salt. Shamil might, in fact, neither have anything to do with these rumours nor even have known about them. Such rumours might have had their origins among dissatisfied Georgians. Another target for similar, though much subtler, activity were the Cossacks of the Line.

Muhājirūn

Two of the aims in the activity discussed above were to divert the Russians from concentrating their efforts on Chechnia and Daghestan, while working towards, and creating the right conditions for, the final unification of the Caucasian tribes. A third aim was to enlist volunteers to reinforce Shamil.[27] All his messengers and *nā'ib*s, including those to the Circassians, were instructed to mobilise volunteers and to send or lead them to the *imām*'s domains. In his search for volunteers and reinforcements the *imām* reached out even to the territories of the Ottomans and the Qājārs. This was done in two ways.

One was the direct dispatch of messengers to Ottoman territory to recruit volunteers. One such case caused a diplomatic incident. In the winter of 1845 Shamil's envoy, Ḥājj Ḥassan Ḥasbī, arrived in Ajāra (the area of Batumi) and started to call for volunteers to join the struggle in Daghestan. The Russians, having learnt about this, remonstrated with the Ottoman authorities. The reaction of the latter pushed Ḥasan Ḥasbī into a coalition with local notables opposed to the *tanẓīmat*. In the end all were arrested, Ḥasan Ḥasbī escaped, and his local allies were sentenced to exile in Saloniki.[28]

What made this '*interlude presque comique*'[29] both a comedy of errors and an instructive lesson in the character of the regime of Nicholas I, was the Russian reaction which, envisaging an Ottoman invasion, put the forces on the border on alert and mobilised all the local militias.[30]

The other way involved what might be called in modern popular parlance the 'Khālidi connection' in Kurdistān. The main leaders involved in the contact with Shamil and Jamāl al-Dīn were al-Shaykh al-Sayyid Ṭaha and after his death his brother and successor, Sāliḥ, both residing on the Ottoman side of the border, and Shaykh Salīḥ's *khalīfa*, Shaykh Ṭāhir, residing on the Qājār side.[31] In addition to a regular exchange of messengers, these persons also dispatched a number of Kurds to join Shamil.[32]

Of course, only a few individuals could have joined Shamil from outside the Caucasus.[33] The overwhelming majority of such reinforcements – *muhājirūn or abreks* – were from the neighbouring tribes: Daghestanīs from Chārtalah and other regions under Russian rule, Ghumuqs, Ghabarṭians, Circassians, and Ossets.[34] In joining Shamil, such people followed a well-established traditional pattern, reinforced now by religious dogma.[35]

A number of *muhājirūn* rose to positions of eminence under Shamil,[36] again continuing a traditional pattern.[37] Perhaps the most famous and prominent *muhājir*, after Daniyāl, was Muḥammad Mīrzā ibn Anzāwr [Anzorov], a Ghabarṭian prince who joined Shamil during the *imām*'s invasion of Ghabarṭa, and followed Shamil with most of his clan on his retreat. Muḥammad Mīrzā was nominated *nā'ib* of Gekhi in August–September 1846 and about six months later he became *mudīr* of Lesser Chechnia. He held this post until his death in June 1851, from wounds received in battle.[38]

Shamil had given much attention to, and invested much effort in favour of, the *muhājirūn*, whether volunteers or people evacuated from border areas.[39] They were allocated lands, given means of existence and supported from the *zakāt* until they could support themselves. The *nā'ib*s were instructed to help them in everything they needed. Small groups were dispersed among existing villages. Large groups, at least in some cases, remained together and on many occasions established their own settlements.

At least in some cases large groups of *muhājirūn* signed agreements with the local population. One such published document specifies the mutual undertakings by both parties, and includes a specific undertaking by the *muhājirūn* to live according to the *sharīʿa* and the *imām*'s *niẓām*.[40]

The *muhājirūn* proved to be a very valuable group for the *imām* and his struggle, apart from the numerical reinforcement they accorded Shamil. Among them were people with much-needed qualifications and expertise. Others had served in, or with, the Russian army and were familiar with Russian tactics, and more important, way of thinking. And there were such people who brought Shamil their personal prestige and valuable influence and connections in the areas under Russian control.

Defectors and Prisoners

Cases of desertion and defection of both soldiers and Cossacks across the lines into the mountains and Ottoman and Qājār territory[41] had been recorded since the arrival of the Russians in the Caucasus. The local Cossacks, familiar with their neighbours, were usually able to join them on an equal basis and participate in their raids.[42] If they converted to Islam they could marry local girls and fully integrate into the community. Soldiers, unfamiliar with the locality and people, were in many cases treated as captives: that is, enslaved.

Shamil had been mindful of the moral and propaganda importance of such defectors even before he became aware of their value as manpower. As early as 1840 the *imām* wrote to all the *nāʾibs*:

> Know that those who have run over from the Russians to us are loyal to us and you should believe them. These people are our sincere friends. By coming over to the believers they have become pure people also. Supply them with all the [needed] aid and means of existence.[43]

Later, aware of their value, Shamil ordered that all deserters (and captives) be brought to him. He personally interrogated them and afterwards designated them for different posts. Artillerymen, smiths and other craftsmen and others of special value or interest stayed with the *imām*.[44]

Shamil tried to convince the captives to enter his service. If they agreed, they were given their freedom. He also did his best to attach all the deserters and the captives who had agreed to serve him to their new place and society.

One such measure was to convert them to Islam. In the case of converts from among the captives-slaves (who thus automatically received their freedom), the *imām* abolished the custom according to which they were retained as serfs.[45] Defectors who converted were put on an equal footing with the mountaineers, their needs were taken care of from the household of the *imām* or the *nā'ibs*, and those retained by Shamil himself were given command over their unconverted comrades. The *imām* made a special point of marrying the converts to local girls. To facilitate this, he even passed a regulation which abolished the punishment of a girl convicted of premarital adultery if she married a convert.[46] So strong was Shamil's involvement in this matter that he himself used to marry converts in his service to girls who had run away to him from their homes.[47]

However, Shamil never tried to force Islam on deserters or captives. That would be contrary to the *sharīʿa*. All those in his service who had not converted were settled in a 'Russian settlement' near the *imām*'s residence, first in Darghiyya and then in New Darghiyya.[48] Here they were given complete freedom to live according to their customs – even to smoke and drink in public. They had their church and priest. Russian women and girls, both captives and defectors, were brought into the settlement and married by a priest to a man of their choice.[49]

In spite of the Russians' initial alarm that the policy adopted by Shamil would cause widespread desertion,[50] the rate of desertion did not increase significantly.[51] Nevertheless, the number of defectors accumulated over the years and reached several hundred at least.[52] It is difficult to overestimate their contribution to the war effort of Shamil and the mountaineers. They manned almost exclusively the artillery and its maintenance services as well as other regular units. They were employed in engineering works and mining. They worked in the factories which produced guns, bombs and shells, gunpowder and other military requirements.

Some of them were employed in propaganda, and called upon

other Russian soldiers to defect. Others, the most trustworthy, served as interpreters and were engaged in translating captured documents and newspapers, in interrogations of captives and in negotiations with the Russians. A few served as spies. Finally, there was the military orchestra, which paraded and played the Russian tattoo for the amusement of the *imām* and his troops, and on so many occasions to the outrage of the Russians.

Other *Ḥarbīs*

Through his dealings with the Russians – captives, defectors and others – Shamil came to know, and subtly make use of, the existence of groups suffering persecution, whether national – like the Poles – or religious – like the 'Old Believers' and other Russian sectarians.[53] To those Russians persecuted for their religious beliefs, their own authorities rather than Shamil and his people were the 'fanatics'. A few among them acted on these views and went over into the mountains, not to join Shamil and fight for him, but to practise their religion in peace and freedom.

The story of one such group of Old Believers from among the Terek Cossacks has been published. They crossed the Terek in December 1849 and asked Shamil to establish a monastic settlement, where they would pray and wait for the coming of the Antichrist, which they believed would happen in the near future. In the spring of 1850 the *imām* allowed them to establish their settlement at any place of their choice. The new settlement was reinforced by new people. But some of the settlers soon lost their faith and confidence. The settlement underwent a series of ups and downs, was transferred to another location and finally dismantled in 1852.[54]

In dealing with this and similar groups, Shamil acted strictly within the boundaries of the *sharīʿa*. Both these groups and the defectors were *ḥarbīs* who came over to the *dār al-islām*, and were therefore treated by him as *mustaʾminūn*. Their classification as *mustaʾminūn* allowed Shamil to grant them a series of privileges – within the confines of their settlements, one should not forget – which would have been impossible had they been treated as *dhimmīs*.

To the *dār al-ḥārb* belonged also two other groups of interest to Shamil – Jews and Armenians. Both dominated the commerce in the mountains.[55] Both suffered traditionally from raids of the mountaineers, though the Jews probably less so because their commerce was on a lesser scale and, more important, because they were part of the mountaineers' society, were armed, were expert fighters and were able and determined to avenge the killing of any member of their family.

From Shamil's point of view both groups were *ḥarbīs*, and as such a legitimate target for attacks and raids. Both communities complained of savage attacks by Shamil's hordes[56] and professed loyalty to the Russian authorities.[57] Again in the case of the Jews, most of the complaints refer actually to the eighteenth century, though they suffered from Shamil's hordes as well.[58] And in spite of some acts in support of the authorities[59] and the Russians rewarding and praising the community for its loyalty,[60] this loyalty was actually rather passive.

The special standing of the Jews and Armenians in commerce and the fact that they were minorities made them of special interest to Shamil. The *imām* was interested in developing commerce inside his dominions as well as with the territories controlled by the Russians.[61] Yet, since direct contact between his people and the Russians, and even with the Muslims under Russian control, was undesirable, the use of Jews and Armenians as middlemen was a logical policy. This explains Shamil's remark to his cousin-in-law when this Armenian merchant came to visit Shu'awana in May 1848: thanked for the permission to enter his realm, the *imām* replied that he 'would give similar permission' to others but no one 'dared to ask for it'.[62]

Shamil's efforts to employ the services of both groups as middlemen seem to have had very limited success at best. There is some scant evidence of Jews engaged in commerce in Shamil's domains.[63] With regard to the Armenians, such evidence is even more rare.

Shamil's attempts at accommodation, alliance and co-operation with non-Muslims, both on the communal and individual level, show him to be a pragmatist and far removed from the image of a 'blind fanatic hater of everything Christian and Russian' drawn by many Russian and Soviet sources. One should not go, however, to the other extreme and accept uncritically 'Abd al-Raḥīm's idealistic apologetic account, according to which the *imām*'s

> devotion to Islam did not hinder him from being tolerant in questions of faith: respecting other religions, Shamil demanded that

> each of his subjects – be he Christian, Jew or Muslim – adhere strictly to the stipulations of his own [religious] law.[64]

Shamil's attitude towards other religions and their believers was strictly within the boundaries of the *sharīʿa*. Accordingly his 'religious tolerance' was in effect only towards 'the People of the Book'[65] and never included pagans. These, as the *imām* wrote to Muḥammad Amīn, had to be converted through the use of force.[66]

Chapter 24

Shamil and the Powers

The Ottomans

As mentioned above,[1] strong historical bonds connected the Daghestanīs and Chechens to the Ottomans. The Ottoman *sulṭān* was held in the highest esteem, as the head of the *Sunnī* world. 'There is,' said Shamil to a Russian officer, 'only one God in Heaven and one *pādishāh* on earth – the Ottoman *sulṭān*.'[2]

In view of this background it was only natural that when Shamil started to look for outside help he turned to İstanbul.[3] The *imām*'s first appeal for help to the Ottomans mentioned in the available sources was made in 1839.[4] This, indeed, falls within the general change of Shamil's strategy which started in 1837.[5] However, neither this nor subsequent requests during the 1840s and early 1850s were answered favourably.

It is true that many messengers were intercepted by the Russians[6] or did not reach their destination because of other reasons.[7] But even those who arrived.[8] 'could get nothing from the *sulṭān*'.[9] The Ottomans had, indeed, tried to stir up the mountaineers a decade earlier, during their war with the Russians.[10] But now, the *sulṭān* was at peace with the tsar and would not violate it by supplying any help to Shamil. Furthermore, during the 1830s Russia had become the *sulṭān*'s main supporter (not to say protector) against Muḥammad ʿAlī,[11] which added an important incentive not to do anything which might irritate the Russians.

This basic policy did not change, even after the successful end of the 'Second Muḥammad ʿAlī Crisis' and the accession of Abdül Mecid, who was less emotionally committed to the Russians than his father had been. It was of primary importance to keep the peace with St. Petersburg. Therefore, no assistance could be given to Shamil, especially as the Russians demonstrated on numerous occasions their extreme sensitivity to any interference in the Caucasus.[12] Furthermore, Shamil's relations with Muḥammad ʿAlī, his Khālidī connection,[13] and the involvement of his messengers with opposition forces in the sensitive north-eastern provinces bordering on Russia and Persia[14] did not make him particularly attractive in the eyes of the Sublime Porte.

The anger and frustration the *imām* must have felt following the Ottoman failure to help him was expressed bluntly in a conversation with a captive Russian officer in 1842:

> Do you really think that the *sulṭān* observes loyally Muḥammad's laws and [that] the Turks [are] true Muslims? They are worse than the *gâvurs* [infidels]. If I only laid my hands on them I would cut them into 24 pieces, beginning with the *sulṭān* [himself]. He sees that we, his coreligionists, have been leading a struggle against the Russians for God and [for] the Faith. [So] why does he not help us?[15]

Whatever the exaggeration for the benefit of the Russian, these feelings were real. But they did not diminish the *sulṭān*'s prestige even in the *imām*'s own eyes.[16] Realising that a major change in Ottoman policy was not imminent and that help on a massive scale would not be available, at least at the moment, Shamil tried to keep in contact with İstanbul until things changed for the better.

Meanwhile, such contacts had their value in keeping up the morale of his people. They were also used for making specific requests for assistance which would be kept on a small scale but would at the same time be important for the mountaineers.[17] These contacts were also used to try to persuade the Ottomans to change their policy. For such attempts at lobbying, other means were used as well. These included the activity of the 'Khālidī connection', and direct appeals from the *imām* and his *murshid* to dignitaries with great religious prestige, like the *şeyhül islam* and the *sharīf* of Mecca to intervene on their behalf with the *sulṭān*.[18]

Always fraught with great danger and difficulties, these contacts were conducted through two routes: The overland roundabout route, in which the Khālidī connection was central; and the Black Sea route to the Circassians, and then across Ghabarṭa to Chechnia. The use of the latter intensified especially following the arrival of Muḥammad Amīn among the Circassians. The defection of Daniyāl made possible the use of his ex-subjects, who in their overwhelming majority remained loyal to him, for such contacts as well. They, on many occasions, used the direct land route to İstanbul.[19]

One of the facts which kept alive Shamil's hope for a change in Ottoman policy was the Porte's continuation and even initiation of contacts with him. The Ottomans' reason for initiating contacts with Shamil was the need to gather information about a movement whose fame and power grew rapidly and which might affect the interests, not to say the peace and security, of their empire. In 1843 a request was sent to supply such information.[20] Shamil sent back detailed information which probably did not reach its destination.[21] In the spring of 1848 a Circassian resident of İstanbul was sent to Shamil to obtain information about the *imām*'s struggle, tactics, aims and successes.[22] This time the replies seem to have arrived at their destination.[23]

By this time the diplomatic horizon had changed. Russo-Ottoman relations had cooled and a war was not unthinkable any more. In these circumstances, the idea of co-operating with Shamil in case of war was naturally explored.[24] In the above-mentioned, or other, contacts, this matter must have been raised with Shamil, since by the beginning of 1850 the *serasker* (Commander-in-Chief) of Erzurum was sure that Shamil would co-operate in such circumstances.[25] If, indeed, there was an understanding of any kind, it must have been at the most general level possible – the level of intentions – without any practical preparations for such co-operation, or for Ottoman assistance, present or future, to the *imām*.

The results of this lack of co-ordination were not slow to appear when the Crimean War broke out. Both sides were unprepared for co-operation. They lacked any real knowledge of each other's strength, plans, capabilities etc. Most important, each hoped and expected the other to do the entire job almost completely on their own.[26] The painful disappointment of Shamil *vis-à-vis* the Ottoman incompetence and defeats explains his bitterness towards them and the *sulṭān* Abdül Mecid in later years.[27]

However, as in many other fields, Shamil managed to turn even this less than positive relationship to his advantage. An alignment with the *hunkâr* (one of the titles of the Ottoman ruler), apart from the obvious meaning for Shamil in terms of prestige and legitimacy, was used by him to boost the morale of his people. The *imām* knew well that his was a small and surrounded people fighting a great power. His supporters understood well that on their own they did not stand a chance of victory. In order to continue to fight and suffer all the deprivations of war they needed to know that other Muslims knew about their struggle, identified with them and were ready to, and would indeed, help them. No success of whatever magnitude could remove this need for a long time.

These were the reasons why the *imām* made his contacts with the Ottomans known; publicised the arrival of messengers – true or supposed – from Istanbul; and put into the widest possible circulation letters from the *sulṭān*.[28] In doing so he was following in the footsteps of Ghāzī Muḥammad. But Shamil went one step further: he frequently referred to his plans to march forward to make contact with an Ottoman army. In the late 1840s a widespread rumour, or 'prophecy', claimed that Shamil would become the *sulṭān*'s *sirdār* in the Caucasus after the Ottomans' arrival.[29] Even if Shamil did not initiate this rumour, he did nothing to stop it.

It is not surprising that such efforts by Shamil increased in the late 1840s and early 1850s when successes became fewer and the hardships experienced by the people greater. In the early 1840s, though much needed, practically no contacts existed with the Ottomans. In the mid-1840s the series of spectacular successes deferred for a while the need for them. Now the *imām* had to play more and more the Ottoman card. This was facilitated by the growth of the contacts with the Ottomans at that time. However, his reliance on the Ottomans was finally to backfire following the Crimean War.

Muḥammad ʿAlī

During the early 1840s any lack of help from the Ottomans was more than compensated for by the support of the *pāshā* of Egypt. Muḥammad ʿAlī's influence on the events of 1840 both in Circassia and in Chechnia had been dealt with above. So was the issue of his letter and that of his son, Ibrāhīm – fake or genuine – supporting Shamil.[30] Contacts between the *pāshā* and the *imām* continued for a few more years,[31] and Shamil used them to boost both his own prestige and legitimacy and his people's morale and confidence, in the very same way he would use his contacts with the Ottomans in later years.[32] Muḥammad ʿAlī's letter of support from 1840, for example, was still used and displayed as late as January 1844.[33]

To understand properly the strength of the support Shamil derived from using the name of the *pāshā* of Egypt, Muḥammad

ʿAlī's enormous prestige has to be emphasised again.[34] 'To the mountaineers', testified a Russian officer who had been Shamil's prisoner,

> Muḥammad ʿAlī stands much higher than the [Ottoman] *sulṭān* because he has conquered an entire kingdom from him [the *sulṭān*], become the supreme ruler of the Muslims, and subdued infidel nations like the *Inglīz* [English] and the *Ifranj* [French].[35]

But Shamil enjoyed more than the moral and prestige-related benefits of associating with Muḥammad ʿAlī. According to some sources the *pāshā* of Egypt supplied the *imām* with more tangible assistance as well. ʿAbd al-Raḥman, the *qāḍī* of Shekī, for example, told the British consul in Tabrīz that he had been sent by Shamil on a mission to both the *sulṭān* and Muḥammad ʿAlī, and that the latter sent 'some money' and 'some native engineers, who still continue at that country'.[36]

There were, indeed, in Shamil's service several people who had at least three things in common: they were natives of the Caucasus or in one case of the Crimea; they had all travelled around the Middle East and had stayed for a period in Egypt; and they had acquired certain skills. Among these were Ḥājj Yaḥyā al-Chirkāwī, who organised and commanded Shamil's artillery; Jaʿfar,[37] a Crimean Tatar by origin, who established and managed one of Shamil's gunpowder mills; Ḥājj Jabrāʾīl al-Unsukuluwī,[38] who built and managed the gun foundry and the gunpowder mill in Anṣāl and later in New Darghiyya; and the one to reach the most important position of them all, Ḥājj Yūsuf Safaroghlū [Safarov],[39] a Chechen from ʿAldī.[40]

Ḥājj Yūsuf served the *imām* as an engineer, cartographer, military commander, administrator, political and legal adviser. In his capacity as engineer he was in charge of most of the fortification works, including those at Girgil, Salṭah and Chōkha. As an ex-officer in Muḥammad ʿAlī's *nizām-ı cedid*, he helped Shamil to build his regular infantry – the *niẓām*. In 1854 he was sent by Shamil into exile because of his contacts with the Russians – or the Ottomans, according to another source. After two years in exile he escaped to the Russians a short while before his death. Yūsuf's last work was the drawing for the Russians of a map of Shamil's dominions.[41]

Whether sent by Muḥammad ʿAlī or not – and the important fact is that many people believed they were – these engineers made an enormous contribution to the war effort of the mountaineers, to their ability to continue the struggle for a long time and to the consolidation of Shamil's power and authority. Thus, the help from Muḥammad ʿAlī – actual or perceived – and especially Shamil's ability to use it to the full, proved of primary importance.

The Qājārs

In contrast to Ghāzī Muḥammad, who was reported to have extensive contacts with the Qājārs,[42] Shamil had almost none. In 1848, not long before his death, *shāh* Moḥammed sent Shamil a message 'studiously concealed from his [chief] minister' in which he expressed 'his sympathy with him in the war in which that chief is engaged, and holding out promises of assistance whenever Persia could afford it'.[43] Shamil answered the letter, but his letter arrived after the death of the *shāh*.[44]

In the same year the governor of Arbīl was arrested, upon Russian protests, for selling gunpowder to Shamil.[45] It is difficult to assess whether the governor had any political motive in addition to his love of money, and if so, whether these two incidents were connected in any way at all. In general, however, they stand isolated in what might be called a non-relationship. Traditional mutual hatred and suspicion between Daghestanīs and Persians, *sunnīs* and *shīʾīs*, contributed to this state of affairs. But the main reason for it lay in the fact that the peace treaty of Turkumānchāy – 'the most humiliating national disaster in recent Persian history' – left Ādhārbāyjān 'under the cold shadow of the Colossus of the North, a fact which has ever since dominated the minds of Persian statesmen'.[46]

According to a contemporary Russian assessment, Shamil's envoys, using the Khālidī connection, were travelling freely 'between Tsargrad [İstanbul], Baghdād and Herāt'.[47] Indeed, Shamil's struggle was known, and sympathised with, all over the Muslim world. But other Muslim rulers even further removed than the Qājārs could not have been expected to be able to give more than sympathy and moral support. All they could do, in fact, was to pray for Shamil's success, as the *amīr* of Bukhāra was reported to have done.[48]

The Western Powers

Of the Western powers interested in the Black Sea basin and the Caucasus, only Britain maintained a high profile. The anti-Russian activity of British agents – authorised or unauthorised – among the Circassians has been mentioned above.[49] France, although the only European power to be represented by a consul in Tiflis, kept a markedly lower profile.[50] During the 1830s, 1840s and early 1850s neither power attempted to contact Shamil.[51] The only European group to try, unsuccessfully, to make such contacts were the expatriate Polish opposition groups.[52]

From Shamil's point of view, both Britain and France were untrustworthy, and not only because they were infidel powers. The *imām* must have heard enough about the promises made in the name of Britain by Urquhart and his colleagues, promises which were never kept.[53] As for France, Shamil must have known – through both the Khālidī connection and captured Russian newspapers – of the war of that power in Algeria against his fellow-Khālidī *shaykh*, ʿAbd al-Qādir.[54] The *imām*, therefore, made no effort of his own to contact any of the Christian powers. The Crimean War would cause changes in the attitudes of both, but only for a short while, and without lasting effects.

Part 9

The End

Chapter 25

The Crimean War

In March 1853 Shamil wrote to the Ottoman *sulṭān*, Abdül-Mecid:

> Gracious and Great *khalīfa*. We, your subjects, having for a very long time fought the enemies of our Faith, have lost our strength. Furthermore, we, your subjects, have been [continuously] hard-pressed year after year [to such an extent that] now we have no force to furnish against our enemies. We are deprived of [all] means and are now in a disastrous position.[1]

Although the *imām* had been appealing for more than 15 years to the Ottomans for help,[2] never before had he used such desperate terms. Even if the language is exaggerated, the letter still demonstrates the physical and moral state of Shamil and his people.

The 'seven bad years' of constant Russian advance in Chechnia – all the Russian blunders notwithstanding – had clearly taken their toll. Although a vast majority of the Chechens were still firmly under his control and ready to continue the struggle, they were hungry, exhausted, frustrated and desperate. Shamil, unlike the Russians and many natives, knew that the Chechens were, in fact, very near their breaking-point. And with their collapse, Daghestan could not resist for long on its own.[3]

The prospect of a war between Russia and the Ottomans was, therefore, for the *imām* and his people, almost like the kiss of life. To start with, the Russians, their attention and main forces now diverted to the Ottoman front, 'were reduced to a defensive war, which was much more troublesome than an active one'.[4] More important, the long-awaited and hoped-for Ottoman help which would relieve and liberate the mountaineers from the Russians was now in view. And neither Shamil nor his people intended to remain passive in the ensuing struggle. During the spring and summer of 1853 the Russians received many reports of Shamil's preparations for a large-scale offensive, but as usual, these reports were conflicting as to his intentions.[5]

On 5 September Shamil appeared with a force of over 10,000 men and four guns on the peak above Zakartalah.[6] He caught the Russians completely by surprise. The following day the mountaineers occupied the empty village. Orbeliani pushed them back to the mountain at the cost of 64 killed and 113 wounded. There Shamil remained for the following nine days. His 'presence alone agitated the minds of the local Muslim population and subjected its dubious fidelity to our government to strong temptation'.[7]

Immobilising Orbeliani at Zakartalah, Shamil 'sent his *murīds* into the villages of the Balagin district',[8] and 'flooded the environs of Zakartalah with small gangs, who, surrounding us completely, started without formalities to make themselves at home in front of our eyes'.[9]

On 17 September Shamil shifted his positon to Mesed el-Kher [Mesedel'ger or Mesel'deger], where the Russians had been building a fort since the spring.[10] Not yet completed, the fort had come under siege on 7 September.[11] Now the *imām* attempted to storm the fort twice, but being unsuccessful retreated into the mountains on 18 September.

The reason for Shamil's move to Mesed el-Kher was the march of Argutinskii with a force of about 6,500 infantry, 2,000 cavalry, and 12 pieces of artillery to Orbeliani's rescue. Receiving the news of the invasion on 7 September, Argutinskii reacted with uncharacteristic speed and set out on the 9th. His ten-day march 'by bridle paths or none over five successive ranges of the snow-covered main chain'[12] was rightly described by Vorontsov as 'historical and almost unprecedented'.[13] However, by the time he joined forces with Orbeliani, all was over.

This was Argutinskii's last deed. Upon his return to Temir-Khān-Shūra, he retired, ill and 'offended for his troops, the hardships of which in the above-mentioned march had not been, in his view, duly recognised'.[14] Soon afterwards he died.

Shamil's invasion caused worry to Vorontsov and the Russian command.[15] His aims were clear: He 'assured the local inhabitants that he was on his way to Tiflis, where he was to meet the Ottoman *sulṭān*'.[16] But the *imām* was a month too early. The Ottomans officially declared war on Russia only on 5 October 1853. Having learned that the war had not yet broken out, and with his supplies dwindling, Shamil preferred to avoid battle with Argutinskii and retreated.

During or immediately before this campaign Shamil 'sent mes-

MAP 20: MESED EL-KHER

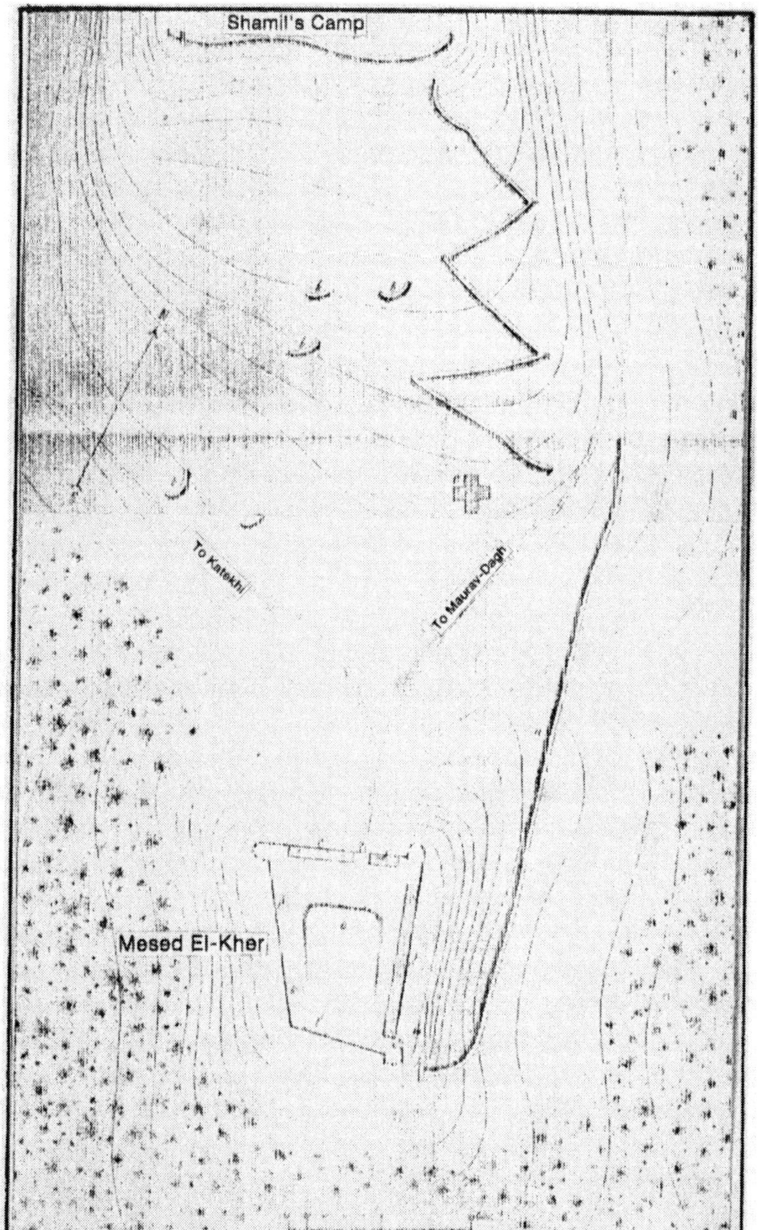

Source: Sbornik Opisanii Osad i Oboron Krepostei i Ukreplenii, Vol.I (St. Petersburg, 1869).

sengers to assure the Turks that they may depend on his co-operation, and that as soon as he learns [that] they are prepared to attack the Russians, he will fall upon them on his side'.[17] At the very same time that Shamil's message reached the Ottomans, he received a letter (or *firmān*) from the *sulṭān*.[18] Contact between the two sides was thus established, and in spite of Russian attempts to stop it[19] and other difficulties,[20] it was to continue.[21]

The autumn of 1853 passed in relative calm, with only a few raids carried out by both sides.[22] But this calm was not tension-free. Frequent reports of large-scale preparations and concentrations in the mountains[23] and intensive propaganda efforts by Shamil among the pacified and semi-pacified Muslim communities[24] kept the Russians constantly on their toes. In mid-December Shamil held a gathering of all his *nā'ibs* in New Darghiyya for four weeks, after which all the Chechens were instructed to be constantly ready for a major campaign.[25]

But Shamil undertook no large-scale campaign during the winter or spring of 1854. At the end of December 1853 Talgik was ordered by Shamil to try to resettle the area of Khān Qalʿa, but his attempt was thwarted by the Russians.[26] After that there were few raids, though the Russians had many alarms.[27] It was only in July that the *imām* undertook another major campaign, which through an accident became the best known of all his campaigns in the West.[28]

In the evening of 14 July Shamil, with a force of 7,000 cavalry and 5,000 infantry, camped on Mount Pakhalis-Tavi overlooking Shildi and the Alazān valley. Again, as in the previous year, the *imām* succeeded in deceiving the Russians, and he 'fell on Shildi like snow on the head'.[29] The following campaign was in many respects a repetition of the previous one with the results, however being much more detrimental to the Russians because their command was in considerably less competent hands.

With Argutinskii's retirement, Orbeliani was nominated commander of the Caspian Province. His place on the Lesghian Line was taken by Melikov, who had already in 1850 shown great incompetence.[30] Also, in Tiflis some changes had occurred. Vorontsov was ill and exhausted, and bitterly disappointed that a political course had been pursued against his advice, which led to war first with the Ottomans and then with Britain and France. He asked for permission to go abroad for treatment. Receiving it, finally, in March 1854, he left immediately.

The emperor intended at first to nominate Murav'ev in Vorontsov's stead. However, out of deference to the outgoing viceroy – Murav'ev and Vorontsov had been personal enemies for some time – he agreed to defer nomination of a new viceroy. Vorontsov was thus officially given temporary leave[31] and replaced by a reluctant Nikolai Andreevich Read as temporary commander with powers of the commander-in-chief of the Caucasian Separate Infantry Corps in time of war. Having served about 30 years in the cavalry in Russia proper, Read joined Vorontsov's staff in 1851 as an expert on cavalry.[32] In addition to his inexperience in Caucasian affairs, Read displayed hesitancy, reluctance to take decisions and a disposition to panic.[33]

On 15 July Shamil sent his son, Ghāzī-Muḥammad, with part of his force to raid the valley. Encountering no serious resistance – the Russians were extremely slow and confused in their reactions – the mountaineers raided on that and the following days both banks of the river, pillaging and burning all the villages. On 17 July they returned to Shamil's camp with unprecedented numbers of prisoners and quantities of booty.

The mountaineers' sudden appearance, great numbers and swift movements created panic among the local population,[34] and even in Tiflis. According to an Italian merchant who was there at the time, the Russians 'were in the greatest alarm. Shamil was close by and there were not above 2,000 soldiers in the city and it apparently was in his power to plunder it'.[35] But the *imām* did not move from his place. Much more realistic about his own strength and capabilities than many Russian and Western observers,[36] he waited to see whether the Ottoman army was advancing. On 22 July Shamil retreated into the mountains. There, he waited for three more weeks. Finally, he dispersed his force and returned to New Darghiyya in mid-August.

While his people celebrated what they regarded as an exceptionally successful raid, Shamil was reported to have said 'this is joy after which one will have to grieve'.[37] He was among the very few to grasp the significance of this campaign. Before embarking on it, the *imām* informed the Ottoman command in Kars that he would march on Tiflis to meet them.[38] No doubt informed of the Ottoman defeats during the winter,[39] Shamil 'requested the *müşir* to co-operate with him if he felt confidence in his troops, but if he did not, [Shamil] advised him not to risk defeat but to await the results of his own attack'.[40] The obvious conclusion from the Ottomans' failure to move was soon reinforced by the news of their defeats on the river Çolok (15 June), at Çengel (15 July) and at Kurudere (5 August 1854):[41] no help could be expected from that quarter.

In the beginning of Muḥarram 1271 (towards the end of September 1854), Shamil made another major effort. This time he concentrated his forces in Chechnia, aiming at a juncture with his *nā'ib* in Circassia, Muḥammad Amīn. However, receiving no reply from the *nā'ib*, he had to abandon this plan as well.[42] Thus, during the remainder of the war, the *imām*, stayed passive, limiting himself to 'frequent mobilisations' and 'raids on our frontiers'.[43]

What gave the raid on the Alazān Valley such a renown was the fact that among the hundreds of captives were Prince Tchavtchavadze's wife, her sister – both grand-daughters of the last king of K'art'lo-Kakhet'i, Giorgi XII, – and their children with their French governess, captured on Tchavtchavadze's estate at Tsinandali.[44] This event, which sent waves of shock not only into Russia but into the West as well, had three consequences for Shamil.

The most personal and immediate one was the return to him of Jamāl al-Dīn, the son whom he had had to give as a hostage to Grabbe in 1839.[45] On 22 March 1855, after complicated negotiations, the princesses and their families were exchanged for Jamāl al-Dīn and 40,000 silver rubles as part of a deal involving a general exchange of prisoners.[46] Among the people returned to Shamil were the hostages given to Faesy in 1837 – including Shamil's nephew – and those taken prisoner in the storm of Akhulgoḥ in 1839. The *imām*'s joy in having his son back was short-lived; Jamāl al-Dīn's health deteriorated and in 1857 he died of consumption according to a Russian source. In the mountains, however, it was widely believed that he died of a slowly acting poison administered to him by the Russians before the exchange.[47]

The second and in the long run the most important consequence of the raid on Tsinandali was its impact on Shamil's relations with the Ottoman Empire and its Western allies. Both Britain and France entered the war with little knowledge of the Caucasus, but with the intention to co-operate with Shamil, the romantic 'Chief of the Circassians' who had become so popular in Europe in the late 1840s and early 1850s.[48] For his co-operation some, like Palmerston, were even ready to establish an independent Circassian state after the war, to be headed by the *imām*.[49]

Both the French and the British tried to contact Shamil.[50] However, soon the difficulties of even reaching the *imām*, not to speak of co-operating with him, began to become clear.[51] Thus, more attention was given to reports by 'men in the field', who had claimed all along that co-operation with Shamil was very difficult to achieve.[52]

Lord Stratford de Redcliffe, the powerful British ambassador to the Sublime Porte,[53] had never been enthusiastic about Shamil and the prospect of co-operating with him.[54] Now, upon receiving news of the capture of the princesses, he concluded that Shamil 'is a fanatic and a barbarian with whom it will be difficult for us, and even for the Porte, to entertain any credible or satisfactory relations'.[55]

In his outrage, de Redcliffe sent a 'private letter' to Colonel Williams, the British commissioner to the Ottoman forces in Anatolia,[56] and instructed him to send a letter to Shamil by one of the *imām*'s messengers to the Ottoman commander.[57] In this letter Williams was to tell Shamil in no uncertain terms that one should not fight women and children and to ask the *imām* to release the captive princesses at once. Williams sent Shamil the required letter and received a reply.[58] Lord Clarendon, the foreign secretary, shared de Redcliffe's outrage about this 'atrocious and revolting outrage' and 'entirely approved' all of the ambassador's steps.[59] The influence of this outrage could be felt in the lack of enthusiasm and half-heartedness of further British attempts to contact Shamil.[60]

This was not all. The British ambassador, with London's approval, 'convinced' the Porte to send a strongly worded letter to Shamil, reprimanding him for fighting women and children and ordering him to release them immediately.[61] Four years later Shamil gave his version of the events:

> At the very beginning of the [Crimean] War he [Shamil] received an offer to prepare to meet the allied forces at Imeret'i. Expressing his agreement Shamil immediately took steps to carry out this plan . . . In the spring of 1854 he marched towards the district of Chārtalah . . . He intended to march on Tiflis, but in order to act more freely, he sent to inform the [Ottoman] commanders in Kars and in Abkhazet'i of his intentions. Awaiting an answer he sent his son [Ghāzī Muḥammad] with all the cavalry and some infantry into Kakhet'i, while himself with the rest of his force camping near one of our [Russian] forts . . . Soon he received an answer, the

> contents of which were extremely insulting. Instead of being grateful for his expressed readiness to co-operate with the plans of the allies and for the speed with which he had carried out his promise, he was reproached and told off as [if he were] a common subject.[62]

Shamil could, and did, ignore his personal feelings, as his letter to Williams demonstrated.[63] But they were not forgotten, especially as Britain (and France) seemed to be willing to do little to help him. In August 1855, for example, the Russians received word to the effect that Shamil was not enthusiastic about the alliance between the Ottoman Empire and the Western powers.[64]

As for İstanbul, the *imām* soon realised that it was a 'broken reed'. All the Ottomans could do for him was to send medallions and flags – and promises.[65] Such messages and mementos proved useful to keep up the spirits of the people – and Shamil made full use of them[66] – but could not allay the *imām*'s worries.

The third consequence of Tsinandali – the most unexpected and one that might have been the most meaningful had it been realised – was an attempt at re-opening, after a pause of 12 years, the negotiations between the Russians and the *imām*.[67] The prospect was considerably brightened by the nomination, on 11 December of a new viceroy and commander-in-chief to the Caucasus. The tsar, his patience at an end due to Read's disposition to panic and his endless disagreements with Bebutov, the commander of the acting forces on the Anatolian front, decided to replace him.

Nikolai Nikolaevich Murav'ev had by then had a distinguished career. *Inter alia*, he was sent on a diplomatic mission to Khiva by Ermolov. At the conquest of Kars in 1828 he was cited for bravery. In 1833, at the height of 'the First Muḥammad ʿAlī Crisis', he was sent as an extraordinary envoy to the *pāshā* of Egypt and later that year he commanded the Russian troops on the Bosphorus. A strict disciplinarian and a critic of the lavish luxury introduced by his predecessor, he soon became very unpopular among the Russian officers and officials in the Caucasus.[68]

The new viceroy wondered

> whether it might not be possible to end the Caucasian war or, at least, to suspend it, through conducting negotiations with Shamil, with the prospect of prompting him to submit on conditions advantageous to his self-respect. To achieve such an aim it was necessary

to act with extreme caution: and for this it was desirable, at the beginning, to establish somewhat friendly relations [with] Shamil, which could be used, at a *suitable moment*, as a springboard for more serious suggestions.[69]

The first thread for such a relationship[70] had in fact been established during the negotiations which had led to the exchange of prisoners. Leontii Pavlovich Nicolaÿ [Nikolai], the commander of the Ghumuq plain,[71] struck up a friendship with Jamāl al-Dīn and gained Shamil's trust. After his return, Jamāl al-Dīn kept in contact with Nicolaÿ, mainly requesting Russian books.

Now Nicolaÿ was instructed by Murav'ev through Bariatinskii to start such proceedings.[72] Nicolaÿ had to keep this attempt in complete secrecy and to report over the heads of his superiors directly to Bariatinskii. Apart from these three, only the minister of war, Gorchakov, and the emperor were parties to this secret. In May 1855 Bariatinskii left Tiflis because of his worsening relationship with Murav'ev.[73] He was replaced by Nicolaÿ's brother, Aleksandr Pavlovich – a senior official in Tiflis – as the recipient of the reports. In February 1856, when Evdokimov took over the command of the Left Flank, all the reports went through him.

Nicolaÿ proceeded very cautiously. He deemed this necessary because of the 'unfavourable opinion, which for unknown reasons Shamil and his followers formed, of our integrity'.[74] The Russians deemed it best to proceed at first by developing commercial relations. They found Shamil much more forthcoming than expected, and by the end of 1855 an agreement was concluded to establish regular commercial relations between the *imām*'s domain and Khasav-Yūrt. This was to be the first step in a long process of pacification by peaceful means.[75]

Contrary to his expectations, Nicolaÿ found out very soon that Shamil understood that 'the present circumstances provided [him with] an apt opportunity to obtain an accommodation with the Russians on conditions favourable to him'. However, being 'an experienced actor', the *imām* 'will cover up his intentions until he is sure that it is possible to step on the path of peace [with the Russians] without any danger to his influence over the population'. Furthermore, 'as a true Muslim, he [Shamil] does not reject the hope' that the powerful anti-Russian coalition 'will triumph to the Glory of Islam. Therefore, he will try to linger, taking no decisive step (knowing that such [a step] cannot remain a secret from his followers).'[76]

The Russians, for their part, could not afford to initiate such negotiations either. Nicolaÿ was specifically instructed that his 'first concern is to keep [our] mountain neighbour from [initiating any large-scale] hostilities, *until he decides to submit any offers*'.[77] Under such limitations no progress could have been made beyond the commercial agreement.

In September 1856, six months after the conclusion of the peace treaty of Paris, Shamil finally made an attempt to break the deadlock. He told Jamāl al-Dīn that 'if the *sulṭān* Abdül Mecid, [who] has made peace [with the Russians], suggests to us to do the same, I shall have no right to reject it'.[78] This was, however, too late. By then the Russians were no longer interested in a negotiated settlement.

Chapter 26

Ghunīb

The Crimean War clearly demonstrated to the Russians how precarious their hold on the country was as long as pockets of resistance remained.[1] It was clear, therefore, that this problem would be given first priority after the end of the war.

Already in the autumn of 1854 a memorandum was submitted to Nicholas suggesting the use of the augmented strength of the Caucasian Corps due to wartime reinforcements 'to undertake decisive actions to subdue the mountaineers'.[2] The author of the memorandum, Dmitri Alekseevich Miliutin, the future minister of war and executant of the military reforms of the 1860s, was one of the most brilliant officers in the empire. Starting his service in 1833, Miliutin served twice in the Caucasus and participated in the siege of Akhulgoḥ in 1839. Since 1845 he had been an instructor in the military academy and since 1848 an officer for special assignments to the minister of war.[3]

Two weeks before the conclusion of the peace treaty of Paris[4] (signed on 30 March 1856) the new emperor, Alexander II, instructed the minister of war, Prince Dolgorukov, to seek the view of a few 'old Caucasian hands' on Miliutin's memorandum. All those consulted – Vorontsov, Murav'ev Kotzebue, Wolf and Bariatinskii – were in favour of it.[5] Thus, by the summer of 1856 the decision was reached to use the 200,000-man army in the Caucasus[6] to crush Shamil and then subdue the Circassians while the impact caused by the peace treaty of Paris lasted.[7]

Indeed, the peace treaty of Paris had a tremendous impact:

> Delegations from all over Chechnia and from almost all the mountain tribes gathered to the *imām* and in unison demanded peace. They said to Shamil: 'if the *sulṭān* with the French and the English who had promised us so much could not defeat Russia and did not help us at all, then it is time for us to think of our own security. What hope have we left?' They were so strong in this opinion that Shamil had no choice but to agree [with them] and only asked for

> a delay of two months in order to enquire whether any stipulation in the mountaineers' favour had been included in the general peace [treaty].[8] It was possible [now], without any know-how, just by [using] common sense, to achieve in one moment all that we had struggled for with such futility for fifty years.
>
> At this crucial moment the following happened: it was decided that for the [complete] pacification of the Caucasus it was necessary to transfer the submitting population to Vologda Province or any other empty land and it was decided, in a council in Stavropol', to send all the Chechens to Manych . . .[9] Can one believe that this was not a fantasy of a politically-minded high-school student but [an official] decree?
>
> This madness was [officially] transmitted to the Chechen elders. Shamil was resurrected. He gathered again all the delegations and asked whether they knew about the decree of the Russian command. All said they knew. 'This is God's finger,' said Shamil. 'I could never invent such a punishment for those Chechens who had betrayed us as their Russian masters did. Would you like to go to Manych as well?' There was no reply [to this question] and the people dispersed in silence.
>
> The pacified Chechens stated that they would never part with their homeland, whatever the cost. The subjugated population in Chechnia and Daghestan has been brought again to the same mood as in 1843. Luckily, the Chechens tried a peaceful approach first: they sent an appeal to the emperor through Bariatinskii and [in reply] a messenger arrived prohibiting any further action on this issue. But the impression has already been made and the only favourable moment to be used has been wasted.[10]

This act of folly contributed to Murav'ev's replacement, though a much more important motive was his rivalry with Bariatinskii.[11]

Prince Aleksandr Ivanovich Bariatinskii was a childhood friend of the tsarevich, later Emperor Alexander II. He chose to serve in the Caucasus where he was quickly promoted to command a battalion (1845), a regiment and the Ghumuq plain (1850), the Left Flank (1852) and finally became chief-of-staff of the Caucasian Corps (1853). Very well-connected and of independent means, in fact wealthy, Bariatinskii possessed an independent mind and was not usually obedient to authority. This was the main reason for his clash with Murav'ev and his departure from the Caucasus on 6 June 1855.[12]

Now, with the new emperor on the throne, it was clear that

Bariatinskii would play a decisive role in the affairs of the Caucasus. On 17 June 1856 Murav'ev submitted his resignation.[13] The emperor accepted it and named Bariatinskii as his successor.[14] Bariatinskii's first step was to secure Miliutin's nomination as his chief-of-staff.[15] The two immediately made plans, based on Miliutin's 1854 memorandum, for a final assault on Shamil.[16]

Thus, for Shamil, and for the mountaineers in general, it was to be a desperate battle, without any hope, to the end. And desperate it was. Already in the winter of 1856–57 the new energetic commander of the Left Flank, Evdokimov,[17] embarked upon a campaign in Greater Chechnia.[18] By April 1857 Bariatinskii could report to St. Petersburg that 'the lowland of Greater Chechnia has finally been wrenched away from Shamil's possessions' – a return, in fact, to the *status quo* of spring 1853.

Before embarking on this final assault, however, Bariatinskii and Miliutin carried out a reorganisation of the Caucasian Corps, now renamed 'the Caucasian Army', upon more rational lines. This included a new division of the Caucasian line into left and right 'wings'; the redrawing of the boundaries between different regional commands; the relocation of units in such a way that each was concentrated in a specific area; and, following that, the establishment of a single, clear-cut chain of command.

In May 1857 Bariatinskii carried out an inspection tour of Northern Daghestan and the Left Wing. Following that tour it was finally decided to carry out a double-pronged attack from the north-west and north-east by the forces of the Left Wing and the Caspian Province respectively, with a third diversionary campaign on the Lesghian Line.[20]

In accordance with the orders he was given, Orbeliani, with a force of 8,500 infantry, 400 dragoons, 1,400 irregular cavalry and ten cannon, set out to Salaṭawh on 28 June 1857. Despite strong resistance led by the *imām* himself, the Russians cleared avenues through the forests, paved roads and established a new fort at Burtinah, whence the headquarters of the Daghestan regiment was transferred on 11 November. Orbeliani also stormed and destroyed Shamil's fort opposite Burtinah (17 October) and received the submission of part of the population of Salaṭawh, including Jamāl al-Chirkawī.

Vrevskii, the commander of the Lesghian Line[21] started his campaign on 14 July, and during the following three weeks he destroyed the entire south-western part of the Dido community, consisting of 11 villages.[22] On 25 August, he started again for the north-eastern part of Dido. Notwithstanding the fact that he had at his disposal about 10,000 men against Ghāzī Muḥammad's 2,000, the expedition almost ended in disaster.[23]

Completing the fort at Burtinah, Orbeliani between 12 and 28 November destroyed Zandaq, Dilim and all the country in between them.[24] This was a diversion in favour of Evdokimov, who in December 1857 started his winter campaign. Evdokimov destroyed all the villages along the Jalka, Shavdon and Khūlkhulaw rivers and transferred their population beyond the Sunja.[25] After a month's rest, which he used to deceive Shamil by false movements, Evdokimov dealt his master-blow: on 28 January 1858 he conquered the Argūn defile, where Vorontsov's son had been repelled with huge losses in 1852.[26]

Strategically the Upper Argūn defile was of great importance, being the very centre of Shamil's dominions. By taking possession of it, the Russians expected to cut them in two and to subdue easily the part of Chechnia lying to the west of it. By this, the *imām*'s threat to the Georgian Military Highway would be eliminated as well. In addition, positioned in the defile, the Russians could, as they indeed did, threaten Shamil's residence at New Darghiyya from the flank and rear.

During the following nine weeks the Russians built fort Argunskoe in the fork between the Shārō and Chantī Argūn. They felled the forest and paved roads, against desperate resistance led by Ghāzī-Muḥammad. Evdokimov carried out several attacks, the most important of which was the seizure, on 12 March, of Mount Dargin Duk, which controls the rear of Greater Chechnia.

Ending the winter campaign on 12 April, Evdokimov immediately moved to Lesser Chechnia, where between 13 and 28 April he received the submission of 96 villages inhabited by 15,000 people.[27] Ten weeks later he started his summer campaign.

According to the plans, Wrangel, the new commander of the Caspian Province,[28] carried out a campaign in Salaṭawh between 31 May and 31 July 1858.[29] Vrevskii also carried out an expedition, in which he was killed.[30] Neither campaign had any significance, but they served as diversions for Evdokimov's summer campaign. Evdokimov, however, was not satisfied with these diversions. He engaged again in feints between 10 and 15 July. Thus, deceiving the *imām*, the Russian general captured the valley of the Lesser Varanda on 11 July.[31] The following day he captured Zunūh and established there a fort on the 22nd.

Although encountering bitter resistance, the Russians

Vrevskii's body is taken away, 1858

The Russians storm an *awul*, 1858

advanced step by step, continually clearing the forest and cutting through roads. On 12 August Shubūt was captured and fort Shatoevskoe was established there on the 20th. On 26 August the community of Shubūt submitted. It was followed by that of Chantī on 27 August. There the fort of Itum Qalʿa was renamed Evdokimovskoe. On 28 August the *nāʾib* Batoqa surrended. By 12 September, when Evdokimov terminated his summer campaign, 15 Chechen communities had submitted to the Russians.

The rest of the year brought no large-scale operations.[32] However, when on 22–25 December Shamil tried to take the initiative, Evdokimov moved again. On 2 January 1859 he conquered Bāsim Birdī [Basym Berdi] and established himself in the defile of the Bās.[33] Ten days later he captured the entirety of the defile. Completing the clearance of forests and the paving of roads, Evdokimov contemplated his next move which, contrary to the general plan, was towards New Darghiyya.[34]

On 27 January Evdokimov captured Tawzen. On 8 February ʿAlīṣanji [Ali Standzhi] was conquered. On 19–20 February New Darghiyya was invested. This soon forced Shamil to retreat, leaving his son in charge. Without hurry, Evdokimov completed the construction of his lines of communications. On 22 February he established the fort of New Vedān near New Darghiyya. A week later the siege started and lasted until 12 April. On 13 April a small bastion outside New Darghiyya was stormed, and on that night Ghāzī-Muḥammad with the garrison retreated.

The fall of New Darghiyya had a tremendous effect on morale, as Shamil himself explained in a message to the Sublime Porte.[35] Following it Chārbi [Charbeloi] and its *nāʾib* offered their submission. Ichkerī followed suit in May.[36] ʿAwkh submitted in June to Wrangel,[37] who between 13 March and 21 April conducted there a campaign as a diversion, and support to Evdokimov.[38] In Southern Daghestan, Antsukh submitted in May.[39]

Contrary to Baddeley's opinion,[40] Shamil did not remain inactive for a moment. The *imām* did everything possible to check the Russian advance. He concentrated his forces and fortified his positions on the estimated Russian routes of advance. He continually harassed the Russians on all sides, and especially the expeditionary forces. He tried diversionary attacks. Finally, he led in person the forces which confronted Evdokimov in July 1858. This resulted in such bitter fighting by the mountaineers 'that even artillery fire did not stop them'.[41]

In June[42] and again in August 1858[43] Shamil tried unsuccessfully

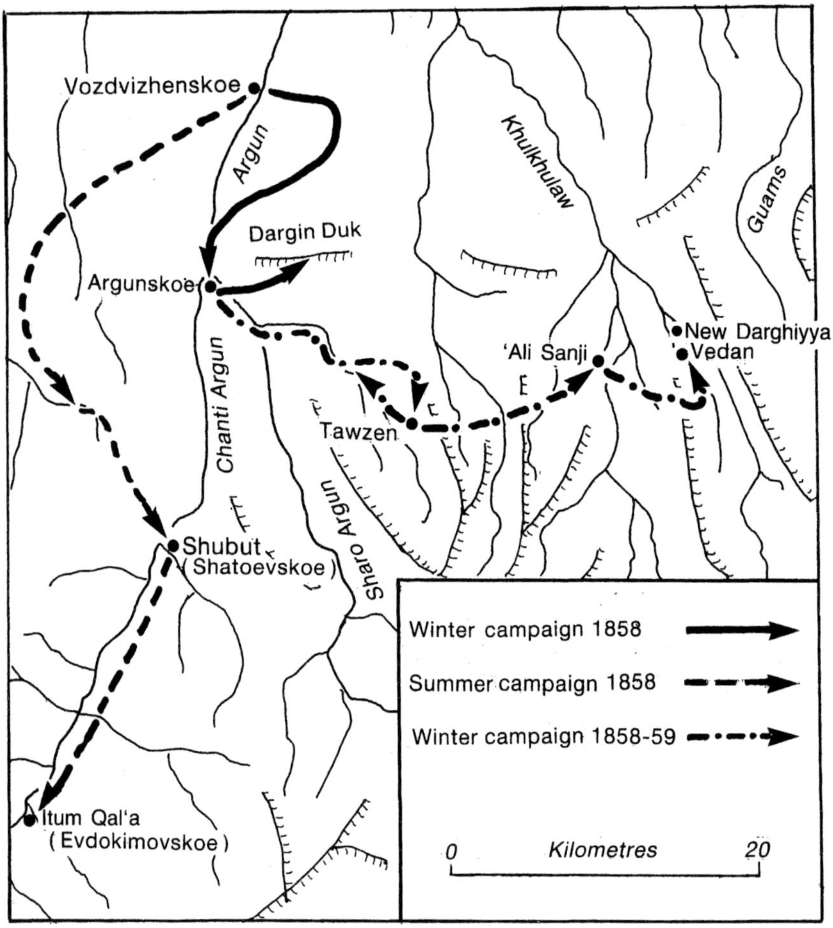
Vozdvizhenskoe
Argun
Khulkhulaw
Guams
Dargin Duk
Argunskoe
New Darghiyya
Vedan
'Ali Sanji
Chanti Argun
Tawzen
Sharo Argun
Shubut
(Shatoevskoe)
Itum Qal'a
(Evdokimovskoe)
Winter campaign 1858
Summer campaign 1858
Winter campaign 1858-59
0
Kilometres
20

to invade Lesser Chechnia and the area of Naṣrān. He did so in response to the appeal of the population, which revolted because it had been ordered by the Russians to abandon its small hamlets and concentrate in a few large villages. In his first attempt the *imām* 'pre-empted and deceived Evdokimov, who could by no means expect such a decisive move on his part'.[44] In the second one Shamil was, according to his own testimony, told that Mūsā Kundukh, the commander of the Osset district, had invited him and promised his co-operation.[45] His failure underlined the overwhelming Russian strategic and tactical superiority.

In his despair the *imām* took an unprecedented step and approached the Western powers directly on his own initiative. In February 1857 he wrote letters to the French[46] and British[47] ambassadors in İstanbul asking for help. The letter to the French ambassador seems never to have reached its destination. The letter to his British counterpart did reach the Foreign Office, but if it was answered – no such answer has survived in the archives – it must have been the same flat refusal given to Muḥammad Amīn.[48] Disappointed with Shamil and with the Circassians, and 'long aware that the struggle [in the Caucasus] was virtually concluded',[49] Britain was resigned to its conquest by Russia.

After the fall of New Darghiyya Shamil sent a man to İstanbul and asked

> to be informed if the Sublime Porte has any expectations of a war with Russia, to create a diversion in his favour, within a reasonable period of time, say a few years, in which case he will still hold on in the hope of giving and receiving support, but that otherwise he will be forced to put an end to the bloody war.[50]

What Shamil meant by these words was demonstrated soon enough. In July 1859 his agent in İstanbul approached the Russian Embassy and stated that he was empowered to open negotiations with the Russians.[51] The emperor, who in May had asked Bariatinskii whether there was a possibility to end the war by negotiations,[52] was inclined to accept the offer.[53] But the viceroy, a strong opponent of anything short of total military victory, would not hear of it. Negotiations at the very moment when he was ready to launch his final assault and knew well of Shamil's desperate situation from intercepted messages,[54] was tantamount to letting the trapped game free.

The final assault started simultaneously by Evdokimov and Wrangel on 26 July.[55] Bariatinskii himself led Evdokimov's force.

Shamil fortified Ichichalī [Ichichale] and prepared to take his stand there against either of the Russian generals, or both.[56] But he was outmanoeuvred again. On 27–28 July Wrangel crossed the ʿAndī Koyṣū in an unexpected place, and after preparing the road, stormed Akhkent Dāgh on 2 August. Shamil had to abandon Ichichalī.

The mountaineers' resistance collapsed suddenly. By 19 August all the area under Shamil's control had submitted to the Russians. The collapse was so instant that Shamil was transformed within a few days from the comander of (still) thousands of warriors into a refugee whose wagons were robbed by the population. The *imām*, with his family and 400 followers, took position on top of Mt. Ghunīb, determined to fight to the end.

On 11 August Wrangel reached Bariatinskii's headquarters, thus establishing a link between his force and that of Evdokimov. Communications with the third force were established on 17 August, when Melikov reached the headquarters. On 21 August the Russian forces reached Ghunīb and encircled it the next day.

During the following two weeks Bariatinskii, eager to capture Shamil alive,[57] tried to negotiate with the *imām* but to no avail. On the night of 5–6 September the Russians stormed the mountain and surrounded the village.[58] Shamil was finally persuaded to surrender in order to save the lives of the children and women, which he did that day, 6 September (25 August Old Style) 1859.

According to Bariatinskii, 'a proper system of [conducting the] war, skillful orders by the chief commanders and the dissemination of rifles among the troops – reduced our losses in the Caucasian war to an insignificant number. This reduction in losses, in turn, together with deciding engagements by tactical movements, was one of the chief causes for our success'.[59]

The first reason is mainly to the credit of Miliutin, whose role in the final conquest is under-appreciated.[60] It was Bariatinskii's good fortune (and judgment) to be one of the only two viceroys in the Caucasus to have an outstanding chief-of-staff – the other being Ermolov.

On the importance of the use of rifles all Russian sources agree unanimously.[61] This, however, might be exaggerated. The mountaineers had shown in the past great ability to deal with new weapons and tactics – artillery, rockets, mining, the use of dragoons etc. – and would no doubt have probably adjusted to the rifles as well. Furthermore, rifles were still comparatively

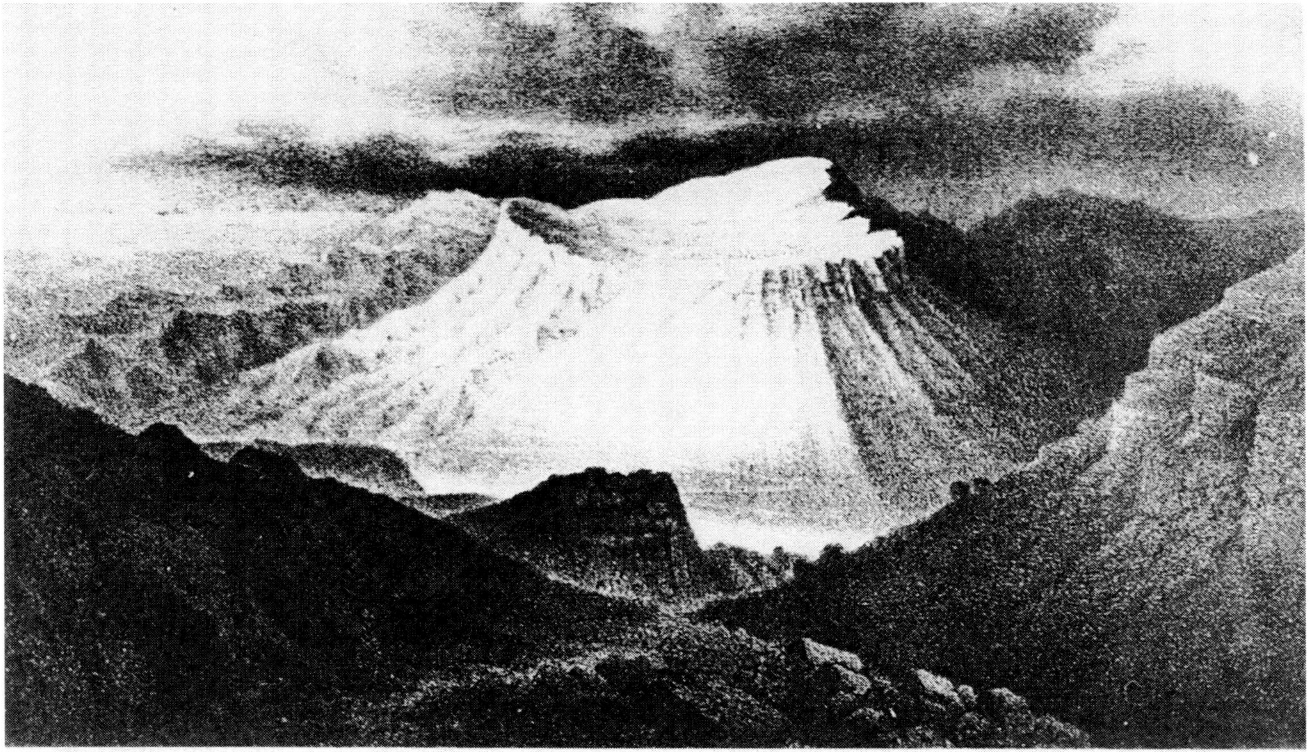

Mount Ghunīb: Shamil's last stand

Shamil's surrender

MAP 22: GHUNĪB

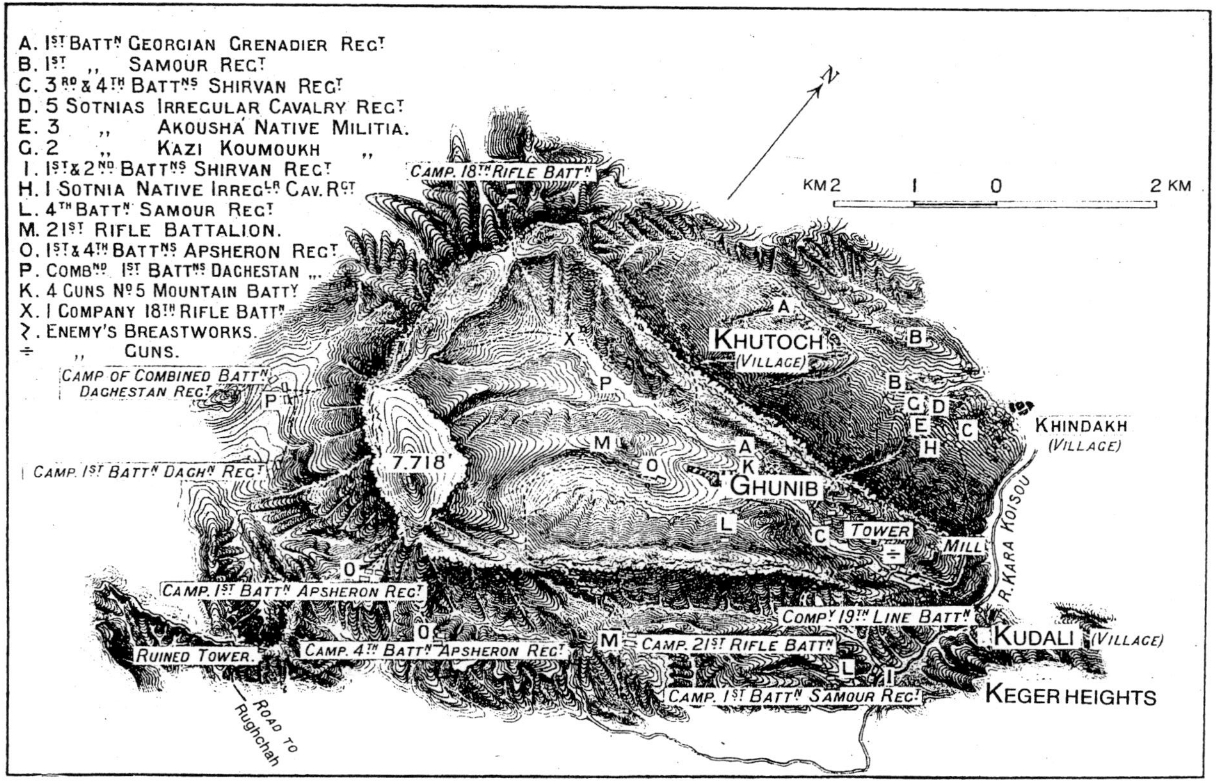

Source: John F. Baddeley, *The Russian Conquest of the Caucasus* (London, 1908).

rare – one battalion per regiment was equipped with them – which minimised their effect.

The second reason, refers almost entirely to Evdokimov. Unlike his counterparts in Daghestan – (Orbeliani and Wrangel) and on the Lesghian Line – (Vrevskii and Melikov), Nikolai Ivanovich Evdokimov spent all his service in the Caucasus and held a series of commands and administrative posts.[62] Not educated or well born and connected, he became very experienced in the affairs of Chechnia and Daghestan. Cunning and courageous, he was not afraid of taking the initiative and carrying out his own designs, knowing at the same time how to avoid the appearance of insubordination to his superiors. As Bariatinskii wrote:

> Evdokimov never once gave the mountaineers a chance of fighting us where they had prepared themselves and where it might have been advantageous for them. The strongest positions held by Shamil's hordes fell almost without resistance as a result of well-planned movements.[63]

Bariatinskii was right in naming this way of warfare a major cause of Shamil's collapse:

> The mountaineers could not be frighened by fighting. Constant warfare had given them such confidence, that a few score men would engage without fear a column several battalions strong, and returning one shot to our hundred would occasion us much more loss than we them. Fighting underlines equality between forces, and, as long as the mountaineers could fight, they entertained no thought of submission. But when, time after time, they found that they were not even given a chance to resist, their weapons started to fall from their hands. Defeated, they would have gathered again on the morrow. Circumvented and forced to disperse without fighting, while seeing their valleys occupied without opposition, they came in the next day and offered their submission. Shamil's power was undermined by nothing so much as by the gathering of useless hordes which had to disperse to their homes without anywhere offering serious resistance.[64]

To these causes others must be added, which are not usually mentioned in Russian sources: the Russians' 'loads of red and white [gold and silver], which captivated the hearts of the people and enslaved the free',[65] the hunger exacerbated by two successive years of drought;[66] the war-fatigue after 30 years of incessant fighting and blockade; and the greatly increased number of Russian troops operating in the Caucasus.

Another significant cause was the disillusionment with the results of the Crimean War. People can endure many hardships and privations as long as they have a hope to win. So did the mountaineers, in their hope to receive help against, and be delivered from, the Russians by the strongest Muslim power – the Ottoman Empire (and for a few years Muḥammad ʿAlī). Once this hope proved to be unrealistic, the resistance started to collapse. That the mountaineers in general – Shamil with a small number of devotees excepted, since they would have resisted to the end anyway – continued to struggle for three more years was the result, as on so many occasions in the past, mainly of Russian blunders and inflexibility.

Conclusion

Wilhelm Steinitz, the first official world champion in modern chess, used to say: 'You do not lose because of the inspired play of your opponent, but because you make mistakes.'[1] According to this line of thought, Shamil's and the mountaineers' ability to resist the Russians for more than a quarter of a century was at least partly, the result of their opponents' mistakes. In many cases the Russians resembled the Austrians facing Napoleon in his Italian campaign:

> Even if the Austrians win a battle, all that is necessary is to wait until their routine obliges them to return to their quarters for afternoon tea, so to speak, and win it back from them.[2]

However, one's opponents' mistakes are not a sufficient guarantee of victory. One has to be able to discern these mistakes and take advantage of them. Shamil, as shown throughout the narrative above, was extremely good at spotting and using the Russians' mistakes. He was usually successful even in turning Russian victories into hollow ones and deriving advantages from his own reverses.

This was not his only talent. Shamil was a born leader, commander, diplomat and politician. He repeatedly outmanoeuvred the Russians in battles, intrigues and negotiations. Contrary to Russian propaganda, he was far from extremism or blind fanaticism. He tended to use force sparingly and tried to come to an accommodation with both his internal rivals and the Russians. Furthermore, while engaged continually in these battles, intrigues and negotiations, he managed to unite a multiplicity of tribes and forge them into a unified state.

The fact that he erected his state on the fundaments built by his predecessors does not detract from his achievement. While continuing the policies, strategies and tactics of his predecessors, Shamil improved and adjusted them to the changing circumstances. Neither does the fact that many of Shamil's deeds might have originated with his aides and advisers diminish his stature. It is less important for a leader to possess an original mind than to be able to detect and choose those with such minds, and to listen to their advice. The greatest gift a leader may possess is the ability to appoint the right person to each position. Shamil's ability to do so was far from negligible, though his ability to keep such persons in key positions lagged quite markedly behind.

In the end, however, Russian mistakes, the mountaineers' steadfastness and Shamil's talents could not prevent the Russians from conquering Chechnia and Daghestan. After all, Russia was a mighty European power, and Nicholas I, like Napoleon, could boast of 'an annual income of 100,000 heads'.[3] Shamil and his predecessors were aware from the very beginning of this basic imbalance of power. This understanding that the mountaineers on their own stood no chance was behind the different strategies they pursued alternately and sometimes simultaneously. When it became clear that they were left to fight the Russians on their own,

> the struggle was virtually concluded. The constant and persevering efforts by the Russian Governors, supported by the whole strength of the Empire, made the extinction of national resistance merely a question of time.[4]

Even then, it should not be forgotten, it took the support of 'the whole strength of the Empire' finally to subdue Chechnia and Daghestan.

Shamil's submission signified the collapse of the mountaineers' resistance all over the Caucasus. By 1865 all the tribes were either pacified or expelled. Shamil's long rule and the state he established, admitted many Russian sources, had accustomed the mountaineers to a regular state machinery and would, therefore, make it easier for the Russians to rule. Shamil himself, when asked about the possibility of a renewal of the resistance in the Caucasus, replied: 'The Caucasus is now in Kaluga.'[5]

Whatever he meant by this, the mountaineers soon proved that they had been forced to submit, but were not resigned to Russian rule. Uprisings broke out whenever there seemed to be a chance to overthrow Russian rule – during the Polish revolt of 1863,[6] during the Russo-Ottoman War of 1877–78[7] and after the 1917 Revolution and during the civil war that followed it.[8] In the 40-year interval between the latter two conflicts, the discontent of the mountaineers, especially the Chechens and Ingush, found its vent in widespread banditry – always aimed at 'unbelievers' (Russians, Georgians, Ossets and other foreigners) – which rendered the Caucasus the most insecure area in the Russian Empire.[9] In the Second World War the population of places reached by the Germans co-operated with them willingly.[10] At the time of Shamil's surrender, however, this could not be anticipated; and the Russian pacification of the Caucasus seemed to be a success. Others, particularly the Austrians, even tried to learn and use its lessons when faced with Muslim resistance.[11]

Shamil was far away geographically and mentally from these developments. From Ghunīb he was taken across Russia to St. Petersburg, to meet Alexander II.[12] Afterwards he was allocated a house in Kaluga, about 150 kilometres south-west of Moscow. Shamil and his family lived there in a golden cage for several years.[13] In 1866 he was allowed to move to Kiev and two years later to perform the *ḥajj*. In 1871 the *imām* died and was buried in Medina. Of his three surviving sons, the eldest, Ghāzī Muḥammad, became an Ottoman general and led a force of Caucasian volunteers in the war of 1877–78. Shamil's grandson by his youngest son, Kāmil, Saʿīd (Sait Şamil), continued this tradition and participated in the fighting in Daghestan in the 1920s. The *imām*'s other son, Muḥammad Shāfiʿ, became a Russian general.

Shamil was soon almost completely forgotten in the West[14] and in the Muslim world. But in Chechnia and Daghestan, as well as among the large Caucasian (mainly Circassian) diaspora,[15] Shamil continued to be the hero of their struggle for freedom. This was the main reason for the prolonged controversies over his description in Soviet historiography.[16] These, in turn, served only to spread Shamil's fame. Within the USSR, he is now regarded as a hero by Muslims far away from the Caucasus. Outside, he became the hero of Muslims confronting,[17] or even actually fighting, the Soviets.[18]

Describing an imaginary conversation between Shamil and Bariatinskii, a Soviet Avār poet put in the *imām*'s mouth words to the effect that his (Shamil's) struggle would remain forever in the memory of the people and that his main achievement had been the forging of a unified Daghestan.[49] The poet is more than correct. Shamil's long rule and struggle played a crucial role in the shaping of the Chechnia and Daghestan of today, if not always in the direction desired by the *imām*. His deeds and misdeeds, for example, helped to consolidate the self-consciousness and thus assist the self-determination of both Daghestanis and Chechens as two separate entities. Yet to both, Shamil and the struggle he led are central components of their communal identity, and the *imām* and some of his *nā'ibs* are worshipped as heroes and 'saints'.[20]

Another result is the continuing influence of the *Ṣūfī ṭā'ifas* in Chechnia and in Daghestan. In both, the organisation of the *ṭā'ifas* is interwoven with the social, economic and political structure, and influences daily life.[21] So strong was the effect of Shamil's 25-year rule that even though the Chechens, in reaction to it, rejected the Naqshbandiyya, they still turned to another *ṭā'ifa* – the Qādiriyya, different branches of which are now dominant in the Chechen-Ingush ASSR.[22] These two results might prove in the long run to be Shamil's most important legacy.

Notes

Preface

1. Bernard Lewis, *The Middle East and the West* (New York, 1966), Ch. 5.
2. For which see, for example, Raphael Danziger, *Abd al-Qadir and the Algerians: Resistance to the French and Internal Consolidation* (New York, 1977).
3. For example, Qeyamuddin Ahmad, *The Wahabi Movement in India* (Calcutta, 1966). For a comparison between the two, see Jameela Maryam, *Two Great Mujahedin in the Recent Past and Their Struggle against Foreign Rule* (Lahore, 1976).
4. For example, C. S. Hourgronje, *The Achenese* (London, 1906); K. van der Maaten, *Snouck Hourgronje en de Atje Oolrog* (Leiden, 1948).
5. The Mahdiyya in the Sudan, the Wahhābī movement in the Arabian Peninsula and a series of movements against the Chinese penetration of eastern Turkestan can be included in this category even if they were not aimed directly against Western powers.
6. John F. Baddeley, *The Russian Conquest of the Caucasus* (London, 1908) (hereafter: Baddeley).
7. David Lodge, *Out of the Shelter* (London, 1985), p. 185.

Introduction: The Russian Conquest of Transcaucasia

1. This summary is based on the following sources: W. E. D. Allen, *A History of the Georgian People from the Beginning to the Russian Conquest in the Nineteenth Century* (London, 1932), pp. 131–218; Ali Arslan, 'Russya'nın Kırım ve Gürcistan'ı, İlhakindan Sonra Osmanli Develeti'nin Çerkes Kabileleri ile Münasebetleri (1784–1829)', in Mehmet Saray *et al.* (eds.), *Kafkas Araştirmalari*, Vol. I (İstanbul, 1988), pp. 46–51 (hereafter: *KA*); Muriel Atkin, *Russia and Iran, 1780–1828* (Minneapolis, 1980); Baddeley, pp. 1–72; M. Bagration, 'The Caucasus and Russia in the Historical Past', *The Caucasus*, No. 6–7 (11–12) (June-July 1952), pp. 14–20; N. N. Beliavskii and V. A. Potto, *Utverzhdenie Russkogo Vladychestva na Kavkaze* (Tiflis, 1901–4); S. A. Belokurov (ed.), *Snosheniia Rossii s Kavkazom. Materialy Izvlechennye iz Moskovskogo Glavnogo Arkhiva Ministerstva Inostrannykh Del*, Vol. I, *1578–1613 GG* (Moscow, 1889); N. T. Dubrovin, *Istoriia Voiny i Vladychestva Russkikh na Kavkaze* (St. Petersburg, 1871–88); Semen Ésadze, *Istoricheskaia Zapiska ob Upravlenii Kavkazom* (Tiflis, 1907); pp. 1–32; W. F. von Freygan, *Letters from the*

Caucasus and Georgia (London, 1823); V. N. Gamrekeli (ed.), *Dokumenty po Vzaimootnoshenii Gruzzii s Severnym Kavkazom v XVIII V.* (Tbilisi, 1968); A. A. Gordeev, *Istoriia Kazakov* (Paris, 1970); *Istoricheskii Ocherk Kavkazskikh Voin ot Ikh Nachala do Prisoedineniia Gruzii* (Tiflis, 1899); Sema Işıktan, '1787–1792 Osmanlı-Rus Harbı Sırasında ve Sonrasında Osmanlı Devlet'inin Dağıstan Hânları ile Münasebetleri', *KA*, Vol. I, pp. 34–45; 'Istoricheskii Ocherk Raspostraneniia Russkogo Vladychestva Pod Kavkazom', *Kavkazskii Kalendar*, 1851, Otdel III, pp. 43–51; P. Khutsunov, 'Snosheniia Rossii s Severnoi Chastiu Kavkaza', *Sbornik Gazety Kavkaz* (1846), pp. 203–19; N. S. Kiniapina, M. M. Bliev and V. V. Degoev, *Kavkaz i Sredniaia Aziia vo Vneshnei Politike Rossii. Vtoraia Polovina XVIII – 80-e Gody XIX V.* (Moscow, 1984); P. I. Kovalevskii, *Kavkaz*, Vol. II; *Istoriia Zavoevaniia Kavkaza* (St. Petersburg, 1915, 3rd ed.); D. M. Lang, *The Last Years of the Georgian Monarchy, 1658–1832* (New York, 1957) (hereafter: Lang, *Last Years*); idem, *A Modern History of Georgia* (London, 1962), pp. 34–41 (hereafter: Lang, *Modern History*); O. P. Markova, *Rossiia, Zakavkaz'e i Mezhdunarodnye Otnosheniia v XVIII Veke* (Moscow, 1966); R. G. Marshaev, *Russko-Dagestenskie Otnosheniia XVII-Pervoi Chetverti XVIII VV. (Dokumenty i Materialy)* (Makhachqala, 1958); W. Monteith, *Kars and Erzeroum. With the Campaigns of Prince Paskiewitch in 1828 and 1829 and an Account of the Conquests of Russia beyond the Caucasus from the Time of Peter the Great to the Treaty of Turcuman Chie and Adrianople* (London, 1856), pp. 1–28; V. A. Potto, *Kavkazskaia Voina* (St Petersburg, 1887–97); N. A. Smirnov, *Politika Rossiina Kavkaze v XVI-XIX Vekakh* (Moscow, 1958); Muzaffer Ürekli, 'Rus Yayilması Karşısında Kırım Hânlığı ve Kafkasya', *KA*, Vol. I, pp. 12–24; Ibrahim Yüksel, 'Çarlık Rusyası'nın Azerbaycan'ı İstilâsi ve Osmanlı Devleti'nin Tutumu', ibid, pp. 25–33; L. B. Zasedateleva, *Terskie Kazaki (Seredina XVI-Nachalo XX V.). Istoriko-Ētnograficheskie Ocherki* (Moscow, 1974).

2. Baddeley, p. 5.
3. The Grebentsy contributed 800 men to this expedition, of which only two survived. For the expedition to Khiva, see M. S. Anderson, *Peter the Great* (London, 1978), p. 155; B. H. Sumner, *Peter the Great and the Emergence of Russia* (London, 1950), pp. 174–5; Michael Rywkin, *Russia in Central Asia* (New York, 1963), pp. 16–17.
4. For these events, see L. Lockhart, *The Fall of the Safavi Dynasty and the Afghan Occupation of Persia* (Cambridge, 1958).
5. In addition to the above sources, see Anderson, op. cit., p. 155; Sumner, op. cit., pp. 175–9, 195.
6. Baddeley, p. 25. Also, see idem, *The Rugged Flanks of the Caucasus* (London, 1940), Vol. I, p. 82 (hereafter: Baddeley, *Rugged Flanks*).
7. Baddeley, p. 10, quoting, in fact, A. P. Bergé in *Akty Sobrannye Kavkazskoi Arkheograficheskoi Kommissiei* (hereafter: *AKAK*), Vol. I, p. X.
8. In addition to the above sources (note 1), see D. M. Lang, 'Count Todtleben's Expedition to Georgia 1769–1771, according to a French Eyewitness', *Bulletin of the School of Oriental and African Studies*, Vol. XIII, Part 4 (1951), pp. 878–901.
9. Baddeley, p. 19. For the text of the peace treaty of Küçük Kaynarca, see

J. C. Hurewitz (ed.), *The Middle East and North Africa in World Politics: A Documentary Record*, Vol. I, *European Expansion, 1533–1914* (New Haven, 1975, 2nd ed.), pp. 92–101, document No. 32 (hereafter: Hurewitz).

10. Alan W. Fisher, *The Russian Annexation of the Crimea* (Cambridge, 1970). Also see N. T. Dubrovin, *Prisoedinenie Kryma k Rossii*, 4 Vols (St. Petersburg, 1885–89).
11. Baddeley, pp. 38–9.
12. Suvorov summoned the Nogay to Eisk, on the shores of the Sea of Azov, and read to them Shāghīn Girey's manifesto, in which he abdicated in favour of Catherine. The Nogay, for centuries subjects of the Crimean *khāns*, took the oath of allegiance to the empress. Later, however, when it became known that the Russians planned to resettle them between the Volga and the Ural (an area depopulated by the Pugachev rebellion and the migration of the Qalmuqs to Central Asia and the borders of China in 1771), the Nogay tried to resist, but found the Russian forces ready and waiting for such a move. The nomads, driven into marshy ground and having no possibility of escape, preferred to kill their wives and children and die rather than surrender – a scene to be repeated again and again during the war in the Caucasus. Of the survivors, 'an irreconcilable minority settled amongst the Circassians; the remainder made their submission and were transferred to the Crimea' (Baddeley, p. 45).
13. Baddeley, p. 45.
14. For the negotiations leading to this treaty and its stipulations, see Lang, *Last Years*, pp. 182–5, and plate opposite p. 209; Allen, op. cit., pp. 210–11.
15. A cousin of Catherine's lover.
16. Baddeley, p. 20.
17. Ibid., p. 21 and cf. Lang, *Last Years*, pp. 205–9.
18. John Malcolm, *History of Persia*, Vol. II (London, 1829), p. 191, as quoted by Lang, *Last Years*, p. 217. Also see Riḍā Qūlī Khān Hidāyāt, *Ta'rīkh-i rawḍat al-Ṣafā-yi Nāṣiri*, Vol. IX (Tehrān, 1961–62), pp. 273–4.
19. In 1775 Medem captured Derbend without authorisation, and was ordered by Catherine to retreat.
20. Mark Osipovich Kosven and Khadzhi-Murat Omarovich Khashaev (eds.), *Istoriia, Geografiia i Ētnografiia Dagestana XVII-XIX VV. Arkivnye Materialy* (Moscow, 1958), pp. 200–8; Petr Grigor'evich Butkov, 'Proekt Otcheta o Persidskoi Ekspeditsii v Vide Pisem' (excerpts) (1796); Baddeley, p. 57.
21. Succeeded Erekle II in 1798.
22. *AKAK*, Vol. I, pp. 105–6, document No. 21, Knorring to the Emperor, 22 June [4 July] 1800.
23. Ibid, pp. 106–7, document No. 22, Paul to Knorring, 10 [22] July 1800.
24. Ibid, pp. 168–9, document No. 109, Lazarev to Knorring, 8 [20] November 1800, No. 67.
25. *Polnoe Sobranie Zakanov Rossiiskoi Imperii s 1649 G*, Vol. XXVI, No. 19721 (St. Petersburg, 1830–84).
26. Ibid, Vol. XXVI, No. 20007.
27. For the negotiations with Paul and the (internal) Russian deliberations

under Alexander I, see Lang, *Last Years*, pp. 235–51. Also see Z. D. Avalov, *Prisoedinenie Gruzii k Rossii* (St. Petersburg, 1906, 2nd ed.); A. P. Bergé, 'Prisoedinenie Gruzii k Rossii', *Russkaia Starina* (1880), No. 5, pp. 1–34, No. 6, pp. 159–77; N. T. Dubrovin, *Georgii XII Poslednii Tsar Gruzii* (St. Petersburg, 1867).

28. Ēsadze, op. cit., p. 29; Lang, *Last Years*, pp. 244–54; Lang, *Modern History*, pp. 43–45; A. Züssermann, 'Otryvki iz Moikh Vospominanii', *Russkii Vestnik* (1876), No. 3, pp. 67, 68; No. 4, pp. 428–9, No. 12, p. 502 (1878), No. 2, p. 568 (hereafter: Züssermann, 'Otryvki' and No. of *RV*).
29. For this plot, see Stephen Jones, 'Russian Imperial Administration and the Georgian Nobility: The Georgian Conspiracy of 1832', *Slavonic and East European Review*, Vol. LXV, No. 1 (January 1987), pp. 53–76. See also N. B. Makharadze, *Vosstanie v Imeretii 1819–22 GG.* (Tbilisi, 1942).
30. France, Ministère des Relations Extérieures, Archives Diplomatiques, Correspondance Politique des Consuls (hereafter: MRE, CPC) Russie, Tiflis, Vol. I, ff. 53–55. Extrait d'une Lettre de M. le Consul de France à Tiflis, 22 September 1840.
31. For which, see G. Khachapuridze, *Guriis Ajankheba 1841 Tsels* (Tpilisi, 1931).
32. Ēsadze, op. cit., p. 29.
33. Ibid., loc. cit. Emphasis added.
34. Ibid., loc. cit.
35. Baddeley, pp. 61–2.
36. Ibid., p. 64.
37. See, for example, E. Pakravan, *Abbas Mirza Prince Reformateur*, Vol. I (Tehrān, 1958), p. 80, as quoted by Hamid Algar, *Religion and State in Iran, 1785–1906: The Role of the Ulama in the Qajar Period* (Berkeley, 1969), p. 75, note 12.
38. For the possible involvement of Fatḥ ʿAlī Shāh in Tsitsianov's murder, see Algar, op. cit., p. 65.
39. Ēsadze, op. cit., p. 32. See also Baddeley, pp. 71–2; N. T. Dubrovin, *Zakavkaz'e ot 1803 do 1806 Goda* (St. Petersburg, 1866); Lang, *Last Years*, p. 260; Lang, *Modern History*, p. 51; Monteith, op. cit., pp. 45–6.
40. Baddeley, p. 68.
41. Lang, *Modern History*, p. 52. For the events of 1805–13, see Algar, op. cit., pp. 79–81; Baddeley, pp. 73–90; Dubrovin, op. cit., Vol. IV, pp. 432–528; Vol. V, pp. 1–486, Vol. VI, pp. 1–166; Lang, *Last Years*, pp. 259–70; Monteith, op. cit., pp. 46–106; Potto, op. cit., Vol. I, pp. 129–309, Vol. II, pp. 1–425; O. P. Markova, *Vosstanie v Kakhetii 1812 G.* (Moscow, 1951); V. Sollohub [Sollogub], *Biografiia Generala Kotliarevskogo* (St. Petersburg, 1856, 2nd ed.).
42. For the text of the treaty, see Hurewitz, pp. 193–7, document No. 54.
43. For the text of the treaty, see ibid, pp. 197–9, document No. 55.
44. For the submission of different local rulers in Daghestan and for the events in this period, see G. E. Grümberg [Griumberg] and S. K. Bushuev (eds.), *Materialy po Istorii Dagestana i Chechni*, Vol. III, Part I, *1801–1839*, pp. 57–9. 93–101, 104–16, 148–9, document Nos. 4, 25, 26, 28, 29, 30, 32, 34, 35, 36, 37, 38, 66, Lashkarev to Engel, 25 April [7 May] 1801, Bulgakov to Gudovich, 30 November [12 December] 1806,

No. 494, 'List of Daghestani Rulers who Accepted Russian Suzerainty (not before December 1801)', Repin to Tormasov, 19 [31] March, No. 353, Maʿṣūm Bek Shāmkhāl to Zhmenskii, Surkhāy Khān to Zhmenskii, (both) 19 [31] March 1811, Khatuntsov to Paulucci 9 [21] January, 5 [17] March 1812, Nos. 13, 136, 144, Khatuntsov to Rtishchev, 29 May [10 June], 23, 27 July [4, 8], 26 August [7 September] 1812, Nos. 337, 433, 208, 230, Repin to Tormasov, 28 January [9 February] 1811, No. 128 respectively (hereafter: *Materialy*).

45. For the wars of 1826–29, see Algar, op. cit., pp. 82–93; Baddeley, pp. 154–222; Dubrovin, op. cit., Vol. VI, pp. 512–714; Monteith, op. cit., pp. 120–330; Potto, op. cit., Vols. IV–VIII, *passim*.
46. For the text of the treaty, see Hurewitz, pp. 231–7, document No. 65.
47. For the text of the treaty, see Monteith, op. cit., pp. 305–16, Appendix. And cf. M. S. Anderson, *The Great Powers and the Near East* (London, 1970), p. 34.
48. Anapa had been captured twice before and Akhalk'alak'i once. But they had been returned to the Ottomans in the peace treaties of Jassy (1791) and Bucharest (1812).

Chapter 1: The Theatre

1. Georges Jorré, *The Soviet Union: The Land and Its People* (London, 1961, 2nd ed.), p. 338.
2. Some geographers regard the Manych depression as the dividing line, e.g. ibid, p. 326; Theodore Shabad, *Geography of the USSR: A Regional Survey* (New York, 1951), p. 210.
3. In addition to the above-quoted books, the following textbooks and studies were used for the geographical description: Lev Semonovich Berg, *Natural Regions of the USSR* (New York, 1950); Britain, the Foreign Office, the Historical Section, *Caucasia: A Handbook* (London, 1920); Şerafeddin Erel, *Dağıstan ve Dağıstanlılar* (İstanbul, 1961); I. Erhorn, *Kaukasien* (Berlin, 1942); Nikolai Andreevich Gvozdetskii, *Fizicheskaia Geografiia Kavkaza. Kurs Lektsii* (Moscow, 1954); Idem, *Kavkaz. Ocherk Prirody* (Moscow, 1963); E. S. Levin, *Perevaly Tsentral'nogo Kavkaza* (Moscow, 1938); M. Litvinov, 'Kavkaz. Voenno-Geograficheskii Ocherk', *Voennyi Sbornik* (1884), No. 2, pp. 304–20, No. 3, pp. 149–64, No. 4, pp. 328–46; E. P. Maslov, A. I. Gozulov and S. N. Riazantsev (eds.), *Severnyi Kavkaz* (Moscow, 1957); P. P. Nadezhdin, *Kavkazskii Krai, Priroda i Luidi* (Tula, 1895); Walerian Tewzadze, *Kaukaz. Skic Geograficzno-Opisowy* (Warsaw, 1933); A. E. Viktorov, P. L. Himmelreich [Gimmel'reikh], P. L. L'vov, I. N. Mikulich and M. M. El'darov, *Dagestanskaia ASSR. Fiziko-Geograficheskii i Ekonomiko-Geograficheskii Obzor* (Makhachqala, 1958). For travellers' accounts, guides and reference books used here as well, see list of sources.
4. 'Orographically the front range is not a distinct chain. In general it is composed of the northern spurs of the main range' – Berg, op. cit., p. 203.
5. Ibid, p. 204.
6. Jorré, op. cit., p. 327.
7. I. S. Shchukin, as quoted by Gvozdetskii, op. cit., p. 127.

8. Berg, op. cit., p. 203.
9. In addition to the above sources, see A. P. Bergé, *Chechnia i Chechentsy* (Tiflis, 1859) (hereafter: Bergé, *Chechnia*).
10. Baddeley, *Rugged Flanks*, Vol. I, p. 55.
11. *Dağ* is 'mountain' in Turkish.
12. Gvozdetskii, op. cit., p. 197.
13. Ibid., p. 196; Berg, op. cit., p. 230. In addition to the above-listed sources, see A. P. Bergé, 'Materialy dlia Opisaniia Nagornogo Dagestana', *Kavkazskii Kalendar*, 1859, Otdelenie III, pp. 249–88 (hereafter: Bergé, 'Materialy'); A. A. Neverovskii, 'Kratkii Vzgliad na Severnyi i Srednii Dagestan v Topograficheskom i Statistitechskom Otnosheniiakh', *Voennyi Zhurnal* (1847), No. 5, pp. 1–64.
14. Gvozdetskii, op. cit., p. 197.
15. The average elevation of the plateaus is 1,900 metres; that of the rivers, 700 metres.
16. I. S. Shchukin, as quoted by Gvozdestskii, op. cit., p. 197.
17. Marlinksii, as quoted by Baddeley, *Rugged Flanks*, Vol. II, p. 43.
18. Ibid, p. 19.
19. *Derbend* in Persian means 'narrow pass', 'canyon', or 'bolt for a door'.
20. During the 1830s the Russians, in fact, listed them as part of Daghestan.
21. A. Iurov, '1844-i God na Kavkaze', *Kavkazskii Sbornik*, Vol. VII, p. 169; Idem, '1840, 1841 i 1842-i Gody na Kavkaze', ibid, Vol. X, pp. 305–6; K., 'Levyi Flang Kavkazskoi Linii v 1848 Godu', ibid, Vol. IX, p. 379; N. A. Volkonskii, 'Okonchatel'noe Pokorenie Kavkaza (1859-i God)', ibid, Vol. IV, pp. 51–2, 79, 284–5.
22. A. Anoev, 'Vospominaniia o Boevoi Sluzhbe na Kavkaze', *Voennyi Sbornik* 1877, No. 6, p. 403. The lightest gun, the use of which was, therefore, the most widespread, was the ¼-*pud* long-barrelled mountain gun (1 *pud* = 16.380 kg.), which weighed 106.47 kg. Each bomb weighed about 1.5 kg., each grapeshot grenade about 4.5 kg., and the explosive charge needed to shoot them approximately 0.3 kg. (See also note 2 to Chapter 3). Four such guns with their ammunition and other baggage easily exceeded a (metric) ton. The daily food ration [*poek*] of a soldier on the march consisted of 716 g. of biscuits, 94 g. of meat and 2.2 g. of salt. Since according to regulations any force on the march had to carry enough food to last for six days (the soldiers themselves had to carry four-day rations), three battalions, with an average of 800 soldiers in each, had to carry at least 10,310.4 kg. of biscuits, 1353.6 kg. of meat and 31.68 kg. of salt, or a total of c. 11.7 tons of food. To these must be added other kinds of baggage and equipment (ammunition in huge quantities – see the following note – office equipment, kitchens, barrels of alcohol) belonging to the units, the luggage of the officers, each of whom had a pack-horse, the merchandise of the sutler [*markitant*], etc. There was, thus, an enormous train of carts (*ʿarabas*) and/or pack-horses following and bogging down each unit on the march because it had to be protected and helped over obstacles. In some areas of Inner Daghestan logistics were further complicated by the need to bring along firewood and fodder for the horses.
23. One tactic the Chechens learned to employ against the Russians was 'to occupy some of the gigantic beech-trees. Room was found in each for from thirty to forty men, who poured deadly fire on the approaching

Russians. The volleys of whole battalions failed to dislodge the garrisons from these improvised towers of defence' – Baddeley, p. 358, note 1. The ineffectiveness of these volleys is not at all surprising, when one takes into account that the effective range of Russian muskets probably did not exceed 30–50 metres when shooting horizontally, and here they were used to shoot upwards, and, more important, the Russian army, more than its other European counterparts, preferred the bayonet to the almost complete exclusion of shooting. The result was that soldiers were not instructed in aiming and shooting properly, and usually shot in the air without taking aim at all. Thus, such volleys may have been very impressive acoustically, but as far as results go they were a huge waste of ammunition. The Russian response to this was to rely on artillery (grapeshot) for anti-personnel fire, and to carry huge amounts of ammunition, which only exacerbated their enormous logistical problems.

24. Blanch, p. 100. And cf. Anoev, op. cit., p. 395; Constantine Benckendorff, *Souvenirs Intimes d'une Campagne au Caucase pendant l'Été de 1845* (Paris, 1858), pp. 63–5.

Chapter 2: The People

1. The following sources are among those used in this section: Amidei B. Barbiellini, *Elementi per uno Studio Linguistico e Politico del Caucaso* (Naples, 1938); Adolphe P. Bergé, *Chechnia*; idem, 'Ētnograficheskoe Obozrenie Kavkaza', in V. V. Grigoriev (ed.), *Trudy Tret'ego S"ezda Orientalistov v S.-Peterburge 1876*, Vol. I. (St. Petersburg, 1879–80), pp. 291–326; Idem, 'Materialy'; Ernest Chantre, *Recherches Anthropologiques dans le Caucase* (Paris, 1885–87); G. F. Chursin, *Ocherki po Ētnografii Kavkaza* (Tiflis, 1913); R. von Erckert, *Der Kaukasus und Seine Völker* (Leipzig, 1887); Erel, op. cit.; A. P. Ippolitov, 'Ētnograficheskie Ocherki Argunskogo Okruga', *Sbornik Svedenii o Kavkazskikh Gortsakh*, Vol. I, 52 p.; Mark Osipovich Kosven et. al., *Narody Kavkaza* (Moscow, 1960); Idem and Kh. M. Khashaev (eds.), *Narody Dagestana. Sbornik Stat'ei* (Moscow, 1955); Idem and idem (eds.), *Istoriia, Geografiia i Ētnografiia Dagestana XVIII–XIX VV. Arkhivnye Materialy* (Moscow, 1958); Evgenii P. Kovalevskii, 'Ocherki Ētnografii Kavkaza', *Vestnik Evropy*, 1867, No. 3, pp. 75–140, No. 4, pp. 1–29; Konstantin Minovich Kurdov, 'K Antrpologii Lezgin: Kiurintsy', *Russkii Antropologicheskii Zhurnal* Vol. VII–VIII, pp. 165–75; Idem, 'K Antropologii Lezgin: Tabasarantsy', ibid, Vol. XXI–XXII, pp. 129–34; Idem, 'Taty Dagestana', ibid, Vol. XXVII–XXVIII, pp. 56–66; Idem, 'Taty Shemakhinskogo U. Bakinskoi G.', ibid, Vol. XXXIII–XXXIV, pp. 162–72; Umalat Laudaev, 'Chechenskoe Plemia', *Sbornik Svedenii o Kavkazskikh Gortsakh*, Vol. VI, 62 p.; I. P. Linevich, 'Karta Gorskikh Narodov Podvlastnykh Shamiliu (s Prilozheniem)', ibid, Vol. VI, 4 + II p.; N. Ia. Marr, *Plemennyi Sostav Naseleniia Kavkaza. Klassifikatsiia Narodov Kavkaza (Rabochii Prospekt)* (Petrograd, 1920); Evgenii Maksimov, 'Chechentsy. Istoriko-Geograficheskii i Statistiko-Ēkonomicheskii Ocherk', *Terskii Sbornik*, Vol. III, No. 2 (1893), Otdel I, pp. 3–100; Neverovskii, op. cit.; Bruno Plaetschke, *Die Tschetschen. Forschungen zur Völkerkunde der Nordöstlichen Kauka-*

zus auf Grund von Reisen in den Jahren 1918–20 und 1927–8 (Hamburg, 1929); V. P. Pozhidaev, *Gortsy Severnogo Kavkaza. Ingushi, Chechentsy, Khevsury, Osetiny i Kabardintsy. Kratkii Istoriko-Ētnograficheskii Ocherk* (Moscow and Leningrad, 1926); N. Semenov, *Tuzemtsy Severo-Vostochnogo Kavkaza. Rasskazy, Ocherki, Issledovaniia, Zametki o Chechentsakh, Kumykakh i Nogaitsakh i Poezii Etikh Narodov* (St. Petersburg, 1895); Galina Aleksandrovna Sergeeva, *Archintsy* (Moscow, 1965); Starozhil (pseud.), *Kavkaz. Spravochnaia Kniga*, Vol. III, *Ētnograficheskii i Istoricheskii Ocherki* (Tiflis, 1888); P. F. Sviderskii, 'K Antropologii Archintsev, *Russkii Antropologicheskii Zhurnal*, Vol. XXXV–XXXVI, pp. 32–44; S. P. Tolstov *et al.* (eds.), *Ocherki Obshchei Ētnografii. Aziatskaia Chast' SSSR* (Moscow, 1940); Natal'ia Grigorievna Volkova, *Ētnicheskii Sostav Naseleniia Severnogo Kavkaza v XVIII-Nachale XX Veka* (Moscow, 1974); Platon Zubov, *Kartina Kavkazskogo Kraia Prinadlezhashchego Rossii i Sopredel'nykh Onomu Zemel' v Istoricheskom, Statisticheskom, Ētnograficheskom, Finansovom i Torgovom Ostnosheniiakh* (St. Petersburg, 1834–35).

2. In pre-twentieth-century sources, all the inhabitants of Southern – and in many cases all of – Daghestan were indiscriminately called Lesghians. In Persian sources in particular Southern Daghestan was called Lesghistān.
3. Alexandre Benningsen and Enders S. Wimbush, *Muslims of the Soviet Empire: A Guide* (London, 1985), p. 189.
4. The most important work on the customs of the mountaineers is Maksim Kovalevskii, *Zakon i Obychai na Kavkaze* (Moscow, 1890). In addition to the above-listed sources, see 'Adaty Darginskikh Obshchestv', *Sbornik Svedenii o Kavkazskikh Gortsakh*, Vol. VII, 128 p.; 'Adaty Iuzhno-Dagetanskikh Obsheshestv', ibid., Vol. VIII, 72 p.; 'Adaty Kumykov', *Dagestanskii Sbornik*, Vol. III, pp. 73–101; Chakh Akhriev, 'Ingushi (Ikh Predaniia, Verovaniia i Poveriia)', *Sbornik Svedenii o Kavkazskikh Gortsakh*, Vol. VIII, 40 p.; N. N. Khurzin, 'Zametki o Iuridicheskom Byte Chechentsev i Ingushei', *Sbornik Materialov po Ētnografii Izdavaemyi pri Dashkovskom Ētnograficheskom Muzee*, Vol. III, pp. 115–42; A. V. Komarov, 'Adaty i Sudoproizvodstvo po Nim. (Materialy dlia Statistiki Dagestanskoi Oblasti)', *Sbornik Svedenii o Kavkazskikh Gortsakh*, Vol. I, 88 p.; A. I. Lilov, 'Ocherki iz Byta Gorskikh Musul'man', *Sbornik Materialov dlia Opisaniia Mestnostei i Plemen Kavkaza*, Vol. V, Otdel II, pp. 1–36; Idem, 'Ocherki Byta Kavkazskikh Gortsev', ibid, Vol. XIV, Otdel I, pp. 1–57; G. Moliavkin, 'Ocherki Obshchinnogo Zemlevladeniia v Chechne', *Terskie Vedomosti*, 25, 27 November [7, 9], 4 [16] December 1892, 13 [25], 15 [27] January 1893 (Nos. 141, 142, 145, 6, 7), pp. 3, 4, 4, 2–3, 3 respectively; P. Przewlacki [Przhevlatskii], 'Dagestan, Ego Nravy i Obychai', *Vestnik Evropy* (1867), No. 3, pp. 141–92; S. Svechin, 'Ocherk Narodonaseleniia, Nravov i Obychaev Dagestantsev', *Zapiski Kavkazskogo Otdela Imperatorskogo Geograficheskogo Obschestva*, Kn. II, pp. 54–65.
5. Lewis J. Luzbetac, *Marriage and the Family in Caucasia: A Contribution to the Study of North Caucasian Ethnology and Customary Law* (Vienna-Mödling, 1951).
6. In addition to the sources already mentioned, some Soviet studies are very useful in spite of the narrow framework within which they had to be

written. See, for example, P. A. Briukhanov, 'Gosudarstvennoe Ustroistvo i Administrativnoe Upravlenie Vol'nykh Obshchestv Dagestana v Pervoi Chetverti XIX V.', *Sbornik Trudov Piatigorskogo Gosudartsvennogo Pedagogicheskogo Instituta*, Vol. I.; Anatolii Vsevolodovich Fadeev, 'Vopros o Sotsial'nom Stroe Kavkazskikh Gortsev XVII–XIX VV. v Novykh Rabotakh Sovetskikh Istorikov', *Voprosy Istorii* (1958), No. 5, pp. 130–7; A. I. Ivanov, 'Sotsial'no-Ekonomicheskoe i Politicheskoe Polozhenie Dagestana do Zavoevaniia Tsarkoi Rossiei', *Istoricheskii Zhurnal* (1940), No. 2, pp. 62–72; Kh. M. Khashaev, *Kodeks Umma-Khana Avarskogo (Spravedlivogo)* (Moscow, 1948); Rasul M. Magomedov, *Obshchestvenno-Ekonomicheskii i Politicheski Stroi Dagestanna v XVIII-Nachalo XIX Vekov* (Makhachqala, 1957); Il'ia Pavlovich Petrushevskii, *Dzharo-Belakanskie Vol'nye Obshchestva v Pervoi Tret'i XIX Stoletiia. Vnutrennii Stroi i Bor'ba s Rossiiskim Kolonial'nym Nastupleniem* (Tiflis, 1934); Idem, 'Sotsial'naia Struktura Dzharo-Belokanskikh Vol'nykh Obshchestv Nakanune Rossiisskogo Zavoevaniia', *Istoricheskii Sbornik*, No. 1, pp. 191–228; A. Tamai, 'Materialy k Voprosu o Feodalizme v Istorii Dagestana', *Revoliutsionnyi Vostok* (1935), No. 5. See also, A. K., 'Kazikumukhskie i Kiurinskie Khany', *Sbornik Svedednii o Kavkazskikh Gortsakh*, Vol. II, 4 p.; I. P. Linevich, 'Byvshee Elisuiskoe Sultanstvo', ibid, Vol. VII, 54 + p.; 'Mekhtulinskie Khany', ibid, Vol. II, 17 p.; 'Shamkhaly Tarkovskie (Istoricheskaia Zapiska, Sostavlennaia Vremennoi Kommissiei, Nariazhennoi dlia Opredeleniia Lichnykh i Pozemel'nykh Prav Tuzemtsev Temir-Khan-Shuringskogo Okruga)', ibid, Vol. I. pp. 54–89. For lists and descriptions of the different communities, see Bergé, *Chechnia*; Idem, 'Materialy'; K., 'Obzor Sobytii na Kavkaze v 1846 G.', *Kavkazskii Sbornik*, Vol. XII, pp. 191–2; N. A. Volkonskii, 'Trekhletie na Lezginskoi Kordonnoi Linii (1847–1849)', ibid, Vol. IX, Appendix I, p. 1 (separate pagination).

7. These *qāḍīs* had nothing in common with *sharʿī* judges but the title.
8. For Nādir Shāh's invasion of Daghestan and defeat in Aqūsha, see Laurence Lockhart, *Nadir Shah: A Critical Study based Mainly upon Contemporary Sources* (London, 1938), pp. 215–50; Baddeley, *Rugged Flanks*, Vol. II, pp. 39–42, 247–51.
9. Kurāh was originally part of Ghāzī-Ghumuq. It was created as a separate Khanate by the Russians to repay Aslān Khān for his services and loyalty. And see *Materialy*, Vol. III, Pt. I, pp. 101–4, document No. 31, Khatuntsov to Paulucci 9[21] January 1812; *AKAK*, Vol. V, pp. 150, 156–9, 631, document Nos. 218, 224, 772, Paulucci to Mogilevskii, 4 [16] January, No. 3, Paulucci to Minister of War, 9 [28] February, No. 38, Patent of Investiture to Aslān Bek the Ruler of Kurāh, 10 [22] June 1812, Vol. VI, Pt. II, pp. 35–6, document No. 76, Ermolov to Gur'ev, 5 [17] March 1818, No. 40.
10. *Ṭawh* is 'mountain' in Chechen.
11. The degree of Islamisation varied from area to area, the Chechens being the most recently converted and therefore the least Islamicised. All over Daghestan and Chechnia, however, the customary law (*ʿādat*) was in force, and in some Khanates it was even codified in writing.
12. Thus, a Daghestani scholar could find enough material to write about these connections – Ch. M. Hashimov [Gashimov], 'Iz Istorii Dagestano

– Severokavkazskikh Kul'turnykh Sviazei', *Voprosy Istorii i Etnografii Dagestana*, Vol. I (1970), pp. 67–78; Idem, 'O Sovmestnykh Poseleniiakh Gortsev Dagestana i Severnogo Kavkaza (XVI–XVIII VV.)', ibid, pp. 79–84. And cf. Volkova, op. cit., pp. 204–10.

13. Even the Circassians who, unlike the Chechens, lived in a stratified society, were described by an Englishman who had lived among them for a year as 'soon tir[ing] of authority in the hands of the same individual'. And he added: 'So jealous, indeed, is this sovereign people of their power, that no individual will trust his share of it out of his own hands or even formally delegate it to any particular or any given number of representatives for a moment' – J. A. Longworth, *A year among the Circassians* (London, 1840), Vol. II, p. 307, Vol. I, p. 103 respectively. And cf. Baddeley, *Rugged Flanks*, Vol. I, p. 218.
14. See, e.g., P., 'O Posledstviiakh Ubiistv i Poranenii Mezhdu Gortsami Vostochnogo Kavkaza', *Sbornik Svedenii o Kavkazskikh Gortsakh*, Vol. VIII, 14 p.; A. Runowski, 'Kanly v Nemirnom Krae', *Voennyi Sbornik* (1860), No. 7, Otdel Neoffitsial'nyi, pp. 199–216; T., 'Razboi i Samorasprava na Kavkaze', *Vestnik Evropy* (1885), No. 12, pp. 617–46.
15. For admiring descriptions of the mountaineers' qualities as warriors see, for example, Vel'iaminov's memorandum of 1828 printed in N. Sh., 'General Vel'iaminov i Ego Znachenie dlia Istorii Kavkazskoi Voiny', *Kavkazskii Sbornik*, Vol. VII, pp. 78–144 (hereafter: 'Vel'iaminov'), extensively translated in Baddeley, pp. 112–120; *AKAK*, Vol. XII, pp. 1275–1394, Bariatinskii's Report for the years 1857–59, especially p. 1286; A. Anoev, 'Vospominaniia o Boevoi Sluzhbe na Kavkaze', *Voennyi Sbornik* (1877), No. 5, pp. 197, 201; V. A. Heimann, '1845 God', *Kavkazskii Sbornik*, Vol. II, pp. 366–7; K., 'Zimniaia Ēkspeditsiia 1852 G. v Chechne (Vospominaniia Ochevidtsa)', ibid, Vol. XIII, p. 459; N. A. Volkonskii, 'Lezginskaia Ēkspeditsiia (v Didoiskoe Obshchestvo) v 1857 Godu', ibid, Vol. I, p. 404; Idem, 'Trekhletie v Dagestane. 1849-i God: Osada Ukrepleniia Chokh', ibid, Vol. VIII, p. 285.
16. For comparative colonial warfare and the Russian army at that period, see Victor G. Kiernan, *European Empires from Conquest to Collapse, 1815–1960* (London, 1982) and John Shelton Curtiss, *The Russian Army under Nicholas I, 1825–1855* (Durham, N.C., 1965) respectively. Both leave much to be desired. Much better works are Dietrich Beyrau, *Militär und Gesellschaft in Vorrevolutionäre Russland* (Köln, 1984); John L. H. Keep, *Soldiers of the Tsar: Army and Society in Russia, 1462–1874* (Oxford, 1985). All the following data on the Russian army, unless otherwise stated, are taken from these two books and from *Voennaia Enstikplolediia*. As explained above (note 23 to Chapter 1), the Russians relied solely on the bayonet. For the artillery used by them, see below, note 2 to Chapter 3.

Chapter 3: The Russians

1. See above, note 22 to Chapter 1.
2. The following are the different artillery pieces in use then by the Russian army:

Type of Artillery	Official Name of Gun	Weight in kg.	Weight of bomb in kg.	Weight of explosive charge in kg.	Furthest distance in km.
Field Artillery	12-*funt* battery gun	802.62	6.04	1.638	1.9197
	12-*funt* lightened gun	532.35	4.5045	1.126	1.9798
	6-*funt* light gun	352.17	2.8605	0.819	1.0665
	½-*pud* long-barrelled gun	806.75	8.9066	1.638	1.2795
	¼-*pud* long-barrelled gun	368.55	4.5045	0.819	1.0665
	¼-*pud* long-barrelled mountain gun	106.47	4.5045* 1.5015†	0.3071	0.6399
Siege Artillery	24-*funt* gun	2784.6	12.080	3.276	2.7729
	18-*funt* gun	2031.12	8.8042	2.457	2.7729
	1-*pud* long-barrelled gun	2278.21	18.4275	2.8665	2.3463
	5-*pud* mortar	1082.08	94.185	2.8665	2.069
	2-*pud* mortar	589.68	36.4455	2.0475	2.4316
	½-*pud* mortar	94.185	8.7359	2.0475	0.9598

* grapeshot; † bomb

The gun used more than others was, for obvious reasons, the ¼-*pud* long-barrelled mountain gun. On most occasions it was used to fire grapeshot. On such instances it is doubtful whether its effective range was more than 150–200 metres. In fact, on many occasions the Russians used it in very close range – 50 metres and less – so close that the mountaineers were able to hit the artillerists with their musket-fire. It should be remembered that the mountaineers used muskets, even Russian ones, from far greater distances, and very effectively. They even used to load captured Russian muskets with more gunpowder than the regulations allowed for, doubling, in effect, their range. The range of the mountaineers' small-arms fire was, thus, about 60–80 metres, and almost none of their bullets missed its target. And see note 33 to Chapter 21.
3. The best description of the Caucasian Corps is the (unpublished) report by Lt. Hiller von Gaertringen, Potsdam, August 1844, now in the possession of Dr Fr. von Gaertringen in Gärtringen, Germany (herafter: Gaertringen archive). Lt. Hiller von Gaertringen was one of three Prussian officers attached to the Caucasian Corps from 1842 to 1844.
4. Benckendorff, op. cit., p. 49. See also N. A. Volkonskii, 'Lezginskaia Ēkspeditsiia (v Didoiskoe Obshchestvo) v 1857 Godu', *Kavkazskii Sbornik*, Vol. I, pp. 374–80.
5. In fact these crafts were essential to the soldiers. Each soldier was issued with an overcoat [*shinel'*] once in three years, a jacket once in four years, a pair of woollen trousers once in two years, and a pair of boots, a pair of linen trousers and enough linen to make two shirts annually. But the need for tailors (and shoemakers) was great. The quality of the fabric and

leather of the uniforms was quite bad and they wore out fairly quickly even in peacetime. The uniforms of soldiers on constant campaigns and marches needed, of course, frequent repairs and patching.

6. Again, as with clothing, these were essential. 'Food and drink were important to the Russian soldier psychologically as well as physically: preparing, cooking and consuming food was one of his few leisure activities, and the problem of filling his stomach usually loomed large' – Keep, op. cit, p. 183. With a food ration of 807 g. of flour (716 g. of biscuits on a march), 161 ml. of grist, 94 g. of meat and 2.2 g. of salt per day, and a cup of alcohol (vodka or beer) three times a week, these gardens and herds supplied meat, vegetables and fruit – an essential supplement to the soldiers' diet. Such supplement of food was also one of the reasons for the soldiers' enthusiasm for raids into the mountains. Apart from the distraction such raids gave from the routine and hard work of camp life, the soldiers returned from them with loads of fresh vegetables, fruit, grain, cattle and sheep, as well as other booty which could be used or exchanged.
7. See, for example, N. Akhshamurov, 'Smert' Sleptsova. "Kavkazskaia Byl",' *Russkii Vestnik* (1888), No. 10, p. 59.
8. See, for example, Vel'iaminov's memoir quoted above, note 15 to Chapter 2. The Don Cossacks had the so-called 'mounted artillery', which consisted of some light small-calibre pieces. It was used to fire grapeshot and its effective range did not exceed 50–100 metres.
9. See, e.g., Züssermann, 'Otryvki,' (1876), No. 12, p. 540.
10. 'The Russian Failure', *New York Tribune*, 11 July 1854, as republished in *The Oriental Question* (London, 1969), pp. 397–8.
11. N. A. Volkonskii, '1858 God v Chechne', *Kavkazskii Sbornik*, Vol. III, p. 503.
12. Liubitel' Kavkaza i Zakavkaz'ia (pseud.), 'Nikolai Nikolaevich Murav'ev', *Russkaia Starina* (1874), No. 5, p. 143. This attitude to the soldiers by their officers and their great load of physical work, coupled with improper diet and clothing (on many occasions because of corruption), the extremities of weather, bad sanitary conditions and the lack of properly trained medics and physicians in sufficient numbers, all resulted in the fact that battle casualties accounted for only one in 11 deaths. 'In Russia,' wrote Vorontsov's physician, 'it is already understood that a general must have, if not an acquired knowledge, at least some talents and quick thinking, but as far as military physicians go, it is still thought that he may have no knowledge nor talent at all' – S. L. Avaliani (ed.), *Iz Arkhiva K. Ē. Andrevskogo*, Vol. I, *Zapiski Ē. S. Andreevskogo* (Odessa, 1913), p. 184. The medical services were in such a poor state that many officers preferred to be treated by native healers, who reportedly were much more successful.
13. For a lively description of these 'pheasants' and the season of their arrival to Stavropol', see E. G. Weidenbaum [Veidenbaum], 'Prodelki na Kavkaze', *Kavkazskie Etiudy. Issledovanniia i Zametki* (Tiflis, 1901), p. 310.
14. Thomas à Kempis, *De Imitatione Christi*, Book I, Chapter IX, (de Oboedientia et Subjectione), paragraph 1.
15. K., 'Levyi Flang Kavkazskoi Linii v 1848 Godu', *Kavkazskii Sbornik*, Vol. XI, p. 419.

16. See, for example, Lesley Blanch. *The Sabres of Paradise* (London, 1960), pp. 14, 83, 93 (hereafter: Blanch); Zoë Oldenbourg, *Catherine the Great* (New York, 1966), pp. 268, 292, 300; Benjamin Schwartz (ed.), *Letters from Persia Written by Charles and Edward Burges, 1828–1855* (New York, 1942), pp. 56, 98; Karl Marx, *The Oriental Question* pp. 21, 24–5, 75, 146, 209.
17. See, for example, Züssermann, 'Otryvki' (1877), No. 3, p. 82.
18. Don Simpson and Leslie Fisch, 'Serpent's Reach' song.

Chapter 4: Ermolov

1. The tribes subdued before Ermolov's period were the Georgian mountaineers – the T'ushes, the P'shavs and the Khevsurs – and the partly Christianised Ossets living astride the Georgian Military Highway. For the latter's subjugation, see V. Chudinov, 'Okonchatel'noe Pokorenii Osetii', *Kavkazskii Sbornik*, Vol. XIII, pp. 1–114.
2. Ermolov being an idol for successive generations of nationalist Russians until 1917, a tremendous amount of material by and about him was published. His biographies (none of them critical) include: 'Aleksei Petrovich Ermolov (Materialy dlia Biografii, Ego Razskazy i Perepiska)', *Russkaia Starina* (1896), No. 10, pp. 97–120, No. 12, pp. 565–83; Aleksandr Ermolov, *Aleksei Petrovich Ermolov, 1777–1861. Biograficheskii Ocherk* (St. Petersburg, 1912); 'Novye Podrobnosti iz Molodoi Zhizni A. P. Ermolova', *Russkii Arkhiv* (1878), No. 8, pp. 475–82; M. Pogodin, *Aleksei Petrovich Ermolov, Materialy dlia Ego Biografii* (Moscow, 1863); M. Whittock, 'Ermolov: Proconsul of the Caucasus', *The Russian Review*, Vol. XVIII, No. 1 (January 1959), pp. 53–60 (This essay may be called a 'latter-day eulogy'); V. P. Zhelikovskaia, *Ermolov na Kavkaze* (St. Petersburg, n.d.). Ermolov's own notes and memoirs were published in: 'Zametki A. P. Ermolova ob Ego Molodosti', *Russkii Arkhiv* (1867), No. 3, pp. 366–75; *Zapiski Alekseia Petrovich Ermolova. Materialy dlia Istorii Voiny 1812 Goda* (Moscow, 1863); N. V. Ermolov (ed.), *Zapiski Alekseia Petrovicha Ermolova (s Prilozheniiami)*, 2 Vols. (Moscow, 1865–68). His letters were published in: A. P. Bergé, 'Aleksei Petrovich Ermolov v Ego Pis'makh k Kn. M. S. Vorontsovu, 1816–1852', *Russkaia Starina* (1885), No. 12, pp. 523–50; 'Pis'mo A. P. Ermolova Grafu D. A. Gur'evu 17 Iiunia 1822 G.', *Russkaia Starina* (1892), No. 10, p. 215; 'Pis'ma A. P. Ermolova k Petru Andreevichu Kikinu, 1817–1832', *Russkaia Starina* (1872), No. 11, pp. 502–37; 'Iz Pisem A. P. Ermolova k Denisu Davydovu', *Voennyi Sbornik* (1906), No. 12, pp. 245–50; 'Dva Pis'ma A. P. Ermolova k Grafu (Kniaziu) M. S. Vorontsovu (1814)', *Russkii Arkhiv* (1905), No. 2, pp. 314–19; 'Doneseniia i Pis'ma A. P. Ermolova', *Russkaia Starina* (1872), No. 11, pp. 453–501; 'A. P. Ermolov k Pav. Nik. Ushakovu', *Russkaia Starina* (1872), No. 11, p. 538; 'A. P. Ermolov k Nik. Ger. Ustroialovu', *Russkaia Starina* (1872), No. 9, pp. 290–2; 'Aleksei Petrovich Ermolov v Pis'makh k Byvshym Svoim Ad'iutantam', *Russkii Arkhiv* (1906), No. 9, pp. 38–88; 'Aleksei Petrovich Ermolov. Pis'ma Ego k Kniaziu V. O. Bebutovu', *Russkaia Starina* (1873), No. 3, pp. 431–56; 'Aleksei Petrovich Ermolov' [Letter to R. I. Hooven], *Russkaia Starina*

(1876), No. 10, pp. 225–50. See also S. I. Khramovitskii, 'Znakomstvo s Ermolovym', *Russkaia Starina* (1872), No. 11, pp. 530–42; N. Berg, 'Vstrechna Moia s A. P. Ermolovym', *Russkii Arkhiv* (1872), No. 5, pp. 985–92.

3. Ermolov's letter to Davydov, 10 [22] February 1819, in 'Iz Pisem A. P. Ermolova k Denisu Davydovu', *Voennyi Sbornik* (1906), No. 12, p. 247. Hence the title of Whittock's article. And see K. Borozdin, 'Vospominaniia o N. N. Murav'eve', *Istoricheskii Vestnik* (1890), No. 2, p. 309.
4. Whittock, op. cit., p. 54.
5. Baddeley, pp. 94–5.
6. Ibid., p. 99.
7. Ēsadze, op. cit., p. 35.
8. Potto, *Kavkazskaia Voina*, Vol. II, Part I, p. 14.
9. 'My grim visage,' wrote Ermolov, 'always expressed pretty clearly what I felt, and when I spoke of war conveyed the impression of a man ready to sink his teeth in their throats. Unluckily for them I noticed how little they liked this, and consequently, whenever more reasonable arguments were wanting, I relied on my wild beast's muzzle, gigantic and terrifying figure and extensive throat; for they were convinced that any one who could shout so vociferously must have good and weighty reasons.' (Pogodin, p. 241, as quoted in Baddeley, p. 102) For Ermolov's mission to Tehrān, see in addition to the above-listed sources A. P. Bergé, 'Posol'stvo A. P. Ermolova v Persiiu: Istoricheskii Ocherk', *Russkaia Starina* (1877), No. 6, pp. 255–74, No. 7, pp. 383–427; Moritz von Kotzebue, *Reise nach Persien mit der Russisch Kais. Gesandschaft in Jahre 1817* (Weimar, 1819). (English translation: *Narrative of a Journey into Persia in the Suite of the Imperial Russian Embassy in the Year 1817* [London, 1819]).
10. For Russo-Persian relations during the Ermolov era from a Persian point of view, see Mahmoud Afschar, *La Politique Européenne en Perse. Quelques Pages de l'Histoire Diplomatique* (Tehrān, 1973, 2nd ed.); Fereydoun Adamiyat, 'The Diplomatic Relations of Persia with Britain, Turkey and Russia, 1815–1830' (unpublished Ph D. thesis, London, 1949).
11. *AKAK*, Vol. VI, Part II, pp. 498–9, 447–8, document Nos. 873, 795, Ermolov to the Emperor, November 1817, 14 [26] May 1818 respectively. The latter document has also been published in a 'completer version' in V. G. Hadziev [Gadzhiev] and Kh. Kh. Ramazanov (eds.) *Dvizhenie Gortsev Severo-Vostochnogo Kavkaza v 20–50 GG. XIX Veka. Sbornik Dokumentov* (Makhachqala, 1959) (hereafter: *Dvizhenie*), pp. 23–6, as document No. 4, where its date is given as 20 May [1 June] 1818; *Materialy*, pp. 149–52, document No. 67, Ermolov to the Emperor, 20 May [1 June] 1818.
12. *AKAK*, Vol. VI, Pt. II, p. 498.
13. *Dvizhenie*, p. 25.
14. Ibid., loc. cit.. Translation based on Baddeley, pp. 106–7.
15. *AKAK*, Vol. VI, Pt. II, p. 498.
16. *Dvizhenie*, p. 25.
17. N. A. Volkonskii, F. von-Kliemann and P. Bublitskii, 'Voina na Vostochnom Kavkaze s 1824 po 1834 G. v Sviazi s Miuridizmom', *Kavkazskii Sbornik*, Vol. XV, p. 524 (hereafter: 'Voina' + Vol. of *K.S.*). Translation

based on Baddeley, p. 112. The entire memorandum is given in 'Vel'iaminov', pp. 78–144.

18. Baddeley, pp. 109–11.
19. For Vel'iaminov's biography, see 'Vel'iaminov', pp. 1–77.
20. In addition to the above-mentioned sources, the following items were used in this narrative: Jean François Gamba, *Voyages dans la Russie Méridionale et Particulièrement dans les Provinces au delà du Caucase, Faits depuis 1820 jusq'en 1824* (Paris, 1826, 2nd ed.); Eduard Eichwald, *Reise auf dem Kaspischen Meere und in dem Kaukasus Internommen in den Jahren 1825–1826* (Stuttgart and Tübingen, 1834–37); Juan van Halen, *Narrative of Don Huan van Halen's Imprisonment in the Dungeons of the Inquisition at Madrid and His Escape in 1817 and 1818, to which Are Added His Journey to Russia, His Campaigns with the Army of the Caucasus and His Return to Spain in 1821* (London, 1827), Vol. II. (The Spanish edition 'omits the whole of the Russian part' – Baddeley, p. 123, note 1); Prushanovskii, 'Proisshestviia v Kaitakhe ot 1820 do 1836 [misprint for 1826] Goda', *Sbornik Gazety Kavkaz* (1846), pp. 170–80; N. I. Tsylov, *Epizody iz Boevoi Zhizni Alekseia Petrovicha Ermolova na Kavkaze v 1818, 1819 i 1820 Godakh. Zapiski Ochevidtsa Sluzhivshego pod Ego Nachal'stvom* (St. Petersburg, 1878); 'Voina', Vol. X, pp. 1–41.
21. Baddeley, p. 123; *Materialy*, pp. 116–19, document Nos. 39, 40, 'Ādil Khān 'Utsmī and Mahdī Khān Shāmkhāl to Ermolov [18 and 30 March 1819] respectively.
22. Baddeley, p. 124; *Materialy*, pp. 153–5, document Nos. 68, 69, Wrede to Ermolov, 25 May [6 June], Ermolov to Wrede, 31 May [12 June] 1819, Nos. 10, 6, respectively.
23. *Dvizhenie*, pp. 27–8, document No. 5, Ermolov to Muṣṭafā Khān of Shirvān (with copies to Mīrzā Ḥasan Khān of Ṭālish, Ismāʿīl Khān of Shekī, Mahdī Qūlī Khān of Qarābāgh and the *sulṭān* of Iliṣū), 2[14] January 1819.
24. Baddeley, p. 129. For Madatov's biography, see *Zhizn'General-Leitenanta Kniazia Madatova* (St. Petersburg, 1837); 'Kn V. G. Madatov', *Russkaia Starina* (1872), No. 12, p. 669.
25. *Dvizhenie*, pp. 31–2, document No. 9, Volkonskii to Ermolov, 18 [30] December 1819; *Materialy*, p. 121, document No. 42, Ermolov to Mahdī Khān Shāmkhāl, 19 [31] January 1820.
26. *Dvizhenie*, p. 31, document No. 8, Ermolov to the Inhabitants of Chirkah, 13 [25] October 1819.
27. *AKAK*, Vol. VI, Part II, p. 79, document No. 177, Ermolov to Vel'iaminov, 22 December 1819 [3 January 1820].
28. *Dvizhenie*, pp. 32–3, document No. 10, Ermolov to Zuḥūm, 23 December 1819 [4 January 1820].
29. 'Voina', Vol. X, p. 12.
30. See above, note 9 to Chapter 2.
31. *AKAK*, Vol. VI, Part II, p. 41, document No. 93, Ermolov to the Emperor, 7 [19] July 1820. Translation based on Baddeley, pp. 137–8.
32. For what may be called economic warfare against the mountaineers at this period, see *Dvizhenie*, pp. 29–30, 33–4, 35–9, document Nos. 7, 11, 13, 14, 15, 16, 17, 18, Wrede to Vel'iaminov, 29 September [11 October] 1819, Peters to Vel'iaminov, 19 [31] July 1820. Aslān Khān of Kurāh to

Wrede, not later than January, 'List of Auctioned Goods Confiscated from Merchants from ʿAndi, 14 [26] May,' Vel'iaminov to Zuḥūm Qāḍī of Aqūsha, 5 [17] June, Vel'iaminov (the CoS) to Vel'iaminov (Chief Civilian Administrator), 7 [19] June, Vysotskii to Vel'iaminov, 15 [27] September, Ermolov to Governor of Georgia, not later than December 1821.

33. 'Voina', Vol. X, p. 19.
34. Quoted by Whittock, p. 58.
35. Quoted by Baddeley, p. 97.
36. Ibid., loc. cit.
37. Ibid., loc. cit.
38. Prushanovskii, pp. 175–7.
39. For the description of this massacre, see Baddeley, pp. 130–2, translating Potto.
40. This throws a rather cynical light on the Russian argument that one of the aims of their pacification of the Caucasus was to stop the slave trade.
41. Baddeley, p. 145. Ermolov himself fathered a daughter who remained for all her life an object of curiosity and pilgrimage for Russian officers passing near her village. The shocking effect of this licentious behaviour of infidels towards Muslim women can be easily imagined.
42. Ibid, p. 132.
43. Quoted by Blanch, p. 93. Over a century later a Yugoslav diplomat wrote that 'for the Russians a conciliatory attitude is a sign of weakness, just as the violence of the language used in the articles published in their press and the arrogance of their behaviour are signs of strength – Veljko Mićunovic, *Moscow Diary* (London, 1980), p. 375.
44. *Dvizhenie*, pp. 345–7. document No. 192, Ladyński to Golovin, 16[28] July 1842, p. 346.
45. Baddeley, p. 99.
46. Tsitsiianov to the Emperor, as quoted in ibid, p. 65.
47. For example, see Ēsadze, op. cit., pp. 34–5.
48. Evgenii Kozubskii, 'Dagestanskie Vospominaniia o Ermolove', *Russkii Arkhiv* (1900), No. 9, pp. 137–42.
49. 'Such a convincing proof of our rights,' wrote Ermolov of his use of artillery, 'could not fail to give me the advantage. It is very interesting to see the first effect of this innocent means on the heart of man, and I learnt how useful it was to be in possession of the one when unable all at once to conquer the other' – Ermolov to Davydov, 10 [22] February 1819, in 'Iz Pisem A. P. Ermolova k Denisu Davydovu', *Voennyi Sbornik* (1906), No. 12, p. 247. Translation based on Baddeley, p. 125. In this, again, he was not at all original. Already Tsitsianov was 'making music with bombshells and bullets, constraining every *khān* to dance to his piping' – Baddeley, p. 68.
50. 'So said the iron to the magnet: "I hate you the most because you pull, but are not strong enough to draw close to you" ' – Friedrich Nietzsche, 'Von Alten und Jungen Weiblein', *Also Sprach Zarathustra*.
51. For his biography, see 'Voina', Vol. X, pp. 42–3; *Voennaia Entsiklopedia*, Vol. VIII, p. 467.
52. 'Voina', Vol. X, p. 44.
53. Baddeley, pp. 147–8. For the events of 1818–24 in Chechnia, see 'Voina',

Vol. X, pp. 8–46; *Materialy*, pp. 155–78, document Nos. 70, 71, 72, 73, 74, 76, 77, 78, 79, Grekov to Stahl [Stal'] 24 February [8 March], Grekov to Ermolov 6[18], 17[29] July, Grekov to Vel'iaminov, 5[17] October, Nos. 26, 42, 46, 70, 78 respectively, Grekov's Manifesto to the Chechens, 30 October [11 November] 1819, Ermolov to the Emperor, 24, 25 January [5, 6, February], Diebitsch to Ermolov, 11 [23] February, No. 243, Alexander I to Ermolov, 15 [27] February 1824.

54. Baddeley, p. 148.
55. Not to be confused with *shaykh* Muḥammad al-Yarāghī.
56. According to some Russian sources the village fool.
57. Here *imām* has probably a religious rather than temporal meaning. It is difficult to establish from the available sources the nature of this movement, though it seems to have contained some messianic and millenarian features. The Russian sources demonstrate complete ignorance of all such movements and call all their leaders from Shaykh Manṣūr to Shamil 'false prophets' [*lzheproroki*].
58. He was insulted and mistreated by Grekov when he came to offer his congratulations on the occasion of Grekov's nomination to command the Sunja Line – 'Voina', Vol. X, p. 44. For his biography, see F. Serov, 'Naezdnik Beibulat Taimazov', *O Tekh Kogo Nazyvali Abrekami* ([Groznyi], 1925), pp. 125–39.
59. The description of the following events is based on: *AKAK*, Vol. VI, Part I, pp. 508–16, document Nos. 893, 894, 896, 897, 895, Ermolov to the Emperor, 23 January [4 February], 23 February [7 March], 20, 28 May [1, 9 June], Ermolov to Laptev, 1 [13] May 1826; *Dvizhenie*, pp. 53–5, document Nos. 26, 27, 28, Letter from the People of Enderī to the People of Chirkah, not before May 1825, Ermolov to ?, 28 August [9 September] 1825, Disterlo to Goboretskii, 10 [22] September 1826; *Materialy*, pp. 179–80, 182–4, document Nos. 80, 83, 84, Ermolov to the Emperor, 28 August [9 September] 1825, Ermolov to Tatishchev, 11 [23] January, Ermolov to Diebitsch, 30 March [11 April] 1826, Nos. 114, 16 respectively; 'Voina', Vol. X, pp. 52–220 and 221–4, Appendices II, III, IV, Alexander to Ermolov, 18 [30] August 1825, Nicholas to Ermolov, 16 [28] February 1826, Ermolov's proclamation to the Chechens, 1826; N. N. Beliavskii and V. A. Potto, *Utverzhdenie Russkogo Vladychestva na Kavkaze*, Vol. III, Part 2 (Tiflis, 1904), pp. 207–28; Kuzanov, No. 2, pp. 36–7; Eichwald, op. cit., Vol. I, pp. 81–2; Baddeley, pp. 148–53.
60. Ibid., pp. 148–9.
61. Ibid., p. 153.
62. Ibid., loc. cit.
63. Perhaps Ermolov, in spite of his warnings of a possible war with the Qājārs (not to say his contribution to its outbreak), was so strongly convinced of his ability to hold them in terror that the attack came as a shock.
64. For his biography, see Shcherbatov, *General-Fel'dmarshal Kniaz' Paskevich. Ego Zhizn'i Deiatel'nost'*, 7 Vols. (St. Petersburg, 1888–1904); his activities in the Caucasus are described in Vols. 2 and 3.
65. 'Ermolov, Dibich i Paskevich, 1826–1827', *Russkaia Starina* (1872), No. 5, pp. 706–26, No. 7, pp. 39–69, No. 9, pp. 243–80; 'Ermolov, Dibich i Paskevish, 1827', *Russkaia Starina* (1880), No. 11, pp. 617–26; M. N.

Pokhvisnev, 'Aleksei Petrovich Ermolov (Po Povodu Pomeshchennykh v "Russkoi Starine" Materialov pod Zaglaviem: "Ermolov, Dibich i Paskevich")', *Russkaia Starina* (1872), No. 11, pp. 475–92; V. Andreev, 'Ermolov i Paskevich', *Russkii Arkhiv* (1873), No. 8, cc. 1571–83 (an altered version of this article appeared in *Kavkazskii Sbornik*, Vol. I. pp. 197–213); E. G. Weidenbaum, 'Ermolov i Paskevich', in *Kavkazskie Etiudy*, pp. 216–32; 'Voina', Vol. XI, pp. 7–9, 14–20, 51–3.

Chapter 5: The Naqshbandiyya-Khalidiyya

1. Ṣufism (*taṣwwuf* in Arabic) is Muslim mysticism. *Ṭarīqa* (literally, way, path) is a mystical method, system or school. *Ṭāʾifa* (literally, group) is a *ṣūfī* order. For these and other terms mentioned below, see appropriate entries in the *Encyclopedia of Islam* (*EI*), and J. Spencer Trimingham, *The Sufi Orders in Islam* (Oxford, 1971) (hereafter: Trimingham).
2. Literally; the way of the masters.
3. Western scholarship has only very recently started to deal seriously with the Naqshbandiyya. Thus, although its importance in the history of the Muslim world has been recognised in the past, no comprehensive studies of this *ṭarīqa* were published. This narrative is based on *EI* and Trimingham, pp. 14, 62–4, 92–6, 99, 124, 127, 202–4. For an appraisal of the Naqshbandiyya's role in Muslim history, see Hamid Algar, 'The Naqshbandi Order: A Preliminary Survey of Its History and Significance', *Studia Islamica*, Vol. 44 (1970), pp. 123–52 (hereafter: Algar). For its influence on resistance to Western encroachment and on fundamentalist movements, see Bernard Lewis, *The Middle East and the West* (New York, 1966), pp. 97–100 (hereafter: Lewis).
4. Its 'orthodoxy' is stressed by the fact that two of the three *silsilas* (chains of initiation leading back to Muḥammad through one of the first four caliphs – al-khulafāʾ al-rashīdūn) go back to Abū Bakr and only one – to ʿAlī-Algar, p. 124. And see Trimingham, pp. 149–50; Al-Shaykh al-Sayyid Jamāl al-Dīn al-Ghāzī-Ghumuqī al-Dāghistānī, *Al-Ādāb al-Marḍiyya fī al-Ṭtarīqa al-Naqshbandiyya* (Petrovsk, 1323/1905), p. 77 (hereafter: Sayyid Jamāl al-Dīn).
5. Trimingham, p. 63.
6. Lewis, p. 96. For Sirhindī's biography and teaching, see Yohanan Friedmann, *Shaykh Ahmad Sirhindi* (Montreal, 1971).
7. Lewis, p. 97. Trimingham's (p. 95) definition: 'a somewhat bigoted Sunni movement', would probably solicit the same reaction from Muslims, as another of his phrases (p. 49) has done: in one of the copies of his book in the SOAS Library someone has written in red ink on the margin: 'Dirty missionary joke.'
8. Literally, the Reformer of the Second Millennium.
9. Berezin, *Puteshestvie*, p. 82; I. R-v, 'Nachalo i Postepennoe Razvitie Miuridizma na Kavkaze', *Russkii Khudozhestvennyi Listok*, 20 November [2 December] 1859, No. 33, p. 113.
10. The most comprehensive work on Shaykh Manṣūr is Alexandre Bennigsen, 'Un Mouvement Populaire au Caucase du XVIIIe Siècle: La "Guerre Sainte" du Sheikh Mansur (1785–1794). Page Mal Connue et Controversée

des Relations Russo-Turques', *Cahiers du Monde Russe et Soviétique*, Vol. V, No. 2 (April–June 1964), pp. 159–205. Baddeley (pp. 47–52, 55–6) summarised all the works available at that time, including Ottino's claim that Shaykh Manṣūr was in fact an Italian Dominican monk, which Baddeley rejected. Two articles published after Baddeley are P. Iudin, 'Lzheprorok Ushurta-Shikh Mansur (Iz Istorii Religioznykh Dvizhenii na Kavkaze)', *Russkii Arkhiv* (1914), No. 10, pp. 217–28; M. Ia Korol'kov, 'Sheikh Mansur Anapskii (Epizod iz Pervykh Let Zavoevaniia Kavkaza)', *Russkaia Starina* (1914), No. 5, pp. 410–17. In addition, three Soviet works can be added – S. B. Akhmadov, 'Ob Istokakh Antifeodal'nogo i Antikolonial'nogo Dvizheniia v Chechne v Kontse XVIII V.', *Izvestiia Checheno-Ingushkogo Nauchno-Issledovatel'skogo Instituta*, Vol. IX, Part 3, Vypusk 1 (1974); Z. Sheripov, 'Sheikh Mansur. (Kratkii Istoriko-Biograficheskii Ocherk)', *O Tekh Kogo Nazyvali Abrekami* ([Groznyi], 1925), pp. 151–8; Nikolai Aleksandrovich Smirnov, 'Sheikh Mansur i Ego Turetskie Vdokhnoviteli', *Voprosy Istorii* (1950), No. 10, pp. 19–39. Caucasian expatriate literature includes E. Kaval, 'Sheikh Mansur', *United Caucasus*, No. 8(25) (August 1953), pp. 23–7; Tarik Cemal Kutlu, *İmam Mansur* (İstanbul, 1987). The romantic nature of Shaykh Manṣūr and the events surrounding him inspired at least two novels – V. I. Savinov, *Shikh Mansur. Vostochnyi Roman v Chetyrekh Chastiakh* (St. Petersburg, 1853); Edmund Spencer, *The Prophet of the Caucasus: An Historical Romance of Krim-Tartary*, 3 Vols. (London 1840).

11. Baddeley, p. 47.
12. For Shaykh Khālid, see Butrus Abu-Manneh, 'The Naqshbandiyya-Mujaddidiyya in the Ottoman Lands in the Early 19th Century', *Die Welt des Islams*, Vol. XII (1982), pp. 1–12 (hereafter: Abu Manneh); Albert Hourani, 'Sufism and Modern Islam: Maulana Khalid and the Naqshbandi Order', in idem. *The Emergence of the Middle East* (London, 1981), pp. 75–89.
13. Makhmudbekov, 'Miuridicheskaia Sekta na Kavkaze', *Sbornik Materialov dlia Opisaniia Mestnostei i Plemen Kavkaza*, Vol. XXIV, Part I, p. 22 (hereafter: Makhmudbekov); Muḥammad ibn Sulaymān al-Baghdādī, *al-Ḥadīqa al-Nadiyya fī Ādāb al-Ṭarīqa al-Naqshbandiyya* (Cairo, 1313 [1895]), pp. 79–80.
14. Sayyid Jamāl al-Dīn, p. 80. Similarly A. Runowski [Runovskii] 'Dnevnik Polkovnika Runovskogo Sostoiavshego Pristavom pri Shamile vo Vremia Prebyvaniia Ego v Gor. Kaluge s 1859 po 1862 God', *AKAK*, Vol. XII (hereafter: Runowski's Diary), pp. 1490–6, entry for 3 [15] July 1860.
15. E.g., Mirza Aleksandr Kazem-Bek, 'Miuridizm i Shamil', *Russkoe Slovo* (1859), No. 12, Otdel 1, pp. 182–242; N. V. Khanykov, 'O Miuridakh i Miuridizme', *Sbornik Gazety Kavkaz* (1847) Vol. 1, pp. 136–56 (resumée in *Moskovskie Vedomosti* 18 [30] 21 October [2 November] 1847, Nos. 125, 126, pp. 912–13, 970–1 respectively); Kuzanov, 'Miuridizm v Dagestane', *Raduga* (1861), No. 1, pp. 1–8, No. 2, pp. 28–37, No. 3, pp. 50–7, No. 4, pp. 65–71 (hereafter: Kuzanov + No. of *Raduga*); Makhmudbekov, pp. 14–40; A. A. Neverovskii, *O Nachale Bezpokoistv v Severnom i Srednem Dagestane* (St. Petersburg, 1847) (hereafter: Neverovskii, *O Nachale*); [Prushanovskii] 'Kazi Mulla (Gazi Magomet), (Iz Zapisok Kapitana Prushanovskogo)', *Sbornik Gazety Kavkaz* (1847), Vol. II, p. 22; T.,

'Razvitie Miuridizima na Kavkaze', *Odesskii Vestnik*, 29 September [4 October] 1859, No.103, pp. 447–9; I. R-v 'Nachalo i Postepennoe Razvitie Miuridizima na Kavkaze', *Russkii Khudozhestvennyi Listok*, 10 [22], 20 November [2], 1 [13], 10 [22], 20 December 1859 [1 January 1860], pp. 104–10, 113–16, 117–19, 123–8, 129–30; Romanowski [Romanovskii], *Kavkaz i Kavkazskaia Voina. Publichnye Lektsii Chitannye v Zale Pasazha v 1860 Godu* (St. Petersburg, 1860); 'Voina', Vol. X. pp. 19–30.

16. E.g., Semen Kuzmin Bushuev, 'O Kavkazskom Miuridizme', *Voprosy Istorii* (1956), No. 12, pp. 72–9; Anatolii Vsevolodovich Fadeev, 'Vozniknovenie Miuridistskogo Dvizheniia na Kavkze i Ego Sotsial'nye Korni', *Istotriia SSSR* (1960), No. 5, pp. 37–58; Nikolai Aleksandrovich Smirnov, *Miuridizm na Kavkaze* (Moscow, 1963); Andarbek Dudaevich Iandarov, *Sufizm i Ideologiia Natsional'no-Osvoboditel'nogo Dvizeniia. (Iz Istorii Razvitii Obshchestvennykh Idei v Chechneno-Ingushetii v 20–70-e Gody XIX V.)* (Alma-Ata, 1975).
17. From *murīd* – disciple of a *ṣūfī shaykh*. Accordingly, all the mountaineers who fought the Russians under the banner of the *imāms* are called indiscriminately *murīds [miuridy]*. Unfortunately, many Western scholars and Caucasian expatriates, who should have known better, have adopted this terminology. E.g. Allen and Muratoff, op. cit.; Aytek Kunduh, *Kafkasya Müridizmi (Gazavat Tarihi)* (İstanbul, 1987); Mohyieddin Izzat Quandor, 'Muridism: A Study of the Caucasian Wars of Independence, 1819–1859', (Ph. D. thesis, Claremont, Ca., 1964).
18. A very notable exception was the great Russian orientalist V. V. Barthold [Bartol'd]. See, for example, his *Islam* (Petrograd, 1918), p. 15.
19. In extreme cases 'Muridism' was given the attributes of a new religion separate from Islam. The cause for such descriptions was, in addition to political interests, the ignorance of Russian authors with regard to both Islam and the Caucasus. Some of the accounts of the Naqshbandī-Khālidī *silsila* in the Caucasus, for example, read like an incredible combination of factual errors, misunderstanding and fantasy. That contemporary and even later Western authors – even Baddeley – accepted these descriptions is understandable; after all they depended exclusively on Russian sources. But it is quite incredible to find Western scholars in the 1960s subscribing to such a theory, like, for example, Irène Mélikoff, 'L'Idéologie Religieuse du Muridisme Caucasien', *Bedi Kartlisa*, Vol. XXV (1968), pp. 27–45.
20. Baddeley, p. 234.
21. *Nemirnye*, literally, unpeaceful.
22. For which see above, note 32 to Chapter 4.
23. *Mirnye*, literally, peaceful.
24. *Dvizhenie*, pp. 312–24, document No. 168, 'Excerpt from Survey of the Disastrous Situation in Northern Daghestan, with a Short Outline of Preceding Events', [by Klüge-von-Klugenau], 31 December 1841 [12 January 1842], p. 323. And see ibid., pp. 307–8, document No. 165, 'Excerpts from Report by the Office of Mountaineers Administration', not before July 1840; A. Iurov, '1843-i God na Kavkaze', *Kavkazskii Sbornik*, Vol. VI, pp. 39–40; Idem, '1840, 1841 i 1842-i Gody na Kavkaze', ibid., Vol. XI, p. 195 (note).
25. For this process, which forced the Grebentsy and the Terek Cossacks back to the northern bank of the Terek, see Volkova, op. cit., pp. 168–93.

26. This expulsion and the extremely cruel and brutal way in which it was carried out (see above, p. 34) must be considered as a major initial reason for the Chechens' more vociferous hatred of the Russians than that of the Daghestanis.
27. The introduction of alcoholic drinks seems, in fact, not to have been planned, at least not by the authorities. But neither can it be regarded as accidental, being of such a central importance in Russian, indeed in European, social behaviour. Later it was the ban on drinking imposed by 'Muridism' which elicited the strongest emotional reaction among the Russians. For example, Ivchenko to von Krabbe, 21 January [2 February] 1830, No. 22, as quoted in 'Voina', Vol. XI, p. 149.
28. Baddeley, p. 134.
29. See below, p. 44.
30. Atkin, op. cit., p. 165.
31. See, for example, Kakhanov to Pankrat'ev, 9 [21] June 1831, No. 245, as quoted in 'Voina', Vol. XIII, p. 287.
32. V. Soltan, 'Obzor Sobytii v Dagestane v 1855 i 1856 Godakh', *Kavkazskii Sbornik*, Vol. XII, pp. 503–5.
33. This description is based on Abu-Munneh, pp. 12–17.
34. Shaykh Khālid's disciples developed this notion further. Muḥammad al-Yarāghī is reported to have stated that 'a Muslim should be no one's slave [but God's] and should not pay any taxes, not even to a Muslim [ruler]. A Muslim must be a free man and equality must reign among the believers', Neverovskii, *O Nachale*, p. 5.
35. Quoted in Abu Manneh, p. 15. Shaykh Khālid also exhorted 'his disciples to finish the *Khatm al-Khawjakān* (i.e. the ending prayers which close the *dhikr* in the Naqshbandī practice) by a prayer (*du'a'*) for God to 'annihilate (*ahlik*) the Jews, Christians, fire worshippers (*majus*) and the Persian Shiites (*rawafid al-A'jam*)' – ibid., loc. cit.
36. Baddeley, p. 242.
37. In addition to *EI*, see A. I. Agronomov, *Dzhikhad. Sviashchennaia Voina Mukhammedan* (Qazan, 1877); N. V. Khanykov, 'Perevod Musul'manskikh Postanovlenii o Voine', *Sbornik Gazety Kavkaz* (1846), pp. 282–98. (Originally appeared in *Kavkaz* (1846), Nos. 20, 21.) Reprinted by the Turkestan Military District as *Dzhikhad ili Gazavat, to est' Sviaschennaia Voina Musul'man s Nevernymi* (Tashkent, 1899).
38. E.g., Lewis, pp. 96–100; Trimingham, pp. 240–1.
39. For which, see *Dvizhenie*, pp. 42–8, document Nos. 22, 23, 24, Ermolov to ?, 25 January [6 February], Ermolov to Bekovich-Cherkasskii, 5 [17] February, Ermolov to Jakubowskii, 19 February [3 March] 1829; 'Voina', Vol. X, pp. 175–83.
40. For which, see above, pp. 36–7.
41. A speech by Muḥammad al-Yarāghī as given by Neverovskii, *O Nachale*, pp. 5–6. A somewhat different and shorter version was published in 'Voina', Vol. X, p. 20. Yet another, longer version was printed in Kuzanov, No. 2, pp. 32–3.
42. Neverovskii, *O Nachale*, p. 6.
43. Muḥammad al-Yarāghī to the people of Chirkah, as published in 'Voina', Vol. X, p. 28. Neverovskii (pp. 13–14) attributes this speech to Ghāzī Muḥammad.

44. E.g., ibid, pp. 8–9, 11–12; Kuzanov, No. 2, pp. 33–4, 35–6.
45. Thus both the Capuchins and the Scottish missionaries were expelled from the Caucasus.
46. For Russian missionary activities see, for example, *AKAK*, Vol. VI, Part II, pp. 501, 507, documents Nos. 880, 890, 891, Ermolov to Commander of Vladikavkaz, 24 May [5 June] 1819, Golitsyn to Ermolov, 26 July [7 August], Ermolov to Golitsyn, 19 September [1 October] 1822, Nos. 1701, 2579, 194, Vol. VIII, pp. 704–7, 708, 710–11, document Nos. 599, 600, 602, 598, 605, 607, Shirokii to Rosen, 17 [29] February, 5 [17], 19 [31] March, 14 [26] April, Rosen to Shirokii, 20 February [9 March], Rosen to Malinovskii, 30 April [12 May], Rosen to Chernyshev, 21 May [2 June] 1836, Nos. 386, 529, 637, 884, 255, 391, 496; Vol. IX, pp. 340–42, document No. 303, Golovin to Chernyshev, 6 [18] August 1840, No. 871, Vol. X, pp. 239–40, document No. 241, Vorontsov to Prokurov, 31 December 1852 [12 January 1853], No. 519, Vol. XII, pp. 1069–70, 1080, document Nos. 940, 949, Bariatinskii to Vel'iaminov, 12 [24] April, Zotov to Miliutin, 22 May [3 June] 1859, No. 129; *Dvizhenie*, pp. 555–8, document No. 308, Vorontsov to Commander Caucasian Line, 3 [15] November 1847; [Mūsā Kundukh,] 'Memuary Gen. Musa-Pashi Kundukhova (1837–1865)', *Kavkaz* (Paris), 1937, No. 10 (46), pp. 23–5, Appendix, Bariatinskii to Alexander II (n.d.) (hereafter: Kundukh + No. of *Kavkaz*); Züssermann, 'Otryvki', 1878, No. 11, pp. 56–66, 79–85, 1879, No. 2, pp. 689, 693.
47. *Dvizhenie*, pp. 41–2, document No. 21, Vel'iaminov to Area Commanders, not later than September 1822. And see Ēsadze, op. cit, p. 35; Neverovskii, *O Nachale*, p. 10; V[asilii] N[ikolaevich] N[oro]v, 'Kavkazskaia Ekspeditsiia v 1845 Godu. Razskaz Ochevidtsa', *Voennyi Sbornik* (1906), No. 11, p. 10. For the importance of the *ḥajj* to Caucasian Muslims, see Baddeley, *Rugged Flanks*, Vol. II, p. 65.
48. Mark Osipovich Kosven and Khadzi-Murat Omarovich Khashaev (eds.), *Istoriia, Geografiia i Etnografiia Dagestana XVIII-XIX VV. Arkhivnye Materialy* (Moscow, 1958), pp. 362–8, 'Historical Survey of the Samur District' by André de Simon [Andrei Frantsevich Desimon], 1839. Quotation from p. 367.
49. Baddeley, *Rugged Flanks*, Vol. II, pp 12–18. This intolerance prevented the Russians from using the *ṣufī* order of the Qādiriyya against Shamil. When it first started to spread in the Caucasus, the Qādiriyya (called by the Russians, *zikrizm*) was very peaceful, and preached accommodation with the Russian authorities. The Russians, nevertheless, persecuted it – e.g. *AKAK*, Vol. X, p. 245, document No. 251, Chernyshev to Vorontsov 3 [15] January 1848, No. 5 (secret). For the Qādiriyya, see Trimingham, pp. 40–4.
50. See, for example, Réoute to Pankrat'ev, 5 [17] August 1831, No. 145, as quoted in 'Voina', Vol. XIV, p. 194. Thus, the Russians tried to fight the *sharīʿa* all along. One of the ways was to re-establish the *ʿādat* by using them in local courts – e.g. Georges Wl[ast]offl, *Ombres du Passé*, pp. 151–60.
51. For the events of these years in Chechnia and Daghestan, see *Materialy*, pp. 199–201, document No. 89, Paskiewicz to Suhtelen, 28 January [9 February] 1830, No. 52; 'Voina', Vol. XI, pp. 1–107, 127–45.

52. Baddeley, pp. 244–5, paraphrasing, in fact, 'Voina', Vol. XI, pp. 108–9. After setting out the Russians' view, Baddeley gives, as if in an afterthought, a far better reason: 'No doubt also the fact the Persians were Shiites had much to do with their non-success' – ibid, p. 245. For Ottoman activity among the mountaineers in those years, see M. M. Gabrichidze (ed.) *Shamil' – Stavlennik Sultanskoi Turtsii i Angliiskikh Kolonizatorov. Sbornik Dokumental'nykh Materialov* (Tbilisi, 1953) (hereafter: *Shamil*), pp. 1–7, 9–12, document Nos. 8, 12, 1, 2, 3, 5, 6, 7, 13, 14, 11. Two manifestos by the Serasker in Erzurum to the people of Daghestan and Shirvān, February-March and June 1829, Tausch to Sysoev, 5 [17] (two), 27 September [9 October] 1826, Bekovich-Cherkasskii to Sipiagin (secret), 9 [21] April, Chief-of-Staff Caucasian Corps to Paskiewicz, 9 [21] July, Emmanuel to Paskiewicz, 17 [29] July 1828, 11, 14 [23, 26], April 1830, Hess to Strekalov, 24 June [1 July] 1829, Nos. 50, 54, 57, 293, 126, 80, 373, 398 respectively; 'Voina', loc. cit. (as in previous note). For the attempts of 'Abbās Mīrzā to stir up the mountaineers, see *Materialy*, p. 181, document No. 81, Vel'iaminov to Hooven, 24 September [6 October] 1825.
53. 'Voina', Vol. XI, pp. 175–82; 'Stsena iz Pokoreniia Dzharo-Belakan', *Sbornik Gazety Kavkaz* (1846), pp. 15–20.
54. See, for example, *Shamil*, pp. 12–13, document No. 15, Summary of a Debriefing of Georgians Returning from Captivity in Daghestan, 25 April [7 May] 1830, No. 548.
55. For the events of 1829 in Chārtalah, see 'Voina', Vol. XI, pp. 127–37. For the Russian plans for 1830, see *Dvizhenie*, pp. 60–2, 68–72, document Nos. 35, 39, Paskiewicz to Nesselrode, 18 February [2 March], Paskiewicz to the Emperor, 6 [18] May 1830; 'Voina', Vol. XI, pp. 150–2, Vol. XII, pp. 63–9.
56. *AKAK*, Vol. VII, pp. 517–18, document No. 470, Meddox to Paskiewicz, 8 [20] February 1831, No. 19.
57. Proclamation by Ghāzī Muḥammad, as quoted in 'Voina', Vol. XI, pp. 158–9.

Chapter 6: The First Imām

1. Different sources mention different years as the date of birth of Ghāzī Muḥammad. All that can be conclusively established is that he was a few years older than Shamil, which points to the early 1790s. In addition to the above-mentioned sources, the following were used in this chapter: Muḥammad Ṭāhir al-Qarākhī, *Bāriqat al-Suyūf al-Dāghistāniyya fī Ba'ḍ al-Ghazawāt al-Shāmiliyya* (Moscow and Leningrad, 1946), pp. 9–28 (hereafter: Qarākhī): Hadzhi Ali syn Abdul Meleka Efendi, 'Skazanie Ochevidtsa o Shamile', *Sbornik Svedenii o Kavkazskikh Gortsakh*, Vol. VII, pp. 6–8 (hereafter: Ḥājj 'Alī); Timofei Astakhov, 'Vospominaniia o Zhizni i Boevoi Deiatel'nosti Kizliaro-Grebenskogo Kazach'ego Polka so Dnia Sform irovaniia Ego do 1879 Goda', *Terskie Vedomosti*, 23 May [4], 2 [14], 9 [21] June 1891 (Nos. 41, 44, 46), pp. 3–4, 2, 3–4 respectively; N. Dubrovin, 'Iz Istorii Voiny i Vladychestva Russkikh na Kavkaze (Kazi Mulla kak Rodonachal'nik Miurdizma i Gazavata)', *Voennyi Sbornik*,

(1890), No. 10, pp. 197–240, (1891), No. 3, pp. 5–39, No. 4, pp. 177–206, No. 5, pp. 5–38, No. 6, pp. 197–217; 'Dva imana [*sic*!], ili Isterblenie Doma Avarskogo. Istoricheskoe Povestvovanie o Kavkaze', *Russkii Arkhiv* (1915), No. 1, pp. 116–46, No. 2, pp. 231–58, No. 3, pp. 358–85; S. Filonov and V. Tomkeev, 'Kavkazskaia Liniia pod Upravleniem Generala Emmanuelia', *Kavkazskii Sbornik*, Vol. XV, pp. 327–450, Vol. XIX, pp. 120–220, Vol. XX. pp. 142–249; Izidor Grzegorzewski [Grzhegorzhevskii], 'General-Leitenant Kliuki-fon-Klugenau. Ocherk Voennykh Deistvii i Sobytii na Kavkaze, 1818–1850', *Russkaia Starina* (1842), No. 11, pp. 508–15 (hereafter: Grzegorzewski + year and No. of *RS*); Ivan Karakin, 'Vozrazhenie na Stat'iu G. Zissermana "Osada Burnoi i Derbenta Kazi-Mulloi v 1831 G." ', *Russkii Vestnik* (1865), No. 12, pp. 648–71; 'Mesiats Voennopokhodnoi Zhizni Mirnogo (v Severnom Dagestane v 1832 Godu.)', *Moskvitiannin* (1843), No. 11, pp. 79–108; Prushanovskii, 'Kazi Mulla (Gazi Magomet). (Iz Zapisok Kapitana Prushanovskogo)', *Sbornik Gazety Kavkaz* (1847), Vol II, pp. 22–39; Pawel Przewłacki [Przhevlatskii], 'Vospominanie o Blokade Goroda Derbenta v 1831 Godu', *Voennyi Sbornik* (1864), No. 2, Otdel Neoffitsial'nyi, pp. 155–78; T., 'Vospominaniia o Kavkaze i Gruzii', *Russkii Vestnik* (1869), No. 1, pp. 1–36, No. 2, pp. 401–43, No. 3, pp. 102–55, No. 4, pp. 658–707; Arnold Züssermann, 'Osada Burnoi i Derbenta Kazi Mulloi v 1831 G.' *Russkii Vestnik* (1864), No. 12, pp. 698–732 (hereafter: Züssermann, 'Osada'); A. M., 'Guerre des Russes dans le Daghestan', *Nouveau Journal Asiatique* (1832), No. 9, pp. 466–72 (hereafter: 'Guerre'); Eichwald, op. cit., Vol. II, pp. 675–740.

2. Ḥājj ʿAlī, p. 11 (note 9).
3. Baddeley, p. 240.
4. *Dvizhenie*, pp. 55–6, document Nos. 29, 30, The *Shāmkhāl*'s Letter to Ghāzī Muḥammad, and Ghāzī Muḥammad's Reply, both 1827; 'Voina', Vol. XI, pp. 108–26; Neverovskii, *O Nachale*, pp. 14–16 (quotation from p. 14); Prushanovskii, pp. 31–2; Kuzanov, No. 3, p. 51.
5. See, for example, Shaykh ʿAbdallah al-ʿAshilṭī's speech to the Chechens as mentioned and ridiculed in 'Voina', Vol. XII, p. 62. *Rābiṭa* (literally: bond) in *ṣūfī* usage is the mystical communication of thoughts between a disciple and his *murshid*, invoked by the disciple's concentration on the image of his master.
6. Ibid, Vol. XI, p. 152. See also Qarākhī, pp. 11–14.
7. Here in the usual meaning of 'leader'.
8. For example, 'Voina', Vol. XI, pp. 148–9.
9. Runowski's Diary, pp. 1496–98, entry for 3 [15] July 1860; Al-Sayyid Jamāl al-Dīn's letter to Korganov (from March 1830?) in 'Voina', Vol. XII, pp. 9–10; *Dvizhenie*, pp. 412–23, document No. 221, Excerpts from the Testimony of Lt. Orbeliani, Who Had Been in Shamil's Captivity in 1842, 1843, p. 419.
10. Qarākhī, pp. 13–14.
11. Ibid., loc. cit., *Dvizhenie*, pp. 62–5, 129–30, document Nos. 36, 79, Excerpts from Paskiewicz's War Diary, 1 [13]–16 [28] March 1830, Saʿīd al-Harakānī's Letter to Aslān Khān, September 1833; 'Voina', Vol. XI, pp. 153–8. Saʿīd al-Harakānī was one of the most prominent *ʿulamāʾ* in Daghestan and the instigator of the revolt of 1819. Afterwards he became

reconciled to Russian rule (according to some sources in an all-night conversation with Ermolov—e.g., Potto, and Beliaev, op cit., Vol. III, Part I, pp. 519–20) and one of the main opponents of the Naqshbandiyya-Khālidiyya. Among other things, he opposed their imposition of the *sharīʿa* and the abolition of the *ʿādat*. He also opposed their ban on smoking and drinking, interpreting the *quarʾānic* ban on wine as not inclusive of other spirits.

12. Ibid., pp. 158–61.
13. *AKAK*, Vol. VII, p. 515, document No. 468, Korganov to Paskiewicz 15 [27] March 1830, No. 15; *Dvizhenie*, pp. 66–7, document Nos. 37, 38, Letters from Nūsal Khān to Strekalov, March, and from Aslān Khān to Abū Sultān Nūsal Khān, 21 March [2 April] 1830; *Materialy*, pp. 202–13, document Nos. 90, 91, 92, 94, 93, Paskiewicz to Chernyshev, 25 February [9], 11 [23], 13 [25], 27 March [8 April], Chernyshev to Paskiewicz, 21 March [2 April] 1830 (secret), Nos. 125, 136, 140, 174, 9 respectively; *Shamil*, pp. 12–13, document No. 15, 'Summary of Debriefing of Georgians Returned from Captivity in Daghestan', 25 April [7 May] 1830, No. 548; Qarākhī, pp. 14–16.
14. 'Voina', Vol. XI, p. 181.
15. For which, see above, note 53 to Chapter 5.
16. For details see 'Dokumenty o Dvizhenii Gortsev Severo-Vostochnogo Kavkaza 20–50 GG. XIV V. pod Rukovodstvom Shamilia', *Uchenye Zapiski*, Dagestanskii Filiial Akademii Nauk SSSR, Institut Istorii, Iazyka i Literatury Imeni G. Tsadasy, Vol. II, pp. 264–8, document Nos. 1, 2, Strekalov to Paskiewicz, 15 [27] October (secret), Paskiewicz to Strekalov 8 [20] November 1830 (secret) (hereafter: 'Dokumenty') (both published in *Dvizhenie*, pp. 81–6, as document Nos. 46, 47 respectively); *Dvizhenie*, pp. 78–81, 86–7, document Nos. 43, 45, 48, Excerpt from Paskiewicz's War Diary, 16 [28] July–1 [13] August, Strekalov to Paskiewicz, 9 [21] October, Paskiewicz's War Diary, 1 [13]–16 [28] December 1830; *Shamil*, pp. 13–16, 19–23, documents Nos. 16, 17, 18, 19, 23, 24, 25, 26, Bekovich-Cherkasskii to Paskiewicz, 27 April [9 May], Sergeev to Strekalov, 6, 16 [18, 28] June, Paskiewicz to Chernyshev, 9 [21] July, Commander of Signakhi to Strekalov, 6 [18] October, Sergeev to Strekalov, 7 [19] November, Strekalov's War Diary for 5 [17] November, Strekalov to Paskiewicz, 14 [26] November 1830, Nos. 250, 185, 234, 26, 1637, 1188, 530 respectively; 'Voina', Vol. XII, pp. 35–6, 106–205; Qarākhī, p. 16.
17. See, for example, *Dvizhenie*, pp. 78–9, document No. 43, Excerpts from Paskiewicz's War Diary, 16 [28] July–1 [13] August 1830 and 'Voina', Vol. XII, pp 46–9, for appeals by different communities to Pakhu Bike to join an anti-Russian defensive agreement. See also 'Voina', Vol. XIII, pp. 154–5, for such an agreement between the Chechens, the ʿAndīs and the Avārs.
18. Ibid, Vol. XII, p. 135. And see *Dvizhenie*, pp. 106–7, document No. 64, Muḥammad al-Yarāghī to the *Shāmkhāl*, not later than 14 April 1832 (also printed in *Materialy*, pp. 262–3, as document No. 113), where he called Ghāzī Muḥammad 'the renewer of the law [i.e. the *Sharīʿa; vozobnovitel' zakona*]'. Two unconnected events, a strong earthquake in March 1830 and an epidemic of cholera later that year, also served to enhance

Ghāzī Muḥammad's prestige among the mountaineers – not, one would guess, without his indirect encouragement – e.g., Qarākhī, p. 16.

19. *Dvizhenie*, pp. 72–6, document No. 40, Excerpts from Paskiewicz's War Diary, 1 [13]–16 [28] May 1830; 'Voina', Vol. XII, pp. 17–24, 36–8.
20. Ibid., loc. cit., and pp. 206–11, Appendix VII, Proclamation of Mūlā Muṣṭafā the *Qāḍī* of Germenchuk to the Chechen People (n.d.).
21. *Dvizhenie*, pp. 79–80, document No. 44, Excerpts from Paskiewicz's War Diary, 16 [28] August–1 [13] September 1830; 'Voina', Vol. XII, pp. 61–3, 72.
22. Ibid, pp. 73–7.
23. Züssermann, 'Osada', p. 701.
24. For the Russian reactions, see *AKAK*, Vol. VII, pp. 514–15, 535–7, document Nos. 467, 496, Paskiewicz to Korganov (secret), 3 [15] March, Paskiewicz to Nesselrode, 27 March [8 April] 1830, Nos. 11, 174 respectively; *Dvizhenie*, pp. 72–8, document Nos., 40, 42, 41, Excerpts from Paskiewicz's War Diaries, 1 [13]–16 [28] May, 1 [13]–16 [28] June, Rodofinik to Paskiewicz, 20 May [1 June] 1830; 'Voina', Vol. XII, pp. 1–17, 24–5, 38–59, 80–103, Vol. XIII, pp. 174, 179, 187.
25. For which, see *Dvizhenie*, pp. 60–2, 68–72, document Nos. 35, 39, Paskiewicz to Nesselrode, 18 February [2 March], Paskiewicz to the Emperor, 6 [18] May 1830; 'Voina', Vol. XI, pp. 150–2, Vol. XII, pp. 63–9.
26. For his nomination, see *AKAK*, Vol. VII, pp. 514–15, document No. 467, Paskiewicz to Korganov (secret), 3 [15] March 1830, No. 11.
27. For which, see ibid, Vol. VII, pp. 507–11, document No. 462, Paskiewicz to Nesselrode, 13 [25] September 1828, No. 683, Vol. VIII, pp. 567–69, document No. 445, Rosen to Nesselrode, 6 [18] April 1833, No. 249; *Materialy*, pp. 129–38, document Nos. 44, 45, 46, 48, 50, 53, 54, 41, 49, 56, 57, 59, Abū Sulṭān Nūsal Khān's Oath to the Emperor, 9 [21] September, Emmanuel to Chernyshev, 11 [23] October 1828, No. 1315, Lashkarev to Volkonskii, 8 [20] January, No. 6, Kankrin to Nesselrode, 24 January [5 February], No. 389, Volkonskii to Nesselrode, 8 [20] March, No. 1410, Request of Nūsal Khān's Messengers to Nicholas I, 1829, not later than December, Appeal of Nūsal Khān to Paskiewicz, 1829, Appeal of Nūsal Khān to Nicholas I, 1829, Note by the Foreign Ministry Archives about Russia's Relations with the Avār Khāns, not before 21 December, 1829, Notes on Avāristān by Skalon, February 1829, Nesselrode to the Emperor, not later than 3 April 1830, Nicholas I's Answer to Nūsal Khān, 26 April [8 May], Paskiewicz to Nūsal Khān 4 [16] June 1830, No. 2492; Marks Osipovich Kosven and Khadzi-Murat Omarovich Khashaev (eds.), *Istoriia, Geografiia i Etnografiia Dagestana XVIII-XIX VV. Arkhivnye Materialy* (Moscow, 1958), pp. 353–61, 'Zapiska o Snosheniiakh Nashykh s Avarskimi Khanami s 1800 Goda do Nastoiashchego Vremeni', 1838; 'Voina', Vol. XX, pp. 135–41.
28. For Korganov's activities, see *Materialy*, pp. 213–19, document Nos. 95, 96, Paskiewicz to Chernyshev, 10 [22] April, 7 [19] May 1830, Nos. 205, 262; 'Voina', Vol. XII, pp. 80–103.
29. Ibid., Vol. XII, pp. 8–9, 17, 51, Vol. XIII, pp. 174, 179, 187; *Materialy*, document No. 96 quoted in the previous note.
30. 'Voina', Vol. XII, pp. 43–59.
31. Ibid., p. 4.

32. Ibid., pp. 3, 27–8, 42–3, 82.
33. Ibid., Vol. XIII, pp. 174, 179, 187. This was part of a conscious Russian policy to try to buy local leaders. Soon, however, it proved to be another half-measure which backfired – ibid., Vol. XIV, pp. 177–8, 181, 188, 196, 198–9, Vol. XVII, pp. 326–34.
34. Robert Rosen [Roman Fedorovich Rozen], not to be confused with Grigorii Vladimirovich Rosen. For his biography see *AKAK*, Vol. VII, p. IX.
35. According to Rosen's explanation, they died of cholera and the heat. For the entire expedition, see *Materialy*, pp. 224–33, document Nos. 98, 99, 100, Paskiewicz to Chernyshev, 8 [20] May, 6 [18], 21 June [3 July] 1830, Nos. 270, 362, 379 respectively; 'Voina', Vol. XII, pp. 43–59.
36. Qarākhī, p. 16.
37. *AKAK*, Vol. VII. p. 473, document No. 425, Pankrat'ev to Paskiewicz (in French), 7 [19] May 1831, No. 239, Vol. VIII, pp. 527–8, document No. 401, Pankrat'ev to Chernyshev, 7 [19] May 1831, No. 467; *Dvizhenie*, pp. 88–94, document Nos. 50, 51, 52, Rosen to Chernyshev, 24 March [5 April], Paskiewicz to Chernyshev, 27 April [9 May], Emmanuel to Paskiewicz, 6 [18] June 1831; 'Voina', Vol. XIII, pp. 174–209; Qarākhī, p. 17.
38. Pankrat'ev to Paskiewicz, 28 May [9 June] 1831, No. 585, as quoted in 'Voina', Vol. XIII, p. 209.
39. *AKAK*, Vol. VII, pp. 475, 519–20, document Nos. 428, 473, Pankrat'ev to Nesselrode, 9 [21] July 1831, No. 352, Pankrat'ev to Nesselrode (draft, n.d.), Vol. VIII, pp. 528–30, document Nos. 403, 404, 405, Excerpt from the War Diary of the Siege of Burnaia, Pankrat'ev to Chernyshev, 11 [23] June, No. 675, Pankrat'ev to Paskiewicz, 18 [30] June 1831, No. 726; *Dvizhenie*, p. 95, document No. 53, Nūsal Khān's Letter to the Elders of Qarākh, n.d., probably the beginning of June 1831; *Materialy*, pp. 247–9, document Nos. 102, 103, Paskiewicz to Chernyshev, 19 [31] March, 27 April [9 May] 1831, Nos. 228, 443 respectively; 'Voina', Vol. XIII, pp. 263–79, 286–90; Züssermann, 'Osada', pp. 701–19; Karakin, op. cit., pp. 648–71; 'Guerres', pp. 466–71; Qarākhī, pp. 17–18.
40. 'Voina', Vol. XIII, p. 286.
41. Ibid., pp. 326 (the quotation), 295–300, 304.
42. Ibid., pp. 159–74, 177.
43. 'Dokumenty', p. 269, document No. 3, Emmanuel to Chernyshev (excerpt), not before 28 June [10 July] 1831 (published also in *Dvizhenie*, pp. 95–6, as document No. 54); 'Voina', Vol. XIII, pp. 210–36; Qarākhī, pp. 18–19.
44. 'Voina', Vol. XIII, p. 223.
45. Ibid., pp. 236–40; Qarākhī, p. 19.
46. 'Voina', Vol. XIV, pp. 116–97.
47. Ibid., Vol. XIII, pp. 240–61.
48. *AKAK*, Vol. VIII, pp. 533–4, document No. 407, Pankrat'ev to Paskiewicz, 13 [25] August 1831, No. 793; 'Voina', Vol. XIII, pp. 290–6, 301–4.
49. *AKAK*, Vol. VIII, pp. 534–5, document Nos. 408, 409, Kakhanov to Pankrat'ev, 30 August [11 September], Pankrat'ev to Chernyshev, 5 [17] September 1831, Nos. 521, 1310 respectively; 'Dokumenty', pp. 269–70, document No. 4, Nūsal Khān to Pankrat'ev 14 [26] September 1831; *Dvizhenie*, pp. 96–9, document No. 56, Excerpt from Pankrat'ev's War

Diary, 28 August [9]–15 [27] September 1831; 'Voina', Vol. XIII, pp. 305–22; Qarākhī, p. 19; Züsserman, 'Osada', pp. 721–32; 'Guerre', pp. 471–2 [Lettre de Village de Goubden, 6 September 1831]; Przeclawski, op. cit., pp. 155–78.

50. 'Voina', Vol. XIII, p. 309. (The same texts are also published as Appendices 1 and 2 to Züssermann, 'Osada'.) The letter to the commander and garrison of Derbend is in strict observance of the *sharʿī* stipulations on *jihād*.

51. 'Voina', Vol. XIII, pp. 262, 322–7.

52. Ibid., Vol. XIV, p. 173.

53. *AKAK*, Vol. VIII, pp. 535, 536–9, document Nos. 410, 413, 414, 416, 412, 415, 417, Pankrat'ev's Manifestos to 'the Free Muslim Communities and the Different Tribes Inhabiting Daghestan', 15 [27] September, to 'the Inhabitants of Ṭabarsarān and Qarāqaytāq', 6 [18], 8 [20] October, and to 'the *Beks* and Inhabitants of Ṭabarsarān', 18 [30] October, Pankrat'ev to Chernyshev, 3 [15], 10 [22], 19 [31] October 1831, Nos. 1079, 1091, 1108 respectively; *Dvizhenie*, pp. 99–100, document No. 57, Pankrat'ev's Manifesto to 'the people of Daghestan', 16 [28] September 1831; 'Voina', Vol. XIV, pp. 81–99. The dates of the manifestos printed or mentioned in all three sources do not match.

54. Ibid, p. 89.

55. Ibid., pp. 86–7; *Materialy*, pp. 254–7, document Nos. 105, 106, Pankrat'ev to Rosen, 24, 29 October [5, 10 November] 1831, Nos. 1119, 1123.

56. 'Voina', Vol. XIV, p. 106.

57. *AKAK*, Vol. VIII, pp. 538–40, 542–8, document Nos. 417, 418, 421, 425, 423, 424, Pankrat'ev to Chernyshev, 19 [31] October, Vel'iaminov to Rosen, 21 October [2 November], Pankrat'ev to Rosen, 11 [23], 26 November [8 December], Rosen to Chernyshev, 12 [24], 19 November [1 December] 1831, Nos. 1108, 1002, 1155, 1190, 135, 161 respectively; *Dvizhenie*, pp. 101–3, document No. 59, Rosen to Chernyshev, 12 [24] November 1831; *Materialy*, pp. 258–9, document No. 108, Rosen to Chernyshev, 28 January [9 February] 1832, No. 72; 'Voina', Vol. XIV, pp. 99–116; Qarākhī, p. 19.

58. *AKAK*, Vol. VIII, pp. 541–2, 669–71, 673, 675–77, document Nos. 419, 568, 569, 470, 577, 572, Rosen to Chernyshev, 5 [17], 12 [24], 26 November [8 December], Vel'iaminov to Rosen, 5 [17] November 1831, 26 May [7 June], Chernyshev to Rosen, 13 [25] March 1832, Nos. 106, 135, 190, 1034, 60, 423 respectively; 'Voina', Vol. XIV, pp. 116–29, 133; Qarākhī, pp. 19–20.

59. 'Voina', Vol. XIV, p. 123.

60. Ibid., p. 128.

61. Ibid, p. 123.

62. *AKAK*, Vol. VIII, pp. 341–2, 545, 548–51, document Nos. 253, 428, 424, 426, 430, 427, Autographed Letter from Rosen to Chernyshev, 13 [15] December, Pankrat'ev's Manifesto to 'the People of Daghestan', n.d. [December], Rosen to Chernyshev, 26 November [8], 2 [14], 10 [22], 14 [26] December, Pankrat'ev to Rosen, 4 [16] December 1831, Nos. 189, 218, 234, 249, 1207 respectively; 'Voina', Vol. XIV, pp. 133–53, Vol. XVI, pp. 406–7; Qarākhī, p. 20.

63. Among them Colonel Miklashevskii, one of the bravest Russian commanders.
64. 'Voina', Vol. XIV, p. 153. In Pankrat'ev's own words, 'the uprising in Daghestan stirred up by the traitor Ghāzī Muḥammad is now completely terminated' – *AKAK*, Vol. VIII, pp. 542–3, document No. 421, Pankrat'ev to Rosen, 11 [23] November 1831, No. 455.
65. *Dvizhenie*, pp. 104–6, document Nos. 62, 63, Rosen to Chernyshev, 14 [26] January, 17 [29] March 1832; 'Voina', Vol. XIV, pp. 154–60, Vol. XVI, pp. 405–38. Reporting these attempts, the Russian source felt the need to justify or explain them. 'Obviously,' he wrote, 'the Caucasian authorities did not know what to do, and comparing Ghāzī Muḥammad to big criminals, who are denied the protection of the law, did not regard it a sin to "eliminate" him. Luckily . . . Ghāzī Muḥammad died not at the hand of an assassin, but in battle' ('Voina', Vol. XVI, p. 428).
66. *AKAK*, Vol. VIII, pp. 672–73, 674–5, document Nos. 570, 571, 573, Rosen to Chernyshev, 11 [23] February, 10 [22] March, Chernyshev to Rosen, 5 [17] April 1832, Nos. 109, 175, 544 respectively; 'Voina', Vol. XV, pp. 549–60.
67. *AKAK*, Vol. IX, p. XXVII.
68. For which, see ibid, Vol. VIII, pp. 674–5, 340–1, document Nos. 574, 252, Chernyshev to Rosen, 5 [17] April 1832, Rosen to Chernyshev, 12 [24] November 1837, Nos. 544, 137 respectively; *Dvizhenie*, pp. 103–4, document No. 61, Chernyshev to Rosen, 11 [23] January 1832; *Materialy*, pp. 263–9, document No. 114, Rosen to Chernyshev, 5 [17] May 1832, No. 16; 'Voina', Vol. XIV, pp. 132–3, Vol. XV, pp. 506–48, 561–76.
69. Report quoted (without date) in ibid, Vol. XV, p. 512. And see Vel'iaminov's statement that 'the mutiny of Ghāzī Muḥammad could have been stopped promptly, if [proper] measures against him were taken without delay. However, he had been allowed to grow stronger, and then unsuccessful military operations further encouraged the people to join this mutiny' – Vel'iaminov to Rosen, n.d., as quoted in ibid, Vol. XIII, p. 261.
70. Ibid, Vol. XIV, p. 132.
71. *Materialy*, pp. 275–6, document No. 119, Chernyshev to Rosen, 27 May [8 June] 1832, No. 761 (secret).
72. Ibid., pp. 259–61 document Nos. 109, 110, 111, Rosen to Chernyshev, 10 [22], 24, 31 March [5, 12 April] 1832, Nos. 176, 203, 226; 'Voina', Vol. XVI, pp. 438–54; Qarākhī, pp. 21–2. For Russian intelligence of such intentions by Ghāzī Muḥammad, see *AKAK*, Vol. VIII, p. 541, document No. 419, Rosen to Chernyshev, 5 [17] October 1831, No. 106.
73. For a good analysis of Ghāzī Muḥammad's possible intentions and the reasons for his retreat, see 'Voina', Vol. XVI, pp. 447–51.
74. *AKAK*, Vol. VIII, p. 675, document No. 575, Rosen to Chernyshev (excerpt), 7 [19] April 1832, No. 254; *Materialy*, pp. 270–3, document No. 116, 'Note on the Activities of Ghāzī Muḥammad' by Rosen, 11 [23] May 1832; 'Voina', Vol. XVI, pp. 454–7.
75. Ibid, pp. 456–7. For Ghāzī Muḥammad's subsequent activity in Daghestan, see *Materialy*, pp. 274–7, document Nos. 117, 118, 120, Rosen to Chernyshev, 18 [30] May, 2 [14] June 1832, Nos. 431, 432, 502 respectively.
76. For the events of 1831 in Chārtalah, see *AKAK*, Vol. VIII, pp. 535–6,

document No. 411, Pankrat'ev to Chernyshev, 3 [15] September 1831, No. 358; *Shamil*, pp. 24–5, document Nos. 28, 29, 30, Strekalov to Paskiewicz, 8 [20] January, Rosen to Paskiewicz, 23 January [4 February], Paskiewicz to Strekalov, 22 May [3 June] 1831, Nos. 1, 141, 528 respectively; 'Voina', Vol. XIV, pp. 161–211.

77. *AKAK*, Vol. VIII, pp. 551–2, document No. 431, Rosen to Chernyshev, 17 [29] March 1832, No. 190; 'Voina', Vol. XVII, pp. 336–46.
78. *AKAK*, Vol. VIII, pp. 553, 554–6, 961, document Nos. 432, 434, 435, 903, Rosen to Chernyshev, 15 [27], 31 July [12], 6 [18], 28 August [9 September] 1832, Nos. 63, 64, 76, 132 (the last three documents were reprinted in *Shamil*, pp. 28–31, as Nos. 36, 37, 38); *Dvizhenie*, pp. 109–11, 114–17, document Nos. 69, 70, 72, 73, Kakhanov to Rosen, 22 July [3 August], Karpov to Rosen, 31 July [12 August], Rosen to Chernyshev, 6 [18], 27 August [8 September] 1832; *Shamil*, pp. 27–8, 32–6, document Nos. 34, 35, 40, Tchavtchavadze to Rosen, 28 July [9 August], Nos. 37, 38, 'Short Description of Military Activities, 14 [26]–30 July [11 August]' 1832; 'Voina', Vol. XVII, pp. 346–58, Vol. XVIII, pp. 288–309.
79. *Dvizhenie*, pp. 107–8, document No. 65, Rosen to Chernyshev, 5 [17] July 1832; 'Voina', Vol. XVII, pp. 358–79.
80. His instructions were 'to act decisively against any horde appearing in his area in order to destroy it at the very beginning' – ibid, p. 365.
81. For the events in Daghestan between July and September, see *Dvizhenie*, pp. 108–9, 111–13, document Nos. 66, 71, 67, Rosen to Chernyshev, 9 [21], 31 July [12 August] 1832; 'Voina', Vol. XVIII, pp. 333–6, 338–41.
82. *AKAK*, Vol. VIII, pp. 677–82, document Nos. 578, 579, 580, 581, 582, Rosen to Chernyshev, 15 [27], 21, 29 July [2, 10 August] 1832, Nos. 17, 20, 21, 42, 43; *Materialy*, pp. 269–70, document No. 115, Rosen to Chernyshev, 5 [17] May 1832, No. 334; 'Voina', Vol. XVII, pp. 379–409; Baddeley, *Rugged Flanks*, Vol. I, pp. 110, 205, 211.
83. There are no precise data for the strength of both forces in the Russian sources. For the expedition, see *AKAK*, Vol. VIII, pp. 682–95, 556–8, document Nos. 583, 584, 585, 586, 587, 588, 589, 438, 436, 437, Rosen to Chernyshev, 17 [29], 22, 27 August [3, 8], 3 [15], 20, 22, 27 September [2, 4, 9], 4 [16] October, Nos. 91, 111, 131, 147, 173, 184, 192, 218 respectively, Rosen's Manifestos to the Communities of ʿAndī and Salaṭawh, 17 [29], 20 September [2 October] 1832 respectively; *Dvizhenie*, pp. 117–8, document No. 74, Shumskii to Vel'iaminov, 29 August [10 September] 1832; *Materialy*, pp. 279–82, document No. 123, Rosen to Chernyshev, 10 [22] August 1832, No. 86; 'Voina', Vol. XVIII, pp. 309–32, Vol. XX, pp. 97–101; [Evdokim Emel'ianovich Lachinov] 'Otryvok iz "Ispovedi" Lachinova', *Kavkazskii Sbornik*, Vol. II, pp. 75–115; Qarākhī, pp. 21–2.
84. 'Vel'iaminov regarded the destruction of houses and fields as the strongest means to force the Chechens into obedience' – 'Voina', Vol. XVII, p. 381.
85. These cannon were recaptured by the Russians on 22 September 1832.
86. *AKAK*, Vol. VIII, pp. 557–8, document No. 438, Rosen to Chernyshev, 4 [16] October 1832, No. 218; 'Voina', Vol. XVIII, pp. 337–8, where extensive quotations are printed from the *shāmkhāl*'s and Nūsal Khān's reports.
87. 'Voina', Vol. XVIII, p. 343. The letter is badly written in poor colloquial

Russian, the writer being a simple soldier, probably a Pole. For the entire episode, see *AKAK*, Vol. VIII, pp. 695, 557–8, document Nos. 589, 438, 439, Rosen to Chernyshev, 27 September [9 October], 4 [16], 12 [24] October 1832, Nos. 192, 218, 281 respectively. 'Voina', Vol. XVIII, pp. 343–7, gives quotations from the correspondence. Ḥājj ʿAlī, (p. 7) gives a completely different version.

88. 'Voina', Vol. XVIII, p. 344.
89. Texts in ibid, pp. 345–7.
90. *AKAK*, Vol. VIII, p. 558, document No. 439, Rosen to Chernyshev, 12 [24] October 1832, No. 281; 'Voina', Vol. XVIII, pp. 341–2.
91. *AKAK*, Vol. VIII, pp. 558–67, 695–6, 351, document Nos. 440, 441, 442, 443, 591, 259, Vel'iaminov to Rosen, 21 October [2 November], Rosen to Chernyshev, 22 October [3 November], Rosen to 'the *Qāḍīs*, Elders and all the Community of Hindāl', 25 October [6 November], Rosen to Chernyshev, 26 October [7 November] (including Chernyshev to Rosen, 6 [18] July), Rosen to Chernyshev, 31 October [12 November], Nos. 680, 303, 302, 306 (incl. 902), 349 respectively, the Emperor's Order to the Caucasian Troops, 16 [28] November 1832; *Materialy*, pp. 282–4, document No. 124, Rosen to Chernyshev, 25 October [6 November] 1832; 'Voina', Vol. XX, pp. 102–25; 'Mesiats Voennopokhodnoi Zhizni Mirnogo (v Severonom Dagestane v 1832 Godu)', *Moskvitianin*, 1843, No. 11, pp. 79–108; Qarākhī, pp. 24–8; Baddeley, *Rugged Flanks*, Vol II, pp. 24, 59–60. For the inscription on the grave of Ghāzī Muḥammad in Targhū, see *Ēpigraficheskie Pamiatniki Severnogo Kavkaza*, Vol. II, pp. 97–8, Inscription No. 640.
92. One of them would become the third *imām*, and see Chapter 8.

Chapter 7: The Second *Imām*

1. Very little, relatively speaking, has been published on Ḥamza Bek. This chapter is based, in addition to the document collections named above, on Qarākhī, pp. 31–8; Ḥājj ʿAlī, pp. 8–10; 'Voina', Vol. XX, pp. 125–34; Ēsadze, pp. 38–9; Grzegorzewski, 1875, No. 3, pp. 545–7; Kuzanov, No. 3, pp. 56–7; 'Nachalo' 1 [13], 10 [22] December 1859 (Nos. 34, 35), pp. 117–19, 123–5 respectively; J. Kostenecki [Kostenetskii], *Zapiski ob Avarskoi Ekspeditsii na Kavkaze 1837 Goda* (St. Petersburg, 1851), pp. 5–7 (hereafter: Kostenecki); A. A. Neverovskii, *Istreblenie Avarskikh Khanov v 1834 Godu* (St. Petersburg, 1848) (also published in *Voennyi Zhurnal*, 1848, No. 3) (hereafter: Neverovskii, *Istreblenie*).
2. 'Nachalo', No. 34, p. 117.
3. R-v's date for this meeting, 1829, (ibid, loc. cit.), seems to be too late.
4. 'Voina', Vol. XI, pp. 34, 136.
5. See above, note 16 to Chapter 6.
6. Qarākhī, p. 16. For the Russian version, see *AKAK*, Vol. VIII, pp. 581–4, document No. 467, Rosen to Chernyshev, 31 July [12 August] 1834, No. 719; 'Voina', Vol. XIV, pp. 165, 180, 195.
7. *Dvizhenie*, pp. 87–8, document No. 49, Declaration of Ghāzī Muḥammad and Ḥamza Bek to the People of Daghestan, January 1831.

8. 'Voina', Vol. XVII, p. 361. For the battle see above, note 79 to Chapter 6.
9. For which, see above, note 78 to Chapter 6.
10. See above, note 91 to Chapter 6.
11. Qarākhī, p. 31. And see also Ḥājj ʿAlī, p. 8; 'Voina', Vol. XX, pp. 131–2; Kuzanov, No. 3, p. 56; 'Nachalo', No. 34, p. 118.
12. Ḥājj ʿAlī, p. 8. And see Qarākhī, p. 31.
13. *AKAK*, Vol. VIII, pp. 569–74, 581–4, document Nos. 446, 448, 450, 452, 454, 455, 456, 458, 467, 453, 457, Rosen to Chernyshev, 21 June [3], 6 [18] July, 24, 31 August [12, 14], 21, 28 September [3, 10], 12 [24] October, 23 November [5 December] 1833, 31 July [12 August] 1834, 14 [26] September, 9 [21] October 1833, Nos. 377, 418, 593, 606, 689, 702, 730, 855, 719, 654, 831 respectively (the two last documents were published also in *Dvizhenie*, pp. 128–9, 130–1 as document Nos. 78, 80 respectively); *Shamil*, pp. 39–40, 42–6, document Nos. 44, 47, 'Excerpt from Intelligence on Activities in Transcaucasia, 1 [13] January–1 [13] August 1833', Governor of T'elavi to Palavondov, 6 [18] April 1834, No. 509; 'Voina', Vol. XX, pp. 130–2; 'Nachalo', No. 34, pp. 118–19; Qarākhī, pp. 31–3; Ḥājj ʿAlī, p. 8.
14. In August a planned expedition against the Circassians had to be abandoned because of the activity of Ḥamza Bek's messengers in Chechnia – *AKAK*, Vol. VIII, p. 571, document No. 452, Rosen to Chernyshev, 31 August [12 September] 1833, No. 606.
15. 'Voina', Vol. XX, pp. 132–4.
16. Ibid, p. 132.
17. See its translation in ibid, p. 133.
18. Translation of letters in ibid, pp. 132–3 (quotation from p. 132).
19. Ibid, p. 133.
20. Ibid, p. 134.
21. Not that any negotiations had a chance of success, the two sides working at cross-purposes.
22. *AKAK*, Vol. VIII, pp. 569–72, document Nos. 449, 451, 453, Rosen to Nūsal Khān, 19 [31] August, Rosen to Nesselrode, 24 August [5 September], Rosen to Chernyshev, 14 [26] September 1833, Nos. 592, 594, 654 respectively; 'Voina', Vol. XX, pp. 125–9.
23. *AKAK*, Vol. VIII, pp. 573–4, document Nos. 457, 458, Rosen to Chernyshev, 9 [21] October, 23 November [5 December] 1833, Nos. 831, 855 (the former document is also published in *Dvizhenie*, pp. 130–1, as No. 80).
24. *AKAK*, Vol. VIII, pp. 575–6, document Nos. 460, 461, Rosen to Chernyshev, 23 February [3 March], 12 [24] April 1834, Nos. 135, 240 respectively.
25. Ibid, p. 576. And see Qarākhī, p. 36.
26. *AKAK*, Vol. VIII, pp. 567–9, 584–5, document Nos. 462, 463, 464, 465, 468, Rosen to Chernyshev, 14 [26], 21 June [3], 5 [17], 19 [31] July, 9 [21] August 1834, Nos. 459, 494, 546, 609, 738; *Dvizhenie*, pp. 132–6, document Nos. 82, 86, 83, 84, 85, Rosen to Chernyshev, 20 June [1 July], 8 [20] August, Letter from 'the *Qāḍīs*, '*Ulamā*', Notables and People of Khunzakh to the Communities Siding with Ḥamza Bek', not before June, Aslān Khān's Letter to Vol'khovskii, 10 [22] July, Aḥmad Khān's Letter

to the Elders of Khunzakh, July 1834; *Materialy*, pp. 287–9, document Nos. 128, 129, 131, Aslān Khān to Rosen, 10 [22] July, Rosen to Chernyshev, 9 [21] August, No. 739, Chernyshev to the Emperor, 1 [13] September 1834, No. 301; Neverovskii, *Istreblenie*; Kuzanov, No. 3, pp. 56–7; 'Nachalo', No. 34, pp. 118–9, No. 35, pp. 123–4; Kostenecki, p. 5; Qarākhī, pp. 33–6; Ḥājj ʿAlī, pp. 8–9.

27. For example, Ḥājj ʿAlī, p. 10. So widespread was this belief, even in the mountains, that Shamil found it necessary to swear that there had been no intention to kill anyone (Qarākhī, p. 34) and that, on the contrary, the two brothers were the ones who had planned to assassinate Ḥamza Bek and some of his lieutenants (ibid, p. 36).
28. *AKAK*, Vol. VIII, pp. 584–5, document No. 468, Rosen to Chernyshev, 9 [21] August 1834, No. 738.
29. Ibid, pp. 585–6, document No. 469, Rosen to Chernyshev, 16 [28] August 1834, No. 763 (also published in *Shamil*, pp. 50–1, as document No. 53, where its number is given as 769); Qarākhī, pp. 33, 36.
30. *AKAK*, Vol. VIII, pp. 586–7, 587–8, document Nos. 471, 472, 475, Rosen to Chernyshev, 23, 30 August [4, 11], 13 [25] September 1834, Nos. 783, 812, 843; Qarākhī, p. 37.
31. *AKAK*, Vol. VIII, pp. 585–6, document No. 469, Rosen to Chernyshev, 16 [28] August 1834, No. 763 (also published in *Shamil*, pp. 50–1, as document No. 53). For the events in Chechnia during this period, see *AKAK*, Vol. VIII, pp. 695–9, document Nos. 590, 591, 592, 593, Rosen to Chernyshev, 31 October [12 November] 1832, 27 July [8], 10 [22], 24 August [5 September] 1833, Nos. 349, 512, 86, 596 respectively.
32. Ibid, pp. 581–4, 585–6, 587, document Nos. 467, 469, 471, 470, 473, Rosen to Chernyshev, 31 July [12], 16 [28], 23 August [9 September], Chernyshev to Rosen, 19 [31] August, 5 [17] September 1834, Nos. 719, 763, 783, 6476, 6871 respectively; *Materialy*, pp. 289–95, document No. 130, Rosen to Lanskoi, 11 [23] August 1834, No. 748.
33. *AKAK*, Vol. VIII, p. 588, document No. 476, Rosen to Chernyshev, 25 September [7 October] 1834, No. 906 (also published in *Dvizhenie*, pp. 136–7, as document No. 87); 'Nachalo', No. 35, p. 125; Kostenecki, p. 7; Qarākhī, p. 38; Ḥājj ʿAlī, p. 9. For the inscription on Ḥamza Bek's grave in Khunzakh, see *Ēpigraficheskie Pamiadtniki*, pp. 100–3, inscription No. 649.
34. 'Voina', Vol. XVI, p. 462.
35. Ibid, pp. 469–70. For a shrewd analysis of such measures during the *imām*'s campaign in Naṣrān, see ibid, pp. 447–51.
36. Sorochan to Vel'iaminov, 8 [20] April 1832, No. 115, as quoted in ibid, p. 458.
37. Ibid, p. 458–9. For the entire analysis of Ghāzī Muḥammad's long-range measures, see pp. 457–70.
38. See ibid, p. 463.
39. Ḥājj ʿAlī, p. 8.

Chapter 8: The Third *Imām*

1. Qarākhī, p. 42; Ḥājj ʿAlī, pp. 10–11; Blanch, p. 46; I. Drozdov, 'Nachalo Deiatel'nosti Shamilia (1834–1836 G.)' *Kavkazskii Sbornik*, Vol. XX, p. 251 (hereafter: Drozdov).
2. That is, Samuel.
3. Because of its pronunciation many – though never Shamil himself – spelled his name Shāmil. Later, in his captivity, Shamil explained the two versions of his name by claiming to have changed his name twice in imitation of the Prophet (Muḥammad). However, as he himself always used the form Shamūyil, this explanation must be rejected.
4. Qarākhī (p. 21), mentions a woman to whom Ghāzī Muḥammad was a maternal cousin and Shamil a paternal one.
5. Ḥājj ʿAlī, p. 11 (note 9).
6. But not necessarily his right-hand man, as his official biography, acepted without challenge by all the sources, claims.
7. For what became the accepted Russian description of the proclamation of Shamil *imām*, see Baddeley, pp. 279–80. For Shamil's account, see Qarākhī, pp. 25–7. A much less dramatic version is given in Mīrzā Ḥasan ibn ʿAbdalla al-Qadarī al-Dāghistānī, *Kitap Asar-ı Dağıstan* (Bāqū, 1903), p. 130 (hereafter: *Asar-ı Dağıstan*). See also Blanch, pp. 73–9. For a hostile version, see Ḥājj ʿAlī, p. 11.
8. The first time Shamil was seriously wounded and 'left for dead' was in his childhood, when he was attacked by other children in his village – for details, see Blanch, pp. 47–8. All in all, Shamil was severely wounded 19 times. On four occasions he was left for dead – 'Razgovor Peterburgskogo Korrespondenta *le-Nord* s Shamilem'. *Sovremennaia Letopis*' (1866), No. 40, p. 15.
9. The *qur'ānic* verse (XIII, 18): 'And whatever is useful to the people remains on the earth' (*wa'amma ma yanfaʿ al-nās fayamkuth fī'l-arḍ*) was widely applied in this sense to Shamil's miraculous survivals. Qarākhī, for example, quotes it repeatedly.
10. Qarākhī, p. 38.
11. Ibid, p. 35. It does not seem to be a mere coincidence that Shamil, refusing his nomination as *imām*, suggested the same people in exactly the same order as they were listed here. Also, see Drozdov, p. 255; Mateusz Gralewski, *Kaukaz. Wspómnienia s Dwunastoletniej Niewoli* (Lwów, 1877), pp. 464–6 (hereafter: Gralewski).
12. Indeed, one of the first Russian reports described the 'head *murīd* Shamil' as the 'chief [*starshina*] of Gimrāh' – *AKAK*, Vol. VIII, pp. 589–90, document No. 477, Rosen to Chernyshev, 10 [22] October 1834, No. 949.
13. Baddeley, p. 289.
14. Runowski's Diary, p. 1418, entry for 6 [18] March 1860.
15. Friedrich Bodenstedt, *Die Völker der Kaukasus und Ihre Freihats-Kämpfe Gegen die Russen. Ein Beitrag zur Neusten Geschichte des Orients* (Frankfurt am Main, 1849, 2nd ed.), p. 419 (hereafter: Bodenstedt); J. Milton Mackie, *Life of Schamyl and Narrative of the Circassian War of Independence Against Russia* (Boston, 1856), p. 193 (hereafter: Mackie).
16. Runowski's Diary, p. 1472, entry for 16 [28] January 1861. For more

detailed and dramatic descriptions, see Drozdov, pp. 254–5, and Gralewski, pp. 464–6.

17. Qarākhī, p. 38.
18. Shamil's nomination to *imām* is strongly reminiscent of Temuchin's (Jenghiz Khān) nomination as *khān* of the Mongols, as described by Michael Prawdin [pseud.], *The Mongol Empire: Its Rise and Legacy* (London, 1940) pp. 50–1. Of course, Shamil could not claim originality in staging and playing his part in this ceremony. Many leaders and rulers before and after him preferred – as so many contemporary politicians do – to 'submit to the will of the people' and 'reluctantly' accept a nomination, which they had done everything in their power to secure beforehand. There is, however, no need to regard this cynically. First, personal ambition was not the only motive behind Shamil's actions. As in the case of so many leaders before and after him, dedication to his cause and society was no less strong a driving force. Second, and more important, the nomination was not merely a rubber stamp. In a way it reflected popular will, and by the mere fact of proclaiming Shamil *imām* it showed the limits to his power and authority. Also, one should not forget that such a ceremony was – and still is – in many cases part of etiquette and the political culture.
19. In fact, Nūsal Khān's wife was spared because she was pregnant. She gave birth to a son. However, at the time, Būlach Khān, as the only survivor of the ruling family, was a threat not so much in himself as because he was a potential focus for intrigues.
20. Lanskoi started his new command in the beginning of September – *AKAK*, Vol. VIII, p. 487, document No. 474, Rosen to Chernyshev, 11 [23] September 1834, No. 842. His command lasted little more than a month, however. According to Russian sources, he contracted jaundice during the expedition to Gimrāh and died a few days after his return to Temir-Khān-Shūra – ibid, p. XIV.
21. Drozdov, pp. 254–5. For the description of the raid, see ibid, pp. 256–7 and *AKAK*, Vol. VIII, pp. 588–90, document Nos. 477 and 478, Rosen to Chernyshev, Nos. 949 and 951, both of 10 [22] October 1834; *Materialy*, pp. 329–49, document No. 133, 'Description of Lanskoi's Expedition against Ḥamza Bek with a Short Historical Survey of the Conquest of Daghestan', by Sub-Lt Kuzminskii, 1834; Grzegorzowski, 1875, No. 3, pp. 547–9; Kostenecki, pp. 77–9.
22. Qarākhī, p. 39. Russian sources confirm that the rearguard was attacked on its way back, and that an officer was killed – *AKAK*, Vol. VIII, pp. 588–90, document No. 477, Rosen to Chernyshev, 10 [22] October 1834, No. 949; Drozdov, p. 257; Lanskoi's death so short a while after this expedition makes it an intriguing question whether he indeed contracted jaundice or died of wounds received during the expedition.
23. Bodenstedt, p. 420. Ḥājj ʿAlī calls it just a 'small-fire exchange' (p 12).
24. The intended commander of the expedition was Lanskoi. But he died and Réoute was ill. For details about Klugenau and Réoute, pp. 74–5 and note 42 to this chapter.
25. *AKAK*, Vol. VIII, p. 589, document No. 477, Rosen to Chernyshev, 10 [22] October 1834, No 949.
26. Drozdov, p. 258; Grzegorzewski, 1875, No. 3, p. 550.

27. *AKAK* Vol. VIII, pp. 588–94, document Nos. 477, 479, 480, 481, 484, 482, Rosen to Chernyshev, 10 [22], 25 October [6], 1 [13], 8 [20], 15 [27] November, Rosen to Aslān Khān of Ghāzī-Ghumuq and Kurāh and Ruler of the Avār Khanate, 11 [23] November 1834, Nos. 949, 995, 1011, 1024, 1051 1034 respectively; *Materialy*, pp. 329–49, document No. 133 'Description of Lanskoi's Expedition against Ḥamza Bek, with a Short Historical Survey on the Conquest of Daghestan' by Sub-Lt. Kuzminskii, 1834; Drozdov, pp. 257–62; Grzegorzewski, 1875, No. 3, pp. 549–53; Ḥājj ʿAlī, pp. 13–14.
28. Drozdov's lamentation of the lost opportunities in Daghestan because 'the general attention was then aimed at the line of the Black Sea, on which our military forces were used up to the detriment [*raskhodovalis' v ushcherb*] of other, more important parts of the Caucasus' (p. 268), disregards contemporary realities and sensitivities.
29. The peace treaty of Adrianople stipulated that 'those [territories] situated north and east of the said line towards Georgia, Imeretia and Gouriel, as well as the littoral of the Black Sea from the mouth of the Kuban to the port of St. Nicholas inclusive shall remain in perpetuity under the domination of the Emperor of Russia' – Anderson, p. 34.
30. For British activity among the Circassians, see below, pp. 116–17.
31. For such plans, see *AKAK* Vol. VIII, pp. 353–54, document No. 261, Chernyshev to Rosen, 26 February [10 March] 1835, No. 1389; Drozdov, p. 267.
32. Ibid, pp. 264–79. Quotation from p. 266.
33. *AKAK*, Vol. VIII, p. XIII. For a detailed biography, see Isidor A. Grzegorzewski [Grzhegorzhevskii], 'General-Leitenant Kliuki-fon-Klugenau. Ocherk Voennykh Deistvii i Sobytii na Kavkaze, 1818–1850', *Russkaia Starina* (1874), No. 9, pp. 131–52, No. 11, pp. 497–515, (1875), No. 3, pp. 545–54, (1876), No. 1, pp. 144–62, No. 2, pp. 377–87, No. 3, pp. 646–58, No. 6, pp. 351–82.
34. One description of Klugenau runs as follows: 'Very tall, stoutly built, brusque in manner and fiery-tempered to the verge of insanity, but good natured withal, honest and generous' – N. Okol'nichii, 'Perechen' Poslednikh Sobytii v Dagestane (1843 god)', *Voennyi Sbornik* (1859), No. 3, Otdel Neoffitsial'nyi, p. 11, as translated by Baddeley, p. 308, note 1.
35. According to Okol'nichii, 'he understood very well how to carry on the war, and was successful in command of expeditions. But he was quite incapable to direct affairs in such a crisis as that of 1843' (ibid, p. 11 – Baddeley, p. 365, note 1). Golovin gave of him the following opinion: 'Without denying the military qualities of Klugenau on the battlefield, I have acquired the conviction by long experience that he is not sufficiently to be trusted as administrator of the country confided to his care' – *AKAK*, Vol. IX, pp. 348–50, document No. 317, Golovin to Chernyshev, 15 [27] February 1842, No. 4 (secret), p. 348. (Translation based on Baddeley, p. 365, note 1). For Rosen's opinion of Klugenau in the summer of 1836, see the quotation in Drozdov, p. 289 and Grzegorzewski, 1876, No. 2, pp. 378–9. Réoute, his immediate superior in 1835–36, had a different opinion of Klugenau, and wholeheartedly recommended him as his (Réoute's) successor – Drozdov, p. 285.
36. Grzegorzewski, 1876, No. 2, p. 378.

37. Ibid, p. 379.
38. Ibid, 1876, No. 1, p. 149, No. 2, pp. 378–9.
39. Shaykh Muḥammad, the *qāḍī* of Gimrāh, and Yūsuf Bek, the headman of Qaranay, and a lieutenant in the Russian service.
40. This agreement, the way it was reached, and (at least some of) its stipulations are mentioned in the following sources: *AKAK*, Vol. VIII, pp. 596–7, 601–2, document Nos. 491, 504, 505, 506, 508, Shamil to Réoute, n.d., Shamil to Jamāl the Headman of Chirkah, [22 July 1836], Shamil to Klugenau, n.d., Shamil to Klugenau [2 August 1836], Shamil to 'the General in [Temir-Khān-] Shūra' [Klugenau], n.d.; *Dvizhenie*, pp. 140–2, 151–2, document Nos. 90, 91, 98, 99, Shamil to Klugenau, received 23 June [6 July] 1836, Shamil to Réoute [26 August 1836] (published also in Grzegorzewski, 1876, No. 1, pp. 155–6 and Drozdov, pp. 286–7, where its date is given as 16 [28] August), Shamil to Réoute and Shamil to Klugenau, both not before 4 December 1836; Drozdov, pp. 270, 279, 286, The Elders of Five Villages to the *Shāmkhāl*, received 14 [26] April 1835, Shamil to Klugenau, April 1836, Shamil to Réoute [19 August 1836]; Qarākhī, pp. 50–1, paraphrase of Shamil to Klugenau, n.d.; Grzegorzewski, 1876, No. 1, p. 160, paraphrase of Shamil to Aḥmad Khān and Mīrzā Muḥammad Khān, n.d. And see Runowski's Diary, p. 1483, entry for 22 February [6 March] 1861.
41. For such accusations and denials see, for example, Grzegorzewski, 1876, No. 2, pp. 378–80; Drozdov, p. 289.
42. Iosif Antonovich Réoute [Reutt] was an old Caucasian hand who had served throughout his military career, since his graduation from the Cadet Corps, in the Caucasus. He was too experienced in local politics, and too acquainted with Klugenau, who had served under him for a long time, not to know about the agreement, even without Shamil's references to it in his letters to this general. For Réoute's biography, see *AKAK*, Vol. VII, p. IX, Vol. VIII, p. XV.
43. If indeed Klugenau realised these implications, it might point to the fact that for him this agreement with Shamil was just the first step to lure him into the Russian orbit. It might point to a line of thought arguing that it would be preferable for the Russians to deal with one strong leader, who could pacify and control the entire country, than with a multitude of tribes in a state of constant warfare and anarchy. Shamil appeared to be the best candidate for this role, being the least 'fanatic' among his colleagues, or, in other words, the most pragmatic and the most ready to come to terms with the Russians.
44. *AKAK*, Vol. VIII, pp. 601–2, document No. 505, Shamil to Klugenau, n.d. [1836]; Drozdov, p. 286, Shamil to Réoute [19 August 1836].
45. The above two letters; *AKAK*, Vol. VIII, p. 601, document No. 504, Shamil to Jamāl the Headman of Chrikah [22 July 1836]; Qarākhī, pp. 50–1, paraphrase of Shamil to Klugenau, n.d.
46. But then the loss of legitimacy was small anyway. After all, Shamil must have enjoyed the support of Sayyid Jamāl al-Dīn on this matter, in which he merely followed the line taken by both his predecessors. Furthermore, the legitimacy of his rule was based upon the propagation and enforcement of the *sharīʿa* rather than, or more than, upon *jihād*. Still, the agreement must have caused some damage.

47. D. M. Miliutin, 'Opisanie Voennykh Deistvii 1839 Goda v Severnom Dagestane', *Voenyyi Zhurnal* (1850), No. 1, p. 20 (hereafter: Miliutin); N. Pokrovskii, 'Miurdizm u Vlasti ('Teokraticheskaia Derzhava Shamilia')', *Istorik Marksist* (1934), No. 2 (36), p. 70 (hereafter: Pokrovskii); Bodenstedt, pp. 418–19; Mackie, pp. 193, 201; Grzegorzewski, 1876, No. 1, p. 147. And see *Asar-ı Dağıstan*, p. 140.
48. For Qibid Muḥammad's behaviour, see Grzegorzewski, 1876, No. 1, p. 148; Pokrovskii, pp. 69–70.
49. Qarākhī, p. 39. And see Ḥājj ʿAlī, p. 12.
50. Qarākhī, p. 40; Drozdov, pp. 270, 271.
51. For the events of 1835 and 1836, see Qarākhī, pp. 45–52; *AKAK*, Vol. VIII, pp. 599–609, document Nos. 500, 518, 520, 509, 511, 512, 514, Rosen to Chernyshev, 21 May [2 June], 12 [24], 22 October [3 November], Rosen to Adlerberg, 23, 30 July [4, 11], 6 [18], 20 August [1 September], 1836, document Nos. 497, 1115, 1144, 835, 860, 883, 932 respectively; ibid, p. 597, document No. 492, Rosen to Chernyshev, 19 [31] March 1836, No. 233, (published also in *Dvizhenie*, pp. 139–40, as No. 89); *AKAK*, Vol. VIII. pp. 600–1, document Nos. 502, 503, Rosen to Adlerberg, 2 [14], 9 [21] July 1836, Nos. 728, 748 (published also in *Shamil*, pp. 78, 83, as Nos. 70, 74 respectively); *Materialy*, pp. 360–63, document No. 141, Internal GHQ Report by Schubert, 4 [16] August 1836, No. 75; Grzegorzewski, 1876, No. 1, pp. 146–57, 161–2.
52. *AKAK*, Vol. VIII, pp. 596–7, document No. 491, Shamil to Réoute, n.d.
53. Ibid, pp. 601, 603–4, 358, document Nos. 504, 511, 263, Shamil to Jamāl the Headman of Chirkah [22 July], Rosen to Adlerberg, 30 July [12 August] 1836, No. 860, 'Note on the Ways to Pacify the Caucasian Mountaineers', written probably by Rosen, 1837(?). And see Grzegorzewski, 1876, No. 1, p. 153.
54. Drozdov, p. 264.
55. *AKAK*, Vol. VIII, pp. 596–7, document No. 491, Shamil to Réoute, n.d. (1836?).
56. Grzegorzewski, 1876, No. 1. p. 147.
57. For Ḥājj Tāshō's biography, see R. Sh. Sharafutdinova, 'Pis'mo Naiba Tashev Khadzhi k Shamiliu', *Pis'mennye Pamiatniki Vostoka* (1972), pp 86–7. For further details, see below, note 3 to Chapter 22.
58. Drozdov, pp. 273–4; Mackie, p. 193.
59. Grzegorzewski, 1876, No. 1. p. 148.
60. The stages of Ḥājj Tāshō's acceptance of Shamil's superiority and authority, for example, can be clearly seen in his letters: in 1836 he still tried to appear, at least in Chechnia, on an equal footing with Shamil. Thus, a joint letter by him and Shamil to the Kenak community is addressed – if the awkward Russian translation can be trusted – from 'The *imām* Tāshō and Shamil' (*AKAK*, Vol. VIII, p. 712, document No. 609, also printed in *Shamil*, pp. 91–2, as document No. 82). Soon enough, however, he described himself as the *imām*'s *wazīr* – his letter to Tāz al-Dīn ibn Muṣṭafā, part of which is quoted by Drozdov, p. 292.
61. Grzegorzewski, 1876, No. 1. p. 148.
62. Drozdov (p. 271), for example, stated that Shamil's lieutenants 'terrorised' the population and treated it 'with real beastly ruthlessness'.
63. Ibid, p. 255. Shamil's growing power is reflected clearly in his letters to

the Russian generals. While his early letters contained complaints against his opponents' attacks on him and professed that all he wanted was to be left in peace, by April 1836 the *imām* felt strong enough to ask Klugenau 'not [to] prevent us from fighting amongst ourselves. The bravest among us will, naturally, win, the uncontrolled will be pacified, authority and order will triumph and then, God willing, there will be general peace' – Drozdov, p. 279. More or less at that time Shamil openly stated that the *sharīʿa* was to be implemented either willingly or by force [*'tawʿan aw kurhan'*] – Qarākhī, pp. 50–1. By July he could inform Klugenau that 'this time . . . no one dared to oppose me any more' – *AKAK* Vol. VIII, pp. 601–2, document No. 505, Shamil to Klugenau, n.d. (1836). The same trend appears in his letters to local communities, where from mildly reproaching his correspondents and reminding them of God's wrath towards sinners – ibid, p. 595, document No. 487, Shamil to Maḥmūd-oghlū, April 1835 (published also by Drozdov, pp. 272–3) – he moved to explicit threats to personally punish them – e.g. *AKAK* Vol. VIII, pp. 711, 712, document Nos. 608, 609, Shamil to the Chechen People and Shamil and Ḥājj Tāshō to the Community of Kenak, n.d. (1836) (also published in *Shamil*, pp. 90–2, as Nos. 80, 82).

64. Baha-Eddin Khoursch, *Obrona Twierdzy Achulgo przez Imama Szamila* (Warsaw, 1939), p. 18 (hereafter: Khoursch).
65. E.g. the appointment of *murtāziqs* in Ihalī, as reported in *AKAK*, Vol. VIII, pp. 606–7, document No. 517, Rosen to Chernyshev, 5[17] October 1836, No. 1098.

Chapter 9: Ṭiliq

1. Drozdov, pp. 280–1. For an elaborate exposé of Rosen's views of Shamil, see *AKAK*, Vol. VIII, pp. 603–4, document No. 511, Rosen to Adlerberg, 3 [15] July 1836, No. 860.
2. See his answer to Klugenau's suggestion to negotiate with Shamil, as quoted in Grzegorzewski, 1876, No. 2, p. 378.
3. For the *shāmkhāl*'s illness, death and succession, see *AKAK*, Vol. VIII, pp. 597–600, document Nos. 493, 494, 495, 497, 498, 499, 500, 501, Rosen to Nesselrode, 2 [14] April, Gimbut to Rosen, 8 [20] April, Rosen to Nesselrode, 9 [21] April, Nesselrode to Rosen, 28 April [10 May], Rosen to Nesselrode, 7 [19] May (two dispatches), Rosen to Chernyshev, 21 May [2 June], Nesselrode to Rosen, 23 June [5 July] 1836, Nos. 230, 15, 242, 861, 328, 429 [329?], 497, 1240 respectively; *Materialy*, pp. 139–40, document No. 140, The Imperial Patent to Abū Muslim, 20 June [2 July] 1836.
4. For the death of the *khān* and his succession, see *AKAK*, Vol. VIII, pp. 606–7, document Nos. 515, 516, 517, 519, Rosen to Chernyshev, 10 [22] September, Rosen to Nesselrode, 16 [28] September, Rosen to Chernyshev, 5 [17] October, Nesselrode to Rosen, 13 [25] October 1836, Nos. 1008, 747, 1098, 2302 respectively; *Dvizhenie*, p. 147, document No. 93, Rosen to Chernyshev, 11 [23] September 1836; *Materialy*. pp. 140–1, document No. 63, Imperial Patent to Muḥammad Mīrzā, 27 October [8 November] 1836.

5. Drozdov, p. 275.
6. Ibid., loc. cit. For the events in this theatre of operations, see *AKAK*, Vol. VIII, pp. 699–704, 707–11, 383–98, document Nos. 594, 595, 596, 601, 603, 604, Rosen to Chernyshev, 22 February [6], 2 [14] March, 21 November [3 December] 1835, 2 [14], 23 April [5], 7 [19] May 1836, Nos. 20, 832, 788, 287, 364, 431 respectively, 'Survey of the Military Operations against the Mountain Peoples in the Years 1835, 1836 and 1837' [most probably written by Rosen], specifically p. 388; *Dvizhenie*, pp. 137–8, 142–6, document Nos. 88, 92, Rosen to Chernyshev, 4 [16] July 1835, Pullo to Petrov, 27 August [8 September] 1836. And see Drozdov, pp. 273–7, 280–1.
7. *Materialy*, pp. 351–6, 359–60, document Nos. 136, 140, Rosen's Instructions to Tāz al-Dīn ibn Muṣṭafā, 28 May [9 June], Rosen to Adlerberg, 2 [14] July 1836, Nos. 523, 698 respectively; Drozdov, pp. 290–2. In addition to money, Tāz al-Dīn was rewarded by being appointed *muftī* and *shaykh al-Islām* of the Caucasus. A Russian translation of his proclamation to the mountaineers was published in *Dvizhenie*, p. 167, document No. 106. Part of a letter to him by Ḥājj Tāshō was quoted by Drozdov, p. 292.
8. Ibid, p. 282.
9. *Shamil*, pp. 80–1, document No. 72, Rosen to Réoute, 8 [20] July 1836, No. 728; *AKAK*, Vol. VIII, pp. 601, 603, document Nos. 503, 510, Rosen to Adlerberg 2 [14], 28 July [9 August] 1836, Nos. 748, 854 respectively (the former was also published in *Shamil*, p. 83, as document No. 74); Drozdov, p. 282.
10. Ibid, pp. 282–4; *AKAK*, Vol. VIII, pp. 712–14, document No. 610, Rosen to Chernyshev, 10 [22] September 1836, No. 106; Grzegorzewski, 1876, No. 1, p. 158. That it indeed happened and Shamil's rule was re-established immediately upon Russian withdrawal, was reported in *AKAK*, Vol. VIII, pp. 715–16, document No. 613, Rosen to Chernyshev, 10 [22] December 1836, No. 1307.
11. Ibid., pp. 604–6, document No. 513, Rosen to Adlerberg, 13 [25] August 1836, No. 919; Drozdov, pp. 285–6; Grzegorzewski, 1876, No. 1, pp. 154–5.
12. *AKAK*, Vol. VIII, pp. 607–9, document Nos. 520, 521, Rosen to Chernyshev, 22, 29 October [3, 10 November] 1836, Nos. 1144, 1164 respectively; *Dvizhenie*, pp. 148–9, document No. 95, Rosen to Chernyshev, 19 [31] October 1836; Drozdov, pp. 284–9; Grzegorzewski, 1876, No. 1, pp. 157–60.
13. Drozdov, p. 290. Indeed, Shamil's rule spread into new areas. And see Grzegrozewski, 1876, No. 1, pp. 154–7, 161–2.
14. *AKAK*, Vol. VIII, p. 602, document Nos. 506, 508, Shamil to Klugenau [2 April] 1836 and n.d.; *Dvizhenie*, pp. 140–2, document Nos. 90, 91, Shamil to Klugenau, received 23 June [6 July], Shamil to Réoute [26 August] 1836; Drozdov, p. 286; Qarākhī, pp. 50–1.
15. *AKAK*, Vol. VIII, p. 602, document No. 508, Shamil to 'the General in [Temir-Khān-] Shūra', n.d. (1836).
16. E.g. *Shamil*, pp. 90–1, document No. 81, Shamil's Appeal to the Community of Ankraṭl.
17. *Dvizhenie*, pp. 149–50, 151–2, document Nos. 96, 98, 99, Letter from Klugenau to Jamāl, the Headman of Chirkah, 28 October [9 November]

1836 (obviously a misprint for 28 December 1836 [9 January 1837]), Shamil to Klugenau and to Réoute, both not before 22 November [9 December] 1836 respectively. And see ibid., pp. 150–1, document No. 97, 'Conditions to be Imposed on Submitting Mountaineers', not later than 19 November [1 December] 1836.

18. This measure was introduced due to Rosen's suspicion that Klugenau had private dealings with Shamil, for which see Grzegorzewski, 1876, No. 2, pp. 378–80.
19. *Dvizhenie*, pp. 150–1, document No. 97, 'Conditions to Be Imposed on Submitting Mountaineers' not later than 19 November [1 December] 1836. The quotation is from p. 150.
20. Ibid, p. 166, document No. 105, Klugenau to Réoute, 5 [17] April 1837. Shamil might have been prompted to this initiative by the devastating defeat dealt to Klugenau about a month previously, for which see below, note 27.
21. Iurov, Vol. VIII, pp. 3–6.
22. *AKAK*, Vol. IX, p XXIX.
23. Baddeley, p. 304.
24. Vel'iaminov to Ermolov, Stavropol', 19 [22] January 1838, as quoted by E. G. Weidenbaum, 'Bergengeim i Gordeev', in *KavKazskie Etiudy*, p. 290. And see A. I. Gagarin, 'Zapiski o Kavkaze', *Voennyi Sbornik* (1906), No. 2, p. 30 (hereafter: Gagarin + No. of *VS*).
25. For this expedition, see *AKAK*, Vol. VIII, pp. 716–22, document No. 618, Rosen to Chernyshev, 11 [23] February 1837, No. 186; Iurov, Vol. VIII, pp. 7–13. For a few raids conducted by the Russians before Faesy's arrival, see *AKAK*, Vol. VIII, pp. 716–18, document Nos. 614, 615, 616, 617, Rosen to Chernyshev, 7 [19], 21, 29 January (two reports), [2, 10 February] 1837, Nos. 13, 54, 97, 116 respectively; *Dvizhenie*, pp. 153–5, document No. 102, Rosen to Chernyshev, 9 [21] January 1837; Iurov, Vol. VIII, pp. 6–7.
26. For this campaign, see *AKAK*, Vol. VIII, pp. 722–8, document Nos. 619, 620, 621, 622, 623, 624, 625, Rosen to Chernyshev, 23 February [7], 4 [16], 11 [23], 25, 31 March [6. 11], 12 [26] April, 30 May [11 June] 1836, Nos. 224, 273, 315, 374, 413, 466, 652 respectively; *Dvizhenie*, pp. 155–6, 162–5, document Nos. 102, 104, 'Evidence by the Elder ʿAlī Ghāzī ibn Muḥammad from ʿAndī, Captured at the Battle near the Village of Avtiri' 10 [22] February, Faesy to Vel'iaminov, 15 [27] March 1837; Iurov, Vol. VIII, pp. 13–20, 30–7; Grzegorszewski, 1876, No. 2, pp. 380–1, 383–7.
27. To assist Faesy, Klugenau was ordered to carry out a diversion against Shamil in Daghestan. This ended in disaster, though through no fault of Klugenau, when his advance guard, consisting of no more than 240 men, was routed, resulting in 71 men killed and captured and 17 wounded – *Dvizhenie*, pp. 156–62, document No. 102, Rosen to Chernyshev, 15 [27] March 1837; Iurov, Vol. VIII. pp. 20–30; Grzegorzewski, 1876, No. 2, pp. 381–3. For a good English summary, see Baddeley, pp. 289–94. Faesy did not lose time in accusing Klugenau in this disaster – in his report of 19 [31] March 1837, No. 240, quoted in Iurov, Vol. VIII, pp. 29–30 – thereby starting their feud. For a further development in the feud between the two, see 'Iz Proshlogo Dagestanskoi oblasti. (Po Mestnym Arkhivnym Dannym)', *Dagestanskii Sbornik*, Vol. II, pp. 203–7.

28. Iurov, Vol. VIII, p. 38.
29. Baddeley, p. 294.
30. See above, p. 82. The words within quotation marks are from Iurov, Vol. VIII, p. 39.
31. For details see ibid., pp. 39–40;; Baddeley, pp. 294–5. And see Ḥājj ʿAlī, pp. 14–15.
32. Iurov, Vol. VIII, p. 40. Translation based on Baddeley p. 295. In parallel, Rosen asked St. Petersburg's approval for this move – *Materialy*, pp. 363–8, document No. 142, Rosen to Chernyshev, 29 January [10 February] 1837, No. 99.
33. Rosen to Klugenau (secret), 6 [18] February 1837, No. 153, as quoted in Iurov, Vol. VIII, p. 41. Translation based on Baddeley, pp. 295–6.
34. Initially Klugenau was intended to command the expedition, but his political approach did not match Rosen's. *Inter alia*, Klugenau suggested that on reaching Khunzakh it should be explained to the local population that the occupation 'has been undertaken in reply to the wish of the population itself, because the Russian government, disregarding any expenses and trouble, is always ready to defend those who remain loyal to it, and that, finally, *our troops will stay in Khunzakh for a limited period of time only, just until peace and the authority of Aḥmād Khān are re-established*' – Iurov, Vol. VIII, pp. 41–2, (emphasis added). Rosen, therefore, decided to nominate Faesy as commander of the expedition. Klugenau, 'rather than serve under [Faesy] pleaded sickness and took a leave of absence for the summer' – Baddeley, p. 294. How correct Klugenau's approach had been was testified to by Kostenecki, pp. 57 and 98.
35. Iurov, Vol. VIII, pp. 44–51 (quotation from p. 51); Kostenecki, pp. 9–57. Faesy chose the roundabout road because he had information that Shamil intended to block the direct road from Temir-Khān-Shūra to Khunzakh – Qarākhī, pp. 51–2; Iurov, Vol. VIII, pp. 43–4. 'The difficulties of the route may be imagined from the fact that it had taken this picked corps – with heavy transport it is true – twenty days to cover 100 miles' – Baddeley, p. 297.
36. For its description, see Iurov, Vol. VIII, pp. 51–4; Baddeley, pp. 297–8.
37. It took two days for all the units to assemble.
38. For the description of the battle, see Iurov, Vol. VIII, pp. 58–63; Kostenecki, pp. 65–70. For a good English summary, see Baddeley, pp. 299–301.
39. Iurov, Vol. VIII, p. 63. Translation based on Baddeley, p. 301.
40. For the description of the conquest of Akhulgoḥ, see Iurov, Vol. VIII, pp. 63–5; Kostenecki, pp. 73–4, 79–81; Baddeley p. 301.
41. Iurov, Vol. VIII, pp. 65–7; Kostenecki, pp. 81–5; Baddeley, pp. 301–2. According to another Russian general, Faesy was 'in a desperate situation from which he extricated himself with a huge loss, leaving part of his camp' – Pavel Khristoforovich Grabbe, 'Iz Dnevnika i Zapisnoi Knizhki Grafa P. Kh. Grabbe. 1839-i God. (Komandovanie na Kavkazskoi Linii i v Severnom Dagestane)', *Russkii Arkhiv*, (1888) No. 6, p. 110, entry for 8 [20] June 1839 (hereafter: Grabbe). And see A[natolii Vladimirovich] O[rlov]-D[avydov]. 'Chastnoe Pis'mo o Vziatii Shamilia', *Russkii Arkhiv* (1869), No. 6, c. 1056; Gagarin No. 2, p. 31.
42. Iurov, Vol. VIII, pp. 70–2. For the description of the battle and the

negotiations, see ibid., pp. 67–71; *AKAK*, Vol. VIII, p. 617, document No. 530, Rosen to Chernyshev, 12 [24] August 1837, No. 816; *Dvizhenie*, pp. 168–9, document No. 107, Rosen to Cherneyshev, 31 July [12 August] 1837; Grzegorzewski, 1876, No. 3, pp. 645–9; Gagarin, No. 2, p. 31; Kostenecki, pp. 90–6; Bodenstedt, pp. 422–30; Baddeley, pp. 302–4; Ḥājj ʿAlī, pp. 15, 17; Britain, Public Record Office, Foreign Office Archives (hereafter: PRO), FO/65/235, Milbank to Palmerston, St. Petersburg, 10 July, 23 August 1837, Nos. 9, 23, respectively, summarising the reports of the French consul in Tiflis.

43. Faesy to Rosen, 12 [24] July 1837, No. 45, as quoted by Iurov, Vol. VIII, p. 75.
44. *AKAK*, Vol. VIII, p. 618, document No. 512, Faesy to Rosen, 30 August [11 September] 1837, No. 73.
45. Iurov, Vol. VIII, p. 72. Translation based on Baddeley, p. 304. According to Vel'iaminov, 'last year he [Faesy] was sent to Daghestan, where he lost all his horses of exhaustion and, due to his awkward orders, sustained a considerable loss of men. But since he shamelessly lied in his report he was decorated' – Vel'iaminov to Ermolov, Stavropol', 10 [22] January 1838, as quoted in Weidenbaum, 'Bergengeim i Gordev', in *Kavkazski Etiudy*, pp. 290–1. And see Kostenecki, p. 96. The breakdown of the Russian casualties is reported as follows: in Shamil's attempt to break out of Ṭiliq (the night of 19–20 June) – 94 killed and 187 wounded; in the conquest of 'Ashilṭa – 28 killed and 158 wounded; in the conquest of Akhulgoḥ – 8 killed and 15 wounded; in the battle of 27–28 June – 33 killed and 134 wounded; during the storm of Ṭiliq – 92 killed and 256 wounded. In addition, it is reported that 5 wounded and 55 sick men were left in Khunzakh when Faesy marched on 'Ashilṭa (17 June).
46. *AKAK*, Vol. VIII, p. 618, document No. 512, Faesy to Rosen, 30 August [11 September] 1837, No. 72. And see Bodenstedt, pp. 425–6.
47. Iurov, Vol. VIII, Appendix No. 1, p. 1 (separate pagination). Translation based on Baddeley, p. 305. (Also printed in *AKAK*, Vol. VIII, p. 602, as document No. 507, where it is placed between documents dated 21 and 28 July [2 and 9 August] 1836, and in Grzegorzewski, 1876, No. 3, pp. 647–48.)
48. Iurov, Vol. VIII, Appendix No. 2, pp. 1–2 (separate pagination). Translation based on Baddeley pp. 305–6. (Also published in Grzegorzewski, 1876, No. 3, pp. 648–9.)
49. 'The acceptance by General Faesy,' analysed a Russian author, 'of such letters attesting to the conclusion of *peace* with Shamil was a political mistake; it officially consolidated in the eyes of the natives the *imām*'s title as the worldly and religious sovereign of the unsubmitting communities, whereas up until then no one but himself had considered him to be their ruler' – Iurov, Vol. VIII, p, 71. Translation based on Baddeley, p. 303. And see the criticism in A. A. Gordeev, *Istoriia Kazakov*, Vol. III (Paris, 1970), p. 226.
50. And see Rasul Hamzatov [Gamzatov], *Moi Dagestan* (Moscow, 1972), p. 297 (hereafter: Hamzatov).
51. Bodenstedt, pp. 430–4. Translation by Mackie, pp. 202–6. And see the inscription on the grave of Ḥamza Bek in Khunzakh, *Epigraficheskie Pamiatniki*, pp. 100–3, inscription No. 649.

52. Such an interpretation of a sudden relief is not uncommon in history, and cf. II Kings; 19; 35–6.
53. *AKAK*, Vol. VIII, p. 618, document No. 532, Faesy to Rosen, 30 August [11 September] 1837, No. 73.
54. Text in ibid., pp. 617–8, document No. 531.
55. Ibid., p. 618, document 532.
56. 12 [24] July 1837, No. 732, as quoted in Iurov, Vol. VIII, p. 77.
57. Adlerberg to Rosen, 10 [22] August 1837, No. 159, as reprinted in Iurov, Vol. VIII, pp. 76–8. Also see *AKAK* Vol. VIII, pp. 620–1, document No. 536, Rosen to Adlerberg, 25 September [7 October] 1837, No. 275; *Materialy*, pp. 371–2, document No. 145, Rosen to Chernyshev, 4 [16] October 1837, No. 1099.
58. Rosen to Faesy, 21 August [2 September] 1837, as printed in Grzégorzewski, 1876, No. 3, pp. 650–1.
59. This was, of course, a great personal and political victory for Klugenau.
60. Text of letter in Iurov, Vol. VIII, pp. 79–80, and Grzegorzewski, 1876, No. 3, p. 652.
61. Shamil's letter to Klugenau, 28 September 1837, in Iurov, Vol. VIII, p. 80; Grzegorzewski, loc. cit.; Klugenau's letter to Shamil of the same date, in Iurov, Vol. VIII, pp. 80–1; Grzegorzewski, 1876, No. 3, p. 653.
62. Iurov, Vol. VIII, pp. 81–2: Grzegorzewski, 1876, No. 3, pp. 653–4. Shamil, indeed, sent on 1 October messengers to consult the abovementioned persons.
63. Iurov, Vol. VIII, p. 82. When, at the end of the meeting, Klugenau stretched out his hand to greet Shamil, one of the *imām*'s bodyguards prevented this handshake. Klugenau in anger had to be restrained from drawing his sword. For a longer and more dramatic description of the meeting, see Baddeley, pp. 307–10.
64. Iurov, Vol. VIII, p. 83.
65. Ibid., pp. 83–4; Grzegorzewski, 1876, No. 3, pp. 654–5.
66. Iurov, Vol. VIII, p. 84; Grzegorzewski, 1876, No. 3, p. 656.
67. Iurov, Vol. VIII, p. 85; Grzegorzewski, 1876, No. 3, pp. 655–6.
68. For the emperor's visit to the Caucasus, see A. P. Bergé, 'Imperator Nikolai na Kavkaze v 1837 G.', *Russkaia Starina* (1884), No. 8. pp. 377–98; Kundukh, 1936, No. 1 (25), pp. 14–16.
69. Iurov, Vol. VIII, pp. 85–6.
70. Ibid., p. 86. (Also published in *Materialy*, p. 371 under No. 144 and Grzegorzewski, 1876, No. 3, p. 657.) Translation based on Baddeley, pp. 310–11.
71. *AKAK*, Vol. VIII, p. 618, document No. 532, Faesy to Rosen, 30, August [11 September] 1837, No. 73. The only exception was Klugenau, of whom Shamil 'spoke with special praise' and in whom 'he has great trust' – *Dvizhenie*, pp. 412–23, document No. 221, 'Excerpts from the Debriefing of Lt. Orbeliani, Who Had Been in Shamil's Captivity in 1842'. Quotation from p. 422.
72. His letter to Shamil, 19 September [1 October] 1837, reproduced by Iurov, Vol. VIII, p. 83; Grzegorzewski, 1876, No. 3, pp. 654–5.

Chapter 10: Akhulgoḥ

1. For Golovin's biography, see Iurii Tolstoi, 'Ocherk Zhizni i Sluzhby E. A. Golovina', in Petr Bartenev (ed.), *Deviatnadtsatyi Vek. Istoricheskii Sbornik*, Vol. I (Moscow, 1872), pp. 1–64 (pp. 43–58 deal with the period of his command in the Caucasus). For a comment on it, see M. Shcherbinin, 'Zametka po Povodu Ocherka Zhizni i Sluzhby E. A. Golovina', *Russkii Arkhiv* (1879), No. 3–4, cc. 707–17. Additional material is supplied in an extensive editorial note in *Arkhiv Raevskikh*, Vol. II, pp. 418–21 (note to letter No. 549, Golovin to N. N. Raevskii, Tiflis, 5 May 1838).
2. [Evgenii Aleksandrovich Golovin,] 'Ocherk Polozheniia Voennykh Del na Kavkaze s Nachala 1838 do Kontsa 1842 Goda', *Kavkazskii Sbornik*, Vol. II, p. 5 (hereafter: Golovin). For the situation of the Caucasus in the beginning of 1838, see ibid., pp. 1–8; Iurov, Vol. VIII, pp. 159–61.
3. For this revolt, see *AKAK*, Vol. VIII, pp. 610–11, 612–17, 618–20, 621–22, document No. 523, 525, 526, 527, 528, 529, 533, 535, 537, 538, 539, Réoute to Rosen, 14 [21] February, Rosen to Chernyshev, 8 [20] May, Potocki to Rosen, 10 [22] May, Rosen to Réoute, 11 [23] May, Potocki to Rosen, 15 [27] May, Olenich to Rosen, 27 June [9 July], Rosen to Adlerberg 9 [21], 10 [22], 26 September [3 October], Adlerberg to Rosen 5 [17], 11 [23] October 1837, Nos. 4, 167, 25, 298, 29, 1, 921, 985, 931, 288, 398, 452, respectively, Vol. IX, pp. 204–9, document No. 222, Golovin to Chernyshev (secret), 7 [19] April 1838, No. 454 and annexed to it, Rosen to Chernyshev, 10 [22] December 1837, No. 981; *Dvizhenie*, p. 178, document No. 913, Rosen to Chernyshev, 14 [26] March 1838; MRE, CPC, Russie, Tiflis, Vol. 1, ff. 19–21, Ratti-Menton to the Foreign Minister, Tiflis, 15/27, 24 September/16 October 1837, Nos. 35, 36 respectively; Iurov, Vol. VIII, pp. 103–17; A. S. Sumbatzade, *Kubinskoe Vosstanie 1837 G.* (Bāqū, 1962) (hereafter: Sumbatzade).
4. For these hostilities, see *AKAK*, Vol. VIII, pp. 704–8, 710, 711, document Nos. 597, 598, 599, 600, 602, 605, 607, Shirokii to Rosen, 17 February [1 March], Rosen to Shirokii, 20 February [4 March]; Shirokii to Rosen, 5 [17], 19 [31] March, Rosen to Malinovskii, 30 April [12 May], Rosen to Chernyshev, 21 May [2 June] 1836, Nos. 386, 1255, 529, 637, 884, 391, 496 respectively.
5. *AKAK*, Vol. VIII, pp. 518–25, document Nos. 396, 397, 398, 399, 400, Bebutov to Rosen (with appendices), 5 [17], 24 June [6 July], Rosen to Chernyshev (secret), 13 [25] July, Adlerberg to Rosen, 31 August [12 September] 1837, Bebutov to Rosen, 12 [24] March 1838, Nos. 4000, 4492, 37, 278, 1838 respectively.
6. The expedition 'weakened the mountaineers to such an extent that they could initiate nothing particular against us in 1838' – Iurov, Vol. VIII, pp. 75–6. For the situation in the later part of 1837, see *AKAK*, Vol. VIII, pp. 622–5, document Nos. 540, 541, 542, 543, 545, Rosen to Chernyshev, 24, 25 October [5, 6 November] (two despatches), 9 [21] December 1837, 19 [31] January 1838, Nos. 1057, 1059, 1195, 1252, 80 respectively; *Dvizhenie*, pp. 172–5, document No. 110, Rosen to Chernyshev, 29 October [10 November] 1837; *Materialy*, pp 376–9, document No. 147, Rosen to Chernyshev, 29 December 1837 [10 January 1838], No. 1361.
7. Iurov, Vol. VIII, pp. 164–6. For the situation in Southern Deghestan, see

AKAK, Vol. IX, pp. 209–12, document Nos. 223, 224, 225, Golovin to Chernyshev, 12 [24], 19 [31], 20 May [1 June] 1838 (secret), Nos. 612, 635, 122.

8. For a detailed description of this campaign, see *AKAK*, Vol. IX, pp. 213–17, document Nos. 227, 228, 229, 230, 231, 232, 233, Golovin to Chernyshev, 2 [14] June, Faesy to Golovin, 5 [17] June, (published also in *Dvizhenie*, pp. 181–3, as document No. 155, where its date is given mistakenly as 5 July), 8 [20], 10 [22], 15 [27] June, Golovin to Chernyshev, 11 [23], 24 August [5 September], 1838, Nos. 753, 243, 3, 4, 48, 1212, 1335 respectively; Iurov, Vol. VIII, pp. 206–11. A brief summary is given in Golovin, pp. 10–11.
9. *AKAK*, Vol. IX, pp. 217–18, 318–21, documents Nos. 234, 285, 286, Golovin to Chernyshev, 9 [21], 13 [25], 14 [26] September 1838, Nos. 1491, 1538, 1544 respectively. Again, so 'successful' was Faesy that the following year Golovin himself had to mount a major campaign in that area.
10. This 'campaign' is described in *AKAK*, Vol. IX, pp. 315–18, document Nos. 283, 284, Golovin to Chernyshev, 18 [30], 26 August [7 September] 1836, Nos. 1290, 1375 respectively. (The former report is published also in *Dvizhenie*, pp. 184–6, as document No. 117); Iurov, Vol. VIII, pp. 211–17; Golovin gives a brief resumé on p. 11. And see Qarākhī, p. 59.
11. For this campaign, see Iurov, Vol. VIII, pp. 219–21.
12. Baddeley, p. 313. For the situation in Daghestan during the first half of 1838, see *AKAK*, Vol. IX, pp. 212–13, 308–9, 312–14, 315, document Nos, 226, 276, 277, 279, 280, 281, 282, Golovin to Chernyshev, 25 May [6 June] (published also in *Dvizhenie*, pp 178–81, as document No. 114), Chernyshev to Golovin 6 [18] February, Faesy to Rosen, 16 [28] March, Golovin to Chernyshev, 25 April [7] , 9 [21] May, Faesy to Golovin 23 June [6], 4 [16] July, 1838, Nos 692, 91, 77, 517, 770, 60, 67 respectively; *Dvizhenie*, pp. 176–7, document No. 112, Rosen to Chernyshev, 16 [28] February 1838; *Materialy*, pp. 385–93, document Nos. 149, 150, Rosen to Chernyshev, 1 [13] February, 4 [16] March 1838, Nos. 151, 264 respectively. For the events there after Faesy's withdrawal, see *AKAK*, Vol. IX, pp. 221–2, 321, document Nos. 238, 239, 288, Kotzebue to Chernyshev, 27 October [8 November], Golovin to Chernyshev, 10 [22], 19 November [1 December] 1838, Nos. 1872, 1958, 2026 respectively; *Dvizhenie*, pp. 186–7, document No. 118, Golovin to Chernyshev, 2 [14] December 1838; *Materialy*, pp. 393–7, document No. 151, Grabbe to Chernyshev, 31 October [12 November] 1838.
13. Qarākhī, pp. 57–8. Khoursch's (p. 11) assertion that this meeting was held at the beginning of 1835 is contradicted by all the available sources.
14. Khoursch, p. 12.
15. Sumbatzade, p. 111.
16. Khoursch, p. 25. The author, in his enthusiasm, overevaluates Shamil's influence on the events in Southern Daghestan during this entire period (1837–39).
17. Quoted by Sumbatzade, pp. 111–12.
18. For Shamil's relations with the Ottomans and with Muḥammad ʿAlī, see below, pp. 257–61.

19. Miliutin, p. 20. Translation by Baddeley, p. 313.
20. *AKAK*, Vol. IX, p. 321, document No 287, Golovin to Pullo (secret), 17, [29] November 1838, No. 2008/28. The sum offered was 3,000 *rubles*.
21. Iurov, Vol. IX, p. 3. Similarly, Golovin, p. 15. For a full elaboration of the planning, with the emperor's changes in it, see *AKAK*, Vol. IX, pp. 227–39, document Nos. 245, 246, Golovin to Chernyshev, 15 [27] December 1838, Chernyshev to Golovin, 15 [27] January 1839, Nos. 2161, 296 respectively. (These documents were also published in Iurov, Vol. IX, Appendices XII A and XII B, pp. 1–9 [separate pagination].) For the campaign itself, see *Dvizhenie*, pp. 197–208, document No. 125, 'Excerpts from the War Diary of the Main Force Operating against the Mountaineers of the Samur Valley, from 27 May [8] to 12 [24] June [1839]'; Iurov, Vol. IX, pp. 92–115; Golovin, pp. 18–21; Baddeley, p. 343; Khoursch, pp. 147–50. Also see *AKAK*, Vol. IX, pp. 222–5, 239–41, document Nos. 240, 241, 242, 247, 248, Golovin to Chernyshev, 23 July [4 August]; Chernyshev to Golovin, 19 [31] August; Golovin to Chernyshev, 24 August [5 September], 21 March [2 April] (two reports), Nos. 207, 5038, 1440, 558, 566 respectively; *Dvizhenie*, pp. 193–4, document No. 123. Proclamation of Golovin to the Mountaineers of the Samur Valley, 26 May [7 June] 1839 (also published in Iurov, Vol. IX, Appendix XXII, pp. 17–19 [separate pagination]); Orders of the Day by Golovin and Simborskii, 25 May [6], 11 [23] June 1839, ibid., Appendices XXI, XXIII, pp. 16–17, 18–20 (separate pagination) respectively; *Arkhiv Raevskikh*, Vol. III, pp. 156–63, letter Nos. 686, 687, 688, Mend, Golovin and Kotzebue to Raevskii, 8, [20], 11 [23], 12 [24] June 1839 respectively.
22. Iurov, Vol. IX, p. 3. Similarly, Golovin, pp. 15–16; Miliutin, pp. 21–3. And see the documents mentioned in the previous note.
23. *AKAK*, Vol. IX, pp. XVIII-XIX.
24. Miliutin, p. 47. Similarly, Iurov, Vol. IX, pp. 23–4.
25. Ibid., p. 10; Miliutin, pp. 26–7. The conditions of surrender offered to Shamil are detailed in *AKAK*, Vol. IX, p. 326, document No. 294, Golovin to Chernyshev, 27 April [9 May] 1839, No. 875.
26. Miliutin, p. 27. Similarly, Iurov, Vol. IX, p. 10.
27. For the transfer of the population of three such villages, see Khoursch, pp. 30–1; Miliutin, pp. 27–8; Iurov, Vol. IX, pp. 10–12. For the activities of both sides during the first four months of 1839, see *AKAK*, Vol. IX, pp. 321–6, document Nos, 289, 290, 291, 292, 293, Golovin to Chernyshev, 17 February [1 March], Kotzebue to Chernyshev, 24 February [8 March] (also published in *Dvizhenie*, pp. 189–90, as document No. 121), 3 [15], 9 [21] March, Golovin to Chernyshev, 31 March [12 April] 1839, Nos. 295, 390, 435, 476, 674 respectively; *Dvizhenie*, pp. 187–9, document Nos. 119, 120, Panteleev to Pullo, 7 [19] February, Kotzebue to Chernyshev, 15 [27] February 1839 respectively.
28. Iurov, Vol. IX, pp. 13–14; Miliutin, pp. 29–31; Khoursch, pp. 26–7, 30–2; Grabbe, p. 102, entry for 6 [18] May 1839.
29. Golovin, p. 22. For a detailed description of the campaign, see *Materialy*, pp. 414–15, document No. 157, Grabbe to Chernyshev, 18 [30] May 1839; Iurov, Vol. IX, pp. 14–22; Miliutin, pp. 35–42. And see Grabbe, pp. 103–4; Baddeley p. 316.
30. This account is based on the following sources: *AKAK*, Vol. IX,

pp. 326–38, document Nos. 296, 297, 298, 299, Grabbe to Chernyshev, 26 May [7], 1 [13] June, Grabbe to Golovin, 24, 28 August [5, 10, September] 1839, Nos. 86, 97, 456, 498 respectively; *Dvizhenie*, pp. 194–6, 208–13, document Nos. 124, 126, War Diaries of the Force Operating on the Left Flank from 1 [13] to 10 [22] June and from 25 June [7] to 5 [17] July 1839; *Materialy*, pp. 415–24, document Nos. 158, 160, 159, Excerpts from the War Diary of the Left Flank, 4 [16]–14 [26] July, 29 August [10]–9 [21] September, Grabbe to Chernyshev, 29 August [10 September] 1839, No. 497; MRE, CPC, Russie, Tiflis, Vol. 1, ff. 31–6, Rivoire to the Foreign Minister, Tiflis, 1/13 June, 25 June/11 July, 1/13 September 1839, Nos. 7–9, 10, 11 respectively; PRO, FO/65/251, Clarricard to Palmerston, St. Petersburg, 4 February, 29 August/10 September, 30 November 1839, Nos. 16, 21, 107 respectively, FO/65/255, Yeames to Palmerston, Odessa, 19 April, 16 July, 12 October 1839, Nos. 1, 2, 7 respectively, FO/78/366, f. 31, Brant to Palmerston, Erzeroom, 22 April 1839, No. 8; Grabbe, pp. 104–26; Golovin, pp. 22–4; Miliutin, pp. 45–121; Iurov, Vol. IX, pp. 24–83; Gagarin, No. 2, pp. 32–3; Baddeley, pp. 317–41; Ḥājj ʿAlī, p. 18; Qarākhī, pp. 60–71; Khoursch, pp. 42–134; Bodenstedt, pp. 437–52.

31. Miliutin, pp. 48–9; Iurov, Vol IX, pp 24–5. Khoursch (p. 45) states that Shamil had at his disposal c. 1,000 men.
32. Miliutin, pp. 51–2; See also Iurov, Vol. IX, pp. 24–8.
33. According to Russian sources 16,000 men. Khoursch (p. 50) details Shamil's forces and their positions and totals them at 2,900 men.
34. Golovin, p. 22. And see Grabbe, p. 107; Miliutin, p. 57; Iurov, Vol. IX, p. 30. The 'masses' were the bands of Ḥājj Tāshō and Murtaḍā-ʿAlī [Murtazali] Muḥammad – Khoursch, p. 51.
35. Golovin, p. 22.
36. The Russian losses numbered 646, including one general killed. The mountaineers' losses approximated, according to Khoursch (p. 62), 600.
37. Grabbe, p. 111, entry for 11 [23] June 1839. And see pp. 105, 106, 109, 110, entries for 23, 27 May [4, 8], 5 [17], 9[21], 10 [22] June respectively; Miliutin, pp. 61–7; Iurov, Vol. IX, p. 37; Baddeley, p. 322.
38. Golovin, p. 23. And see Miliutin, p. 75. Two attempts to storm Old Akhulgoḥ, on 25 and 31 June, were completely unsuccessful – Grabbe, pp. 111 and 112 respectively. How considerable the losses were can be learnt from the fact that in spite of an addition of a few units, most notably an infantry battalion (the one which had accompanied the supplies from Temir-Khān-Shūra), the Russian forces' strength dropped from a total of 8,513 men before the storm of Irghin to 7,672 men at the beginning of the siege of Akhulgoḥ – Miliutin, Appendices 4 and 5, pp. 137–9. The militias of the Khanates which now joined Grabbe totalling c. 3,600 men were, as always, completely unreliable, and Grabbe had to ask Golovin for reinforcements – Miliutin, pp. 81–2; Iurov, Vol. IX, pp. 46–7.
39. According to Khoursch (p. 82), Akhbirdi Muḥammad and Galbats Dibīr crossed the river to Akhulgoḥ on the night of 29–30 June to receive instructions from Shamil.
40. Miliutin, p. 84.
41. Baddeley, p. 326. The 'reconnaissance in force' was, in fact, a full-fledged attack – Grabbe, p. 112, entry for 19 June [1 July} 1839.

42. Baddeley, pp. 323–4.
43. Miliutin, Appendix 6, p. 140.
44. Golovin, pp. 23–4. One can, however, understand – though not justify – Grabbe's decision. In this kind of warfare, in which will-power and stamina are of prime importance, the protagonists' spirits seem to change swiftly from one extremity to the other. Exasperated by this war of nerves, they often tend to take high risks and make attempts at what looks to them like short-cuts to victory.
45. Grabbe, p. 118, entry for 20 July [1 August] 1839.
46. Miliutin, p. 108.
47. Grabbe, pp. 119–20, entries for 1, 2 [13, 14] August 1839.
48. Ibid., p. 113, entry for 27 June [9 July] 1839.
49. Ibid., p. 118, entry for 24 July [5 August] 1839.
50. Reproduced in Miliutin, Appendix 7, pp. 140–1; Iurov, Vol. IX, Appendix XIV, p. 12 (separate pagination).
51. Grabbe, p. 119, entry for 27 July [8 August] 1839.
52. Miliutin, p. 112. 'He spoke with the dignity becoming a leader of a fighting party' – Iurov, Vol. IX, p. 74.
53. Ibid., pp. 73–4.
54. Grabbe, p. 119, entry for 28 July [9 August] 1839.
55. Ibid., p. 121, entry for 7 [19] August 1839.
56. Ibid., p. 122–3, entries for 12, 15 [24, 27] August 1839.
57. Ibid., p. 123, entry for 16 [28] August 1839.
58. Miliutin, p. 133; Iurov, Vol. IX, p. 74.
59. Ibid., pp. 76–7.
60. What is meant here is Faesy's 1837 agreement with Shamil.
61. *AKAK*, Vol. X, p. 505, document No. 456, Affidavit by Major-General Wolf [Vol'f], 9 [26] July 1850.
62. Russian translations in Miliutin, Appendices 7, 8, pp. 140–3, and in Iurov, Vol. IX, Appendices XVII A, XVII B, pp. 12–14 (separate pagination).
63. Grabbe, p. 123, entry for 19 [31] August 1839.
64. Qarākhī, pp. 66–7.
65. Iurov, Vol. IX, p. 78.
66. E.g. Qarākhī, p. 64; Khoursch, pp. 118–19.
67. Grabbe was so determined that 'before the final attack he had already decided that in case of failure, he would continue the siege even throughout the *entire* winter' – Miliutin, p. 123 (emphasis in original).
68. E.g. Khoursch, pp. 118–22; Qarākhī, pp. 64–71.
69. Two bodies, which had been preserved in one of the caverns, became later a focus of pilgrimage until the Russians authorities felt compelled to forbid entry to the area – Baddeley, *Rugged Flanks*, Vol. II, p. 32.
70. For the details of his escape, see Qarākhī, pp. 81–8; Millutin, pp. 120–1; Baddeley, pp. 341–2.
71. *AKAK*, Vol. IX, p. 333, document No. 298, Grabbe to Golovin, 24 August [5 September] 1839, No. 456.
72. Iurov gives the following numbers of casualties: Grabbe's campaign in Chechnia – 26 killed and 152 wounded; the battle near Burtinah – 4 killed and 35 wounded; the conquest of Irghin – 140 killed and 506 wounded; the battle with Akhbirdi Muḥammad – 9 killed and 84 wounded; first storming of Shulatl ul-guḥ – 36 killed, 279 wounded; second storming of

Shultatl ul-Guḥ – 11 killed and 94 wounded; first storming of Akhulgoḥ – 160 killed and 716 wounded; second storming of Akhulgoḥ – 102 killed and 400 wounded; third storming of Akhulgoḥ – 156 killed and 512 wounded; the battle of Chirkah – 55 killed and 95 wounded; the total number of losses for the siege of Akhulgoḥ – 3,069. The total number of casualties during the entire campaign was (according to Iurov) 3,913. One should remember that those who died or became indisposed because of illness, though not counted here, were much more numerous.

73. See Golovin's criticism (p. 29).
74. Ibid., p. 25. Characteristically, Grabbe attributed this to his finding 'no benefit in destroying a rich village, populated by 4,000 people who cultivate vineyards covering almost ten square *versts*', to his unwillingness 'to increase the number of homeless *abreks*', and to his hope 'to change in the future the attitudes of the villagers by building a fort above the village' – Iurov, Vol. IX, p. 89. For the entire episode, see ibid., pp. 85–9; Millutin, pp. 126–31; Golovin, pp. 24–6; Grabbe, pp. 126–7; Grzegorzewski, 1876, No. 6, p. 353; Gargarin, No. 2, p. 34; Khoursch, pp. 144–7.
75. Iurov, Vol. IX, p. 91. Also his special appendix, 'Review of the Administration of the Left Flank of the Caucasian Line, Submitted by Adjutant-General Grabbe to the Emperor through the Commander of the Corps in 1839', pp. 21–32 (separate pagination); *Materialy*, pp. 425–36, Grabbe's Memorandum attached to Grabbe to Chernyshev, 14 [26] October 1839, No. 648.

Chapter 11: Chechnia

1. Qarākhī, p. 83. And see *Shamil*, p. 191, document No. 146, Grabbe to Golovin, 2 [14] December 1839, No. 990.
2. A. Iurov, '1840, 1841 i 1842-i Gody na Kavkaze', *Kavkazskii Sbonik*, Vol. X, p. 330, (hereafter: Iurov, '1840–1842' + Vol. of *KS*). Similarly, Golovin, p. 40.
3. Iurov, '1840–1842', Vol. X, p. 276.
4. Grabbe to Golovin, 19 [31] January 1840, No. 73, as quoted by Iurov, '1840–1842', Vol. X, p. 272. Translation based on Baddeley, p. 345.
5. They were installed and secured in their places during two expeditions undertaken by Pullo in January and February 1840 – Iurov '1840–1842', Vol. X, pp. 268–9.
6. *Dvizhenie*, pp. 280–91, document No. 154, 'Memorandum on the Situation on the Left Flank of the Caucasian Line between 1834–1840 and the Necessary Measures to Strengthen the Russian Rule There', written by Pullo in 1840. Quotation from p. 285.
7. Iurov, '1840–1842', Vol. X, p. 271. During Pullo's two expeditions in the beginning of 1840, for example, 6,242 *rubles* and 1,000 muskets were collected. In addition, the soldiers fed on sheep confiscated as fines.
8. Runowski's Diary, p. 1513, entry for 3 [15] January 1862.
9. For the importance of their weapons to the mountaineers, see Baddeley, *Rugged Flanks*, Vol. II, pp. 21, 78–9. How grossly the Russians misunderstood the mountaineers can be seen from Pullo's boast that by confiscating muskets 'the mountaineers have for the first time been inculcated upon

with the idea that the authorities have the right to deny weapons to those who misuse them' – document quoted in note 6 above, p. 285.

10. Many of these rumours originated in threats made by *pristavs*, who wanted to cow people into obedience – Iurov, '1840–1842', Vol. X, pp. 272–3; Qarākhī, pp. 85, 92. And see Kundukh, 1936, No. 1 (25), pp. 14, 16.
11. Baddeley, *Rugged Flanks*, Vol. II, p. 78.
12. *AKAK*, Vol. IX, pp. 424–5, 428–33, document Nos. 373, 377, Grabbe to Chernyshev, 23 March [4 April] 1840, No. 483, 'Suggestions for [Ways to] Subdue the Tribes Inhabiting the Left Flank of the Caucasian Line', written by Grabbe in 1840; *Dvizhenie*, pp. 241, 246, 252–4, 264–5, document Nos. 128, 133, 138, 139, 146, Grabbe to Klugenau, 28 February [12 March], Grabbe to Kotzebue, 20 March [1 April], Grabbe to Galafeev, 8 [20] April, Klugenau to Grabbe 9 [21] April, 19 June [1 July] 1840; the above quoted document in note 6, p. 285; 'Dokumenty', p. 274, document No. 7, Pullo to Grabbe, 28 February [12 March] 1840.
13. Iurov, '1840–1842', Vol. X, p. 272, quoting Galafeev to Grabbe, 22 April [4 May] and Grabbe to Chernyshev, 18 [31] May 1840, Nos. 70, 759 respectively. And see Gagarin, No. 2, p. 34; Grzegorzewski, 1876, No. 6, p. 354. For Pullo's biography, see *AKAK*, Vol. IX, p. XXV, Vol. X, p. XXIX. For a venomous description of Pullo's career, see Gagarin, No. 2, pp. 31–2. And see Kundukh, 1936, No. 1 (25), p. 15.
14. Document quoted above, note 6, p. 283.
15. Iurov, '1840–1842', Vol. X, p. 272.
16. For the 'First Muḥammad ʿAlī Crisis' of 1831–32, see Jacques Ancel, *Manuel Historique de la Question d'Orient, 1792–1923* (Paris, 1931), pp. 104–7 (hereafter: Ancel); M. S. Anderson, *The Eastern Question, 1774–1923: A Study in International Relations* (London, 1966), pp. 77–87 (hereafter: Anderson); René and Georges Cattaoui, *Mahomet-Aly et l'Europe* (Paris, 1950); pp. 25–113 (hereafter: Cattaoui); Pierre Crabitès, *Ibrahim of Egypt* (London, 1935) pp. 134–87 (hereafter: Crabitès); Henry Dodwell, *The Founder of Modern Egypt: A Study of Muhammad Ali* (Cambridge, 1967), pp. 106–24 (hereafter: Dodwell); Gabriel Enkiri, *Ibrahim Pacha (1789–1848)* (Cairo, 1948), pp. 173–276 (hereafter: Enkiri); John Arthur R. Marriott, *The Eastern Question: An Historical Study in European Diplomacy* (Oxford, 1956, 4th ed.), pp. 231–35 (hereafter: Marriott); Muhammad Sabry, *L'Empire Egyptien sous Mohamed-Aly et la Question d'Orient (1811–1849)* (Paris, 1930), pp. 191–249 (hereafter: Sabry); Harold Temperley, *England and the Near East: the Crimea* (London, 1936), pp. 63–5 (hereafter: Temperley); Kingsley Webster, *The Foreign Policy of Palmerston, 1830–1841: Britain, the Liberal Movement and the Eastern Question* (London, 1951), pp. 278–300 (hereafter: Webster).
17. For the 'Second Muḥammad ʿAlī Crisis' of 1839–41, see Ancel, pp. 112–20; Anderson, pp. 88–109; Cattaoui, pp. 139–217, 247–73; Crabitès, pp. 202–50; Dodwell, pp. 154–91; Enkiri, pp. 325–420; Marriott, pp. 238–45; Vernon John Puryear, *International Economics and Diplomacy in the Near East, 1834–1853* (n.p., 1969), pp. 146–80 (hereafter: Puryear); Sabry, pp. 441–540; Temperley, pp. 87–153; Webster, pp. 596–737, 753–76.
18. How strong Muḥammad ʿAlī's image of invincibility was all over the

Muslim world and among all strata can be learnt from the fact that 'when the capture of Acre was first reported in Persia, it was scarcely believed by the *shāh*.' In fact, according to the Russian consul-general in Erzurum, the *shāh* called in the Russian minister and asked him 'as a friend' to swear that the report was true – PRO FO/78/366. f. 13, Brant to Palmerston, Erzeroom, 15 April 1841, No. 6. And see *Letters from Persia*, p. 46, Edward to George Burges, Tabreez, 15 June 1840.

19. Iurov, '1840–1842', Vol. X, p. 250.
20. Golovin, p. 39. Similarly, *AKAK*, Vol. IX, p. VI (preface), translation in Baddeley, p. 348. Also, MRE, CPC, Russie, Tiflis, Vol. I, ff. 53–5, 'Extrait d'une Lettre de M. le Consul de France à Tiflis', 2 September 1840. According to the consul, 'Ibrāhīm Pāshā is the hero of the natives, Christian and Muḥammadan alike, who equally detest the Russian authorities. They regard him [Ibrāhīm] as a liberator and will make use of any opportunity to join him' (f. 53 b). And see PRO, FO/65/262, Bloomfield to Palmerston, St. Petersburg, 10 October 1840, No. 78, where he reports that the Russians could not send more than 10,000 troops to the Bosphorus due to this threat.
21. Ḥājj Muḥammad Efendī was especially active in distributing these messages among the Chechens – *Dvizhenie*, pp. 243–5, document No. 131, Pullo to Grabbe, 13 [25] March 1840; *AKAK*, Vol. IX, pp. 424–5, document No. 373, Grabbe to Chernyshev, 23 March [5 April] 1840, No. 483.
22. Ibid., p. VI. Also published in *Dvizhenie*, pp. 428–9, as document No. 228, annexed to Neidhardt to Chernyshev, 7 [19] October 1844. Translation based on Baddeley, p. 348–9.
23. Iurov, '1840–1842', Vol. X, pp. 400–1, Appendix A.
24. Not only was Russia the power most hostile to him, but he had reasons to believe that Russian agents were stirring up the inhabitants of Syria and Palestine – Asad Jibra'il Rustum, *The Royal Archives of Egypt and the Disturbances in Palestine, 1834* (Beirut, 1938), pp. 31–5; Halford Lancaster Hoskins, *British Routes to India* (London, 1928), p. 267. A pressure group on the *pāshā* of Egypt to take such a course were the Polish officers in his service – e.g. Adam Georges Benis (ed.), *Une Mission Militaire Polonaise en Egypte* (Cairo, 1938), Vol. II, pp. 85–9, 114–19, document Nos. 237, 250, 'Memorandum by Prince Czartoryski Transmitted to M. R. C. Ferguson, M.P.'. Paris, 12 April 1834, L. Bystrzawsky to General Dembinski, 20 May 1834 respectively. For the activity of Polish emigrées in Caucasian affairs in general, see Ludwik Widerszal, *Sprawy Kaukazkie w Politice Europejskej w Latach 1834–1864* (Warsaw, 1934), (hereafter: Widerszal).
25. Thus, for example, he said to Rif'at Bey: 'If the European powers ever implement . . . the[ir] decision to blockade the port of Alexandria, I shall immediately order Ibrāhīm to march, and you know [well] that once he advances . . . he will not have the slightest difficulty in stirring up [*soulever*] Arabia, Persia and *the inhabitants of Daghestan, not to say Circassia*.' [emphasis added] – René Cattaoui (ed.), *Le Règne de Mohamed Aly d'après les Archives Russes en Egypte*, Vol. III (Rome, 1936), pp. 447–9, document No 288, 'Protocol of the Second Interview Granted by Muḥam-

mad ʿAlī to Rifʿat Bey on 18 Jumāda al-Ākhir [17 August]' annex No. 2 to Medem to Nesselrode, 25 August 1840. Quotation from p. 447.

26. Anderson, p. 91. Also see John Howes Gleason, *The Genesis of Russophobia in Great Britain: A Study in the Interaction of Policy and Opinion* (Cambridge, Mass., 1950), *passim*, (hereafter: Gleason); Norman Luxemburg, 'The Russian Expansion into the Caucasus and the British Relationship Thereto' (Ph.D. thesis, Ann Arbor, Mich., 1956), pp. 67–150 (hereafter: Luxemburg); Widerszal, *passim;* Puryear, pp. 49–53. In fact 'during much of the period in question [1815–41] Great Britain's policy was, in the main, more provocative than Russia's. British nationals laboured in the Balkans, in the Caucasus, in Afghanistan and Persia as well as in Constantinople, Syria and Egypt, far more efficaciously than did their Russian counterparts, and it was the British, not the Russian, sphere of influence which advanced. British statesmen insisted that their aims were defensive, but had the Russians appealed to the criteria of deeds rather than words, which their British contemporaries applied against them, an impartial judge must probably have produced a verdict in their favour.' (Gleason, p. 3).

27. For his biography, see Gertrude Robinson, *David Urquhart: Some Chapters in the Life of a Victorian Knight-Errant of Justice and Liberty* (Oxford, 1920); Idem., *Some Account of David Urquhart* (Oxford, 1921); And see Gleason, pp. 153–7, 173–80, 190–204, 257–66, 274; Temperley, pp. 407–9, note 68.

28. James Stanislaus Bell, *Journal of a Residence in Circassia during the Years 1837, 1838 and 1839* (London, 1840). The book was translated into French and published in Paris in 1841; John Augustin Longworth, *A Year among the Circassians* (London, 1840); Edmund Spencer, *Travels in Circassia, Krim Tartary, etc.* (London, 1837); Idem., *Travels in the Western Caucasus* (London, 1838).

29. According to a Russian source, in 1836 Urquhart even tried to contact Shamil, through the above-mentioned Ḥājj Muḥammad Efendī – *AKAK*, Vol. VIII, p. 768. Butenev to Vel'iaminov, annexed to pp. 767–9, document No. 671, Vel'iaminov to Chernyshev, 21 August [2 September] 1837, No. 120. Naturally the activities of Urquhart and his agents were extensively monitored and reported by the Russians – e.g. *AKAK*, Vols. VIII and IX and *Shamil, passim*; *Arkhiv Raevskikh*, Vol. II, pp. 422–3 (note 2); Golovin, pp. 2–3; Iurov, Vol. VIII, pp. 154–8. And see Gleason, pp. 179–80, 191–204, 230–1, 245–6.

30. Iurov '1840–1842', Vol. X, p. 251. In fact by then the British agents had been promising Muḥammad ʿAlī's intervention in the Caucasus for a few years – *Arkhiv Raevskikh*, Vol. II, p. 423 (note 2). It is another of so many ironies of history that while in Circassia British agents were joining hands with agents of Muḥammad ʿAlī, their government was taking an opposite course in leading other European powers in resisting and then expelling Muḥammad ʿAlī from the Levant. No less ironic is the fact that one of the reasons for that course was a fear shared by some British officials and agents that the *pāshā* of Egypt might eventually join hands with the Russians in invading and dividing Mesopotamia and Persia – e.g. Anderson, p. 97; Gleason, pp. 151, 228–9, 261; Temperley, pp. 93–6, 423

(note 148); M. Veretė, 'Palmerston and the Levant Crisis, 1832', *Journal of Modern History*, Vol. XXIV, No. 2 (June 1932), p. 149.

31. The attacked forts were: Fort Vel'iaminovskoe (12 March), Fort Mikhailovskoe (2 April), Fort Nikolaevskoe (15 April), and Fort Navaginskii. The last-named was partly taken (6 May), but the attackers were eventually repulsed. The last attack on Fort Abin (7 June) was unsuccessful – Iurov, '1840–1842', Vol. X, pp. 229–66; Golovin, p. 30–1; *AKAK*, Vol. IX, pp. 468–70, 480–90, 493–4, document Nos. 413, 417, 418, 421, 415, 419, 420, 422, 423, 416, Chernyshev to Golovin, 29 February [12], 29, 30 March [10, 11], 12 [24] April, Grabbe to Chernyshev, 16 [28] March, 8 [20] April, Chernyshev to Grabbe, 11 [23] April, Golovin to Chernyshev, 12 [24] May, 8 [20] August, Raevskii to Vorontsov, 25 May [6 June], Nos. 1253, 174, 1091, 2192, 430, 574, 207, 212, 876, 619 respectively, 'Evidence of Vasilii Kornenko of the Azov Cossack Regiment' 24 March [5 April] 1840; MRE, CPC, Russie, Tiflis, Vol. 1, ff. 49–52, 60–5, de la Chapelle to Guizot, Tiflis, 8/20 August, 5/17 September, 13/25 September 1840, 8/20 January 1841. Nos. 4, 5, 8, 1 respectively; PRO FO/65/260, Clanricard to Palmerston, St. Petersburg, 1, 7, 20 April, 6, 26 May 1840, Nos. 31, 43, 45, 54, 69, FO/65/261 Bloomsfield to Palmerston, St. Petersburg, 6, 20 June, 26 July, 1 August 1840, Nos. 7,14, 26, FO/65/264, Yeames to Palmerston, Odessa, 29 March, 11, 22, 25 April, 9, 26 May, 4. 16, 20 June, 4, 13, 18, 25 July, 9, 14 August, 8 September 1840, Nos. 1, 2, 3, 4, 5, 6, 7, 8, 9, 10, 11, 12, 13, 17, 18, 22, FO/78/393 f. 15, Ponsonby to Palmerston, Therapia, 29 April 1840, No. 92, FO/78/394, f. 36, Ponsonby to Palmerston, Therapia, 13 May 1840, Separate and Secret, FO/78/397, f. 145, Ponsonby to Palmerston, Therapia, 4 October 1840, No. 224.
32. Miliutin, p. 132 (note).
33. Qarākhī, p. 73; Iurov, '1840–1842', Vol. X, p. 273.
34. Ibid., p. 274.
35. Qarākhī, pp. 85–6; Iurov, '1840–1842', Vol. X, pp. 274–5; Kundukh, 1936, No. 2 (26), pp. 13–14.
36. See above, pp. 36–7.
37. See notes 21 and 29 above.
38. Millutin, p. 132 (note).
39. Iurov, '1840–1842', Vol. X, p. 51, Appendix B, Letter from Shamil and Ḥājj Muḥammad to the Yandir community.
40. *Dvizhenie*, pp. 255–8, document No. 141, 'Excerpts from the War Diary of the Chechen Force 18 [30] – 25 April [7 May] 1840'. The reference is to p. 257, entry for 21 April [3 May].
41. Qarākhī, p. 86; Ḥājj ʿAlī, pp. 18–20; Iurov, '1840–1842', Vol. X, p. 275.
42. Ibid, p. 276.
43. Ibid., loc. cit.; 'Dokumenty', pp. 274–6, document No. 8, Grabbe to Golovin, 18 [30] March 1840.
44. Baddeley, p. 364.
45. Iurov, '1840–1842', Vol. X, p. 286.
46. Yisra'el Ber, *Biṭḥon Yisra*'el – *Etmol, Hayom, Maḥar* (Tel Aviv, 5726 [1966]), pp. 18, 264–5.
47. See above, p. 90.
48. *Dvizhenie*, pp. 243–9, document Nos. 130, 131, 132, 133, 134, Pullo to Grabbe, 9 [21], 13 [25] March, Piriatinskii to Grabbe, 14 [26] March,

Grabbe to Kotzebue, 20 March [1 April], Pushkin to Traskin, 23 March [4 April] 1840; *AKAK*, Vol. IX, pp. 248–51, document No. 255, Grabbe to Chernyshev, 30 March [11 April] 1840, No. 527; Iurov, '1840–1842', Vol. X, p. 287; Qarākhī, p. 88.

49. For Galafeev's biography, see *AKAK*, Vol. IX, p. XVII.
50. *Dvizhenie*, pp. 252–4, document No. 138, Grabbe's Instructions to Galafeev, 8 [20] April 1840.
51. Gagarin, No. 2, p. 34. For Galafeev's expeditions to ʿAwkh (9–17 May), Salaṭawh (29 June–5 July), Greater and Lesser Chechnia (7–26 July), Northern Daghestan (29 July–29 August) and again to Greater Chechnia (9–31 October), see Iurov, '1840–1842', Vol. X, pp. 285–319, 344. And see PRO, FO/65/264, Yeames to Palmerston, Odessa, 18 July 1840, No. 12.
52. Mikhail Iurevich Lermontov, 'Valerik', *Polnoe Sobranie Sochinenii* (St. Petersburg, 1901, 2nd ed.), Vol. I, pp. 46–53. For an English translation see Mikahil Lermontov, *Major Poetical Works*, trans. Anatoly Liberman (London, 1983), pp. 295–307. Lermontov was cited for bravery in this battle but the tsar crossed his name off the list. For a full description of the battle, see Iurov, '1840–1842', Vol. X, pp. 302–8. And see PRO FO/65/264, Yeames to Palmerston, Odessa, 30 July, 9 August 1840, Nos. 14, 17 respectively. Also, see Liberman's commentary, pp. 568–72.
53. Golovin, pp. 33–7 (quotation from pp. 33–4). And see *Dvizhenie*, pp. 267–73, document No. 149, Golovin to Grabbe, 17 [29] August 1840.
54. The battle on the river Valerik, for example, was so costly, *inter alia*, because Galafeev had not bothered to reconnoitre the ford in advance.
55. Iurov, '1840–1842', Vol. X, p. 308.
56. Ibid, p. 289; *Dvizhenie*, p. 262, document No. 143, Golovin to Chernyshev, 6 [18] June 1840; and see pp. 249–51, document No. 125, Grabbe's Instructions to Labyntsev, 25 March [6 April] 1840.
57. For the attempt, see Iurov, '1840–1842', Vol. X, pp. 290–2; Baddeley, p. 350; Qarākhī, pp. 88–90; Runowski's Diary, pp. 1513–16, entry for January 1862. And see Hamzatov, pp. 301–3. Shamil's miraculous escape added to his prestige. The *imām*'s absence did not prevent his *nāʾibs* from their activity, though. And see Iurov, '1840–1842', Vol. X, pp. 292–3; *Shamil* pp. 192–3, document No. 148, 'Excerpts from the War Diary of the Chechen Force, 7 [19] – 13 [25] June 1840'.
58. *AKAK*, Vol. IX, pp. 338–42, document Nos. 300, 301, 302, 303, 304, Golovin to Chernyshev, 17 [29], 24, 28 July [5, 9], 6 [18] August, 9 [15] October 1840, Nos. 784, 814, 9, 821, 1112 respectively; *Dvizhenie*, pp. 259–61, 273–4, 292–8, 265, document Nos. 142, 150, 157, 147, Klugenau to Grabbe, 25 May [6 June], 20 August [1 September] 1840, 30 January [11 February] 1841, Klugenau to Golovin, 5 [17] July 1840, respectively; *Shamil*, p. 194, document No. 150, 'Excerpt from the War Diary of the Caucasian and Black Sea Lines, 21–28 September [3–10 October] 1840'; Iurov, '1840–1842', Vol. X, pp. 308, 332–4, 345–60; Grzegorzewski, 1876, No. 6, pp. 355–7; Qarākhī, pp. 90–5.
59. One of the women, a daughter of an Armenian merchant subsequently became Shamil's most beloved wife. For the raid, see Iurov, '1840–1842', Vol. X, pp. 312–14; MRE, CPC, Russie, Tiflis, Vol. I, ff. 56–7, de la

Chapelle to Guizot, Tiflis, 20 October 1840, No. 6. For a folk legend about the capture of the girl, see Baddeley, *Rugged Flanks*, Vol. I, p. 213.

60. Iurov, '1840–1842', Vol. X, p. 314.
61. Gagarin, No. 2, p. 34; Golovin, p. 37. For the campaigns, see Iurov, '1840–1842', Vol. X, pp. 318–30. The Russian losses in both campaigns were 92 killed and 117 wounded, and 15 killed and 99 wounded respectively.
62. *Materialy*, pp. 423–4, 'Excerpt from the War Diary of the Force Acting on the Left Flank, 29 August [10]–9 [21] September 1839'; Grabbe, p. 126, entry for 5 [17] September 1839; Miliutin, p. 132.
63. Iurov, '1840–1842', Vol. X, p. 369. At the same time Golovin instructed his aide 'to obtain by bloodless means the submission of Chirkah'.
64. Shamil's Letter to the Inhabitants of Chirkah, translated in ibid, p. 371.
65. *AKAK*, Vol. IX, p. 346, document No. 313, Excerpts from Golovin's Letter to Chernyshev, Camp Near Chirkah, 2 [14] July 1841, No. 66. Translation based on Baddeley, p. 355. And see Iurov, '1840–1842', Vol. XII, pp. 245–6.

Chapter 12: Daghestan

1. Golovin, p. 50. The most notable raids were the one carried out by Akhbirdi Muḥammad, Shuʿayb and Jawād Khān on the Cossack *stanitsa* Porbacheva on 8 January, which caused the Russians 93 losses; the one by Akhbirdi Muḥammad on 21–22 February in the area of Vladikavkaz, which caused 'a terrible panic among the Qarābulāqs and Ingush' (Iurov, '1840–1842', Vol. XI, p. 209); the storming of Chiryūrt by Shamil on 20 March, which created 'a strong impression upon the Ghumuqs' (ibid, p. 212); and the *imām*'s invasion of the area of Naṣrān between 13 and 19 April. But the raid which caused such a shock and consternation among the Russians that the emperor ordered an inquiry into it was carried out by Akhbirdi Muḥammad on 10 May against the military settlement Aleksandrovskoe on the Georgian Military Highway. The result was that 'our best military settlement, which had just begun to prosper' was 'almost completely destroyed, losing many of its farmers and all its livestock' (ibid, p. 218). The mountaineers 'cut to pieces or abducted' 119 men, women and children, carried away 1,126 goats, 769 sheep, 125 horses, 77 muskets and 58 axes, and burnt a few dozen stacks of wheat and barley. Akhbirdi Muḥammad had become such a danger that Golovin instructed Grabbe to arrange for his assassination – *Dvizhenie*, p. 292, document No. 156, Golovin to Grabbe, 29 January [10 February] 1841. For this period, see Iurov, '1840–1842', Vol. XI, pp. 198–220, Vol. XII, pp. 225–7 (from Vol. XII onwards the author is identified as 'N. V'; however, in order not to create confusion he will continue to be quoted as Iurov): Golovin, pp. 41–2; *AKAK*, Vol. IX, pp. 265–6, document No. 266, Order of the Day by Golovin, 24 January [2 February] 1841, No. 24; Qarākhī, p. 96.
2. Ḥajimurād's older brother ʿUthmān was a 'milk brother' (*imchek*, or *shaqīq*) of Nūsāl Khān. For the importance of this institution, see, for example, Baddeley, *Rugged Flanks*, Vol. II, p. 18.

3. His first letter to Klugenau, published in Iurov, Vol. X, pp. 366–7. There is an abundance of material about Ḥajimurād. See, for example, V. Potto, 'Gadzhi Murat. (Biograficheskii Ocherk)', *Voennyi Sbornik* (1870), No. 11, Otdel I, pp. 159–82; S. N. Shul'gin, 'Predanie o Shamilevskom Naibe Khadzi Murate', *Sbornik Materialov dlia Opisaniia Mestnosteii Plemen Kavkaza*, Vol. XL, Otdel I, pp. 54–70 (French resumé in Ibrahimoff, 'Hadji-Mourat, Le Naïb de Chamyl', *Revue du Monde Musulman*, No. 11 ([May 1910], pp. 100–4); 'Predaniia o Khadzi Murate'. *Dagestanskii Sbornik*, Vol. III, pp. 7–49; G. Kvinitadze, 'Khadzhi Murat', *Kavkaz* (Paris), 1934, No. 7, pp. 8–12. The best description of Ḥajimurād's biography and personality is, nevertheless, that by Lev Nikolaevich Tolstoi, 'Khadzhi Murat', in *Posmertnye Khudozhestvennye Proizvedeniia*, Vol. III (Moscow, 1912), pp. 3–125 (hereafter: Tolstoi, 'Khadzhi Murat'); (For an English translation, see, e.g. *The Works of Leo Tolstoy* [London, 1934], Vol. XV, pp. 227–384). Even though his work is fiction, Tolstoi had engaged in meticulous research before writing it, and tried to be as accurate as possible. He even quoted long passages from official despatches. And see, e.g. V. Chertkov's note in ibid, pp. 190–4, and V. A. D'iakov, 'Istoricheskie Realii "Khadzhi Murata" ', *Voprosy Istorii* (1973), No. 1, pp. 135–48.
4. His second letter to Klugenau, published in Iurov, '1840–1842', Vol. X, p. 368.
5. See, for example, the questions posed by the elders of Tsatanikh to Evdokimov, appended to Evdokimov to Klugenau, 8 [20] August 1841, No. 189, as quoted in Iurov, '1840–1842', Vol. XII, p. 253. And see the letters of ʿAddāl Muḥammad-Oghlū from the village of Shebakho to Schwartz and of Nūrichī the elder of Tokita to Talyzin as published in ibid, pp. 234, 249–50 respectively; Kundukh, 1936, No. 1 (25), p. 13, No. 2 (26), pp. 14–19, No. 4 (28), pp. 22–3, No. 5 (29), pp. 20–1.
6. His first letter to Klugenau, in Iurov, '1840–1842', Vol. X, p. 366.
7. His second letter to Klugenau, ibid, p. 368.
8. Ibid., loc. cit.
9. For which, see ibid, pp. 365–8. Also, see Grzegorzewski, 1876, No. 6, pp. 357–8.
10. See above, pp. 93–5.
11. Of course, officially the reconciliation was presented as having been initiated by Ḥajimurād and Shamil's proclamation, published to announce it, included the Avār leader's letter to the *imām* and Shamil's reply. A German translation of both was published in Bodenstedt, p. 614.
12. Golovin to Aḥmad Khān, 27 January [8 February] 1841, No. 150, as quoted by Iurov, '1840–1842', Vol. XI, p. 221. For the situation in Daghestan and Ḥajimurād's activity, see *AKAK*, Vol. IX, pp. 342–4, document Nos. 305, 306, 307, Golovin to Chernyshev, 21 January [2 February], Chernyshev to Golovin (secret), 25 January [6 February], Golovin to Chernyshev, 15 [27] February 1841, Nos. 107, 109, 278 respectively.
13. Bakunin to Klugenau, 18 February [2 March] 1841, No. 13, as quoted by Iurov, '1840–1842', Vol. X, p. 223.
14. Forty-eight were killed, among them Bakunin himself, and 142 wounded, which amounted to nearly a third of the force.
15. Golovin, p. 40. In a note on the same page Golovin calls the entire

expedition 'a badly conceived search'. For differing views on this statement see Iurov, '1840–1842', Vol. XI, pp. 228–9 and Vol. XII, p. 219 (the latter being the view of 'N.V.'); Grzegorzewski, 1876, No. 6, p. 358. For a detailed description of the expedition, see Iurov, '1840–1842', Vol. XI, pp. 221–8; *AKAK*, Vol. IX, pp. 344–5, document Nos. 308, 309, Golovin to Chernyshev, 20 February [4], 3 [15] March 1841, Nos. 278, 299 respectively; *Dvizhenie*, pp. 298–303, document No. 158, Golovin to Chernyshev, 24 February [8 March] 1841.

16. Published in Iurov, '1840–1842', Vol. XII, p. 236.
17. Ibid, p. 239.
18. Ibid, p. 220.
19. Mend to Khvostov, 2 [14] April, No. 430, as quoted in ibid, p. 220.
20. Iurov, '1840–1842', Vol. XI, p. 187.
21. Ibid, Vol. XII, pp. 246–7.
22. A. B., 'Dagestan 1841 Goda', *Sbornik Gazety Kavkaz* (1846), p. 74 (hereafter: 'Dagestan'); Iurov, '1840–1842', Vol. XI, pp. 190–8, 232. For the new plans, see *AKAK*, Vol. IX, pp. 345–6, document Nos. 311, 312, Golovin to Grabbe (excerpt), 6 [18] April, Grabbe to Golovin, 12 [24] May 1841, Nos. 378, 626 respectively; *Dvizhenie*, pp. 298–303, document No. 158, Golovin to Chernyshev, 24 February [8 March] 1841; Iurov, '1840–1842', Vol. XI, pp. 230–1; Golovin (p. 42) describes the altered plan without mentioning the fact that it was changed.
23. *AKAK*, Vol. IX, pp. 266–8, document No. 267, Autographed Note by the Emperor, 1841. And see PRO, FO/65/264, Yeames to Palmerston, Odessa, 22 September 1840, No. 23.
24. Showing typical Russian fascination with size, Golovin stated that 'the impression made on the minds of the mountaineers was very noticeable – never before had they seen such huge forces . . . and never had they been struck by such a terror' – Golovin, p. 44.
25. For the campaigns in both Daghestan and Chechnia between May and November 1841, see *AKAK*, Vol. IX, pp. 268–78, 346, 433–6, document Nos. 269, 270, 313, 314, 378, 379, 278, Orders of the Day by Golovin and Grabbe, 6 [18], 24 May [5 June] respectively, Golovin to Chernyshev, 2 [14] July, 7 [19] October, Grabbe to Golovin (secret), 30 May [11 June], Golovin to Chernyshev, 7 [19] October 1841, Nos. 66, 1018, 921, 1071 respectively, 'Survey of Military Activities on the Left Flank of the Caucasian line during 1841', written by Grabbe; Golovin, pp. 42–8, 52–3; 'Dagestan', pp. 72–81; Iurov, '1840–1842', Vol. XI, pp. 232–311, Vol. XII, pp. 240–41; Qarākhī, pp. 90–6.
26. Gagarin, No. 2, pp. 35–6. During this expedition Grabbe's force lost 39 killed and 487 wounded. All in all, the Russians lost during the campaign in Daghestan and Chechnia 231 killed and 1,185 wounded; 848 of the losses (70 killed and 778 wounded) were sustained by Grabbe's force.
27. Gzregorzewski, 1876, No. 6, pp. 358–9.
28. For which, see Iurov, '1840–1842', Vol. XII, pp. 242–5, 248–57.
29. For which, see ibid, pp. 229–33, 258–60; *Dvizhenie*, pp. 305–6, document No. 163, Civil Governor of Georgia-Imeret'i to Braiko, 26 May [7 June] 1841; *Shamil*, pp. 199–202, document Nos. 158, 159, 160, 162, Commander of T'elavi to Civil Governor of Georgia-Imeret'i, 26 June [8 July], Schwartz to Kotzebue, 2 [14] July, Civil Governor of Georgia-Imeret'i to

Braiko, 5 [17] July, 27 August [8 September] 1841, Nos. 708, 78, 434, 550 respectively.

30. For which, see Iurov, '1840–1842', Vol. XII, pp. 261–9; *Dvizhenie*, pp. 324–7, document Nos. 169, 170, 171, 172, 173, 174, Qibid Muḥammad to Lt. Alibkachbek, Qibid Muḥammad to Muḥammad the *Pristav* and *Qāḍī* of ʿAndāl, the *Qāḍī* of Tsudaqār to Lt. Alibkachbek, Muḥammad the *Qāḍī* of Aqūsha to Lt. Alibkachbek, Maḥmūd Bek, Regent of Ghāzī-Ghumuq, to Lt. Alibkachbek, Alibkachbek to Klugenau, the *Qāḍīs* and Honourable People of Chōkha and Sughūr to Klugenau (all n.d.).
31. Iurov, '1840–1842', Vol. XII, pp. 288–9. For this campaign, see 'Dokumenty', pp. 277–84, document No. 10, 'General Survey of the Continuing Military Operations in Northern Daghestan' [by Klugenau?], 17 [29] November 1841, especially pp. 277–80; *Dvizhenie*, pp. 309–11, 312–24, document Nos, 166, 168, Klugenau to Golovin, 16 [28] November, 'Survey of the Disastrous Situation of Northern Daghestan with a Short Outline of Preceding Events' (excerpt), written, or at least signed, by Klugenau, 31 December 1841 [12 January 1842], especially pp. 314–16, (hereafter: Klugenau). [The editors of *Dvizhenie* were 'unable to identify the author of the document', but according to Iurov, who quoted extensively from it ('1840–1842', Vol. XII, pp. 314–15, 327–30), it was written by Klugenau.]; Grzegorzewski, 1876, No. 6, p. 359; Iurov,' 1840–1842', Vol. XII, pp. 269–90; Qarākhī, pp. 98–9.
32. Iurov, '1840–1842', Vol. XII, p. 284.
33. Klugenau even withdrew the reinforcements sent to Avāristān in October. Even this relatively short period of calm did not pass without another folly. Aḥmad Khān wanted to recover Hulāl [Golotl']. In order to assist him, 'it was decided to compel [the villagers] to do so by a bombardment, without using troops' (Iurov, '1840–1842', Vol. XII, p. 291). After two days of bombardment (14 and 15 November), a messenger was sent to demand surrender, but was not allowed into the village. Unable to storm the village, the Russian commander and Aḥmad Khān decided to retreat. But 'in order to prevent the population of Hulāl from attributing our retreat to lack of success, a proclamation was sent to the village signed by Aḥmad Khān.' (ibid, p. 293. The proclamation is printed on p. 294).
34. Golovin, p. 53. For more elaborate descriptions, see *AKAK*, Vol. IX, pp. 436–40, document No. 380, Olszewski to Grabbe, 14 [26] November 1841; Iurov, '1840–1842', Vol. XIII, pp. 335–49. And see Gagarin, No. 3, p. 18.
35. Iurov, '1840–1842', Vol. XII, p. 298. For a detailed description of this campaign, see ibid, pp. 297–314; *AKAK*, Vol. IX, pp. 346–8, document Nos, 315, 316, Golovin to Chernyshev, 12 [24] December 1841, 3 [15] March 1842, Nos. 1221, 5 respectively; Golovin, pp. 53–4; Klugenau, pp. 316–20; Grzegorzewski, 1876, No. 6, p. 359; Qarākhī, pp. 98–9.
36. Iurov, '1840–1842', Vol. XII, p. 307.
37. Ibid, p. 308. Similarly, p. 306.
38. *AKAK*, Vol. IX, p. 348, document No. 316, Golovin to Chernyshev, 3 [15] January 1842, No. 5.
39. On 9 December the Lesghians raided T'ushet'i, (for this and other events, see Iurov, '1840–1842', Vol. XII, pp. 332–41). On 14 December Akhbirdi Muḥmmad raided Cossack *stanitsas* along the Line (ibid, Vol. XIII,

pp. 350–4). For the events in Daghestan, see ibid, Vol. XII, pp. 317–26, 330–2.
40. Ibid., p. 326.
41. Ibid, pp. 323, 324. On 15 December, for example, a small Russian force was ambushed and routed. Out of 88 only 34 soldiers reached their base.
42. Ibid, p. 326.
43. Klugenau, p. 321.
44. Quoted by Iurov, '1840–1841', Vol. XII, p. 327. Also see Grzegorzewski, 1876, No. 6, p. 360, where Klugenau's request to resign is mentioned; Gagarin, No. 3, pp. 25–6.

Chapter 13: Ghāzī-Ghumuq and Ichkerī

1. Golovin, p. 47.
2. E.g. ibid., *passim*; Golovin's reprimand to Klugenau in November 1841, quoted by Iurov, '1840–1842', Vol. XII, pp. 289–90; *AKAK*, Vol. IX, pp. 269–78, 345–50, 377–81, 391–2, 395–8, 433–4, document Nos, 287, 317, 335, 336, 348, 352, 353, 378, 'Survey of the Military Operations on the Left Flank of the Caucasian Line during 1841', written by Grabbe, Golovin to Chernyshev (secret), 15 [27] February, Golovin to Grabbe, 16 [28] April, Golovin to Chernyshev, 17 [29] April, Golovin to Kleinmichel, 17 [29] June (secret), 16 [28], 24 July [5 August] 1842, Grabbe to Golovin (secret), 30 May [11 June] 1841, Nos. 4, 389, 390, 660, 812, 21, 921 respectively. And see Gagarin, No. 3, pp. 17–18.
3. *AKAK*, Vol. IX, pp. 266–8, document No. 267, Autographed Note by the Emperor, 1841.
4. For which, see Golovin, pp. 54–6.
5. By that time the Russians might have already had reasons to believe that an appearance of a large force in ʿAndī would be followed by the organised submission of that community. Also see, for example, Iv[an] Zagorskii, 'Vosem Mesiatsev v Plennu u Gortsev', *Kavkazskii Sbornik*, Vol. XIX, p. 299 (hereafter: Zagorskii) for the 'coolness' of the people of ʿAndī towards Shamil's rule.
6. [Constantin Benckendorff,] 'Vospominaniia Grafa Konstantina Konstantinovicha Benkendorfa o Kavkazskoi Letnei Ekspeditsii 1845 Goda', ed. B. M. Koliubakin, *Russkaia Starina* (1911), No. 1, p. 110 (editor's note).
7. *AKAK*, Vol IX, p. 355, document No. 322, Golovin to Chernyshev, 9 [21] March 1842, No. 8. By then the feuds among the four generals – Golovin, Grabbe, Faesy and Klugenau – intertwined and drew Golovin and Faesy in a common front against Grabbe and Klugenau. It seems that the direct reason for Klugenau's removal was Golovin's exasperation with the former's gloomy and alarming reports and constant demands for reinforcement and for increase of his (Klugenau's) authority. Golovin demanded that Klugenau take 'energetic measures', i.e. lead an expedition against Qibid Muḥmmad, storm Ṭiliq and 'punish' the communities of Hindāl, ʿAndāl and Qarākh. When Klugenau answered that he was unable to do it with his present, diminished means and sent his above-mentioned memorandum of 31 December 1841 [12 January 1842] (see note 31 to

chapter 12), Golovin decided to accept his resignation – Grzegorzewski, 1876, No. 6, pp. 359–60.

8. For Faesy's campaign, see *AKAK*, Vol. IX, pp. 351–62, 363–89, document Nos. 319, 322, 326, 320, 321, 323, 324, 325, 329, 330, Golovin to Chernyshev, 2 [14], 13 [25], 30 March [11 April], Faesy to Golovin, 3 [15], 8 [20], 13 [25], 15 [27], 20 March [1 April], Nos. 175, 229, 232, 9, 10, 13, 16, 17, respectively, 'Survey of the Winter Campaign in Daghestan from 6 [18] February to 20 March [1 April]', 'Excerpt from the War Diary of the Winter Campaign in Daghestan under the Command of Lieutenant-General Faesy from 6 [18] February to 6 [18] April', both annexed to Faesy's report of 5 [17] April 1842, No. 28; *Dvizhenie*, pp. 330–31, document No. 177, Faesy to Golovin, 22 February [6 March] 1842; Golovin, p. 58; N. Okol'nichii, 'Perechen' Poslednikh Voennykh Sobytii v Dagestane (1843 God)',*Voennyi Sbornik* (1859), No. 2, pp. 389–90 (hereafter; Okol'nichii + No. of *VS*); Qarākhī, p. 100. Indeed, all the Russian sources testify to his success in creating the right impression.

9. *AKAK*, Vol. IX, pp. VII-VIII, 'Shamil's Proclamation to the Chechen People Following the Capture of Ghāzī-Ghumuq', 20 May [5 June] 1842 (20 March [5 April]?). And see ibid, pp. 360–1, 369–72, document Nos. 327, 331, Golovin to Chernyshev, 30 March [11 April], No. 232, 'Survey of the Events in Ghāzī-Ghumuq in March 1842' annexed to Faesy's Report of 5 [17] April 1842, No. 28; 'Dokumenty', pp. 271–2, document No. 5, Buchkiev to Golovin, 28 March [9 April] 1842; *Dvizhenie*, pp. 332–3, document Nos. 178, 180, Faesy to Golovin, 24 March [5 April], Skalon to Golovin, 29 March [10 April] 1842; Golovin, p. 59; Okol'nichii, No. 2, pp. 390–2; Qarākhī, pp. 100–2; Hājj ʿAlī, pp. 20–1; MRE, CPC, Russie, Tiflis, Vol. I, ff. 97–101, Monnot-Arbilleux to Guizot, Tiflis, 18/6 April, 13/1 May 1842, Nos, 4, 5.

10. Jamāl al-Dīn, however, denied afterwards that he had prodded Shamil to invade Ghāzī-Ghumuq.

11. *AKAK*, Vol. IX, pp. 391–2, document No. 348, Golovin to Chernyshev, 17 [29] June 1842, No. 660, (secret). Quotation from p. 391. Also, Golovin, p. 59.

12. *AKAK*, Vol. IX, pp. 373–5; 382–4, document Nos. 333, 337, 338, 340, Golovin to Chernyshev, 10 [22] April, 6 [18] May, Golovin to Kleinmichel, 24 April [6], 10 [22] May 1842, Nos, 357, 450. 405, 466 respectively; *Dvizhenie*, p. 335, document No. 183, Daniyāl *Sulṭān* to Schwartz, 12 [24] April 1842; 'Richinskoe Delo 1-go Maia 1842 Goda', *Sbornik Gazety Kavkaz* (1846), pp. 103–8; Golovin, pp. 59–60; Okol'nichii, No. 2, pp. 392–3; Qarākhī, p. 103.

13. See, e.g. *Shamil*, pp. 212–13, document No. 16 [misprint for 15], Skalon to Captain of Nobility in Georgia-Imeret'i, 19 [31] March 1842, No. 634; *AKAK*, Vol. IX, pp. 362–6, document No. 328, Golovin to Chernyshev, 3 [15] April 1848 [should be 1842], No. 276. For the detention of residents of the two Khanates in other parts of the Caucasus, see *Dvizhenie*, pp. 333, 335–6, document Nos. 181, 184, 185, Skalon to Chief Administrator of the Caucasus, 31 March [12 April], Shakhovskii to Grabbe, 13 [25] April, Grabbe to Prianishnikov, 16 [28] April 1842.

14. Fedor Fedorovich Tornauw [Tornov], 'Gergebil', *Russkii Arkhiv* 1881, No. 4, p. 436 (hereafter: Tornauw). For Argutinskii's biography, see

'Kratkii Obzor Sluzhebnoi Deiatel'nosti General-Ad''iutanta Kniazia Argutinskogo-Dolgorukugo', *Kavkaszskii Kalendar* (1856), Otdelenie IV, pp. 565–81; Okol'nichii, No. 4, pp. 310–11 (note); *AKAK*, Vol. IX, pp. XV-XVI.

15. *Dvizhenie*, pp. 338–41, 342–3, document Nos. 187, 190, Argutinskii to Golovin, 13 [25], 19 [31] May 1842 respectively; Golovin, p. 61; Okol'nichii, No. 2, pp. 393–4.
16. *Dvizhenie*, p. 344, document No. 191, Argutinskii to Golovin, 26 May [7 June] 1842; *AKAK*, Vol. IX, p. 384, document Nos. 341, 342, Argutinskii to Golovin (secret), 30 May [11 June], Argutinskii to Schwartz, 31 May [12 June] 1842, Nos. 339, 344 respectively; Golovin, p. 63; Okol'nichii, No. 2, pp. 394–5.
17. *AKAK*, Vol. IX, pp. 384–5, 388–90, document Nos. 343, 345, 346, Argutinskii to Golovin, 3 [15], 9 [21] June 1842, Nos. 346, 364 (both of the same date), 369 respectively. Quotation from p. 385; Golovin, pp. 63–4; Okol'nichii, No. 2, pp. 395–6; Qarākhī, pp. 103–5; MRE, CPC, Russie, Tiflis, Vol. I, ff. 104–5, Monnot-Arbilleux to Guizot, Tiflis, 11 July/29 June 1842, No. 7.
18. E.g. Golovin, pp. 64, 71.
19. Qarākhī, p. 105.
20. See, e.g., *AKAK*, Vol. IX, pp. 390–5, document Nos. 347, 348, 349, 350, 351, Argutinskii to Golovin (secret), 13 [25] June, Golovin to Kleinmichel (secret), 17 [29] June, Argutinskii to Kotzebue (secret), 21 June [3 July], Wolf to Chernyshev (secret), 25 June [7 July], Argutinskii to Golovin, 5 [17] July 1842, Nos. 405, 660, 500, 19, 603 respectively.
21. This is a 'blow below the belt' by Golovin. Not only was it the only success of Grabbe's expedition – in the fact that it compelled Shamil to retreat from Ghāzī-Ghumuq – but Golovin himself urged Grabbe to start his expedition as soon as possible – ibid, pp. 377–80, document No. 335, Golovin to Grabbe, 16 [28] April 1842, No. 389.
22. Golovin, pp. 65–7. Translation based on Baddeley, pp. 356–9. Also, see *AKAK*, Vol. IX, pp. 390–2, 440–4, document Nos. 347, 348, 382, Argutinskii to Golovin (secret), 13 [25] June, Golovin to Kleinmichel (secret), 17 [29] June, No. 405, 'War Diary of the Chechen Force from 30 May [11] to 8 [20] June, Annexed to Grabbe to Chernyshev, 10 [22] June 1842, Nos. 405, 405, 253 respectively; Gagarin, No. 3, pp. 15–17; Grzegorzewski, 1876, No. 6, pp. 360–1; Okol'nichii, No. 2, pp. 396–8; Qarākhī, pp. 105–7; MRE, CPC, Russie, Tiflis, Vol. 1, ff. 102–7, la Chapelle to Guizot, 24/12 June, 11 July/29 June, 29/17 August 1842, Nos. 6, 7, 8 respectively; PRO, FO/65/282, Bloomfield to Aberdeen, St. Petersburg, 2 July 1842, No. 25, FO/65/286, Yeames to Aberdeen, Odessa, 22 July 1842, No. 3; *Leipziger Allgemeine Zeitung*, 10 August 1842 (No. 222) p. 2358 (n.d. [no No.]), p. 2618, von Gaertringen archive. For Vorontsov's reaction to Golovin's description, see 'Pis'ma Kniazia Mikhaila Semenovicha Vorontsova k Alekseiu Petrovichu Ermolovu', *Russkii Arkhiv* (1890), No. 3, pp. 346–7, Vorontsov to Ermolov, Tiflis, 17 [29] March 1849 (hereafter quoted by details of letter + No. of *RA*). Within a decade and a half the soldiers' oral tradition described Grabbe 'sitting on a drum, with his eyes full of tears', dictating the following order of the day: 'Boys [*rebiata*], we have suffered a defeat' – N. A. Volkonski,

'1858 God v Chechne', *Kavkazskii Sbornik*, Vol. III, p. 424. Here, the popular memory combined the picture of Galafeev after the battle of Valerik with the more famous Grabbe at the greater disaster in the forests of Ichkerī.

23. As a mark of distinction, Shamil gave the two *nā'ibs* two flags, given by Alexander I to Aslān Khān, which he had seized in Ghāzī-Ghumuq – Zagorskii, p. 236.
24. *AKAK*, Vol. IX, pp. 393–5, document No. 350, Wolf to Chernyshev (secret), 25 June [7 July] 1842, No. 19.
25. Golovin, pp. 67–8. Translation based on Baddeley, p. 359. Also, see *AKAK*, Vol. IX, pp. 395–8, document Nos. 352, 353, Golovin to Kleinmichel, 16 [28], 24 July [5 August] 1842, Nos. 812, 21 respectively; Gagarin, No. 3, p. 17; A[natolii Vsevolodovich] O[rlov]-D[avydov], 'Chastnoe Pis'mo o Vziatii Shamilia', *Russkii Arkhiv* (1869), No. 6, c. 1051; Qarākhī, p. 107.
26. *AKAK*, Vol. IX, pp. 444–5, 278, document Nos. 383, 384, 274 Grabbe's Autographed Letter to the Emperor [n.d.], Kleinmichel to Grabbe, 20 June [2 July], Kleinmichel to Golovin 7 [19] August 1842, No. 5295.
27. He was given a vacation to recover in Germany and in 1845 was appointed governor of the Baltic provinces with his seat in Riga.

Chapter 14: Avāristān

1. E.g., Weidenbaum, 'prodelki na Kavkaze', in *Kavkazskie Etiudy*, p. 312 (hereafter: Weidenbaum, 'Prodelki na Kavkaze').
2. Ibid., pp. 313–14.
3. *Dvizhenie*, pp. 360–1, document No. 202, Hurko to Commander of Vladikavkaz, 7 [19] January 1843. Quotation from p. 361.
4. 'The scene was terrible, and it created a strong effect on Prince Chernyshev' – Gagarin, No. 3, p. 17.
5. *Dvizhenie*, pp. 345–7, document No. 192, Ladyński to Golovin, 16 [28] June 1842. Quotation from p. 345.
6. Ibid., document No. 202, p. 362.
7. Ibid., pp. 352–3, document No. 195, Chernyshev to Golovin, 19 [31] July 1842. Quotation from pp. 352, 353.
8. Ibid, p. 352. Similarly, document No. 192, p. 346. For a list of possible partners for secret negotiations, see ibid., pp. 353–6, document No. 196, Golovin to Chernyshev, 28 August [9 September] 1842.
9. See, e.g., *AKAK*, Vol. IX, pp. 137, 350–1, document Nos. 172, 318, Golovin to Perovskii, 24 March [4 April] (secret), Chernyshev to Golovin, 20 February [4 March] 1842, Nos. 12, 1386 respectively.
10. *Dvizhenie*, document No. 195, p. 352.
11. *AKAK*, Vol. IX, p. XXIV.
12. A. Iurov, '1844-i God na Kavkaze', *Kavkazskii Sbornik*, Vol. VII, p. 159 (hereafter: Iurov, '1844').
13. P. Il'in, 'Iz Sobytii na Kavkaze. Nabegi Shamilia v 1843 Godu', *Russkii Arkhiv* (1872), No. 7, p. 216 (hereafter: Il'in); *Dvizhenie*, document No. 202, pp. 361–3; A. Iurov '1843-i God na Kavkaze', *Kavkazskii Sbornik*, Vol. VI, p. 16 (hereafter: Iurov, '1843').

14. Ibid, pp. 5–31 and Appendix I, pp. 1–13 (separate pagination); *AKAK*, Vol. IX; pp. 744–7, document Nos. 627, 628, Neidhardt to Chernyshev, 1 [13] August, Chernyshev to Neidhardt, 21 August [2 September] 1843, Nos. 1391, 7239 respectively.
15. *Dvizhenie*, pp. 394–401, document No. 218, Chernyshev to the Emperor, 16 [28] November 1843; Grzegorzewski, 1876, No. 6, pp. 365–6.
16. Ibid., loc. cit. Quotation from p. 366. The echoes of this reached the British vice-consul in Batumi – PRO, FO/78/564, Guarracino to Canning, Batoom, 18 November, No. 16, annexed to Canning to Aberdeen, Buyukdery, 9 December 1844, No. 275.
17. *Shamil*, p. 222, document No. 172, Avalov to Chief Administrator Transcaucasia, 15 [27] June 1843, No. 1210; MRE, CPC, Russie, Tiflis, Vol. I, f. 142, de Castillone to Guizot, 2 July 1842, No. 16.
18. For the events of this period, see *AKAK*, Vol. IX, pp. 754–6, document Nos. 642, 643, Klugenau to Neidhardt (secret), 3 [15] May, Neidhardt to Chernyshev, 17 [29] May 1843, Nos. 79, 1139 respectively; *Dvizhenie*, pp. 368–74; 387–91, document Nos. 204, 205, 206, 207, 208, 209, 212, 213, 214, 215, Neidhardt to Chernyshev, 13 [25] January, Orbeliani to Argutinskii, 14 [26] January, Klugenau to Neidhardt, 18 [30] January, Tarakanov to Kotzebue, 13 [25] February, Klugenau to Neidhardt 1 [13] March, Neidhardt to Chernyshev, 12 [24] March, 1 [13] April, Tarakanov to Kotzebue, 6 [18] May, Neidhardt to Chernyshev, 10 [22] May, Neidhardt to Chief Administrator Transcaucasia, 4 [16] June 1843 respectively; *Shamil*, pp. 221–4, document Nos. 171, 173, 174, Avalov to Skalon, 10 [22] June, Avalov to Chief Administrator Transcaucasia, 19 June [1 July], Avalov to Commander T'ush-P'shav-Khevsur Command, 30 July [11 August] 1843, Nos. 1114, 1213, 1510 respectively; Iurov, '1843', pp. 49–53; Il'in, pp. 216–17; Qarākhī, p. 112.
19. Baddeley, p. 364. For the strength and positions of the Russian forces in Daghestan, see Appendix to Okol'nichii, No. 3, pp. 51–4, and Iurov, '1843', Appendix III, pp. 14–16 (separate pagination). For the strength of Shamil's forces and his plans, see Khursh [Khoursch], 'Voennaia Operatsiia v Dagestane v 1843 Godu', *Gortsy Kavkaza*, No. 39, pp. 8–11 (hereafter: Khursh + No. of *GK*).
20. During the campaign of Faesy, for which see above, note 8 to Chapter 13.
21. How bitter the fighting was could be seen from the casualties sustained by Shamil's force – 120 killed and 1,520 wounded (Qarākhī, p. 116).
22. For details, see *Dvizhenie*, pp. 460–8, document No. 243, Neidhardt to Chernyshev, 5 [17] April 1844 (especially pp. 465–6); Iurov, '1843', pp. 55, 61, 63–5; Okol'nichii, No. 3, pp. 17–18, 22–5; Il'in, pp. 217, 223, 235–6; Gagarin, No. 3, p. 26; Grzegorzewski, 1876, No. 6, p. 366; Qarākhī, pp. 113–16; Hājj ʿAlī, pp. 22–3; Khursh, No. 39, pp. 11–13: MRE, CPC, Russie, Tiflis, Vol. I, ff. 155–6, de Castillon to Guizot, Akhti, 27 September 1843, No. 20.
23. *AKAK*, Vol. IX, pp. 757–8, 767–74, document Nos. 645, 654, Klugenau to Neidhardt, 30 August [11 September], Klugenau to Hurko (secret), 29 September [11 October] 1843, Nos. 1488, 184 respectively. (Annexed to the latter is Veselitskii to Klugenau, 28 August [9 September] 1843, No. 2002, which is also published in Iurov, '1843', Appendix IV, pp. 16–17

(separate pagination); Okol'nichii, No. 3, pp. 18–22; Iurov, '1843', pp. 56–7, 59–60; Il'in, pp. 219–23; Gagarin, No. 3, pp. 26–7; Grzegorzewski,1876, No. 6, p. 366; Baddeley, p. 366; Qarākhī, p. 116; Khursh, No. 39, p. 13. Lieutenant-Colonel Vasilevskii, the Commander of the fort of Tsatanikh who attempted this rescue was later blamed for all the following Russian failures. He proved to be an excellent scapegoat, since, being dead, he could not counter-blame others.

24. Iurov, '1843', pp. 66–9; Okol'nichii, No. 3, pp. 28–32; Il'in, pp. 233–5; Grzegorzewski, 1876, No. 6, pp. 366–7; Khursh, No. 39, p. 14; MRE, CPC, Russie, Tiflis, Vol. I, ff, 59–60, Castillon to Guizot, Kouba, 6 October 1843, No. 21. Kosovich now became the second scapegoat.

25. Ṭānūs and Okoda on 18 September, Tsatanikh on 18–19 September, Akhalchi on 19 September, Mohokh and Siyukh on 21 September and Hutsāl on 22–24 September - *AKAK*, Vol. IX, p. 758, document No. 646, Klugenau to Neidhardt, 8 [20] October 1843; *Dvizhenie*, pp. 460–8, document No. 243, Neidhardt to Chernyshev, 5 [17] April 1844; Iurov, '1843', pp. 70–81; Okol'nichii, No. 3, pp. 33–46; Il'in, pp. 236–50; Gagarin, No. 3, pp. 27–9; Grzegorzewski, 1876, No. 6, pp. 366–7; [Samoila Riabov,] 'Rasskaz Byvshego U[nter] O[fitsera] Apsheronskogo Polka, Samoily Riabova, o Svoei Boevoi Sluzhbe na Kavkaze', ed. Andrei Vasil'ev Derzhavin, *Kavkazskii Sbornik*, Vol. XVIII, pp 356–62; Qarākhī, pp. 117–19; Ḥājj ʿAlī, pp. 23–5; Khursh, No. 39, pp. 14–16; MRE, CPC, Russie, Tiflis, Vol. I, ff. 159–60, Castillon to Guzot, Tiflis, 29 October 1843, No. 22; *Bresslauer Zeitung*, 9 September, 3 October 1843 (No. 211, 231), pp. 1648, 1888 respectively (von Gaertringen archive).

26. For his biography, see *AKAK*, Vol. IX, p. XXVII.

27. For their activities see Iurov,'1843', pp. 112–22; Okol'nichii, No. 4, pp. 328–34; Il'in, p. 263; Khursh, No. 48, pp. 10–11.

28. *AKAK*, Vol. IX, pp. 759–63, document Nos. 648, 649, Neidhardt to Chernyshev 15 [27] September (and annexed to it Argutinskii to Neidhardt, 8 [20] September), Argutinskii to Neidhardt, 17 [29] September 1843, Nos. 1629 (and 1353), 1380 respectively; Iurov, '1843', pp. 84–95; Okol'nichii, No. 4, pp. 305–22; Qarākhī, pp. 119–20; Ḥājj ʿAlī, p. 25; Khursh, No. 39, p. 17. To defend Ghāzī-Ghumuq, Schwartz marched there from the Lesghian Line – *AKAK*, Vol. IX, pp. 758–9, 765–6, 775–6, 780–1, document Nos. 647, 652, 656, 659, Schwartz to Neidhardt, 11 [23] September, Neidhardt to Chernyshev, 24, 30 September [6, 11], 24 October [6 November] 1843, Nos. 1332, 1676, 1737, 1874 respectively; Iurov, '1843', pp. 102–12; Okol'nichii, No. 4, pp. 330–1.

29. *AKAK* Vol. IX, pp. 763–4, document No. 649, Klugenau to Neidhardt, 18 [30] September 1843, No. 111; Iurov, '1843', pp. 95–8; Okol'nichii, No. 4, pp. 322–5; Il'in, pp. 250–60; Gagarin, No. 3, pp. 31–2; Grzegorzewski, 1876, No. 6, pp. 367–8; Tornauw, p. 427; Qarākhī, pp. 120–1; Ḥājj ʿAlī, pp. 25–6; Khursh, No. 39, pp. 17–18.

30. *AKAK*, Vol. IX, pp. 765–6, document No. 651, Neidhardt to Chernyshev, 24 September [6 October] 1843, No. 1676; Iurov, '1843', pp. 28–101; Okol'nichii, No. 4, pp. 325–8, 334–5; Il'in pp. 260–1; Szimanski [Shimanskii], 'Delo na Gotsatlinskikh Vysotakh 21-go Sentiabria 1843 Goda. (Iz Pokhodynkh Zapisok.)', *Voennyi Sbornik* (1869); No. 7, pp. 5–9; Qarākhī, p. 121; Khursh, No. 39, pp. 18–20, No. 40, pp. 10–11.

31. *AKAK*, Vol. IX, pp. 879–81, document No. 723, Freytag to Hurko, 16 [28] October 1843, No. 307; Iurov, '1843', pp. 123–7; Okol'nichii, No. 4, pp. 336–7.
32. For the Russian losses, see Iurov, '1843', Appendix V, pp. 17–18 (separate pagination).
33. Tornauw, p. 432. For Hurko's biography, see *AKAK*, Vol. IX, p. XIX.
34. Tornauw, p. 430. And see Il'in, p. 256.
35. *AKAK*, Vol. IX, pp. 764–5, 766–7, document Nos. 651, 653, Hurko to Neidhardt, 24 September [6 October], Neidhardt to Chernyshev, 26 September [8 October] 1843, Nos. 144, 1694 respectively; Klugenau to Neidhardt, 20 September [2 October] 1843, No. 114, as quoted by Okol'nichii, No. 4, pp. 339–40, 344–5; Il'in, p. 267; Iurov, '1843', pp. 127–8; Okol'nichii, No. 4, pp. 338–45; Grzegorzewski, 1876, No. 6, pp. 368–9; Tornauw, pp. 430–2, 436–7.
36. Iurov, '1843', pp. 128–30; Okol'nichii, No. 4, pp. 345–8; Grzegorzewski, 1876, No. 6, pp. 369–70.
37. Iurov, '1843', p. 130.
38. Five letters addressed to Hurko and Klugenau from: (1) the '*Ulamā*', *Beks*, Honourable and Wise People and the Communities of Tsunta (Dido), Tindal, Baqgulal, Chindal, Karalal, 'Andi, Kindal, Keleb, Kakhib, 'Andāl, Hindāl (Koyṣūbū), Khunzakh, Chechnia and Others; (2) The '*Ulamā*' and Honourable and Wise People of Darghī (Aqūsha) and Other Communities; (3) The '*Ulamā*', Elders and All the People of ʿAndāl; (4) The '*Ulamā*', *Beks*, and All the Inhabitants of the Lowlands; (5) Jamāl and Taymāz Khān Qāḍi, published in Iurov, '1843', as Appendices VIII C, VIII D, VIII E, VIII F and VIII G, pp. 21–5 (separate pagination) and in *Dvizhenie*, pp. 424–8, as document Nos. 223, 227, 225, 226, 224 respectively. The first letter is published also in Okol'nichii, No. 5, pp. 313–14. Also, see letter from the '*Ulamā*', *Beks*, and All the Inhabitants of Daghestan to the *Shāmakhāl*, Hurko and Klugenau, and Klugenau's reply, published in Iurov, '1843', as Appendices VIII A, VIII B respectively, p. 20 (separate pagination); *Dvizhenie*, p. 423, document No. 222, Neidhardt to Chernyshev, 3 [15] January 1844. For a different version, see Khursh, No. 40, pp. 12–13.
39. *AKAK*, Vol. IX, pp. 776–7, 783–4, document Nos. 657, 663, Hurko to Neidhardt, 2 [14] October, Neidhardt to Chernyshev, 11 [23] November 1843, Nos. 178, 1942 respectively; Iurov, '1843', pp. 130–7; Okol'nichii, no. 5, pp. 314–18; Tornauw, pp. 437–8; Gagarin, No. 4, pp. 13–18; Grzegorzewski, 1876, No. 6, pp. 370–1; Qarākhī, pp. 121–2; Khursh, No. 48, pp. 12–14, No. 49, pp. 12–13.
40. Iurov, '1843', p. 137. Also, see Tornauw, p. 444. Hurko had c. 2,000 troops and 5 cannons, against what he estimated as Shamil's 4,700 men and 6 cannons.
41. The protocol of this council is published in Iurov, '1843', as Appendix IX, pp. 25–8 (separate pagination). According to Tornauw, then Hurko's chief-of-staff (pp. 456–7), this is an 'edited' version. A reconstruction of the original version is given by him on pp. 445–6. This passivity had, naturally, a disastrous effect on the morale of the besieged garrison.
42. Ibid, p. 447.

43. Ibid, p. 449. See especially his note there, in which he disputes Okol'nichii (and Iurov), who gave 20 November as the date of the fort's fall.
44. Ibid, pp. 450–1. For the entire affair, see *AKAK*, Vol. IX, pp. 781–3, 784–8, document Nos. 661, 662, 664, 665, 666, 667, 668, Argutinskii to Hurko, 5 [17] November, Neidhardt to Chernyshev, 8 [20] November, Hurko to Neidhardt (secret), 12 [24] November, Neidhardt to Chernyshev, 14 [26] November, Argutinskii to Neidhardt, 16 [28] November, Neidhardt to Chernyshev, 17 [29], 25 November [7 December] 1843, Nos. n.a., 1928, 254, 1962, 1840, 1972, 2026 respectively; Iurov, '1843', p. 137–47; Okol'nichii, no. 5, pp. 318–30; Il'in, pp. 267–9; Tornauw, pp. 439–54; Gagarin, No. 4, pp. 18–21; Grzegorzewski, 1876, No. 6, pp. 371–2; Züssermann, 'Otryvki', 1876, No. 3, pp. 93–4; Qarākhī, p. 122; Ḥājj ʿAlī, pp. 26–7; Khursh, No. 49, p. 14; MRE, CPC, Russie, Tiflis, Vol. I, ff. 161–6, Castillon to Guizot, 29/17 November, 6 December/14 November 1843, Nos. 23, 24.
45. Already on his way from Girgil, Hurko 'did not dare to return by the way by which he had come . . . because of unrest in the Khanate of Mekhtulī' – Okol'nichii, No. 5, p. 329. And see Tornauw, pp. 454–7.
46. Baddeley, p. 372. For the siege of Temir-Khān-Shuīa, where Hurko and Klugenau with the bulk of the forces were locked, see *AKAK* Vol. IX, pp. 787–9, documents Nos. 667, 668, 669, 672, 673, 674, Neidhardt to Chernyshev, 17 [29], 21, 25 November [3, 7] 6, [18], 16 [28] December 1843, Nos. 1972, 2007, 2026, 25, 26, 75 respectively; Hurko to Neidhardt, 15 [27] November 1843, No. 258, as published in Aleksandr Volotskoi, 'General Freitag i ego Boevye Tovarishchi. Tri Epizoda iz Zavoevaniia Kavkaza', *Russkaia Starina* (1873), No. 6, pp. 835–8 (hereafter: Volotskoi); Iurov, '1843', pp. 149–50, 152–6, 161–4; Okol'nichii, No. 5, pp. 333–9, 346–7, 349–53; Il'in, pp. 269–71, 281, 285–6, 289, 302–5; Gagarin, No. 4, pp. 21–32; Gzregorzewski, 1876, No. 6, pp. 372–3; Qarākhī, pp. 122–3, 124–5; Ḥājj ʿAlī, pp. 27–8; Khursh, No. 49, pp. 15, 16, 17; MRE, CPC, Russie, Tiflis, Vol. I, ff. 167–9, Castillon to Guizot, 11 December 1843, No. 25. For the evacuation of the forts on the Ṣūlaq and their concentration in Evgenievskoe, see *Dvizhenie*, pp. 364–8, document No. 203, 'Excerpts from Debriefings of Officers and Soldiers Returning from Shamil's Imprisonment', 12 [24] January 1843 [obvious misprint for 1844]; Iurov, '1843', pp. 150–1; Okol'nichii, No. 5, p. 131; Qarākhī, pp. 125–6; Khursh, No. 49, p. 15. For Passek's stay in Khunzakh, subsequent retreat to Balakhin and his stay under siege there, see Passek, 'Otstuplenie iz Khunzakha (1843 God)', *Kavkazskii Sbornik*, Vol. I, pp. 215–35. (This is the text of Passek's report to Klugenau, 11 [23] January 1844, No. 1, which was published also in Okol'nichii, No. 5, p. 353–66 and in *AKAK*, Vol. IX, pp. 798–805, as document No. 679); *AKAK*, Vol. IX, pp. 792–7, document No. 672, Neidhardt to Chernyshev, 6 [18] December 1843, No. 25; Iurov, '1843', pp. 180–98; Okol'nichii, No. 5, p. 349; Osip Ivanov, 'Rasskaz Soldata', *Kavkaz*, 7 [19] October 1853 (No. 74), pp. 321–3; Tornauw, p. 470; Qarākhī, pp. 123–4; Khursh, No. 49, p. 15. And see *Bresslauer Zeitung*, 14 December 1843, 5, 20 January, 6, 7, 10, 13 February 1844 (Nos. 223, 4, 17, 31, 32, 35, 37), pp. 2329, 32–3, 143, 269, 274, 298, 319 respectively (von Gaertringen archive).
47. According to Okol'nichi, (No. 5, p. 335), Shamil called Shuʿayb to Ghaz-

ānish for political rather than military reason: the *imām* wanted the Chechens to see that his proclamations about his conquests were true.

48. Volotskoi, pp. 817–27, 'War Diary of the Left Flank of the Caucasian Line, 14 [26] – 23 November [5 December] 1843' (secret), written by Freytag, Volotskoi to Freytag, 24 November [6 December] 1843; Iurov, '1843', pp. 156–61, 164–70; Okol'nichii, No. 5, pp. 339–45; Qarākhī, p. 123; Khursh, No. 49, pp. 15–16; MRE, CPC, Russie, Tiflis, Vol. I, f. 170, Castillon to Guizot, 14 December 1843, No. 26.
49. *AKAK* Vol. IX, p. XXIX.
50. Volotskoi, pp. 827–34, 838–9, 'Notes by a Witness on the Battle of 15 [27] December', Volotskoi to Hurko, 23 July [4 August] 1844, No. 203; *AKAK*, Vol. IX, pp. 790–2, 793–4, documents Nos. 671, 673, Neidhardt to Chernyshev, 1 [13], 6 [18] December 1843, Nos. 7, 26; Iurov, '1843', p. 174; Okol'nichii, No. 5, pp. 366–71; Qarākhī, p. 125; Khursh, No. 49, pp. 16–17.
51. *AKAK* Vol. IX, pp. 795–6, document No. 675, Hurko to Neidhardt, 19 [31] December 1843, No. 272; Iurov, '1843', pp. 174–180; Okol'nichii, No. 5, pp. 371–6; Il'in, pp. 305–8, 311; Qarākhī, pp. 124, 125; Khursh, No. 49, pp. 17–19; MRE, CPC, Russie, Tiflis, Vol. I, ff. 171–8, Castillon to Guizot, 18, 28 December 1843, 5, 13 January 1844, Nos. 27, 28, 29, 30 respectively; PRO, FO/65/294, Yeames to Aberdeen, Odessa, 10, 20 December 1843, Nos. 1, 2, FO/65/298, Yeames to Rothesay, Odessa, January 1844, No. 1, attached to Rothesay to Aberdeen, St. Petersburg, 8 March 1844, No. 38.
52. Qarākhī, p. 125.
53. Iurov, '1843', pp. 206–7; Khursh, No. 49, p. 19.
54. Iurov, '1843', p. 139.
55. When Freytag reported that Shamil possessed four guns, 'they laughed heartily in Stavropol' [the HQ of the Caucasian Line] – Gagarin, No. 3, p. 19. Shamil, in fact, used artillery for the first time on 13 August 1843, i.e. about a month *before* his campaign in Daghestan – ibid, pp. 20–1, and Zagorskii, p. 240.
56. Iurov, '1843', pp. 204–6.
57. *AKAK*, Vol. IX, pp. 797–8, 805–8, document Nos. 678, 680, 681, 682, 683, Neidhardt to Chernyshev, 3 [15], 21, 25 January [2, 6], 3 [15], 10 [22] February 1844, Nos. 4, 70, 93, 130, 161 respectively (the last document was printed also in *Dvizhenie*, pp. 449–51, as document No. 234); *Dvizhenie*, pp. 430–8, document Nos. 229, 230, Neidhardt to Chernyshev, 7 [19] January, Bebutov to Neidhardt, 19 [31] January 1844; Iurov, '1844', pp. 172–6.

Chapter 15: Darghiyya

1. *Dvizhenie*, pp. 393–4, document No. 217, Nicholas I to Golovin [should be to Neidhardt], 14 [26] November 1843; Iurov, '1844', p. 158 and Appendix I, p. 375.
2. Ibid, p. 157.
3. The Emperor's Rescript to Neidhardt, 18 [30] December 1843, No. 130, as quoted by ibid, p. 158. Translation based on Baddeley, p. 379.

4. Iurov, '1844', loc. cit, emphasis added. Translation based on Baddeley, p. 380.
5. *Dvizhenie*, p. 444, document No. 232, Chernyshev to Neidhardt, 1 [13] February 1844.
6. The above Rescript to Neidhardt (note 3) – Iurov, '1844', pp. 158–9. Translation based on Baddeley, pp. 379–80.
7. See, e.g., *AKAK*, Vol. IX, pp. 822, 851–2, 857, document Nos. 693, 706, 707, 711, Chernyshev to Neidhardt, 8 [20] April, 2 [14], 7 [19], 17 [29] July 1844, Nos. 3373, 6089, 6957, 6604 respectively.
8. Rzewuski, Vol. IV, pp. 223–4; A-D, G., 'Pokhod 1845 Goda v Dargo', *Voennyi Sbornik* (1859), No. 5, Otdel Neoffitsialnyi, p. 3 (hereafter 'Pokhod').
9. Baddeley, p. 382. For the drawing of the plans and their final version, see *AKAK*, Vol. IX, pp. 748–9, 808–11, 816–18, 820–2, document Nos. 630, 684, 689, 691, 692, Autographed Letter from Nicholas I to Neidhardt, 2 [14] February, Excerpt from an Internal Report [Ministry of War] (secret), 12 [24] February, Argutinskii to Neidhardt, 18 [30] March (secret), Neidhardt to Chernyshev, 27 March [8 April], No. 410, Neidhardt to Chernyshev (top secret), 5 [17] April 1844, No. 453; Iurov, '1844', pp. 157–69.
10. Chernyshev to Neidhardt (confidential), 18 [30] November 1843, No. 557, as quoted in Iurov, '1844', pp. 159–60. Translation based on Baddeley, p. 380.
11. This policy originated probably from both the need in reinforcement and the doctrinal prohibition to live under the rule of unbelievers, to which the *imāms* had adhered. Such transfers of population were started by Ghāzī Muḥammad (e.g. Qarākhī, p. 19) and continued by Shamil on a small scale in the 1830s. Only in the 1840s did Shamil engage in what Pinson called 'demographic warfare' (Marc Pinson, 'Russian Expulsion of Mountaineers from the Caucasus, 1856–66 and Its Historical Background. Demographic Warfare – An Aspect of Ottoman and Russian Policies, 1854–1866', PhD thesis, Harvard University, 1970). Shamil's massive population transfers from the border areas into the heartland of his domains created, in effect, a ring of scorched earth around them which 'very markedly increased the obstacles we face in achieving our aim' (Golovin, p. 34). And see *AKAK*, Vol. IX, pp. 841–4, document No. 702, Neidhardt to Chernyshev, 19 June [1 July] 1844, No. 69 (secret).
12. *AKAK*, Vol. IX, pp. 883–6, document No. 728, Neidhardt to Chernyshev (top secret), 19 [31] May 1844, No. 16; *Dvizhenie*, pp. 468–9, document No. 244, Neidhardt to Nesterov, 5 [17] April 1844; Iurov, '1844', pp. 219–21, 227–40.
13. For raids carried out by the mountaineers during this time, see *AKAK*, Vol. IX, pp. 815–16, 881–3, document Nos. 688, 726, 727, Neidhardt to Chernyshev, 5 [17] March, 28 April [10], 1 [13] May 1844, Nos. 265, 59, 85 respectively; *Shamil*, p. 231, document No. 182, 'Excerpt from Survey of the Most Important Military Events in the Caucasus, 1 [13] January–1 [13] March 1844'; Iurov, '1844', pp. 222–6.
14. *Dvizhenie*, pp. 457–60, document No. 242, Neidhardt to Chernyshev, 2 [14] April 1844. Indeed at the time, two of his *nā'ibs* were already operating in Ghāzī-Ghumuq – *AKAK*, Vol. IX, pp. 811–15, 818–20, 822, document

Nos. 685, 686, 687, 690, 693, Neidhardt to Chernyshev, 20, 24 February [4, 8], 1 [13] March, Nos. 211, 222, 254, Argutinskii to Neidhardt, 18 [30] March (secret), Chernyshev to Neidhardt, 8 [20] April 1844, No. 3373 respectively; *Dvizhenie*, pp. 453–5, document Nos. 237, 238, 239, Shamil to Muḥammad the *Qāḍī* of Aqūsha, not later than 13 March, Argutinskii to Neidhardt 6 [18] March, Proclamation of Lüders to the People of Aqūsha and Tsudaqār, 15 [27] March 1844 respectively; Iurov, '1844', pp. 176–83; Qarākhī, pp. 126–8.

15. *Dvizhenie*, pp. 457–60, document No. 242, Neidhardt to Chernyshev, 2 [14] April 1844. For Shuʿayb's murder and Shamil's reaction to it, see below, p. 244.
16. *AKAK*, Vol. IX, pp. 822–32, document Nos. 694, 697, 695, 696, Neidhardt to Chernyshev, 23 April [5] (secret), 15 [27] May, Argutinskii to Neidhardt, 24 April [6 May], Lüders to Neidhardt, 11 [23] May 1844, Nos. 9, 787, 837, 1844 respectively; Iurov, '1844', pp. 183–98.
17. *AKAK*, Vol. IX, pp. 841–4, document No. 702, Neidhardt to Chernyshev (secret), 19 June [1 July] 1844, No. 69; *Dvizhenie*, p. 477, document No. 250, Report by HQ Caucasian Corps, 9 [21] June 1844; Iurov, '1844', pp. 240–2, 246–8. For the activities of Lüders, see *AKAK*, Vol. IX, pp. 834–41, document Nos. 699, 700, 701. 'Detailed Description of the Battle of 3 [15] June 1844 Near Qarā Shūra' by Passek, Lüders to Neidhardt, 5 [17], 15 [27] June 1844, Nos. 342, 402 respectively; *Dvizhenie*, pp. 477–8, document No. 250, Report by HQ Caucasian Corps, 9 [21] June 1844; Iurov, '1844', pp. 198–204, 242–6; A. Vrankin, 'Odno iz Del General-Maiora Passeka: Delo pri Gilli 5-go Iiunia 1844 Goda', *Sbornik Gazety Kavkaz* (1846), pp. 21–7.
18. *AKAK*, Vol. IX, pp. 841–4, document No. 702, Neidhardt to Chernyshev (secret), 19 June [1 July] 1844, No. 69; Iurov, '1844', pp. 248–50.
19. The above-quoted document from *AKAK* (previous note), p. 842. Shamil, according to Neidhadt's information, intended to 'act on our communications' – ibid, pp. 736–9, document No. 624, Neidhardt to Chernyshev, 26 June [8 July] 1844, No. 78 (secret). Quotation from p. 738.
20. Ibid, p. 849, document No. 704, Neidhardt to Chernyshev, 26 June [8 July] 1844, No. 83 (top secret).
21. Ibid, the above document, and pp. 852–3, document No. 708, Chernyshev to Neidhardt, 10 [22] July 1844, No. 428 (secret); Iurov, '1844', pp. 265–6.
22. *AKAK*, Vol. IX, pp. 844–51, 853–7, document Nos. 703, 705, 709, 710, Argutinskii to Neidhardt, 20 June [2 July], Lüders to Neidhardt, 2 [14], 14 [26] (two reports) July 1844 (all three secret), Nos. 1545, 83, 481, 482 respectively; Iurov, '1844', pp. 204–13, 252–60, Ḥājj ʿAlī, pp. 28–9.
23. The official relations reported that Shamil had run away – e.g. *AKAK*, Vol. IX, pp. 849–51, document No. 705, Lüders to Neidhardt, 2 [14] July 1844, No. 60 (secret).
24. Rostislav Andreevich Fadeev to his father, Temir-Khān-Shūra, 14 [26] July 1844, in 'Pis'ma Rostislava Andreevicha Fadeeva k Rodnym', *Russkii Vestnik* (1897), No. 8, p. 4 (hereafter: details of letter + No. of *RV*). The bridge referred to is the one near Qurūdah.
25. *AKAK*, Vol. IX, pp. 857–65, document Nos. 712, 713, 714, Neidhardt to Chernyshev, (top secret) 22 July [6 August] 1844, Nos. 160, 19, 457 respectively; Iurov, '1844', pp. 265–6. Fadeev remarked: 'The military

operations in Daghestan for this year are finished (many assert that they have never started)' – to his father, Piatigorsk, 4 [16] September 1844, No. 8, p. 5. For two small expeditions, see *AKAK*, Vol. IX, pp. 874–6, 886–8, document Nos. 720, 721, 730, Neidhardt to Chernyshev, 22 September [4 October], Passek to Neidhardt, 5 [17] October (secret), Kowalewski to Neidhardt, 9 [21] September 1844, Nos. 1084, 402, 241, respectively; Iurov, '1844', pp. 267–9.

26. For Argutinskii's campaign, see *AKAK*, Vol. IX, pp. 871–4, document No. 719. Argutinskii to Neidhardt, 21 September [3 October] 1844, No. 2296; Iurov, '1844', pp. 270–80. For that of Schwartz, see *AKAK*, Vol. IX, pp. 869–71, document No. 718, Schwartz to Neidhardt, 6 [18] September 1844, No. 2015; *Dvizhenie*, pp. 481–3, document No. 255, Neidhardt to Chernyshev, 12 [24] October 1844; Iurov, '1844', pp. 339–60.
27. *AKAK*, Vol. IX, p. 886, document No. 729, Neidhardt to Chernyshev, (secret), 28 August [9 September] 1844, No. 218 (excerpt); Iurov, '1844', pp. 284–310; G. Vertepov, 'Po Povodu Piatidesiatiletii Kreposti (Nyne Slobody) Vozdvizhenskoi', *Terskie Vedomosti*, 6 [18], 8 [20] April, 1894 (Nos. 41, 42), pp. 3–4 respectively. The Chechens in order to block Freytag's advance, resorted *inter alia* to setting ablaze the dry grass on 31 August, and to diverting the stream to deny his force drinking water on 1 September.
28. Fadeev to his father, Piatigorsk, 4 [16] September 1844, No. 10, p. 6. And see Züssermann, 'Otryvki', 1876, No. 3, p. 95. For a completely opposite view, *viz.* that Neidhardt 'had enough courage to refuse to attack', see Dondukov-Korsakov, Vol. V, p. 207.
29. See, e.g., Grzegorzewski, 1876, No. 6, p. 375, for Klugenau's objection to the plans for the campaign of 1844.
30. 'Lüders has gone now [to St. Petersburg] to put the blame on Neidhardt; upon his return, Neidhardt will go to put the blame on him; then Hurko will put the blame on both' – Fadeev to his father, Piatigorsk, 4 [16] September 1844, No. 10, p. 6.
31. In an autographed memorandum to Chernyshev (published in *Russkaia Starina* (1855), No. 10, pp. 202–12 and in Rzewuski, Vol. VI, pp. 235–9, neither source, unfortunately, gives its date), the emperor stated the aims of the 1844 campaign as:

    1. to rout, *if possible*, Shamil's hordes [emphasis added];
    2. to penetrate into the heart of his dominions;
    3. to consolidate [the Russian hold] there.

32. Tolstoi, 'Khadzi Murat', p. 44. Translation by Aylmer Mode. *The Works of Leo Tolstoy*, Vol. XV (Oxford and London, 1934), pp. 276–7. Pushkin described Vorontsov differently:

    Half hero and half ignoramus
    Let's add half villain to the toll.
    However, there is still a hope
    That he will presently be whole.

    Translation by Blanch, p. 227. For Vorontsov's biography, see *AKAK*, Vol. X, p. XVII; M. P. Shcherbinin, *Biografiia General-Fel'dmarshala Kniazia Mikhaila Semenovicha Vorontsova* (St. Petersburg, 1858) (hereafter: Shcherbinin); Alexander Wald, *Kurze Biographie der Fürsten Michail Simeonowitsch Woronszow* (Odessa, 1863) (hereafter: Wald).

33. [Nikolai Vasil'evich Isakov,] 'Iz Zapisok N. V. Isakova. Kavkazskie Vospominaniia (Period Voiny s Gortsami 1846 i 1848 Godov)', *Russkaia Starina* (1917), No. 2, p. 175 (hereafter: Isakov + No. of *RS*).

34. Rzewuski, Vol. VI, pp. 231–50, 279–80; 'Pokhod', pp. 2–7, 9–11, 16–17; [Vasillii Nikolaevich Norov,] 'Kavkazskaia Ēkspeditsiia v 1845 Godu. Rasskaz Ochevidtsa N.V. N-va', *Voennyi Sbornik* (1906), No. 11, pp. 13–19 (hereafter: Norov + No. of *VS*).

35. *AKAK* Vol. X, pp. 362–4, document Nos. 365, 366, 367, Vorontsov to Chernyshev, 5 [17], 15 [27] (secret), 19 [31] May 1845, Nos. 5, 351, 11 respectively; [Mikhail Semenovich Vorontsov] 'Vypiski iz Dnevnika Svetleishego Kniazia M. S. Vorontsova s 1845 po 1854 G', *Starina i Novizna*, Vol. V, pp. 74–78 (hereafter: Vorontsov's Diary); Rzewuski, Vol. VI, pp. 278, 283–5.

36. For these and other events during the first four months of 1845, see *AKAK*, Vol. IX, pp. 876–7, document No. 722, Argutinskii to Neidhardt, 26 March [7 April] 1845, No. 51; *Dvizhenie*, pp. 492–7, document No. 268, 'Excerpt from the War Diary of the Commander of Northern Daghestan, Lieutenant-General Bebutov, 12 [24] March–15 [27] December 1845'; *Shamil*, pp. 236–44, 254–68, document Nos. 189, 190, 191, 202, 192, 193, 194, 196, 197, Neidhardt to Chernyshev, 25 January [6 February] 1845, No. 15, 'Excerpts from Short Survey of the Most Important Military Events in the Caucasus' from 1 [13] November 1844 to 1 [13] January 1845, from 1 [13] January–1 [13] March and from 1 [13] March–1 [13] June 1845, Vorontsov to Chernyshev, 4 [16] (secret), 11 [23], 22 March [3 April] (secret), 28 April [10 May] (secret), 9 [21] May 1845 (secret). Nos. 24, 27, 33, 222, 247 respectively; Rzewuski, Vol. VI, pp. 250–61, 270–7, 286, 396–419; Vol. VII, pp. 383–7; Norov, 1906, No. 11, pp. 20–3; 'Pokhod', pp. 11–14; Qarākhī, pp. 133–6. Quotations from Rzewuski, Vol. VI, pp. 273, 253 respectively.

37. Vorontsov's campaign of 1845 is the most widely described episode in the Caucasian War. This description is based on the following sources: *AKAK*, Vol. X, pp. 364–77, 380–1, 385–91, 396–418, document Nos. 368, 369, 370, 372, 375, 378, 379, 382, 371, 373, 383, 384, Vorontsov to Chernyshev, 8 [20] (secret), 19, 26 June [1, 8], 1 [13], 9 [21], 21, 24 July (secret) [2, 5 August], Nos. 21, 25, 31, 32, 33, 42, 44, Vorontsov to Chernyshev, 5 [17] August, Chernyshev to Vorontsov, 27 June [9 July], No. 6509, Freytag to Vorontsov, 5 [17] July, Bellegarde to Hurko, 19 [31] July, No. 2055, Adlerberg to Vorontsov, 4 [16] September, No. 317, 'Military Operations in the Caucasus in 1845', respectively; *Shamil*, pp. 245–6, 252–4, document Nos. 195, 200, 201, Civilian Governor Georgia-Imeret'i to Captain of Nobility, 16 [28] April, No. 499, Vorontsov's Orders of the Day, 15 [27], 16 [28] June 1845, Nos. 51, 53, respectively; Austria, Haus-, Hoff- und Staatsarchiv (hereafter: HHSA), Toskana 66/Varia Vorontsov to Marechal Marmont, Tiflis, 10/22 December 1845 (copy); MRE, CPC, Tiflis, Vol. 2, ff. 45–54, Castillon to Guizot, Tiflis, 4/16 May, 8 August/27 July, 16/28 September 1845, Nos. 4, 5, 6, CPC, Turquie, Erzeroum Vol. 2, ff, 137–8, 156–7, Clairambault to Guizot, Trebizonde, 20 July, 9 September 1845, Nos. 12, 16; PRO, FO/78/613, Brant to Aberdeen, Erzeroom, 13

March, 12 June, 11 July, 1 October 1845, Nos. 4, 8, 11, 12, FO/60/117, Abott to Aberdeen, Tabreez, 7 July, 6, 29 August, 5 September, 3 November 1845, Nos. 14, 16, 17, 18, 24, Abott to Sheil, Tabreez, 14, 25 July 1845, Nos. 49, 51 respectively, FO/65/315, Yeames to Aberdeen, Odessa, 21 March, 30 June, 26 September 1845, Nos. 2, 3, 4 (the latter was published in M. Gammer, 'Vorontsov's 1845 Expedition against Shamil: A British Report', *Central Asian Survey*, Vol. IV, No. 4 [Autumn 1985], pp. 13–33 [hereafter: Gammer]); The Benckendorff/Lieven/Cröy archive found in a trunk in the loft of Lime Kiln, Claydon, Ipswich, Suffolk in August 1984 (hereafter: Benckendorff Archive), private letters from Constantin Benckendorff to Princess Lieven (his aunt), Tasch Kitschou, 27 May/3 June and Piatigorsk, 18/30 August, Nos. 9, 12, [Ernest?] to Benckendorff, St. Petersburg 3/14 [*sic*] August 1845; S. L. Avaliani (ed.), *Iz Arkhiva K. Ē. Andreevskogo*, Vol. I. *Zapiski Ē. S. Andreevskogo* (Odessa, 1913), pp. 1–37, 60–1, 63–6, 213 (hereafter: Andreevskii); [Nikolai Beklemishev,] 'Ēpizod iz Ēkspeditsii v Dargo v 1845 Godu. Pis'mo s Kavkaza ot 25 Iiunia 1845 Goda', in V. Kashpirev (ed.), *Pamiatniki Novoi Russkoi Istorii. Sbornik Istoricheskikh Stat'ei i Materialov*, Vol. I (St Petersburg, 1871), pp. 312–16 (hereafter: Beklemishev); Fadeev, No. 8, pp. 7–14; Nikolai Gorchakov, 'Ēkspeditisiia v Dargo (1845 G.) (Iz Dnevnika Ofitsera Kurinskogo Polka)', *Kavkazskii Sbornik*, Vol. II, pp. 117–41 (hereafter: Gorchakov); Vorontsov's Diary, pp. 78–9; [Mikhail Semenovich Vorontsov] Pis'ma Kniazia Mikhaila Semenovicha Vorontsova k Alekseiu Petrovichu Ermolovu', *Russkii Arkhiv* (1890), No. 2, pp. 162–83 (hereafter; Vorontsov to Ermolov + date and No. of *RA*); *Arkhiv Kniazia Vorontsova*, Vol. XXXVI (Moscow, 1890), pp. 256–70; 'Ēkspeditsiia v Dargo 1845 Goda', *Voennyi Zhurnal* (1855), No. 4, Part II, 'Voenaia Istoriia', pp. 27–44; 'Ēkspeditsiia v Dargo 1845 Goda', *Zhurnal dlia Chteniia Vospitannikam Voenno-Uchebnykh Zavedenii*, Vol. CXXIII; Qarākhī, pp. 136–50; Ḥājj ʿAlī, pp. 29–32; Rzewuski, Vol. VI, pp. 221–395, 13–16 (separate pagination); Michał Butowt Andrzejkowicz, *Skice Kaukazu* (Warsaw, 1859), pp. 55–180 (hereafter: Andrzejkowicz); Constantin Benckendorff, *Souvenirs Intimes d'une Campagne au Caucase Pendant l'Été de 1845* (Paris, 1858), (hereafter: Benckendorff); Nikolai Delwig, 'Vospominaniia ob Ēkspeditsii v Dargo', *Voennyi Sbornik* (1864), No. 7, pp. 189–230 (hereafter: Delwig); Dondukov-Korsakov, Vol. VI, pp. 92–160, 208–15; [V. A. Heimann,] '1845 God. Vospominaniia V. A. Geimana', *Kavkazskii Sbornik*, Vol. III, pp. 251–375 (hereafter: Heimann); Isakov, No. 2, pp. 171–7; Kalinowski, pp. 25–31; Aleksandr Pavlovich Nicolaÿ, 'Iz Vospominanii o Moei Zhizni: Darginskii Pokhod, 1845', *Russkii Arkhiv* (1890), No. 6, pp. 249–78 (hereafter: Nicolaÿ); Norov, 1906, No. 11, pp. 1–34, No. 12, pp. 15–52, 1907, No. 1, pp. 31–64, No. 2, pp. 1–42, No. 3, pp. 1–28, No. 4, pp. 16–46; 'Stseny iz Voennoi Zhizni', *Sbornik Gazety Kavkaz* (1846), pp. 410–11; Baddeley, pp. 385–410; Grzegorzewski, 1876, No. 6, pp. 376–80; Shcherbinin, pp. 220–48; Züsserman, 'Otryvki', 1876, No. 4, pp. 418–23; 'Darginskaia Ēkspeditsiia', *Terskie Vedomosti* 12 [24] August 1893 (No. 93), pp. 3–4; 'Important if True', *The Times*, 20 August 1845, p. 6, c. 4.

38. The jesters in Vorongsov's camp called this affair 'bataille en chimère' – Delwig, p. 193.

39. This move by Passek was controversial in Russian pre-revolutionary historiography, but even Passek's supporters admitted that he had acted 'in the spirit' of Vorontsov's instructions rather than upon an explicit command.
40. These were left behind to guard the route of supplies.
41. 'Pokhod', p. 32.
42. Grzegorzewski, 1876, No. 6, p. 377.
43. Norov, 1907, No. 4, pp. 44, 45. The number of effectives, however, was 7,940 infantry, 1,218 cavalry and 342 artillery – Rzewuski, Vol. VI, p. 328.
44. Nicolaÿ, p. 263.
45. Delwig, p. 209. Translation based on Baddeley, pp. 397–98 (who mistakenly atributes his quotation to Heimann). Also, Norov, 1907, No. 2, p. 16; Gorchakov, p. 124.
46. The neglect to occupy the forest was another point of criticism raised later against Vorontsov.
47. 'Pokhod', p. 42; Rzewuski, Vol. VI, p. 333.
48. Gorchakov, p. 136.
49. Messengers had been sent to Freytag before Vorontsov left Darghiyya.
50. Gammer, p. 30. For Argutinskii's operations, see *AKAK*, Vol. X, pp. 377–80, 381–5, 391–6, document Nos. 374, 376, 380, 381, Argutinskii to Vorontsov, 6[18], 10 [22], 27, 28 July [8, 9 August] 1845, Nos. 176, 183, 204 (the last one had no number); Rzewuski, Vol. VI, pp. 431–67; Norov, 1906, No. 12, p. 38, 1907, No. 4, pp. 32–4; 'Ēkspeditsiia', p. 39; Qarākhī, pp. 150–1. For Schwartz's campaign, see Rzewuski, Vol. VII, pp. 387–419; Norov, 1906, No. 12, pp. 36–8, 1907, No. 4, pp. 32–4; 'Ēkspeditsiia', pp. 37–9; Arnold Züssermann, 'Iz Moikh Zapisok. 6-go Iiunia 1845 Goda', *Sbornik Gazety Kavkaz* (1846), pp. 306–11.
51. For which, see Rzewuski, Vol. VI, pp. 424–7, 467–76; *Dvizhenie*, pp. 490–2, document No. 265, Argutinskii to Bebutov, 15 [27] September 1845.
52. See, e.g., the cold reception he accorded Freytag, who had voiced criticism of the entire idea of the campaign (Heimann, p. 262), and his reaction to Benckendorff's remarks about the disorders during the march of the column (Benckendorff, p. 36).
53. Thus, Klugenau, who had fought for 12 years in the mountains of Daghestan, was nominated to head the 'biscuit expedition', which needed commanders experienced in forest warfare, while Labyntsev, who had such experience of forest warfare in Chechnia, was sent to storm the heights opposite Darghiyya. The same misuse of experience happened with Caucasian troops at the column, when units experienced in mountain warfare in Daghestan were used in the forest, and units stationed in Chechnia and experienced in forest warfare were sent to attacks in the mountains.
54. Passek's advance to the 'Cold Mountain' and Bariatinskii's attack at 'Andī are but two examples.
55. These included, *inter alia*, Prince Alexander von Hesse-Darmstadt (the emperor's brother-in-law), Prince Wittgenstein, Prince Paskiewicz Junior, Prince Bariatinskii and Count Benckendorff.

56. Dondukov-Korsakov, Vol. VI, p. 109.
57. This, of course, does not diminish the validity of the above and other points of criticism, and that it was one of the reasons for Vorontsov's inattentiveness to military matters could explain, but by no means justify, the viceroy's conduct.
58. *AKAK*, Vol. X, pp. 867–8, document No. 717, '[The Required] Disposition towards the General Offensive by All Participating Forces from Northern Daghestan and the Left Flank of the Caucasian Line', 13 [25] August 1844. (emphasis added). An official history of the campaign of 1845 mentioned the same aim: 'To supply the natives, who have been forcibly transported by Shamil, with an opportunity to cross over to our side' – 'Ēkspeditsiia', p. 35.
59. Benckendorff, p. 9, Similarly, pp. 89–90; Rzewuski, Vol. VI, p. 289; 'Pokhod', p. 16; Gammer, p. 20.
60. This must be the real meaning of his letters to Chernyshev, 25 May [6 June] (Rzewuski, Vol. VI, pp. 281–2) and to Ermolov, Tash Kichu, 26 May [7 June] 1845 (No. 2, pp., 163–5).
61. Vorontsov's Diary, pp. 76–7, entries for 4 [16], 6 [18] May 1845; Rzewuski, Vol. VI, pp. 283–4, 289–90; Norov, 1906, No. 11, pp. 23–6; Kundukh, 1936, No. 3 (27), p. 15; Gammer, p. 15. Also, see *Dvizhenie*, pp. 486–8, document No. 262, Vorontsov to the Emperor, 12 [24] April 1845.
62. Runowski's Diary, pp. 1419–20, entry for 16 [28] March 1860.
63. Vorontsov to Chernyshev, 25 May [6 June] 1845, as quoted by Rzewuski, Vol. VI, pp. 281–2. Also, Vorontsov to Ermolov, Tash Kichu, 26 May [7 June] 1845, No. 2, pp. 163–5.
64. *Dvizhenie*, pp. 501–2, document No. 275, Shamil's letter to the *Qāḍī* and the Entire Community of ʿAndī [spring 1845?].
65. The *imām* seems to have mistrusted the people of ʿAndī all along, and before the beginning of the campaign took a special oath from the *nāʾib* and all the community to obey his orders – Qarākhī, p. 137.
66. How painfully he struck at the people of ʿAndī can be seen from the fact that they tried to resist the burning of their villages – ibid., p. 138. And see also his remark (p. 139): 'This skirmish is like a plague to the renegades, who have thought that the unity of Islam has been broken. Their minds have become transparent.'
67. 'Pokhod', p. 36. Also, Benckendorff, p. 90.
68. Ibid., loc. cit. Also, Gammer, p. 20.
69. Qarākhī, pp. 139–40. As one should expect, the Daghestani source claims that Vorontsov approached Shamil and was rejected. But the entire logic of the situation testifies to the opposite.
70. Norov, 1907, No. 1, p. 37.
71. Gammer, p. 20.
72. Ibid., loc. cit; Qarākhī (p. 140) hinted at it when he mentioned that some *nāʾibs* asked Shamil to make peace with Vorontsov. These communications must have been the reason behind Vorontsov's 'patrol' of 2–3 July. One of the declared aims of Vorontsov was 'by the sudden appearance of our troops to supply the neighbouring mountain tribes with a means to join us' (Norov, 1907, No. 1, p. 40). But only one family joined the Russians (ibid., 1907, No. 2, p. 2).

73. Qarākhī, p. 140.
74. Ibid, pp. 140–1.
75. Delwig, p. 201; Benckendorff, p. 121.
76. Ibid, p. 118.
77. Ibid, p. 121. Two events demonstrate how right he was. When Vorontsov finally decided to march on Darghiyya, the local spies he used gave him completely wrong descriptions of the roads leading there (Norov, 1907, No. 2, p. 2); and then, an hour before the force started to march, one of the native spies escaped on Vorontsov's favourite stallion to warn Shamil (Delwig, p. 202; Gammer, p. 23; Nicolaÿ, p. 259, Rzewuski, Vol. VI, p. 333). The thief was caught by the Russians two years later during the siege of Salṭah (Vorontsov's Diary, p. 85, entries for 4 [16], 5 [17] August 1847).
78. Gammer, p. 20. This last demand must have added to their credibility because the Russians had been aware of Shamil's contacts with Muḥammad ʿAlī.
79. This is clearly demonstrated by the fact that the guards were ordered to allow in two natives who were expected to come from the right flank of the camp and wave their hats – Norov, 1907, No. 2, p. 199.
80. The emperor, who had originally wanted to withdraw the Fifth Corps in December 1845, was persuaded by Vorontsov to delay it to the spring of 1846.

Chapter 16: Ghabarṭa

1. K., 'Obzor Sobytii na Kavkaze v 1846 Godu', *Kavkazskii Sbornik*, Vol. XIV, pp. 474–598; Vol. XV, pp. 453–6, 481–505; Vol. XVI, pp. 279–93 (hereafter: '1846' + Vol. of *K S*); MRE, CPC, Russie, Tiflis, Vol. II. ff. 75–8, Castillon to Guizot, 14/2 February, 7/19 March 1846, Nos. 5, 6; Baddeley, pp. 411–12.
2. *AKAK*, Vol. X, pp. 421–2, document No. 388, Vorontsov to Chernyshev, 20 April [2 May] 1846, No. 18; '1846', Vol XVI, pp. 312–14.
3. Baddeley, p. 415.
4. *Arkhiv Raevskikh*, Vol. III (St. Petersburg, 1910), pp. 350–1, letter No. 775, N. N. Raevskii to Grabbe (draft), probably end of February 1840. Also, see Iurov, '1840–1842', Vol. XI, p. 188.
5. *AKAK*, Vol. IX, pp. 147–52, document Nos. 177, 178, 179, Golovin to Chernyshev, 26 September [8], 3 [15] October 1840, 8 [20] January 1841, Nos. 1095, 1113, 15 respectively; Iurov, '1840–1842', Vol. XI, p. 188.
6. Iurov, '1840–1842', Vol. XI, p. 189.
7. Ibid, p. 220. And see above, p. 120.
8. Iurov, '1843', pp. 48–9; Rzewuski, Vol. VII, 442–3.
9. MRE, CPC, Russie, Tiflis, Vol. I, f. 139, Castillon to Guizot, 22 May 1843, No. 13; Iurov '1843', p. 48.
10. Sources as in note 8 above.
11. Norov, 1906, No. 11, p. 26.
12. Iurov, '1844', p. 308.

13. Rzewuski, Vol. VII, pp. 423–6, 432–7, 439–40, 442–3, 444, 445–51, 454–5, 459–61, 463–5; G. N. Prozritelev, 'Posol'stvo ot Shamilia k Abadzekham', *Dagestanskii Sbornik*, Vol. III, pp. 125–9; Also, see Shamil's (undated) Proclamation to the Ghabarṭians, as published in Mackie, pp. 266–71.
14. The following description is based on: *AKAK*, Vol. X, pp. 578–86, document Nos. 531, 534, 532, 533, 535, 536, Vorontsov to Chernyshev, 21 April [3], 1 [13] May, Nos. 22, 60, Vorontsov's Proclamation to the Ghabarṭians, 27 April [9 May], 'Journal of the Military Events from 11 [23] to 30 April [12 May]' (secret) by Freytag, Kovalevskii to Zavodovskii, 6 [18] May, No. 2145 (reprinted in *Shamil* p. 279, as No. 214), Adlerberg to Vorontsov, 15 [27] May 1846, No. 352; *Dvizhenie*, pp. 504–10, document Nos. 275, 280, 281, 282, Golitsyn to Beklemishev, 18 [30] April, Shamil to Ḥājj Misostov, 20 April [2 May], Vorontsov to the Emperor, 30 April [12 May], Kodiakov to Golitsyn, April 1846; Vorontsov to Ermolov, Nal'chik, 5 [17] May 1846, No. 2, pp. 183–6; MRE, CPC, Russie, Tiflis, Vol. II, ff. 79–98, 103–11, Castillon to Guizot, 15/22 April, 2, 7, 10, 16, 20, 25 May, 8/20 September 1846, Nos. 7, 8, 9, 10, 12, 13, 13 [*sic*], 16 respectively; PRO, FO/65/321, Bloomfield to Aberdeen, St. Petersburg, 23, 26 May 1846, Nos. 84, 87, FO/65/325 Yeames to Aberdeen, Odessa, 10 June 1846, No. 1, FO/78/653 Brant to Aberdeen, Erzeroom, 4 July 1841, No. 17; '1846', Vol. XVI, pp. 312–51, Vol. XVII, pp. 175–86, 192–6, 209–14; Nikolai Gorchakov, 'Vtorzhenie Shamilia v Kabardu v 1846 Godu. Iz Zapisok Ofitsera Kurinskogo Polka', *Kavkazskii Sbornik*, Vol. IV, pp. 19–37 (hereafter: Gorchakov, 'Vtorzhenie'); Isakov, No. 2, pp. 177–80; Kundukh, 1936, No. 3 (27), p. 16; Baddeley, pp. 411–26; Qarākhī, pp. 152–3; Ḥājj ʿAlī, pp. 35–6.
15. '1846', Vol. XVI, pp. 336–7. Seeing this position, Freytag grasped the meaning of a sentence in Shamil's letter to Bata and Talgik: 'I want to position the guns near the enemy's road.' The letter, shown to Freytag on 21 April by one of his spies, was published in ibid, p. 313.
16. A letter from Shamil to Talgik and Duba, intercepted by Freytag on 21 October 1846 – ibid, p. 304.
17. It is sufficient to see the quantity of Shamil's letters intercepted by Freytag's spies which are quoted or mentioned in '1846' to be impressed by this intelligence network.
18. Baddeley, pp. 416–17.
19. Ibid, p. 421. Similarly, '1846', Vol. XVI, p. 345; Gorchakov, 'Vtorzhenie', pp. 31–2.
20. '1846', Vol. XVI, p. 341. Translation based on Baddeley, p. 422.
21. '1846', Vol. XVI, p. 342.
22. Baddeley, p. 421.
23. '1846', Vol. XVI, p. 343. Translation based on Baddeley, p. 423.
24. '1846', Vol. XVI, p. 346. In fact a Russian patrol witnessed the beginning of Shamil's retreat but failed to comprehend its meaning – Gorchakov, 'Vtorzhenie', p. 30.
25. Baddeley, p. 424. And see for details, '1846', Vol. XVI, pp. 347–8; Gorchakov, 'Vtorzhenie', pp. 26–9, 35–6.
26. '1846', Vol. XVI, p. 348.
27. Baddeley, p. 425.
28. '1846', Vol. XVII, p. 184. Two other persons who joined Shamil, Ismāʿīl

Sasikov and Edik Alborev, are mentioned in B. A. Gordanov (ed.), *Materialy po Obychnomu Pravu Kabardintsev. Pervaia Polovina XIX V.* (Nalchik, 1956), pp. 261–70, 300–5, document Nos. 32, 39 respectively. Also see below, p. 251. Four others who joined Shamil – Muḥammad Kazhokhov, Muḥammad Titlerov, Muḥammad Kudenetov Efendī and Ḥājjī Bartsov – were mentioned in Vorontsov to Ermolov, Nal'chik, 5 [17] May 1846, No. 2, p. 186.

29. Ibid., loc. cit. '1846', Vol. XVII, pp. 184–5.
30. Ibid, Vol. XVI, p. 321.
31. Ibid, Vol, XVII, p. 180.
32. Ibid, p. 183.
33. Ibid, Vol. XVI, p. 324. This inactivity, however, did not prevent him from reaping the honours due, in fact, to Nesterov.
34. John Shelton Curtiss, *The Russian Army under Nicholas I, 1825–1855* (Durham, N. C., 1965). p. 301.
35. After all, many held (privately) the opinion that Vorontsov's 'victory' over Napoleon in Krasnoe in 1814 was due to his timely rescue by Saaken – Isakov, No. 2, p. 175.
36. Baddeley, p. 417.
37. '1846', Vol. XVII, p. 179.
38. E.g., *AKAK*, Vol. X, pp. 418–19, document No. 385, Shamil's Proclamation to the Circassians and Ghabarṭians, September 1845.
39. See, e.g., *Dvizhenie*, pp. 528–9, document No. 293, Khliupin to Nesterov, 6 [18] September 1846; MRE, CPC, Russie, Tiflis, Vol. II, ff. 112–13, Castillon to Guizot, 30 September/12 October 1846, No. 17; '1846', Vol. XV, pp. 456–8, Vol. XVII, pp. 186–90.
40. Shamil's letter to Talgik and Duba, intercepted by Freytag, as quoted in '1846', Vol. XVI, p. 304.
41. *AKAK*, Vol. X, pp. 432–41, document Nos. 393, 395, 396, 397, 394, 398, 399, 400. Bebutov to Vorontsov, 16 [28] (secret), 26, 31 (two dispatches), October [7, 12 November] Nos. 9, 221, 223, 224, Bebutov to the Head of the Community of Aqūsha, Lieutenant Zuḥūm, the *Qādīs* the Elders and the *Jamā'a*, 19 [31] October, Vorontsov to Chernyshev, 8 [20] (two dispatches), 25 November [7 December] 1846, Nos. 108, 109, 126 respectively; *Dvizhenie*, pp. 529–31, document Nos. 295, 296, The *Qādī* of Tsudaqār to Argutinskii, October, Verevkin to Kotzebue, 25 October [6 November] 1846; Vorontsov's Diary, p. 82, entries for 17 [29], 23 October [4 November] 1846; Vorontsov to Bebutov, Vladikavkaz, 24 30 October [5, 11 November], Tiflis 9 [21], 18 [30] November 1846, in 'Kniaz' M. S. Vorontsov. Pis'ma Ego k Kn. V. E. Bebutovu,' *Russkaia Starina* (1871), No. 1, pp. 104–8 (hereafter details of letter + No. of *RS*); MRE, CPC, Russie, Tiflis, Vol. II, ff. 115–18, Castillon to Guizot, 9, 18 November 1846, Nos. 19, 20; PRO, FO/60/139, Abott to Palmerston, Tabreez, 3 April 1847, No. 9; '1846', Vol. XIV, pp. 529–48; Qarākhī, pp. 153–4; Ḥājj 'Alī, pp. 32–4.
42. Vorontsov's Diary, pp. 80–2, entries for 15 [27]–21 June [3 July], 13 [25]–14 [26] August 1846; Vorontsov to Ermolov, Vladikavkaz, 1 [13] July 1846, No. 2, pp. 193–4; '1846', Vol. XV, pp. 456–78, Vol. XVI, pp. 293–310; Isakov, No. 2, pp. 181–6; MRE, CPC, Tiflis, Vol. II, ff.

99–111, Castillon to Guizot, 23 June, 7 July, 8/20 September 1846, Nos. 14, 15, 16.

43. Baddeley, p. 426; '1846', Vol. XIV, pp. 552–3. This raid created such waves of shock that the tsar himself ordered an investigation into it, for which see, *AKAK*, Vol. X, pp. 441–2, 443–4, document Nos. 402, 404, Chernyshev to Vorontsov, 12 [24] January, Vorontsov to Chernyshev, 14 [26] March 1847 (secret), Nos. 468, 51 respectively.
44. Benckendorff Archive, Vorontsov to Benckendorff, Tiflis, 27 December 1846.

Chapter 17: Lesser Chechnia

1. Vorontsov to Ermolov, Tiflis, 2 [14] January 1846, Temir-Khān-Shūra, 1 [13] August 1845, No. 2, pp. 181, 171 respectively. Similarly, Vorontsov to the Emperor, Kislovodsk, early September 1845, as printed in Rzewuski, Vol. VI, pp. 379–90, especially p. 381.
2. Vorontsov's Diary, p. 79, entries for 1 [13], 19 September [1 October] 1845; Shcherbatov, p. 249.
3. *AKAK*, Vol. X, pp. 311–13, document No. 312, Vorontsov to Chernyshev, 5 [17] August 1845, No. 384; Vorontsov to the Emperor (note 1 above) pp. 386–7.
4. *AKAK*, Vol. X, pp. 318–19, document Nos. 315, 317, Vorontsov to Chernyshev, 16 [28] May, Chernyshev to Vorontsov, 11 [23] June 1846, Nos. 220, 3354 respectively; Vorontsov to Ermolov, Nal'chik, 5 [17] May, Vladikavkaz, 1 [13] July 1846, No. 2, pp. 189, 193 respectively.
5. Vorontsov to the Emperor (note 1 above) pp. 381–3; Vorontsov to Ermolov, Nal'chik, 5 [17] May 1846, No. 2, pp. 186–7, 188–9; K., 'Levyi Flang Kavkazskoi Linii v 1848 Godu', *Kavkazskii Sbornik*, Vol. IX, pp. 447–9 (hereafter: 'Levyi Flang' + Vol. of *KS*).
6. In 1848 five more *stanitsas* were established which formed the Second Sunja Cossack regiment.
7. 'Voenno-Akhtynskaia Doroga ot S. Shina do Perevala chrez Goru Bol. Salavat', *Sbornik Gazety Kavkaz* (1847), Vol. II, pp. 134–5; N. A. Volkonskii, 'Trekhletie v Dagestane. 1847 God. Osada Gergebilia i Vziatie Salty', *Kavkazskii Sbornik*, Vol. VI, pp. 479–80 (hereafter: Volkonskii, '1847'); Vorontsov to Ermolov, Vladikavkaz, 1 [13] July 1846, No. 2, pp. 197–8.
8. Züssermann, 'Otryvki', 1876, No. 4, p. 424; Kundukh, 1936, No. 3 (27), pp. 16–17, No. 4 (28), pp. 19–20. For analyses of Vorontsov's strategy, see HHSA, Russland III. 139/Konv. II, Calloredo to Meternich, St. Petersburg, 8 February/27 January 1847, No. 5; A. Benningsen, 'Un Témoignage Français sur Chamil et les Guerres de Caucase', *Cahiers du Monde Russe et Soviétique*, Vol. VII, No. 4 (October–December 1965), pp. 311–22; S. K. Bushuev, 'Pis'ma Vikonta Kastil'ona k Gizo (24 Aprelia 1844–4 Marta 1846)', *Istorik Marksist* (1936), No. 5 (57), pp. 105–23; '1846', Vol. XIV, pp. 445–51.
9. Vorontsov to the Emperor (note 1 above), p. 384. Similarly, Vorontsov to Ermolov, Tiflis, 2 [14] January 1846, No. 2, p. 182.

10. Vorontsov to the Emperor, p. 384; Vorontsov to Ermolov, Tiflis, 2 [14] January 1846, No. 2, p. 182.
11. Vorontsov to the Emperor (note 1 above), p. 382.
12. Another example of psychological warfare was the transmission to Shamil of a letter from his son in St. Petersburg – *AKAK*, Vol. X, pp. 468–9, document No. 426, 4 [16] November 1847.
13. *Dvizhenie*, pp. 519–20, 521–2, 525–7, document Nos. 285, 287, 290, Labyntsev to Vorontsov, 26 June [8], 22 July [3], 10 [22] August 1846; Vorontsov's Diary, p. 82, entry for 18 [30] September 1846' Vorontsov to Ermolov, Vladikavkaz, 1 [13] July 1846, No. 2, p, 192. Also see *Dvizhenie*, pp. 486–8, document No. 262, Vorontsov to the Emperor 12 [24] April 1845; Vorontsov to Bebutov, Tiflis, 28 March [9 April] 1847, No. 2, p, 255.
14. *Dvizhenie*, pp. 484–5, document No. 261, Vorontsov to the Emperor, 13 [25] March 1845.
15. 'Opisanie Postupkov Shamilia Protivnykh Musul'manskomu Shariatu, Kotorye Byli Zamecheny Suleiman-Efendiem vo Vremia Ego Nakhozhdeniia pri Nem', *Sbornik Gazety Kavkaz* (1847), Vol. I, pp. 30–5. (Excerpts were also published in *Shamil*, pp. 280–2, as document No. 216.)
16. *Dvizhenie*, pp. 561–3, document No. 317, Muḥammad the *Qāḍī* of Aqūsha to Shamil, 1847.
17. Vorontsov's letter to the Emperor (note 1 above), p. 385.
18. Ibid, pp. 385–6; *Kolonial'naia Politika*, Vol. II, *passim*; Khadzhimurat Omarovich Khashaev (ed.), *Feodal'nye Otnosheniia v Dagestane XIX – nachalo XX V. Arkhivnye Materialy* (Moscow, 1969), pp. 9–10, document No. 1, the Emperor's Rescript to Vorontsov, 6 [18] December 1846.
19. Thus, for example, he initiated the investment of the *shāmkhāl* with the title 'Prince of Targhū' (*Kniaz'* Tarkovskii) – *AKAK*, Vol. X, pp. 493–4, 496, document Nos. 446, 451, Vorontsov to Chernyshev, 20 July [1 August] 1849, No. 199, 'Decree to the Ruling Senate' (by the emperor), 21 December 1849 [2 January 1850]. And see Züssermann, 'Otryvki', 1876, No. 12, pp. 480–7.
20. For this process of co-optation, see Lawrence Hamilton Rhinelander, 'The Incorporation of the Caucasus into the Russian Empire: The Case of Georgia, 1801–1854', Unpublished PhD. thesis, Columbia University, 1972.
21. Rzewuski, Vol. VI, pp. 427–33, 481–505; Vorontsov to Ermolov, Tiflis, 19 [22] December 1845, 2 [14] January 1846, No. 2, pp. 175, 182.
22. Vorontsov's Diary, pp. 80–2, entries for 15 [27]–21 June [3 July], 13 [25] – 14 [26] August 1846; Vorontsov to Ermolov, Vladikavkaz, 1 [13] July 1846, No. 2, pp. 193–4; '1846', Vol. XV, pp. 456–78.
23. *AKAK*, Vol. X, pp. 471–4, document No. 430, 'Note on Chechnia' by [Leontii Pavlovich] Nicolaÿ, March 1848; *Dvizhenie*, p. 533, document No. 301, Shamil to the *Nā'ibs* and People of Chechnia, not later than 22 January 1847; 'Izvestiia s Kavkaza', *Sbornik Gazety Kavkaz* (1847) Vol. I, pp. 28–30; MRE, CPC, Russie, Tiflis, Vol. II, ff. 121–33, Castillon to Guizot, 5, 16 January, 9 February, 6 March, 9 April 1847, Nos. 22, 23, 24, 25, 26 respectively.
24. 'Levyi Flang', Vol. XI, p. 349.

25. Thus, for example, Nesterov in his 1847 clearing operation suffered five killed and 59 wounded, while Freytag on his raid sustained 13 killed and 137 wounded.
26. Vorontsov to Ermolov, Tiflis, 3 [15] November 1847, No. 2, p. 211. For the cholera epidemic, see below, note 14 to Chapter 18.
27. *AKAK*, Vol. X, pp. 471–4, document No. 430, 'Note on Chechnia' by Nicolaÿ, March 1848, p. 474; 'Levyi Flang', Vol. IX, pp. 380–420; Vorontsov to Ermolov, Tiflis, 20 December 1847 [1 January 1848], No. 2, p. 214.
28. *AKAK*, Vol. X, p. 474. In his typical excessive optimism, Vorontsov wrote: 'One can say that Lesser Chechnia is in our hands and without it Greater [Chechnia] will not resist for long' – Vorontsov to Ermolov, Tiflis, 25 March [6 April] 1848, No. 3, p. 331.
29. *AKAK*, Vol. X, pp. 411–12, document No. 437, Vorontsov to Chernyshev, 15 [27] July 1848, No. 703; Vorontsov's Diary, pp. 89–90, entries for June, 12 [24], 29 July [10 August] 1848; Vorontsov to Ermolov, Vozdvizhenskoe, 11 [23] June 1848, No. 3, pp. 334–5; Benckendorff Archive, Vorontsov to Benckendorff, Vozdvizhenskoe, 2 [14] July, Nicolaÿ to Benckendorff, Vozdvizhenskoe, 3 [15] July 1848. On the night of 31 August–1 September, the Chechens raided and burnt the bridge and the tower.
30. For which see below, pp. 188–90.
31. See, for example, his letters to all the *Nā'ibs* of Lesser and Greater Chechnia, and to Talgik, printed in 'Levyi Flang', Vol. X, p. 494, Vol. XI, pp. 345–6 respectively.
32. Vorontsov to Ermolov, Vozdvizhenskoe, 11 [23] June 1848, No. 3. p. 335.
33. Ibid., loc. cit.
34. Benckendorff Archive, Vorontsov to Benckendorff, Tiflis, 21 March 1849; Vorontsov to Ermolov, Tiflis, 23, 28 January [4, 9 February], 17 [29] March 1849, No. 3, pp. 344, 345, 348 respectively. (Quotation from p. 345.)
35. Vorontsov to Ermolov, Vozdvizhenskoe, 1 [13], Kislovodsk 10 [22] June 1849, No. 3, pp. 349, 345 respectively.
36. Vorontsov to Ermolov, Tiflis, 5 [17] November 1848, 23 January [4 February] 1849, No. 3, pp. 340, 344 respectively (quotation from p. 344).
37. De-Saget [de-Sazhe], 'Pokorenie Galashek. Iz istorii Kavkazskoi Voiny', *Voennyi Sbornik* (1902), No. 2, pp. 47–54, and Appendix on pp. 54–7, Vorontsov to Chernyshev, 19 [31] December 1849, No. 1755 (hereafter: de-Saget).
38. *AKAK*, Vol. X, pp. 486–99, document No. 452, Sleptsov to Il'inskii, 12 [24] January 1850, No. 80; Vorontsov to Ermolov, Tiflis, 25 January [6 February] 1850, No. 3, p. 353; K., 'Letuchii Otriad v 1850 i 1851 Godakh', *Kavkazskii Sbornik*, Vol. XII, pp. 348–58 (hereafter: 'Letuchii Otriad').
39. *AKAK*, Vol. X, pp. 499–501, document No. 453, Sleptsov to Il'inskii, 9 [21] February 1850, No. 287; 'Letuchii Otriad', pp. 358–66; de-Saget, p. 54.
40. Following these attempts, Sleptsov took measures to strengthen Russia's rule in these communities and to prevent further incursion by the mountaineers. These measures included the concentration of the population in large villages, the establishment of a local militia and the rendering of all

the roads leading to Shamil's domains impassable. On both counts, however, these and other measures fell short of their aim.

41. De-Saget, p. 54.
42. E.g., *AKAK*, Vol. X, pp. 501–2, document No. 454, 'Il'inskii's War Diary, 16 [28] - 25 February [9 March] 1850'; 'Letuchii Otriad', pp. 366–77.
43. *AKAK*, Vol. X, pp. 509–10, document No. 460, Slepstov to Il'inskii, 4 [16] October 1850, No. 2871; 'Letuchii Otriad', pp. 407–12.
44. Runowski's Diary, p. 1419, entry for 16 [28] March 1860.
45. For an example of such a permission, see *Dvizhenie*, p. 575, document No. 329, Shamil to Qurbān al-Muḥammad, July 1848.
46. For the events of 1847 in Chechnia, see *AKAK*, Vol. X, pp. 471–4, document No. 430, 'Note on Chechnia' by Nicolaÿ, March 1848; *Dvizhenie*, pp. 533–4, document Nos. 302, 303, Nesterov to Kotzebue, 24 March [5 April], Freytag to Nesterov, 19 April [1 May] 1847; 'Izvestiia s Kavkaza', *Sbornik Gazety Kavkaz* (1847), Vol. I, pp. 109–12, 156–8, 180–2, Vol. II., pp. 40–2, 57–8.
47. 'Levyi Flang', Vol. XI, p. 357. For the events of 1848 in Chechnia, see *AKAK*, Vol. X, pp. 470–1, 481–2, document Nos. 427, 437, Sleptsov to Nesterov, 12 [24] March, Vorontsov to Chernyshev, 15 [27] July 1848, Nos. 439, 730 respectively; 'Levyi Flang', Vol. IX, pp. 406–7, 421–43, Vol. X, pp. 434–5, 444; Vol. XI, pp. 433–41, 443–6, 449–60.

Chapter 18: Central Daghestan

1. See above, pp. 170–1.
2. Vorontsov to Bebutov, Vladikavkaz, 30 October [11 November] 1846, No. 1, p. 105.
3. *AKAK*, Vol. X, pp. 442–3, document No. 403, Vorontsov to Chernyshev (top secret), 12 [24] February 1847, No. 52; Volkonskii, '1847', pp. 481–9; MRE, CPC, Russie, Tiflis, Vol. II, ff, 130–3, Castillon to Guizot, 9 April 1847, No. 6. (The quotations are from *AKAK*, p. 443 and Volkonskii, p. 485 respectively.) Vorontsov might have hoped, as some hints indicate, to be able to capture Ghunīb and to carry out an offensive into Avāristān – MRE, CPC, Russie, Tiflis, Vol. II, ff. 152–9, Castillon to Guizot, Paris, 22 September 1847, (reference to f. 153b). And see hints to this in Vorontsov to Ermolov, Camp on Turchīdāgh, 1 [13] July, Ermolov to Vorontsov, Moscow, January 1847, No. 2, pp. 208–9, 203 respectively. In these plans, Vorontsov followed in the footsteps of previous suggestions, e.g. – *AKAK*, Vol, IX, pp. 764, 864–5, document Nos. 651, 714, Hurko to Neidhardt, 24 September [6 October] 1843, Chernyshev to Neidhardt, 25 July [6 August] 1844 (secret), Nos. 144, 457 respectively.
4. Vorontsov to Ermolov, Tiflis, 5 [17] November 1848, Ermolov to Vorontsov, 5 [17] January 1848, No. 3, pp. 340, 329 respectively.
5. Vorontsov to Ermolov, Camp on Turchīdāgh, 1 [13] July, Ermolov to Vorontsov, Moscow, January 1847, No. 2, pp. 207, 202 respectively.
6. Vorontsov, for example, confiding to Ermolov his plans, wrote him twice within two days to keep them 'in complete secrecy' – Vorontsov to Ermolov, Tiflis, 15 [27], 17 [29] December 1846, No. 2, pp. 199–200.
7. Baddeley, p. 429.

8. Volkonskii, '1847', p. 499.
9. According to the plans he had to take possession of Girgil by 17 May and start to build there a fort – Volkonskii, '1847', p. 483.
10. Ibid, p. 513. The description of this campaign is based on the following sources: *AKAK*, Vol. X, pp. 450–4, document Nos. 410, 411, 412, Order of the Day by Vorontsov, 7 [19] June, Vorontsov to Chernyshev, 7 [19], 12 [24] June 1847, Nos 176, 202 respectively; Vorontsov's Diary, pp. 83–4; Vorontsov to Ermolov, Camp on Turchīdāgh, 1 [13] July 1847, No. 2, pp. 207–10; N. A. Volkonskii, 'Trekhletie na Lezginskoi Kordonnoi Linii (1847–1849)', *Kavkazskii Sbornik*, Vol. IX, Appendices V, VII, pp. 4–5, 6 (separate pagination), Vorontsov to Schwartz, Khōjā al-Makhī, 27 May [7 June], Camp near Girgil, 5 [17] June respectively (hereafter: Volkonskii, 'Trekhletie'); Benckendorff Archive, Vorontsov to Benckendorff, Camp near Ulluchar, 14 June, Tiflis, 18/30 December 1847 respectively; MRE, CPC, Russie, Tiflis, Vol. II, ff. 137–40, Castillon to Guizot, 18, 22 June, 17, 5 [*sic*] July, Nos. 30, 31, 32, 33, ff. 146–7, Lauxerrois to Guizot, 23 August, No. 3, ff. 152–9, Castillon to Guizot, Paris, 22 September 1847; Volkonskii, '1847', pp. 512–44 and Appendices I-VI, pp. 1–4 (separate pagination); 'Izvestiia s Kavkaza', *Sbornik Gazety Kavkaz* (1847), Vol. I, pp. 260–1, Vol. II, pp. 39–40; Isakov, No. 3, pp. 328–34; Baddeley, pp. 428–33; Qarākhī, p. 158.
11. Volkonskii, '1847', p. 515.
12. The force comprised ten infantry battalions, a company of tirailleurs, two dragoon squadrons, three and a half hundreds of Cossacks, 16 hundreds of militiamen (both mounted and infantry), 12 cannon, two mortars, a rocket platoon and two platoons of fortress guns.
13. Volkonskii, '1847', pp. 520–1.
14. This is the same epidemic which attacked Russia proper in 1848–49, and which repeatedly prevented the Russians from erecting a tower on the Goyta (see previous chapter, p. 178 and note 26). For the origin and spread of the epidemic, see Volkonskii, '1847', pp. 527–9. The epidemic persisted and broke out again the following year – e.g. Ērast Stepanovich Andreevskii, 'Neskol'ko Slov o Kholere Poiavivsheisia na Kavkazskoi Linii v 1848 Godu', *Kavkazskii Kalendar* (1849), Otdelenie III, pp. 41–50.
15. Only later did the Russians learn that the force protecting the gardens had been dispersed because of the epidemic.
16. Isakov, No. 3, p. 330.
17. Volkonskii, '1847', p. 521.
18. Baddeley, p. 432.
19. Volkonskii, '1847', p. 534.
20. Ibid., p. 537.
21. Baddeley, p. 433.
22. Volkonskii, '1847', p. 543.
23. Vorontsov to Ermolov, Camp on Turchīdāgh, 1 [13] July 1847, No. 2, p. 207. And see *AKAK*, Vol. X, pp. 453–4, document No. 412, Vorontsov to Chernyshev, 12 [24] June 1847, No. 202; Benckendorff Archive, Vorontsov to Benckendorff, Tiflis, 18/30 December 1847.
24. Already on 6 June, while arriving at Khōjā al-Makhī, Vorontsov found out that cholera had broken out among Bebutov's troops (Vorontsov's Diary, p. 83, entry for 25 May [6 June] 1847). A week later, when Argutin-

skii arrived in Girgil, Bebutov's troops were 'considerably decimated' by the epidemic (Isakov, No. 3, p. 328). By 15 June, almost all the shells and bombs – 1,423 in all – had been used, and 'the force had been already melting from the cholera, [other] diseases and hardships' (ibid., p. 331). But, 'to leave the village intact and retreat would have meant to let the mountaineers get acquainted with our weakness, [and] it would have badly impressed our troops. [Furthermore], after the expedition to Darghiyya this [such a retreat] would not have counted in Prince Vorontsov's favour in St. Petersburg' (ibid., pp. 331–2). Vorontsov, therefore, pointed to the feeble fire from within the village as proof that the garrison was weak (Volkonskii, '1847', p. 527), and ordered to storm it. Even when on the eve of the attack he found out that the garrison was much stronger than he had thought, and that the breach in the wall had been partially patched and refortified, he still ordered to go on with the attack (ibid., p. 531; Isakov, No. 3, pp. 330–1). After the attempted storm, Vorontsov 'agreed that another attempt was impossible. Then, to stay longer near Girgil without shells was aimless, and the decision to leave was inevitable' (ibid., p. 333).

25. Volkonskii, '1847', p. 541.
26. Ibid., pp. 549–50; Vorontsov's Diary, p. 84, entries for 14 [26] June, 14 [26], 17 [29] July 1847; Vorontsov to Ermolov, Camp on Turchīdāgh, 1 [13] July 1847, No. 2, pp. 209–10.
27. The force consisted of eight infantry battalions, two companies of tirailleurs, a squadron of dragoons, two hundreds of Cossacks, 1,500 local levies (both mounted and infantry), 15 cannons (three of them heavy), rockets, fortress guns, a company of sappers and a platoon of engineers. This force was later joined by three and a half infantry battalions with one cannon.
28. This description is based on the following sources: *AKAK*, Vol. X, pp. 454–68, document Nos. 414, 415, 416, 419, 420, 423, 424, 422, 417, 418, 421, Vorontsov to Adlerberg, 3 [15], 8 [20], 12 [24] August, Nos. 367, 387, 400, Kotzebue to Chernyshev, 13 [25], 15 [27] September, Nos. 535, 543, Vorontsov to Chernyshev, 29 September [11 October], Nos. 597, 599, Vorontsov to Schwartz, 20 September [2 October], Vorontsov's Orders of the Day, 27 August [8], 10 [22], 15 [27] September 1847, respectively; *Dvizhenie*, pp. 534–45, document Nos. 304, 305. War Diaries of the Samur Force (excerpts), 25 July [6] – 5 [17] August, 4 [16] August – 23 September [5 October] 1847; Vorontsov's Diary, pp. 84–8; Vorontsov to Ermolov, Tiflis, 3 [15] November 1847, No. 2, pp. 210–12; Volkonskii, 'Trekhletie', Appendices IX, X, pp. 7–10, 11–12 (separate pagination), Kotzebue and Vorontsov to Schwartz, Camp near Salṭah, 30 and 31 July [11 and 12 August], Vorontsov to Schwartz, Camp near Salṭah, 12 [24] August 1847 respectively; Benckendorff Archive, Nicolaÿ to Benckendorff, Tiflis, 20 October, Vorontsov to Benckendorff, Tiflis, 18/30 December 1847; 'Izvestiia s Kavkaza', *Sbornik Garety Kavkaz* (1847), Vol. II, pp. 49–51, 56–7, 90–2; Isakov, No. 4–6, pp. 46–62; Volkonskii, '1847', pp. 442–666; Züssermann, 'Otryvki', 1876, No. 12, p. 494; MRE, CPC, Russie, Tiflis, Vol. II, ff. 148–51, 160–6, Lauxerrois to Guizot, 30, 31 August, 8, 18 October 1847, Nos. 4, 5, 6, 7; PRO, FO/78/751, Brant to Palmerston, Erzeroom, 18, 19 January 1848, Nos. 4, 5; Qarākhī, pp. 158–61; Ḥājj ʿAlī, pp. 36–7.

29. Volkonskii, '1847', pp. 551–2.
30. Ibid., p. 578.
31. Isakov, No. 4–6, p. 47.
32. Volkonskii, 'Trekhletie', Appendix IX, p. 7 (separate pagination), Kotzebue to Schwartz, Camp near Salṭah, 30 July [11 August] 1847.
33. Isakov, No. 4–6, p. 54.
34. Ibid., p. 50. For Burnod's biography, see *Voennaia Entsiklopediia*, Vol. V (St. Petersburg, 1911), pp. 203–4.
35. Volkonskii, '1847', p. 577.
36. Isakov, No. 4–6, p. 51. The Russian losses were 143 killed and 212 wounded.
37. Vorontsov's Diary, pp. 87–8, entries for 26, 27 August [7, 8 September] 1847; Volkonskii, '1847', pp. 607–8; Isakov, No. 4–6, pp. 50–1.
38. Vorontsov's Order of the Day, 23 September [5 October] 1847, as quoted in Volkonskii, '1847', p. 608; Qarākhī, p. 160.
39. Volkonskii, '1847', pp. 652, 656. Among the wounded was Argutinskii. Vorontsov, who had not expected such huge losses, stopped the storming troops.
40. *Dvizhenie*, pp. 545–55, document No. 307, Vorontsov to Chernyshev, 25 October [6 November] 1848; N. A. Volkonskii, 'Trekhletie v Dagestane. 1848-i God. Vziatie Gergebilia i Geroiskaia Zashchita Ukrepleniia Akhty', *Kavkazskii Sbornik*, Vol. VII, pp. 482–3 (hereafter: Volkonskii, '1848'); MRE, CPC, Russie, Tiflis, Vol. II, ff. 184–5, Lauxerrois to Guizot, 17 December 1847, No. 14, CPC, Turquie, Erzeroum, Vol. III, ff. 106–13, Barrière to Guizot, 26 April 1848, No. 7, quoting Sidi Paşa, the governor of Kars.
41. Isakov, No. 7–9, p. 11.
42. Volkonskii, '1848', pp. 485–6.
43. Ibid., p. 487.
44. The description is based on the following sources: *AKAK*, Vol. X, pp. 474–80, 481, 482–4, document Nos. 431, 432, 433, 438, 435, 436, Argutinskii to Vorontsov, 29 June [11], 7 [19], 9 [21], 21 July [2 August], Nos. 227, 307, 331, 428 respectively, Vorontsov to the Emperor, 10 [22] July, Vorontsov to Chernyshev, 15 [27] July 1848, No. 715, respectively; *Dvizhenie*, pp. 570–4, document No. 327, Vorontsov's Order of the Day, 12 [24] July 1848; Vorontsov's Diary, p. 90; Vorontsov to Ermolov, Vozdvizhenskoe, 11 [23] July 1848, No. 3, p. 339; Benckendorff Archive, Vorontsov to Benckendorff, Vodvizhenskoe, 2 July 1848; Volkonskii, '1848', pp. 481–536; Eduard Ivanovich Todtleben, 'Osada Ukreplennogo Seleniia Gergebil v Dagestane v 1848 G.', *Sbornik Opisanii Osad i Oboron Krepostei i Ukreplenii*, Vol. I (St. Petersburg, 1869), pp. 50–73 (hereafter: Todtleben); N. Schilder, *Graf Eduard Ivanovich Totleben. Ego Zhizn' i Deiatel'nost'. Biografiecheskii Ocherk* (St. Petersburg, 1885), Vol. I, pp. 25–44 (hereafter; Schilder); Isakov, No. 7–9, pp. 12–22; MRE, CPC, Russie, Tiflis, Vol. II, ff. 212, 217–18, Leuxerrois to Guizot, 26 July, 2 November 1848, Nos. 28, 29; PRO, FO/78/792, Brant to Palmerston, Erzeroom, 16 January 1849; Qarākhī, pp. 161–2.
45. Fourteen and a half infantry battalions, two squadrons of dragoons, ten hundreds of mounted militia and five hundreds of infantry militia.
46. Isakov, No. 7–9, p. 13.

47. Ibid., p. 14; Todtleben, p. 57; Schilder, p. 30, quoting Todtleben's diary; Volkonskii, '1848', pp. 498, 502, 503, 504.
48. Schilder, pp. 33–4.
49. Ibid., pp. 33–4, quoting from Todtleben's diary.
50. Volkonskii, '1848', pp. 509–15; Isakov, No. 7–9, pp. 13–14; Schilder, p. 36. The total Russian losses were 53 killed and 216 wounded.
51. Isakov, No. 7–9, p. 15. The Russians suffered up to 15 losses per day – Schilder, p. 36.
52. Volkonskii, '1848', p. 518.
53. Isakov, No. 7–9, p. 15.
54. Volkonskii, '1848', p. 518.
55. Isakov, No. 7–9, p. 15.
56. Ibid., loc. cit.
57. Vorontsov to Ermolov, Tiflis, 5 [17] November 1848, 23 January [4 February], Vozdvizhenskoe, 1 [13] June 1849, No. 3, pp. 340–1, 344, 349 (quotation from p. 341); N. A. Volkonskii, 'Trekhletie v Dagestane. 1849-i God. Osada Ukrepleniia Chokh', *Kavkazskii Sbornik*, Vol. VIII, pp. 252–7 (hereafter: Volkonskii, '1849').
58. Vorontsov to Ermolov, Tiflis, 5 [17] November 1848, p. 341. It was out of this consideration that Vorontsov had not allowed in previous years to stop the trade of Tsughūr with Georgia and the district of Chārtalah – Volkonskii, '1849', pp. 252–3, 256–7.
59. This description is based on the following sources: *AKAK*, Vol. X, pp. 494–5, document No. 448, Argutinskii to Vorontsov, 28 August [9 September] 1849, No. 197; Vorontsov to Ermolov, Tiflis, 26 November [8 December] 1849, No. 3, p. 353; Kotzebue to Chiliaev, Kodzhory, 27 July [8 August] 1849, in Modzalevskii, p. 166; Eduard Ivanovich Todtleben, 'Osada i Bombardirovanie Ukreplenniia Chokh v Dagestane v 1849 G.', *Sbornik Opisanii Osad i Oboron Krepostei i Ukreplenii*, Vol. I (St. Petersburg, 1869), pp. 107–25 (hereafter: Todtleben; this is a report written by Todtleben immediately after the siege. An abridged version of it was published without Todtleben's knowledge or name in *Inzhenernyi Zhurnal* (1857), No. 4, Part I, Doneseniia i Ofitsial'nye Stat'i, pp. 205–27); Volkonskii, '1849', pp. 250–95; Schilder, pp. 63–76; Züssermann, 'Otryvki', 1877, No. 2, p. 565; Nikita Sergeevich Trubetskoi, 'Osada Aula Chokh', *Russkii Voenno-Istoricheskii Vestnik*, No. 6 (Paris, 1950), pp. 9–12; Qarākhī, pp. 169–74; Ḥājj ʿAlī, pp. 38–9.
60. Volkonskii, '1849', p. 261.
61. Todtleben, p. 108. The number of losses reported that day was 17 killed and 57 wounded.
62. Ibid., pp. 109–10, including note.
63. Volkonskii, '1849', p. 268.
64. Todtleben, p. 110.
65. *AKAK*, Vol. X, pp. 494–5, document No. 448, Argutinskii to Vorontsov, 28 August [9 September] 1849, No. 197.
66. During the campaign the Russians lost 104 killed and 581 wounded.
67. Volkonskii, '1849', p. 242.
68. For which see below, pp. 197, 199, 201.
69. Kundukh, 1936, No. 3, pp. 17–18 (quotation), No. 4, p. 20.
70. Vorontsov to Ermolov, Tiflis, 3 [15] November 1847, No. 2, p. 210.

71. Benckendorff Archive, Vorontsov to Benckendorff, Tiflis, 18/30 December 1847.
72. E.g. Volkonskii, '1848', p. 536.
73. *AKAK*, Vol. X, pp. 479–80, 481, document Nos. 433, 436, Argutinskii to Vorontsov, 9 [21] July, Vorontsov to Chernyshev, 15 [27] July 1848, Nos. 331, 715, respectively; Volkonskii, '1848', pp. 536–8. Vorontsov to Ermolov, Tiflis, 18 [30] November 1848, No. 3, p. 340. And see *AKAK*, Vol. X, pp. 491–3, Vorontsov to the Emperor, 6 [18] October 1848.
74. The breakdown of the Russian losses is as follows: Girgil (1847) – 133 killed and 538 wounded; Salṭah – 535 killed and 1,888 wounded; Girgil (1848) – 86 killed and 475 wounded; Chōkha – 104 killed and 685 wounded. These figures do not include the victims of cholera and other diseases or those killed and wounded by accidents.
75. And see Züssermann, 'Otryvki', 1876, No. 4, pp. 426–7.
76. Vorontsov to Ermolov, Tiflis, 18 [30] November 1848, No. 3, p. 340. And see *AKAK*, Vol. X, pp. 491–3, document No. 444, Vorontsov to the Emperor, 6 [18] October 1848.
77. E.g. Vorontsov to Ermolov, Tiflis, 18 [30] November 1848, No. 3, p. 341.
78. Ibid., loc. cit.
79. *AKAK*, Vol. X, pp. 493, 495–6, document Nos. 445, 449, Daniyāl to Vorontsov, the beginning of Shaʿbān 1265 [end of June 1849] (published also in *Rzewuski*, Vol. VI, as Appendix AI), Chernyshev to Vorontsov, 22 September [4 October] 1849, No. 664 respectively; Rzewuski, Vol. VI, pp. 2–3 (separate pagination), Appendix AII, Vorontsov's letter to Bebutov, Odessa, 11 [23] August 1849.
80. See, for example, note 16 to Chapter 19, and Vorontsov to Bebutov, Tiflis, 28 March [9 April] 1847, No. 2, p. 255.
81. Volkonskii, '1849', pp. 241, 242.
82. Iurov, '1840–1842', Vol. X, p. 267.

Chapter 19: The South

1. *AKAK*, Vol. X, p. 468, document No. 425, Shamil's Proclamation to the Villages of Ghāzī-Ghumuq, 1847; *Shamil*, p. 283, document No. 217, 'Notice on Military Events in the Caucasus' (excerpt), 31 January [12 February] 1847; 'Izvestiia s Kavkaza', *Sbornik Gazety Kavkaz* (1847), Vol. I, pp. 27–8; Volkonskii, '1847', pp. 492–504.
2. Ibid., p. 496. While the local commanders took this too seriously, Vorontsov usually tended to disregard them altogether, suspecting ulterior motives behind the local commanders' warnings – e.g. Vorontsov to Ermolov, Nal'chik, 5 [17] May 1846, Tiflis, 22 April [4 May] 1847, No. 2, pp. 185, 205 respectively; Vorontsov to Bebutov, Tiflis, 23 December 1846 [4 January], 18 [30] April 1847, No. 2, pp. 254, 255–6 respectively.
3. Dobrovol'skii-Evdokimov, 'Ēkspeditsiia 1850 go Goda na Lezginskoi Linii', *Kavkazskii Sbornik*, Vol. VII, p. 618 (hereafter: Dobrovol'skii, '1850').
4. For his investiture see N. G. Bogdanova and I. M. Priatykin (eds.), *Kolonial'naia Politika Rossiiskago Tsarizma v Azerbaidzhane* (Moscow and Leningrad, 1936), (hereafter: *Kolonial'naia Politika*), Vol. I,

pp. 67–9, document No. 3 I, Paskiewicz to Daniyāl, 14 [26] February 1831, No. 838, (also published in Iurov, '1844', as Appendix III, pp. 377–9.)

5. For a description of his domain, see I. P. Linevich, 'Byvshee Elisuiskoe Sultanstvo (s Kartoi)', *Sbornik Svedenii o Kavkazskikh Gortsakh*, Vol. VII, 54 + 2 pp. (separate pagination).
6. Runowski's Diary, pp. 1481–2, entry for 22 February [6 March] 1861. Significantly, these contacts started in 1841, i.e. *after* the limitations put on Daniyāl's power in September 1840.
7. *Kolonial'naia Politika*, Vol. I, pp. 69–70, document No. 3 II, Golovin to Daniyāl, 6 [18] September 1840, No. 5727.
8. Ibid., pp. 70–5, document Nos. 3 III, 3 IV, 3 V, Daniyāl's Appeals to Golovin, the Emperor and Chernyshev, 19 [31] October 1840, 23 March [4 April], 1 [13] June 1842 respectively. (The latter is published also in *Dvizhenie*, pp. 350–3, as document No. 194, where its date is given as 1 [13] July 1842.) In fact, Daniyāl's appeal to the emperor was under investigation – *Kolonial'naia Politika*, Vol. I, pp. 75–9, document Nos. 3 VI, 3 VII, Rosen to the Emperor, 27 March [8 April] 1843, 3 [18] March 1844 respectively – but he had no way of knowing it.
9. *AKAK*, Vol. IX, p. XXX.
10. Dobrovol'skii, '1850', pp. 618–19; Dondukov-Korsakov, Vol. VI, pp. 46–7; Il'ia Pavlovich Petrushevskii, *Dzharo Belakanskie Vol'nye Obshchestva v Pervoi Tret'i XIX Stoletiia. Vnutrennii Stroi i Bor'ba s Rossiiskim Kolonial'nym Nastupleniem* (Tiflis, 1934), p. 115; Züssermann, 'Otryvki', 1876, pp. 84–6, 1877, No. 2, pp. 545–9.
11. Baddeley, p. 384. See also Rzewuski, Vol. VI, pp. 261–6 and Appendix B, pp. 3–13 (separate pagination), Daniyāl's letter to *Le Journal de St. Petersburg*, February 1861, in response to a report in *Le Journal du Midi*. For Shamil's reaction to it, see Runowski's Diary, pp. 1481–2, entry for 22 February [6 March] 1861. And see ibid., p. 1451, entry for 10 [22] August 1860.
12. This description is based on the following sources: *AKAK*, Vol. IX, pp. 729–32, 734–41, 865–7, document Nos. 618, 619, 620, 623, 624, 625, 715, Schwartz to Neidhardt, 6 [18], 10 [22], 15 [27] June, Neidhardt to Chernyshev, 21 June [3 July], Schwartz to Neidhardt, 25 June [7 July], Neidhardt to Chernyshev, 26 June [8 July] (secret), 3 [15] July (top secret), 29 July [10 August] 1844 (secret), Nos. 376, 397, 443, 71, 586, 78, 99, 164 respectively (document No. 618 was also published in *Dvizhenie*, pp. 476–7, as No. 249; document No. 624 was also published in *Kolonial'naia Politika*, Vol. I, pp. 79–80, as Nos. 3 VIII and 3 VIIIa); *Dvizhenie*, pp. 478–9, 480, document Nos. 251, 253, Markov to Hurko, 10 [22] June, HQ Caucasian Corps to Nesterov, 2 [14] July 1844; *Kolonial'naia Politika*, Vol. I, pp. 80–1, document Nos. 3 IX, 3 X, Chernyshev to Neidhardt, 9 [21], 11 [23] July 1844 respectively; *Shamil*, pp. 232–4, document No. 185, 'Excerpt from a Short Survey of the Most Important Military Events in the Caucasus from 1 [13] May to 1 [13] November 1844'; Iurov, '1844', pp. 310–39; Rzewuski, Vol. VI, pp. 262–3, 266–7.
13. Text in *AKAK*, Vol. IX, p. 730, annexed to document No. 618, Schwartz to Neidhardt, 6 [18] June 1844, No. 376, and in Rzewuski, Vol. VI, pp. 263–6.
14. Text in ibid., pp. 262–3. Quotation from p. 263.

15. Runowskii's Diary, p. 1451, entry for 10 [22] August 1860.
16. Ibid., loc. cit. In April 1845, with the arrival of the new *Sardār* in Tiflis, Daniyāl approached him, enquiring what terms the Russians would offer for his redefection to their camp. After consultation with St. Petersburg, the viceroy replied that Daniyāl would be granted a state pension and be allowed to live in the Caucasus. But Daniyāl would be denied what he wanted most – the restoration of his rights in the sultanate of Ilis̩ū. Hence the negotiations had no results – *AKAK*, Vol. X, pp. 347–8, document Nos. 351, 352, 353, Vorontsov to Chernyshev, 13 [25] April, Chernyshev to Vorontsov, 30 April [12 May], Vorontsov to Schwartz, 29 September [11 October] 1845, Nos. 33, 291, 102 respectively (document No. 351 was also published in *Dvizhenie*, pp. 488–9, as No. 263); *Kolonial'naia Politika*, Vol. I, pp. 81–3, document No. 3XI, Vorontsov to the Emperor, 12 [24] April 1845 (also published in *Dvizhenie*, pp. 486–8, as document No. 262); Rzewuski, Vol. VI, pp. 267–70, Vol. VII, p. 394. In following years Daniyāl entered intermittently into contacts with the Russian authorities, again without any results. As in the case of his pre–1844 contacts with Shamil, these seem to have been aimed at maintaining an 'insurance policy' with the Russians rather than at achieving concrete results.
17. Baddeley, p. 384.
18. Runowski's Diary, pp. 1444–5, entry for 6 [18] July 1860.
19. Volkonskii, 'Trekhletie', p. 157.
20. 'The main communities – Dido, Antsukh, Kapucha and Jurmūt – ' had, until 1847, 'recognized their dependence upon us, accepting our *pristavs* among them. Although they did not lose an opportunity to fall out, secretly fight against us and raid our territory, they still assured us of their friendship and submission. Since 1847 we lost even this, and confronted instead of dependent and so-called submitted [communities], open enemies in arms' – ibid., p. 161.
21. Dobrovol'skii, '1850', p. 619. And see Modzalevskii, pp. 145–8, 165–6, 160–3, Koliubakin to Chiliaev, Tiflis, 19 February [3 March], Kotzebue to Chiliaev, Tiflis, 27 July [8 August] 1849, Vorontsov to Chiliaev, Tiflis, 29 September [11], 14 [26] October 1850, respectively; Züssermann, 'Otryvki', 1877, No. 2, p. 531.
22. Volkonskii, 'Trekheltie', pp. 168–9.
23. The following description is based on these sources: *AKAK*, Vol. X, pp. 352–3, 445–50, document Nos. 357, 407, 406, 408, 409; Schwartz's War Diaries, 6 [18] – 13 [25] May, 13 [25] – 20 May [1 June], Schwartz to Vorontsov, 11 [23], 15 [27] May, Burnod to Vorontsov, 16 [28] May 1847, Nos. 935, 960, 96 respectively; Volkonskii, 'Trekhletie', pp. 174–216; Ibid., Appendix VI, p. 5 (separate pagination), Daniyāl's Proclamation to the Rutul Community, 16 Jumāda al-Ākhira 1263 [1 June 1847]; Volkonskii, '1847', pp. 504–12; MRE, CPC, Russie, Tiflis, Vol. II, f. 136, Castillon to Guizot, 6 June 1847, No 29; Dobrovol'skii, 'Ēkpspeditsiia', p. 621; Züssermann, 'Otryvki', 1877, No. 2, p. 531.
24. Volkonskii, 'Trekhletie', p. 188.
25. Schwartz's letter to Gogol', Tsarskie Kolodtsy, 6 [18] May 1847, as quoted in ibid., p. 187.
26. Ibid., loc. cit.

27. Autographed letter by Schwartz (to Vorontsov?), Zakartalah, 11 [23] May 1847, as quoted in ibid., p. 204.
28. Ibid., loc. cit. He had already asked Argutinskii directly for help on 28 May – Volkonskii, '1847', p. 509.
29. Volkonskii, '1847', pp. 509–10; Volkonskii, 'Trekhletie', p. 211.
30. Daniyāl's Declaration to the Rutul Community, 16 Jumāda al-Ākhira 1263 [1 June 1847], ibid., Appendix VI, p. 5 (separate pagination).
31. For these and other events, see 'Izvestiia s Kavkaza', *Sbornik Gazety Kavkaz* (1847), Vol. II, p. 40; Volkonskii, '1847', pp. 552–3; Volkonskii, 'Trekhletie', pp. 219–45 and Appendix XII, pp. 12–15 (separate pagination), 'List of the Most Outstanding Attacks by the Mountaineers and Skirmishes with Them on the Line and on the Plain in 1847'.
32. *AKAK*, Vol. X, p. 468, document No. 425 (reprinted in *Dvizhenie*, p. 559, as document No. 312). A somewhat different translation is rendered in Volkonskii, '1847', pp. 667–8.
33. *AKAK*, Vol. X, pp. 469–70, document No. 427, Vorontsov to Chernyshev (secret), 15 [27] December 1847, No. 140; Volkonskii, '1847', pp. 667–82; Vorontsov to Ermolov, Tiflis, 20 December 1847 [1 January 1848], No. 2, pp. 212–14.
34. The siege and defence of Akhdī entered the canon of Russian military heroic traditions. Everything was done to make the public aware and proud of it and future generations of officers and soldiers were raised on its example. Accordingly there is an abundance of narratives as well as published primary sources dealing with the siege of Akhdī and with the campaign in the Upper Samur Valley in general. In contrast, Western diplomatic and consular agents did not pay attention to this campaign. The following description is based on: Eduard Vladimirovich Brümmer [Brimmer], 'Sluzhba Artileriiskogo Ofitsera, Vospityvavshegosia v l Kadetskom Korpuse i Vypushchennogo v 1815 Godu', *Kavkazskii Sbornik*, Vol. XIX, pp. 371–427 (Appendices), Roth [Rott] to Brümmer, 10 [22] September (secret and urgent), No. 791, letters from Roth to Brümmer (in French), 29 September [11], 18 [30], 3 [15] October respectively, 'War Diary of the Siege of Akhdī', by Roth, 3 [15] October (printed also in *AKAK*, Vol. X, pp. 487–90, as document No. 441), 'Diary by Captain Novoselov, Written during the Siege of Akhdī', Brümmer to Argutinskii, 11 [23] September, Nos. 1003, 1004, Vorontsov's Order of the Day, 11 [23] November, No. 132, 'Description of the Siege of Akhdī' (reprinted from *Zakavkazskii Vestnik*, 1848, No. 45), Vorontsov's Order of the Day, 6 [18] October 1848, No. 117 (also printed in *Dvizhenie*, pp. 578–83, as document No. 352), 'Description of, and Anecdotes Relating to, the Siege of Akhdī by Shamil in 1848' (reprint of the brochure *Zashchita Ukrepleniia Akhty i Samurskogo Okruga* [Tiflis, 1850], published upon Vorontsov's instructions. The second part of it was also reprinted as 'Zashchita Ukrepleniia Akhty v 1848 Godu', in *Sbornik Opisanii Osad i Oboron Krepostei i Ukreplenii*, Vol. I [St. Petersburg, 1869], pp. 74–106); *AKAK*, Vol. X, pp. 490–3, document Nos. 442, 443, 444, Vorontsov to Wrangel, 3 [15] October, No. 1073, Argutinskii to Vorontsov, 4 [16] October, No. 1073, Vorontsov to the Emperor, 6 [18] October (with Argutinskii to Vorontsov, 25 September [7 October] 1848, No. 1069); *Dvizhenie*, p. 578, document No. 331, Daniyāl to Shamil, [20 September] 1848; 'Zashchita Ukrepleniia

Akhty v 1848 Godu', *Chteniia dlia Soldat* (1860), Book 3, pp. 13–42; Vorontsov's Diary, p. 92, entries for 28 September [10], 6 [18], 12 [24] October 1848; Vorontsov to Ermolov, Tiflis, 18 [30] October, 5 [17] November 1848, 23 January [4 February] 1849, No. 3, pp. 340–4; Dobrovol'skii-Evdokimov, 'Iz Kavkazsloi Zhizni. 1848-i God v Dagestane', *Kavkazskii Sbornik*, Vol. VI, pp. 683–727 (hereafter: Dobrovol'skii, '1848'). The editorial board of *KS* remarked (note on p. 683) that 'despite a note on the manuscript that this [article] was intended for publication in *Voennyi Sbornik*, it has not been printed there yet'. In fact, a professionally edited version of it appeared in *Ruskii Vestnik* (1862), No. 7, pp. 35–66, under the pseudonym 'Kavkazets'. The former version is, however, used here because it seems to reflect the unedited manuscript. Isakov, No. 10–12, pp. 13–32; Semen Novoselov, 'Rasskaz ob Osade Ukrepleniia Akhty', *Khudozhestvennyi Listok*, 20 May [1], 20 June [2 July] 1851 (Nos. 15, 18); Volkonskii, '1848', pp. 542–612; Volkonskii, 'Trekhletie', pp. 283–99; Schilder, pp. 46–58; Qarākhī, pp. 162–9; Ḥājj ʿAlī, pp. 37–8.

35. Volkonskii, '1848', p. 550.
36. Ibid. p. 551
37. *Dvizhenie*, p. 578, document No. 331, Daniyāl to Shamil, [20 September 1848]. That the population joined the mountaineers is also confirmed by Qarākhī (p. 162) and by the Russian sources.
38. Afterwards, the Russians deduced from the positions of the corpses that they were overwhelmed while trying to escape – Dobrovol'skii, '1848', p. 703. Only two soldiers survived and escaped to Khazry.
39. Volkonskii, '1848', p. 558.
40. Vorontsov to Ermolov, Tiflis, 23 January [4 February] 1849, No. 3, p. 343.
41. Vorontsov to Ermolov, Vozdvizhenskoe, 11 [23] June 1848.
42. Dobrovol'skii, '1850', p. 621.
43. Volkonskii, 'Trekheltie', p. 294.
44. Volkonskii, '1848', p. 609.
45. Ibid. pp. 556–7.
46. Dobrovol'skii, '1848', p. 688.
47. Isakov, No. 10–12, pp. 16, 17.
48. During the eight-day siege, the garrison lost 91 killed and 150 wounded – almost half (48 per cent) of its defenders.
49. It seems that the wound was not the only reason for Roth's relinquishment of his command. He must have been strongly affected by Shamil's psychological masterblow of promising Roth's daughter to the first of the *imām*'s followers to break into the fort, and letting Roth know of his promise through his spies.
50. Dobrovol'skii, '1848', p. 694.
51. Isakov, No. 10–12, p. 17; Todtleben's diary, quoted by Schilder, p. 53.
52. Todtleben's diary, quoted by Schilder, p. 57; Dobrovol'skii, '1848', pp. 707, 719–20, 722–3.
53. Vorontsov to Ermolov, Tiflis, 23 January [4 February] 1849, No. 3, pp. 343–4.
54. And see note 50 above.
55. Todtleben's diary, quoted by Schilder, p. 52.
56. Dobrovol'skii, '1848', pp. 702–3. And see Isakov, No. 10–12, pp. 19–20, on the conduct of the native militia at Meskīnjī.

57. This phrase – 'resolute movement' – used by Vorontsov to describe Argutinskii's action does not at all correspond to what really happened – *AKAK*, Vol. X, pp. 491–3, document No. 444, Vorontsov to the Emperor, 6 [18] October 1848. Not only was Argutinskii slow to rescue the fort, but he missed an opportunity to block Shamil's retreat after the battle of Meskīnjī – Dobrovol'skii, '1848', pp. 725–7.
58. The conduct of the generals apart, the disorder and confusion were such that afterwards it was 'impossible to find out' whether the garrison of fort Tiflisskoe 'consisted of members of different units or formed an organic unit. Equally it is impossible to find out how many people were there and from which unit[s]. The latter [two] questions cannot be answered also because fort Tiflisskoe does not appear at all in the lists for 1848 of fortified places manned by infantry in the Caucasus' (Volkonskii, '1848', p. 564). Still, not everything could be covered up and a scapegoat was needed. Schwartz, the commander of the nearest considerable force, had enough excuses for his non-intervention. Furthermore, he was then Vorontsov's 'favourite in every sense of the word' (Volkonskii, 'Trekhletie', p. 172). Thus everyone, including Schwartz, turned the accusing finger on another favourite of Vorontsov – Burnod. This general, constructing the Akhdī Military Highway, had at his disposal a bare 1,000 bayonets without cavalry or artillery. First, Burnod concentrated all his force at Borch. But realising that his force was not a match for the mountaineers, he retreated from that position on 25 September, i.e. on the day that Daniyāl entered Akhdī and started to besiege the nearby fort. Burnod was now unanimously accused of a 'blunder' which opened the way to Akhdī for Shamil, who no longer needed to fear attack at his rear and flank. Furthermore, it was claimed now that Burnod's retreat exposed the Shemākha and Balagin districts to the mountaineers, which prevented Schwartz from moving to the help of Akhdī. The fact that Burnod had been cautious enough to have the decision to retreat made by a council of senior officers did not help him, and all his explanations were dismissed as 'stupid excuses'. He was court-martialled, and although found not guilty on this count, released from service, though not dishonourably – Vorontsov to Ermolov, Tiflis, 5 [17] November 1848, No. 3, p. 341 (from where the quotations are taken); Volkonskii, 'Trekhletie', p. 292; Volkonskii, '1848', pp. 555, 559, 609; *AKAK*, Vol. X, pp. 490–1, document No. 442, Vorontsov to Wrangel, 3 [15] October 1848, No. 1152 (Volkonskii, '1848', note on p. 556 quotes its No. as 11,329); Vorontsov's Diary, p. 92, entry for 12 [24] November 1848; *Voennaia Entsiklopediia*, Vol. V (St. Petersburg, 1911), p. 204.
59. Volkonskii, 'Trekhletie', p. 265.
60. For the year's events on the Lesghian Line, see: *AKAK*, Vol. X, pp. 480–1, document No. 434, Schwartz to Vorontsov, 9 [21] July 1848, No. 544; *Dvizhenie*, pp. 566–70, 574–5, 583–5, document Nos. 321, 322, 323, 324, 326, 328, 333, Kwiatkowski to Schwartz, 14 [26] March, Schwartz to Vorontsov, 31 March [12 April], No. 679 (published also in *Shamil*, p. 289, under No. 225), Schwartz to Kotzebue, 2 [14] March, Schwartz to Vorontsov, 3 [15] April, Korganov to Vorontsov, 5 [17] June, Schwartz to Vorontsov, 30 July [11 August], 'War Diary of the Lesghian Line, 1 [13] April–13 [25] November 1848 (excerpts)', respectively; *Shamil*, pp. 285,

288–9, 290–5, 296–308, document Nos. 228, 233, 235, 236, 238, 239, 240, 241, 243, 244, 245, 246, 247, 248, 249, 250, 220, 224, 230, 231, 232, 234, 237, 242, 251, 'War Diaries of the Lesghian Line', 2 [14]–15 [27] April, 21–28 May [2–9 June], 29 May [10]–2 [14], 18 [30]–24 June [5], 8 [20]–15 [27], 15 [27]–21 July [2 August], 28 July [9]–4 [16], 5 [17]–12 [24], 19 [31]–26 August [7 September], 26 August [7]–2 [14], 2 [14]–9 [21], 9 [21]–16 [28], 23–30 September [5–12 October], 30 September [12]–7 [19], 22–29 October [3–10], 5 [17]–19 November [1 December], Schwartz to Vorontsov, 28 February [12], 20 March [1], 30 April [12 May] (two dispatches), 15 [27] May (two dispatches), 29 May [10 June], Nos. 400, 624, 928, 929, 1050, 1051, 273 respectively, C.O. Don Cossack Regiment to Khreshchiatinski, 16 [28] July, No. 457, Bykov to Gogel', 21 August [2 September], No. 1575, Chiliaev to Vorontsov, 24 December 1848 [5 January 1849], No. 1578 respectively; Volkonskii, 'Trekhletie', pp. 255–304 and Appendix XIII, pp. 15–17 (separate pagination), 'List of the Most Important Attacks and Skirmishes on the Lesghian Line in 1848'; Modzalevskii, pp. 139–40, Schwartz to Chiliaev, Mesed el-Kher, 16 [28] July 1848.

61. Schwartz was accused, and found guilty, of causing the death of a Cossack during an investigation into a theft from his safe (in which Schwartz himself was not clear of suspicion). For details, see *AKAK*, Vol. IX, pp. XXX-XXXI; Vladimir Tolstoi, 'Iz Vospominanii o Gruzii (1847). Delo Generala Shvartsa', *Russkii Arkhiv* (1877), No. 5, pp. 37–41; Züssermannn, 'Otryvki', 1876, No. 12, pp. 500–1, 1877, No. 1, pp. 163–4 (note).
62. Volkonskii, 'Trekhletie', pp. 307, 315–16.
63. *Shamil*, pp. 308–9, document No. 252, Governor of T'elavi to Ermolov [Chief Civilian Administrator] 22 June [4 July] 1849, No. 442; Volkonskii, 'Trekhletie', pp. 305–24; Modzalevskii, p. 165, Kotzebue to Chiliaev, Kodzhory, 27 July [8 August] 1849.
64. Dobrovol'skii, '1850', p. 622. And see Züssermann, 'Otryvki', 1877, No. 2, p. 541. For a detailed description based on Chiliaev's reports, see Volkonskii, 'Trekhletie', pp. 325–35. This version mentions 16 killed and 59 wounded. For Vorontsov's first reaction to Chiliaev's report, see Modzalevskii, p. 155, Vorontsov to Chiliaev, Tiflis, 29 July [10 August] 1849.
65. For the events of the second half of 1849 on the Lesghian Line, see Volkonskii, 'Trekhletie', pp. 335–64.
66. Out of 200 militiamen, only a few escaped and 14 were taken prisoner. For details, see *Dvizhenie*, pp. 594–7, document No. 352, Vorontsov's Order of the Day, 3 [15] October 1850; *Shamil*, pp. 314–15, 317–22, document Nos. 258, 261, 262, 263, 264, Chiliaev to Vorontsov, 9 [21] May, Andronikov [Andronikashvili] to Military Governor of Tiflis, 18 [30] May, Commander of T'ushet'i-P'shavet'i-Khevsuret'i to Military Governor of Tiflis, 6 [18] June, Vorontsov's Order of the Day, 12 [24] June 1850, Nos. 273, 2248, 998, 106 respectively; Vorontsov to Bebutov, Tsarskie Kolodtsy, 13 [25] May 1850, No. 2, pp. 257–8; Dobrovol'skii, '1850', pp. 622–4; A. Z. [Arnold Züssermann?], 'Desiat' Let na Kavkaze', *Sovremennik* (1854), No. 11, pp. 19–20 (hereafter: '10 Let'); Züssermann, 'Otryvki', 1877, No. 3, pp. 85–7, 89–90.
67. Dobrovol'skii, '1850', pp. 623–4, 646–7; Vorontsov's Diary, p. 104, entry for 8 [20] November 1850; Modzalevskii, pp. 157, 150–1, Vorontsov to

Chiliaev, Tiflis, 7 [19] April, Koliubakin to Chiliaev, 19 April [1 May] 1850 respectively; Züssermann, 'Otryvki', 1877, No. 3, p. 9.

68. For these, see the sardonic description in Dobrovol'skii, '1850', pp. 624–43. And see Züssermann, 'Otryvki', 1877, No. 3, pp. 94–113, 126–35. For the official version of the events, see *Dvizhenie*, pp. 597–8, document No. 353, Vorontsov's Order of the Day, 3 [15] October 1850; Vorontsov to Ermolov, Kislovodsk, 24 August [5 September] 1850, No. 3, p. 361; Modzalevskii, pp. 158–61, 170, 172, Vorontsov to Chiliaev, Kislovodsk, 24 August [5], 4 [16], 29 September [11], 6 [18] October, Orbeliani to Chiliaev, Luchek, 28 September [10 October], Tchavtchavadze to Chiliaev, Kakh, 7 [19] October 1850; '10 Let', pp. 19–23.
69. *Dvizhenie*, pp. 598–601, document No. 354, Melikov to Vorontsov, 16 [28] October 1850; Dobrovol'skii, '1850', pp. 643–6.
70. For his biography, see *AKAK*, Vol. X, p. XXVIII, Vol. XI, p. X.

Chapter 20: Greater Chechnia

1. Vorontsov to Ermolov, St. Petersburg, 24 January [5 February] 1845, No. 2, p. 162. He suffered especially from an eye disease. And see Andreevskii, pp. 50–1.
2. Volkonskii, 'Trekhletie', Appendix VII, p. 6 (separate pagination), Vorontsov to Schwartz, Camp near Girgil, 5 [17] June 1847.
3. Vorontsov to Ermolov, Vozdvizhenskoe, 11 [23] April 1848, No. 3, p. 336.
4. Ibid., loc. cit.
5. Vorontsov's Diary, p. 94. Quotations from entry for 26 July [7 August] 1849.
6. E.g. Dobrovol'skii, '1850', p. 641.
7. In the battle of 1 February the Russians lost 40 killed and 200 wounded. For the expedition, see *AKAK*, Vol. X. pp. 502–5, document No. 455, Kozlowski to Zavodovskii, 12 [24] April 1850, No. 332; Vorontsov to Ermolov, Tiflis, 25 January [6 February], 20 February [4 March], 9 [21] May 1850, No. 3, pp. 353, 354; Modzalevskii, pp. 156, 149, Vorontsov to Chiliaev, Tiflis 28 February [12 March], Koliubakin to Chiliaev, Tiflis 7 [19] March 1850, respectively; Georges Wl . . . off [Georgii Vlastov], *Ombres du Passé. Souvenirs d'un Officier du Caucase* (Paris, [1899]), pp. 47, 67, 74–90 (hereafter: *Ombres du Passé*); Qarākhī, p. 175. Vlastov's is by far the best and most detailed description.
8. 'Letuchii Otriad', pp. 388–9.
9. In March 1850 Nesterov became insane. He was transferred to Tiflis and was treated by Vorontsov's physician. Having recovered, he returned to his command in the summer, only to relapse into madness again in April 1851. He was then relieved of his position and sent to Moscow. For further details, see *AKAK*, Vol. X. p. XXVII; Vorontsov's Diary, pp. 96–7, 98, 105, 106, entries, for 21, 22, 24, 28, 30, 31 March [2, 3, 5, 9, 11, 12], 2 [14], 5 [17], 27 April [9], 2 [14] May, 14 [26] August 1850, 1 [13] April, 11 [23] May 1851; Vorontsov to Ermolov, Tiflis, 9 [21] May, Kislovodsk, 24 August [5 September] 1850, No. 3, pp. 354, 362 respectively; Modzalevskii, p. 148, Koliubakin to Chiliaev, Tiflis, 7 [19] March 1850; Dondukov-Korsakov, Vol. V, pp. 203–4.

10. The Caucasian Corps was too busy in preparations and parade-drilling for the visit to engage in any large-scale fighting ('Letuchii Otriad', p. 385). For Alexander's visit, see Meletii Iakovlevich Olszewski [Ol'shevskii], 'Tsesarevich Aleksandr Nikolaevich na Kavkaze s 12 Sentiabria po 28 Oktiabria 1850 G.', *Russkaia Starina* (1884), No. 9, pp. 576–88; Vorontsov's Diary, pp. 98, 100–4, 105, entries for 3–5 [15–17], 24 July [5 August], 1 [13], 15 [27], 17 [29] September–31 October [12], 23 November [5 December] 1850, 1 [13] January 1851; Vorontsov to Ermolov, Kislovodsk, 24 August [5 September] (and the annexed reply of Ermolov, Moscow, 15 [27] November), Tiflis, 6 [18] December 1850, No. 3, pp. 359–60, 362–5 respectively; Vorontsov to Bebutov, Piatigorsk, 21 September [3 October], Vladikavkaz, 23 September [5 October] 1850, No. 5, pp. 693–4; Modzalevskii, pp. 167–9, 151–3, 160, 172, Gogel' to Chiliaev, Tiflis, 8 [20] September, M. E. to B. G. Chiliaev, Tiflis 28 September [10 October], Koliubakin to Chiliaev, Vorontsov to Chiliaev, (both) Tiflis, 29 September [11 October], Orbeliani to Chiliaev, Luchek, 22 October [3 November] 1850, respectively; Züssermann, 'Otryvki', 1877, No. 6, pp. 507–16.
11. 'Letuchii Otriad', pp. 374–7. For the viceroy's journey, see Vorontsov's Diary, p. 98.
12. Vorontsov to Ermolov, Kislovodsk, 24 August [5 September] 1850, No. 3, p. 360; 'Letuchii Otriad', pp. 382–7 (quotations from pp. 384, 383 respectively.)
13. Vorontsov to Ermolov, Kislovodsk, 24 August [5 September] 1850, No. 3, pp. 360–1; Vorontsov to Bebutov, Kislovodsk, 26 August [7 September] 1850, No. 5, pp. 692–3, (including Sleptsov's letter to Kozlowski, Shalī, 22 August [3 September] 1850). (This letter was also published in *AKAK*, Vol. X, p. 506, as document No. 458.); Vorontsov's Diary, p. 99, entries for 25, 26, 29 August [6, 7, 10 September] 1850; *AKAK*, Vol. X. pp. 506–9, document No. 459, Vorontsov to Chernyshev, 2 [14] September 1850, No. 724; 'Letuchii Otriad', pp. 387–407.
14. Ibid, p. 387.
15. Vorontsov to Ermolov, Kislovodsk, 24 August [5 September] 1850, No. 3, p. 361. Similarly, 'Letuchii Otriad', pp. 404–5.
16. Vorontsov's Diary, p. 98, entry for 14 [26] August 1850.
17. See note 9 above.
18. Vorontsov to Ermolov, Tiflis, 7 [19] February 1851, No. 4, pp. 442–3; Vorontsov's Diary, pp. 105–6, entries for 1 [13], 4 [16], 5 [17] March, 7 [19] April 1851; Runowski's Diary, p. 1450, entry for 2 [14] August 1860; *Ombres du Passé*, pp. 113–25; K., 'Obzor Sobytii na Kavkaze v 1851 Godu', *Kavkazskii Sbornik*, Vol. XIX, p. 16, Vol. XXI, pp. 28–9 (hereafter: 'Obzor Sobytii' + Vol. of *KS*); Qarākhī, pp. 176–7.
19. Vorontsov to Ermolov, Tiflis, 7 [19] February 1851, No. 4, pp. 442–3; 'Letuchii Otriad', pp. 421–4.
20. Ibid., p. 424; [Nikolai Pavlovich Sleptsov], 'Pis'ma N. P. Sleptsova k Kniaziu Bariatinskomu. 1851', *Russkii Arkhiv* (1892), No. 2, pp. 263–7, Camp near Alkhān Yūrt (28 April [10 May]?), 6 [18], 14 [26], 19 [31], 20, 22 May [1, 3], 14 [26] June 1851.
21. For Ḥajimurād's attempts and the Russians' countermoves, see 'Letuchii Otriad', pp. 424–7, 471–3, Appendix II, Vorontsov to Chernyshev, 19

[31], 30 March [11 April], Chernyshev to Vorontsov, 10 [22] March, 7 [19] April 1851, Nos. 373, 449, 2317, 3432 respectively; Vorontsov to Ermolov, Tiflis, 7 [19] February 1851, No. 4, pp. 442–3; 'Obzor Sobytii', Vol. XXI, pp. 23–4.

22. The only published description of it is given in *Ombres du Passé*, pp. 122–5.
23. Runowski's Diary, p. 1450, entry for 2 [14] August 1860.
24. Vorontsov's Diary, p. 105, entry for 4 [16] March 1851.
25. *AKAK*, Vol, X. pp. 511–19, 523–4, document Nos. 462, 464, 463, 465, 471, Sleptsov to Il'inskii, 20 June [2 July], Vorontsov's Order of the Day, 6 [18] July, Bariatinskii to Zavodovskii, 20 June [11 July], 18 [30] September, Kozlowski to Zavodovskii, 21 November [3 December] 1851, Nos. 1884, 97, 1079, 1503, 1948 respectively; 'Obzor Sobytii', Vol XIX, pp. 17–37, Vol. XXI, pp. 22–51; 'Letuchii Otriad', pp. 415–21, 428–51; Meletii Iakovlevich Olszewski, 'Kniaz' Aleksandr Ivanovich Bariatinskii na Levom Flange Kavkazskoi Linii, 1851–1853', *Russkaia Starina* (1897), No. 7, pp. 424–6 (hereafter: Olszewski, 'Bariatinskii' + No. of *RS*).
26. 'Obzor Sobytii', Vol. XXI, p. 21.
27. Vorontsov to Ermolov, Tiflis, 6 [18] December 1850, No. 3, p. 364; Runowski's Diary, p. 1450, entry for 2 [14] August 1860. This disavowal, however, was not total. Occasionally the mountaineers continued to fight in 'a correct order', as on 19 February 1852 – K., 'Zimniaia Ēkspeditsiia 1852 G. v Chechne', *Kavkazskii Sbornik*, Vol. XIII, p. 558 (hereafter: 'Zimniaia Ēkspeditsiia').
28. 'Levyi Flang', Vol. XI, p. 433. In some cases a visit by a neighbouring unit was deemed a good enough reason for a raid – e.g. ibid., pp. 433–9.
29. Some Russian sources try to paint an idyllic picture of these two being good friends. However, there are enough indications to point to the fact that theirs was more than a friendly competition. Sleptsov and Bariatinskii, it seems, hated and detested each other behind the façade of comradeship. In one thing only did they have a common feeling – they both equally hated and detested Meller-Zakomel'ski, another, though less probable, candidate to command the Left Flank. For these raids, see *AKAK*, Vol. X, pp. 510–11, document No. 461, Vorontsov's Order of the Day, 23 April [5 May] 1851; Fadeev to his father, Kusary, 29 April [11 May] 1851, No. 9, p. 3; 'Obzor Sobytii', Vol. XVIII, pp. 132–44.
30. *AKAK*, Vol. X. pp. 517–18, document No. 464, Vorontsov's Order of the Day, 6 [18] July 1851, No. 97; 'Obzor Sobytii', Vol. XVIII, pp. 144–55; Qarākhī, p. 177; Ḥājj ʿAlī, pp. 40–1.
31. *Dvizhenie*, pp. 603–4, document No. 355, Letter from Ḥājjī Khalīl to Shamil, 13 [25] July 1851; Vorontsov to Ermolov, Kislovodsk, 20 July [1], 4 [16] August, Camp on [the river] Belaia, 9 [21] August 1851, No. 4, pp. 443–4, 446 respectively; Vorontsov's Diary, p. 107, entries for 2 [14], 3 [15], 10 [22] August 1851; Fadeev to his father, Camp on Turchīdāgh, 5 [17] July, Ṭabarsarān, 20 July [1 August], Ghāzī-Ghumuq, 1 [13] August 1851, No. 9, pp. 3–5; 'Obzor Sobytii', Vol. XVIII, pp. 155–79; V. Soltan, 'Ocherk Voennykh Deistvii v Dagestane v 1852 i 1853 Godakh', *Kavkazskii Sborning*, Vol. IX, p. 478 (hereafter: Soltan, '1852–1853'); Züssermann, 'Otryvki', 1877, No. 6, pp. 554–8, 1878, No. 2, pp. 540–63; Qarākhī, pp. 177–8; Ḥājj 'Alī, p. 41.

32. *AKAK*, Vol. X, pp. 544–5, document No. 490, War Diary of the Caspian Province, 19 [31] – 26 October [7 November 1852; '10 Let', pp. 35, 39–40; Soltan, '1852–1853', pp. 486–94.
33. Vorontsov to Ermolov, Kodzhory, 25 July [6 August 1852], No. 4, pp. 456–7.
34. 'Obzor Sobytii', Vol. XVIII, pp. 182–3. And see Hamzatov, pp. 304–5. For folk-tales related to the relationship between Shamil and Ḥajimurād, see ibid. pp. 284, 303–4, 370, 398.
35. *AKAK*, Vol. X, pp. 519–23, 524–30, 538–40, document Nos. 466, 468, 467, 469, 470, 471, 473, 476, 485, 486, Argutinskii to Vorontsov, 24 September [6], 27 October [8 November], Argutinskii to Kotzebue, 13 [25] October (secret), No. 1179, Chernyshev to Vorontsov, 28 October [9 November], No. 319, Kozlowski to Kotzebue, 12 [24] November, No. 1877, Vorontsov to Chernyshev, 26 November [8 December], No. 596, Excerpt from the War Diary of the Left Flank by Kozlowski, 22–29 November [4–11 December] 1851, 'Summary of Ḥajimurād's Debriefing by Loris-Melikov' (without date), Smitten to Bebutov, 27 April [9 May], No. 574, Vorontsov to Chernyshev, 30 April [12 May] 1852, No. 725; Vorontsov's Diary, pp. 108–10, entries for 27, 29 November [9, 11], 8 [20], 9 [21], 18 [30] December 1851, 21 January [2 February], 30 March [11], 12 [24], 25, 27 April [7, 12 May] 1852; Vorontsov to Ermolov, Temir-Khān-Shurā, 7 [19] November 1851, Tiflis, 2 [14], April 1852, No. 4, pp. 447, 454; 'Kn. M. S. Vorontsov i N. N. Murav'ev v Pis'makh k M. T. Loris-Melikovu, 1852–1856 GG.', *Russkaia Starina* (1884), No. 9, pp. 589–92. Vorontsov to Loris-Mekilov, Tiflis 14 [26], 21 January [2], 18, 20 February [1, 3], 17 [29], 30 March [11 April], 1852; Andreevskii, pp. 46–7; A. Züssermann, 'Khadzhi Murat. Pis'ma o Nem Kn. M. S. Vorontsova i Rasskazy Kavkaztsev, 1851–1852 GG.', *Russkaia Starina* (1881), No. 3, pp. 655–80; Idem, 'Otryvki', 1877, No. 6, pp. 518–19, 1878, No. 2, pp. 574–81; 'Obzor Sobytii', Vol. XVIII, pp. 184–8, Vol. XXI, pp. 43–4; V. Potto , 'Gadzhi Murat (Biograficheskii Ocherk)', *Voennyi Sbornik* (1870), No. 11, pp. 159–87; '10 Let', pp. 28–32; Tolstoi, 'Khadzhi Murat'; Qarākhī, pp. 178–9; S. N. Shul'gin, 'Predanie o Shamilevskom Naibe Khadzhi Murate', *Sbornik Materialov dlia Opisaniia Mestnostei i Plemen Kavkaza*, Vol. XL, Part I, pp. 54–70; A Takh-Gedi, 'Predaniia o Khadzhi Murate', *Dagestanskii Sbornik*, Vol. III, pp. 7–49; G. Kvinitadze, 'Khadzhi Murat', *Kavkaz* (Paris), 1934, No. 7, pp. 8–12; HHSA, PA. X. 34/Konv. VIII Lebzelder (?) to Schwarzenberg, St. Petersburg, 3 January 1852/22 December 1851, No. 2, PA. X. 34/Konv. IX, ? to Buol-Schanenstein, St. Petersburg, 29/17 May 1852, No. 7. For the inscription on Ḥajimurad's grave in Qipchāq [Kypchak], see *Epigraficheskie Pamiatniki*, p. 100, inscription No. 647. And see Hamzatov, pp. 370–2.
36. Olszewski, 'Bariatinskii', No. 6, p. 318; 'Zimniaia Ēkspeditsiia', pp. 483–4 and Appendix on pp. 613–16; 'Levyi Flang', Vol. XI, p. 317; N. A. Volkonskii, 'Pogrom Chechni v 1852 Godu', *Kavkazskii Sbornik*, Vol. V, pp. 23–5 (hereafter: Volkonskii, 'Pogrom').
37. 'Obzor Sobytii', Vol. XVIII, pp. 183–4; Soltan, '1852–1853', p. 478.
38. *AKAK*, Vol. X. p. 536, document No. 428, War Diary of the Caspian Province by Argutinskii, 24 February–2 [7–14] March 1852; Soltan, '1852–1853', pp. 478–86; Andreevskii, p. 39; Qarākhī, pp. 180–1.

39. The commander of the First Brigade of the 21st Infantry Division.
40. In the summer of 1851 Sleptsov suggested a plan to subdue the upper part of Lesser Chechnia by what would be in fact the construction of a new, advanced line. Vorontsov approved the plan, and it was decided to carry it out in the winter. On 14 December 1851, Sleptsov took to the upper Gekhī with a force of 4,000 infantry, 1,100 cavalry and ten cannon. On 15 December he occupied and destroyed all the hamlets in the vicinity, and on the following day started to clear the forest. The clearing proceeded in face of mounting opposition and on 22 December the Russians had to fight a hard battle, in which Sleptsov himself was killed. For these and further events, see *AKAK*, Vol. X, p. 525, document Nos. 474, 475, Vorontsov to Chernyshev, 14 [26] December, Chernyshev to Vorontsov, 20 December 1851 [1 January 1852], Nos. 1636, 13,296 respectively (also published as Appendices III and IV to 'Letuchii Otriad', p. 474); 'Obzor Sobytii', Vol. XIX, pp. 38–9, Vol. XXI, pp. 47–9; 'Letuchii Otriad', pp. 451–69; N. Akhshamurov, 'Smert' Sleptsova. Kavkazskaia Byl', *Russkii Vestnik* (1888), No. 10, pp. 52–74.
41. Volkonskii, 'Pogrom', p. 20. And see Andreevskii, p. 213.
42. *AKAK*, Vol. X, pp. 530–7, document Nos. 477, 478, 479, 480, 481, 483, Vorontsov to Chernyshev, 12 [24] January, Vorontsov's Orders of the Day, 15 [27], 31 January [12], 8 [20], 26 February, [9], 15 [27] March 1852, Nos. 2, 7, 24, 27, 36, 54 respectively: *Dvizhenie*, pp. 605–10, document No. 363, Bariatinskii to Zavodovskii, 19 February [2 March] 1852; Vorontsov's Diary, pp. 109–10, entries for 11 [23], 12 [24], 21 January [2], 22 February [5 March] 1852; Vorontsov to Ermolov, Tiflis, 17 [29] January, 18 February [2 March] 1852, No. 4, pp. 448–9, 451; *Ombres du Passé*, pp. 132–42; Volkonskii 'Pogrom', pp. 8–142; 'Zimniaia Ēkspeditsiia', pp. 452–612; Olszewski, 'Bariatinskii', No. 6, pp. 317–332; HHSA, PA XXXVIII, 97/Odessa, 29 March 1852, No. 225; Qarākhī, p. 177.
43. Volkonskii, 'Pogrom', p. 8. Emphasis in the original.
44. 'Zimniaia Ēkspeditsiia', pp. 442–54. Quotations from pp. 446, 452.
45. Ibid., p. 491; Volkonskii, 'Pogrom', p. 53.
46. 'Zimniaia Ēkspeditsiia', p. 478.
47. 'Prince Bariatinskii, having enemies among the confidants of the commander-in-chief [Vorontsov], was cautious enough in spite of his young age not to mention to the viceroy the details of the catastrophe on the Goyta in a letter. But he described it to him at a personal interview in Tiflis . . . after the dismissal of the force' – ibid. p. 524.
48. Ibid., p. 533.
49. Ibid., p. 550.
50. Ibid., pp. 587–8.
51. Ibid., pp. 576, 578, 580.
52. Ibid., p. 579.
53. Ibid., p. 601. Nevertheless, the Chechens found the grave and afterwards mocked the Russians about it.
54. Baklanov was clearing the forests along the Michik, one of his aims being to divert the neighbouring communities from acting against Bariantinskii – ibid. pp. 593–4, 608.
55. Volkonskii, 'Pogrom', p. 132.
56. *AKAK*, Vol. X, pp. 437–8, 540–4, 545, document Nos. 484, 487, 488,

489, 491, Vorontsov to Chernyshev, 4 [16] April, Vorontsov's Order of the Day, 18 [30] June, Bariatinskii to Zavodovskii, 21 August [2 September], Vorontsov to Chernyshev (secret), 23 August [4 September], Vorontsov to Dolgorukov, 21 December 1852 [2 January 1853], Nos. 15, 106, 1286, 263, 1691 respectively; *Dvizhenie*, pp. 611–14, 615–19, document Nos. 366, 368, 369, War Diaries of the Chechen Force, 16 [28]–28 June [10], 6 [18]–16 [28] July, Vorontsov to Chernyshev, 30 August [11 September] 1852 respectively; Vorontsov's Diary, pp. 110, 111, entries for 30 March [11 April], 19 [31], 21–31 August [3–12 September] 1852; Vorontsov to Ermolov, Tiflis, 2 [14] April, Eisk, 13 [25] September 1852, No. 4, pp. 453, 458–9; Vorontsov to Bebutov, Groznaia, 30 August [11 September] 1852, No. 5, p. 694; *Ombres du Passé*, pp. 127–30, 142–3, 160–4; Volkonskii, 'Pogrom', pp. 144–228; Olszewski, 'Bariatinskii', No. 7, pp. 426–36.

57. Volkonskii, 'Pogrom', p. 166.
58. Ibid., p. 164.
59. Ibid., p. 204. For the topographical difficulties in assaulting this place, see Baddeley, *Rugged Flanks*, Vol. I, pp. 84–5.
60. Volkonskii, 'Pogrom', p. 172.
61. Ibid., p. 190.
62. *Ombres du Passé*, (pp. 127–9) places this action a year earlier, naming it Bariatinskii's first operation after becoming the commander of the Left Flank.
63. Volkonskii, 'Pogrom', p. 192.
64. For the winter campaign, see *AKAK*, Vol. X, pp. 545–7, 549–51, document Nos. 492, 493, 501, 494, 500, Vorontsov's Orders of the Day, 5 [17], 31 January [12 February], 7 [19] October, Bariatinskii to Dolgorukov, 10 [22] February, Nos. 2, 12, 207, 298, War Diaries of the Left Flank, 25–31 August [6–12], 22–29 September [4–11 October] 1853 respectively; Vorontsov's Order of the Day, 14 [26] February, *Kavkaz*, 18 February [2 March] 1853 (No. 123), p. 54; Vorontsov to Ermolov, Tiflis, 22 January [3 February] 1853, No. 4, pp. 460–1; M. Egorov, 'Deistviia Nashikh Voisk v Chechne s Kontsa 1852 Goda po 1854 God', *Kavkazskii Sbornik*, Vol. XVI, pp. 352–404 (hereafter: Egorov); *Ombres du Passé*, pp. 172–81; Volkonskii, 'Pogrom', pp. 229–34; I. Iu. Krachkovskii and A. N. Genko, 'Arabskie Pis'ma Shamilia v Severo-Osetii', *Sovetskoe Vostokovedenie*, Vol. III, pp. 41–2, letter No. V, Shamil to the People of Dachin Barzī [Dachu Barzoy] and Uluskert, [winter, 1852–53] (hereafter: Krachkovskii and Genko).
65. Egorov, p. 377.
66. Vorontsov to Ermolov, Tiflis, 22 January [3 February] 1853, No. 4, p. 461.
67. For these plans, see Egorov, pp. 358–9, 360–1.
68. *AKAK*, Vol. X, p. 547, document No. 495, Vorontsov's Order of the Day, 20 June [2 July] 1853, No. 123; *Shamil*, pp. 324–36, document Nos. 267, 268, 269, 270, 272, 274, 275, 276, 277, 278, 279, 282, 271, 273, 281; War Diaries of the Lesghian Line, 20–27 February [4–11 March], 27 February–6 [11–18], 13 [25]–20 March [1 April], 20–27 March [1–18], 3 [15]–10 [22] April, 1 [13]–8 [20], 8 [20]–15 [27] May, 5 [17]–12 [24], 12 [24]–19 June [1 July], 19–26 June [1–18], 3 [15]–10 [22] July, 7 [19]–14 [26] August, Orbeliani to Vorontsov, 3 [15] April, Wolf to Orbeliani, 14 [26] April, Melikov to Orbeliani, 21 July [2 August] 1853, Nos. 219, 480,

1315 respectively; Vorontsov's Diary, p. 113, entry for 21 June [3 July] 1853; Soltan, '1852–1853', pp. 495–503.

Chapter 21: Shamil's State

1. See *AKAK*, Vol. VIII, pp. 543–4, document No. 422, Rosen to Chernyshev, 12 [24] November 1831, No. 136, and 'Voina', Vol. XIV, p. 103, for the nomination by him of Ummalat Bek as the new *shāmkhāl*, and 'Voina', Vol. XIII, p. 307, for the nomination of 'Umar Bek as *'uṣmī*. This is in contrast to Shamil's habit of nominating members of the ruling houses as *nā'ibs* – e.g. *AKAK*, Vol. IX, pp. 375–7, document No. 334, Golovin to Chernyshev, 13 [25] April 1842, No. 376.
2. See above, pp. 65, 69–70.
3. For which, see above, p. 62.
4. This description is based on the following sources: *AKAK*, Vol. X, pp. 525–30, document No. 476, Loris-Melikov's Report of the Debriefing of Ḥajimurād (n.d.) (hereafter: Ḥajimurād); *Dvizhenie*, pp. 357–9, document No. 198, Neidhardt to Chernyshev, 12 [24] December 1842 (hereafter: Neidhardt, 1842); ibid., pp. 381–6, document No. 211, Klugenau to Neidhardt, 22 March [3 April] 1843, No. 39 (secret) (also published in *Shamil* pp. 211–21, as document No. 170) (hereafter: Klugenau); *Dvizhenie*, pp. 401–8, document No. 219, Neidhardt to Chernyshev, 20 November [2 December] 1843 (hereafter: Neidhardt, 1843); Ibid., pp. 412–23, document No. 221, 'Excerpts from the Report of Lieutenant Orbeliani, Who Was in Shamil's Captivity in 1842', 1843 (hereafter: Orbeliani); Ibid., pp. 492–7, document No. 266, 'Excerpts from the War Diary of Bebutov', 12 [24] March–15 [27] December 1845 (hereafter: Bebutov); Runowski's Diary, *passim;* 'Nizam Shamilia (Material dlia Istorii Degestana)' *Sbornik Svedenii o Kavkazkikh Gortsakh*, Vol. II, 18 pp. (separate pagination) (reprinted in *Severenyi Kavkaz* [Warsaw], No. 53) [1938], pp. 30–3 (hereafter: 'Niẓām'); R. Sh. Sharafutdinova, 'Eshche Odin "Nizam" Shamilia', *Pis'mennye Pamiatniki Vostoka* (1975), pp. 168–71, 331 (hereafter: 'Another Niẓām'); Iurov, '1843', pp. 42–8; Iurov, '1844', pp. 215–17; 'Shamil' i Chechnia', *Voennyi Sbornik* (1859), No. 9, pp. 121–64; de Saget, 'O Grazhdanskikh, Voennykh i Dukhovnykh Postanovleniiakh Shamilia', ibid. (1900), No. 3, pp. 210–14; S. K. Bushuev, 'Gosudarstvennaia Sistema Imamata Shamilia', *Istorik Marksist* (1937), No. 5–6, (63–4), pp. 77–104 (hereafter: Bushuev); N. Pokrovskii, 'Miuridizm u Vlasti ("Teokraticheskaia Derzhava" Shamilia)', ibid. (1934), No. 2 (36), pp. 30–75 (hereafter: Pokrovskii).
5. For a more detailed discussion, see below, pp. 232–8.
6. *Dvizhenie*, pp. 619–20, document No. 371, Shamil to Talhin Hayirbek, the *Muftīs* and the *Qāḍīs* [November 1852]; R. Sh. Sharafutdinova, 'Arabskie Pis'ma Shamilia iz Arkhiva B. A. Dorna', *Pis'mennye Pamiatniki Vostoka* (1970), p. 209, Letter No. II, Shamil to Duba, 1 Muḥarram 1262 [30 December 1845] (also published in *Dvizhenie*, p. 484, as document No. 259).
7. For such letters, see *Dvizhenie*, pp. 449, 502, 510, 532, 545, 558, 559, 585, 588, 589, 590, 591, 601, 604, 621, 625, 652–3, 658, 667, 672, document

Nos. 271, 277, 283, 299, 306, 309, 310, 311, 334, 335, 341, 342, 343, 347, 348, 355, 359, 360, 374, 379, 380, 382, 403, 411, 421, 427, and the facsimiles of five letters as published in Şerafeddin Erel, *Dağıstan ve Dağıstanlılar* (İstanbul, 1961) p. 144, and Mustafa Zihni Hizaloğlu, *Şeyh Şamil. Şimalı Kafkasya İstiklal Mucadedeleri* (Ankara, 1958), pp. 25, 27.

8. See above, p. 92. According to Shamil, the *diwān* was established at a time when he was seriously ill and there was a good chance that he would die – Runowski's Diary, p. 1417, entry for 6 [18] March 1860.
9. See, e.g. Sharafutdinova, 'Pis'ma', pp. 209–10, letter No. III, Shamil to Duba, 6 Rabiʿ al-Awwal 1262 [4 March 1846]; Krachovskii and Genko, pp. 39–40, letter Nos. II, III, Shamil to Batoqa, 3 Ramaḍān [21 June], 21 Dhū al-Qaʿda 1267 [6 September 1852].
10. For examples of such letters, see *Dvizhenie*, pp. 492, 527, 598, 610, document Nos. 267, 292, 350, 364; Sharafutdinova, 'Pis'ma', p. 214, letter No. VII, Shamil to the People of Kalay and ʿArshtkhī, 13 Dhū al-Oaʿda 1266 [20 September 1850]; Krachkovskii and Genko, pp. 38, 40–1, letter Nos. I, IV, Shamil to the People of Shubūt, 2 Rabīʿ al-Awwal 1266 [16 January 1850], Shamil to the People under Atabay, 21 Dhū al-Qaʿda 1267 [6 September 1852].
11. Qarākhī, p. 126.
12. Linevich, 'Karta Gorskikh Narodov Podvlastnykh Shamiliu', *Sbornik Svedenii o Kavkazskikh Gortsakh*, Vol. VI, 4 pp. (separate pagination) and 2 maps (Arabic original and Russian translation).
13. See, for example, Sharafutdinova, 'Pis'ma', letter No. III, Shamil to Duba, 6 Rabīʿ al-Awwal [4 March 1846].
14. *Muḥtasib* was an officer appointed to see that the precepts of Islam were obeyed, to detect offences and to punish offenders.
15. E.g., *Dvizhenie*, p. 628, document No. 386, Shamil to the *Nāʾibs* Ramaḍān, Muḥammad ʿAlī, Ismāʿīl, Muḥammad Amīn, Al-Būrī, Abākār Ḥājjī and Ibrāhīm, November 1853.
16. Klugenau, p. 383.
17. 'Niẓām', p. 10.
18. *Khuṭba* is the sermon given at Friday noon prayers by the ruler, or usually in his name. It became one of the two symbols of sovereignty in Islam, the other being coinage.
19. 'Niẓām, p. 11.
20. This is distinctly different from the usual designation of the two offices in the Muslim world, where *qāḍī* is a *sharʿī* judge, while *muftī* is the interpreter of the *sharīʿa*.
21. See, e.g., *Dvizhenie*, pp. 499–501, document No. 273, Shamil's Letter to all the '*Ulamā*' and *Qāḍīs* 1845.
22. According to Bushuev (p. 88), the *muftī* was appointed by the *nā'ib*.
23. See 'Niẓām,' p. 11, where the *muftīs* are instructed not to attack the *nāʾib*'s acts directly or indirectly in their *khuṭbas*.
24. Runowski's Diary, pp. 1398, 1399, 1521–2, entries for 12 [24], 17 [29] November, 6 [18] December 1859.
25. None the less, the *nāʾibī murīds* included many *ṣūfī* ones.
26. Runowski's Diary, p. 1474, entry for 25 January [6 February] 1861.
27. Ibid., loc. cit.
28. According to ibid, loc. cit. the institution of *murtāziqs* was limited to

Chechnia only. This is contradicted, however, by all the rest of the available evidence. For the beginning of this institution see above, p. 80.

29. Khursh's claim (*Osada Twiardzy Achulgo*, p. 18) that it existed already in the late 1830s is not supported by the available documentation.
30. Runowski's Diary, p. 1450, entry for 2 [14] August 1860. And see above, p. 212.
31. 'Levyi Flang', Vol. XI, p. 309.
32. *Shamil*, pp. 227–8, document No. 179, Shamil's Letter to the Ottoman *Sultan*, 1843(?); Runowski's Diary, pp. 1398, 1399–1400, 1521, entries for 15 [27], 17 [29] November, 3 [15] December 1859; Qarākhī, p. 175; Volkonskii, '1859', p. 365; Orbeliani, p. 416.
33. See, for example, Dzierzyński, No. 10, p. 46. The mountaineers used great quantities of captured Russian weapons, including muskets, which they loaded with more gunpowder than Russian regulation allowed and, therefore, could shoot for longer distances – Volkonskii, '1857', Vol. I, p. 404. And see note 2 to Chapter 3.
34. *Shamil*, pp. 227–8, document No. 179, Shamil's Letter to the Ottoman *Sultan* 1843[?]; Dzierzyński, No. 10, pp. 45–6; Ignatius, pp. 21–2.
35. Orbeliani, p. 416.
36. For both, see below, p. 261.
37. For their production and the Russians' impression of them, see *Shamil*, pp. 227–8, document No. 179, Shamil's Letter to the Ottoman *Sultan*, 1843 [?]; Runowski's Diary, pp. 1399, 1400, entries for 15 [27], 18 [30] November 1859; Qarākhī, pp. 111–12; Baddeley, *Rugged Flanks*, Vol. II, p. 35; Volkonskii, '1847', pp. 548–9; Volkonskii, '1858', p. 571; Volkonskii, '1859', p. 365.
38. For a discussion of these deserters, see below, pp. 252–4.
39. 'Pokhod,' pp. 14–15.
40. See, for example, Rzewuski, Vol. VI, p. 448, for the grant of two cannon to the people of Ṭiliq (i.e. to Qibid Muḥammad) for their steadfastness and bravery in battle.
41. Volkonskii, '1849', p. 145 (note).
42. For which see, for example, *Dvizhenie*, pp. 341–2, document Nos. 188, 189, Grabbe to [Chernyshev?] and an annexed 'List of Marks of Distinction', 14 [26] May 1842; Klugenau, pp. 383–4; Bushuev, pp. 97–8.
43. E.g., ibid., loc. cit.; Klugenau, p. 384; 'Niẓām', pp. 8–10, 12–13.
44. See above, p. 71. For the existence of the treasury already in Ghāzī Muḥammad's time, see Qarākhī, p. 19.
45. The exact percentage or amount of taxation on different items is difficult to establish because the numbers differ from source to source. And see, for example, Orbeliani, pp. 415–16, and Bushuev, pp. 99–100.
46. Ḥājj 'Alī, p. 74.
47. Runowski's Diary, pp. 1398, 1399, entries for 12 [24], 17 [29] November 1859.
48. See, for example, Klugenau, p. 384; Rzewuski, Vol. VI, p. 409.
49. To this category belongs Shamil's most beloved wife, the Armenian Shu'awana [Shuanet], who came to him as one of the captives of Akhbirdi Muḥammad's raid on Muzlik in 1840. See above, p. 120, and Hamzatov, pp. 375–9.
50. Ḥājj 'Alī, p. 75.

51. Klugenau, p. 384.
52. A. Runowski, 'Kodeks Shamilia', *Voennyi Sbornik* (1862), No. 2, p. 373. (hereafter:Runowski, 'Kodeks'). This article is an edited version concentrating all the material dealing with Shamil's legislating activity in Runowski's Diary. Also, see *Shamil*, pp. 200–1, 214, 234–5, 285, 288, document Nos. 159, 166, 187, 221, 224, Schwartz to CoS Caucasian Corps, 2 [14] July 1841, Governor of T'elavi to Governor of Georgia-Imeret'i, 13 [25] May 1842, 'Excerpts from Note by Viktorov', 1844, Schwartz to Vorontsov, 28 February [12], 20 March [1 April] 1848, Nos. 78, 614, 400, 624 respectively; Züssermann, 'Otryvki', 1876, No. 4, p. 445. Also some Ghumuq and other villages paid such a tax – see, e.g., Iurov '1840–1842', Vol. XI, pp. 188–9.
53. E.g., Runowski, 'Kodeks', pp. 368, 377, 378.
54. Bushuev's conclusion (p. 100) that 'all the collected money went to Shamil's treasurer while the income in kind was left to the *nā'ibs*' disposal and was used by them according to the *imām*'s instructions' seems to be oversimplified.
55. Runowski, 'Kodeks', pp. 331, 370.
56. See note 51 above.
57. S. Shul'gin, 'Rasskaz Ochevidtsa o Shamile i Ego Sovremennikakh', *Sbornik Materialov dlia Opisaniia Mestnostei i Plamen Kavkaza*, Vol. XXXII, p. 11 (hereafter: ʿAbd al-Raḥīm); Runowski, 'Kodeks', pp. 374–6.
58. Ibid, pp. 368, 377–8. *Inter alia* Shamil did not usually allow people to go on the *ḥajj*, because the conditions were not right – see, for example, *Dvizhenie*, p. 653, document No. 404, Shamil to 'Umar Muḥammad [1854]. The fifth intended to be used for this purpose was used for others.
59. E.g., 'Niẓām', p. 14.
60. Runowski, 'Kodeks', p. 368.
61. See, for example, *Dvizhenie*, pp. 498, 604, 626, document Nos. 270, 361, 384, Shamil to the *Qāḍī* Muḥammad, 1845, Shamil to the *Qāḍī* and Community of 'Andī, 1850, Shamil to the *Nā'ib* Ḥādis, 17 [29] October 1853 respectively.
62. E.g., *Dvizhenie*, p. 498, document No. 270, Shamil to the *Qāḍī* Muḥammad, 1845. And see below, p. 251.
63. A side effect of this prohibition was that it became an efficient tool in discovering people engaged in illegal contacts with the Russians, since a man smelling of tobacco or alcohol could have consumed it only in Russian territory – '1852', p. 438, note 7.
64. 'Another Niẓām', p. 169; Runowski, 'Kodeks', pp. 369–70.
65. See, for example, A Runowski, 'Kanly', *Voennyi Sbornik* (1860), No. 7, pp. 199–216, which is an edited version of the relevant entries from his diary.
66. E.g., 'Niẓām', p. 14; ʿAbd al-Raḥīm, p. 16.
67. 'Another Niẓām', p. 169; Neidhardt, 1843, p. 403.
68. Runowski's Diary, pp. 1459–60, entry for 20 September [2 October] 1860.
69. In the Ottoman Empire the *qawānīn* (plural of *qānūn*) were the regulations issed by the *sultans*, mainly in the domains of administrative, financial and penal law.
70. 'Niẓām'.
71. E.g., ibid, pp. 2–3; 'Another Niẓām', p. 169; Bushuev, pp. 92–4.

72. E.g., 'Another Nizām'; *Dvizhenie*, pp. 494–5, 499–501, 531–32, 560, 601–2, 619–20, document Nos. 268, 273, 298, 314, 356, 371, 'Excerpts from Bebutov's War Diary, 12 [24] March – 15 [27] December 1845', Shamil to All the *'Ulamā'* and *Qāḍīs*, 1845, Shamil's instructions to All the *Nā'ibs* and *Qāḍīs*, 1846, Shamil to All the *Nā'ibs* and *Qāḍīs* 1847, The *Diwān's* Appeal to All the Population, 1850, Shamil to the *Muftīs* and *Qāḍis*, November 1852.
73. See, for example, Neidhardt, 1843, p. 404; Qarākhī, p. 117.
74. Neidhardt, 1843, p. 404.
75. 'Another Niẓām', p. 169. For such permissions, see *Dvizhenie*, p. 575, document No. 329, Shamil to Qurbān al-Muḥammad [July 1848].
76. 'Another Niẓām', p. 169; 'Abd al-Raḥīm, p. 17.
77. 'Niẓām', p. 14.
78. Runowski, 'Kodeks', pp. 378–80. And see *Dvizhenie* p. 385, document No. 417, Shamil to the *Nā'ib* 'Umar [27 March 1857].
79. Qarākhī, p. 117.
80. Runowski, 'Kodeks', pp. 344–54. And see *Dvizhenie*, p. 619, document No. 370, Shamil to Ḥājjī [27 November 1852].
81. Runowski, 'Kodeks', pp. 342–44.
82. Ibid, pp. 338–9.
83. Ibid., p. 384.
84. Ibid, pp. 384–5.
85. G.V. Tsereteli, 'Vnov' Naidennye Pis'ma Shamilia', *Trudy Pervoi Sessii Arabistov* (Moscow and Leningrad, 1937), p. 104, Shamil to Nicolaў, 8 Ramaḍān 1271 [25 May 1855] (hereafter: Tsereteli).
86. E.g., Zagorskii, pp. 231–8.
87. Runowski, 'Kodeks', p. 385.
88. Ibid, p. 384, 'Another Niẓām', p. 169.
89. Runowski, 'Kodeks', pp. 345–9.
90. See, e.g., Sharafutdinova, 'Pis'ma', p. 216, letter No IX, Shamil to Muḥammad Mīrzā [n.d].
91. E.g., 'Shamil' i Chechnia', *Voennyi Sbornik* (1859), No. 10, p. 142.
92. Runowski's Diary, p. 1398, entry for 10 [22] November 1859.
93. See, for example, Neidhardt, 1843, p. 403; Orbeliani, p. 414.

Chapter 22: The Ruler and the Ruled

1. Qarākhī, p. 63: 'I am the *imām* [here] like the *hunkâr* and this village is like İstanbul'.
2. See above, pp. 76–7, 79–80, 118.
3. For Ḥājj Tāshō's biography, see above, note 57 to Chapter 8. At a certain stage in the early 1840s, it seems, Tāshō had been deposed and sent a letter requesting Shamil to return him to his post – text in Sharafutdinova, 'Pis'mo', pp. 87–8. He seems to have been reinstated and then, after a while, his name disappeared from the documents. Also, see Pokrovskii, p. 70.
4. Runowski's Diary, pp. 1401, 1452–3, entries for 26 November [8 December] 1859, 25 August [6 September] 1860.

5. For which, see below, p. 243.
6. See above, pp. 82, 177.
7. Runowski, 'Kodeks', p. 353. For the wedding, see also Zagorskii, p. 243. Whether such a divorce helped Shamil's standing among the Chechens is a different question.
8. See above, pp. 232–5.
9. E.g. *Dvizhenie*, pp. 601–2, document No. 356, Manifesto of the *Diwān* to All the People, 1850.
10. See above, p. 177.
11. See, for example, his good treatment, which converted Muḥammad the *Qāḍī* of Sughūr into a devotee - Iurov, '1844', p. 272 (note). And see Rzewuski, Vol. VI, p. 404.
12. E.g., ʿAbd al-Raḥīm, p. 11; Rzewuski, Vol VI, p. 404. For the Khālidiyya's special reverence for the descendants of the Prophet, see Abu Manneh, p. 16.
13. See, for example, his public speech as reported by Orbeliani, p. 419.
14. See above, p. 131.
15. See, e.g., Neidhardt, 1843, p. 403.
16. Zagorskii, pp. 241, 243–4.
17. See above, p. 71.
18. See, for example, his public speech as reported by Orbeliani, pp. 419–20. And see Volkonskii, 'Trekhletie', pp. 169–70.
19. E.g., *Dvizhenie*, p. 589, document No. 344, Jamāl al-Dīn to the Abadzekhs [9 August 1849].
20. See, for example, ibid, pp. 602–3, document No. 357, Jamāl al-Dīn to Aghālār Bek, 1850. For Jamāl al-Dīn's influence among the local rulers, see Iurov, '1840–1842', Vol. XII, pp. 220–3.
21. E.g., *Dvizhenie*, pp. 575–8, document No. 310, Jamāl al-Dīn to *Şeyhül İslam* [August 1848]; *Shamil*, pp. 312–13, document Nos. 256, 257, Jamāl al-Dīn to the Ottoman *Sultan*, 1849, and to the Grand *Vezir*, Hacci Mehmet Ali Paşa [9 August 1849].
22. Runowski's Diary, pp. 1410–12, 1414, 1424, entries for 11 [23] January, 14 [26], 24 February [7 March], 18 [30] April 1860.
23. Ibid, p. 1402, entry for 28 December 1859 [9 January 1860].
24. See Orbeliani, p. 413; Rumiantsev, pp. 83–7.
25. See, for example, Runowski's Diary, pp. 1402, 1405–7, entries for 28 December 1859 [9], 4 [16] January 1860. Runowski regarded Shamil's passing out and the other symptoms as pointing to the fact that Shamil suffered from catalepsy - p. 1407, entry for 4 [16] January 1860.
26. E.g., Klugenau, p. 385; 'Shamil' i Chechnia', p. 130; Zagorskii, pp. 242–3; Volkonskii, '1847', pp. 502–3.
27. 'Odin iz Fanaticheskikh Postupkov Shamilia', *Kavkaz*, 30 May [11 June] 1853 (No. 40), pp. 103–5. For another, distorted version preserved in the popular memory, see Hamzatov, pp. 372–4.
28. Volkonskii, '1847', pp. 502–3.
29. E.g., Friedrich Wagner, *Schamyl als Feldherr, Sultan und Prophet und der Kaukasus* (Leipzig, 1854). The mistake is repeated throughout practically all the Western literature up to Blanch (p. 125). For a recent Soviet repetition of this claim, see A. M. Khalilov, 'Shamil' v Istorii i Pamiati Naroda', *Sovetskii Dagestan* (1988), No. 5 (September–October), p. 34.

30. Zagorskii, pp. 241–2.
31. For a short, though hostile, biography of Shuʿayb, see Neidhardt, 1843, pp. 407–8.
32. See, for example, Vorontsov to Ermolov, Temir-Khān-Shūra, 7 [19] November 1851, No. 4, p. 447; Qarākhī, p. 111.
33. E.g., 'Levyi Flang', Vol. X, pp. 494–7; '1850–1851', pp. 350–1.
34. See, e.g., Volkonskii, 'Trekhletie', pp. 244–55; Sharafutdinova, 'Pis'ma', pp. 212–13, letter No. VI, Shamil to Duba, undated; *Dvizhenie*, pp. 502–3, 587, document Nos. 278, 338, Daniyāl to Shamil [24 May 1846] and to the *ʿUlamā'* of Sughūr, 1848.
35. In addition to all the cases mentioned above, *passim*, see *Dvizhenie*, pp. 631–2, document No. 392, Predemirov to Vrevskii, 6 [18] April 1854.
36. See, for example, Baratov, 'Opisanie Nashestvia Skopishch Shamilia v Kakhetiiu v 1854 Godu', *Kavkazskii Sbornik*, Vol. I, pp. 240–1, 246–7; Soltan, '1854', p. 542; Volkonskii, 'Trekhletie', pp. 249–55.
37. E.g., Iurov, '1840–1842', Vol. XI, p. 354.
38. See, for example, 'Niẓām', p. 13; *Dvizhenie*, pp. 501, 531–2, 560, 601–2, 619–20, document Nos. 274, 298, 314, 356, 371, Shamil to Galbats, 1845, Shamil to All the *Nā'ibs* and *Qāḍīs*, 1846, the *Diwān* to All the People, 1850, Shamil to Talhin Hayirbek, the *Muftīs* and *Qāḍīs* [November 1852] respectively; Rzewuski, Vol. VI, p. 397.
39. For examples of such instances of removal of a *nā'ib*, see '1846', Vol. XVI, p. 303; '1851', Vol. XVIII, p. 153; Volkonskii, '1847', p. 663–4, 668; Volkonskii, '1848', pp. 483–5; Volkonskii, '1849', p. 302; 'Levyi Flang', Vol. XI, p. 317.
40. E.g., Iurov, '1840–1842', Vol XII, p. 243; R. Sh. Sharafutdinova, 'Arabskii Dokument iz Arkhiva Adademika B. A. Dorna (Materialy k Istorii Osvoboditel'nogo Dvizheniia Gortsev na Severnom Kavkaze v 20–50kh Godakh XIX V.)', *Pis'mennye Pamiatniki Vostoka* (1971), pp. 166–7 (hereafter: Sharafutdinova, 'Dokument'). For places of exile used by Shamil, see Runowski's Diary, p. 1456, entry for 8 [20] September 1860. Interestingly, unauthorised contacts with the Russians did not lead automatically to capital punishment.
41. See notes 33 and 38 above. Also, see Vorontsov to Bebutov, Tiflis, 13 [25] February 1849, No. 2, p. 257.
42. 'Levyi Flang', Vol XI, p. 315.
43. 'Niẓām', p. 13.
44. Rzewuski, Vol. VI, pp. 405–6.
45. Daniyāl did not have a power base of his own inside Shamil's area and did not really belong to this group. But his continuing influence on his previous subjects and in Chārtalah made him important to the *imām* and justified his inclusion in this category. For Daniyāl's continued influence in the aforementioned areas, see, for example, Volkonskii, 'Trekhletie', p. 178 (third note).
46. E.g., Pokrovskii, pp. 70–1; Volkonskii, '1847', pp. 663–4, 668; Volkonskii, '1848', pp. 483–5. And see Runowski's Diary, p. 1396, entry for 3 [15] November 1859. Rumiantsov (pp. 32–3 and ff.) witnessed another confrontation between Shamil and Qibid Muḥammad, but related a story closer to the *Arabian Nights* than to facts.
47. E.g., *Dvizhenie*, pp. 502–3, 587, 631, document Nos. 278, 338, 391, Dani-

yāl to Shamil [24 March 1846], Daniyāl to the '*Ulamā*' of Sughūr, 1848, Shamil to Daniyāl [24 January 1854]; Vorontsov to Ermolov, Tiflis, 5 [17] November 1848, No. 3, p. 341, Kodzhory, 25 July [6 August] 1852, No. 4, p. 457; Volkonskii, '1849'. p. 302; Runowski's Diary, p. 1451, entry for 10 [22] August 1860.

48. See above, note 3.
49. See above, p. 118.
50. According to some sources, this marriage was not entirely to Shamil's liking.
51. The eldest son, Jamāl al-Dīn, had been given as a hostage to the Russians in Akhulgoḥ (see above, p. 106), and was then, therefore, in Russia.
52. Qarākhī, pp. 175–6; Ḥājj ʿAlī, p. 34; Runowski's Diary, pp. 1417, 1472, entries for 6 [18] March 1860, 16 [28] January 1861; Vorontsov to Ermolov, Tiflis, 25 March [6 April] 1848, No. 3, p. 331; Volkonskii, '1848', pp. 484–5. According to Shamil, it was during his dangerous illness, when the *diwān* was established (see above, note 8 to Chapter 21), that a decision was secretly reached that in case he died, the seven- or eight-year-old Ghāzī-Muḥammad would succeed him and that Albāz Dibīr would be the regent. (Runowski's Diary, loc. cit.). The act of 1848 was thus in a way only an act of announcing publicly what had already been decided years before.
53. See above, p. 216.
54. Runowski's Diary, p. 1417, entry for 6 [18] March 1860. Also see Pokrovskii, p. 71. One of two letters, now in the Princeton University Library, seems to be a direct response to this refusal. It is addressed from Shamil 'to his dear son ʿAlī [an obvious mistake for Ghāzī] Muḥammad'. In it the *imām* tells his son that 'now I have come to know you' and promises him the succession 'if Allah grants us victory' over 'that People of the unbelievers'. This letter is undated, but the other, also addressed from Shamil to Ghāzī Muḥammad, is dated 9 Shaʿbān 1273 [4 April 1857].
55. Runowski's Diary, p. 1448, entry for 23 July [4 August] 1860.
56. E.g., Volkonskii, '1852', pp. 142–4.
57. Iurov, '1840–1842', Vol. X, pp. 319–20; Vol XI, pp. 205–8.
58. '1852', p. 435, note 5.
59. Runowski's Diary, p. 1448, entry for 23 July [4 August] 1860. For one such particular resistance to the nomination of a *nā'ib*, see S. Farforovskii, 'Shamil' i Chechentsy (Neizvestnyi Eshche Ēpizod iz Zavoevaniia Kavkaza)', *Russkii Arkhiv* (1913) , No. 6, pp. 770–4.
60. Volkonskii, '1857', Vol. II, pp. 376–7; Volkonskii '1858', pp. 567–8. One of Shamil's reasons for nominating Ḥamza over Mazha seems to have been a response to local intrigues in which a potential local rival to Mazha's candidacy had been assassinated – A. Volkonskii, 'Sem Let v Plenu na Kavkaze (1849–1856)', *Russkii Vestnik* (1882), No. 5, pp. 222–3 (hereafter: Volkonskii, 'Sem Let'). Also the community of Shubūt went over to the Russians at the same time because of dissatisfaction with its *nā'ib* – Volkonskii, '1858', p. 583.
61. Iurov, '1840–1842', pp. 207–8.
62. Ibid, pp. 198–9, 206.
63. *AKAK*, Vol. IX, p. 881, document Nos. 724, 725, 'Excerpts from the War Diary of the Sunja Line', annexed to Freytag to Chernyshev, 11 [23]

March, No. 1561, 'Excerpt from the War Diary of the Caucasian Line, 17 [29]–21 March [2 April] 1844'; *Shamil*, pp. 232, document No. 184, 'Excerpt from Review of the Most Important Military Events in the Caucasus, 1 [13] March – 1 [13] May 1844'.

64. Volkonskii, '1858', p. 583.
65. For one such occasion, when there was a widespread refusal to go on a campaign, see Volkonskii, 'Trekhletie', pp. 169–70.
66. For a discussion of Shamil's system as opposed to that of the Russians, see Runowski's Diary, p. 1467, entry for 17 [29] November 1860.
67. Ibid., p. 1448, entry for 23 July [4 August] 1860.
68. For a few out of many such instances, see *Ombres du Passé*, p. 200; Iurov, '1844', pp. 304, 417; '1846', Vol. XV, p. 494; '1852', pp. 529–30; Volkonskii, '1852', pp. 174–5; Volkonskii, '1858', p. 526.
69. See, for example, Volkonskii, '1858', pp. 265–90.
70. In addition to sources already mentioned above, see *Dvizhenie*, pp. 620–1, 668, document Nos. 373, 422, Shamil to the Community of Argūn [12 May 1853] and to the People of Tsughūr, 1858, respectively.
71. E.g., '1846', Vol. XVI, p. 292; 'Levyi Flang', Vol. XI, p. 317.
72. For example, Rzewuski, Vol. VI, pp. 228–9, 267; Runowski's Diary, pp. 1500–3, entry for 3 [15] August 1861. For a similar Soviet approach, see, e.g., Pokrovskii, pp. 38–41.
73. Like in Runowski's Diary, loc. cit.
74. This of course, does not exclude the existence of social undercurrents to the movement he led and to his own personal feelings towards the *khāns* and *beks*. What is rather suggested here, is that such evidence should not be carried to extreme interpretations.
75. E.g., *AKAK*, Vol. IX, pp. 369–72, document No. 331, 'Review of the Events of March 1842 in Ghāzī-Ghumuq', annexed to Faesy's Report, 5 [17] April 1842, No. 28; Iurov, '1840–1842', Vol. XII, pp. 265–7. And see Runowski's Diary, pp. 1502–3.
76. Ibid, pp. 1486–7, entry for 10 [22] March 1861.
77. Ibid, loc. cit.
78. See above, p. 230.
79. Again, there was not much new in this fact since it followed a traditional local pattern.
80. An analysis of the 'class origin' of the *nā'ibs* was done, for example, by Bushuev, op. cit.
81. E.g., *Dvizhenie*, pp. 533, 620–1, document Nos. 301, 373, Shamil to the *Nā'ibs* and All the Chechen People, not before 10 January 1847, Shamil to the Community of Argūn [12 May 1853]. And see above, pp. 90, 131.
82. E.g., Egorov, pp. 403, 404; Volkonskii, '1858', p. 492.

Chapter 23: The *Imām* and His Neighbours

1. For Ghāzī Muḥammad's activity among the Circassians and Ghabarṭians, see 'Voina', Vol. XIII, pp. 251, 253, Vol. XVI, pp. 459–60, and Vel'iaminov to Rosen, n.d. [not before the end of September 1831], as quoted in ibid, Vol. XIII, p. 261.
2. See above, p. 98.

3. Above p. 157. See also *Dvizhenie*, pp. 328–9, 449–51, document Nos. 175, 234, Commander of the Sunja Line to Olszewski, 9 [21] January 1842, Neidhardt to Chernyshev, 10 [22] February 1844 respectively.
4. Above, pp. 213, 215–16. In addition, see *AKAK*, Vol. IX, pp. 789–90, 794–5, document Nos. 670, 674, Argutinskii to Neidhardt, 27 November [9 December], Neidhardt to Chernyshev, 19 [31] December 1843, No. 272.
5. E.g., *AKAK*, Vol. IX, pp. 147–8, document No. 177, Golovin to Chernyshev, 26 September [8 October] 1840, No. 1025; '1851', Vol. XIX, pp. 34–5.
6. See, for example, *Shamil*, p. 236, document No. 188, 'Excerpt from a Note about the Political Situation in Transcaucasia', by Viktorov [1844].
7. For the mutual effect of the Circassians' attacks on the Black Sea Line and the Chechens' uprising, see above, p. 117. Also, see *Dvizhenie*, pp. 251–2, document No. 137, Shamil's Letter to the Circassians [1 April 1840]; Iurov, '1840–1842', Vol. XI, pp. 188–9.
8. Bushuev, *Iz Istorii*, p. 50. According to Zagorskii (p. 239), Shamil started on such a campaign, but had to cancel it 'due to the high level of water in the Sunja'.
9. For Shamil's activities in Ghabarṭa until 1846, see, *inter alia, AKAK*, Vol. IX, pp. 261–3, 410–16, document Nos. 260, 364, Golovin to Chernyshev, 9 [21] July, Grabbe to Chernyshev, 18 [30] May 1840, Nos. 260, 760 respectively; *Dvizhenie*, pp. 303, 304–5, 475–6, 499, 504–5, 510, document Nos. 159, 160, 162, 248, 272, 280, 282, Anastas'ev to Piriatinskii, 9 [21] March (two reports), Golovin to Chernyshev, 10 [22] May 1841, Neidhardt to Commander of Force in Naṣrān, 24 May [5 June] 1844, Shamil's Letter to the Ghabarṭians, [1845], Shamil's Letter to Ḥājj Misostov and Other Ghabarṭians [20 April 1846], Kodiakov to Golitsyn, April 1846 respectively; *Shamil*, p. 215, document No. 168, Letter Received by Golitsyn on 20 January [1 February] 1843; Orbeliani, p. 417.
10. For Ḥājj Muḥammad's activity, see, *inter alia, AKAK*, Vol. IX, pp. 890, 897–901, document Nos. 732, 738, Neidhardt to Chernyshev, 28 April [10 May], 8 [20] July 1843, Nos. 8, 1307 respectively; *Dvizhenie*, pp. 445–8, 451, 473–5, document Nos. 233, 235, 247, Commander of Caucasian Line to Neidhardt, 7 [19] February, Chernyshev to Neidhardt, 22 February [6 March], Neidhardt to Chernyshev, 28 April [10 May] 1844 respectively; *Shamil*, pp. 215–16, document No. 160, Report by Zergel', 24 February [8 March] 1843, No. 118 (secret).
11. *Dvizhenie*, pp. 480–1, 483, document Nos. 254, 257, Riechter to Krukowski, 24 September [6], 13 [25] October 1844.
12. For Sulaymān Efendī's activities, see, apart from the appropriate documents in *AKAK*, *Shamil*, pp. 245–52, document Nos. 198, 199, Commander of Black Sea Line to Vorontsov, 30 May [11 June], No. 62 (secret), 'Excerpt from the War Diary of the Black Sea Line, 29 May [10]–6 [18] June 1845'; G. N. Prozritelev, 'Posol'stvo ot Shamilia k Abadzekham', *Dagestanskii Sbornik*, Vol. III, pp. 125–9; Bushuev, *Iz Istorii*, pp. 51–4.
13. *AKAK*, Vol. IX, p. 892, document No. 734, Letter from the Circassians to Neidhardt, 28 Rabīʿ al-Ākhir 1260 [17 May 1844], annexed to Neidhardt to Chernyshev, 27 June [9 July] 1844, No. 82.

14. Ibid., Vol. X, p. 590, document No. 543, Letter from Ḥājjī Yandaroghlū [Iandarov] to Zavodovskii, [1847].
15. For which, see above, pp. 162–9.
16. *Dvizhenie*, p. 560, document No. 282, Kodiakov to Golitsyn, April 1846.
17. For Shamil's contacts with, and activities among, the Ghabarṭians, see, in addition to the appropriate documents in *AKAK, Shamil*, pp. 286–7, 290, document Nos. 222, 227, Head *Pristav* to the Trans-Kuban Tribes to Zavodovskii, 3 [15] March, Serebriakov to Kotzebue, 3 [15] April 1848 (secret), Nos. 158, 21 respectively; '1851', Vol. XIX, pp. 34–5; Kundukh, 1936, No. 4 (28), pp. 22–3.
18. *Shamil*, loc. cit.
19. Runowski's Diary, pp. 1522–3, entry for 12 [24] December 1859. According to Shamil, the *nā'ib*'s real name was Muḥammad Asiyalō. The name Muḥammad Amīn was given to him by the Circassians and the Ottomans because they misunderstood the *imām*'s letters, which were addressed 'to the loyal Muḥammad' (*ilā Muḥammad al-amīn*) – ibid, p. 1417, entry for 4 [16] March 1860.
20. Unfortunately, no thorough research has yet been done on Muḥammad Amīn, or on the Circassians' struggle with the Russians in general.
21. For Muḥammad Amīn's activities, see *inter alia, AKAK*, Vol. X, pp. 268–79, 590–1, 593, 621–4, document Nos. 279, 287, 569, 280, 284, 288, 281, 282, 283, 285, 290, 291, 292, 544, 546, 571, 572, Vorontsov's Letter to Sharvashidze, September 1853, Sharvashidze's Letter to Read, 4 [16] May 1854, 'Excerpts from Evdokimov's War Diary, 24 June [6 July] – 1 [13] August 1853', Dolgorukov to Read, 29 March [10 April] (secret), 21 April [3], 4 [16], 7 [19] May, Dolgorukov to Sharvashidze, 29 March [10 April], Read to Dolgorukov, 9 [21], 13 [25], 22 April [4], 4 [16] 29 May [5], 9 [21] June, 24 July [5 August] 1854, Vorontsov to Chernyshev, 8 [20] November 1847 (secret), Kowalewski to Zavodovskii, 17 [29] January 1849, Evdokimov to Zavodovskii, 12 [24], 13 [25] July 1853, Nos. 4903, 6308, 8840, 4905, 101, 106, 115, 123, 185, 219, 316, 117, 183, 42, 43 respectively; *Dvizhenie*, pp. 589–90, 593–4, 620, 652, 653–4, document Nos. 344, 345, 351, 372, 402, 405, Jamāl al-Dīn's Letter to the Abadzekhs, [9 August], Shamil's Letter to the Abadzekhs, [21 August] 1849, 'Evidence of Lieutenant Muḥammad Tambiev', 16 [28] May 1850, Zavodovskii to Vrevskii, 30 March [11 April] 1853, Intelligence Report, 25 December 1854 [6 January 1855], Predemirov to Vrevskii, 25 [misprint for 29] January [8 February] 1855 respectively; *Shamil*, pp. 316–17, document Nos. 259, 260, Muḥammad Amīn to Kan Mirsize, Kan Mirsize to the Ottoman *Sultan*, both 15 Shaʿbān 1266 [26 June 1850]; Vorontsov to Bebutov, Kusary, 22 May [3 June] 1850, No. 2, p. 254; Vorontsov to Ermolov, Kislovodsk, 10 [22] June 1849, Tiflis, 24 August [5 September] 1850, No. 3, pp. 350, 361 respectively; '1851', Vol. XIX, pp. 34–5; Lapiński, *Die Borgovölker der Kaukasus* (Hamburg, 1863), Vol. II, *passim*; Bushuev, *Iz Istorii*, pp. 54–63.
22. *AKAK*, Vol. XII, p. 872, document No. 704, Shamil's Letter to Muḥammad Amīn, Kaluga, 27 November [9 December] 1859.
23. The frequent Russian alarms over a possible 'spillover' of Shamil's influence into the areas populated by *Shīʿīs* only demonstrated their ignorance of the population under their rule. Only one Russian source appreciated

the differences between the two sects correctly, and even he might have done it only in retrospect – *Ombres du Passé*, p. 191.

24. See above, p. 231.
25. *Shamil*, pp. 200–1, 214, 285, 288, document Nos. 159, 166, 221, 224, Schwartz to CoS Caucasian Corps, 2 [14] July 1841, Governor of T'elavi to Governor of Georgia-Imeret'i, 13 [25] May 1842, Schwartz to Vorontsov, 28 February [2], 20 March [1 April] 1848, Nos. 78, 614, 400, 624 respectively.
26. Ibid., p. 236, document No. 188, 'Excerpt from a Note on the Political Situation in Transcaucasia', by Viktorov, 1844.
27. See above, note 11 to Chapter 15.
28. Pertev Boratav, 'La Russie dans les Archives Ottomanes. Un Dossier Ottoman sur l'*Imâm* Chamil', *Cahiers du Monde Russe et Soviétique*, Vol. X, pp. 524–35; *Shamil*, pp. 272–4, document Nos. 207, 208, Iurkovskii to Setkov (secret), 21 September [3 October], Governor of Akhaltsikhe to Chief Civilian Administrator, 22 September [4 October] 1845, Nos. 78, 349 respectively; PRO, FO/78/613, Brant to Aberdeen, Erezeroom, 6, 24 November 1845, Nos. 14, 15 FO/78/653, Brant to Aberdeen, Erezeroom, 8 January 1846, No.3, FO/78/602, Canning to Aberdeen, Constantinople, 24 November 1845, No. 269, FO/78/642, Wellesley to Palmerston, Buyukdery, 1, 7, 18 August 1846, Nos. 4, 16, 17, 23 and annexed consular reports, FO/78/643, Wellesley to Palmerston, Constantinople, 19 October 1846, No. 91; MRE, CPC, Turquie Erzeroum. Vol. II, ff. 165, 176–7, Garnier to Guizot, Erzeroum, 24 October, 15 December 1845, Nos. 4, 9, ff. 178, 183–7, de Clairambault to Guizot, Trebizonde, 19 December 1845, 3, 10 March 1846, Nos. 28, 2, 3 respectively.
29. Boratav, p. 525.
30. *Shamil*, pp. 270–4, document Nos. 204, 206, 205, 207, 208, 209, CoS Caucasian Corps to Chief Civil Administrator, 16 [28] (secret), 18 [30] September, Chief Civil Administrator to Governor of Alexandropol' (Gumri) District, 17 [29] September, Iurkovskii to Setkov, 21 September [3 October] (secret), Governor of Akhaltsikhe to Chief Civil Administrator, 22 September [4 October], HQ Caucasian Corps to Setkov, 24 September [6 October] 1845, Nos. 187, 441, 86, 78, 349, 446 respectively.
31. *AKAK*, Vol. XI, pp. 504–5, document No 495, Anichkov to Vorontsov, Dilmān, 17 February [1 March] 1854, No. 138; Bushuev, *Iz Istorii*, p. 54, quoting an official report: PRO, FO/60/147, Stevens to Palmerston, Tabreez, 5 January 1849, No. 2; Maarten Maartinus van Bruinessen, 'Agha, Shaikh and State: On the Social and Political Organization of Kurdistan', PhD thesis, Utrecht, 1978, pp. 292–344. For the existence of another network used for recruitment, see *Dvizhenie*, pp. 614–15, document No. 367, Daniyāl's Letter to Ḥājjī Yūsuf [June 1852].
32. See, for example, the mention of Qarākhān al-Hulukī al-Kurdistānī by Qarākhī (p. 180), and of Muḥammad al-Kurdistānī by Ḥājj ʿAlī (pp. 72–3).
33. Despite the difficulties created by the Russians in free passage to and from their territories, such movement still existed in both directions, and individuals arrived to Shamil even from Bukhāra and Herāt – Qarākhī, p. 118, and Ḥājj ʿAlī, pp. 42–3 respectively. Traditionally, the *dār al-islām* had been one world and political borders had not been obstacles to the

free movement of people all over it, including the Caucasus. In the period under review, the introduction of border controls by the Russians was still too recent an innovation to stop such movement completely. Just one example out of many for such movements can be seen in the family history of ʿAzīz al-Maṣrī, the Arab nationalist leader. One of his ancestors, a merchant from Baṣra, married a Circassian and emigrated to the Caucasus. His descendants lived there until the Russo-Ottoman War of 1877–78, following which the family emigrated to İstanbul.

34. For one such example, see '1851', Vol. XIX, pp. 34–5.
35. *Hijra* (literally, migration) was Muḥammad's emigration from Mecca to Medina (AD 622). The stricter schools of Muslim law require the believers to follow the Prophet's example and emigrate from *dār al-ḥarb* to *dār al-islām*.
36. Shamil might have even preferred to nominate *muhājirūn*, because they lacked any power base in his territory.
37. It would suffice to mention here the names of two such *muhājirūn* who had risen to eminence in the years before Shamil became *imām*: Ḥājj Tāshō (see above, note 57 to Chapter 8 and note 3 to Chapter 22), and Mūlā Ramaḍān from Chārtalah, who became the head of the community of Qarākh (for whose biography, see *AKAK*, Vol. VIII, pp. 599–600, document No. 500, Rosen to Chernyshev, 21 May [2 June] 1836, No. 497).
38. For a short biography of Muḥammad Mīrzā, see Sharafutdinova, 'Dokument', pp. 166–7. And see Sharafutdinova, 'Pis'ma', pp. 210, 214, 215, 216, letter Nos. IV, VII, VIII, IX, Shamil to Duba, 9 Rabīʿ al-Thānī 1265 [4 March 1849], Shamil to the people of Kalay and ʿArshtkhoy, 13 Dhū al-Qaʿda 1266 [20 September 1850], Shamil to Ḥājj Yaḥyā, 21 Rabīʿ al-Thānī 1265 [16 March 1849], Shamil to Muḥammad Mīrzā (undated) respectively; '1846', Vol. XVI, p. 303; '1851', Vol. XVIII, p. 199.
39. E.g., Sharafutdinova,'Pis'ma', pp. 208, 211–12, letter Nos. IV, V, Shamil to Duba, Rabīʿ al-Ākhir 1261 [April–May 1845], and undated [1848] respectively (the latter was also published in *Dvizhenie*, p. 586, as document No.337); *Dvizhenie*, pp. 498, 565, document Nos. 270, 320, Shamil to the *Qāḍī* Muḥammad [1845], Shamil to Daniyāl [4 March 1848], respectively.
40. Sharafutdinova, 'Dokument', pp 162–4, 23 Dhū al-Ḥijja 1262 [12 December 1846].
41. Both the Ottomans and the Qājārs established and used special units manned by Russian deserters.
42. Some such cases of Terek Cossacks were published by Fedor Chernozubov, 'Ocherki Terskoi Stariny. I: Pobegi k Nepokornym Gortsam. Zhizn' u Shamilia (1832-1859 GG)', *Russkii Arkhiv* (1912), No. 1, pp. 66–79.
43. *Dvizhenie*, pp. 291–2, document No. 155, Shamil to All the *Nāʾibs* [1840].
44. ʿAbd al-Raḥīm, p. 18.
45. Runowski's Diary, p. 1486, entry for 10 [22] March 1861.
46. Ibid., p. 1398, entry for 10 [22] November 1859.
47. Ibid., loc. cit.
48. For a (hostile) eye-witness account of this settlement in the early 1850s, see Rumiantsev, pp. 102–9.

49. ʿAbd al-Raḥīm, p. 18.
50. *Dvizhenie*, pp. 329–30, document No. 176, Olszewski to Grabbe, 9 [21] January 1842 (top secret). Interest in the defectors did not subside. The issue was raised from time to time in the correspondence and occasional attempts were made to entice them back – e.g., *AKAK*, Vol. XII, pp. 1167–8, document No. 1041, Bariatinskii to Sukhozanet, 4 [16] August 1859, No 265; *Dvizhenie*, pp. 356–60, 486, document Nos. 197, 261, Chernyshev to Golovin, 6 [18] September 1842, Vorontsov's Manifesto to the Deserters, 14 [26] March 1845 respectively. (For the latter see HHSA, St. K. Konsulate 33/Odessa, unsigned, undated [April 1845?] report.) Vorontsov to Bebutov, Vladikavkaz, 30 October [11 November], Tiflis, 9 [21] November, No. 1, pp. 105, 106 respectively.
51. This corresponds to other cases in history. Military discipline, it seems, is obeyed even by members of dissatisfied minorities. Only the total collapse of the chain of command and military discipline leads to desertions on a massive scale.
52. The following is an incomplete list of sources mentioning the defectors, their employment by Shamil, their way of life, etc.: *AKAK*, Vol. IX, pp. 832–4, document No. 698, 'Debriefing of NCO Moisei Kuznetsov, Who Returned from Captivity in Exchange for [Native] Hostages', 26 May [8 June] 1844, Vol. XII, pp. 139–43, document No. 840, 'Observations [Made] during 1860 in Different Localities in the Terek District', by Captain Gilev; *Dvizhenie*, pp. 364–8, 470–1, document Nos. 203, 245, 'Debriefings of Soldiers and Officers Returning from Shamil's Captivity', 12 [24] January 1843 [misprint for 1844], 'Testimony of Shams al-Dīn Amīn-Oghlū from Irpilī', 18 [30] April 1844 respectively; Anoev, No. 6, p. 407; A. Anoev, 'Iz Kavkazshikh Vospominanii', *Istoricheskii Vestnik* 1906, No. 9, pp. 810–11; Dzierzyński, 'Iz Kavkazskoi Voiny. Po Povodu 50-ti letii Osady Shamilem Mesel'degerskogo Ukrepleniia v 1853 Godu', *Voennyi Sbornik* (1903), No. 9, p. 62, No. 10, p. 43; Ignatius, p. 7; Isakov, No. 4–6, p. 54, No. 7–9, pp. 8–10; 'Levyi Flang', Vol. XI, pp. 327–9; Olszewski, 'Kavkaz', pp. 309–10, 317; *Ombres du Passé*, pp. 99–108; A O[rlov]-D[avydov], 'Chastnoe Pis'mo o Vziatii Shamilia', *Russkii Arkhiv* (1896), No. 6, cc. 1046–7; P. K., 'Iz Dnevnika Dagestantsa', *Kavkazskii Sbornik*, Vol. VIII, pp. 249, 252–3, 265–8, 270, 272, 275; 'Rasskaz Byvshego U.O. Apsheronskogo Polka Samoily Riabova o Svoei Sluzhbe na Kavkaze', *Kavkazskii Sbornik*, Vol. XVIII, p. 353–81; Rumiantsev, *passim*; '1850–1851', pp. 372–3; '1852', Vol. XVIII, p. 199; Volkonskii, '1847', pp. 502–3; Volkonskii, 'Sem Let', pp. 222–3; Zagorskii, *passim*.
53. For the latter groups in the Caucasus, see *AKAK*, Vol. X, pp. 281–9, document No. 293, 'Note on the Russian Settlers – Sectarians in the Caspian Province', n.d.
54. Fedor Chernozubov, 'Ocherki Terskoi Stariny, Pobegi v Gory. Istoriia Odnoi Raskol'nich'ei Obiteli u Shamilia (1849–1859)', *Russkii Arkhiv* (1911), No. 10, pp. 249–61; (1912), No. 1, pp. 64–79, No. 6, pp. 218–25. Ḥājj ʿAlī, pp. 41–2, refers either to this group or to another.
55. Baddeley, *Rugged Flanks*, Vol. I, p. 55; 'Levyi Flang', Vol. X, p. 415.
56. E.g., I. Sh. Anisimov, 'Kavkazskie Evrei-Gortsy, *Sbornik Materialov po Ētnografii Izdavaemyi pri Dashkovskom Ētnograficheskom Muzee*, Vol. III, pp. 195–8: Chernyi, 'Kavkazskie Evrei', *Sbornik Svedenii o Kavkaz-*

skikh Gortsakh, Vol. III (separate pagination), *passim*; Tsvi Kasday, *Mamlakhot Ararat* (Odessa, 5672 [1912]), pp. 13, 26, 28, 31–2, 78–9.

57. See, for example, R[abbi] Yaʿaqov ben Yitsḥaq Yitsḥaqovich [Yitsḥaqi] and Dr. Sharbat ben Nissim Anisimov, *Sefer Toldot Yehudey Daqestan ha-Mada'im ha-Nimtsa'im be-Harey Qawqaz ʿad Henna* (Jerusalem, 5654 [1894], p. 14. For an exposition of these complaints based mainly on Jewish sources, see Mordekhay Altshuler, *Yehudey Mizraḥ Qawqaz* (Jerusalem, 5750 [1990]), p. 61–70.
58. For example, *Shamil*, p. 213, document No. 217, 'Summary of Military Events in the Caucasus', 31 January [12 February] 1847; 'Izvestiia s Kavkaza', *Sbornik Gazety Kavkaz* (1847), Vol I, pp. 27–8; Volkonskii, '1847', pp. 493–5, for a raid on the Jewish suburb of Targhū on 27 January that year. See also Rumiantsev, p. 144, for the mention of the fact that the wife of Yūnus, one of the closest confidants of Shamil, was a Jewess captured in one of the raids.
59. See, e.g., Avraham Firqovich, *Avney Zikkaron* (Vil'na, 5632 [1872]), pp. 102–4, (text of) 'Appeal from the Jews of Derbend to the Emperor Submitted through Golovin, 14 [26] November 1840', for the mention of the Jewish participation in the defence of Enderī against Ghāzī Muḥammad. Also see *AKAK*, Vol. VIII, pp. 610–11, document No. 523, Réoutte to Rosen, 14 [26] February 1837, No. 4, for the mention of a Jew acting as a spy for the Russians.
60. *Igrot u-Te'udot me-Arkhiyon ha-Rav Yaʿ*aqov ben ha-Rav Yitsḥaq Yitsḥaqi (Jerusalem 5734 [1974]) pp. 8, 10, Nomination of Rav Yitsḥaq ben ha-Rav Yaʿaqov to the Post of Religious Judge in Derbend, 22 Ṭevet 5605 [1 January 1845]. Decoration [Granted] to Rav Yitsḥaq ben ha-Rav Yaʿaqov, 23 May [4 June] 1860 respectively.
61. E.g., *Dvizhenie*, pp. 610–11, document No. 365, Shamil to the People of Sughūr [March 1852]; Runowski's Diary, pp. 1521–22, entry for 6 [18] December 1859.
62. V. Sollohub, 'Rasskaz Mozdokskogo Grazhdanina, 3-i Gildii Kuptsa Minaia Shaeva Syna Atarova, o Poezdke Svoei v Dargy-Vedenno, Mestoprebyvanie Shamilia', *Kavkaz*, 14 [26] November 1853 (No. 85), p. 368.
63. '1852', p. 494; A. P. Nicolaÿ, 'Ēpizod iz Istorii Kavkazskoi Voiny', *Russkaia Starina* (1882), No. 11, pp. 267, 258, 270.
64. ʿAbd al-Raḥīm, p. 16.
65. *Ahl al-kitāb* (literally the People of the Book) are the believers of other monotheistic religions, mainly Jews and Christians, who possess scriptures recognised by Islam as earlier divine revelations.
66. As quoted by Bushuev, *Iz Istorii*, p. 57.

Chapter 24: Shamil and the Power

1. See above, p. 21.
2. Orbeliani, p. 422.
3. Strangely enough, there is little mention in the available sources of the first *imām*'s attempts to contact the Ottomans, though according to the late Professor Benningsen, there are letters from Ghāzī Muḥammad in the Ottoman archives in İstanbul. One such appeal might be, *Dvizhenie*,

pp. 591–2, document No. 349, Letter from the *Qādīs, ʿUlamāʾ*, Honest, Distinguished and Other Persons to the Ottoman *Sulṭān* [January 1850], if 1850 is, indeed, a misprint for 1830.

4. Shamil's Letter to the Ottoman *Sulṭān*, quoted in Bushuev, *Iz Istorii*, pp. 38–9.
5. See above, pp. 82–3.
6. For such letters, see *Shamil*, pp. 226–30, 367, document Nos. 178, 179, 180, 181, 302, Shamil to İbrahim Paṣa, Shamil to the Ottoman, *Sulṭān*, Map of Shamil's Domains, Plans of Shamil's Residence [all 1843], Shamil to the Ottoman *Sulṭān* [1853] respectively.
7. See, for example, Qarākhī, pp. 108–11.
8. For reports about such contacts, the passage of messengers, their capture and for intercepted letters, see *Dvizhenie*, pp. 614–15, document No. 367, Daniyāl to Ḥājjī Yūsuf [June 1852]; *Shamil*, pp. 247–52, 290, 309–11, 316–17, document Nos. 198, 199, 227, 253, 259, 260, Commander of Black Sea Line to Vorontsov, 30 May [11 June] 1854, No. 62 (secret), 'Excerpts from the War Diary of the Black Sea Line, 29 May [10]–6 [18] June 1854'; Serebriakov to Kotzebue, 3 [15] April 1848 (secret), Zavodovskii to Vorontsov, 28 October [9 November] 1849, No. 2345, Muḥammad Amīn al-Dāghistānī to Kan Mirsize and the latter to the Ottoman *Sulṭān* both 15 Shaʿbān 1266 [26 June 1850]. For texts of letters which were intercepted by the Russians, translated and then allowed to continue to İstanbul, see *Shamil*, pp. 311–13, document Nos. 254, 255, 256, 257, Shamil to the *Sulṭān* Abdül Mecid, Shamil to Olayaçı İbrahim Paşa (part of this letter was published in *Dvizhenie*, p. 590, as document No. 346), Jamāl al-Dīn to the *Sulṭān* Abdül Mecid, Jamāl al-Dīn to Olayaçı İbrahim Paşa, all not later than 4 October 1849. For a reported mission which arrived in İstanbul according to Russian sources but denied by Ottoman ones, see PRO, FO/78/702, Brant to Palmerston, Erzeroom, 10 March 1847, No. 31, FO/78/679, Holmes to Wallesely, Batoum 3 December 1846, No. 7 annexed to Wallesely to Palmerston, Constantinople, 2 January 1847, No. 8. For evidence by someone who professed to have taken part in such a mission, see FO/60/133 ff. 66–69, Abott to Palmerston, Tabreez, 22 July 1847, No. 27, quoting the *Qāḍī* of Shekī.
9. Ibid, f. 66.
10. For such attempts, see, for example, *KA*, Vol. I, pp. 234–5 (and 127–31), document No. 42, Letter from the *Sulṭān* to the Daghestanis and Circassians, n.d.; *Shamil*, p. 5–7, 10–11, document Nos. 8, 12, Manifestos of the *Serasker* of Erzurum to the People of Daghestan and Shirvān [February-March and June 1829] respectively.
11. See above, note 24 to Chapter 11.
12. The affair of Ḥassan Ḥasbī (see above, pp. 250–1) was but one such case. The Russian obsession, in fact paranoia, about foreign intervention in the Caucasus is well documented. One such example, as quoted by Bushuev (*Iz Istorii*, p. 61) will suffice. The Russian envoy in İstanbul showed to the Grand *vezir* an intercepted letter from Muḥammad Amīn addressed to the *sulṭān*. Reşit Paşa, no doubt exasperated by frequent similar allegations, tried to dismiss it by 'an insidious joke' and 'asked whether we would like the *sulṭān* to confirm the *maḥkama* [court of law] established

by Shamil's *nā'ib*', which the suspicious, humourless Russian diplomat interpreted as a confirmation of the Russian allegations.

13. For which, see above, p. 251.
14. As demonstrated by the affair of Ḥasan Ḥasbī, for which see above p. 250.
15. Orbeliani, p. 422. For a similar expression, see Runowski's Diary, p. 1521, entry for 2 [14] December 1859. And see ʿAbd al-Raḥīm, p. 23.
16. See note 2 above.
17. E.g. *Shamil*, p. 226, document No. 178, Shamil to İbrahim Paşa [1843]. Also see *Dvizhenie*, pp. 614–15, document No. 367, Daniyāl to Ḥājjī Yūsuf [June 1852].
18. *Dvizhenie*, pp. 575–8, 585–7, document Nos. 330, 336, Jamāl al-Dīn's Letter to *Şeyhül İslam* [August 1848], Shamil's Letter to the *Sharīf* of Mecca [1848]. Such a request for intervention contains a hint to the attitude that the *sulṭān* was not implementing properly the stipulations of the *sharīʿa*.
19. In addition to the sources quoted above, see also Runowski's Diary, pp. 1444–5, entry for 6[18] July 1860.
20. *Shamil*, document Nos. 178, 179, 180, 181 quoted above (note 6), were a response to this request.
21. One copy was intercepted by the Russians. Other copies might not have survived.
22. *Shamil*, p. 290, document No. 227, Serebriakov to Kotzebue, 3[15] April 1848, No. 21 (secret). Document Nos. 254, 255, 256, 257 quoted above (note 8) were answers to this request brought by the same, or another, messenger.
23. The Russians intercepted the letters, translated them, and then let the messenger carry on.
24. MRE, CPC, Turqie, Erzeroum, Vol. III, ff. 31–4, Wiett to Foreign Minister, 16 November 1848, No. 3. And see ibid., ff. 104–7, Wiett to Foreign Minister, 4 March 1850, No. 21; *KA*, Vol. I, pp. 236 (and 131), document No. 43, Memorandum by Dağıstanı Hasan Efendi, 1269 [1852–53].
25. The above report of 4 March 1850.
26. For the developments during the Crimean War, see Chapter 25.
27. E.g., ʿAbd al-Raḥīm, p. 23; Runowski's Diary, pp. 1449, 1521, entries for 21 July [9 August] 1860, 2[14] December 1859 respectively.
28. For such use by Shamil of his contacts with the Ottomans, see *inter alia* *AKAK*, Vol. X, pp. 336–8, document No. 340, Vorontsov to Chernyshev, 9[21] October 1853, No. 635; *Dvizhenie*, pp. 370–2, 625, document Nos. 206, 381, Klugenau to Neidhardt, 18 [30] January 1843, Commander of Force at Naṣrān to Uslar, 9 [21] August 1853; *Shamil*, pp. 286–7, document No. 222, Chief *Pristav* to Trans-Kuban Tribes to Kowalewski, 3 [15] March 1848, No. 158; Iurov, '1843', p. 48.
29. Runowski's Diary, p. 1484, entry for 22 February [6 March] 1861.
30. See above, pp. 115, 116.
31. *Shamil*, pp. 247–52, document Nos. 198, 199, Commander of Black Sea Line to Vorontsov, 30 May [11 June] 1845, No. 62 (secret), 'Excerpts from the War Diary of the Black Sea Line, 29 May [10]–6 [18] June 1845' respectively; PRO, FO/60/133, ff. 60–9, Abott to Palmerston, Tabreez, 22 July 1847, No. 27.
32. For such use by Shamil of his contacts with Muḥammad 'Alī, see, for

example, *Dvizhenie*, pp. 306, 428–9, document Nos. 164, 228, Talyshin to Klugenau, 25 June [7 July] 1841, Neidhardt to Chernyshev, 7 [19] January 1844; Iurov, '1843', p. 48; Orbeliani, pp. 417, 421.

33. *Dvizhenie*, pp. 428–9, document No. 228, Neidhardt to Chernyshev, 7 [19] January 1844.
34. See above, p. 115 and note 18 to Chapter 11.
35. Orbeliani, p. 421.
36. PRO, FO/60/133, Abott to Palmerston, Tabreez, 22 July 1847, No. 27, ff. 67–8.
37. About him, see, for example, Runowski's Diary, p. 1521, entry for 3 [15] December 1859.
38. See, for example, ibid, p. 1399, entry for 15 [27] November 1859; ʿAbd al-Raḥīm, p. 17; Qarākhī, p. 151; Volkonskii, '1847', pp. 548–9.
39. For his biography, see A. N. Genko, 'Arabskaia Karta Chechni Ēpokhi Shamilia', *Zapiski Instituta Vostokovedenia Akademii Nauk SSSR*, Vol. II, pp. 31–6. And see ʿAbd al-Raḥīm, pp. 17–18; *Dvizhenie*, p. 483, document No. 257, Commander of the Kislovodsk Line to Krukowski, 13 [25] October 1844; *Shamil* pp. 215–16, document No. 160, Report by Zergel', 24 February [18 March] 1843, No. 118 (secret); Neidhardt, 1843, p. 408; Ḥājj ʿAlī, pp. 21–2.
40. The birthplace of Shaykh Manṣūr.
41. This map was published by Linevich in *Sbornik Svedenii o Kavkazskikh Gortsakh*, Vol. VI.
42. E.g., 'Voina', Vol. XIII, pp. 279–80, 285 and Bekovich-Cherkasskii to Paskiewicz, 2 [14] May 1831, No. 37, as quoted in ibid, p. 195. It seems that Ghāzī Muḥammad used his contacts with the Qājārs the way Shamil used his contacts with the Ottomans and Muḥammad ʿAlī.
43. PRO, FO/60/147, Stevens to Palmerston, Tabreez, 5 January 1849, No. 2, ff. 56–7.
44. For the translation of Shamil's letter to the *shāh*, see ibid, ff. 63–67.
45. *Dvizhenie*, pp. 563, 569, document Nos. 318, 325, Dolgorukii to Vorontsov, 2 [14] March, Vorontsov to Dolgorukii, 3 [15] April 1848 respectively; PRO, FO/60/140, Stevens to Palmerston, Tabreez, 5 March, 5 May 1848, Nos. 4, 15 respectively, FO/65/349, Bloomfield to Palmerston, St. Petersburg, 9 May 1848, No. 137.
46. Adamiyat, op. cit, p. 234.
47. Bushuev, *Iz Istorii*, p. 54, quoting a memorandum by Khanykov.
48. Qarākhī, p. 80.
49. See above, pp. 116–17.
50. For a thorough description of French interests and policy in the Caucasus, see Michel Lesure, 'La France et le Caucase à l'Époque de Chamil à la Lumière de Dépêches des Consuls Français', *Cahiers du Monde Russe et Soviétique*, Vol. XIX, No. 1-2 (January–June 1978), pp. 5–65 (hereafter: Lesure). Also, see Surkhāy, 'Kavkaz i Derzhavy v XIX V.', *Kavkaz* (Paris), 1938, No. 4 (52), pp. 17–21, No. 5 (53), pp. 13–17, No. 7 (55), pp. 4–8, No. 10 (58), pp. 26–8, 1939, No. 1 (61), pp. 21–4, No. 2 (62), pp. 18–21, No. 5 (65), pp. 8–11.
51. If a Russian report was correct there was one possible exception. In 1837 it was reported that in the previous year Urquhart had sent Shamil 'letters

and promises' – *AKAK*, Vol. VIII, pp. 767–9, document No. 671, Vel'iaminov to Chernyshev, 21 August [2 September] 1837, No. 120.

52. The most thorough description of Polish activities in and regarding the Caucasus is Widerszal, op. cit. Also see *Dvizhenie*, p. 529, document No, 294, CoS Caucasian Line to Nesterov, 7 [19] September 1846; *Shamil* p. 280, document No. 215, Budberg to Vorontsov, 13 [25] August 1846, No. 125; Rzewuski, Vol. VII, pp. 451–2; *Ombres du Passé*, pp. 174–5; Lapiński, Vol. II, pp. 148–9.
53. Again, if the above Russian report (note 51) was correct, Shamil experienced this breach of promise personally.
54. For the initiation of ʿAbd al-Qādir and his father into the Naqshbandiyya by Shaykh Khālid and their consequent nomination as *khalīfas*, see Raphael Danziger, *Abd al-Qadir and the Algerians: Resistance to the French and Internal Consolidation* (New York, 1977), p. 56.

Chapter 25: The Crimean War

1. *Shamil*, p. 367, document No. 302, Shamil's Letter to the *Sulṭān* 1853, [not later than 7 April].
2. For which, see above, pp. 257–8.
3. *AKAK*, Vol. X, pp. 92–100, document No. 72, Vorontsov to the Emperor, 1 [13] March 1854.
4. *Ombres du Passé*, p. 189.
5. See, for example, *AKAK*, Vol. X, pp. 547–9, 551–3, document Nos. 496, 497, 498, 502, 503, 504, 505, Vrevskii to Vorontsov, 17 [29] July, No. 21, Wrangel to Vrevskii, 19 [31] July, No. 1618, 'Excerpts from the War Diary of the Vladikavkaz Command, 5 [17] July – 19 [31] August', Wrangel to Bariatinskii, 15 [27] October, No. 2071, Vrevskii to Vorontsov, 29 October [10 November], No. 2424, Vrevskii to Szyszyński [Shishinskii], 29 October [10 November], No. 2425, Vorontsov to Vrevskii, 31 October [12 November] 1853, No. 655 respectively; *Dvizhenie*, pp. 620, 622–4, 625, 626, document Nos. 372, 375, 376, 377, 378, 381, 383, Zavodovskii to Vrevskii, 30 March [11 April], Kozlov to Vrevskii, 10 [22] June, Vrevskii to Vorontsov, 25 June [7 July], Wrangel to Vrevskii, 19 [31] July, Gramotin to Vrevskii, 25 July [6 August], C.O. Naṣrān to Uslar, 9 [21] August, Vrevskii to Zavodovskii, 17 [29] August 1853; *Shamil*, p. 337, document No, 283, Orbeliani to Bariatinskii, 14 [26] August 1853, No. 626; Soltan, '1852–1853', p. 503.
6. This description is based on the following sources: *Shamil*, pp. 341–50, 353–61, 362–3, 423–4, 429–30, document Nos. 286, 287, 289, 290, 291, 293, 294, 295, 296, 298, 299, 342, 345, Andronikov to HQ Caucasian Corps (secret), 28 August [9 September], Andronikov to Vorontsov, 31 August [12 September], Andronikov to HQ Caucasian Corps (secret), 2 [14] September, Andronikov to Bariatinskii, 5 [17] September, Vorontsov to Dolgorukov, 9 [21] September, No. 421, Orbeliani to Vorontsov, 11 [23] September, No. 725, 'War Diary of the Lesghian Line 21 August [1] –11 [23] September', Andronikov to Chief Civilian Administrator, 11 [23] September, No. 93, Vorontsov's Order of the Day, 6 [18] October, No. 204, Orbeliani to Bariatinskii, 11 [23] October, Andronikov to Chief

Civilian Administrator, 29 October [10 November] 1853, No. 1707, Shamil's Letters to Hacci İbrahim Paşa and to Mustafa Zârif Paşa, both 20 Şafar 1271 [12 November 1854]; Vorontsov's Diary pp. 114–17, entries for 26, 28, 29, 30, 31 August, [7, 9, 10, 11, 12], 1 [13], 3 [15], 4 [16], 5 [17], 7 [19], 8 [20], 9 [21], September 1853; Vorontsov to Ermolov, Tiflis, 20 September [2 October] 1853, No. 4, p. 465; M. Shcherbinin, 'Iz Pisem Kniazia Mikhaila Semenovicha Vorontsova k Mikhailu Pavlovichu Shcherbininu', *Russkii Arkhiv* (1870), No. 12, cc. 2149–54, Vorontsov to Shcherbinin, Kodzhory, 29, 30 August [10, 11 September] 1853; Gleb Struve, 'An Anglo-Russian Medley: Woronzows, Pembrokes, Nicolaÿs and Others. Unpublished Letters and Historical Notes', *California Slavic Studies*, Vol. 5 (1970), pp. 120–1; N. P. Nicolaÿ to Sidney Herbert, St. Petersburg, 15/27 November 1853; Andreevskii, pp. 59–60; V. S. Dzierzyński [Dzerzhinskii], 'Iz Kavkazskoi Voiny. Po Povodu 50-ti Letiia Osady Mesel'degerskogo Ukrepleniia Shamilem v 1853 Godu', *Voennyi Sbornik* (1903), No. 10, pp. 31–61 (hereafter: Dzierzyński + No. of *VS*); Nikolai Ignatius, 'Osada Shamilem Mesedel'gerskogo Ukrepleniia v 1853 G.', *Inzhenernyi Zhurnal* (1868), No. 1, Otdel Neofitsial'nyi, pp. 1–30 (reprinted in *Sbornik Opisanii Osad i Oboron Krepostei i Ukreplenii* Vol. I, pp. 126–51; the former copy is the one used here) (hereafter: Ignatius); S. Porębski [Porembskii] 'Vtorzhenie Shamilia v Dzharo – Belokanskii Okrug v 1853 Godu', *Kavkazskii Sbornik*, Vol. XI, pp. 499–523 (hereafter: Porębski); Soltan, '1852–1853', pp. 503–21; Züssermann, 'Otryvki', 1878, No. 6, pp. 722–7; Qarākhī, pp. 181–2; Ḥājj ʿAlī, pp. 43–5; PRO, FO/78/955, Brant to Clarendon, Erzeroum, 24 October 1853, No. 3, FO/78/940, Extract from Brant to de Redcliffe, Erzeroum, 10 November, appended to de Redcliffe to Clarendon, Therapia, 24 November 1853, No. 356, FO/60/186, Stevens to Clarendon, Tabreez, 24 September, 20 October 1853, Nos. 42, 45 respectively; HHSA PA XXXVII 107/Trapezunt, 24 March 1854, No. 225.

7. Porębski, p. 508.
8. Soltan, '1852–1853', p. 514.
9. Porębski, p. 512.
10. Dzierzyński, No. 9, pp. 50–68, No. 10, pp. 27–31.
11. In this siege, 'the mountaineers showed us in practice how unfortunately and inconsiderately had the location of the fort been chosen' – ibid, No. 10, p. 36. And see Züssermann, 'Otryvki', 1876, No. 4, p. 433, about the fort at Kodor.
12. Baddeley, p. 449.
13. Excerpt from Vorontsov's Order of the Day, 19 [31] October 1853, No. 191, in Ignatius, pp. 28–30. (Quotation from p. 30.) Also, Dzierzyński, No. 10, pp. 59–60. (Quotation from p. 60.)
14. Soltan, '1852–1853', p. 521.
15. Vorontsov's Diary (pp. 114–17) is full of expressions of extreme worry – e.g. entries for 29, 30, 31 August [10, 11, 12], 3 [15], 7 [19], 8 [20] September 1853 and his underlined 'Thank God' on 9 [21] September 1853. And see Züssermann, 'Otryvki', 1878, No. 6, p. 727.
16. Vorontsov to Ermolov, Tiflis, 20 September [2 October] 1853, No. 4. p. 465. And see *Shamil*, p. 337, document No. 283, Orbeliani to Bariatinskii, 14 [26] August 1853, No. 626.

17. PRO, FO/78/955, Brant to Clarendon, Erzeroom, 17 October 1853, No. 3. And see FO/78/939, de Redcliffe to Clarendon, Therapia, 25 October 1853, No. 313. Also, see Runowski's Diary, p. 1444, entry for 6 [18] July 1860.
18. *AKAK* Vol. X, pp. 551–2, document No. 502, Wrangel to Bariatinskii, 15 [27] October 1853, No. 2071. This may be the letter published in *Dvizhenie*, pp. 627–8, document No. 385, *Sulṭān* Abdül Mecid Hān to Shamil, not before October 1853. Also see *KA*, Vol. I, pp. 132–33, document No. 45, Draft of [Imperial] Letter to Shamil, 6 Muḥarram 1270 [9 October 1853]); Masayuki Yama'uchi, 'Sheikh Shamil and the Ottoman Empire in the Period of the Crimean War Enlightened by the ATASE Archives in Ankara', *Orient* (Tokyo), Vol. XXII (1986), pp. 146–7, document No. IV, Draft of a Letter to Shamil, October (?) 1853, (English translation in idem, 'From Ottoman Archives', *Central Asian Survey*, Vol. IV, No. 4 [1985], p. 9) (hereafter: Yama'uchi); FO/78/955 Brant to de Redcliffe, Erzeroum, 28 October 1853, No. 64 (copy), where a *firmān* from the *sulṭān* to the *imām* is mentioned, 'naming Shamil *vizir* of the provinces he might wrest from the Russians'. For a 'prophecy' that Shamil would be the *sulṭān*'s *vâli* see Runowski's Diary, p. 1500, entry for August 1861.
19. Aware of the significance of such a link, the Russians took measures already in the summer of 1853 to intercept Ottoman messengers to Shamil and to stop any correspondence between the Ottoman consul in Tiflis and the *imām* – *Shamil*, pp. 334–5, 337–8, document Nos. 280, 284, Anichkov to Vorontsov, Nemet-Abād, 16 [28] July, Andronikov to Orbeliani (top secret), 19 [31] August 1853, Nos. 506, 125 respectively. During the first year and a half of the Crimean War, the Russians arrested a number of messengers on their way to or from Shamil with a number of letters – *Shamil*, pp. 368–86, 417–34, document Nos. 304, 305, 306, 307,308, 309, 312, 310, 311, 338, 339, 340, 341, 346, 342, 343, 344, 345, 347, 348, Bebutov to Bariatinskii (secret), 10 [22], 15 [27] March, Hacci İbrahim Bey to Shamil, Zârif Mustafa Paşa to Shamil, Hacci İbrahim Bey to Ḥājj İsmā'īl Bek, Zârif Mustafa Paşa to Ḥājj İsmā'īl Bek, March 1854, Bebutov to Read (secret), 8 [20] May 1854, No. 68 (for this affair see also FO/78/1026, Brant to Clarendon, Erzeroom, 18 April 1854, No. 22), 'Excerpt from the Protocol of the Interrogation of Hacci Ismail Loman-Oğlu', 24 April [6 May], '[Full] Protocol of the Interrogation of Hacci İsmail Loman-Oğlu' (secret), 1854 [probably the same date], Melikov to Bariatinskii, 7 [19] December 1854, Nos. 5967, 5968, Daniyāl to Süleyman Nur-Oğlu, to Seyyit Mehmet Âref and to Hacci Athân, all three 23 Ṣafar [15 November], Shamil to Hacci İbrahim Paşa, Shamil to Hacci İbrahim Paşa, Hacci Halil Paşa and Hacci Hüseyin Bey, Shamil to Şeyh Hacci Yahya Efendi, Shamil to Mustafa Zârif Paşa, all four 20 Ṣafar 1271 [12 November 1854] and envelope of Shamil's above-mentioned Letter to Hacci İbrahim Paşa, Shamil's Letter to Mustafa Zârif Paşa, 1854 [most probably February]; *AKAK*, Vol. XI, pp. 618–19, 652, document Nos. 638, 649, Military Governor of Shemākha to Réoute, 10 [22] May, Shcherbinin to Read (secret), 18 [30] August 1854, Nos. 479, 332 respectively. In other cases the Russians knew of messengers, but failed to intercept them – e. g., *AKAK*, Vol. X, pp. 551–2, document No. 502. Wrangel to Bariatinskii,

15 [27] October 1853, No. 2071, Vol. XI, pp. 619–20, document No. 640, Réoute to Read (secret), 1 [13] June 1854, No. 26; *Dvizhenie*, pp. 652, 653–4, document Nos. 402, 405, 'Information Received from the Mountains', 25 December 1854 [6 January 1855] (published also in *Shamil*, pp. 367–8, as document No. 303), Predemirov to Vrevskii, 25 January [6 February] 1855; *Shamil*, p. 397, document No. 320, Melikov to Read (top secret), 10 [22] July 1854, No. 537 and note 1, Commander of the Force at Akhaltsikhe to HQ Caucasian Corps, 19 [31] July 1854.

20. One difficulty lay in the fact that the mountaineers were not familiar with Ottoman Turkish language and calligraphy, in which, naturally, the Ottoman messages were written. Daniyāl, for example, asked on a few occasions that his correspondents write either in Arabic or in 'Turkish as it is written in Shekī' (i.e. Azeri Turkish) – *Shamil*, pp. 421–2, 431–3, document Nos. 341, 346, Daniyāl to Seyyit Mehmet Ârif and to Hacci Athân, 23 Ṣafar 1271 [15 November 1854], quotation from the latter letter.

21. In addition to the sources listed in note 19 above, see also *KA*, Vol. I, pp. 134–5 (and 239–40), document No. 46, Abstract of Shamil's Letter to the *Sulṭān*, 22 Jumādī al-Awwal 1270 [20 February 1854]; PRO FO/78/1026, Brant to Clarendon, Brant to Raglan, Erzeroum, 8, 30 May 1854, Nos. 27, 2 respectively, FO/352/39/3, ff. 97–100, Williams to de Redcliffe, Private, Camp near Kars, 7 October 1854, FO/78/1004, de Redcliffe to Clarendon, Therapia, 30 October 1854, No. 636, FO/78/1042. Williams to Hammond, 27 November 1854; MRE, CPC, Turquie, Trebizonde, Vol. I, ff. 217–9, Poncharra to Walewski, Trebizonde, 2 June 1854; Ḥājj ʿAlī, pp. 47–8; Runowski's Diary, pp. 1405, 1444, 1521, entries for 3 [15] January, 6 [18] July 1860, 2 [14] December 1859 respectively. For the Ottoman side of the relations, see Mustafa Budak, '1853–1856 Kırım Harbı Başlarında Doğu Anadolu-Kafkas Cephesi ve Şeyh Şamil', *KA*, Vol. I, pp. 52–2, and ibid, pp. 131–6 (and 236–41) document Nos. 43, 44, 42, Memorandum by Dağıstanı Hasan Efendi 1263 [1852–53], Memorandum, 4 Dhū al-Qaʿda [9 August] and (Imperial) Decree, 8 Dhū al-Qaʿda 1269 [13 August 1853], Memorandum, 26 Shaʿbān [24 May] and Imperial Decree, 27 Shaʿbān 1270 [25 May 1854] respectively. And see Hamphry Sandwith, *A Narrative of the Siege of Kars and of the Six Months' Resistance by the Turkish Garrison under General Williams to the Russian Army together with a Narrative of Travels and Adventures in Armenia and Lazistan with Remarks on the Present State of Turkey* (London, 1856), p. 143.

22. *AKAK*, Vol. X, pp. 549–51, document Nos. 499, 500, 501, War Diaries of the Left Flank, 25–31 August [6–12 September], 2–29 September [4–11 October], Vorontsov's Order of the Day, 7 [19] October 1853, No. 207 (reprinted in *Shamil*, pp. 361–2, as document No. 297); *Ombres du Passé*, pp. 187–9.

23. *AKAK*, Vol. X, pp. 551–3, document Nos. 502, 503, 504, 505, Wrangel to Bariatinskii, 15 [27] October, Vrevskii to Vorontsov, 29 October [10 November], Vrevskii to Stiszyński, 29 October [10 November], Vorontsov to Vrevskii, 31 October [12 November] 1853, Nos. 2071, 2424, 2425, 655 respectively.

24. Ibid. pp. 553–5, document No. 506, 'Excerpt from the War Diary of the Vladikavkaz Command, 7 [19] November–6 [18] December 1853';

Dvizhenie, pp. 629–30, document Nos. 388, 389, Letter from the *Shāmkhāl* Abū Muslim to Qazān ʿĀlim Bek, Shamil's Letter to 'the People of Qaytāq and Ṭabarsarān and to Their Neighbours', both from late 1853; Soltan, '1852–1853', p. 496.

25. *AKAK*, Vol. X, pp. 555–7, document No. 507, Wrangel to Vorontsov, 22 December 1853 [3 January 1854], No. 2543.
26. Ibid., loc. cit.; Vorontsov to Ermolov, Tiflis, 24 December 1853 [5 January 1854], No. 4, p. 467; O.K., 'Vesti s Linii. (Pis'mo k Priiateliu.)', *Kavkaz*, 19 [31] January 1854 (No. 6), pp. 21–3.
27. *AKAK*, Vol. X, pp. 557–8, 559–60, document Nos. 508, 510, Vorontsov's Order of the Day, 5 [17] January, Read's Order of the Day, 26 April [8 May] 1854, Nos. 1, 81 respectively; *Dvizhenie*, pp. 636–44, document No. 386, War Diary of the Caspian Province, 21 March [2]–4 [16] April 1854; V. Soltan, 'Ocherk Voennykh Deistvii v Dagestane v 1854 Godu', *Kavkazskii Sbornik*, Vol. XI, pp. 525–36 (hereafter: Soltan, '1854').
28. This raid rivals Vorontsov's 1845 campaign for the amount of material published about it. This description is based on the following sources: *AKAK*, Vol. X, pp. 560–4, 565–6, document Nos. 511, 512, 513, 514, 515, 516, 520, Read to Dolgorukov, 7 [19], 9 [21], 12 [24], 15 [27] July, Dolgokurov to Read, 17 [29] July, Andronikov to Read, 21 August [2 September], Nos. 266, 270, 283, 295, 494, 664 respectively, Read's Letter to Dolgorukov, 19 [31] July 1854, Vol. XI, pp. 679–82, document No. 373, 'List of Losses in Lives and Property' [n.d.]; *Dvizhenie*, pp. 633–6, document Nos. 393, 394, 395, 'Shamil's Letter to Turkey', not later than May 1854 (it seems to be a draft, and its date is most probably Shawwāl 1270 [July 1854]), Read to Dolgorukov, 16 [28] July, 20 August [1 September] 1854; *Shamil*, pp. 387–93, 403–4, 405–10, 412–13, 418–19, 423–4, 429–32, 435–44, 394–6, 400–1, document Nos. 313, 314, 315, 316, 317, 318, 327, 329, 332, 339, 342, 345, 346, 350, 319, 324, Head of T'elavi Police to Military Governor of Tiflis, 3 [15] July, No. 10, Grishchenko to Andronikov, 5 [17] July, No. 836, Deputy Chief of Staff Caucasian Corps to Commander of Vladikavkaz, 5 [17] July, No. 2070, Governor of T'elavi to Military Governor of Tiflis, 5 [17] July, No. 22, President Trans-Caucasian Treasury Committee to HQ Caucasian Corps, 5 [17] July, No. 454, Makaev to Military Governor of Tiflis, 7 [19] July, No. 481, 'Information Gathered by Spies', 21 July [2 August], Governor of T'elavi to Military Governor of Tiflis, 25 July, [6 August] No. 3044, Report by Gamurashvili, Resident of the Village of Kisiskhevi, to Read, 3 [15] August 1854, Shamil's Letters to Hacci İbrahim Paşa and to Mustafa Zârif Paşa, 20 Şafar [12 November], Daniyāl's Letter to Hacci Athān, 23 Şafar 1271 [15 November 1854], 'List of the Losses by the Population of T'elavi', 1854, Melikov to Read, 8 [20] July 1854, No. 517, Read to Dolgorukov, 15 [27] July 1854, No. 292 (the two last documents are referred to as reprints from *AKAK*, but their references are incorrect and the documents could not be found there); Andreevski, pp. 96–7, 100–2; Baratov, 'Opisanie Nashestviia Skopishch Shamilia na Kakhetiiu v 1854 Godu', *Kavkazskii Sbornik*, Vol. I, pp. 237–67; Soltan, '1854', pp. 537–57; Züssermann, 'Otryvki', 1878, No. 6, pp. 749–50; Runowski's Diary, p. 1444, entry for 6 [18] June 1860; Qarākhī, pp. 182–6; Ḥājj ʿAlī, pp. 45–8; PRO FO/78/1207, Brant to Clarendon, Erzeroom, 26 September 1854, No. 59, FO/

60/196, Stevens to Clarendon, Tabreez, 31 July (via Russia) [no No.], 3 August 1854, No. 55. The latter is based on the report of the Persian consul in Tiflis; HHSA, PA XXXVIII, 107/Trapezunt, 22 August 1854, No. 357, PA XXXVIII, 106/Odessa, 1 [13] August 1854, No. 817.

29. Soltan, '1854', p. 544. For financial assistance to the population after the raid, see *Shamil*, pp. 416–17, 445–6, document Nos. 337, 352, Koliubakin to Chief Civilian Administrator of the Caucasus, 5 [17] November 1854, Chief Civilian Administrator to Clerk for Special Assignments, 21 February [5 March] 1855, Nos. 1428, 443 respectively.
30. Dobrovl'skii, '1850', pp. 635–9, 644–6. For Melikov's biography, see *AKAK*, Vol. X, p. XXV.
31. K. A. Borozdin, 'Vospominaniia o N. N. Murav'eve', *Istoricheskii Vestnik* (1890), No. 1, pp. 88–9, 90–1, 93 (hereafter: Borozdin + No. of *IV*); Andreevskii, pp. 85–6, 87, 89–91.
32. For Read's biography, see *AKAK*, Vol. X, p. XXIX.
33. Thus, for example, in view of the prospect of the Qājārs joining the anti-Russian coalition, Read suggested evacuating all Russian forces from Daghestan. For the emperor's indignant reaction, see *AKAK*, Vol. X, pp. 558–9, document No. 509, Dolgorukov to Read, 24 April [6 May] 1854, No. 6474. For another instance of panic, see A. Züssermann. 'Po Povodu Vospominanii o N. N. Murav'eve', *Russkii Arkhiv* (1892), No. 4, p. 514. For the disagreements between Read and Bebutov, see A. P. Bergé, 'Nikolai Nikolaevich Murav'ev vo Vremia Ego Namestnichestva na Kavkaze, 1854–1856', *Russkaia Starina* (1873), No. 10, p. 599 (hereafter: Bergé). And see the mocking rhymes composed by Sollohub, given in Züssermann, 'Otryvki', 1876, No. 6, p. 751, and their censored version in *Russkii Biograficheskii Slovar'*, Vol. XVII, p. 145.
34. Soltan, '1854', pp. 547–8.
35. PRO, FO/78/1207, Brant to Clarendon, Erzeroom, 26 September 1854, No. 54. See also the polemic in Borozdin, No. 1, pp. 91–2; A. Züssermann, 'Po Povodu Vospominanii o N. N. Murav'eve', *Russkii Arkhiv* (1892), No. 4, pp. 510–13; Idem, 'Eshche Neskol'ko Slov po Povodu Stat'i G-na Borozdina o N. N. Murav'eve-Karskom', *Russkii Arkhiv*, (1892), No. 7, pp. 392–3. How dangerous the situation was for the Russians can be learnt from the fact that immediately upon entering his duties, on 13 March 1855, Murev'ev conducted *personally* an investigation into this raid – Bergé, p. 605. Furthermore, following this raid, and less than a year after changes had been made in the Lesghian Line, it underwent a complete reappraisal – 'Izmeneniia na Lezginskoi Linii', *Zapiski Kavkazskogo Otdela Imperatorskogo Geograficheskogo Obshchestva*, Vol. II (1853), pp. 224–8; *AKAK* Vol. XI, pp. 950–62, document Nos. 856, 857, Memorandum by Melikov Addressed to Bariatinskii, 3 [15] January, with an Addition dated 5 [17] January, Memorandum by Lieutenant-Colonel Uslar, 7 [19] February, with Complementary Notes dated 22 June [4 July] 1855.
36. Among those, Marx was one of the most enthusiastic towards Shamil. See, for example, *The Eastern Question*, pp. 47, 153–7, 160, 202, 222–4, 364–6, 385, 443; Karl Marx and Friedrich Engels, *Polnoe Sobranie Sochinenii*, (Moscow, 1955–1966, 2nd ed.), Vol. IX, pp. 149, 337–425, 440–2, 449–53, 469–75, 491–6, Vol. X, pp. 28–33, 289–93, 521–6, Vol. XII,

pp. 294–7, Vol. XVII, pp. 200–5, Vol. XX, p. 550, Vol. XXX, p. 335. Also, see Paul B. Henze, 'Marx on Russians and Muslims', *Central Asian Survey*, Vol. 6, No. 4 (1987), pp. 33–45.

37. Ḥājj ʿAlī, p. 48.
38. PRO, FO/78/1026, Brant to Clarendon and to Raglan, Erzeroom, 8 and 30 May 1854, Nos. 27 and 2 respectively. The latter dispatch was shown to the French Consul in Trabzon, and reported by him to Paris – MRE, CPC, Turquie, Trebizonde, Vol. I, ff. 217–9, Poncharra to Walewski, Trebizonde, 2 June 1854. It is ironic that the Russians learnt about this letter and the messenger carrying it on the very day of Shamil's withdrawal – *Shamil*, p. 397, document No. 320, Melikov to Read, 10 [22] July, No. 537, and note 1, Commander of the Force at Akhaltsikhe to HQ Caucasian Corps, 19 [31] July 1854.
39. The Ottomans suffered three defeats on 10, 13 November and 1 December 1853. In addition, on 30 November the Ottoman Black Sea flotilla was destroyed at Sinop by the Russian navy. This was the event that triggered the entry of France and Britain into the war. For the Caucasian front in the war, see W. E. D. Allen and Paul Muratoff, *Caucasian Battlefields: A History of the Wars on the Turco-Caucasian Border, 1828–1921* (Cambridge, 1953), pp. 57–102 (hereafter: Allen and Muratoff).
40. PRO, FO/78/1026, Brant to Raglan, Erzeroom, 30 May 1854, No. 2.
41. For which see Allen and Muratoff, pp. 73–80.
42. *Shamil*, pp. 423–4, 429–32, document Nos. 342, 345, 346, Shamil's Letters to Hacci İbrahim Paşa and to Mustafa Zârif Paşa, 20 Ṣafar [12 November], Daniyāl's Letter to Hacci Athān, 23 Ṣafar 1271 [15 November 1854]; Ḥājj ʿAlī, pp. 48–9. Also see *AKAK*, Vol. XI, pp. 355–6, 371–2, document Nos. 357, 376, Bebutov to Murav'ev, Tiflis, 17 [29] June, Murav'ev to Gorchakov, Camp on the River Kars Çay, 12 [24] July 1855, No. 27; Soltan, '1854', pp. 569–70.
43. Soltan, '1854', pp. 570–1. For the events of this period, see *AKAK* Vol. XI, pp. 62–3, 135–8, 339–40, 353–6, 371–2, document Nos. 51, 104, 342, 354, 357, 376, Murav'ev's Order of the Day, 12 [24] July, No. 8, Bebutov to Dolgorukov, 28 October [9 November], No. 374, Murav'ev to Dolgorukov, 29 May [10 June], No. 5, Murav'ev's Letter to Bebutov, 15 [27] June (top secret), Bebutov's Letter to Murav'ev, 17 [29] June, Murav'ev to Gorchakov, 12 [24] July 1855, No. 27 respectively; *Dvizhenie*, pp. 644–51, 654–5, 656–8, 659–63, document Nos. 397, 398, 400, 410, 399, 401, 406, 407, 408, War Diaries of the Caspian Province, 1 [13]–8 [20] April [a misprint for August], 22–29 August [3–10 September], 29 August [10]–5 [17] September 1855, 19–26 February [3–10 March] 1856, Predimirov to Vrevskii, 31 August [12 September], Dodd to Vrevskii, 25 September [7 October], Forsten to di Starlo, 20 August [1 September], Wrangel to Vrevskii, 30 August [12 September], the *Shāmkhāl* Abū Muslim to His Son, Shams al-Dīn, 5 [17] September 1855 respectively; *Shamil*, pp. 397, 399–400, 401, document Nos. 321, 323, 325, Vrevskii to Deputy Chief-of-Staff Caucasian Corps, 10 [22] July, Vrevskii to Kozlowski, 12 [24] July, Wrangel to Kozlowski, 16 [28] July 1855, Nos. 464, 489, 88, respectively; O. K., 'Vest' s Kavkazskoi Linii (Pis'mo k Priiateliu)', *Moskovskie Vedomosti*, 5 [17] March (No. 27); 'Pis'mo iz Kurinskogo Ukrepleniia', *Odesskii Vestnik*, 26 April [8 May] 1855 (No. 47); Soltan, '1854', pp. 557–71; V.

Soltan, 'Obzor Sobytii v Dagestane v 1855 i 1856 Godakh', *Kavkazskii Sbornik* Vol. XII, pp. 488–508 (hereafter: Soltan, '1855–1856'); Züssermann, 'Otryvki', 1878, No. 6, pp. 762–3, 767–87.

44. For the French efforts to find out who was Mme Drancey and what had happened to her, see MRE, CPC, Russie, Consulats Divers, Vol. 4, ff. 178–86, Steyert to Walewski, Batoum, 22 November, 1, 4 December 1854, Nos. 2, 3, 4 respectively. For the princesses' account of their captivity and release, see E. A. Verderevskii, *Plen u Shamilia* (St. Petersburg, 1856; 2nd ed., *Kavkazskie Plennitsy ili Plen u Shamilia* [Moscow, 1857]. English translation of the first edition by H. Sutherland Edwards, *Captivity of Two Princesses in the Caucasus* [London, 1857]). For Mme Drancey's account, see Edouard Merlieux, *Les Princesses Russes Prisonnières au Caucase. Souvenirs d'une Française Captive de Chamyl* (Paris, 1857; 2nd ed., Paris, 1860. Russian translation of the first edition by Kiril Dziubinskii, *Plennitsy Shamilia. Vospominaniia G-zhi Dranse* [Tiflis, 1858].)

45. The only attempt at a biography of this tragic figure is Viktor Gertsyk, 'Dzhemal'-Ēddin: Starshii Syn Shamilia', *Russkii Arkhiv* 1890, No. 9, pp. 111–12.

46. *AKAK*, Vol. XI, pp. 60–2, document No. 49, 'Description of the Exchange of the Captive Families of Colonel Prince Tchavtchavadze and Major-General Prince Orbeliani', attached to Murav'ev to Dolgorukov, 30 March [11 April], 1855, No. 398; *Odesskii Vestink*, 9 [21] April 1855 (No. 40), p. 190 (reprinted from *Kavkaz*); *Moskovskie Vedomosti*, 21 April [3 May] 1855 (No. 48), pp. 390–2; *Sanktpeterburgskie Vedomosti*, 30 April [12 May] 1855 (No. 85), pp. 424–5 (reprinted from *Russkii Invalid*); A. Annoev, 'Vospominaniia o Voennoi Sluzhbe na Kavkaze', *Voennyi Sbornik*, 1887, No. 4, p. 409; *Ombres du Passé*, pp. 202–10; [Bünting,] *Ein Besuch bei Schamyl. Brief eines Preussen* (Berlin, 1855; English translation, *A Visit to Schamyl* [London, 1857]); Soltan, '1855–1856', pp. 483–8; Qarākhī, pp. 186–9; Ḥājj ʿAlī, pp. 49–50. For the negotiations, see *AKAK*, Vol. X, pp. 565, 566–8, document Nos. 519, 521, 522, 523, 524, Tchavtchavadze's Plea to the Emperor [n.d.], Tchavtchavadze's Letter to Read, Khasav Yūrt, 11 [23] September, Read to Dolgorukov, 6 [18] October, No. 47, 'Excerpts from the Diary of the Caucasian Committee', 26 October [2 November], Lieutenant [Jamāl al-Dīn] Shamil to Major-General Rachett, Warsaw, 8 [20] November 1854, Vol. XI. pp. 62, 651, document Nos. 50, 700, Dolgorukov to Tchavtchavadze, 31 March [12 April], No. 5033, Indrenius to Shcherbinin, 9 [21] October 1855, No. 1541; *Shamil*, pp. 398–9, 445, document Nos. 322, 351, Melikov to Read, 11 [23] July 1854, Orbeliani to Bariatinskii, 4 [16] January 1855, No. 16; Soltan, '1855–1856', pp. 480–3. For the fate of other prisoners, see *Shamil*, pp. 414–15, 454, 456–60, document Nos. 335, 364, 366, 367, 369 [misprint for 368], 369, 'Appeal by State Serf Vasilii Toradzeshvili to Read', 12 [24] October 1854, Prince Gurgenidze to Bebutov, 11 [23] July, Solomon Kenkadze to Bebutov, 1 [13] October 1855, 'Appeal by the Residents of Shildy' (n.d.), 'Letter from One of the Captives to His Family', 1853 [misprint for 1855], 'Appeal by Church Serf Zurab Guramashvili to Murav'ev', 6 [18] March 1856; Aleksandr Pavlovich Nicolaӱ, 'Ēpizod iz Istorii Kavkazskoi Voiny, 1855–1857', *Russkaia Starina* (1882), No. 11, pp. 257, 272, 279–81, L. P. Nicolaӱ to Bariatinskii,

27 April [9 May] 1855, L. P. Nicolaÿ to A. P. Nicolaÿ, 9 [21] March 1856, Shamil to L. P. Nicolaÿ, 8 Ramaḍān 1271 [25 May 1855], L. P. Nicolaÿ to Shamil, 15 [27] May, 8 [20] July 1855, Shamil to L. P. Nicolaÿ, July 1855, 6 Muḥarram 1272 [18 September 1855] (hereafter: Nicolaÿ).

47. Runowski's Diary, p. 1442, entry for 4 [16] April 1860; Ḥājj ʿAlī, p. 50. And see Hamzatov, pp. 379–85.

48. For this trend, see Lesure, pp. 29–38. And see Sh. Beridze, 'Shamil' v Evropeiskom Predstavlenii', *Kavkaz* (Paris, 1937), No. 5 (41), pp. 39–40; Idem, 'Shamil' vo Frantsuzskoi Literature', ibid (1934), No. 8–9, pp. 30–2.

49. For the British especially Palmerston's, initial war aims, see E. Ashley, *The Life of Henry John Temple*, Vol. II (London, 1876), pp. 61–2; Herbert C. F. Bell, *Lord Palmerston*, Vol. II (London, 1936), pp. 105–49; Kenneth Bourn, *The Foreign Policy of Victorian England* (Oxford, 1970), pp. 78, 321; Brian Connel, *Regina vs. Palmerston: The Correspondence between Queen Victoria and the Foreign and Prime Minister, 1837–1865* (London, 1962), p. 174. For the French initial war aims, see Lesure, pp. 38–41.

50. The French and some British attempts are fully described in Lesure, pp. 42–52. See also PRO, FO/78/1336, Stevens to de Redcliffe, Trebizonde, 1 October, No. 68 (copy), appended to de Redcliffe to Clarendon, Therapia, 9 October, 1854, No. 574, FO/78/986, Clarendon to de Redcliffe, 8 November 1854 (draft). For an interesting report of one of the British attempts, see HHSA, PA XXXVIII 107/Trapezunt, 10 June 1854, No. 245; *Shamil*, pp. 334–5, document No. 280, Anichkov to Vorontsov, Nemet-Abād, 16 [28] July 1853, No. 506; Yama'uchi, pp. 150–2, document Nos. VII, VIII, Circular of the Ministry of War to the Sublime Porte, 18 Şevval [14 July] and undated response to it, Letter to Shamil, 21 Şevval 1270 [17 July 1854].

51. See, for example, Atwel Lake, *Kars and Our Captivity in Russia* (London, 1856), p. 348 (hereafter: Lake).

52. For such reports, see, e.g., PRO, FO/78/939, Brant to de Redcliffe, Erzeroom, 8 October, appended to de Redcliffe to Clarendon, Therapia, 22 October 1853, No. 311, FO/78/1026, Brant to Clarendon, Erzeroom, 8 May 1854, No. 27.

53. For his biography, see Stanley Lane-Poole, *The Life of the Right Honourable Stratford Canning, Viscount Stratford de Redcliffe, K.G., G.C.B., D.C.L., L.L.D., etc.* (London, 1888).

54. See, for example, HHSA, PA XII 50, Buyukdere, 19 June 1854, No. 50.

55. PRO, FO/78/1042, de Redcliffe to Williams, Private, Therapia, 23 September 1854 (copy).

56. For Williams' biography, see *Dictionary of Canadian Biography*, Vol. XI (Toronto, 1982), pp. 931–3.

57. PRO, FO/78/1042, de Redcliffe to Williams, Private, Therapia, 23 September 1854 (copy).

58. Ibid, Williams to Shamil, Turkish Camp near Kars, 12 October 1854, appended to Williams to Hammond, Erzeroom, 27 November 1854, separate. This letter is mentioned also in Ḥājj ʿAlī, p. 42–8. Also see Williams to de Redcliffe, Camp near Kars, 12 October 1854, No. 33 (copy), appended to the same report, and FO/352/39/3, ff. 97–100, Williams to de Redcliffe, Private, Camp near Kars, 7 October 1854. A translation of

Shamil's reply was published in Lake, pp. 340–1 (pp. 342–3 in the second edition).

59. PRO, FO/78/986, Clarendon to de Redcliffe, 13 November 1854, No. 699 (draft).
60. There was only one attempt to reach Shamil afterwards, that by Longworth. For details, see PRO, FO/78/1243, Longworth to Clarendon, Sokoom Kale, 6 October 1855; Murav'ev to Bebutov, 14 [26] October 1855, as quoted in Bergé, p. 625.
61. Text in PRO FO/78/1004, translation of Vizirial Letter to Shamil, 15 October 1854, appended to de Redcliffe to Clarendon, Therapia, 30 October 1854, No. 636.
62. Runowski's Diary, p. 1444, entry for 6 [18] July 1860.
63. Lake, loc. cit.
64. *AKAK*, Vol. XI, pp. 390–1, document No. 391, Murav'ev to Dolgorukov, 19 [31] August 1855, No. 38.
65. One such consignment of medallions and flags for Ghāzī Muḥammad arrived in May 1855, accompanied by a letter, in which Shamil was promised the post of *vâli* of Tiflis after its conquest – Nicolaÿ, p. 276, Jamāl al-Dīn to L. P. Nicolaÿ, 5–6 [17–18] October 1855. For other such letters, see ibid, pp. 260, 274, 277, L. P. Nicolaÿ to A. P. Nicolaÿ, 2 [14] June 1855, No. 2, 30 March [11 April] 1856, Jamāl al-Dīn to L. P. Nicolaÿ, 4 [16] May 1856.
66. *AKAK*, Vol. XI, pp. 355–6, 371–2, document Nos. 357, 376, Bebutov to Murav'ev, 17 [25] June (top secret), Murav'ev to Gorchakov, 12 [24] July 1855, No. 27. Also see the curious report about a letter from the Qājārs to Shamil received in April 1855 (i.e. *six months after* the conclusion of the secret treaty which guaranteed Tehrān's neutrality in the Crimean War in return for St. Petersburg's disavowal of the rest of the war indemnities due to it according to the peace treaty of Turkumānchāy) inviting him to join their intended war against Russia – Soltan, '1855–1856', p. 489.
67. Although 24 documents and letters related to this attempt were published (Nicolaÿ, op. cit.) in 1882 in a central historical periodical, it remained unreferred to by historians for over a century. Tsereteli (op. cit.), a linguist, published the Arabic text and a new, good, translation of Shamil's letters in ibid, 55 years later. Again, no historian referred to them.
68. For Murav'ev's biography, see I. I. Evropeus, 'Nikolai Nikolaevich Murav'ev', *Russkaia Starina* (1874), No. 9, pp. 181–4; Dmitrii Osten-Saken, 'Nikolai Nikolaevich Murave'ev v 1828–1856 GG.', *Russkaia Starina* (1874), No. 11, pp. 535–43; *AKAK*, Vol. VII, pp. VII-VIII, Vol. X, p. XXVI, Vol. XI, p. IX. His activity as viceroy of the Caucasus was and remained in controversy in Russian pre-revolutionary historiography. For example, see Bergé, op. cit.; F. Timiriazev, 'Po Povodu Stat'i Berzhe [Bergé] o N. N. Murav'eve-Karskom', *Russkii Arkhiv* (1873), No. 12, cc. 2530–40; Liubitel' Kavkaza Zakavkaza (pseud.), 'Nikolai Nikolaevich Murav'ev, 1854–1856', *Russkaia Starina* (1874), No. 5, pp. 139–51 (the latter two are reactions to the former); Borozdin, No. 1, pp. 86–101, No. 2, pp. 307–23; A. Züssermann, 'Po Povodu Vospominanii o N. N. Murav'eve', *Russkii Arkhiv* (1892), No. 4, pp. 510–25; Idem, 'Eshche Neskol'ko Slov po Povodu Stat'i G-na Borozdina o N. N. Murav'eve-Karskom', *Russkii Arkhiv* (1892), No. 7, pp. 392–6 (the two latter are,

again, reactions to the preceding one); M. P. Shcherbinin, 'Kn. M. S. Vorontsov i N. N. Murav'ev. (Iz Sluzhebnykh Vospominanii)', *Russkaia Starina* (1874), No. 9, pp. 99–114; [Murav'ev,] 'Zemlianka A. P. Ermolova. Vyderzhka iz Zapisok N. N. Murav'eva', *Russkii Arkhiv* (1888), No. 10, pp. 247–8; 'Otvet Kavkazskogo Ofitsera na Obvineniia N. N. Murav'eva (Pis'mo k General-Leitenantu Kx.)', *Russkaia Starina* (1872), No. 11, pp. 544–6.

69. Nicolaÿ, p. 255. Emphasis added.
70. Ibid., loc. cit.
71. For his biography, see Tsereteli, pp. 99–100.
72. Nicolaÿ, pp. 255–66, Bariatinskii to L. P. Nicolaÿ, 17 [29] March, 16 [30] April 1855.
73. In addition to the sources mentioned above (note 68), see I. S. Kravtsov, 'Kavkaz i Ego Voenachal'niki. N. N. Murav'ev, Kn. A. I. Bariatinskii i Gr. N. I. Evdokimov, 1854–1864', *Russkaia Starina* (1886), No. 6, pp. 563–92, No. 7, pp. 109–50.
74. Nicolaÿ, pp. 257–8, L. P. Nicolaÿ to Bariatinskii, 27 April [9 May] 1855. Nicolaÿ was like all the high command of the Caucasus: too young, or recently arrived in the Caucasus to know about Faesy's and Grabbe's negotiations with Shamil, which explain the *imām*'s complete mistrust of the Russians.
75. Ibid., p. 268, Gorchakov to Murav'ev (copy), December 1855.
76. Ibid., pp. 259–60, L. P. Nicolaÿ to A. P. Nicolaÿ, 2 [14] June 1855, No. 2.
77. Ibid, p. 259, A. P. Nicolaÿ to L. P. Nicolaÿ, 20 May [1 June] 1855. Emphasis added.
78. Ibid., p. 278, Jamāl al-Dīn to L. P. Nicolaÿ, 12 [24] September 1856.

Chapter 26: Ghunīb

1. Efforts by agents of Shamil and the Ottomans helped to exacerbate an existing state of unrest in Ṭabarsarān to such an extent that the Russians were forced to stage three successive annual expeditions there. In the Erivan province an expedition was needed as well, while in Shekī a messenger of the *imām* to the Ottomans, having been discovered by the Russians, escaped arrest and led a band of raiders. For these events see, for example, *AKAK*, Vol. XI, pp. 339–40, 618–20, document Nos. 342, 638, 640, Murav'ev to Dolgorukov, 29 May [10 June] 1855, Military Governor of Shemākha to Réoute, 10 [22] May, Réoute to Read (secret), 1 [13] June 1854, Nos. 5, 479, 121 respectively; Soltan, '1854', pp. 526–36; Soltan, '1855–1856', pp. 494–501, 526–628.
2. P. Bobrovskii, 'Imperator Aleksandr II i Ego Pervye Shagi k Pokoreniiu Kavkaza. (Ēpizod iz Istorii Velikoi Kavkazskoi Voiny.),' *Voennyi Sbornik* (1897), No. 4, pp. 204–5 (hereafter: Bobrovskii).
3. For a short biography of Miliutin, see P. A. Zajączkowski [Zaionchkovskii], 'D. A. Miliutin. Biograficheskii Ocherk', (preface to) idem (ed.), *Dnevnik D. A. Miliutina, 1873–1875*, Vol. I (Moscow, 1947), pp. 5–72. Also see *AKAK*, Vol. X, p. XXV.
4. For the text of which, see Hurewitz, pp. 319–21, document No. 105.

5. Bobrovskii, pp. 205–9.
6. For the Russian battle order in the Caucasus, see Olszewski, 'Kavkaz', p. 298, note 1. And see France, Ministère de la Guerre, État-Major de l'Armée de la Terre, Archives Historiques, Série Mémoires et Reconnaissances, Boîte 1479, 'Note sur l'Armée Russe en 1856', f. 52: 'Corps Détaché, ou Armée du Caucase'; MRE, CPC, Russie, Consulats Divers, Vol. 5, ff. 21–2, Finot to Walewski, Tiflis, 28 July 1857, No. 6.
7. *AKAK*, Vol. XII, pp. 1275–1394, Bariatinskii's Report for the Years 1857–1859, pp. 1278, 1282. Also see Züssermann, 'Otryvki', 1879, No. 2, pp. 703–6.
8. Indeed, Shamil wrote a letter to the *serasker*, for the translation of which, see *Dvizhenie*, pp. 663–4, document No. 414.
9. See *AKAK*, Vol. XI, pp. 64–7, document No. 54, Murav'ev to Dolgorukov, 23 April [5 May] 1856, No. 15; A. Züssermann, 'Po Povodu Vospominanii o N. N. Murav'eve', *Russkii Arkhiv* (1892), No. 4, p. 518.
10. Fadeev to his father, Groznaia, 2 [14] July 1856, No. 10, pp. 63–4.
11. For Murav'ev's biography and his dispute with Bariatinskii in 1855, see above, notes 68, 73 to Chapter 25.
12. For Bariatinskii's biography, see A. L. Züssermann, *Fel'dmarshal Kniaz' Aleksandr Ivanovich Bariatinskii, 1815–1879* (Moscow, 1888–91; also serialised in *Russkii Arkhiv* (1888–89) under the title 'Fel'dmarshal Kniaz' Bariatinskii. Ego Biografiia'); Dmitrii Il'ich Romanovskii, 'General-Fel'dmarshal Kniaz' Aleksandr Ivanovich Bariatinskii i Kavkazskaia Voina, 1815–1876 GG.', *Russkaia Starina* (1881), No. 2, pp. 247–318, 444; 'Plenitel' Shamilia. (Pamiati General-Fel'dmarshala Kniazia A. I. Bariatinskogo.)', *Istoricheskaia Letopis*' (1914), Vol. VIII, pp. 934–42; *AKAK*, Vol. X, pp. XIV-XV. Also see P. D. Gagarin, 'Vospominaniia o Fel'dmarshale Kniaze Aleksandre Ivanoviche Bariatinskom', *Russkii Vestnik* 1888, No. 7, pp. 126–42; P. Nikolaev, 'Vospominania o Kniaze A. I. Bariatinskom', *Istoricheskii Vestnik* (1885), No. 12, pp. 618–44; N. Volkonskii, 'Okonchatel'noe Pokorenie Vostochnogo Kavkaza (1859-i God)', *Kavkazskii Sbornik*, Vol. IV, pp. 71, 73–5 (hereafter: Volkonskii, '1859').
13. 'Nikolai Nikolaevich Murav'ev 5-go Iunia 1856 G.', *Russkaia Starina* (1890), No. 11, p. 456.
14. *AKAK*, Vol. XII, pp. 613, 614–5, document Nos. 538, 540, 541, 542, 543, 544, Bariatinskii to Sukhozanet, 10 [22] September, No. 201, Bebutov's Order of the Day, 15 [27] September, No. 545, Bariatinskii's Orders of the Day, 12 [24] October, 5 [17], 9 [21], 22 November [4 December] 1856; Olszewski, 'Kavkaz', pp. 292–300.
15. *AKAK*, Vol. XII, pp. 613–14, 625, 627–8, document Nos. 539, 548, 550, Bariatinskii's Order of the Day, 15 [27] September 1856, Bariatinskii to Sukhozanet, 12 [24] January, 2 [14] February, 1857, Nos. 82, 37 respectively; Bobrovskii, pp. 210–12.
16. *AKAK*, Vol. XII, pp. 615–29, document Nos. 545, 546, Bariatinskii to Sukhozanet, 4 [16] December 1856, No. 116, 'Suggested Plan of Operations for the Winter of 1856–1857 and the Year 1857' [n.d.]; Alfred J. Rieber, *The Politics of Autocracy: Letters of Alexander II to Prince A. I. Bariatinskii, 1857–1864* (Paris, 1966), p. 101, Alexander [the Emperor] to Bariatinskii, St. Petersburg, 2 [14] January 1857 (hereafter quoted by details of letter and page in the book).

17. For Evdokimov's biography, see *AKAK*, Vol. X, pp. XX-XXI, Vol. XI, p. VII; Isakov, No. 10–12, pp. 14–15; Volkonskii, '1859', p. 83.
18. *AKAK*, Vol. XII, pp. 1028–38, document Nos. 907, 909, 911, 908, 910, 'War Diaries of the Chechen Force', 15 [27] January–14 [26] February, 3 [15]–23 March [4 April], 23–30 March [4–11 April], 'War Diaries of the Ghumuq Force', 28 January [9]–4 [16] February, 3 [15]–17 [29] March 1857; Alexander to Bariatinskii, Tsarskoe Selo, 20 May [1 June] 1857, pp. 104–6; V. Soltan, 'Zaniatie Salatavii v 1857 Godu', *Kavkazskii Sbornik*, Vol. XV, p. 340 (hereafter: Soltan, '1857'); MRE, CPC, Russie, Consulats Divers, Vol. 5, ff. 9–10, Finot to Walewski, Tiflis, 19 January, 6/18 February 1857, Nos. 4, 8 respectively. For the military events during 1856, see *AKAK*, Vol. XII, p. 1027, document No. 906, 'War Diary of the Caspian Province', 21–28 September [2–9 November] 1856; *Dvizhenie*, pp. 660–3, document No. 413, 'War Diary of the Caspian Province', 22–29 April [4–11] May 1856; Arnold Züssermann, 'Pis'mo iz Groznoi', *Kavkaz*, 7 [19] June 1856 (No. 44), pp. 176–8; Soltan, '1855–1856', pp. 488–530.
19. *AKAK* Vol. XII, pp. 1039–40, document No. 912, Bariatinskii to Sukhozanet, 17 [29] May 1857, No. 121; Soltan, '1857', pp. 335–46.
20. *AKAK*, Vol. XII, pp. 1041–2, 1043–44, 1047, 1049–50, 1053–4, 1055, document Nos. 917, 921, 927, 931, 914, 923, 'War Diaries of the Caspian Province', 7 [19]–14 [26], 14 [26]–21 July [2 August], 29 September [11]–6 [18], 20–27 October [1–8 November] 1857, Orbeliani to Bariatinskii, 26 June [8 July], 3 [15] August 1857, Nos. 50, 1229 respectively; *Dvizhenie*, p. 666, document No. 419, 'War Diary of the Caspian Province', 25 August [6]–1 [13] September 1857; Soltan, '1857', pp. 347–84; Qarākhī, pp. 190–1.
21. For his biography, see *AKAK*, Vol. X, pp. XVII-XVIII.
22. *AKAK*, Vol. XII, pp. 1043, 1044–7, 1047–9, 1050, document Nos. 916, 918, 920, 922. 'War Diaries of the Lesghian Force', 2 [14]–9 [21], 9 [21]–16 [28], 16 [28]–21 July [2 August], 21–27 July [2–8 August] 1857; Volkonskii, '1857', Vol. I, pp. 383–409, Vol. II, pp. 223–62.
23. This did not prevent the Russian sources from describing the results as 'a considerable punishment [inflicted upon] more than half of the Dido community and [the establishment of] a solid base for the conquest of that tribe' – *AKAK*, Vol. XII, pp. 1050–3, document Nos. 924, 926, 925, 'War Diaries of the Lesghian Force', 4 [16]–13 [25] August, 13 [25] August–15 [27] September, Vrevskii to Bariatinskii, 22 August [3 September] 1857, No. 502; Volkonskii, '1857', Vol. II, pp. 273–338 (quotation from p. 337). For subsequent events during the winter and spring of 1857–58, see *AKAK*, Vol. XII, pp. 1071–72, document No. 941, Bariatinskii to Sukhozanet, 22 February [6 March] 1858, No. 380; Volkonskii, '1857', Vol. II, pp. 338–86 (Epilogue).
24. *AKAK* Vol. XII, pp. 1058–60, document Nos. 933, 934, 935, 'War Diaries of the Caspian Province', 20–31 October [1–12], 3 [15]–10 [22], 10 [22]–17 [29] November 1857; Soltan, '1857', pp. 384–93.
25. *AKAK*, Vol. XII, pp. 1055–7, 1060–5, document Nos. 930, 932, 936, Evdokimov to Sukhozanet, 19 [31] October, No. 1879, 'War Diary of the Lesser-Chechnia Force', 20–31 October [1–12 November], 'War Diary of the Left Wing', 31 October [12 November]–17 [29] December 1857; N. Volkonskii, '1858 God v Chechne', *Kavkazskii Sbornik*, Vol. III, p. 378

(hereafter: Volkonskii, '1858'); Alexander to Bariatinskii, Tsarkoe Selo, 22 November [4 December] 1857, p. 110.

26. *AKAK*, Vol. XII, pp. 1065–9, 1072–6, 1080, document Nos. 937, 938, 939, 942, 948, 943, 945, Evdokimov to Sukhozanet, 18 [30], 29 January [10], 6 [18], 27 February [11 March], Bariatinskii to Sukhozanet, 21 May [2 June], Nos. 99, 107, 126, 380, 808 respectively, 'War Diaries of the Chechen Force', 28 February [12]–21 March [2 April], 21 March [2]–2 [14] April 1858; Alexander to Bariatinskii, St. Petersburg, 9 [21] February, 22 March [3 April] 1858, pp. 114, 116; Volkonskii, '1858', pp. 380–455; K. Didimov, 'Ēkspeditsiia v Argunskoe Ushchel'e s 15-go Ianvaria po 18e Aprelia 1858 Goda', *Voennyi Sbornik* (1859), No. 7, Chast' Neofitsial'naia, pp. 89–112; MRE, CPC, Russie, Consulats Divers, Vol. 5, ff. 52–3, 95–6, Finot to Walewski, Tiflis, 3/15 January, 17/29 March 1858, Nos. 12, 13 respectively. For the topographic difficulties the Russians had to overcome, see Baddeley, *Rugged Flanks*, Vol. I, pp. 84–5.

27. *AKAK*, Vol. XII, pp. 1076–80, document Nos. 946, 947, Evdokimov to Sukhozanet, 19 April [1], 12 [24] May 1858, Nos. 251, 453 respectively; Alexander to Bariatinskii, Peterhoff, 7 [19] July 1858, p. 119; Volkonskii, '1858', pp. 456–60; Qarākhī, p. 191.

28. For his biography, see *AKAK*, Vol. X, p. XVII.

29. *AKAK*, Vol. XII, pp. 1080–81, 1085–86, document Nos. 950, 956, 'War Diaries of the Caspian Province', 18 [30]–25 May [6 June], 15 [27]–22 June [4 July] 1858; Dobrovol'skii-Evdokimov, 'Ēkspeditsiia v Salataviiu v 1858 Godu', *Kavkazskii Sbornik*, Vol. IV, pp. 39–50. For subsequent events in Daghestan to the end of 1858, see *AKAK*, Vol. XII, pp. 1101–2, 1106–7, document Nos. 966, 970, 'War Diaries of the Caspian Province', 10 [22]–17 [29], 24–31 August [5–12 September] 1858; *Dvizhenie*, p. 667, document No. 420, 'War Diary of the Caspian Province', 21–28 October [2–9 November] 1858; A. Annoev, 'Vospominaniia o Boevoi Sluzhbe na Kavkaze', *Voennyi Sbornik* (1871), No. 4, pp. 398–412.

30. *AKAK*, Vol. XII, pp. 1091–4, 1096–8, 1102–6, 1107–10, document Nos. 961, 963, 967, 968, 972, 'War Diaries of the Lesghian Force', 15 [27]–29 July [10 August], 29 July [10]–8 [20] August, Vrevskii to Bariatinskii, August 1859 [remained unsigned, undated and unnumbered because of Vrevskii's death], de Saget to Vrevskii, 23 August [4 September], Korganov to Bariatinskii, 2 [14] September 1858, Nos. 152, 472 respectively; Alexander to Bariatinskii, Warsaw, 18/30 September 1858, p. 123.

31. *AKAK*, Vol. XII, pp. 1088–90, 1094–5, 1098–101, 1110–17, document Nos. 959, 962, 964, 976, 965, 973, 974, 979, 'War Diaries of the Chechen Force', 1 [13]–15 [27], 15 [27] July–1 [13], 1 [13]–9 [21] August, 8 [20] September–9 [21] October, Bariatinskii to Vasil'chikov, 15 [27] August, Evdokimov to Bariatinskii, 8 [20] September, Bariatinskii to Vasil'chikov, 17 [29] September, Evdokimov to Sukhozanet, 3 [15] November 1858, Nos. 55, 350, 47, 1896 respectively; Alexander to Bariatinskii, Moscow, 30 August [11 September] 1858, p. 121; Volkonskii, '1858', pp. 468–512, 516–91; K. Didimov, 'Ēkspeditsiia v Chanty-Argunskoe Ushchel'e s 1-go Iulia po 19-e Avgusta 1859 Goda', *Voennyi Sbornik* (1859) No. 8, Chast' Neofitsial'naia, pp. 255–84; HHSA, XII 65. ? to von Ludolf, Trapezunt, 23 November 1858, No. 519 (copy) attached to von Ludolf to von Buol-Schlemerstein, Constantinople, 1 December 1858, No. 913; MRE, CPC,

Russie, Consulats Divers, Vol. 5, ff. 132–3, Finot to Walewski, Tiflis, 17 August 1858, No. 15; Qarākhī, p. 191.

32. *AKAK*, Vol. XII, pp. 1119–20, document No. 984, Sviatopol'k-Mirskii to Evdokimov, 16 [28] December 1858, No. 19; Volkonskii, '1859', pp. 90–1, 97–105.
33. *AKAK*, Vol. XII, pp. 1120–4, 1127–32, 1134–9, document Nos. 985, 987, 988, 992, 995, 996, 1000, 1004, 994, 1003, 1002, 'War Diaries of the Left Wing', 23 November [5]–18 [30], 21 December 1858, [2]–1 [13], 1 [13]–15 [27], 15 [27] January–1 [13], 10 [22]–26 February [10 March], 26 February [10]–8 [20], 8 [20]–20 March [1 April], 21 March [2]–2 [14] April, Bariatinskii to Sukhozanet, 20 February [4 March], 2 [14] April, Nos. 29, 69, Bariatinskii's Order of the Day, 2 [14] April 1859 respectively; [Evdokimov,] 'Voennye Deistviia s Levogo Kryla. Donesenie General-Leitenanta Evdokimova ot 11 [23] Aprelia za No. 212', *Kavkaz*, 25 April [7 May] 1859 (No. 31), pp. 157–8; Alexander to Bariatinskii, St. Petersburg, 1 [13], 20 April [2 May] 1859, pp. 127–8; 'Veden', *Voennyi Sbornik* (1859), No. 4, Chast' Neofitsial'naia, pp. 542–58; I. P., 'Iz Boevykh Vospominanii, Rasskaz Kurintsa', *Kavkazskii Sbornik*, Vol. IV, pp. 51–67; Ia., '1-go Aprelia 1859/94 Goda. (Vospominaniia Veterana.)', *Terskie Vedomosti*, 1 [13] April 1894 (No. 29), pp. 2–3; I. Shabanov, 'Vospominanie o Zimnei Ekspeditsii 1859 G. v Chechne', *Voennyi Sbornik* (1866), No. 10, pp. 297–333; Volkonskii, '1859', pp. 91–7, 105–59, 169–99, 204–20; Qarākhī, p. 192; MRE, CPC, Russie, Consulats Divers, Vol. 5, ff. 141–2, 144, Finot to Walewski, Tiflis, 15/27 January, 8/20 April 1859, Nos. 18, 20.
34. For the plans, see *AKAK*, Vol. XII, pp. 641–4, 649–51, document Nos. 560, 563, Bariatinskii to Vasil'chikov, 29 July [10 August], Sukhozanet to Bariatinskii, 28 September [10 October] 1858, Nos. 37, 8489 respectively; Alexander to Bariatinskii, Tsarskoe Selo, 25 October [6 November] 1858, pp. 124–5; Volkonskii, '1859', pp. 217–19.
35. PRO, FO/78/1435, O'Brian to Bulwer, Private, Constantinople, 4 August (copy), attached to Bulwer to Russell, Therapia, 13 September 1859, No. 151.
36. *AKAK*, Vol. XII, pp. 1139–40, document Nos. 1010, 1011, 'War Diaries of the Left Wing', 11 [23] April–6 [18], 6 [18]–12 [24] May 1859; Volkonskii, '1859', pp. 224–7.
37. *AKAK*, Vol. XII, p. 1143, document Nos. 1013, 1014, 'War Diaries of the Caspian Province', 25–30 May, [6–11 June], 31 May [12]–7 [19] June 1859; Volkonskii, '1859', pp. 228–30.
38. *AKAK*, Vol. XII, pp. 1132–4, 1139, document Nos. 997, 1008, 998, 'War Diaries of the Caspian Province', 1 [13]–8 [20] March, 2 [14]–11 [23] April, Wrangel to Sukhozanet, 11 [23] March 1859, No. 16; A. Annoev, 'Vospominaniia o Boevoi Sluzhbe na Kavkaze', *Voennyi Sbornik* (1877), No. 5, pp. 188–204; Volkonskii, '1859', pp. 151–69, 199–203.
39. *AKAK*, Vol. XII, pp. 1134, 1140–3, document Nos. 999, 1012, 'War Diary of the Left Flank of the Lesghian Line', 8 [20]–20 March [1 April], Korganov to Melikov, 21 May [2 June] 1859, No. 759; Volkonskii, '1859', pp. 289–307.
40. Baddeley, p. 464.
41. Volkonskii, '1858', p. 496.

42. *AKAK*, Vol. XII, pp. 1082–5, 1086–8, document Nos. 951, 952, 954, 953, 955, 957, 958, Zotov to Evdokimov, 26 May [7 June], Evdokimov to Bariatinskii, 27 May [8], 10 [22] June, Bariatinskii to Vasil'chikov, 6 [18] June, Zotov to Vasil'chikov, 23 June [5 July], Vasil'chikov to Bariatinskii, 1 [13] July 1858, Nos. 296, 1835, 883, 775, 1026, 6039 respectively; Alexander to Bariatinskii, Peterhoff, 7 [19] July 1858, p. 120; Grigor'ev, 'Vospominanie o Dele bliz' Ukrepleniia Achkhoi', *Voennyi Sbornik* (1893), No. 2, pp. 347–9; Volkonskii, '1858', pp. 460–7.
43. *AKAK*, Vol. XII, pp. 1090–1, 1106–7, 1116, document Nos. 960, 969, 976, Bariatinskii to Vasil'chikov, 26 July [7 August], Vasil'chikov to Bariatinskii, 23 August [4 September], Evdokimov to Sukhozanet, 3 [15] November 1858, Nos. 172, 350, 2518 respectively; Alexander to Bariatinskii, Moscow, 30 August [11 September] 1858, p. 121; Volkonskii, '1858', pp. 513–16.
44. Ibid, p. 466.
45. Runowski's Diary, p. 1413, entry for 20 February [4 March] 1860.
46. *Dvizhenie*, pp. 664–5, document No. 416, Shamil's Letter to the French Ambassador in Constantinople, February 1857.
47. The British Library, Additional Manuscripts, Mss. 39.055, Layard Papers, Vol. CXXV, Miscellaneous Supplementary Papers, 1834–1883, f. 29, Shamil's Letter to the British Ambassador in Constantinople, 5 Rajab 1274 [19 February 1858] (should read: 5 Rajab 1273 [1 March 1857]). Also, see PRO FO/78/1303, ff. 194, 196, Stevens to Clarendon, and to Allinson (copy), Trebizonde, 24 December 1857, Nos. 46, 59 respectively, FO/196/54, Allinson to Clarendon, Constantinople, 13 January 1858.
48. The British acting consul in Trabzon was instructed to 'inform the *nā'ib* that if the Circassians had cooperated with England during the war with Russia, the good offices of Her Majesty's Government would have been used for them in the negotiations for Peace, but the Circassians would not then join us, and the time is gone by when we would have aided them in their views' – FO/78/1345, FO to Allinson, 21 January 1858, No. 59 (draft). Similarly, FO/78/1347, FO to Allinson, 21 April, 11 May 1858, Nos. 153, 179 (drafts) respectively.
49. *The Times*, 28 September 1859.
50. PRO, FO/78/1435, O'Brian to Bulwer, Private, Constantinople, 4 August (copy), attached to Bulwer to Russell, Therapia, 13 September 1859, No. 151. And see the contents of a message from the *imām* received by Muḥammad Amīn in July 1859, in Lapiński, Vol. II, p. 207.
51. *Dvizhenie*, p. 676, document No. 432, Gorchakov to Bariatinskii, 26 July [7 August] 1859; Alexander to Bariatinskii, Krasnoe Selo, 28 July [9 August] 1859, p. 130; Volkonskii, '1859', p. 401.
52. Alexander to Bariatinskii, St. Petersburg, 20 April [2 May] 1859, p. 129.
53. Sources as above in note 51.
54. PRO, FO/78/1435, O'Brian to Bulwer, Private, Constantinople, 4 August (copy), attached to Bulwer to Russell, Therapia, 13 September 1859, No. 151.
55. *AKAK*, Vol. XII, pp. 1150–80, document Nos. 1025, 1028, 1029, 1036, 1045, 1052, 1046, 1053, 1027, 1031, 1032, 1034, 1037, 1038, 1035, 1033, 1041, 1051, 1056, 1049, 1050, 'War Diary of the Caspian Province', 28 June [10]–18 [30] July, 'War Diaries of the Left Wing', 15 [27]–22 July [3

August], 22–29 July [3–10 August], 29 July [10]–7 [19] August, 'War Diaries of the Lesghian Line', 12 [24]–26 August [7 September], 30 March [11 April]–26 August [7 September], Bariatinskii's Telegrams to the Emperor, 22, 26 August [3, 7 September], Melikov to Miliutin, 19 [31] and ? July, Mamatsev to Korganov and Sumarokov-Elstone [El'ston] to Korganov, both 23 July [4 August], Shalikov to Melikov, 29, 31 July [10, 12 August], Shalikov to Korganov, 23 July [4 August], Tarkhan-Mauravov to Staritskii, 29 July [10 August], Wrangel to Bariatinskii, 23–24 July [4–5 August], Bariatinskii to Sukhozanet, 27 July [8], 4 [16], 7 [19], 22, 27 August [3, 8 September], Bariatinskii's [two] Orders of the Day, 22 August [3 September] 1859, Nos. 58, 79, 12, 36, 5, 15, 17, 5, 150, 197, 265, 295, 379, 465, 381, 382 respectively; Bariatinskii's Order of the Day, No. 419, Special Appendices to *Kavkaz*, 30 August [12] and 3 [15] September 1859 (Nos. 68 and 69); 'Imam Shamil i Fel'dmarshal Kn. Bariatinskii. Prikazy po Voiskam Kn. Bariatinskogo i Pis'ma Shamilia i Ego Zhen', *Russkaia Starina* (1880), No. 4, pp. 801–12; 'Vziatie v Plen Shamilia', *Zhurnal dlia Vospitannikov Voenno-Uchebnykh Zavedenii*, Vol. CXLII, No. 566, pp. 177–87; 'Pokorenie Kavkaza – Shamil', *Raduga* (1860), No. 2, p. 37; 'Vziatie Shamilia', *Odesskii Vestnik*, 24 September [6 October] 1859, pp. 454–5; Fadeev to his father, Groznaia, 9 [21] May, 7 [19] July, Camp in Avāristān, 24 July [5 August], Camp near Konkhidatl', 7 [19] August 1859, No. 12, pp. 67–9; A.-D. G., 'Obzor Poslednikh Sobytii na Kavkaze', *Voennyi Sbornik* (1859), No. 10, Chast' Neofitsial'naia, pp. 475–518; Volkonskii, '1859', pp. 235–88, 308–436; A. Annoev, 'Vospominanie o Boevoi Sluzhbe na Kavkaze', *Voennyi Sbornik* (1877), No. 6, pp. 393–414; Ibid, 'Iz Kavkazskikh Vospominanii', *Istoricheskii Vestnik* (1906), No. 9, pp. 820–51; N. Baratov, 'Okonchatel'noe Pokorenie Vostochnogo Kavkaza – Chechni i Dagestana (1859–1909)', *Voennyi Sbornik* (1909), No. 11, pp. 223–40 (1910), No. 1, pp. 1–16, No. 3, pp. 1–22, No. 4, pp. 51–66, No. 6, pp. 17–32, No. 9, pp. 51–66; Semen Ēsadze, *Shturm Guniba i Plenenie Shamilia. Istoricheskii Ocherk Kavkazsko-Gornoi Voiny v Chechne i Dagestane* (Tiflis, 1909); E. Kozubskii, '25-e Avgusta. 1859–1909', *Russkii Arkhiv* (1909), No. 10, pp. 185–91; A[natoli Vladimirovich] O[rlov]-D[avydov], 'Chastnoe Pis'mo o Vziatii Shamilia', *Russkii Arkhiv* (1896), No. 6, cc. 1045–63 (hereafter: Orlov); M. Ia. Olszewski, 'Kniaz' Aleksandr Ivanovich Bariatinskii v 1859 i 1863 GG.', *Russkaia Starina* (1880), No. 9, pp. 97–108; P. K., 'Iz Dnevnika Dagestantsa', *Kavkazskii Sbornik*, Vol. XVIII, pp. 204–87 (hereafter: P. K.); V. Soltan, 'Na Gunibe v 1859 i 1871 GG.', *Russkaia Starina* (1892), No. 5, pp. 391–408; Ḥājj ʿAlī, pp. 56–69; Qarākhī, pp. 192–9; MRE, CPC, Russie, Consulats Divers, Vol. 5, ff. 155–6, 159, 171–2, Finot to Walewski, 14/16, 22, 31 August/12 September 1859, Nos. 22, 23, 24 respectively; G. Kvinitadze, 'Sdacha Shamilia', *Kavkaz* (Paris), 1934, No. 2, pp. 10–12.

56. See *Dvizhenie*, pp. 671–2, document No. 426, Ghāzī-Muḥammad's Letter to Shamil [11 May 1859], for a report about the completion of the fortification works.
57. Before it became known that Shamil had taken refuge on Mt. Ghunīb, Bariatinskii ordered all the roads to be blocked and patrolled to prevent the *imām*'s escape abroad – Volkonskii, '1859', p. 337. Both then and on the eve of the storm of Ghunīb the viceroy offered 10,000 *rubles* to anyone

who would capture Shamil alive – ibid., loc. cit.: Olszewski, 'Kavkaz', p. 312, note 2; Orlov, c. 1057; P. K., p. 282.

58. According to the local oral folk tradition, the *nā'ib* in charge of the position where the Russians climbed up sold out – Baddeley, *Rugged Flanks*, Vol. II, p. 49. Also, Hamzatov, pp. 270–1. And see ibid, pp. 298, 374–5, for legends about Shamil's last hours in Ghunīb and his surrender.
59. *AKAK*, Vol. XII, pp. 1275–1394, Bariatinskii's Report for the Years 1857–1859 (quotation from p. 1286). Translation based on Baddeley, pp. 471–2.
60. The Russian pre-revolutionary historiography was concerned solely with the question of whether to attribute the final conquest of Chechnia and Daghestan entirely to Bariatinskii or whether he only reaped what Vorontsov had sown. Miliutin was almost completely disregarded by both camps. See, for example, Bobrovskii, pp. 5–35; Olszewski, 'Kavkaz', pp. 289–318; A. P. Nicolaÿ, 'K Istorii Pokoreniia Vostochnogo Kavkza', *Russkii Arkhiv* (1889), No. 8, p. 531–5; A. Züssermann, 'Eshche Neskol'ko Slov o Pokorenii Vostochnogo Kavkaza. (Otvet Baronu Nikolai)', *Russkii Arkhiv* (1869), No. 11, pp. 415–20.
61. See, for example, V. G—n, 'O Vvedenii Nareznogo Oruzhiia v Kavkazskoi Armii', *Voennyi Sbornik* (1859), No. 3, Chast' Neofitsial'naia, pp. 171–6; Bobrovskii, pp. 30–3; Heimann, pp. 366–7; Il'in, pp. 275–9; *Ombres du Passé*, pp. 181–2; P. K., p. 252.
62. See note 17 above.
63. *AKAK*, Vol. XII, pp. 1275–1394, Bariatinskii's Report for the Years 1857–1859 (quotation from p. 1286). Translation based on Baddeley, p. 471.
64. *AKAK*, Vol. XII, pp. 1286–7. Translation based on Baddeley, pp. 471–2. And see Qarākhī, p. 192.
65. Ibid, p. 193. And see Orlov, c. 1053.
66. Qarākhī, p. 193.

Conclusion

1. Moshe Cherniyaq, *Toldot ha-shaḥmaṭ me-Reshito veʿ*ad Yamenu (Tel-Aviv, 1963), p. 51.
2. Bernard Shaw, *The Man of Destiny*, Introduction.
3. This was reportedly Napoleon's reply when someone mentioned the huge losses in the battle of Austerlitz.
4. *The Times*, 28 September 1859.
5. Runowski's Diary, p. 1397, entry for 4 [16] November 1859.
6. K. A. Borozdin, 'Lezginskoe Vosstanie v Kakhetii v 1863 G.,' *Russkii Vestnik* (1890), No. 7, pp. 51–77, No. 9, pp. 172–92; 'Po Povodu Vosstaniia v Zakatal'skom Okruge v 1863 Godu', *Kavkazskii Sbornik*, Vol. X, pp. 585–607.
7. Vasilii S. Krivenko, 'Vosstanie v Dagestane v 1877 Godu', *Russkii Vestnik* (1892), No. 3, pp. 167–84; 'Ochevidets', 'Lezginskii Miatezh v Iuzhnom Dagestane', ibid (1880), No. 12, pp. 663–700; N. Semenov, 'Khronika Chechenskogo Vosstaniia 1877 G.', *Terskii Sbornik*, Vol. I, Part I, pp. 1–92; A. I. Ivanov, 'Natsional'no-Osvoboditel'noe Dvizhenie v

Chechne i Dagestane v 60–70kh GG. XIX V.', *Istoricheskie Zapiski*, No. 12 (1941), pp. 165–99; idem, 'Vosstanie v Chechne v 1877 G.', ibid, No. 10 (1941), pp. 280–94.

8. Alexandre Benningsen, 'Muslim Guerrilla Warfare in the Caucasus, 1918–1928', *Central Asian Survey*, Vol. 2, No. 1 (July 1983), pp. 45–56.
9. T., 'Razboi i Samorasprava na Kavkaze,' *Vestnik Evropy* (1885), No. 12, pp. 617–46; Akhmet Ts-ov, 'Russkaia Biurokratiia i Kavkazskie Gortsy', ibid (1909), No. 9, pp. 288–315; G. A. Tkachev, *Ingushi i Chechentsy v Sem'e Narodnostei Terskoi Oblasti* (Vladikavkaz, 1911).
10. This 'treachery' was the reason for the wholesale deportation of the Chechens, Ingush, some other Caucasian Muslim nationalities and the Crimean Tatars to Siberia and Central Asia. For these deportations and rehabilitations after 1956, see Robert Conquest, *The Nation Killers: The Soviet Deportation of Nationalities* (London, 1970).
11. E.g., Markus von Czerlieu, *Unser Kaukasus und Desser Sistematisch Paciefirung* (Vienna, 1882). For the Muslim resistance to the Austrian takeover of Bosnia and Hercegovina, see Robert J. Donia, *Islam under the Double Eagle: The Muslims of Bosnia and Hercegovina, 1878–1914* (New York, 1981); Hamdija Kapidźic, *Hercegovacki Ustanak 1882 Godine* (Sarajevo, 1973).
12. 'Shamil' v Stavrople', *Sanktpeterburgskie Vedomosti*, 29 September [11 October] (No. 210), front page; 'Shamil v Malorossii', ibid, 3 [15] October (No. 213), front page, 'Puteshestvie Shamilia ot Guniba do Sanktpeterburga', *Russkii Mir*, 7 [19] October (No. 54), pp. 941-5; 'Shamil' v Publichnoi Biblioteke', ibid, 14 [26] October (No. 56), p. 975; 'Shamil'v S. Peterburge', *Russkii Khudozhestvennyi Listok*, 1 [13] November, pp. 101–4; I-skii, 'Shamil'v Rossii', *Kavkaz*, 5 [17] November 1859 (No. 87), pp. 483–5; A. Ryndin, 'Imam Shamil'v Rossii', *Istoricheskii Vestnik* (1895), No. 11, pp. 529–42; 'Shamil' Polveka Nazad v Moskve', *Russkaia Starina* (1909), No. 10, p. 310; 'Shamil' Polveka Nazad v Peterburge', ibid, No. 11, p. 576; Hamzatov, p. 270.
13. 'K Biografii Shamilia', *Krasnyi Arkhiv* (1941), No. 2 (105), pp. 115–39; Runowski's Diary, *passim*; idem, 'Znakomstvo s Shamilem', *Voennyi Sbornik* (1859), No. 11, Otdel Neofitsial'nyi, pp. 172–224; idem, 'Shamil' v Kaluge', ibid (1861), No. 1, Otdel Neoffitsial'nyi, pp. 133–201; Pawel Przeclawski, 'Shamil' i Ego Sem'ia v Kaluge. Zapiski Polkovnika P. G. Przhetslavskogo', *Russkaia Starina* (1877), No. 10, pp. 253–76, No. 11, pp. 471–506; (1878), No. 1, pp. 41–64, No. 2, pp. 265–280; Ivan Zakharin (Iakunin), 'Poezdka k Shamiliu v Kalugu v 1860 Godu. Iz Zapisok i Vospominanii', *Vestnik Evropy* (1898), No. 8, pp. 601–40; idem, 'Vstrecha s Synom Shamilia i Ego Rasskaz ob Ottse', *Russkaia Starina* (1901), No. 8, pp. 367–89; D. P. Bogdanov, 'Pamiat' Shamilia v Kaluge', *Istoricheskii Vestnik* (1913), No. 9, pp. 920–35; M. N. Chichagova, *Shamil' na Kavkaze i v Rossii. Biograficheskii Ocherk* (St. Petersburg, 1889).
14. Nowadays when Shamil is mentioned, even to students and graduates of Middle-Eastern history, the typical reaction is 'what (or where) is it?'
15. For expatriate literature on Shamil, see, for example, İsmail Berkok, *Tarihte Kafkasya* (İstanbul, 1958); Burhān al-Dīn al-Dāghistānī, 'Al-Shaykh Shāmil, Za'īm al-Qawqāz wa Shaykh al-Mujāhidīn, 1212–1278 H/ 1797–1871 M.', *Al-Risāla* (Cairo), 16 June 1947 (No. 728), pp. 677–9;

Tarik Mümtaz Göztepe, *İmam Şamil, Kafkasyanīn Büyük Harp ve İhtilal Kahramanı* (İstanbul, 1961); Hamza, 'Maşahid İslam. Şeyh Şamil', *Mihrab* (İstanbul), No. 25 (1341), pp. 32–40; Emir Ḥasan, 'Epokha Shamilia,' *Severnyi Kavkaz*, No. 1 (May 1934), pp. 12–14; idem, 'Şamil Devri', ibid, No. 4 (August 1934), pp. 2–5; Ahmet Hazer Hizal, *Kuzey Kafkasya* (*Hürriyet ve İstiklâl Davası*) (Ankara, 1961); Mustafa Zihni Hizaloğlu, *Şeyh Şamil. Şimalı Kafkasya İstiklâl Mucadeleleri* (Ankara, 1958); Baha Eddin Khoursch, *Obrona Twierdzy Achulgo przez Imama Szamila* (Warsaw, 1939); idem, 'Voennaia Operatsiia v Dagestane v 1843 Godu', *Gortsy Kavkaza*, No. 39, pp. 7–20, No. 40, pp. 10–14, No. 48, pp. 10–14, No. 49, pp. 12–20; Aytek Kundukh, *Kafkasya Müridizmi* (*Gazavat Tarihi*) (İstanbul, 1987); Süleyman Nazıf, 'Şeyh Samil', *Kuzey Kafkasya*, Vol. VIII, No. 47 (February–March 1978), p. 1; Mohyieddin Izzat Quandor, 'Muridism: A Study of the Caucasian Wars of Independence, 1819–1859', PhD thesis, Claremont, Ca., 1964; Samih Nafiz Tansu, *Çarlara Beşeğmeyen Dağlı. Şeyh Şamil* (İstanbul, 1963); Zubeyir Yetik, *İmam Şamil* (İstanbul, 1986).

16. The most comprehensive review of the description of Shamil in Soviet historiography is Lowell R. Tillet, *The Great Friendship: Soviet Historians on the Non-Russian Nationalities* (Chapel Hill N.C., 1969). An update to the mid-1970s is Moshe Gammer, 'Shamil ha-Hisṭoryografiya ha-Sovyeṭit', BA thesis, Tel Aviv University, 1976. For specific turning points, see Bertram D. Wolfe, 'Operation Rewrite: The Agony of Soviet Historians', *Foreign Affairs*, Vol. XXI, No. 1 (October 1951), pp. 39–52; Ramazan Traho, 'The "Rehabilitation" of Imam Shamil', *Caucasian Review*, No. 1 (1955), pp. 145–62; Alexandre Benningsen, 'Les Limites de la Destalinisation dans l'Islam Sovietique', *l'Afrique et l'Asie*, No. 39 (1957), pp. 31–40; Paul B. Henze, ' "Un-Rewriting" History – the Shamil Problem', *Caucasian Review*, No. 6 (1958), pp. 7–29; Lowell R. Tillet, 'Shamil and Muridism in Recent Soviet Historiography', *American Slavic and East European Review*, Vol. XX (1961), pp. 253–69; Anne Sheehy, 'Yet Another Rewrite of the History of the Caucasian War?', *Radio Liberty Research*, RL 39/84, 30 January 1984. And see Hamzatov, pp. 83, 86–92; L. Polonskii, 'Tragediia Talanta', *Bakinskii Rabochii*, 22 September 1988. For a recent attempt to rehabilitate Shamil, see A. M. Khalilov, 'Shamil v Istorii i v Pamiati Naroda', *Sovietskii Dagestan* (1988), No. 5 (September–October), pp. 31–7.
17. Muḥammad Ḥāmid, *'Ālim Islām ke Pahāle Gōrila Lidār: Imām Shāmil Raḥmat Allah 'Alayhi* (Lahore, 1974); Miskin 'Ali Hijazi, *Allah ke Sipahi* (Lahore, 1976).
18. 'Ghāzī Imām Shāmil, Raḥmat Allah 'Alayhi, Avalēn Rahbār-e Jangēhaye Gōrila-ye Islām', *Vatan* (Organ of the Islamic Union of the Provinces of Northern Afghanistan), 20 Jumādi al-Thāni 1402/4 April 1983, front page.
19. Hamzatov, p. 298.
20. The graves of some *nā'ibs* have become centres of pilgrimage; see Alexandre Benningsen and Chantale Lemercier-Quelquejai, *Le Soufi et le Commissaire* (Paris, 1986), p. 217.
21. Ibid, *passim*. Also, Alexandre Benningsen and Enders Wimbush, *Muslims of the Soviet Empire* (London, 1985), pp. 21–3.

22. For the Qādiriyya in Chechnia ('Zikrizm' in the Russian sources), see Alexandre Benningsen, 'The Qadiriyah (Kunta Haji) Tariqah in North-East Caucasus: 1850–1987', *Islamic Culture* (Hyderabad, India), No. 2–3 (April–July 1988), pp. 63–78; A. P. Ippolitov, 'Uchenie Zikr' i Ego Posledovateli', *Sbornik Svedenii o Kavkazskikh Gortsakh*, Vol. II, 17 pp. (separate pagination); G. Vertepov, 'Sud'ba Religiozno-Politicheskikh Uchenii v Chechne', *Terskie Vedomosti*, 1 [13], 6 [18] May 1892 (Nos. 52, 54), pp. 3, 2–3 respectively.

List of Sources

Note: Since an extensive bibliography on the subject has been published in *Central Asian Survey*, Vol. X, No. 1–2 only the archival and unpublished sources are listed here.

1. Archival

Austria, Haus- Hoff- und Staatsarchiv, Vienna, Staatskanzlerei [Foreign Ministry]
  X - Russland, 1830–1918.
  XIII - Türkei, 1848–1918.
  Repertorium P. Abteilung A (PA) [Diplomatic and Consular Reports]
  Staatenabteilung (Vereininkte Diplomatische Akten), Toskana
  Staatskabinets Archiv (St.K.)

Britain, The Public Record Office, London, Foreign Office Archives
  FO/60 - Persia
  FO/65 - Russia
  FO/78 - Turkey
  FO/196 - Register of the Embassy in Constantinople
  FO/352 - Papers of Lord Stratford de Redcliffe.

The Benckendorff/Lieven/Cröy archive, found in a trunk in the loft of Lime Kiln, Claydon, Ipswich, Suffolk, in August 1984.

The British Library, London
  Additional Mss. 39055, Layard Papers, Vol. CXXV. Miscellaneous Supplementary Papers 1834–1883.

The London Library, London
  Baddeley, John Frederick, 'Index Caucasica'
  Photos from the Caucasus.

France, Les Archives Nationales, Paris
  A.E. (Affaires Etrangères) BIII (Consulats, Mémoires et Documents)

Fonds de la Marine, Séries Modernes, BB^3 (Service Général, Lettres Reçues).

Ministère de la Guerre, État-Major de l'Armée de Terre, Archives Historiques, Château de Vincennes

Mémoires et Reconnaissances.
Ministère de Relations Extérieures, Archives Diplomatiques, Paris
Correspondance Politique (CP): Russie, Turquie
Correspondance Politique de Consulats (CPC):
Russie: Tiflis, Odessa, Consulats Divers.
Turquie: Erzeroum, Trebizonde.
Germany, The Hiller-von-Gaertringen papers in the possession of Dr Fr. Hiller von Gaertringen, Gärtringen.

2. Unpublished Works

Adamiyat, Fereydoun. 'The Diplomatic Relations of Persia with Britain, Turkey and Russia, 1815–1830', PhD thesis, University of London, 1949.
Aydemir, Hasan Ali. 'Şeyh Şamil ve Günümize olan Etkiden [Shaykh Shamil and his Significance to our Time]', Graduation thesis, İstanbul University, 1976.
Van-Bruinessen, Maarten Martinus. 'Agha, Shaikh and State. On the Social and Political Organization of Kurdistan', PhD thesis, Utrecht University, 1978.
Duran, Tülay. 'Şeyh Şamil ve Müridizm Hareketi [Shaykh Shamil and the Murid Movement]', Graduation thesis, İstanbul University, June 1966.
Gammer, Moshe. 'Shamil ba Historyografiya ha-Sovyetit [Shamil in Soviet Historiography]', BA thesis, Tel-Aviv University, 1976.
Luxemburg, Norman. 'Russian Expansion into the Caucasus and the British Relationship Thereto', PhD thesis, University of Michigan, 1956.
Pinson, Marc. 'Russian Expulsion of Mountaineers from the Caucasus, 1856–66 and Its Historical Background – Demographic Warfare – An Aspect of Ottoman and Russian Policies, 1854–66', PhD thesis, Harvard University, 1970.
Quandour, Mohyieddin Izzat. 'Muridism: A Study of the Caucasian Wars of Independence, 1819–1859', PhD thesis, Claremont Graduate School, 1964.
Rhinelander, Lawrence Hamilton. 'The Incorporation of the Caucasus into the Russian Empire: The Case of Georgia, 1801–1854', PhD thesis, Columbia University, 1972.

Glossary

Ar. = Arabic; Av. = Avar; C. = Caucasian (unidentified); Ch. = Chechen; Fr. = French; Gr. = Greek; R. = Russian; T. = Turkish; P. = Persian.

Abrek (C., migrant, refugee). In Shamil's terminology, a person who escaped from Russian-controlled territory and settled in the area under Shamil's rule. (See also *Muhājir.*) The Russians adopted this word, giving it the meaning of bandit, robber, outlaw.

ʿĀdat (pl *ʿĀdawāt*; Ar., customs). The traditional justice based on local customs, as opposed to the *sharīʿa.*

Āghā (T., *Ağa* pl. *āghālār, ağalar*), eunuch.

Ahl al-dhimma (Ar., the People of the Covenant). *Ahl al-kitāb* who reside in *dār al-islām* and enjoy protection of life and property on condition of acknowledging the domination of Islam and paying the *jīzya.*

Ahl al-kitāb (Ar., the People of the Book). Adherents of religions – mainly Jews and Christians – who possess holy scriptures recognised by Islam as earlier divine revelations.

Ahl al-sunna (Ar., the People of the *Sunna*). The majority stream in Islam, sometimes called 'Orthodox'. Known also as *sunnīs.*

ʿĀlim (Ar., learned man). Doctor of Muslim (religious) law.

Amān (Ar., safety, protection, quarter). A safe conduct into *dār al-Islām* given to a *ḥarbi* for a specific period of time.

Amīr al-muʾminīn (Ar., Commander of the Believers). Erstwhile official title of the caliphs. Titles of Muslim rulers, especially in areas where Arabic was used, implying full sovereignty.

Aqā (P.), master.

ʿAraba (Ar.), two-wheeled cart.

Awqāf (Ar., pl. of *waqf*). See *Waqf.*

Awul (C.), mountain village.

Bay'a (Ar.). The act of recognition by a certain number of persons, acting individually or collectively, of the authority of another person.

Bayt al-māl (Ar., the House of Wealth). Treasury.

Bek, *Bey* (T., master, ruler). In Daghestan the title of all men of noble or *janka* status.

Bidʿa (Ar., innovation). Bad innovation. Since in principle any innovation has no precedent in the Prophet's *sunna*, all innovations are regarded as *bidʿa*, at least by fundamentalists.

Dāgh, Dağ (T.), mountain.

Dār al-ḥarb (Ar., the abode of War). The areas outside the political control of Islam, which should eventually be conquered by the Muslims.

Dār al-islām (Ar., the Abode of Islam); also known as *dār al-salām* (Ar., the Abode of Peace). The area ruled and controlled by Islam.

Dhikr (Ar., remembrance). In *ṣūfī* terminology the glorifying of God with certain fixed phrases repeated in ritual order, either aloud or in the mind, accompanied by specific breathing and physical movements.

Dhimmī (Ar.). A person belonging to the *ahl al-dhimma*.

Dibīr (P., teacher). In Daghestan another name for *mūlā*. Under Shamil another name for *maʿzūm*.

Diwān (Ar., court, tribunal, council). Shamil's privy council.

Ekzekutsiia (R., from Fr.). Form of punishment in which soldiers were stationed in the offenders' houses at the owners' expense.

Firmān (Ar., decree, edict). In the Ottoman Empire an imperial decree.

Ḥajj (Ar., pilgrimage). The annual pilgrimage to Mecca, which constitutes one of the five 'pillars' (basic commandments) of Islam. Every Muslim must, if circumstances allow it, go once in his lifetime on a *ḥajj*.

Ḥājj (Ar., pilgrim). Title of person who has performed the *ḥajj*.

Ḥarbī (Ar.). A resident of *dār al-ḥarb*.

Hijra (Ar., migration). The emigration of Muḥammad and his followers from Mecca to Medina (AD 622), which is the starting point of the Muslim era. The stricter schools of Muslim law hold that the believers must follow the Prophet's example and emigrate from *dār al-ḥarb* to *dār al-islām*.

Ḥudūd (Ar., limits, borders). Punishments prescribed by the *sharīʿa*.

Hunkâr See *Khunk[y]ār*.

Imām (Ar., one in front, leader). 1. Political and religious leader – in this meaning Ghāzī Muḥammad, Ḥamza Bek and Shamil were proclaimed *imāms*; 2. Leader of the prayer in the mosque; 3. In *shīʿī* Islam *imām* is the true leader of the Muslim *umma*, successor and descendant of the Prophet and endowed with superhuman qualities, including infallibility.

Imchek (T.), milk brother.

ʿIshqallah (Ar., the love of, passion for God). The local Caucasian term for the state of unconsciousness following a period of fasting and prayers in which a *ṣūfī shaykh* sees the Prophet or one of the *ṣūfī* 'saints'.

Janka (C.). A descendant of a noble father and a commoner mother.

Jazm (Ar., cutting off, decision, resolution). A public *dhikr* ceremony in which the *murīds*, strictly supervised by their *murshid*, reach a state of ecstasy.

Jihād (Ar., effort). Holy war against the non-Muslims of *dār al-ḥarb*. Muslim legal literature (*fiqh*) distinguishes between an offensive *jihad* (to conquer parts of *dār al-ḥarb*) which is the obligation and responsibility of the ruler only and a defensive *jihad* when part of *dār al-Islām* is attacked and conquered by unbelievers. In this case participation in the *jihad* is an obligation of all able Muslims in the attacked area.

Kanly (C.), blood feud.

Kânûn (T., from Ar. *qānūn*, from Gr.). Code of regulations or laws, either adopted from non-Muslim origins or enacted by Muslim rulers to regulate areas not covered by the *sharīʿa*.

Kaziasker (T., from Ar. *Qāḍī ʿAskar*: judge of the army). In the Ottoman Empire the two chief *qāḍīs*, one of Rumeli (Thrace) and the other of Anadolu (Anatolia). The institution and title was adopted by the Russians following the annexation of the Crimean Khanate.

Khalīfa (Ar., deputy, replacement). In early Islam, caliph. In *ṣūfī* terminology the deputy of the head of an order in a specific area, authorised to spread the *ṭarīqa*, but not to initiate people into it.

Khalwa (Ar., seclusion). In *ṣūfī* terminology the retirement of a *shaykh* for prayer and reflection.

Khān, Han (T.), ruler, sovereign.

Khānum, Hanım (T.). Feminine of *khān*.

Khawārīj (Ar., pl. of *Khārijī*, one who has gone out). The earliest sect in Islam. Believed that all Muslims ('even black slaves') were eligible to the position of caliph. In later Muslim parlance the term acquired the meaning of anarchists.

Khums (Ar., fifth). The fifth part of the booty, which according to the *sharīʿ*a belongs to the ruler.

Khunk[y]ār, Hunkâr (T. from P. *khudavendegar*, lord, master). Sovereign. One of the official titles of the Ottoman *sulṭān* and the one used by the Caucasian mountaineers.

Khuṭba (Ar., speech). The sermon given at Friday noon prayers by, or in the name of, the ruler.

Kinjāl (C.), dagger.

Maḥāl (Ar., locality). In southern Daghestan the local term for community.

Maʿṣūm (Ar., protected, guarded). The title of the ruler of Ṭabarsarān.

Maʿzūm (Ar., decided, resolved). Under Shamil deputy of a *nā'ib*. Also called *dibīr*.

Mʿer (Av.), mountain.

Mirnye (R., pl. of *Mirnyi*, peaceful). Subdued population.

Mudīr (Ar., head of). Under Shamil the highest military-administrative rank, above that of *nāʾib*.

Muftī (Ar., one who gives a legal opinion). Official interpreter of the *sharīʿa*. Under Shamil head of the religious administration in the area under one *nāʾib*.

Muhājir (Ar., migrant). See *Abrek*.

Muḥtāsib (Ar., one who counts). An officer appointed to see that the commandments of Islam are obeyed, to detect offences and to punish the offenders.

Mūlā (P., master, lord, from Ar. *mawlā*). Religious functionary.

Murīd (Ar., one who desires, strives for). A disciple of a *ṣūfī shaykh*. The Russians used the term indiscriminately to apply to all the mountaineers who fought under the banner of the *imāms* and their movement – 'Muridism'.

Murshid (Ar., teacher, spiritual guide). A *ṣūfī shaykh*.

Murtāziq (Ar., kept, hired). Under Shamil full-time cavalrymen who were kept by nine other families.

Müşir (T., from Ar., *Mushīr*, adviser). Field marshal.

Musta'min (Ar., seeker of protection). A *ḥarbī* who received an *amān*.

Nā'ib (Ar., deputy). The backbone of Shamil's military-administrative structure. Governor and commander of usually one community.

Nakhw (Ar., pride). See *Jazm*.

Nemirnye (R., pl. of *nemirnyi*, unpeaceful). Unsubdued population.

Niẓām (Ar., order, organization, system, law, regulation). Under Shamil the regular infantry unit he established in imitation of Muḥammad ʿAlī's infantry. Also regulations promulgated by Shamil.

Nizam-ı cedid (T., from Ar. *al-niẓām al-jadīd*, the new organization). The European-style army established by Muḥammad ʿAlī and Maḥmūd II.

Pādishāh (P., king). Emperor. One of the titles of the Ottoman *sulṭān* and the one officially used in the empire.

Pristav (R., added, appointed, attached). Police officer, overseer, adjutant.

Qāḍī (Ar., judge). *Sharʿī* judge. In Daghestan before the *imāms*, head of a community, not necessarily an *ʿālim*. Under Shamil, a junior cleric responsible for a single mosque and its parish.

Qur'ān (Ar., from *qara'*, read, recited). Islam's holy book, which contains the divine revelation to Muḥammad.

Rābiṭa (Ar., bond). In *ṣūfī* terminology the mystical communication of thoughts between a disciple and his *murshid*, invoked by the *murīd*'s concentration.

Sayyid (Ar., master, lord). One of the titles of a descendant of the Prophet.

Serasker (T. from P. *Sir* – head and Ar. *ʿAsqar* – army), commander-in-chief.

Şeyhül islam (T., from Ar. *shaykh al-islām*). The chief *muftī* of İstanbul and the Ottoman Empire. Also known in European languages as 'the Grand *Muftī*'.

Shāh (P., king). The popular title of the rulers of Iran.

Shāhinshāh. (P., king of kings). Emperor. The official title of the rulers of Iran.

Shāmkhāl (C.). The title of the rulers of Targhū.

Sharʿī (Ar.). Adjective relating to *sharīʿa*.

Sharīʿa (Ar., approach to a drinking place). The Muslim religious law.

Sharīf (Ar., noble, honourable). See *Sayyid.*

Sharīf of Mecca. In the Ottoman period the autonomous ruler of Mecca, appointed by the Sublime Porte from among the major local families claiming descent from the Prophet.

Shashka (C.), sword.

Shaykh (Ar., old man, elder). 1. Chief of a tribe, village or quarter; 2. Religious scholar; 3. *Ṣūfī* master of an order.

Sirdār (P., head of the army). General.

Stanitsa (R., from *Stan*, camp). Cossack settlement.

Ṣūfī (Ar. from *ṣūf*, wool). A Muslim mystic.

Sulṭān (Ar., ruler). Title of Muslim rulers. One of the titles of the Ottoman ruler, and the one most used in the West.

Sunna (Ar.). Customary practice, norm, tradition.

Sunnat al-nabī (Ar., the *sunna* of the Prophet). The basis of *sunnī* law.

Sunnī (Ar.). A person belonging to *ahl al-sunna.*

Ṭa'ifa (Ar., group). A *ṣūfī* order.

Tanẓīmat (Ar., reorganisations). The common name of the reforms carried out in the Ottoman Empire between 1839 and 1876.

Ṭarīqa (Ar., way, path). Mystical method, system or school.

Taṣawwuf (Ar.). Sufism, Muslim mysticism.

Ṭawh (Ch. from T.), mountain.

Ṭawhlī (Ch., mountaineer). The Chechen name for the Daghestanis.

Tsar (R. from *tsezar*, Caesar). Emperor. Official title of the Russian rulers from Ivan III to Peter I. Continued to be their popular title until the 1917 revolution.

Tsarevich (R. from *tsesarevich*). Title of the Russian crown prince.

'Ulamā' (Ar., pl. of *'ālim*). See *'Ālim.*

Umma (Ar., nation). In Islam the Muslims constitute one nation and all the unbelievers another.

'Utsmī (C.). Title of the ruler of Qaytaq (also known as qarāqaytaq).

Uzden (C., freeman, commoner).

Valī 'ahd (P., from Ar. *walī al-'ahd*, the owner of responsibility). Title of the Qājār crown prince.

Versta (R.). Measure of length equivalent to 1.06 kilometres. Usually rendered in English as *verst*.

Wālī (Ar., protector, benefactor, companion, friend T. Vâli). 1. Governor 2. In twelver *shīʿa* the messenger of the hidden (twelfth) *imām*, who will declare and prepare for the *imām*'s reappearance.

Waqf (Ar., to bring to a stop, to cause to stand). Religious endowment.

Zakāt (Ar., righteousness, charity). Alms.

Ẓulm (Ar.), wrong, injustice, oppression, tyranny.

Zulma (Ar., appearance). The local Daghestani term for the ability of a *ṣūfī shaykh* to know of the approach of people, their identity and purpose before they enter his house.

LIST OF SOURCES

I. PR1MARY SOURCES

1. Archival and Unpublished

Austria, Haus-, Hoff- und Staatsarchiv, Vienna,
Staatskanzlerei [Foreign Ministry]
X Russland, 1830-1918
XIII Turkei, 1848-1918
Repertorium P. Abtellung A (PA) (Diplomatic and Consular Reports)
Staatenabteilung (Vereininkte Diplomatische Akten),Toskana.
Staatskabinets Archiv (St. K.)

France, Les Archives Nationales, Paris
A.E (Affairs Etrangers) BIII (Consulats, Memoirs et Documents)
Fonds de la Marine, Series Modernes, BB3 (Service General, Lettres Recues).
-------- Ministere de la Guerre, Etat-Major de l'Armee de Terre, Archives Historiques, Chateau des Vencennes,
Memoires et Reconnaissances.
-------- Ministere de Relations Exterieurs. Archives Diplomatiques, Paris
Correspondence Politique (CP): Russie, Turquie
Correspondence Politique de Consulats (CPC)
Russie: Tiflis, Odessa, Consulats Divers.
Turquie: Erzeroum,Trebizonde.

Germany, The Hiller-von-Gaertringen Papers in the passession of Dr. Fr. Hiller-von-Gaertringen, Gärtringen.

The United Kingdom, The Public Record Office, London,
Foreign Office Archives
F0/60 - Persia
F0/65 - Russia
F0/78 - Turkey
F0/196 - Register of the Embassy in Constantinople
F0/352 - Papers of Lord Stratford de Redcliffe

-------- The Benckendorff/Lieven/Croy archive found in a trunk in the loft of Lime Kiln, Claydon, Ipswich, Suffolk, in August 1984.

-------- The British Library, London,
Additional Mass. 39055, Layard Papers, Vol. CXXV, Miscellaneous Supplementary Papers 1834-1883.

-------- The London Library, London,
Baddeley, John Frederick, 'Index Caucasica'
------------ Photos from the Caucasus.

2. Published

A. B., 'Dagestan 1841 Goda [Daghestan of 1841]', *Sbornik Gazety Kavkaz*, 1846, pp. 72 - 81.

A.-D. G., 'Obzor Poslednikh Sobytii na Kavkaze [Review ot the Recent Events in the Caucasus]', *Voennyi Sbornik*, 1859, No. 10, Unofficial Part, pp. 475-518.

--------- 'Pokhod 1845 Goda v Dargo [The Expedition of 1845 to Darghiyya]', *Voennyi Sbornik*, 1859, No. 5, Unofficial Part, pp. 1-63.

A.K., 'Kazikumukhskie i Kiurinskie Khany [The Khans of Ghazi-Ghumuq and Kurah]', *Sbornik Svedenii o Kavkazskikh* Gortsakh, Vol. II (1869), 44 pp.

A.M., 'Guerre des Russes dans le Daghestan', *Nouvaue Journal Asiatique*, 1832, No.9, pp. 466-472.

[Abu Muslim Shamkhal Khan,] 'Spisok s Ob"iavleniia ili Vozzvania [Extract from a Manifesto or an Appeal]', *Sbornik Gazety Kavkaz*, 1848, Part 1, pp. 22-30.

'Adaty Darginskikh Obshchestv [The *'Adawat* of the Darghi Communities]', *Sbornik Svedenii o Kavkazskikh Gortsakh*, Vol. VII (1873), 128 pp.

'Adaty Iuzhno-Dagestanskikh Obshchestv [The *'Adawat* of the Communities of Southern Daghestan]', *Sbornik Svedenii o Kavkazskikh Gortsakh*, Vol. VIII (1875), 72 pp.

'Adaty Kumykov [The *'Adawat* of the Ghumuqs]', *Dagestanskii Sbornik*, Vol. III (1927), pp. 73-101.

Agronomov, A.I., *Dzikhad. Sviashchennaia Voina Mukhammedan [Jihad. The Holy War of the Muhammadans]*. Qazan: Tipografiia Kokovina, 1877.

Aitberov, T. M., 'Soglasheniia Avarskikh Obshchin XVIII - Nachala XIX V. [Aggreements of the Avar Communities in the Eighteenth - Beginning of the Nineteenth Centuries]', in: Kh. A. Omarov (ed.), *Pis'mennye Pamiatniki Dagestana XVIII - XIX VV.*, Makhachqala: Dagestanskii Filiial AN SSSR, 1983, pp. 15 - 32.

Alek..., 'Shamil' v Rossii (Pis'mo v Redaktsiiu), Tver' 25 Sentiabria [Shamil in Russia (Letter to the Editor) Tver 25 September [[7 October]]', *Moskovskie Vedomosti*, 29 Sentember [11 October]1859 (No. 231), p. 1678.

Al-Alqadari al-Daghistani, Mirza Hasan ibn 'Abdalla, *Kitâp Asâr-i Dâgistân [The Book of the Antiquities of Daghestan]*, Baqu: Tipografiia 1-go Tipografskogo T-va, 1903.

Anderson, Mathew Smith (ed.) *The Great Powers and the Middle East, 1774-1923.* Documents of Modern History Series, London: Edward Arnold,1970.

Andreevskii, Erast Stepanovich, 'Neskol'ko Slov o Kholere Poiavivsheisia na Kavkazskoi Linii v 1848 Godu [A Few Words About the Cholera which

Appeared on the Caucasian Line in 1848]', *Kavkazskii Kalendar'*, 1849, Part III, pp. 41-50.

Andrzejkowicz, Michal Butowt, *Skice Kaukazu [Sketches of the Caucasus]*, Warsaw: Drukarnia Jana Psurskiego, 1859.

Anoev, A., 'Iz Kavkazskikh Vospominanii [From [[My]] Caucasian Memoirs]', *Istoricheskii Vestnik*, 1906, No. 9, pp. 820-851.

---------- 'Iz Kavkazskoi Stariny [From the Caucasian Past]', *Russkii Arkhiv*, 1913, No.11, pp. 621-646.

---------- 'Vospominaniia o Boevoi Sluzhbe na Kavkaze [Memoirs of [[My]] Military Service in the Caucasus]',*Voennyi Sbornik*, 1887, No. 4, pp. 398-412, No. 5, pp. 188-204, No. 6, pp. 393-414.

Antonov, V. M., 'Epizody iz Kavkazskoi Voiny [Episodes from the Caucasian War]', *Istoricheskii Vestnik*, 1896, No. 6, pp. 798-821.

---------- 'Uzhasnyi Sud. (Epizod iz Minuvshei Kavkazskoi Voiny) [The Terrible Court Martial (An Episode from the Past Caucasian War)]', *Istoricheskii Vestnik*, 1895, No. 8, pp. 327-339.

Ashley, Evelin, *The life and Correspondence of Henry John Temple, Viscount Palmerston*, London: Richard Bentley and Son, 1879.

---------- *The Life of Henry John Temple, Viscount Palmerstone, 1846 - 1865 with Selections from His Speeches and Correspondence*, London: Richard Bentley and Son, 1876.

Astakhov, Timofei 'Vospominaniia o Zhizni i Boevoi Deiatel'nosti Kizliaro-Grebenskogo Kazach'ego Polka so Dnia Sformirovaniia Ego do 1879 Goda [Memoirs of the Life and Military Activity of the Qidhlar- Greben Cossack Regiment from the Day of its Formation to 1879]', *Terskie Vedomosti*, 23 May [14 June] (No. 41), pp. 3-4, 2 [14] June (No, 44), p. 2, 9 [21] June (No. 46), pp. 3 - 4, 20 June [2 July] (No.49), pp. 3-4, 28 July [9 August] 1891, (No. 60), pp, 3-4.

Avaliani, S.L. (ed.), *Iz Arkhiva K. E. Andreevskogo,* Vol. I, *Zapiski E. S. Andreevskogo [From the Archives of Konstantin Erastovich Aadreevskii The Notes of Erast Stepanovich Andreevskii]*. Odessa: Tipografiia Aktsionernogo Iuzhno Russkogo Obshchestva Pechatnogo Dela, 1913.

'Avarskaia Ekspeditsia [The Avar Expedition]', *Zhurnal dlia Chteniia Vospitannikam Voenno-Uchebnykh Zavedenii*, Vol. CXLII, No. 566 (15 [27] January 1860), pp. 142-176.

Al-Baghdadi, Muhammad ibn Sulayman, *Al-Hadiqa al-Nadiyya fi Adab al-Tariqa al-Naqshbandiyya [The Delicate Garden of the Regulations of the Naqshbandi Order]*, printed on the margins of al-Wayli 'Uthman ibn Sa'id, *Asfa' al-Mawarid min Silsal al-Imam Khalid [The Clearest Sources of Pure Water of the Powers of the Imam Khalid]*, Cairo, 1313 [1895].

Bapst, Germain, *Souvenirs de Deux Missions au Caucase*, Paris, 1866.

Baratov, 'Khronika Gruzinskoi Druzhiny [The Chronicle of the Georgian Militia]', *Kavkaz*, 24 June [16 July] *1853* (No. 46), pp. 202-204.

---------- 'Opisanie Nashestvii Skopishch Shamilia na Kakhetiiu v 1854 Godu [Description of the Invasion of K'akhbet'i by Shamil's Hordes in 1854]', *Kavkazskii Sbornik*, Vol. 1 (1876), pp. 237-267.

[Bariatinskii, Aleksandr Ivanovich], 'Imam Shamil i Fel'dmarshal Kn. Bariatinskii. Prikazy po Voiskam Kn. Bariatinskogo i Pis'ma Shamilia i Ego Zhen [The *Imam* Shamil and Fieldmarshal Prince Bariatisnkii. Orders of the Day by Prince Bariatinskii and Letters by Shamil and His Wives]', *Russkaia Starina*, 1880, No. 4, pp. 801 -812.

-----------'Iz Arkhiva Kniazia A. I. Bariatinskogo [From tbe Archives of Prince A. I. Bariatinskii]', *Russkii Arkhiv*, 1889, No. 9, pp. 135-143.

--------- 'Pis'ma Kniazia A.I, Bariatinskogo k N. I. Evdokimovu [Prince A. I. Bariatinskii's Letters to N. I. Evdokimov]', *Russkaia Starina*, 1886, No.10, pp.181 -184.

--------- Prikaz po Kavkazskoi Armii No. 419 [Order of the Day to the Caucasian Army, No. 419]', Special Appendix to *Kavkaz, 30* August [11 September] (No. 68) and 3 [15] September 1859 (No. 69).

Barsukov, Nikolai, 'Prebyvaniie Kniazia A. I. Bariatinskogo v S. - Peterburge i Moskve Posle Pleneniia Shamilia, 1859-1860 GG. [Prince A. I. Bariatinskii's Stay in St. Petersburgh and Moscow After the Capture of Shamil, 1859-1860]', *Russkii Vestnik*, 1902, No.5, pp. 80-92.

[Basargin, N. V.,] 'Vospominaniia N. V. Basargina ob Uchebnom Zavedenii dlia Kolonovozhatykh i ob Uchreditele Ego General-Maiore Nikolae Nikolaeviche Murav'eve [N. V. Basargin's Memoirs of the Educational Institution for Column Leaders and of its Founder, Major-General Nikolai Nikolaevich Murav'ev]', *Russkii Arkhiv*, 1868, No. 4-5, pp. 794-822.

Bartenev, Petr (ed.), *Arkhiv Kniazia Vorontsova [The Archives of Prince Vorontsov]*, XL Vols., Moscow: Tipografiia A. I. Mamontova i Ko., 1870- 1897.

[Beklemishev, Nikolai,] 'Epizod iz Ekspeditsii v Dargo v 1845 Godu. Pis'mo s Kavkaza ot 25-go Iiunia 1845 Goda [An Episode from the Expedition to Darghiyya in 1845. A Letter from the Caucasus Dated 25 June [[7 July]] 1845]', in V. Kashpirev et al (eds.), *Pamiatniki Novoi Russkoi Istorii. Sbornik Istoricheskikh Stat'ei i Materialov*, Vol. I, St. Petersburg: Tipografiia Maikova, 1871, pp. 312-316.

Beliaev, S., 'Deviat' Mesiatsev v Plenu u Chechentsev [Nine Months in the Chechens' Captivity]', *Biblioteka dlia Chteniia*, 1848, Vol. 88, pp. 71 - 108, Vol. 89, pp. 21 - 48.

Bell, James Stanislaus, *Journal of a Residence in Circassia during the Years 1837, 1838 and 1839*, London: Edward Moxon, 1840

French Transl. Louis Vivien, *Journal d'une Residence a Circassie pendant les Annees 1837, 1838 et 1839*, Paris: Arthus Bertrand, 1841.

Belokurov, Sergei Aleksandrovich, *Snosheniia Rossii s Kavkazom. Materialy Izvlechennye iz Moskovskogo Glavnogo Arkhiva Ministerstva Inostrannykh Del [Russia's Relations with the Caucasus. Documents from the Moscow Main Archives of the Ministry of Foreign Affairs]*, Vol. I, *1578 - 1613 GG*, Mosoow: Universitetskaia Tipografiia, 1889.

Benckendorff, Constantine, *Souvenirs Intimes d'une Campagne au Caucase pendant l'Ete de 1845*, ed. Grigorii Gagarin, Paris: Imprimerie de l'Institute Imperial, 1858.

Russian Version: 'Vospominaniia Grafa Konstantina Konstantinovicha Benkendorfa o Kavkazskoi Letnei Ekspeditsii 1845 Goda', ed. B. M. Koliubakin, *Russkaia Starina*, 1910, No. 4, pp. 185-201, No. 5, pp. 291-306, No. 10, pp, 79-94, No, 11, pp. 273-288, No. 12, pp. 518-532, 1911, No, 1, pp. 97-112, No. 2, pp, 270- 284, No. 3, pp. 457-470.

Benis, Adam Georges (ed.), *Une Mission Militaire Polonaise en Egypte*, Societe Royale de Geographie d'Egypte. Publications Speciales Fondee par Sa Majeste le Roi Fouad Ier et Continues sous les Auspices de Sa Majeste le Roi Farouk Ier. Cairo: l'Imprimerie de l'Institute Francaise d'Archeologie Oriental du Cair, 1938.

Benningsen, Alexandre, 'Une Temoignage Française sur Chamil et les Guerres de Caucase', *Cahiers du Monde Russe et Sovietique*, Vol. VII, No. 4 (October-December 1965), pp. 31 1-322.

Berezin, Il'ia Nikolaevich, *Puteshestvie po Vostoku [A Journey Through the Orient]*, Vol. I, *Puteshestvie po Dagestanu [A Journey Through Daghestan]*, Qazan: Universitetskaia Tipografiia, 1849.

Berg, N., 'Vstrecha s A. P. Ermolovym [[[My]] Meeting with A. P. Ermolov]', *Russkii Arkhiv*, 1872, No. 5, cc. 985-992.

Bergé, Adolphe [Berzhe, Adol'f Petrovich], 'Aleksei Petrovich Ermolov v Ego Pis'makh k Kn. M. S. Vorontsovu [Aleksei Petrovich Ermolov in His Letters to Prince M. S. Vorontsov]', *Russkaia Starina*, 1885, No. 12, pp. 523-550.

-------- *Chechnia i Chechentsy [Chechnia and the Chechens]*, Tiflis, 1859.

-------- Etnograficheskoe Obozrenie Kavkaza [An Ethnographic Survey of the Caucasus]', in V. V. Grigor'ev (ed.), *Trudy Tret'ego Mezhdunarodnogo S''ezda Orientalistov v S. - Peterburge, 1876*, St. Petersburg: Tipografiia Brat. Panteleevykh, 1879-1880, Vol. I, pp. 291-326.

-------- 'Materialy dlia Opisaniia Nagornogo Dagestana [Sources for the Description of Upper Daghestan]', *Kavkazskii Kalendar'*, 1859, Part III, pp. 249-289.

-------- 'Nikolai Nikolaevich Murav'ev, 1854-1856', *Russkaia Starina*, 1873 No. 10, pp. 599-632.

Bergé, Adolpbe et al (eds.), *Akty Sobrannye Kavkazskoi Arkheograficheskoi Kommissiei (Arkhiv Glavnogo Upravleniia Namestnika Kavkazskogo) Documents Collected by the Cuacasian Archeographical Commission (The Archives of the Central Administration of the Viceroy to the Caucasus)]*, 12 Vols., Tiflis: Tipografiia Kantselarii Glavnonachal'stvuyushchego Grazhdanskoi Chast'iu na Kavkaze, 1866-1904.

Bobrovskii, P. O., 'Imperator Aleksandr II i Ego Pervye Shagi k Pokoreniiu Kavkaza. (Epizod iz Istorii Velikoi Kavkazskoi Voiny) [The Emperor Alexander II and His First Steps Towards the Conquest of the Caucasus. (An Episode from the History of the Great Caucasian War)]', *Voennyi Vestnik*, 1897, No. 4, pp. 203-215.

-------- 'Uspekhi v Borbe s Miuridami na Vostochnom Kavkaze pri Kniaze M. S. Vorontsove. (Epizod iz Kavkazskoi Voiny) [The Successes in the Struggle with the *Murid*s in the Eastern Caucasus in the Times of Prince M. S. Vorontsov (An Episode from the Caucasian War)]', *Voennyi Sbornik*, 1896, No. 9, pp. 5-35.

Bodenstedt, Friedrich M., *Die Völker der Kaukazus und Ihre Freihatskämpfe gegen die Russen. Ein Beitrag zur Neusten Geschichte des Orients*, Frankfurt-am-Main: Verlag von Karl Bernard Kizius, 1849 (Second Edition).

French Trans. E. de Salus-Kyrburg, *Les Peoples du Caucase et leur Guerre d'Independence contre la Russie. Pour Servir a l'Histoire la plus Recent de l'Orient*, Paris: Dentu, 1859.

Bogdanov, D. P., 'Pamiat' Shamilia v Kaluge [The Memory of Shamil in Kaluga]', *Istoricheskii Vestnik*, 1913, No. 9, pp. 920-935.

Boratav, Pertev, 'La Russie dans les Archives Ottomans. Un Dossier Ottoman sur l'Imam Chamil', *Cahiers du Monde Russe et Sovietique*, Vol. X, No. 3-4 (July-December 1969), pp. 524-535.

Borozdin, K., 'Vospominaniia o N. N. Murav'eve [Reminiscences About N. N. Murav'ev]', *Istoricheskii Vestnik*, 1890, No. 1, pp. 86-101, No. 2, pp. 307-323.

B[ot'ianov], T., *Vospominaniia Sevastopol'tsa i Kavkaztsa 45 Let Spustia [Memoirs of a Veteran of [[the War in]] Sevastopol and the Caucasus Fourty Five Years Later]*, Vitebsk: Gubernskaia Tipolitografiia, 1899.

Bronevskii, Semen Bogdanovich, *Noveishie Geograficheskie i Istoricheskie Izvestiia o Kavkaze [The Most Recent Geofraphical and Historical Information about the Caucasus]*, Moscow:_Tipografiia S. Selivanovskogo, 1823.

Bronevskii, Vladimir, *Poezdka na Kavkaz [A Journey to the Caucasus]*, St. Petersburg: Tipografiia Ekspeditsii Zagotovleniia Gosudarstvennykh Bumag, 1834.

Brümmer, Eduard [Brimmer, Eduard Vladimirovich], 'Sluzhba Artileriiskogo Ofitsera Vospitavshegosia v I Kadetskom Korpuse i Vypushchennogo v 1815 Godu [The Service of an Artillery Officer from the Class of 1815 of the First Cadett Corps]', *Kavkazskii Sbornik*, Vol. XV (1894), pp. 52-260, Vol. XVI (1895), pp. 1-234, Vol. XVII (1896), pp. 1-174, Vol. XVIII (1897), pp. 1-131.

Bünting, *Ein Besuch bei Schamyl. Brief Einer Preussen*, Berlin: Schneider und Co., 1855.

English Trans., *A Visit to Schamyl*, London: John W. Parker & Son, 1857.

Bushuev, Semen Kuzmin, 'Pis'ma Vikonta G. Kastil'ona k Gizo (24 Aprelia 1844 - 4 Marta 1846 G.) [The Letters of the Viscount G. Castillon to Guizot (24 April 1844 - 4 March 1846)]', *Istorik Marksist*, 1936, No. 5 (57), pp. 105-123.

Butkov, Petr Grigor'evich, *Materialy dlia Novoi Istorii Kavkaza s 1722 po 1803 G. [Sources to the Modern History of the Caucasus from 1722 to 1803]*, St. Petersburg: Tipografiia Imperatorskoi Akademii Nauk, 1869.

Canard, M., 'Chamil et Abdel-Kader', *Annales de l'Institute des Etudes Orientales*, Vol. XIV (1956), pp. 231 -256.

Cattaui, Rene (ed.), *Le regne de Mohamed Ali d'Apres les Archives Russe en Egypt*, Vol. I, Cairo: l'Imprimerie de l'Institute Francais d'Archeologie Orientale du Cair, 1931. Vols. II - III, Rome: Instituto Poligrafico dello Stato, 1933-1936.

Chekh, I. S., 'Ocherk iz Staro Kavkazskoi Zhizni [Features from the Old Caucasian Life],' *Russkii Vestnik*, 1891, No. 4, pp. 149-176, No. 9, pp. 96-116, No. 11, pp. 199-218, 1892, No. 4, pp. 54-89, No. 7, pp. 96-114, No. 10, p. 210-230, 1893, No. 5, pp. 194-213, No. 8, pp. 130-140, 1894, No. 7, pp. 114-122.

Chernozubov, Fedor, 'Dar Kavkazu ot Kniazia M. S. Vorontsova [Prince M. S. Vorontsov's Gift to the Caucasus]', *Russkii Arkhiv*, 1912, No. 4, pp, 606-610.

[Chertkov, A. A.,] 'Aleksandr Alekseevich Bashenev (Iz Kavkazskikh Vospominanii A. A. Chertkova) [Aleksandr Alekseevich Bashenev (From A. A. Chertkov's Memoirs from the Caucasus)]', *Russkii Arkhiv*, 1881, No. 3, pp. 191-227.

Chudinov, V., 'Okonchatel'noe Pokorenie Osetii [The Final Conquest of the Ossets]', *Kavkazskii Sbornik*, Vol. XIII (1889), pp. 1 - 114.

Connel, Brian, (ed.), *Regina v. Palmerstone. The Correspondence between Queen Victoria and Her Foreign and Prime Minister, 1837 - 1865* London: Evans Brothers Ltd., 1962.

D. B., 'Nekotorye Biograficheskie Podrobnosti o Shamile [Some Biographical Details about Shamil]', *Voennyi Sbornik*, 1859, No. 12, Non-official Part, pp. 512-524.

'Dagestan i Imam Ego Shamil' [Daghestan and Its *Imam* Shamil]', *Podsnezhnik*, 1859, No. 10, pp. 91-111.

Dagestanskii Filiial Akademii Nauk SSSR, Institut Istorii, Iazyka i Literatury, 'Dokumenty o Dvizhenii Gortsev Severo-Vostochnogo Kavkaza 20-50kh GG. XIX V. pod Rukovodstvom Shamilia [Documents on the Movement of the Mountaineers of the North-Eastern Caucasus in the 1820s-1850s under the Leadership of Shamil]', *Uchennye Zapiski*, Vol. II (1957), pp. 262-287.

Al-Daghistani al-Ghazi-Ghumuqi, Jamal al-Din, *Al-Adab al-Mardiyya fi al-Tariqa al-Naqshbandiyya [The Pleasant Rules of the Naqshbandi Tariqa]*, Petrovsk: Tipo-Litografiia A. M. Mikhailova, 1323/1905

Russian Trans., 'Abdallah 'Umarov, 'Adabul-Marzia (Pravila Dostodolzhnykh Prilichii)', *Sbornik Svedenii o Kavkazskikh Gortsakh*, Vol. II, 22 pp, (separate pagination).

Reprint of the two above: *Al-Adab al-Marziya. A Naqshbandi Treaty*, Reprint Series No. 10, Oxford: The Society for Central Asian Studies, 1986.

Danilevskii, G. P., 'Shamil' v Malorossii [Shamil in Lesser Russia [[i,e the Ukraine]]]', in *idem, Sochineniia [Works]*, Vol. XX, St. Petersburg: Izdanie A.F. Marksa, 1901 (eighth edition).

Danilewski, N., *Der Kaukazus. Physisch-Geographisch, Statistisch, Ethnographisch und Strategisch*, Leipzig: Verlag von J. J. Weber, 1847.

Daragan, 'La Guerre de la Russie dans le Caucase. Le Muridisme et ses Apotres -- Molla Mohammed, Kazy Mahoma, Hamzet Bek et Schamyl (Samuel)', *Revue d'Orient*, 1860, No. 12, pp.17-29, 89-104. French Trans., E. Dulaurier.

D[awid], W[incenty], 'Wspomnienia z Podrozy i Wycieczek po Kaukazie [Memoirs from a Journey and an Excursion in the Caucasus]', *Biblioteka Warszawska*, Vol. III (1854), pp. 28-45.

-------- *Tehe Czyli Zberzenie Aulu Duby. Powiesc Kaukazka [Tehe or the Burning of Duba's Awul. A Caucasian Story]*, Warsaw: Drukarnia Gazety Codziennej, 1860.

Delwig [Del'vig], Nikolai Ivanovich, 'Vospominanie ob Ekspeditsii v Dargo [Memoirs of the Expedition to Darghiyya]', *Voennyi Sbornik*, 1864. No. 7, Non-official Part, pp. 189-230.

Depping, G. *Schamyl, le Prophete du Caucase*, Paris, 1854.

Derzhavin, A., 'Razskaz Byvshego U[nter]-O[fitsera] Apsheronskogo Polka Samoily Riabova o Svoei Boevoi Sluzhbe na Kavkaze [The Story of Samoila Riabov, A Former N.C.O. of the Apsheron Regiment, About His Military Service in the Caucasus]', *Kavkazskii Sbornik*, Vol. XV111 (1897), pp. 352-381.

Didimov, K., 'Ekspeditsiia v Argunskoe Ushchel'e s 15-go Ianvaria po 18-e Aprelia 1858 Goda [The Expedition into the Argun Defile, 15 [[27]] January - 18 [[30]] April 1858]', *Voennyi Sbornik*, 1859, No. 7, Non-official Part, pp. 89- 112.

-------- 'Ekspeditsiia v Chanty-Argunskoe Ushchel'e s 1-go Iiula po 19-e Avgusta 1858 Goda [The Expedition into the Defile of the Chanti-Argun, 1 [[13]] July - 19 [[31]] August 1858]', *Voennyi Sbornik*, 1859, No. 8, Non-official Part, pp. 255-284.

Ditson, Gordon Leighton, *Circassia or a Tour to the Caucasus*, New York: Stringer and Townsend, 1850.

[Dolivo-]Dobrovol'skii-Evdokimov, Viktor Iakovlevich, 'Iz Kavkazskoi Zhizni. 1848 God v Dagestane [From [[Myl] Life in the Caucasus. 1848 in Daghestan]', *Kavkazskii Sbornik*, Vol. VI (1882), pp. 683-722.

Also published in *Russkii Vestnik*, 1862, No. 7, pp 35-66 under the Pseud. 'Kavkazets' (Caucasian).

-------- 'Ekspeditsiia 1850-go Goda na Lezginskoi Linii [The Expedition of 1850 on the Lesghian Line]', *Kavkazskii Sbornik*, Vol. VII (1883], pp. 613-647, Trans. from the French: P.Wolchowski.

-------- 'Ekspeditsiia v Salataviiu v 1858 Godu [The Expedition into Salatawh in 1858]', *Kavkazskii Sbornik*, Vol. IV (1879), pp. 39-50.

Dondukov-Korsakov, A. M., 'Moi Vospominaniia [My Memoirs]', *Starina i Novizna*, Vol. V (1902), pp. 158-223, Vol. VI (1908), pp. 41-215.

Dragun (pseud.), 'Po Povode Stat'i: 'Vospominanie Dragunskogo Ofitsera o Dele 8 Aprelia 1851 Goda [A Reaction to the Article: 'Memoirs of a Dragoons Officer on the Battle of 8 [[20]] April 1851]', *Voennyi Sbornik*, 1860, No. 11, Non-official Part, pp. 81-96.

Drozdov, I., 'Nachalo Deiatel'nosti Shamilia [The Beginning of Shamil's Activity]', *Kavkazskii Sbornik*, Vol. XX (1899), pp. 250-298.

Dumas, Alexandre, *Le Caucase. Impressions de Voyage* Paris: Librairie Theatrale, 1859.

'Dva Imana [*sic*!] ili Istreblenie Doma Avarskogo. Istoricheskoe Povestvovanie o Kavkaze [Two *Imams* or the Annihilation of the Avar Ruling House. A Historical Narrative about the Caucasus]', *Russkii Arkhiv*, 1915, No.1, pp.116-146, No. 2, pp. 231-258, No. 3, pp. 358-385.

Dzierzynski [Dzierzhynskii], V.S., 'Iz Kavkazskoi Voiny. Po Povodu 50-ti Letii Osady Mesel'degerskogo Ukrepleniia Shamilem v 1853 Godu [From the Caucasian War. On the Fiftieth Anniversary of Shamil's Siege of the Fort of Mesed el-Kher]', *Voennyi Sbornik*, 1903, No. 9, pp. 50-68, No. 10, pp. 27-61.

Eichwald, Edward, *Reise auf dem Caspischen Meere und in dem Caucasus Internomen in den Jahren 1825 - 1826*, Stuttgart and Tübingen: Verlag der J.G. COTTA'scher Buchhandlung 1834-1837.

Egorov, M., 'Deistviia Nashikh Voisk v Chechne s Kontsa 1852 po Nachalo 1854 Goda [The Actions of Our Forces in Chechnia from the End of 1852 to the Beginning of 1854]', *Kavkazskii Sbornik*, Vol. XVI (1895), pp. 352-404.

'Ekspeditsiia v Dargo 1845 Goda [The 1845 Expedition to Darghiyya]', *Voennyi Zhurnal*, 1855, No, IV, pp. 27 -44.

Reprinted in *Zhurnal dlia Chteniia Vospitannikam Voenno-Uchebnykh Zavedenii*, Vol. CXXIII, No. 490 (15 [27] November 1856), pp. 182-202.

Erhorn, I., *Kaukasien*, Berlin: Otto Stollberg, 1942.

[Ermolov, Aleksei Petrovich] 'Aleksei Petrovich Ermolov (Materialy dlia Biografii, Ego Razskazy i Perepiska), [Aleksei Petrovich Ermolov (Sources for His Biography, His Reminiscences and Correspondence]', *Russkaia Starina*, 1896, No.10, pp. 97-120, No.12, pp. 565-583.

-------- 'Aleksei Petrovich Ermolov' [Letters to R. I. Hooven], *Russkaia Starina*, 1876, No. 10, pp. 225-250.

-------- 'Aleksei Petrovich Ermolov. Pis'ma Ego k Kniaziu V. O. Bebutovu [Aleksei Petrovich Ermolov. His Letters to Prince V. O. Bebutov]', *Russkaia Starina*, 1873, No. 3, pp. 431 -456.

-------- 'Aleksei Petrovich Ermolov v Pis'makh k Byvshim Svoim Ad"iutantam [Aleksei Petrovich Ermolov in His Letters to His ex-ADCs]', *Russkii Arkhiv*, 1906, No. 9, pp. 38-88.

-------- 'A. P. Ermolov k Nik. Ger. Ustrialovu [A. P. Ermolov to Nik. Ger. Ustrialov]', *Russkaia Starina*, 1872, No. 9, pp. 290-292.

--------- 'A. P. Ermolov k Pav. Nik. Ushakovu [A. P. Ermolov to Pav. Nik. Ushakov]', *Russkaia Starina*, 1872, No.11, p. 538.

--------- 'Doneseniia i Pis'ma A. P. Ermolova [A. P. Ermolov's Reports and Letters]', *Russkaia Starina*, 1872, No. 11, pp. 453-501.

-------- 'Dva Pis'ma A. P. Ermolova k Grafu (Kniaziu) M. S. Vorontsovu (18 I4) [Two Letters from A. P. Ermolov to Count (Prince) M. S. Vorontsov (1814)]', *Russkii Arkhiv*, 1905, No. 2, pp. 314-319.

-------- 'Iz Pisem A. P. Ermolova k Denisu Davydovu [From the Letters of A. P. Ermolov to Denis Davydov]', *Voennyu Sbornik*, 1906, No.12, pp. 245-250.

-------- 'Pis'ma A. P. Ermolova k Petru Andreevichu Kikinu, 1817-1832 [A. P. Ermolov's Letters to Petr Andreevich Kikin, 1817-1832]', *Russkaia Starina*, 1872, No. 11, pp. 502-537.

-------- 'Pis'mo A. P. Ermolova Grafu D. A. Gur'evu 17 Iiunia 1822 G. [A. P. Ermolov's Letter to Count D. A. Gur'ev, 17 [[29]] June 1822]', *Russkaia Starina*, 1892, No. 10, p. 215.

--------'Zametki A. P. Ermolova ob Ego Molodosti [A. P. Ermolov's Remarks about His Youth]', *Russkii Arkhiv*, 1867, No. 3, pp. 366-375.

Ermolov, N. P., *Zapiski Alekseia Petrovicha Ermolova [The Notes of Aleksei Petrovich Ermolov]*, Moscow: Universitetskaia Tipografiia, 1865-1868.

'Ermolov, Dibich i Paskevich, 1826-1827 [Ermolov, Diebitsch and Paskiewicz, 1826-1827]', *Russkaia Starina*, 1872, No. 5, pp. 706 - 726, No. 7, pp. 39-69, No. 9, pp. 243-280.

'Ermolov, Dibich i Paskevich, 1827 [Ermolov, Diebitsch and Paskiewicz, 1827]' *Russkaia Starina*, 1880, No. 11, pp. 617-626.

E--skii, I, 'Vospominaniia Starogo Kavkaztsa [Memoirs of a Veteran of the Caucasus]', *Russkaia Starina*, 1906, No. 9, pp.715-749.

[Evdokimov, Nikolai Ivanovich], 'Voennye Deistviia s Levogo Kryla. Donesenie General-Leitenanta Evdokimova ot 11 Aprelia za No. 212 [Military Actions on the Left Wing. A Report by Lieutenant-General Evdokimov, 11 [[23]] April, No. 212]', *Kavkaz*, 25 April [7 May] 1859 (No. 31), pp. 157-158.

Evropeus, I. I., 'Nikolai Nikolaevich Murav'ev', *Russkaia Starina*, 1874, No. 9, pp. 181-184.

---f ---v, 'Richinskoe Delo 1-go Maia 1842 Goda [The Battle of Richa, 1 [[13]] May 1842]', *Sbornik Gazety Kavkaz*, 1846, pp. 103-108.

[Fadeev, Rostislav Andreevich], 'Pis'ma Rostislava Andreevicha Fadeeva k Rodnym [Rostislav Andreevich Fadeev's Letters to Relatives]', *Russkii Vestnik,* 1897, No. 8, pp. 1-14, No. 9, pp. 1-17, No. 10, pp. 63-69, No. 11, pp. 88-96.

Filonov, S. and Tomkeev, V. 'Kavkazskaia Liniia pod Upravleniem Generala Emanuelia [The Caucasian Line Under the Command of General Emmanuel]', *Kavkazskii Sbornik*, Vol. XV (1894), pp. 327-450, Vol. XIX (1898), pp. 120-220, Vol. XX 11899), pp. 142-249.

Firqovich, Avraham, *Sefer Avney Zikkaron [The Book of the Stones of Memory]*, Vilna: Shmu'el Yosef Fin ve-Avraham Tsvi Rozenqrants, 5632 [1872].

von Freygan, W. P., *Letters from the Caucasus to Which Are Added the Account of a Journey into Persia in 1812 and an Abriged History of Persia Since Nadir Shah*, London: John Murrey, 1823, Trans. from French.

Gabrichidze, M. M. (ed.), *Shamil'-- Stavlennik Sultanskoi Turtsii i Angliiskikh Kolonizatorov. (Sbornik Dokumental'nykh Materialov) [Shamil -- the Stooge of Turkey of the Sultans and the English Colonialists. (A Collection of Documentary Sources)]*, Tbilisi: Gosizdat Gruzinskoi SSR -- Sector Politicheskoi Literatury, 1953.

Gagarin, A.I., 'Zapiski o Kavkaze [Notes About the Caucasus]', *Voennyi Sbornik*, 1906, No. 2, pp. 25-38, No. 3, pp. 15-32, No. 4, pp. 13-32.

[Gagarin, Grigorii Grigorievich,] *Le Caucase Pittoresque. Desine d'Apres Nature par le Prince Gregoir Gagarine avec une Introduction et un Texte Explicatif par le Comte Ernest Stackelberg*, Paris: Gide et J. Bandry, 1849.

-------- *Scenes, Paysage, Moeurs et Costume du Caucase Desines d'Apres Nature par le Prince Gregoire Gagarine et Accompagne d'un Texte par le Comte Ernest Stackelberg*, Paris: A. Houser, 1846.

Gagarin, P. D., 'Vospominaniia o Fel'dmarshale Kniaze Aleksandre Ivanoviche Bariatinskom [Reminiscenoes About Fieldmarshal Prince Alexander Ivanovich Bariatinskii]', *Russkii Vestnik*, 1888, No. 7, pp. 126-142.

Gamba, Jean François, *Voyage Dans la Russie Meridional et Particulierment dans les Provinces au dela du Caucase Fait Depui 1820 Jusqu'a 1824*, Paris: C. J. Trouve, 1826 (Second Edition).

Gammer, Moshe, 'Vorontsov's 1845 Expedition Against Shamil: A British Report', *Central Asian Survey*, Vol. 4, No. 4, (Autumn 1985), pp. 13-33

Gamrekeli, Vakhtang Nikolaevich (ed.), *Dokumenty po Vzaimootnosheniiam Gruzii s Severnym Kavkazom v XVIII V. [Documents on the Relations Between Georgia and the Northern Caucasus in the Eighteens Century]*, Tbilisi: 'Mitsniereba', 1968.

Glinoetskii, I., 'Poezdka v Dagestan (Iz Putevykh Zametok Vedenykh na Kavkaze v 1861 Godu [Journey to Daghestan (Excerpts from Notes Written in the Caucasus in 1861)]', *Voennyi Sbornik*, 1862, No. 1, Non-official Part, pp. 119-164, No. 2, Non-official Part, pp. 387-422, No. 3, Non-official Part, pp. 61-90.

G---n, V., 'O Vvedenii Nareznogo Oruzhiia v Kavkazskoi Armii [On the Introduction of Rifles into the Caucasian Army]', *Voennyi Sbornik*, 1859, No. 3, Non-official Part, pp. 171-176.

[Golovin, Evgenii Aleksandrovich,] *Ocherk Polozheniia Voennykh Del na Kavkaze s Nachala 1838 do Kontsa 1842 Goda [Survey of the Military Activities in the Caucasus from the Beginning of 1838 to the End of 1842]*, Riga: 1846 (printed in a very limited number ofcopies)

Reprint: 'Ocherk Polozheniia Voennykh Del na Kavkaze s Nachala 1838 do Kontsa 1842 Goda [Survey of the Military Activities in the Caucasus from the Beginning of 1838 to the End of 1842]', *Kavkazskii Sbornik*, Vol. II (1877), pp. 1 -74.

Golovin, Ivan, *The Caucasus*, London: Trubner and Co., 1854.

Gorchakov, Nikolai, 'Ekspeditsiia v Dargo (1845 G). (Iz Dnevnika Ofitsera Kurinskogo Polka) [The Expedition to Darghiyya (1845). (From the Diary of an Officer in the Kurin Regiment)]', *Kavkazskii Sbornik*, Vol. II, (1877), pp. 117-141.

-------- 'Vtorzhenie Shamilia v Kabardu v 1846 Godu. Iz Zapisok Ofitsera Kurinskogo Polka [Shamil's Incursion iInto Ghabarta in 1846. From the Notes of an Officer in the Kurin Regiment]', *Kavkazskii Sbornik*, Vol. IV, (1879), pp. 19-37.

Gordanov, B. A. (ed.), *Materialy po Obychnomu Pravu Kabardintsev. Pervaia Polovina XIX V. [Sources on the Customary Law of the Ghabartians. The First half of the Nineteenth Century]*, Nal'chik: Kabardinskoe Knizhnoe Izdatel'stvo, 1956.

Gordon, Jakub, *Kaukaz czyli Ostatnie Dni Szamila. Powiesc Historyczna [The Caucasus or the Last Days of Shamil. An Historical Story]*, Lipsk: F. A. Brockhaus, 1865.

-------- *Turysta z Musu [A Tourist out of Necessity]*, Lwów: Wlasnosc i Naklad H. Bodeka, 1873.

Goriunov, 'Vospominaniia iz Kavkazskoi Voennoi Zhizni [Memoirs of [[My]] Milltary Life in the Caucasus]', *Istoricheskaia Biblioteka*, 1879, No. 8, pp. 39-78, No. 9, pp. 79-122, No. 12, pp. 1-38.

[Grabbe, Paul [[Pavel Khristoforovich]]], 'Iz Dnevnika i Zapisnoi Knizhki Grafa P. Kh. Grabbe [[[Excerpts]] from the Diary and Notebook of Count P. Kh. Grabbe]', *Russkii Akhiv*, 1888, No. 6, pp. 101-132.

Gralewski, Mateusz, *Kaukaz. Wspómnienia z Dwunastoletniej Niewoli [The Caucasus. Memoirs of a Twelve Year Long Imprisonment]*, Biblioteka Historyczna, No. 23. Lwów: Naklad Ksiegarni Polskiej, 1877.

Grümberg [Griumberg], G. E. and Bushuev, Semen Kuzmin, (eds.), *Materialy po Istorii Dagestana i Chechni [Sources to the History of Daghestan and Chechnia]*, Vol. III, Part 1, *1801-1839,* Makhachqala: Dagestanskoe Gosudarstvennoe Izdatel'stvo, 1940.

Grigor'ev, 'Vospominanie o Dele Bliz' Ukrepleniia Achkhoi [Reminiscence About the Battle Near the Fort of Achkhi]', *Voennyi Sbornik*, 1893, No. 2, Non-offocial Part, pp. 347-349.

Grzegorzewski [Grzhegorzhevskii], Isidor A., 'General-Leitenant Kliuki-fon-Klugenau. Ocherk Voennykh Deistvii i Sobytii na Kavkaze, 1818- 1850 [Lieutenant-General Kluge von Klugenau. A Survey of the Military Activities and Events in the Caucasus, 1818- 1850]', *Russkaia Starina*, 1874, No. 9, pp.131-152, No.11, pp. 497-515, 1875, No. 3, pp. 545-554, 1876, No. 1, pp. 144-162, No. 2, pp. 377-387, No. 3, pp. 646-658, No. 6, pp. 351-382.

Güldenstadt, Johann Anton, *Beschreibung der Kaukazischer Länder*, Berlin: Verlag der Stuhischen Buchhandlung, 1834.

Hajiev [Gadzhiev], V. G. and Ramazanov, Kh. Kh. (eds.), *Dvizhenie Gortsev Severo-Vostochnogo Kavkaza v 20 - 50kh GG XIX Veka. Sbornik Dokumentov [The Movement of the Mountaineers of the North-Eastern Caucasus in the 1829s - 1850s. A Collection f Documents]*, Makhachqala: Dagestanskoe Knizhenoe Izdatel'stvo, 1959.

Hajj 'Ali [Gadzhi Ali], 'Skazanie Ochevidtsa o Shamile [A Witness's Testimony about Shamil]', *Sbornik Svedenii o Kavkazskikh Gortsah*, Vol. VII (1873), 76 pp. (separate pagination), Trans. from Arabic.

[van Halen, Juan,] *Narrative of Don Huan van Halen's Imprisonment in the Dungeons of the Inquisition at Madrid and his Escape in 1817 and 1818, to which Are Added his Journey to Russia, his Campaign with the Army of the Caucasus and his Return to Spain in 1821*, London: Henry Colburn, 1827.

von Haxthausen, August, *Tribes of the Caucasus with an Account of Schamyl and the Murids*, Trans. J. E. Taylor, London: Chapman and Hall, 1855.

-------- *The Russian Empire. Its People, Institutions and Resources*, Trans. Robert Earie, London: Chapman and Hall, 1856.

Herzig [Gertsyk], Viktor, 'Dzhemal'-Eddin, Starshii Syn Shamilia [Jamal al-Din, Shamil's Eldest Son]', *Russkii Arkhiv*, 1890, No. 9, pp. 111-112.

Heimann [Geiman], Vasilii Aleksandrovich, '1845 God [The Year 1845]', *Kavkazskii Sbornik*, Vol. III (1879), pp. 251 -375.

Hommaire de Hell, Xavier, *Situations de Russes dans le Caucase*, Paris: Imprimerie de la Societe Orientale, 1844. (Offprint from *Revue de l'Orient.*)

-------- *Travels in the Steppes of the Caspian Sea, the Crimea, the Caucasus etc.*, With Additions from Various Sources, London: Chapman and Hall, 1847.

Hurewitz, Jacob Coleman (ed.), *The Middle East and North Africa in World Politics. A Documentary Record,* Vol I: *European Expansion, 1533 - 1914*, New Haven: Yale Vniversity Press, 1975 (Second, Revised and Enlarged edition.)

Ia., '1-go Aprelia 1859/94 Goda (Vospominaniia Veterana) [1 [[13]] April 1859/94 (A Veteran's Reminiscence)]', *Terskie Vedomosti*, 1 [13] April 1894 (No. 39), pp. 2-3.

I. I. U., 'Karimet, Nevestka Shamilia -- Zhertva Aziatskoi a Zatem Russkoi Politiki [Karima, Shamil's Daughter-in-Law -- the Victim of Asian and Afterwards Russian Politics]', *Istoricheskii Vestnik*, 1910, No. 9, pp. 922-933.

I. P., 'Iz Boevykh Vospominanii. Razskaz Kurintsa [[[Excerpts]] from [[My]] Military Memoirs. The Story of a Soldier in the Kurin Regiment]', *Kavkazskii Sbornik,* Vol. IV, (1879), pp. 51-67.

Ignatius [Ignatsiius], Nikolai, 'Osada Shamilem Mesedel'gerskogo Ukrepleniia v 1853 G. (Sostavlenno po Dokumentam i Razskazam Ochevidtsev) [Shamil's Siege of the Fort of Mesed el-Kher in 1853 (Based on Documents and Eye-witnesses' Accounts]', *Inzhenernyi Zhurnal*, 1860, No. 1 , Non-official Part, pp. 1 -30.

Reprinted in *Sbornik Opisanii Osad Krepostei i Ukreplenii* Vol. 1 (St. Petersburg, 1869), pp. 126-151.

Il'in, P., 'Iz Sobytii na Kavkaze. Nabegi Shamilia v 1843 Godu [From the Events in the Caucasus. Shamil's Raids in 1843]', *Russkii Vestnik*, 1872, No. 7, pp. 216-314.

Iosseliani, P., *Putevye Zapiski po Dagestanu v 1861 Godu [Road-Notes from Daghestan in 1861]*, Tiflis: Tipografiia Glavnogo Upravleniia Namestnika Kavkazskogo, 1862.

Ippolitov, A. P., 'Etnograficheskie Ocherki Argunskogo Okruga [Ethnographic Sketches of the Arghun Area]', *Sbornik Svedenii o Kavkazskikh Gortsakh*, Vol. I (1868), 52 pp. (separate pagination).

-------- 'Uchenie Zikr' i Ego Posledovateli [The Doctrine of *Dhikr* [[i. e. the Qadiriyya]] and Its Followers]', *Sbornik Svedenii o Kavkazskikh Gortsakh*, Vol. II (1869), 17 pp.

Isakov, P. N., 'Iz Zapisok N. V. Isakova. Kavkazskie Vospominaniia. (Period Voiny s Gortsami 1846 i 1848 Godov) [From the Notes of Nikolai Vasil'evich. Isakov. Caucasian Memoirs. (The Period of the War with the Mountaineers in 1846 and 1848)]', *Russkaia Starina*, 1917, No. 2, pp. 161-193, No. 3, pp. 321-336, No. 4-6, pp. 46-62, No. 7-9, pp. 1-22, No 10-12, pp.13-32.

I--skii, V., 'Shamil' v Rossii [Shamil in Russia]', *Kavkaz*, 5 [17] November 1859 (No. 87), pp. 483-485.

Iurov, A., '1843-i God na Kavkaze [The year 1843 in the Caucasus]', *Kavkazskii Sbornik*, Vol. VI (1882), pp. 1-219 (+ 40 pp. of Appendices).

-------- '1844-i God na Kavkaze [The year 1844 in the Caucasus]', *Kavkazskii Sbornik*, Vol. VII (1883), pp. 157-382.

-------- 'Tri Goda na Kavkaze, 1837-1839 [Three Years in the Caucasus, 1837-1839]', *Kavkazskii Sbornik*, Vol. VIII (1884), pp.1-240 (+18 pp. of Appendices). Vol. IX (1885), pp. 1-155 (+32 pp. of Appendices).

Iurov, A. and N. V.,'1840, 1841 i 1842-i Gody na Kavkaze [The Years 1840, 1841 and 1842 in the Caucasus]', *Kavkazskii Sbornik*, Vol. X (1886), pp. 225-404, Vol. XI (1887), pp. 187-301, Vol. XII (1888), pp. 217-344, Vol. XIII (1889), pp. 335-424, Vol. XIV (1890), pp. 303-444.

Ivanov, Osip, 'Razskaz Soldata [A Soldier's Story]', *Kavkaz*, 7 [19] October 1853 (No. 74), pp. 321-323.

Ivanov, S., 'O Sblizhenii Gortsev s Russkimi na Kavkaze [On Rapprochement Between the Mountaineers and the Russians in the Caucasus]', *Voennyi Sbornik*, 1859, No.9, Non-official Part, pp.541 -543.

'Izmeneniia na Lezginskoi Linii [The Changes on the Lesghian Line]', *Zapiski Kavkazskogo Otdela Imperatorskogo Geograficheskogo Obshchestva*, Vol. II (1853), pp. 224-228.

'Izvestiia s Kavkaza [Nesvs from the Caucasus]', *Sbornik Gazety Kavkaz*, 1847, Vol. I, pp. 9-10, 27-30, 109-112, 156-158, 180-182, 260-261, Vol. II, pp. 39-42, 49-51, 56-58, 90-92.

Jaworski, H., *Wspómnienia Kaukazu [Memoirs from the Caucasus]*, Poznan: Naklad I. K. Zupanskiego, 1877.

Al-Jaza'iri, Muhammad ibn 'Abd al-Qadir, *Kitab Tuhfat al-Za'ir fi Ma'athir al-Amir 'Abd al-Qadir wa-Akhbar al-Jaza'ir [The Book of the Exploits of the Amir 'Abd al-Qadir and the Events in Algeria Presented to the Visitor]*, Part II: *Siratuhu al-Qalamiyya [His Literary Biography]*, Alexandria: al-Matba'a al-Tijariyya Gharzuzi wa-Jawish, 1903.

K., 'Letuchii Otriad v 1850 i 1851 Godakh [The Flying Column in the Years 1850 and 1851]', *Kavkazskii Sbornik*, Vol. X11 (1888), pp. 345-478.

-------- 'Levyi Flang Kavkazskoi Linii v 1848 Godu [The Left Flank of the Caucasian Line in 1848]', *Kavkazskii Sbornik*, Vol. IX (1885), pp. 368-475, Vol. X (1886), pp. 405-496, Vol. XI (1887), pp. 303-463.

-------- 'Obzor Sobytii na Kavkaze v 1846 G. [Review of the Events in the Caucasus in 1846]', *Kavkazskii Sbornik*, Vol. XIV (1890), pp. 445-553, Vol. XV (1894), pp. 451-505, Vol. XVI (1895), pp. 279-351, Vol. XVII (1896), pp. 175-255.

-------- 'Obzor Sobytii na Kavkaze v 1851 Godu [Review of the Events in the Caucasus in 1851]', *Kavkazskii Sbornik*, Vol. XVIII (1897), pp. 132-203, Vol. XIX (1898), pp. 16-119, Vol. XX (1899), pp. 1-96, Vol. XXI (1900), Part II, pp. 1-52.

-------- 'Zimniaia Ekspeditsiia 1852 G. v Chechne (Vospominaniia Ochevidtsa) [The Winter Campaign of 1852 in Chechnia (Memoirs of an Eyewitness]', *Kavkazskii Sbornik*, Vol. XIII (1889), pp.425-616.

Kalinowski, Karol, *Pamietnik mojej Zolnierzki na Kaukazie i Niewoli u Szamilia od Roku 1844 do 1854 [Memoirs of My Military Service in the Caucasus and Captivity by Shanil, 1844 - 1854]*, Warsaw: Naklad W. Dawida, 1883.

Karakin, Ivan, 'Vozrazhenie na Stat'iu G. Zissermana 'Osada Burnoi i Derbenta Kazi-Mulloi v 1831 G.' [Reaction to the Article by Mr. Zussermann, 'The Siege of Burnaia and Derbend by Ghazi-Muhammad in 1831']', *Russkii Vestnik*, 1865, No. 12, pp. 648-671.

Kazem-Bek, Mirza Aleksandr Kasimovich, 'Miuridizm i Shamil [Muridism and Shamil]', *Russkoe Slovo*, 1859, No. 12, Part I, pp. 182-242.

-------- 'O Znachenii Imama, Ego Vlast' i Dostoinstvo [About the Significance of the *Imam,* His Rule and Authority]', *Russkoe Slovo*, 1860, No. 3, Part I, pp. 274-306.

'K Biografii Shamilia [[[Additios]] to Shamil's Biography]', *Krasnyi Arkhiv*, 1941, Book 2 (105), pp. 115-139.

Khamar-Dabanov E (Pseud.), *Prodelki na Kavkaze [Tricks in the Caucasus]*, St. Petersburg: Tipofgrafiia K. Zhernakova, 1844.

Khanykov, Nikolai Vladimirovich, 'O Miuridakh i Miuridizme [About tbe *Murids* and Muridism]' *Sbornik Gazety Kavkaz*, 1847, Vol. 1, pp. 136- 156.

Also published in: *Moskovskie Vedomosti*, 18 [30] October (No. 125), pp. 962 -963, 21 October [12 November] 1847, (No. 126), pp. 970-971.

-------- 'Perevod Musul'manskikh Postanovlenii o Voine [Translations of Muslim [[Legal]] Stipulations About War]', *Sbornik Gazety Kavkaz*, 1846, pp. 282-298.

Reprinted as *Dzhikhad ili Gazavat to est' Sviashchennaia Voina Musul'man s Nevernymi [Jihad or Ghazwa that is the Muslims' Holy War Against Unbelievers]*, Tashkent: Tipografiia Shtaba Turkestanskogo Voennogo Okruga, I899.

Khashaev, Khadzhi-Murat Omarovich (ed.), *Feodal'nye Otnosheniia v Dagestane XIX Nachalo XX V. Arkhivnye Materialy [Feudal Relations in Daghestan in the Nineteenth - Begining of the Twentieth Centuries. Archival Sources]*, Moscow: 'Nauka', 1969.

-------- (ed,) *Kodeks Ummu-Khana Avarskogo (Spravedlivogo) [The Code of 'Uma[[r]] Khan of Avaristan (The Just)]*, Moscow: Moskovskii Iuridicheskii Institut, 1948.

-------- (ed.), *Pamiatniki Obychnogo Prava Dagestana XVII - XIX VV. Arkhivnye Materialy [Monuments of the Customary Law of Daghestan in the Seventeenth to Nonteenth Centuries. Archival Sourced],* Moscow: 'Nauka', 1965.

Khripovitskii, S. I., 'Znakomstvo s Ermolovym [[[My]] Acquaintance with Ermolov]', *Russkaia Starina*, 1872, No. 11, pp. 539-542.

'Khronologicheskoe Pokazanie Dostoprimechatel'nykh Sobytii v Kavkazskom i Zakavkazskom Krae i Vazhneishykh Postanovlenii Pravitel'stva Otnosiashchikhsia k Etomu Kraiu [A Chronology of Events Worthy of Mentioning in the Caucasus and Transcaucasia and of the Most Important Decrees of the Government Relating to this Land]', Annually in *Kavkazskii Kalendar'* .

von Klaproth, Julius, *Tableua Historique, Geographique, Ethnographique et Politique du Caucase et des Provinces Limithropes entre la Russie et la Perse*, Paris: Ponthie et Cie., 1827.

-------- *Reise in dem Kaukazus und nach Georgien Unternomen in dem Jahren 1807 und 1808 aus Veranstaltung der Keiserlichen Akademie der Wissenschaften zu St.-Peterburg Enhalten Eine Volstandige Beschreibung der Kaukazischer Lander und Ihren Bewohner*, Berlin: Buchhandlung der Hellische Waisenhauses, 1812 - 1814.

Klinger, Ivan, 'Nechto o Chechne. Zametki o Videnom, Slyshannom i Uznannom vo Vremia Plena u Chechentsev s 24-go Iiulia 1847 po 1-e Ianvaria 1850 [A Bit About Chechnia. Notes of What I Saw, Heard and Learned While in Chechen Captivity from 24 July [[5 August]] 1847 to 1 [[13]] January 1850]', *Kavkaz*, 9 [21] December (No. 97), p. 390, 23 December 1860 [14 January 1861] (No. 101), pp. 404-405.

-------- 'Razskaz Ofitsera Byvshego v Plenu u Chechentsev s 24 Iiulia 1847 po 1 Ianvaria 1850 G. Vkliuchitel'no [The Story of an Officer Who Was in Chechen Captivity from 24 July [[5 August]] 1847 to 1 [[13]] January 1850, Inclusive]', *Kavkaz*, 1 [13] November (No. 86), pp. 344-345, 8 [20] November (No. 88), pp. 352-353, 15 [27] November (No. 90), pp. 361-362, 18 [30] November (No. 913), pp. 364-365, 22 November [4 December] 1856 (No. 92), pp. 368-370.

Kokiev, G. A. (ed.), *Krestianskaia Reforma v Kabarde. Dokumenty po Istorii Osvobozhdeniia Zavisimykh Soslovii v Kabarde v 1867 Godu [The Peasent Reform in Ghabarta. Documents on the History of the Liberation of the Dependent Estates in Ghabarta in 1867]*, Nal'chik: Kabardinskoe Gosuderstvennoe Izdatel'stvo, 1947.

Komarov; A. V., 'Adaty i Sudoproizvodstvo po Nim (Materialy dlia Statistiki Dagestanskoi Oblasti) [The *'Adawat* and the Judgement According to Them. (Sources for the Statistics of the District of Daghestan)]', *Sbornik Svedenii o Kavkazskikh Gortsakh*, Vol. I (1868), 88 pp.

Kosteniecki, Jakub [Kostenetskii, Iakov Ivanovich], *Zapiski ob Avarskoi Ekspeditsii na Kavkaze 1837 G. [Notes on the Campaign in Avaristan in the Caucasus in 1837]*, St. Petersburg: Tipografiia Eduarda Pratsa, 1851

Reprint from *Sovremennik*, 1850, Nos. 10, 11, 12.

Kosven, Marks Osipovich and Khashaev, Kh. V. (eds.), *Istoriia, Geografiia i Etnografiia Dagestana XVIII - XIX VV. Arkhivnye Materialy [The History, Geography and Ethnography of Daghestan in the Eighteenth and Nineteenth Centuries. Archival Sources]*, Moscow: Izdatel'stvo Vostochnoi Literatury, 1958.

von Kotzebue, Moritz [Kotsebu, Mavrikii Avgustovich], *Reise nach Persien mit der Russischen Keiserlichen Gesandschaft im Jahre 1817*, Weimar: Hoffmannische Hoffbuchhandlung, 1817.

Kovalevskii, Evg[enii] P., 'Ocherki Etnografii Kavkaza [Sketches of the Ethnosraphy of the Caucasus]', *Vestnik Evropy*, 1867, No. 3, pp.75-140, No. 4, pp. 1 -29.

Kovalevskii, Maksim, *Zakon i Obychai na Kavkaze [Law and Custom in the Caucasus]*, Moscosv: Tipografiia A. I. Mamonova, 1890.

Kozubskii, Evgenii, 'Dagestanskie Vospominaniia o Ermolove [Daghestani Reminiscences about Ermolov]', *Russkii Arkhiv*, 1900, No. 9, pp. 137- 142.

Krachkovskii, Ignatii Iul'ianovich, 'Neizdannoe Pis'mo Shamilia [An Unpublished Letter by Shamil]', in: *Izbrannye Sochineniia*, Vol. VI, Moscow and Leningrad: Izdatel'stvo Akademii Nauk SSSR, 1960, pp. 551-558.

Krachkovskii, Ignatii Iul'ianovich, and Genko, A. N., 'Arabskie Pis'ma Shamilia v Severo-Osetii [Shamil's Arabic Letters in North-Ossetiia]', *Sovetskoe Vostokovedenie*, Vol. III (1945), pp. 36-58.

'Kratkii Ocherk Sluzhebnoi Deiatel'nosti General-Ad'iutanta Kniazia Argutinskogo-Dolgorukova [A Short Sketch of the Military Activity af Adjutant-General Prince Argutinskii-Dolgorukii]', *Kavkazskii Kalendar'*, 1856, Part IV, pp. 565-581.

Kravtsov, I. S., 'Kavkaz i Ego Voenachal'niki. N. N. Murav'ev, Kn. A. I. Bariatinskii i Gr. N. I. Evdokimov, 1854-1864 [The Caucasus and Its Military Commanders. N. N. Murav'ev, Prince A. I. Bariatinskii and Count N. i. Evdokimov, 1854-1864]', *Russkaia Starina*, 1866, No. 6, pp. 569-592, No. 7, pp. 109-150.

Krikunova, E. O. (ed.), *Dokumenty po Istorii Balkarii 40 - 90 GG XIX V. [Documnets on the History of Balkaria in the 1840s - 1890s]*, Nal'chik: Kabardino-Balkarskoe Knizhnoe Izdatel'stvo, 1959.

[Kundukh, Musa], 'Memuary Gen. Musa-Pashi Kundukhova [The Memoirs of General Musa Pasha Kundukh]', *Kavkaz*, (Paris), 1936, No. 1 (25), pp. 12 -17, No. 2 (26), pp. 13-19, No.3 (27), pp. 14-18, No. 4 (28), pp. 19-23, No. 5 (29), pp. 20-25, No. 8 (32), pp. 31 -34, No. 10 (34), pp. 24-30, No.11 (35), pp. 26-29, No.12 (36), pp. 31 -36, 1937, No. 3 (39), pp. 26-30, No. 5 (41), pp. 24-28, No. 7 (43), pp. 24-27, No. 8 (44), pp. 24-29, No. 10 (46), pp. 22-25.

French version, *Les Memoirs du General Moussa-Pacha Koundoukhov (1837 - 1865)*, Paris: Edition du 'Caucase', 1939.

Turkish transl. Murat Yagan, *General Musa Kundukhov'un Anilari*, Istanbul: 1976

Kurdov, Konstantin Minovich, 'K Antropologii Lezgin: Kiurintsy [On the Anthropology of the Lesghians: The People of Kurah]', *Russkii Antropologicheskii Zhurnal*, Book VII-VIII (1901), pp. 165-176.

-------- 'K Antropologii Lezgin: Tabasarantsy [On the Anthropology of the Lesghians: The Tabarsaranis]', *Russkii Antropologicheskii Zhurnal*, Book XXI-XXII (1905), pp. 129-134.

-------- 'Taty Dagestana [The Tats of Daghestan]', *Russkii Antropologicheskii Zhurnal*, Book XXVII-XXVIII (1908), pp. 56-66.

-------- 'Taty Shemakhinskogo U. Bakinskoi G. [The Tats of the Shemakha District of the Baqu Province]', *Russkii Antropologicheskii Zhurnal*, Book XXXIII-XXXIV(1913), pp. 162-172.

Kuzanov, 'Miuridizm v Dagestane [Tbe *Murid* Movement in Daghestan]', *Raduga*,1861, No. 1, pp. 1-8, No. 2, pp. 28-37, No. 3, pp. 50-57, No. 4, pp. 65-71.

[Lachinov, Evdokim Emel'ianovich,] 'Otryvti iz 'Ispovedi' Lachinova [Excerpts from the 'Confessions' of Lachinov]', *Kavkazskii Sbornik*, Vol. I (1876), pp. 123-195, Vol. II (1877), pp. 75-115.

Lake, Atwell, *Narrative of the Defence of Kars, Historical and Military from Authentic Documents and from Notes Taken by the Several Officers Serving on the Staff of Her Majesty's Commissionair with the Ottoman Army in Asia Minor*, London: Richard Bentley, 1857.

-------- *Kars and Our Captivity in Russia with Letters from Gen. Sir W. F. Williams Bart. of Cars K. C. B., Major Teasdale, C. B. and Late Captain Thompson, C. B.*, London: Richard Bentley, 1856.

Lapinski, Theophil (Sefik Bey), *Die Borgvölker der Kaukazus und ihre Freihetskämpfe gegen die Russen nach Eigener Ausschaung Geschildert*, Hamburg: Hoffmann und Co., 1863.

Laudaev, Umalat, 'Chechenskoe Plemia [The Chechen Tribe]', *Sbornik Svedenii o Kavkazskikh Gortsakh*, Vol. VI (1872), 62 pp.

Lavrov, L. I. (ed.), *Epigraficheskie Pamiatniki Severnogo Kavkaza na Arabskom, Persidskom i Turetskom Iazykakh [Epigraphic Monuments of the Northern Caucasus in the Arabic, Persian and Turkish Languages]*, Vol. II: *Nadpisi XVIII - XX VV. [Inscriptions from the Eighteenth to the Twentieth Centuries]*, Moscow: 'Nauka', 1968.

Lilov, A., 'Ocherki Byta Kavkazskikh Gortsev [An Outilne of the Way of Life of the Caucasian Mountaineers]', *Sbornik Materialov dlia Opisaniia Mestnostei i Plemen Kavkaza*, Vol. XIV (1892), Part I, pp. 1 -57.

-------- 'Ocherki iz Byta Gorskikh Musul'man [Outlines from the Way of Life of the Mountain Muslims]', *Sbornik Materialov dlia Opisaniia Mestnostei i Plemen Kavkaza*, Vol. V (1886), Part II, pp. 1-36.

Linevich, I. P., 'Byvshee Elisuiskoe Sultanstvo (s Kartoi) [The Previous Sultanate of Ilisu (with a Map)]', *Sbornik Svedenii o Kavkazskikh Gortsakh*, Vol. II (1873), 54 pp.

-------- 'Karta Gorskikh Narodov Podvlastnykh Shamiliu [A Map of the Mountain Peoples Under Shamil's Rule]', *Sbornik Svedenii o Kavkazskikh Gortsakh*, Vol. VI (1877), 4 pp.

Litvinov, M. 'Kavkaz. Voenno-Geograficheskii Ocherk [The Caucasus: A Military-Geographical Survey]',*Voennyi Sbornik*, 1884, No. 2, pp. 304-320, No. 3, pp. 149-164, No. 4, pp. 328-346.

Liubitel' Kavkaza i Zakavkaz'ia (pseud.), 'Nikolai Nikolaevich Murav'ev, 1854-1856', *Russkaia Starina*, 1874, No. 5, pp. 134-151.

Longworth, John Augustine, *A Year Among the Circassians*, London: Henry Colburn, 1840.

Mackie, J. Milton, *Life of Schamyl and Narrative of the Circassian War of Independence Against Russia*, Boston: John P. Jewett & Co., 1856.

Markov, T., 'Shamil', Grazhdanski i Voennyi Pravitel', (Otryvok iz Opisaniia Levogo Kryla) [Shamil, a Civil and Military Ruler (Excerpt from a Description of the Left Wing)]', *Kavkaz*, 29 November [11 December] 1859 (No, 94), pp. 525-526.

Marlinskii, A., (pseud. of Bestuzhev, Aleksandr Aleksandrovich) 'Pis'ma iz Dagestana [Letters from Daghestan]', in *Polnoe Sobranie Sochinenii*, Part VI, St. Petersburg: Tipografiia III Otdelenia Sobstvennoi E.I.V. Kantseliarii, 1838 (third ed.), pp. 127-243.

Marshaev, R. G., *Russko-Dagestanskie Otnosheniia XVII - Pervoi Poloviny XVIII VV. (Dokumenty i Materialy) [Russo-Daghestani Relations in the Seventeeth - First Half of the Eighteenth Centuries (Documents and Sources)]*, Makhachqala: Dagestanskoe Knizhnoe Izdatel'stvo,1958.

Marx, Karl, *The Eastern Question. A Reprint of Letters Written in 1853 - 1856 Dealing with the Events of the Crimean War*, Eds. Eleanor Marx-Aveling and Edward Aveling, London: Swan, Connonschein and Co., 1897.

Marx, Karl and Engels, Friedrich, *Polnoe Sobranie Sochinenii [Complete Works]*, Moscow: Gospolitizdat, 1955-1966 (2nd edition).

'Mekhtulinskie Khany [The *Khans* of Mekhtuli]', *Sbornik Svedenii o Kavkazskikh Gortsakh*, Vol.II (1869), 17 pp.

'Memoire de la Province du Sirvan, en Forme de Lettre Adresse au Pere Fleuriau' in: *Lettres Edifientes et Curieuse Ecrites des Missions Etrangeres.* Nouvelle Edition: *Memoirs du Levant*, Toulouse: Noël-Etienne et Auguste Gaude, 1810.

Merlieux, Edouard, *Les Princesses Russes Prisonieres au Caucase. Souvenirs d'Une Française Captive de Schamyl*, Paris: F. Sartorius, 1857.

Second Edition, E. Dentu, Editeur, Librairie de la Societe des Gens de Lettres, 1860.

Russian Trans. Kirill Dziubinski, *Plennitsy Shamilia. Vospominaniia G-azhi Dranse . . . etc...*, Tiflis: Tipograffia Kantselarii Namestnika Kavkazskogo, 1858.

'Mesiats Voennopokhodnoi Zhizni Mirnogo (v Severnom Dagestane v 1832 Godu) [A Month in the Military-Campaign Life of a Layman (in Northern Dagehstan in 1832)]', *Moskvitianin*, 1843, No.11, pp.79-80.

Miliutin, Dmitrii Alekseevich, ‘Opisanie Voennykh Deistvii 1839 Goda v Severnom Dagestane [Description of the Military Actions of 1839 in Northern Daghestan]’, *Voennyi Zhurnal*, 1850, No. l, pp. 1 -144.

Turkish transl. A. Sevket, *1839 Senesinde Simali Dagistanda Yapilan Harp Harekati*, Istanbul: 1931.

Modzalevskii, B. L. (ed.), *Arkhiv Revskikh [The Archives of the Raevskii Family]*, St. Petersburg: Tipografiia M. Aleksandrova, 1908 - 1911.

-------- ‘Kavkaz Nikolaevskogo Vremeni v Pis'makh Ego Voinskikh Deiatelei (Iz Arkhiva B. G. Chiliaeva) [The Caucasus of the Times of Nicholas [[I]] in Letters of Its Military Commanders (From the Archives of B. G. Chiliaev) [[Chilishvli]]]’, *Russkii Arkhiv*, 1904, No. 9, pp. 115-174.

Monteith, William, *Kars and Erzeroum with the Campaigns of Prince Paskiewitch in 1828 and 1829 and an Account of the Conquests of Russia Beyond the Caucasus from the Time of Peter the Great to the Treaty of Turcoman Chie and Adrianople*, London: Longman Brawn, Green and Longmans, 1856.

Moser, Ludwig, *Der Kaukasus, seine Volkerschaften deren Kampfe etc. Nebst einer Charakteristik Schamils*, Vienna: J. B. Wallishauffer, 1854.

[Murav'ev, Nikolai Nikolaevich,] ‘Nikolai Nikolaevich Murav'ev 5-go Iiulia 1856 G. [Nikolai Nikolaesrich Murav'ev on 5 [[17]] July 1856]’, *Russkaia Starina*, No. 11, p. 456.

-------- ‘Zemlianka A. P. Ermolova. Vyderzhka iz Zapisok N. N. Murav'eva [The Hut of A. P. Ermolov. An Excerpt from N. N. Muravev's Notes]’, *Russkii Arkhiv*, 1888, No. 10, pp. 247-248.

Neverovskii, Aleksandr Andreevich, *Istreblenie Avarskiih Khanov v 1834 Godu [The Extermination of the Avar Khans in 1834]*, St. Petersburg: Tipograffia Voenno-Uchebnykh Zavedenii, 1848.

(Offprint from *Voennyi Zhurnal*, 1848, No. 5)

-------- ‘Kratkii Vzgliad na Severnyi i Srednii Dagestan v Topografichesiiom i Statisticileskom Otnosheniiakh [A Short Glance at Northern and Central Daghestan from the Topographical and Statistical Perspectives]’, *Voennyi Zhurnal*, 1847, No. 5, pp. 1-64.

-------- *O Nachale Bezpokoistv v Severnom i Srednem dagestane [On the Beginning of the Unrest in Northern and Central Daghestan]*, St. Petersburg: Tipografiia Voenno-Uchebnykh Zavedenii, 1847.

(Offprint from *Voennyi Zhurnal*, 1847, No. 1.)

[Nicholas I,] ‘Instruktsii Imperatora Nikolaia Pavlovicha Kniaziu Kozlovskomu ot 22 Fevralia 1854 Goda [Instructions by the Emperor Nicholas to Prince Kozlowski, 22 February [[6 March]] 1854]’, *Russkii Arkhiv*, 1904, No. 9, pp. 138-139.

-------- 'Vysochaishii Reskript Dannyi na Imia Namestnika Kavkazskogo, General-Adiutanta Kniazia Vorontsova [An Imperial Rescript to the Viceroy in the Caucasus, Adjutant-General Prince Vorontsov]', *Sbornik Gazety Kavkaz*, 1847, Vol. I, pp. 1 - 4.

-------- 'Zapiska Imperatora Nikolaia I o Voennykh Deistviiakh na Kavkaze (Okolo 1845 G.) [A Note by the Emperor Nicholas I on the Military Operations in the Caucasus (About 1845)]', *Russkaia Starina*, 1885, No. 10, pp. 209-212.

Nicolaÿ, A. Pavlovich, 'Epizod iz Istorii Kavkazskoi Voiny, 1855-1857 [An Episode from the History of the Caucasian War, 1855-1857]', *Russkaia Starina*, 1882, No.11, pp. 251-282.

-------- 'Iz Vospominanii o Moei Zhizni. Darginskii Pokhod, 1845 [From My Memoirs. The March on Darghiyya, 1845]', *Russkii Arkhiv*, 1890, No. 6, pp. 249 -278.

-------- 'K Istorii Pokoreniia Vostochnogo Kavkaza [To the History of the Conquest of the Eastern Caucasus]', *Russkii Arkhiv*, 1889, No. 8, pp. 531-535.

Nikoforov, D. 'Iz Kavkazskik Vospominanii (1854 G.) [From [[My]] Memoirs from the Caucasus (1854)]', *Russkii Vestnik*, 1899, No. 6, pp. 591-603.

Nikolaev, P., 'Vospominania o Kniaze A. I. Bariatinskom [My Reminiscences of Prince A. I. Bariatinskii]', *Istoricheskii Vestnik*, 1885, No. 12, pp. 618-644.

'Nizam Shamllia. (Material dlia Istorii Dagestana) [Shamil's *Nizam* (A Source for the History of Daghestan)]', *Sbornik Svedenii o Kavkazskikh Gortsakh*, Vol. III (1870), 18 pp. (separate pagination).

Reprinted in, *Severnyi Kavkaz*, No. 53 (1938). pp. 30-33.

N[oro]v, V[asilii] N[ikolaevich], 'Kavkazskaia Ekspeditsiia v 1845 Godu. Razskaz Ochevidtsa [The Caucasian Campaign of 1845. An Eyewitness's Story]', *Voennyi Sbornik*, 1906, No. 11, pp. 1-34, No. 12, pp.15-52, 1907, No. 1, pp. 31-64, No. 2, pp.1-42, No. 3, pp. 1-28, No. 4, pp. 15-46.

Novoselov, Semen, 'Razskaz ob Osade Ukrepleniia Akhty [A Story About the Siege of Fort Akhdi]', *Russkii Khudozhestvennyi Listok*, 1851 , 20 May [1], 20 June [2 July] 1851 (Nos.15, 18).

O. K., 'Vest' s Kavkazskoi Linii. (Pis'mo k Priiateliu) [News from the Caucasian Line. (A Letter to a Friend)]', *Moskovskie Vedomosti*, 5 [17] March 1855 (No. 27).

-------- 'Vesti s Linii. (Pis'mo k Priiateliu) [News from the Line. (A Letter to a Friend)]', *Kavkaz*, 19 [31] January 1854 (No. 6), pp. 21-23.

'Odin iz Fanaticheskikh Postupkov Shamilla [One of Shamil's Fanatic Deeds]', *Kavkaz*, 30 May [11 June] 1853 (No. 40), pp.103-105.

Okol'nichii, N., 'Perechen' Poslednikh Sobytii v Dagestane (1843 God) [A List of Recent Events in Daghestan (1843)]', *Voennyi Sbornik*, 1859, No. l, Non-official Part, pp. 107-172, No. 2, Non-official Part, pp. 337 - 406, No. 3, Non-official Part, pp. 1-54, No. 4, Non-official Part, pp. 305-348, No. 6, Non-official Part, pp. 311-380.

Oliphant, Lawrence, *The Trans-Caucasian Campaign of the Turkish Army under Omar Pasha. A Personal Narrtive*, Edinburgh and London: William Blackwood and Sons, 1856.

Olszewski [Ol'shevskii], Meletii Iakovlevich, 'Kavkaz i Pokorenie Vostochnoi Ego Chasti. Kniaz' A. I. Bariatinskii 1856-1861 [The Caucasus and the Conquest of its Eastern Part. Prince A. I. Bariatinskii,1856-1861]', *Russkaia Starina*, 1880, No. 2, pp. 289- 318.

-------- 'Kavkaz s 1841 po 1866 Gody [The Caucasus, 1841-1866]', *Russkaia Starina*, 1893, No. 6, pp. 573-610, No. 7, pp. 89-124, No. 8, pp. 287-319, No. 9, pp. 563-589, 1894, No. l, pp. 133-181, No. 2, pp.131-171, No. 6, pp. 63-94, No. 7, pp. 44-108, No. 9, pp. 22 - 43, No.11, pp. 215-240, No.12, pp.155-197, 1895, No, 3, pp. 167-175, No. 4, pp.179-189, No. 6, pp.171-184, No. 9, pp.115-117, No.10, pp. 129-166.

-------- 'Kniaz' Aleksandr Ivanovich Bariatinskii na Levom Flange Kavkazskoi Linii, 1851-1853 [Prince Aleksandr Ivanovich Bariatinskii on the Left Flank of the Caucasian Line, 1851 - 1853]', *Russkaia Starina*, 1879, No. 6, pp. 307 -332, No. 7, pp. 415-436.

-------- 'Kniaz' Aleksandr Ivanovich Bariatinskii v 1859 i 1863 GG. [Prince Aleksandr Ivanovich Bariatinskii in 1859 and 1863]', *Russkaia Starina*, 1880, No. 9, pp. 97-108.

-------- 'Tsesarevich Aleksandr Nikolaevich na Kavkaze s 12 Sentiabra po 28 Oktiabria 1850 G. [The *Tsarevich* Aleksandr in the Caucasus, 12 [[24]] September- 28 October [[9 November]] 1850]', *Russkaia Starina*, 1884, No. 9, pp. 576-588.

-------- 'Zapiski. 1844 i drugie gody [Notes. The Year 1844 ad other Years],' in: Gordin, Iakov (ed.), *Osada Kavkaza. Vospominaniia uchastnikov kavkazskoi voiny XIX veka [The Siege of the Caucasus. Memoirs of Participants of the Cuacausin War in the Nineteenth Century]*, St. Petersburg: Izdatel'stvo zhurnala *Zvezda*, 2000, pp. 261 - 329.

Omar-oghlu, [Omarov], 'Abdallah, 'Vospominaniia Mutaalima [The Memoirs of a *Muta'alim*]', *Sbornik Svedenii o Kavkazskikh Gortsakh*, Vol. I (1868), 64 pp., Vol. II (1869), 70 pp. (separate pagination).

O[rlov]-D[avydov], A[natolii Vladimirovich], 'Chastnoe Pis'mo o Vziatii Shamilia [A Private Letter About the Capture of Sbamil]', *Russkii Arkhiv*, 1869, No. 6, pp. 1046-1063.

Osten-Saken, Dmitrii Erofeevich, 'Nikolai Nikolaevich Murav'ev v 1828- 1856 GG. [Nikolai Nikolaevich Murav'ev in the Years 1828-1856]', *Russkaia Starina*, 1874, No.11, pp. 535-543, No. 12, pp. 675-691.

'Otvet-Kavkazskogo Ofitsera na Obvineniia N. N. Murav'eva. (Pis'mo k General - Leitenantu K*) [A Caucasian Officer's Answer to the Accusations of N. N. Murav'ev (A Letter to Lieutenant-General K*)]', *Russkaia Starina*, 1872, No. 1 1, pp. 544-546.

P. K., 'Iz Dnevnika Dagestantsa [From the Diary of a Soldier in the Daghestan Regiment]', *Kavkazskii Sbornik*, Vol. XVIII (1897), pp. 204-208.

-------- 'Pokorenie Galashek. Iz Istorii Kavkazskoi Voiny [The Conquest of Galasha. From the History of the Caucasian War]', *Voennyi Sbornik*, 1902, No. 2, pp. 47 -57.

Passek, Diomid Vasil'evich, 'Otstuplenie iz Khunzakha (1843 God) [The Retreat from Khunzakh (1843)]', *Kavkazskii Sbornik*, Vol. I (1876), pp. 215-235.

'Peterburgskaia Letopis' [St. Petersburg Chronicle]', *Sanktpeterburgskie Vedomosti*, 27 September [9 October] 1859 (No. 209), front page.

'Pis'mo iz Kurinskogo Ukrepleniia [A Letter from Fort Kurinskoe]', *Odesskii Vestnik*, 26 April [8 May], 1855 (No. 47).

'Pis'mo iz Moskvy v Provintsiiu [A Letter from Moscow to the Province]', *Russkaia Gazeta*, 30 September [12 October] 1859, No. 39.

'Podrobnoe Opisanie Razmena Plennykh Semeistv Fligel'-Ad'iutanta Kniazia Chavchavadze i General-Maiora Kniaza Orbeliani [A Detailed Description of the Exchange of the Captive Families of the Emperor's A.D.C. Prince Tchavtchavadze and Major-General Prince Orbeliani]', *Odesskii Vestnik*, 9 [21] April 1855 (No. 40), p.190.

Similar reports in: *Moskovskie Vedomosti*, 21 April [3 May] 1855 (No. 48), pp. 390-392, *Sanktpeterburgskie Vedomosti*, 30 April [12 May] 1855 (No. 85), pp. 424 - 425.

Pogodin, M., *Aleksei Petrovich Ermolov. Materialy dlia ego Biografii [Aleksei Petrovich Ermolov. Sources to his Biography]*, Moscow: Universitetskaia Tipografiia, 1863.

'Pokorenie Kavkaza -- Shamil' [The Conquest of the Caucasus -- Shamil]', *Raduga*, 1860, No. 2, p. 37.

Porebski [Porembskii], S., 'Vtorzhenie Shamilia v Dzharo-Belokanskii Okrug v 1853 Godu [Shamil's Invasion of Chartalah in 1853]', *Kavkazskii Sbornik*, Vol.. XI (1887), pp. 499-523.

Potto, V., 'Iz Zapisok Kavkaztsa (Vosem Let v Kurinskom Ukreplenii) [From the Notes of a Caucasian. (Eight Years in Fort Kurinskoe]', *Voennyi Sbornik*, 1871, No. 1, Part I, pp. 127-152.

[Pruszanowski,] 'Kazi Mulla (Gazi Magomet). (Iz Zapisok Kapitana Prushanovskogo) [Ghazi Muhammad. (From the Notes of Captain Pruszanowski)]', *Sbornik Gazety Kavkaz*, 1847, Vol. II, pp. 22-39.

-------- 'Proisshestviia v Kaitakhe ot 1820 do 1836 [Misprint for 1826] Goda [The Events in Qaytaq, 1820-1826]', *Sbornik Gazety Kavkaz*, 1846, pp. 170-180.

Przeclawski [Przhetslavskii], Pawel [Pavel] G., 'Dagestan, Ego Nravy i Obychai [Daghestan, Its Mores and Customs]', *Vestnik Evropy*, 1867, No. 3, pp. 141-192.

-------- 'Shamil i Ego Sem'ia v Kaluge. Zapiski Polkovnika P. G. Przhetslavskogo [Shamil and His Family in Kaluga. Notes by Colonel P. G. Przeclawski]', *Russkaia Starina*, 1877, No. 10, pp. 253-276, No. 11, pp. 471-506, 1878, No. 1, pp. 41-64, No. 2, pp. 265-280.

-------- 'Vospominanie o Blokade Goroda Derbenta v 1831 Godu [[[My]] Memoirs of the Siege of Derbend in 1831]', *Voennyi Sbornik*, 1864, No. 2, Non-official Part, pp. 155-178.

'Puteshestvie Shamilia ot Guniba do Sanktpeterburga [Shamil's Journey from Ghunib to St. Petersburg]', *Russkii Mir*, 7 [19] October 1859 (No. 54), pp. 941-945.

Al-Qarakhi, Muhammad Tahir, *Barikat al-Suyuf al-Daghistaniyya fi ba'd al-Ghazawat al-Shamiliyya [The Glitter of Daghestani Swords in Some of Shamil's Raids]*, ed. A. M. Barabanov, Moscow and Leningrad: Izdatel'stvo Akademii Nauk SSSR, 1946.

Russian Trans. A.M.Barabanov, *Khronika Mukhameda Takhira al-Karakhi o Dagestanskikh Voinakh v Period Shamilia*, Moscow and Leningrad: Izdatel'stvo Akademii Nauk SSSR, 1941.

Russian Trans. G. Mallachikhan, *Tri Imama*, Makhachqala, 1927.

Reprint: Mukhamed Tagir, *Tri Imama*, Reprint Series No, 16, London: Society for Central Asian Studies, 1989.

Ottoman Turkish Trans., Tahirül-Mevlevi, *Kafkasya Mucahidi Seyh Samilin Gazavatii*, Istanbul, 1333 [1914].

Reprint in Modern Turkish, ed. Tarik Cemal Kutlu, *Imam Samil'in Gazavati*, Istanbul: Gözde Kitaplar Yayinevi, 1987.

Ramazanov, Kh. Kh. and Shikhsaidov, A. R. (eds.), *Ocherki Istorii Iuzhnogo Dagestana. Materialy k Istorii Narodov Dagestana s Drevneishikh Vremen do Nachaka XX Veka [An Outline if the History of Southern Daghestan. Sources to the History of the Peoples of Daghestan from the Earliest times to the Beginning of the Twentieth Century*, Makhachqala: Tipografiia Dagestanskogo Filiiala Akademii Nauk SSSR, 1964.

'Razdelenie Kavkazskoi Linii na 4 Otdela [The Division of the Caucasian Line into Four Sectors]', *Kavkazskii Kalendar'*, 1851, Part III, p. 52.

'Razgovor Peterburgskogo Korrespondenta Gazety *le Nord* s Shamilem [The Interview of *le Nord*'s St. Petersburg Correspondent with Shamil]', *Sovremennaia Letopis'*, 1860 (No. 45), pp. 14-15.

Rieber, Alfred J., *The Politics of Autocracy. Letters of Alexander II to Prince A. I. Bariatinskii, 1857 - 1864*, Paris and Hague: Mouton & Co., 1966.

Runowski [Runovskii], Apolon, 'Kanly v Nemirnom Krae [Blood Feuds in the Unpacified Country]', *Voennyi Sbornik*, 1860, No. 7, Non-official Part, pp. 199-216.

-------- 'Kodeks Shamilia [Shamil's Legislation]', *Voennyi Sbornik*, 1862, No. 2. Non-official Part, pp. 327-386.

Excerpt published in: 'Postanovleniia Shamilia o Brake [Shamil's Legislation About Marriage]', *Russkii Khudozhestvennyi Listok*, 10 [22] February 1861, pp. 17-18.

-------- 'Miuridizm i Gazavat v Dagestane po Ob''iasneniiu Shamilia [Muridism and Holy War in Daghestan According to Shamil's Explanation]', *Russkii Vestnik*, 1862, No. 12, pp. 646 - 685.

-------- 'Semeistvo Shamilia [Shamil's Family]', *Voennyi Sbornik*, 1860, No, 5, Non-official Part, pp. 189-218.

Summaries in: 'Nekotorye Svedeniia o Semeistve Shamilia [Some Evidence About Shamil's Family]', *Kievskii Telegraf*, 9 [21] June 1860 (No. 92), pp. 121-172: 'Semeistvo Shamilia [Shamil's Family]', *Russkii Khudozhestvennyi Listok*, 20 March [1 April], pp.22-23, 1 [13] April 1860, pp. 31-33.

-------- 'Shamil', *Voennyi Sbornik*, 1860, No. 2, Non-official Part, pp. 531-582.

-------- 'Shamil' v Kaluge [Shamil in Kaluga]', *Voennyi Sbornik*, 1861, No. 1, Non-official part, pp. 133-200.

Summaries under the same title in: *Moskovskie Vedomosti*, 24 February [5 March] (No. 42), pp. 322-324, 25 February [9 March] 1860 (No. 43), pp. 331-333; *Kavkaz*, 13 [25] March (No. 21), pp. 45-46, 31 March [12April] 1860 (No. 26), pp, 143-146.

-------- *Zapiski o Shamile [Notes about Shamil]*, St. Petersburg: Tipografiia Karla Vol'fa, 1860.

-------- 'Znakomstvo s Shamilem [[[My]] Acquaintance with Shamil]', *Voennyi Sbornik*, 1859, No. 11, Non-official Part, pp. 172-224.

Rumiantsov, I. N., *V Plenu u Shamilia. Zapiski Russkogo [In Shamil's Captivity. Notes of a Russian]*, St. Petersburg: Tipografiia A. N. Bykova, 1877.

Rus-oghlu, 'Neskol'ko Zamechanii po Povodu Sdachi Shamilla [Several Remarks following Shamil's Surrender]', *Moskovskie Vedomosti*, 17 [29] November 1859 (No. 273), pp. 1943-1944.

R -- v, I., 'Nachalo i Postepennoe Razvitie Miuridizma na Kavkaze [The Beginning and Gradual Development of the *Murid* Movement in the Caucasus]', *Russkii Khudozhestvennyi Listok,* 10 [22] November, pp. 104-110, 20 November [2 December], pp. 113-116, 1 [13] December, pp.117-119, 10 [22] December, pp.123-128, 20 December 1859 [1 January 1860], pp. 129-130.

Ryndin, A., 'Imam Shamil v Rossii [The *Imam* Shamil in Russia]l',*Istoricheskii Vestnik*, 1895, No.11, pp. 529-542.

Rzewuski [Rzhevuskii], Adam [Adamovich], '1845 God na Kavkaze [The year 1845 in the Caucasus]', *Kavkazskii Sbornik*, Vol. VI (1882), pp. 221 - 476 (+ 16 pp. Appendices), Vol. VII (1883), pp. 383-479.

Sandwith, Humphrey, *A Narrative of the Siege of Kars and the Six Months of Resistance by the Turkish Garrison under General Williams to the Russian Army, together with a Narrative of Travels and Adventures in Armenia and Lazistan with Remarks on the Present State of Turkey*, London: John Murrey, 1856.

Saray, Mehmet, et al. (eds.), *Kafkas Arastirmalari [Caucasus Studies]*, Vol. 1, Istanbul: Acar Yayinlari, 1988.

Schwartz, Benjamin, (ed.), *Letters from Persia Written by Charles and Edward Burges, 1825 - 1855*, New York: The New York Public Library, 1942.

Seleznev, Mikhail, *Rukovodstvo k Poznaniiu Kavkaza [a Guide to theCaucasus]*, St. Petersburg: Tipografiia Morskogo Kadetskogo Korpusa, 1847-1850.

Shabanov, I., 'Vospominanie o Zimnei Ekspeditsii 1859 Goda v Chechne [Reminiscences of the 1859 Winter Campaign in Chechnia]', *Voennyi Sbornik*, 1866, No. 10, Non-official Part, pp. 297-333.

'Shamkhaly Tarkovskie. (Istoricheskaia Zapiska Sostavlennaia Vremennoi Kommissiei Nariazhennoi dlia Opredeleniia Lichnykh i Pozemel'nykh Prav Tuzemtsev Temir-Khan-Shurinskogo Okruga) [The *Shamkhal*s of Targhi (An Historical Note Composed by the Temporary Committee Formed to Establish the Personal and Land-ownership Rights of the Natives in the District of Temir-Khan-Shura)]', *Sbornik Svedenii o Kavkazskikh Gortsakh*, Vol. I (1868), pp' 54-89.

'Shamil'', *Raduga*, 1860, No. 4, pp. 69-70.

'Shamil'', *Zhurnal dlia Chteniia Vospitannikam Voenno-Uchebnykh Zavedenii*, Vol. CXLI, No. 563 (1 [13] December 1859), pp. 352-363.

'Shamil', Byvshii Imam Chechni i Dagestana' [Shamil the Ex- *Imam* of Chechnia and Daghestan]', *Lastochka*, 1859, No. 9, pp. 465-469.

'Shamil' i Chechnia [Shamil and Chechnia]', *Voennyi Sbornik*, 1859, No. 9, Non-official Part, pp. 121-164.

'Shamil' Polveka Nazad v Moskve [Shamil in Moscow Half a Century Ago]', *Russkaia Starina*, 1909, No. 10, p. 310.

'Shamil' Polveka Nazad v Peterburge [Shamil in St. Petersburg Half a Century Ago]', *Russkaia Starina*, 1909, No.11, p. 576.

'Shamil v Malorossii [Shamil in Lesser Russia [[the Ukraine]]]', *Sanktpeterburgskie Vedomosti*, 3 [15] October, 1859 (No. 213), front page.

'Shamil' v Publichnoi Biblioteke [Shamil in the Public Library]', *Russkii Mir*, 14 [26] October 1859 (No. 56), p. 975.

'Shamil v Stavropole [Shamil in Stavropol]', *Sanktpeterburgskie Vedomosti*, 29 September [11 October], 1859 (No. 210), front page.

'Shamil v S-Peterburge [Shamil in St. Petersburg]', *Russkii Khudozhestvennyi Listok*, 1 [13] November 1859, pp.101-104.

Sharafutdinova, Rukiiat. Sh. (ed.), *Araboiazychnye dokumenty epokhi Shamilia [Arabic Documentrs from Shamil's Period]*, Rossiiskaia Akademiia Nauk, Dagestanskii Nauchnyi Tsentr, Institut Istrorii, Arkheologii i Etnografii, Moscow: Vostochnaia Literatura RAN, 2001.

-------- 'Arabskie Pis'ma Shamilia iz Arkhiva B. A. Dorna [Shamil's Letters in Arabic from the Archive of B. A. Dorn]', *Pis'mennye Pamiatniki Vostoka*, 1970, pp. 204-225, 485-502.

-------- 'Arabskii Dokument iz Arkhiva Akademika B. A. Dorna. (Materialy k Istorii Osvoboditel'nogo Dvizheniia Gortsev na Severnom Kavkaze v 20-50kh Godakh XIX V.) [A Document in Arabic from the Archive of Academician B. A. Dorn. (Sources for the History of the Liberation Movement of the Mountaineers in the Northern Caucasus in the 1820s-1850s)]', *Pis'mennye Pamiatniki Vostoka*, 1971, pp. 162-170, 544-545.

-------- 'Eshche Odin Nizam Shamilia [Yet Another *Nizam* of Shamil]', *Pis'mennye Pamiatniki Vostoka*, 1975, pp. *168-171,33L*

-------- 'Pis'mo Naiba Tashev-Khadzhi k Shamiliu [A Letter from the *Na'ib* Hajj Tasho to Shamil]', *Pis'mennye Pamiatniki Vostoka*, 1972, pp. 86-89, 304.

Shcherbinin, Mikhail Pavlovich, 'Kn. M. S. Vorontsov i N. N. Murav'ev. (Iz Sluzhevykh Vospominanii) [Prince M. S. Vorontsov and N. N. Murav'ev. (From [[My]] Service Memoirs)]', *Russkaia Starina*, 1874, No. 9, pp. 99-114.

-------- 'Zametki po Povodu Ocherka Zhizni i Sluzhby E. A. Golovina [Remarks to the Article on E. A. Golovin's Life and Service]', *Russkii Arkhiv*, 1872, No. 3, cc. 707-717.

Shtab Kavkazskogo Voennogo Okruga, *Istoricheskii Ocherk Kavkazskikh Voin ot ikh Nachala do Prisoedineniia Gruzii. K Stoletiiu Zaniatiia Tiflisa Russkimi Voiskami*

26-go Noiabria 1799 Goda [An Historical Outline of the Caucasian Wars from their Beginning to the Annexation of Georgia. To the Centenial of the Occupation of Tiflis by Russian Troops on 26 November [[6 December]] 1799], Tiflis: Izdanie Voenno-Istoricheskogo Otdela pri Shtabe Kavkazskogo Voennogo Okruga, 1899.

Shul'gin, S. N., 'Razskaz Ochevidtsa o Shamile i Ego Sovremenikakh [An Eyewitness' Account of Shamil and His Contemporaries]', *Sbornik Materialov dlia Opisaniia Mestnostei i Plemen Kavkaza*, Vol. XXXII (1903), Part I, pp. 10-24

French Transl., Ibrahimoff, 'Chamyl le Hero du Caucsse, Jugé par les Siens', *Revue du MondeMusulman,* No.10 (April 1910), pp. 533-541.

-------- 'Predanie o Shamilevskom Naibe Khadzhi-Murate [A Tradition About Shamil's *Na'ib* Hajimurad]', *Sbornik Materialov dlia Opisaniia Mestnostei i Plemen Kavkaza*, Vol. XL (1909), Part I, pp. 54-70.

French Transl., Ibrahimoff, 'Hadji-Mourad, le Naïb de Chamyl', *Revue du Monde Musulman,* No.11 (May 1910), pp.100-104.

[Sleptsov, Nikolai Pavlovich], 'Pis'ma N. P. Sleptsova k Kniaziu Bariatinskomu, 1851 [N. P. Sleptsov's Letters to Prince Bariatinskii, 1851]', *Russkii Arkhiv,* 1889, No. 2, pp. 261-273.

Sollohub [Sollogub] Vladimir Aleksandrovich, *Le Caucase dans la Question d'Orient. Reponse aux Biographes Parisiens de Schamyl*, St. Petersburg: Jacques Issakoff, 1855.

-------- 'Razskaz Mozdokskogo Grazhdanina, 3-i Gildii Kuptsa Minaia Shleva Syna Atarova, o Poezdke Svoei v Dargo-Vedeno, Mestoprebyvanie Shamilia [The Story of the Resident of Muzlik, Merchant of the Third Guild, Minai Atarov the Son of Shlev, About His Journey to Darghiyya-Vedan, Shamil's Residence]', *Kavkaz*, 14 [26] November 1853 (No. 85), pp. 365-368.

Soltan, Viacheslav, 'Na Gunibe v 1859 i 1871 GG. [On [[Mt.]] Ghunib in 1859 and 1871]', *Russkaia Starina*, 1892, No. 5, pp. 390-418.

-------- 'Obzor Sobytii v Dagestane v 1855 i 1856 Godakh [A Review of the Events in Daghestan in the Years 1855 and 1856]', *Kavkazskii Sbornik*, Vol. X11 (1888), pp. 479-532.

-------- 'Ocherk Voennykh Deistvii v Dagestane v 1852 i 1853 Godakh [A Survey of the Military Operations in Daghestan in the Years 1852 and 1853]', *Kavkazskii Sbornik*, Vol. IX (1885), pp. 475-521.

-------- 'Ocherk Voennykh Deistvii v Dagestane v 1854 Godu [A Survey of the Military Operations in Daghestan in 1854]', *Kavkazskii Sbornik*, Vol. XI (1887), pp. 525-571.

-------- 'Zaniatie Salatavii v 1857 Godu [The Occupation of Salatawh in 1857]', *Kavkazskii Sbornik*, Vol. V111 (1884), pp. 335-397.

Spencer, Edmund, *Travels in Circassia, Krim Tartary etc. including a Steam Voyage Down the Danube from Vienna to Constantinople and round the Black Sea in 1836*, London: Henry Colburn, 1837.

-------- *Travels in the Western Caucasus including a Tour through Imeretia, Mingrelia, Turkey, Moldavia, Galicia, Silesia and Moravia in 1836*, London: Henry Colborn, 1838.

-------- *Turkey, Russia the Black Sea and Circassia*, London: George Routledge and Co., 1854.

'Stsena iz Pokoreniia Dzharo-Belakan [A Scene from the Conquest of Chartalah]', *Sbornik Gazety Kavkaz*, 1846, pp. 15-20.

'Stseny iz Boevoi Zhizni [Scenes from [[My][Military Life[', *Sbornik Gazety Kavkaz*, 1846, pp. 410-411.

Struve, Gleb, 'An Anglo-Russian Medley: Woronzows, Pembrokes, Nicolays and Others. Unpublished Letters and Historical Notes', *California Slavic Studies*, Vol. V (1970), pp. 93-135.

[Sulayman Efendi], 'Opisanie Postupkov Shamilia Protivnykh Musul'manskomy Shariatu, kotorye Byli Zamecheny Suleiman-Efendiem vo Vremia ego Nakhozhdeniia pri nem [A Description of Deeds by Shamil Contradicting the *Shari'a* which Were Observed by Sulayman Efendi During his Stay with him]', *Sbornik Gazety Kavkaz*, 1847, Vol. I, pp.30-35.

Svechin, D., 'Ocherk Narodonaseleniia, Nravov i Obycbaev Dagestantsev [Survey of the Population, Mores and Habits of the Daghestanis]', *Zapiski Kavkazskogo Otdela Imperarotorskogo Geograficheskogo Obshchestva*, Book II (1853), pp. 54-65.

Szimanski [Shimanskii], 'Delo na Gotsatlinskikh Vysotakh 21-go Sentiabria 1843 Goda (Iz Pokhodnykh Zapisok) [The Battle on the Hutsal Heights on 21 September [[3 October]] 1843 (From Notes Taken on the March)]', *Voennyi Sbornik*, 1869, No. 7, Part I, pp. 5-9.

T., 'Razvitie Miuridizma na Kavkaze [The Development of the *Murid* Movement in the Caucasus]', *Odesskii Vestnik*, 22 September [4 October] 1859 (No.103), pp. 447-449.

-------- 'Vospominaniia o Kavkaze i Gruzii [Memoirs of the Caucasus and Georgia]', *Russkii Vestnik*, 1869, No.1, pp.1-36, No. 2, pp. 401-443, No. 3, pp. 102 -155, No. 4, pp. 658-707.

Taillander, Saint-Rene, 'La Guere du Caucase. Le Prince Woronzoff et le Prophete Schamyl', *Revue de Deux Mondes*, 1 November 1853, pp. 409-448.

Tewzadze, Walerjan, *Kaukaz. Skic Geograficzno-Opisowy [The Caucasus. A Geographical-Descriptive Sketch]*, Warsaw: Druk Gluwnej Drukarni Wojskowej, 1933.

Timiriazev, F., 'Po Povodu Stat'i Berzhe o N. N. Murav'eve-Karskom [Reaction to Berge's Article on N. N. Murav'ev-Karskii]', *Russkii Arkhiv*, 1873, No. 12, cc. 2530-2540.

Todtleben, Eduard, [Totleben, Eduard Ivanovich], 'Osada i Bombardirovanie Ukrepleniia Chokh v Dagestane v 1849 Godu [The Siege and Bombardment of Fort Chokha in Daghestan in 1849]', *Sbornik Opisanii Osad i oboron Krepostei i Ukreplenii,* Vol. I (1869), pp. 107-125.

Abriged version published in: *Inzhenernyi Zhurnal*, 1857, No. 4, Official Part, pp. 205-227.

-------- 'Osada Ukreplennogo Seleniia Gergebil v Dagestane v 1848 G. [The Siege of the Fortified Village of Girgil in Daghestan in 1848]', *Sbornik Opisanii Osad i Oboron Krepostei i Ukreplenii,* Vol. I (1869), pp. 50-73.

Tolstoi, Lev Nikolaevich, 'Kkadzhi Murat [Hajimurad]l', in *Posmertnye Khudozhestvennye Proizvedeniia*, Vol. III, Moscow: Tipografiia T-va I. D. Sytina, 1912, pp. 3-125.

-------- 'Nabeg. Razskaz Volontera [The Raid. A Volunteer's Story]',in: *Sochineniia*,. Vol. II, Moscow: Tipo-Litogrrafiia T-va I. N. Kushnereva i Ko., 1911 (12th edition), pp. 65-102.

-------- 'Vyrubka Lesa. Razskaz Iunkera [Forest Felling. A Junker's Story]', in *Sochineniia*,. Vol. II, Moscow: Tipo-Litogrrafiia T-va I. N. Kushnereva i Ko., 1911 (12th edition), pp. 423-467.

Tolstoi, Vladimir, 'Iz Vospominanfi o Gruzii (1847). Delo Generala Shvartsa [From [[My]] Memoirs of Georgia (1847). The Affair of General Schwartz]', *Russkii Arkhiv*, 1877, No. 5, pp. 37-41.

Tomai, A. 'Materialy k Voprosu o Feodalizme v Istorii Dagestana [Sources to the Question of Feudalism in the History of Daghestan]', *Revoliutsionnyi Vostok*, 1935, No. 5, pp. 116-137.

[Tornauw, Fedor Fedorovich], 'Gergebil'. (Vospominaniia Barona F. F. Tornova) [Girgil. The Memoirs of Baron Theodor Tornau]', *Russkii Arkhiv*, 1881, No. 4, pp. 425-470.

Tsereteli, Giorgii V., 'Vnov' Naidennye Pis'ma Shamilia [The Found Again Letters of Shamil]', *Trudy Pervoi Sessii Arabistov, 14 - 17 Iiunia 1935 G.*, Moscow and Leningrad: Izdatel'stvo Akademii Nauk SSSR, 1937, pp. 95-112

Tsylov, N. I., *Epizody iz Boevoi Zhizni Alekseia Petrovicha Ermolova na Kavkaze v 1818, 1819 i 1820 Godakh. Zapiski Ochevidtsa Sluzhivshego pod ego Nachal'stvom [Episodes from the Military Life of Aleksei Petrovich Ermolov in the Caucasus in the Years 1818, 1819 and 1820. Notes by a Witness Serving under his Command]*, St. Petersburg: Tipografiia L. Bermana i G. Rabbinovicha 1878.

UK, The Foreign Office, the Historical Section, *Caucasia* (Handbook), London: H. M. Stationary Office, 1920.

V -- ii, A., 'Vospominaniia o Bylom [Reminiscences of the Past]', *Voennyi Sbornik*, 1872, No. 2, Part I, pp. 323-358.

V -- v, A., 'Zimnii Perekhod Cherez Kavkazskie Gory [A Winter Crossing of the Caucasus Mountains]', *Russkii Arkhiv*, 1885, No. 11, pp. 498-509.

'Veden [Vedan]', *Voennyi Sbornik*, 1859, No. 4, Non-official Part, pp. 542- 558.

Verderevskii, Evgenii Aleksandrovich, *Ot Zaural'ia do Zakavkaz'ia. Iumoristicheskie, Sentimental'nye i Kriticheskie Pis'ma s Dorogi [From Tans-Ural to Trans-Caucasus. Humourous, Sentimental and Critical Letters from the Road]*. Moscow: Tipografiia V. Got'e, 1857.

-------- *Plen u Shamilia. Pravdivaia Povest' o Vos'mimesiachnom i Shestidnevnom (v 1854 - 1856 G.) Prebyvanii v Plenu u Sahmilia Semeistv pokoinogo General-Maiora Kniazia Orbeliani i Podpolkovnika Kniazia Chavchavadze Osnovannaia na Pokazaniiakh Lits Uchavstvovavshikh v Sobytii*. St. Petersburg: Tipografiia Koroleva i Komp., 1856.

Second Extended Edition: *Kavkazskie Plennitsy ili Plen u Shamilia. Nevymyshlennaia Povest' o Shestidnevnom (v 1854 - 1856 G.) Prebyvanii v Plenu u Sahmilia Semeistv pokoinogo General-Maiora Kniazia Orbeliani i Polkovnika Kniazia Chavchavadze na Osnovanii Sobstvennykh Pokazaniiakh Lits Uchavstvovavshikh v Sobytii*, Moscow: Tipografiia V.Got'e,1857.

English Transl.: H. Sutherland Edwards, *Captivity of Two Princesses in the Caucasus including a Seven Months Residence in Shamil's Seraglio*, London: Smith, Elder and Co., 1857.

French Summary: H. Delaveau, 'Captivite de Deus Princesses Russes dans le Serail de Schamyl au Caucase en 1855 d'Apres le Recit Russe de M. Verderevski', *Revue de Deux Mondes*, 1 May 1856, pp. 5-48.

Verderevskii, Evgenii Aleksandrovich and Dunkel-Welling, N., *Shamil' v Parizhe i Shamil' Poblizhe [Shamil Viewed from Paris and from Nearby]* Tiflis: Tipografiia Kantseliarii Namestnika Kavkazskogo 1855.

'Voenno-Akhtynskaia Doroga ot S. Shina do Perevala Chrez Goru Bol. Salavat [The Akhdi Military Highway from the Village of Shini to the Pass of Mt. Great Salavat]', *Sbornik Gazety Kavkaz*, 1847, Vol. I, pp.131-132.

Volkonskii, Nikolai A., 'Sem' Let v Plenu na Kavkaze (1849-1856). Ocherk Politicheskogo i Domashnego Byta Kavkazskikh Gortsev [Seven Years in Captivity in the Caucasus (1849-1856). A Sketch of the Political and Private Way of Life of the Caucasian Mountaineers]', *Voennyi Vestnik*, 1882, No. 5, pp. 217-283.

-------- 'Lezginskaia Ekspeditsiia (v Didoiskoe Obshchestvo) v 1857 Godu [The Lesghian Campaign (into the Dido Community) in 1857]', *Kavkazskii Sbornik*, Vol. 1 (1876), pp. 369-409, Vol. II (1877), pp. 215-386.

-------- 'Okonchatel'noe Pokorenie Vostochnogo Kavkaza (1859-i God) [The Final Conquest of the Eastern Caucasus (1859)]', *Kavkazskii Sbornik*, Vol. IV (1879), pp. 69-436.

-------- 'Pogrom Chechni v 1852 Godu [The Defeat of Chechnia in 1852]' *Kavkazskii Sbornik*, Vol. V (1880), pp. 1 -234.

-------- '1858 God v Chechne [The Year 1858 in Chechnia]', *Kavkazskii Sbornik*, Vol. III (1879), pp. 377-591.

-------- 'Trekhletie na Lezginskoi Kordonnoi Linii (1847-1849) [Three Years on the Lesghian Cordonne Line (1847 -1849]]', *Kavkazskii Sbornik*, Vol. IX (1885), pp. 157-366 (+ 22 pp. Appendices).

-------- 'Trekhletie v Dagestane. 1847-i God: Osada Gergebilia i Vziatie Salty [Three Years in Daghestan. 1847: The Siege of Girgil and the Capture of Saltah]', *Kavkazskii Sbornik*, Vol. VI (1882), pp. 477-682 (+ 4 pp. Appendices and map).

-------- 'Trekhletie v Dagestane. 1848-i God: Vziatie Gergebilia i Geroiskaia Zashchita Ukrepleniia Akhty [Three Years in Daghestan. 1848: The Capture of Girgil and thle Heroic Defence of Fort Akhdi]', *Kavkazskii Sbornik*, Vol. VII (1883), pp. 481-612 .

------- 'Trekhletie v Dagestane. 1849-i God: Osada Ukrepleniia Chokh [Three Years in Daghestan. 1849: The Siege of Fort Chokha]', *Kavkazskii Sbornik*, Vol. VIII (1884), pp, 241 -305 (+ 3 pp, Appendices and map).

Volkonskii, Nikolai A,, von Klieman, F. and Bublitskii, P., 'Voina na Vostochnom Kavkaze s 1824 po 1834 G. v Sviazi s Miuridizmom [The War in the Eastern Caucasus, 1824- 1834, in Connection with the *Murid* Movement]', *Kavkazskii Sbornik*, Vol. X (1866), pp. 1-224, Vol. XI (1887), p. 1-185, Vol. XII (1888), pp. 1-216, Vol. XIII (1889), pp. 152-334, Vol. XIV (1890), pp. 1-211, Vol. XV (1894), pp. 506-576, Vol. XVI (1895), pp. 405-480, Vol. XVII (1896), pp. 323-409, Vol. XVIII, (1897), pp. 288-351, Vol. XX (1899), pp. 97-141.

Volotskoi, Aleksandr A., 'General Freitag i Ego Boevye Tovarishchi. Tri Epizoda iz Istorii Zavoevaniia Kavkaza [General Freytag and his Comrades in Arms. Three Episodes from the History of the Conquest of the Caucasus]', *Russkaia Starina*, 1879, No. 6, pp. 815-842.

[Vorontsov, Mikhail Semenovich,] 'Dva Pis'ma Kniazia Vorontsova k Grafu Benkendorfu [Two Letters from Prince Vorontsov to Count Benckendorff]', *Russkii Arkhiv*, 1890, No. 7, pp. 305-310.

-------- 'Iz Pisem Kniazia Mikhaila Semenovicha Vorontsova k Mikhailu Pavlovichu Shcherbininu [From the Letters of Prince Mikhail Semenovich Vorontsov to Mikhail Pavlovich Shcherbinin]', *Russkii Arkhiv*, 1870, No. 12, cc. 2145-2224.

-------- 'Iz Pisem Namestnika Kavkazskogo Kniazia M. S. Vorontsova k Grodonachal'niku Odesskomu A. I. Kaznacheevu [From the Letters of the Viceroy to the Caucasus Prince M. S. Vorontsov to the Administrator of Odessa, A. I. Kaznacheev]', *Russkii Arkhiv*, 1907, No. 3, pp. 452-455.

-------- 'Kn. M. S. Vorontsov i N. N. Murav'ev v Pis'makh k M. T. Loris-Melikovu 1852-1856 GG. [Prince M. S. Vorontsov and N. N. Murav'ev in Their Letters to M. I. Loris-Melikov, 1852-1856]', *Russkaia Starina*, 1884, No. 9, pp. 589-598.

-------- 'Kniaz' M. S. Vorontsov. Pis'ma Ego k Kn. V. O. Bebutovu [Prince M. S. Vorontsov. His Letters to Prince V. O. Bebutov]', *Russkaia Starina*, 1873, No. 3, pp. 431-456.

-------- 'Pis'ma Kniazia Mikhaila Semenovicha Vorontsova k Alekseiu Petrovichu Ermolovu [Letters of Prince Mikhail Semenovich Vorontsov to Aleksei Petrovich Ermolov]', *Russkii Arkhiv*, 1890, No. 2, pp. 161-214, No. 3, pp. 329-365, No. 4, pp. 441-472.

-------- 'Prikaz Po Otdel'nomu Kavkazskomu Korpusu 14 Fevralia 1853 [Order of the Day to the Separate Caucasian Corps, 14 [[26]] February 1853]', *Kavkaz*, 18 February [2 March] 1853 (No. 13), p. 54.

-------- 'Vypiski iz Dnevnika Svetleishego Kniazia M. S. Vorontsova s 1845 po 1854 G. [Excerpts from the Diary of His Serene Highness Prince M. S. Vorontsov, 1845 - 1854]', *Starina i Novizna*, Vol. V (1902), pp. 74-118.

Vrankin, A., 'Odno iz Del General-Maiora Passeka. Delo pri Gilli 5-go Iiunia 1844 Goda [One of the Battles of Major-General Passek. The Battle Near Gilli on 5 [[17]] June 1844]', *Sbornik Gazety Kavkaz*, 1846, pp. 21-27.

'Vziatie Shamilia [The Capture of Shamil]', *Odesskii Vestnik*, 24 September [6 October] 1859, pp. 454-455.

'Vziatie v Plen Shamilla [The Taking Captive of Shamil]', *Zhurnal dlia Chteniia Vospitannikan Voeno-Uchebnykh Zavedenii*, Vol. CXLII, No. 566, pp. 177-187.

Wagner, Friedrich, *Schamyl als Feldherr, Sultan und Prophet und der Kaukazus*, Leipzig: Gustav Memmelmann, 1854.

Wagner, Moritz, *Der Kaukazus und das Land der Kosaken in der Jahren 1843 bis 1846*, Leipzig: Arnoldisch Buchhandlung, 1848.

Warner, *Schamyl, le Prophete du Caucase*, Paris: Librairie Nouvelle, 1854.

Italian Transl. *Sciamyl, il Profera del Caucaso*, Firenze: Pelire le Monnier, 1855.

Watson, Robert Grant, *A History of Persia from the Beginning of the Nineteenth Century to the Year 1858 with a Review of the Principal Events that Led to the Establishment of the Kajar Dynasty*, London: Smith, Elder and Co., 1866.

W[lasto]ff, Georges, [Vlastov, Georgii Konstantinovich,] *Ombres du Passe. Souvenirs d'un Officier du Caucase*, Paris: Artheme Bertrand [1899].

Yama'uchi, Masayuki, 'Sheikh Shamil and the Ottoman Empire in the Period of the Crimean War Enlightened by the ATASE Archives in Ankara', *Orient* (Tokyo), Vol. XXII (1986), pp. 143-158.

English Trans. of some of the documents: 'From the Ottoman Archives', *Central Asian Survey*, Vol. 4, No. 4 (Autumn 1985), pp. 7-12.

[Yitzhaqi, Ya'aqov ben Yitzhaq,] *Igrot u-Te'udot me-Arkhiyon ha-Rav Ya'aqov B[en] Ha-R[av] Yitz[haq] Z[ikhronoh] L[ivrakh], Rabbah ha-Rashi shel Dagestan [Letters and Documents from the Archive of Rabbi Ya'aqov the Son of Rabbi Yitzhaq Yitzhaqi, Blessed Be his Memory, the Chief Rabbi of Daghestan]*, Jerusalem: The Central Archive for the History of the Jewish People, 5734 [1974].

Zagorskii, Ivan, 'Vosem Mesiatsev v Plenu u Gortsev [Eight Months in the Mountaineers' Captivity]', *Kavkazskii Sbornik*, Vol. XIX (1898), pp. 221-247.

Zakharin (Iakunin), Ivan, 'Poezdka k Shamiliu v Kalugu v 1860 Godu. Iz Zapisok i Vospominanii [A Journey to Shamil to Kaluga in 1860. From [[My]] Notes and Reminiscences]', *Vestnik Evropy*, 1898, No. 8, pp. 601-640.

-------- 'Vstrecha s Synom Shamilia i Ego Razskaz ob Ottse [A Meeting with Shamil's Son and His Story About His Father]l', *Russkaia Starina*, 1901, No. 8, pp. 367-389.

'Zakony Shamilia [Shamil's Laws]', *Zhivopisnoe Obozrenie*, 1875, No, 8, pp. 125-126.

'Zashchita Ukrepleniia Akhty v 1848 Godu [The Defence of Fort Akhdi in 1848]', *Chteniia dlia Soldat*, 1860, Book 3, pp.13-42.

'Zashchita Ukrepleniia Akhty v 1849 [*sic!*] Godu [The Defence of Fort Akhdi in 1848]', *Sbornik Opisanii Osad i Oboron Krepostei i Ukreplenii*, Vol. I (1869), pp. 74-106.

'Zemel'nye Otnosheniia v Dorevoliutsionnom Dagestane [Agrarian Relations in Pre-revolutionary Daghestan]', *Krasnyi Arkhiv*, 1936, No, 6 (79), pp. 101-149.

Zubov, Platon, *Kartina Kavkazskogo Kraia Prinadlezhashchim Rossii i Sopredel'nykh Onomu Zemel' v Istoricheskom, Statisticheskom, Etnograficheskom, Finansovom i Torgovom Otnosheniiakh [Description of the Caucasian Region Belonging to Russia and the Neighbouring Lands, in the Historical, Statistical, Ethnographical, Financial and Commercial Aspects]*, St. Petersburg: Tipografiia Konrada Vingebara, 1834-1835.

-------- *Podvigi Russkikh Voinov v Stranakh Kavkazskikh s 1800 po 1834 God [The Achievements of the Russian Soldiers in the Caucasian Lands between 1800 and 1834]*, St. Petersburg: Tipografiia Konrada Vagenberga, 1835-1836.

Züssermann [Zisserman], Arnold L., 'Eshche Neskol'ko Slov o Pokorenii Vostochnogo Kavkaza (Otvet Baronu Nikolai) [A Few More Words on the Conquest of the Eastern Caucasus (An Answer to Count Nicolay)]', *Russkii Arkhiv*, 1889, No. 11, pp. 415-420.

-------- 'Eshche Neskol'ko Slov po Povodu Stat'i G-na Borozdina o N. N. Murav'eve-Karskom [A Few More Words Following Mr. Borozdin's Article on N. N. Murav'ev-Karskii]', *Russkii Arkhiv*, 1892, No. 7, pp. 392 -396.

-------- 'Iz Moikh Zapisok. 6-go Iiunia 1845 Goda [From My Notes: 6 [[18]] June 1845]', *Sbornik Gazety Kavkaz*, 1846, pp. 306-311.

-------- 'Khadzhi-Murat. Pis'ma o Nem Kn. M. S. Vorontsova i Razskazy Kavkaztsev. 1851-1852 GG. [Hajimurad. Prince Vorontsov's Letters and Veteran Caucasians' Stories About Him. 1851-1852]', *Russkaia Starina*, 1881, No. 3, pp. 655-680.

-------- 'Kriticheskie Zametki [Critical Remarks]', *Russkii Arkhiv*, 1885, No. 8, pp. 558-569.

-------- 'Otryvki iz Moikh Vospominanii [Excerpts from My Memoirs]', *Russkii Vestnik*, 1876, No. 3, pp. 50-105, No. 4, pp. 416-461, No. 12, pp. 479-555, 1877, No. 1, pp. 163-213, No. 2, pp. 524-578, No. 3, pp. 80-138, No. 6, pp. 504-559, 1878, No. 2, pp. 529-581, No. 3, pp. 20-52, No. 4, pp. 585-633, No. 6, pp. 722 -788, No. 11, pp. 56-97, 1879, No. 2, pp. 685-734.

Subsequently publisbed as *Dvatsat' Piat' Let na Kavkaze*, St. Petersburg: Tipografiia A. S. Suvorina, 1879.

-------- 'Pis'mo iz Groznoi [A Letter from Groznaia]', *Kavkaz*, 7 [19] June 1856 (No. 44), pp. 176- 178.

-------- 'Po Povodu Razskaza 'Smert' Sleptsova' [Following the Article 'The Death of Sleptsov']', *Russkii Arkhiv,* 1889, No. 1, pp. 153-160.

-------- 'Po Povodu Vospominaniil o N. N. Murav'eve [Following the Memoirs About N. N. Murav'ev]', *Russkii Arkhiv,* 1892, No. 4, pp. 510-525.

II. SECONDARY SOURCES

1. Unpublished

Adamiyat, Fereydoun, 'The Diplomatic Relations of Persia with Britain, Turkey and Russia, 1815- 1830', Ph. D. Dissertation, University of London, 1949.

Atkin, Muriel Ann, "The Khanates of the Eastern Caucasus and the Origins of the First Russo-Iranian War," Yale University, 1976.

Aydemir, Hasan Ali, ' Seyh Samil ve Gunumize olan Etkiden [Shaykh Shamil and his Significance to our Times]', Graduation Thesis, Istanbul University, 1976.

van-Bruinessen, Maarten Martinus, 'Agha, Shaikh and State. On the Social and Political Organization of Kurdistan', Ph. D. Dissertation, Utrecht University, 1978.

Duda, Sadik Tufan, "The Theme of Caucasus in Russian Literature of the Eighteenth-Nineteenth Centuries," Vanderbilt University, 1971.

Duran, Tulay, ' Seyh Samil ve Müridizm Hareketi [Shaykh Shamil and the *Murid* Novement]' Graduation Thesis, Istanbul University, 1976.

Eros, Carol Carbone, "Tolstoj's Tales of the Caucasus and Literary Tradition," The University of Wisconsin - Madison, 1973.

Gammer, Moshe, 'Shamil ba-Historyografiya ha-Sovyetit [Shamil in Soviet Historiography]', B. A. Thesis, Tel-Aviv University, 1976.

Luxenburg, Norman, 'Russian Expansion into the Caucasus and the British Relationship Thereto', Ph. D. Dissertation, Univeristy of Michigan, 1956.

Pinson, Marc, 'Russian Expulsion of Mountaineers from the Caucasus, 1856-66 and Its Historical Background. Demographic Warfare -- An Aspect of Ottoman and Russian Policies, 1854-66', Ph. D. Dissertation, Harvard University, 1970.

Quandour, Mohyieddin Izzat, 'Muridism: A Study of the Caucasian Wars of Independence, 1819-1859', Ph. D. Dissertation, Claremont Graduate School, 1964.

Rhinelander, Lawrence Hamilton, 'The Incorporation of the Caucasus into the Russian Empire: The Case of Georgia, 1801-1854', Ph. D. Dissertation, Columbia University, 1972.

Wixman, Ronald, "Language Aspects of Ethnic Patterns and Processes in the North Caucasus," The University of Chicago, 1978.

Youngblood, Ronald Fred, 'The Amarna Correspondence of Rib-Haddi, Prince of Byblos (E. A. 68-96)', Ph. D. Dissertation, Dropsie College, 1961.

2. Published

Abercromby, John, *A Trip Through the Eastern Caucasus with a Chapter on the Languages of the Country*, London: Edward Stanford, 1889.

Abdullaev, Mahomed Abdullaevich, *Iz Istorii Filosafskoi i Obshchestvenno-Politicheskoi Mysli Narodov Dagestana v XIX V. [From the Philosophical and Socio-Political Thought of the Peoples of Daghestan in the Nineteenth Century]*, Moscow: 'Nauka', 1968.

-------- *Mysliteli Narodov Dagestana XIX i Nachala XX VV. [Thinkers of the Peoples of Daghestan in the Nineteenth and the Beginning of the Twentieth Centuries]*. Makhachqala: Daguchpedgiz, 1968.

Abich, Hermann, *Aus Kaukasischen Landern. Reisebriefe*, Vienna: Alfred Holder, 1896.

Abu-Manneh, Butrus, 'The Naqshbandiyya-Mujadidiyya in the Ottoman Lands in the Early 19th Century' *Die Welt des Islams*, Vol. XII, No. 1 (1982), pp. 1-36.

Adamov, E. and Kutakov, L., 'Iz Istorii Proiskov Inostrannoi Agentury vo Vremia Kavkazskikh Voin [From the History of the Intrigues of Foreign Agents During the Caucasian Wars]', *Voprosy Istorii*, 1950, No. 11, pp. 101-105.

Adighe, R., 'Literature on Daghestan and Its People', *Caucasian Review*, No. 4 (1957), pp. 101-118,

Afschar, Mahmoud, *La Politique Europeene en Perse. Quelques Pages de l'Histoire Diplomatique*, Tehran: Tehran University, 1973 (2nd edition).

Aglarov, M. A., *Sel'skaia Obshchina v Nagornom Dagestane v XVII - Nachale XIX v. [The Rural Community in Upper Daghestan in the Seventeenth - Beginning of the Nineteenth Centuries]*, Moscow: Nauka, 1988.

Ahmad, Qeyamuddin, *The Wahhabi Movement in India,* Calcutta: Firma K. L. Mukhopadhyay, 1966.

Ahmadov [Akhmadov], Yavus. Z., 'Iz Istorii Checheno-Russkikh Otnoshenii [From the History of Checheno-Russian Relations]', *Voprosy Istorii Dagestana*, Vol. III (1975).

Ahmadov, [Akhmadov], Sharpudin. B., *Imam Mansur. (Narodno-Osvoboditel'noe Dvizheniie v Chechne i na Severnom Kavkaze v Kontse XVIII V. [Imam Mansur. The National Liberation Mopvement in Chechnia and the Northern Caucasus at the End of the 18th Century]*, Groznyi: 'Kniga', 1991.

-------- 'Ob Istokakh Antifeodal'nogo i Antikolonial'nogo Dvizhenia Gortsev v Chechne v Kontse XVIII V. [About the Origins of the Anti-Feudal and Anti-Colonial Movement of the Mountaineers in Chechnia at the End of the Eighteenth Century]', *Izvestiia Checheno-Ingushskogo Nauchno-Issledovatel'skogo Instituta*, Vol. IX, Part 3 (1974).

Aitberov, T. M., 'Soglasheniia Avarskikh Obshchin XVIII - Nachala XIX V. [Agreements of the Avar Communities in the Eighteenth - Beginning of the Nineteenth Centuries]', in: Kh. A. Omarov (ed.), *Pis'mennye Pamiatniki Dagestana XVIII - XIX VV.*, Makhachqala: Dagestanskii Filiial AN SSSR, 1983, pp. 15 - 32.

Akhriev, Chakh, 'Ingushi (Ikh Predaniia, Verovaniia i Poveriia) [The Ingush (Their Traditions, Beliefs and Superstitions)]', *Sbornik Svedenii o Kavkazskikh Gortsakh*, Vol. VIII (1875), 40 pp.(separate pagination).

Akhriev, N., 'O Nekotorykh Voprosakh Istorii Dvizheniia Kavkazskikh Gortsev v Pervoi Polovine XIX Veka [On Several Questions in the History of the Movement of the Caucasian Mountaineers in the First Half of the Nineteenth Century]', *Uchenye Zapiski* (Makhachqala), Vol. II (1957), pp. 52-63.

Akiner, Shirin, *Islamic Peoples of the Soviet Union*, London: Kegan Paul, 1983.

Algar, Hamid, 'Bibliograpllical Notes on the Naqshbandi Tariqat', in G. F. Hourani (ed.), *Essays on Islamic Philosophy and Sciences*, New York: Albany State University Press, 1975, pp. 254-259.

-------- 'A Brief History of the Naqshbandi Order,' in: Marc Gaborieau, Alexandre Popovic and Thierry Zarcone (eds.), *Naqshbabdis. Historical Development and Present Situation of a Muslim Mystical Order*. Istanbul and Paris: ISIS Press, 1990, pp. 3 - 44

An Earlier Version: 'The Naqshbandi Order: A Preliminary Survey of Its History and Significance', *Studia Islamica*, No. 44 (1970), pp. 123-152.

-------- 'Political Aspects of Naqshbandi History,' in: Marc Gaborieau, Alexandre Popovic and Thierry Zarcone (eds.), *Naqshbabdis. Historical Development and Present Situation of a Muslim Mystical Order*. Istanbul and Paris: ISIS Press, 1990, pp. 123 - 152.

-------- *Religion and State in Iran, 1785 - 1906. The Role of the Ulama in the Qajar Period*, Berkeley: University of California Press, 1969.

Aliev, Mahomed Hadisovich, Ahmedov, Sharafudin Mahomedovich and Umakhanov, Mahomet-Salam Qurbanovich, *Iz Istorii Srednevekovogo Dagestana [From the History of Medieval Daghestan]*, Makhahqkala: Tipografiia Filiala Akademii Nauk SSSR, 1970.

Allen, William Edward David, *A History of the Georgian People from the Beginning down to the Russian Conquest in the Nineteenth Century*, London: Kegan Paul, Trench, Trubner and Co., 1932.

Allen, William Edward David and Muratoff, Paul, *Caucasian Battlefields. A History of the Wars on the Turco-Caucasian Border, 1828 - 1921*, Cambridge: Cambridge University Press, 1953.

Turkish transl. *Kafkas Harekâti, 1828 - 1921. Türk-Kafkasya Sinirindaki Harplerin Tarihi*, Ankara: 1966.

Altshuler, Mordekhay, *Yehudey Mizrah Qavqaz. Toldot haYehudim haHarariyim meReshit haMe'a haTsha' 'Esre [The Jews of the Eastern Caucasus. History of the Mountain Jews from the Beginning of the Nineteenth Century]*, Jerusalem: Yad Yitzhaq ben-Tzvi, 1990.

Amidei, B. Barbielini, *Elementi per uno Studio Linguistico e Politico del Caucaso*, Naples: Istituto Superiore Orientale, 1938.

Ancel, Jacques, *Manuel Historiqe de la Question d'Orient, 1792 - 1923*, Paris: Librairie de Lagrave, 1931.

Anderson, Matthew Smith, *The Eastern Question, 1774 - 1923. A Study in International Politics*, London: Macmillan, 1966.

-------- *Peter the Great*, London: Thames and Hudson, 1978.

Andreev, N., *Iliustrirovannyi Putevoditel' po Kavkazu [Illustrated guide to the Caucasus]*, Moscow: Tipografiia Poplavskogo, 1912.

Andreev, V., 'Ermolov i Paskevich [Ermolov and Paskiewicz]', *Russkii Arkhiv*, 1873, No. 8, cc. 1571 -1583.

An altered version was published in: *Kavkazskii Sbornik*, Vol, I (1876), pp. 197-213.

Anisimov, I. Sh., 'Kavkazskie Evrei-Gortsy [The Caucasian Jesvs - Mountaineers]', *Sbornik Materialov po Etnografii Izdavaemyi pri Dashkovskom Etnograficheskom Muzee*, Vol. III (1888), pp. 171-322.

Atkin, Muriel, *Russia and Iran, 1780 - 1828*, Minneapolis: University of Minnesota Press, 1980.

Avalishvili, Z., 'Gobino na Kavkate [Gaubinot in the Caucasus]', *Kavkaz* (Paris), 1935, No. 11 (23), pp. 14-18.

-------- 'O Vospominaniiakh Musa-Pashi Kundukhova [About the Memoirs of Musa Pasha Kundukh]', *Kavkaz* (Paris), 1937, No. 8 (44), pp. 11-*17*.

Baddeley, John Erederic, *The Rugged Flanks of the Caucaus*, London: Oxford University Press and Humphrey Milford, 1940.

-------- *The Russian Conquest of the Caucasus*, London: Longmans, Green and Co., 1908.

Arabic transl. Sadiq Ibrahim 'Awda, ed. Taha Sultan Murad, *Al-Ihtilal al-Rusi lil-Qafqas*, Amman: Matba'at al-Iman, 1987.

Turkish transl. Sedat Özden, *Ruslarin Kafkasya'yi Istilasi ve Seyh Samil*, Istanbul: Kayihan Yayinlari, 1989.

Bagirov, Mir Dzhafar, 'K Voprosu o Kharaktere Dvizheniia Shamilia [To the Question of the Character of Shamil's Movement]', *Bol'shevik*, 1950, No. 13, pp. 21 -37.

Bagration, M., 'The Caucasus and Russia in the Historical Past', *The Caucasus*, No. 6-7 (June-July 1952), pp. 14-20.

Bammat, Heidar, '1834-1934', *Kavkaz* (Paris), 1934, No. 7, pp. 1 -3.

Barabanov, A. M., 'Poiasnitel'nye Znachki v Arabskikh Rukopisiakh i Dokumentakh Severnogo Kavkaza [Explanatory Diacritical Signs in the Arabic Manuscripts and Documents of the Northern Caucasus]', *Sovetskoe Vostokovedenie*, Vol. III (1945), pp. 183-214.

Baranowski, Bohdan and Baranowski, Krzysztof, *Historia Azerbajdzanu [History of Adharbayjan]*, Wroclaw: Zaklad Narodowy Imienia Ossoliaskich, 1987.

-------- *Historia Gruzji [History of Georgia]*, Wroclaw: Zaklad Narodowy Imienia Ossoliaskich, 1987.

-------- *Polaków Kaukaskie Drogi [The Poles' Caucasian Roads]*, Lodz: Krajowa Agencja Wydawnicza, 1985.

Baratov, N., 'Okonchatel'noe Pokorenie Vostochnogo Kavkaza -- Chechni i Dagestana (1859-1909 GG.) [The Final Conquest of the Eastern Caucasus -- Chechnia and Daghestan (1859-1909)]', *Voennyi Sbornik*, 1909, No.11, pp. 223-240, 1910, No.1, pp.1-16, No. 3, pp. 1-22, No. 4, pp. 51-66, No. 6, pp. 17-32, No. 9, pp. 51-66.

Barthold [Bartol'd], V. V., *Islam*, Petrograd: 'Ogni', 1918.

-------- *Mesto Prikaspiiskikh Oblastei v Istorii Musul'manskogo Mira [The Place of the Caspian Coastal Districts in the History of the Muslim World]*, Baqu: Obshchestvo Obsledovaniia i Izucheniia Azerbaidzhana, 1925.

Bell, Herbert C. F., *Lord Palmerston*, London: Longmans, Green & Co.,1936.

Bennigsen, Alexandre, 'Les Limites de la Destalinisation dans l'Islam Sovietique', *l'Afrique et l'Asie*, No. 39 (1957), pp. 31-40

-------- 'Mullahs, Mujahidin and Soviet Muslims', *Problems of Communism,* November - December 1984, pp. 28-44.

-------- 'Muslim Guerilla Warfare in the Caucasus (1918-1928)', *Central Asian Survey*, Vol. 2, No. 1 (July 1983), pp. 45-56.

-------- 'The Qadiriyah [Kunta Haji) *Tariqah* in North East Caucasus, 1850-1987', *Islamic Culture* (Hyderabad, India), No. 2-3 (April-]uly 1988), pp. 63-78.

-------- 'Une Mouvement Populaire au Caucase du XVIIIe Siecle. La 'Guerre Saint' du Sheikh Mansur (1785-1794). Page Malconnu et Controversee des Relations Russo-Turques', *Cahiers du Monde Russe et Sovietique*, Vol. V, No. 2, (April-June 1964), pp. 159-205.

Bennigsen, Alexandre and Lemercier-Quelquejay, Chantal, *Le Soufi et le Commissaire. Les Confreries Musulmans en URSS*, Paris: Editions du Seuil, 1986.

English Version: Alexandre Bennigsen and S. Enders Wimbush, *Mystics and Commissars. Sufism in the Soviet Union*, Berkeley and Los Angeles: California University Press, 1985.

Bennigsen, Alexandre and Wimbush, Enders S., *Muslims of the Soviet Empire. A Guide*, London: C. Hurst and Co., 1985.

Ber,Yisra'el, *Bithon Yisra'el -- Etmol, haYom, Mahar [Israel's Security -- Yesterday, Today, Tomorrow]*, Tel-Aviv: Hotsa'at 'Amiqam, 5726 [1966].

Berg, Lev Semonovich, *Natural Regions of the USSR*, Trans., Olga Adler-Titelbaum, New York: The Macmillan Co., 1950.

Bergé, Adolphe P., 'Imperator Nikolai na Kavkaze v 1837 G. [The Emperor Nicholas in the Caucasus in 1837]', *Russkaia Starina*, 1884, No. 8, pp. 377-398.

-------- 'Posol'stvo A. P. Ermolova v Persiiu. Istoricheskii Ocherk [A. P. Ermolov's Embassy to Persia. An Historical Sketch]', *Russkaia Starina*, 1877, No. 6, pp. 255-274, No. 7, pp. 383-427.

-------- 'Samson Iakovlevich Makintsev i Russkie Begletsy v Persii [Samson Iakovlevich Makintsev and the Russian Deserters in Persia]', *Russkaia Starina*, 1876, No. 4, pp. 770-804.

Beridze, Shalva, 'Shamil' v Evropeiskom Predstavlenii [Shamil in the Europeans' Image]', *Kavkaz* (Paris), 1937, No. 5 (41), pp. 39-40.

-------- 'Shamil' vo Frantsuzskoi Literature [Shamil in Erench Literature]', *Kavkaz* (Paris), 1934, No. 8-9, pp. 30-32.

Berkok, Ismail, *Tarihte Kafkasya [The Caucasus in History]*, Istanbul: Istanbul Matbaasi, 1958.

Bestuzhev, I. V., 'Oborona Kavkaza v Krymskoi Voine 1853-56 Godov [The Defence of the Caucasus in the Crimean War, 1853-1856]', *Voprosy Istorii*, 1954, No. 12, pp. 53-66.

Beyrau, Dietrich, *Militär und Gesellschaft in Vorrevolutionäre Russland*. Beitrage zur Geschichte Osteuropas, Band 15, Köln: Bohlan Verlag, 1984.

Blanch, Lesley, *The Sabres of Paradise*, London: John Murrey, 1960.

Turkish transl. Izzet Kantemir, *Cennetin Kiliçlari*, Istanbul: 1978.

Bliev, M. M., 'Kavkazskaia voina: Sotsial'nye istoki, sushchnost' [The Caucasian War: Its Social Roots and Essance],' *Istoriia SSSR*, 1982, No. 2, pp. 54 - 75.

-------- 'K Voprosu o Vremeni Prisoedineniia Narodov Severnogo Kavkaza k Rossii [To the Question of the Time of the Annexation of the Peoples of the Northern Caucasus to Russial', *Voprosy Istorii*, 1973, No. 5, pp.135-148.

Bliev, M. M., Degoev, V. V. and Kiniapina, N. S., 'Sovremennaia Burzhuaznaia Istoriografiia Politiki Rossii na Kavkaze i v Srednei Azii v XIX Veke [Contemporary Bourgeois [[i.e., Western]]l Historiography of Russian Policy in the Caucasus and Central Asia in the Nineteenth Century]', *Voprosy Istorii*, 1988, No. 4, pp. 37-53.

Boguslavskii, L., *Istoriia Apsheronskogo Polka, 1700 - 1892 [History of the Apsheron Regiment, 1700 - 1892]*, St. Petersburg: Tipografiia Ministerstva Putei Soobshcheniia, 1892.

Bol'shaia Sovetskaia Entsiklopediia [The Great Soviet Encyclopedia], Moscow, First Edition, 1929-1938, Second Edition, 1949-1959, Third Edition, 1970-1980.

Bolsover, G. H., 'David Urquhart and the Eastern Question, 1833-1837', *Journal of Modern History*, Vol. VIII (1936), pp. 444-467.

Borozdin, K. A., 'Lezginskoe Vosstanie v Kakhetii v 1863 G. [The Lesghian Uprising in Kakhet'i in 1863]', *Russkii Vestnik*, 1890, No. 7. pp. 51-77, No. 9, pp. 172 -192.

Bourne, Kenneth, *The Foreign Policy of Victorian England, 1830 - 1902*, Oxford: Clarendon Press, 1970.

Briukhanov, P. A., 'Gosudarstvennoe Ustroistvo i Administrativnoe Upravlenie Vol'nykh Obshchestv Dagestana v Pervoi Tret'i XIX V. [The State Structure and Administrative Management of the Free Communities of Daghestan in the First Third of the Nineteenth Century]', *Sbornik Trudov Piatigorskogo Gosudarstvennogo Pedagogicheskogo Instituta*, Vol. I (Stavropol, 1947).

Brutskus, I., 'Di Geshikhte fun di Berg Yid[n] oyf Kavkaz [History of the Mountain Jews of the Caucasus]', Yidisher Visnshaftlikher Institut, *Historishe Shriftn*, Vol. II, pp. 26-42.

Budak, Mustafa, '1853-1856 Kirim Harbi Baslarinda Dogu Anadolu-Kafkas Cephesi ve Seyh Samil [The Headquarters of the East-Annatolian-Caucasian Front in the Crimean War of 1853-1856 and Shaykh Shamil]', in: Mehmet Saray et al (eds.) *Kafkas Arastirmalari*, Vol. I, Istanbul: Acar Yayinlari, 1988, pp. 52-58.

Bugaev, E., 'Kogda Utrachivaetsia Nauchnyi Podkhod [When the Scientific Approach Is Lost]', *Partiinaia Zhizn'*, 1956, No. 14, pp. 62-72.

Bulwer, Henry Lytton, *The Life of Henry John Temple, Viscount Palmerstone with Selections from his Diaries and Correspondence*, London: Richard Bentley, 1870-1874.

Burchuladze, E. E., 'Krushenie Anglo-Turetskikh Planov v Gruzii v 1855-6 Godakh [The Collapse of the Anglo-Turkish Plans in Georgia in 1855-6]', *Voprosy Istorii*, 1952, No. 4, pp.10-24.

[Burdzhalov. E. N.,] 'O Stat'e Tovarishcha E. Bugaeva [About the Article of Comrade E. Bugaev]', *Voprosy Istorii*, 1956, No. 7, pp. 215 - 222.

Burkin, N. 'O Velikoderzhavnykh i Natsionalisticheskikh Tendentsiiakh v Gorskoi Istoricheskoi Literature [About the Great Powerly and Nationalistic Tendencies in the Mountain Historical Literature]', *Istorik Marksist*, 1932, No. 1-2 (23-24), pp. 140-161.

Bushuev, Semen Kuzmin, *Bor'ba Gortsev za Nexavisimost' pod Rukovodstvom Shamilia [The Mountaineers' Strugle for Independence under the Leadership of Shanil]*, Moscow and Leningrad: Izdatel'stvo AN SSSR, 1939.

-------- 'Dagestan i Chechnia v Period ikh Zavoevaniia Russkim Tsarizmom [Daghestan and Chechnia in the Period of their Conquest by Tsarist Russia]', Introduction to G.

E. Grumberg and S. K. Bushuev (eds.) *Materialy po Istorii Dagestana i Chechni*, Vol. III, Part 1, *1801 - 1839*, Makhachqala: Dagestanskoe Knizhnoe Izdatel'stvo, 1939, pp. 3-40.

-------- 'Gosudarstvennaia Sistema Imamata Shamilia [The State System of Shamil's State]', *Istorik Marksist*, 1937, No. 5-6 (63-64), pp. 77-104.

-------- *Iz Istorii Vneshnepoliticheskikh Otnoshenii v Period Prisoedineniia Kavkaza k Rossii (20 - 70 Gody XIX Veka) [From the History of International Relations in the Period of the Unification of the Caucasus with Russia (1820s - 1870s)]*, Moscow: Izdatel'stvo Moskovskogo Universiteta, 1955.

-------- 'O Kavkazskom Miuridizme [On Caucasian Muridism]', *Voprosy Istorii*, 1956, No. 12, pp. 72-79.

Byhan, Arthur, *La Civilisation Caucasienne*, Paris: Payot, 1936.

Cahagi, Wassan Giray, *Kafkas-Rus Mücadedeleri*, Istanbul: 1967.

Cannynghame, Arthur Thurlow, *Travels in the Eastern Caucasus, on the Caspian and Black Seas, especially in Daghestan and on the Frontiers of Persia and Turkey during the Summer of 1871*, London: John Murry, 1872.

Cattaoui, Rene and Cattaoui, Georges, *Mohamed-Aly et l'Europe*, Paris: Librairie Orientaliste Paul Geuthner, 1950.

Cevdet Pasa, *Kirim ve Kafkas Tarihcesi [Historian of the Crimea and the Caucasus]*, Istanbul: Matbaa Abül-Ziya, 1307 [1873].

Chantre, Ernest, *Recherches Anthropologiques dans le Caucase*, Paris: Ch. Reinwald, 1885-1887.

Cherniyaq, Moshe, *Toldot ha-Shahmat me-Reshitoh ve'ad Yamenu [The History of Chess from its Beginning to Our Days]*, Tel Aviv: Hotsa'at Mizrahi, 1963.

Cherniavskii, *Kavkaz v Techenii 25-i Letnego Tsarstvovaniia Gosudaria Imperatora Aleksandra II, 1855 - 1880. Istoricheskii Ocherk [The Caucasus during the 25 Year Long Reign of the Sovereign the Emperor Alexandre II, 1855 - 1880. An Historical Sketch]*, St. Petersburg: Voennaia Tipografiia, 1898.

Chernozubov, Fedor, 'Ocherki Terskoi Stariny [Sketches of the Terek's Past]', *Russkii Arkhiv*, 1912, No. 3, pp. 452-460.

-------- 'Ocherki Terskoi Stariny. Na Staroi Terskoi Linii, 1832 -1843 [Sketches from the Terek's Past. On the Old Terek Line, 1832-1843]', *Russkii Arkhiv*, 1914, No. 6-7, pp. 316-345.

-------- 'Ocherki Terskoi Stariny. 1: Pobegi k Nepokornym Gortsam. Zhizn' u Shamilia (1832 -1859 GG.); Iashka Altapov (1842-1856) [Sketches from the Terek's Past. 1:

Defections to the Unpacified Mountaineers. Life in Shamil's Country (1832-1859); Iashka Altapov (1842-1856)]', *Russkii Arkhiv*, 1912, No. 1, pp. 64-79.

-------- 'Ocherki Terskoi Stariny. Pobegi v Gory. Istoriia Odnoi Raskol'nich'ei Obiteli u Shamilia (1849- 1859) [Sketches from the Terek 's Past. Defections into the Mountains. The History of One Sectarian Settlement in Shamil's Country]', *Russkii Arkhiv*, 1911, No. 10, pp. 249-261, 1912, No. 6, pp. 218-225.

Chernyi Iuda Ia., 'Kavkazskie Evrei [the Caucasian Jews]', *Sbornik Svedenii o Kavkazskikh Gortsakh*, Vol. III (1870),44 pp. (separate pagination).

Chichagova, M. N., *Shamil' na Kavkaze i v Rossii. Biograficheskii Ocherk [Shamil in the Cuacasus and in Russia. A Biographical Outline]*, St. Petersburg: S. Mullas and I. Bogel'man, 1889.

Chursin, G. F., *Ocherki po Etnografii Kavkaza [Sketches on the Ethnography of the Caucasus]*, Tiflis: Tipografiia K. P. Kozlovskogo, 1913.

Cech, Svatopluk, *Cesta na Kavkaz [A Journey to the Caucasus]*, Prague: Ceskoslovenskii Spisovatel, 1952.

Costello, D. P., 'The Murder of Griboyedov', *Oxford Slavonic Papers*, Vol. VIII (1957), pp. 65-89.

Crabites, Pierre, *Ibrahim of Egypt*, London: George Routledge and Sons, 1935.

Curtiss, John Shelton, *The Russian Army Under Nicholas I, 1825 - 1855*, Durham, N. C.: Duke University Press, 1965.

von Czerlieu, Markus, *Unser Kaukazus und Dessen Sistematische Pacifierung*, Vienna: L.W. Seidel und Sohn, 1882.

Dagestanli, 'Khadzhi Murat po Bol'shevistski [Hajimurad According to the Bolsheviks]', *Kavkaz* (Paris), 1935, No. 5 (17), pp. 15-16.

Dagistanli, Ahmet Han, 'Dagistan'in Istiklal Mucadeleleri [Daghestan's Independence Struggles]', *Sebilüresad* (Ankara), Vol. XX (1338 [1922]), No. 513, pp. 224-224, No. 514, pp. 237-240, No. 516, pp. 256-260, No. 517, pp. 275-276.

al-Daghistani, Burhan al-Din, 'Al-Shaykh Shamil Za'im al-Qawqaz wa-Shaykh al-Mujahidin, 1212-1278 H: 1797-1871 M [Shaykh Shamil the Leader of the Caucasus and of the Holy Warriors]', *Al-Risala* (Cairo), 16 June 1947 (No. 728), pp. 677-679.

Dalgat, Uzdiat Bashirovna, *Folklor i Literatura Narodov Dagestana [The folklore and Literature of the Peoples of Daghestan]*, Moscow: 'Nauka', 1967.

Daniialov, A. D., 'Ob Izvrashcheniiakh v Osveshchenii Miuridizma i Dvizhenii Shamilia [On Distortions in the Description of Miuridism and Shamil's Movement]', *Voprosy Istorii*, 1950, No. 3, pp. 3-18.

-------- 'O Dvizhenii Gortsev Dagestana i Chechni pod Rukovdstvom Shamilia [On the Movement of the Mountaineers of Daghestan and Chechnia Under the Leadership of Shamil]', *Voprosy Istorii*, 1966, No. 10, pp. 17-28.

Daniialov, G. D., 'Dvizhushchie Sily i Kharakter Dvizheniia Gortsev pod Rukovodstvom Shamilia [The Motivating Forces and Character of the Movement of the Mountaineers under the Leadership of Shamil]', *Dagestanskaia Pravda*, 14 December 1956.

-------- 'O Dvizhenii Gortsev pod Rukovodstvom Shamilia [On the Movement of the Mountaineers under the Leadership of Shamil]', *Voprosy Istorii*, 1956, No. 10, pp. 67 -72.

Danziger, Raphael, *Abd al-Qadir and the Algerians. Resistance to the French and Internal Consolidation*, New York: Holmes and Meir, 1977.

'Darginskaia Ekspeditsiia [The Expedition to Darghiyya]', *Terskie Vedomosti*, 12 [24] April 1894 (No. 93), pp. 3 -4.

Degoev, Vladimir. V., 'Burzhuaznaia Istoriografiia o Britanskoi politike na Kavkaze vo Vtoroi Treti XIX Veka [Bourgeois [[.ie. Western]] Historiography on Britain's Policy in the Caucasus in the Second Third of the Nineteenth Century]', *Voprosy Istorii*, 1979, No. 2, pp. 53 - 66.

D'iakov, V. A., 'Istoricheskie Realii 'Khadzhi Murata' [The Historical Realities of [[Tolstoi's]] 'Khadzhi Murat']', *Voprosy Istorii*, 1973, No. 1, pp. 135 - 148.

Dictionary of Canadian Biography, Toronto: University of Toronto Press, 1982.

Dirr, Adolf, ' Aus dem Gewohnheitsrecht der Kaukazischer Bergvölker', *Zeitschrift für Vergleichende Rechtswissenschaft* (Stuttgart), Vol. III (1926).

'Diskussiia o Dvizhenii Shamilia [A Discussion on Shamil's Movement]', *Voprosy Istorii*, 1947, No. 11, pp. 134 - 140.

Dodwell Henry Harold, *The Founder of Modern Egypt. A Study of Muhammad 'Ali*, Cambridge: Cambridge University Press, 1967 (reprint).

Dolgorukov, Petr, *Mikhail Nikolaevich Murav'ev*, London: Imprimerie du Prince Pierre Dogorukov, 1864.

Donia, Robert J., *Islam under the Double Eagle. The Muslims of Bosnia and Hercegovina, 1878 - 1914*, New York: Columbia University Press. 1981.

Dubrovin, Nikolai T., 'Deiatel'nost' Tormasova na Kavkaze [The Activity of Tormasov in the Caucasus]', *Voennyi Sbornik*, 1877, No. 9, pp. 5 - 24, no. 10, pp. 169 - 187, No. 11, pp. 5 - 41, No. 12, pp. 189 - 202, 1878, No. 1, pp. 5 - 34, Np. 2, pp. 189 0 209, No. 3, pp. 5 - 18.

-------- *Istoriia Voiny i Vladychestva Russkikh na Kavkaze [History of the Russians' War and Rule in the Caucasus]*, St. Petersburg: Tiografiia Departmenta Udelov, 1871 - 1888.

-------- Iz Istorii Voiny i Vladychestva Russkikh na Kavkaze (Kazi-Mulla kak Rodonachal'nik Miuridizma i Gazavata) [From the History of the Russians' War and Rule in the Caucasus (Ghazi Muhammad as the Founder of the *Murid* Movement and *Jihad*)], *Voennyi Sbornik*, 1890, No.10, pp. 197-240, 1891, No. 3, pp. 5-39, No. 4, pp. 177-206, No. 5, pp. 5-38, No.6, pp.197-217.

Dulaurier, Ed[ouard], 'La Russie dans le Caucase', *Revue de Deux Mondes*, 15 June 1860, 15 April, pp. 947-981, 15 May 1861, pp. 297-335, 15 December 1865, pp. 947-982, 1 January 1866, pp. 41-62.

Dzhakhiev, G. A., 'K Istoriograffi Voprosa 'Dagestan v Kavkazskoi Politike Irana i Turtsii v Pervoi Treti XIX Veka' [On the Historiography of the ouestion of 'Daghestan in the Caucasus Policy of the Qajar and Ottoman Empires in the First Third of the Nineteenth Century']', *Voprosy Istorii i Etnografii Dagestana*, Vol. II (1970), pp. 72-82.

-------- 'K Voprosu 'Dagestan v Russko-Turetskikh Otnosheniiakh v Nachale XIX Veka' [To the Question of 'Dagestan in Russo-Ottoman Relations at the Beginning of the Nineteenth Century']', *Voprosy Istorii i Etnografii Dagestana*, Vol. V (1974).

Ehrnroth, Magnus, *Casimir Ehrnroth. Trogen Tvene Tsarer och en Furste Alexander [Casimir Ehrnroth. The Confidant of two Tsars and One Prince Alexander]*, Helsinki: Svenska Litteratursallskapet i Finland, 1974.

Encyclopedia of Islam, Leiden: First edition, 1913-1938: Second edition, 1960 --.

Enkiri, Gabriel, *Ibrahim Pacha (1789 - 1848)*, Cairo: Imprimerie Française, 1948.

von Erckert R., *Der Kaukazus und seine Völker*, Leipzig: Paul Frohberg, 1887.

Erel, Serafeddin, *Dagistan ve Dagistanlilar [Daghestan and the Daghestanis]*, Istanbul: Istanbul Matbaasi, 1961.

Ermolov, Aleksandr, *Aleksei Petrovich Ermolov, 1771 - 1861. Biograficheskii Ocherk [Aleksei Petrovich Ermolov, 1771 - 1861. A Biographical Outline]*, St. Petersburg: Tipografiia A. S. Suvorina, 1912.

-------- *Rod Ermolovykh [The Genus of the Ermolovs]*, Moscow: Tipografiia V. I. Voronova, 1913.

Esadze, Semen, *Istoricheskaia Zapiska ob Upravlenii Kavkazom [An Historical Outline on the Administration of the Caucasus]*, Tiflis: Tipografiia 'Guttenberg', 1907.

-------- *Shturm Guniba i Plenenie Shamilia. Istoricheskii Ocherk Kavkazsko-Gorskoi Voiny v Chechne i Dagestane [The Storm of Ghunib and the Capture of Shamil. An*

Historical Outline of the Caucasian-Mountain War in Chechnia and Daghestan], Tiflis: Tipografiia Shtaba Kavkazskogo Voennogo Okruga, 1909.

Fadeev, Anatolii Vsevolodovich, 'Miuridizm kak Oruzhie Agressivnoi Turtsii i Anglii na Severo-Zapadnom Kavkaze [The *Murid* Movement as a Weapon of Aggressive Turkey and Britain in the North-Western Caucasus]', *Voprosy Istorii*, 1951, No. 9, pp. 76-96.

-------- *Ocherki Ekonomicheskogo Razvitiia Stepnogo Predkavkaz'ia v Doreformennyi Period [An Outline of the Economic Development of the Steppe Piedmonte of the Caucasus in the Pre-Reform Period]*, Moscow: Izdatel'stvo Akademii Nauk SSSR, 1957.

-------- 'O Vnutrennei Sotsial'noi Baze Miuridistskogo Dvizheniia na Kavkaze v XIX Veke [On the Internal Social Base of the *Murid* Movement in the Caucasus in the Nineteenth Century]', *Voprosy Istorii*, 1955, No. 6, pp. 67-77.

-------- 'Protiv Fal'sifikatsii Istorii Narodov Kavkaza [Against the Falsification of the History of the Peoples of the Caucasus]', *Vestnik Moskovskogo Universiteta (Istoriko-Filosofskaia Seriia)*, 1958, No. 3, PP. 232-236.

-------- *Rossiia i Kavkaz Pervoi Tret'i XIX V. [Russia and the Caucasus in the First Third if the Nineteenth Century]*, Moscow: Izdatel'stvo Akademii Nauk SSSR, 1960.

-------- *Rossiia i Vostochnyi Krizis 20kh Godov XIX Veka [Russia and the Eastern Crisis of the 1820s]*, Moscow: Izdatel'stvo Akademii Nauk SSSR, 1958.

-------- 'Vopros o Sotsial'nom Stroe Kavkazskikh Gortsev XVII-XIX VV. v Novykh Rabotakh Sovetskikh Istorikov [The Question of the Social Structure of the Caucasian Mountaineers in the Seventeenth -- Nineteenth Centuries in New Works of Soviet Historians]', *Voprosy Istorii*, 1958, No. 5, pp. 130-137.

--------'Vozniknovenie Miuridistskogo Dvizheniia na Kavkaze i ego Sotsial'nye Korni [The Emergence of the *Murid* Movement in the Caucasus and its Social Roots]', *Istoriia SSSR*, 1960, No. 5, pp. 37- 58.

Farforovskii, S.. 'Bor'ba Chechentsev s Russkimi [The Chechens' Struggle with the Russians]', *Russkii Arkhiv*, 1914, No. 4, pp. 455-457,

-------- 'Shamil' i Chechentsy. (Neizvestnyi Eshche Epizod iz Zavoevaniia Kavkaza) [Shamil and the Chechens. (An Unknown Episode from the Conquest of the Caucasus)]', *Russkii Arkhiv*, 1913, No. 6, pp. 770-774.

Fibikh, Daniil (pseud. of Luchanov, Daniil Vladimirovich), *Strana Gor. Ocherki Dagestana [Mountainland. Sketches of Daghestan]*, Moscow and Leningrad: Gosudarstvennoe Izdatel'stvo, 1928.

Fishel, Alan W., *The Russian Annexation of the Crimea, 1772 - 1783*, Cambridge: Cambridge University Press, 1970.

Freshfield, Douglas William, *Travels in Central Caucasus and Bashan*, London: Longmans, Green and Co., 1869.

Friedman, Yohanan, *Shaykh Ahmad Sirhindi. An Outline of his Thoughts and a Study of his Image in the Eyes of Posterity*, Montreal: McGill-Queen's University Press, 1971.

Genko, A. N. 'Arabskii Iazyk i Kavkazovedenie. O Znachenii Arabskikh Materialov dlia Izucheniia Istorii Kavkaza [The Arabic Language and the Study of the Caucasus. About the Significance of Arabic Sources to the Study of the History of the Caucasus]', *Trudy Vtoroi Sessii Assotsiiatsii Arabistov, 19 - 23 Oktiabria 1937G.*, Moscow and Leningrad: Izdatel'stvo Akademii Nauk SSSR, 1941, pp. 81-110.

'Ghazi Imam Shamil Rahmat Allah 'Alayhi Avalen Rahbar-e Jangha-ye Ghorila-ye Islam [The Holy Warrior Imam Shamil, God's Mercy Upon His Soul, The First Leader of Islamic Guerrilla Groups]', *Vatan* (Organ of the Islamic Union of the Provinces of Northern Afghanistan), 20 Jumadi al-Thani 1402/4 April 1983.

Giedrojc, Wincenty Gedeon, *Kilka Wspómnien z Kaukazkiego Wygnania [A Few Memories from Exile in the Cuacasus]* [Poetry], Lwów: Karel Piller, 1867.

Gleason, John Howes, *The Genesis of Russophobia in Great Britain. A Study of the Interaction of Policy and Opinion*, Cambridge, Mass.: Harvard University Press, 1950.

Glikhnitskii, N. and Pokrovskii, N., 'Protiv Velikoderzhavnogo Shovinizma v Izuchenii Istorii Gorskogo Natsional'no-Osvoboditel'nogo Dvizheniia [Against Great-Power Chauvinism in the Study of the National Liberation Movement of the Mountaineers]', *Istorik Marksist*, 1934; No. 2 (36), pp. 99-105.

Glinoetskii, N., 'Sluzhba General'nogo Shtaba pri Kavkazskikh Voiskakh s 1832 po 1853 God [The Service of the General Staff in the Caucasian Army, 1832-1853]', *Voennyi Sbornik*, 1888, No. 7, pp. 38-65, No. 8, pp. 249-265, No. 9, pp. 30-59.

Gnucheva, V. P. (ed.), *Materialy dlia Istorii Ekspeditsii Akademii Nauk v XVIII i XIX Vekakh. Khronologicheskie Obzory i Opsanie Arkhivnykh Materialov [Sources to the History of the Expeditions by the Academy of Sciences in the Eighteenth and Nineteenth Centuries. Chronological Surveys and a Discription of the Archival Sources]*, Moscow and Leningrad: Izdatel'stvo Akademii Nauk SSSR, 1940.

Gökçe, Cemal, *Kafkasya ve Osmanli Imperatorlugu'nun Kafkasya Siyaseti [The Caucasus and the Caucasus Policy of the Ottoman Empire]*, Istanbul: Has-Kutulmus Matbaasi, 1979.

Golitsin, N. B., *Zhizneopisaniie Generala-ot-Kavalerii Emanualia [Biography of Cavalry General Emannuel]*, St. Petersburg: Tipografiia N. Grecha, 1851.

Gordeev, A. A., *Istoriia Kazakov [History of the Cossacks]*, Part 3: *So Vremeni Tsarstvovaaiia Petra Velikogo do Nachala Velikoi Voiny 1914 G.[From the Reign of Peter the Great to the Beginning of the Great War of 1914]*, Paris: Societe d'Imprimerie Periodique et d'Editions, 1970.

Göztepe, Tarik Mumtaz, *Imam Samil. Kafkasa'nin Büyük Harp ve Ihtilal Kahramani [Imam Shamil. The Hero of the Great War and Conquest of the Caucasus]*, Istanbul, 1961.

------- *Dagistan Arslani. Imam Samil*, 2 Vols. Istanbul: 1969

Guizetti [Gizetti], A., *Bibliograficheskii Ukazatel' Pechatannym na Russkom Iazyke Sochineniiam i Stat'iam o Voennykh Deistviiakh Rossiiskikh Voisk na Kavkaze [Bibliographical Guide to the Printed Works and Articles inRussian on the Military Operations of the Russian Army in the Caucasus]*, St. Petersburg: Ekonomicheskaia Tipo-Litografiia, 1901.

Gvozdetskii, Nikolai Andreevich, *Fizicheskaia Geografiia Kavkaza [Physical Geography of the Caucasus]*, Moscow: Izdatel'stvo Moskovskgo Universiteta, 1954.

-------- *Kavkaz. Ocherk Prirody [The Caucasus. An Outline of its Nature]*, Moscow: Gosudarstvennoe Izdatel'stvo Geograficheskoi Literatury, 1963.

Hajiev [Gadzhiev], Adil-Girei Saadulaevich, *Rol' Russkogo Naroda v Istoricheskikh Sud'bakh Narodov Dagestana [The Russian People's Role in the Historical Fates of the Peoples of Daghestan]*, Makhachqala: Dagestanskoe Knizhnoe Izdatel'stvo, 1964.

Hajiev [Gadzhiev] Vladilen Hadisovich, *Dvizhenie Kavkazskikh Gortsev pod Rukovodstvom Shamilia v Istericheskoi Literature [The Movement of the Caucasian Mountaineers under the Leadership of Shamil in the Historical Literature]*, Makhachqala: Tipografiia Ministerstva Kul'tury DASSR, 1956.

-------- 'Istoricheskie Sviazi Dagestana s Rossiei [Daghestan's Historical Ties with Russia]', *Istoricheskie Zapiski*, Vol. XIII (1964), pp. 135-154.

-------- *Rol' Rossii v Istorii Dagestana [Russia's Role in the History of Daghestan]*, Moscow: 'Nauka' 1965.

von Hahn, *Bilder aus dem Kaukazus*, Leipzig: Verlag von Duncker und Humbolt, 1900.

-------- *Kaukazische Reisen und Studien*, Leipzig: Verlag von Duncker und Humbolt, 1896.

-------- *Neue Kaukazische Reisen und Studien*, Leipzig: Verlag von Duncker und Humbolt, 1911.

Hambley, Gavin et al., *Central Asia*, London: Weidenfeld and Nicholson, 1969.

Hamid, Muhammad, *'Alim Islam ke Pahale Gorila Lidar. Imam Shamil Rahmat Allah 'Alayhi [The 'Alim who Became a Guerilla Leader: Imam Shamil God's Mercy on his Soul]*, Lahore: Ferozson'st 1974.

Hamza, 'Masahid Islam: Seyh Samil [The Martyrs of Islam: Shaykh Shamil]', *Mihrab*, No. 25, (Istanbul 1341 [1923]), pp. 32-40.

Hamzatov [Gamzatov], Rasul, *Moi Dagestan [My Daghestan]*, Trans. Vl[adimir] Soloukhin, Moscow: Molodaia Gvardiia, 1972.

Hasan, Emir, 'Epokha Shamilia [Shamil's Time]', *Severnyi Kavkaz*, No. 1, (May 1934), pp. 12-14.

Turkish Version: 'Samil Devri', *Severnyi Kavkaz*, No. 4 (Ausust 1934), pp, 2-5.

Hashimov [Gashimov], Ch. M., 'Iz Istorii Dagestano-Severokavkazskikh Kul'turnykh Sviazei [From the History of the Cultural Contacts Between Daghestan and the Northern Caucasus]', *Voprosy Istorii i Etnografii Dagestana*, Vol. I (1970), pp. 67-78.

-------- 'O Sovmestnykh Poseleniiakh Gortsev Dagestana i Severnogo Kavkaza (XVI-XVIII VV.) [On the Joint Settlements of the Mountaineers of Daghestan and of the Northern Caucasus (16th-18th Centuries)]', *Voprosy Istorii i Etnografii Dagestana*, Vol. I (1970), pp. 79-84.

Hatuki, K., 'Great Britain and the Northern Caucasian War', *The Caucasus*, No. 1 (16) (January 1952), pp. 9-11.

Hedin, Sven, *Genom Persien, Mesopotamien ock Kaukasien. Resemimren [A Tour of Persia, Mesopotamia and the Caucasus. Memoirs from a Journey]*, Stockholm: Albert Bonniers Forlag, 1887.

Henze, Paul, 'Circassia in the Nineteenth Century. The Futile Fight for Freedom', in Ch. Lemercier-Quelquejay, G. Weinstein and S. E. Wimbush (eds.), P*asse Turco-Tatar, Present Sovietique. Etudes Offertes a Alexandre Bennigsen*, Louvain: Editions Peeters and Paris: Editions de l'Ecole des Hautes Etudes en Sciences Sociales, 1986, pp. 243-273.

-------- 'Fire and Sword in the Caucasus: the 19th Century Resistance of the North Caucasian Mountianeers', *Central Asian Survey*, Vol. 2, No. 1, (July 1983), pp. 5-44.

-------- 'Marx on Russians and Muslims', *Central Asian Survey*, Vol. 4, No. 4, (1982), pp. 33-45.

-------- '"Un-Rewriting" History -- the Shamil Problem', *Caucasian Review*, No. 6 (1958), pp. 7-29.

Reprint, 'The Shamil Problem', in Walter Z. Laquer (ed.), *The Middle East in Transition. Studies in Contemporary History*, New York: Praeger, 1956, pp. 415-443.

Hizal, Ahmet Hazer, *Kuzey Kafkasya (Hürriyet ve Istiklal Davasi) [The Northern Caucasus (The Call for Freedom and Independence)]*, Ankara: Orkun Basimevi, 1961.

Hizaloglu, Mustafa Zihni, *Seyh Samil. Simali Kafkasya Ilstiklal Mucedeleleri [Shaykh Shamil. The Independence Fighters of the Northern Caucasus]*, Ankara: Ayyildiz Matbaasi, 1958.

Hoffmann, Joachim, 'Die Politik die Mächte in der Endphase der Kaukasuskriege,' *Jahrbucher fur Geschichte Osteuropas*, Vol. 17, No. 2 (1969), pp. 215 - 258.

Holt, P.M., *The Mahdist State in the Sudan, 1881 - 1898. A Study of its Origins, Development and Overthrow*, Oxford: Oxfrod University Press, 1958.

Hoskins, Halford Lancaster, *British Routes to India*, London: Longmans, Green and Co., 1928.

Humuz, K., 'Russian Imperialism', *The Caucasus*, No. 6-7 (June-July 1952), pp.11-14.

Hurgronje, Christiaan Snouck, *The Achenese*, Trans. A. S. S. O'Sullivan, Leiden: E. J. Brill and London: Luzac and Co., 1906.

Iandarov, Andarbek Dudaevich, *Sufizm i Ideologiia Natsional'no-Osvoboditel'nogo Dvizheniia. (Iz Istorii Razvitiia Obshchestvennykh Idei v Checheno-Ingushetii v 20 - 70e Gody XIX V.) [Sufism and the Ideology of the National Liberation Movement. (From the History of the Development of Social Ideas in Checheno-Ingushetiia in the 1820s - 1870s)]*, Alma Ata: Izdatel'stvo 'Nauka' Kazakhskoi SSR, 1975.

Ibrahimbeili [Ibragimbeili], Khadzhi Murat, *Kavkaz v Krymskoi Voine [The Caucasus in the Crimean War]*, Moscow:'Nauka', 1971.

Istoriia Azerbaidzhana [History of Adharbayjan], Baqu: Izdatel'stvo Akademii Nauk Azerbaidzhanskoi SSR, 1960.

Istoriia Dagestana [History of Daghestan], Moscow: 'Nauka', 1967-1969.

Istoriia Russkikh Voin [History of Russia's Wars], Free Appendix to *Russkii Palomnik*, 1915.

'Istoricheskii Ocherk Raspostraneniia Russkogo Vladychestva na Kavkaze [An Historical Outline of the Spread of Russian Rule in the Caucasus]', *Kavkazskii Kalendar'*, 1851, Part III, pp. 43-51.

'Istoriografiia Istorii Narodov Dona i Severnogo Kavkaza. Vtoraia Vserossiiskaia Konferentsiia v Groznom [The Historiography of the History of the Peoples of the Don [[Basin]] and the Northern Caucasus. The Second All-Russian Conference in Groznyi]', *Istoriia SSSR*, 1979, No. 2, pp. 212-214.

Isaev, S. A., 'Agrarnaia Politika Tsarisma v Ploskotnoi Chechne v 50-60kh GG. XIX Veka [Tsarist Agrarian Policy in Lower Chechnia in the 1850s-1860s]', *Voprosy Istorii Dagestana*, Vol. II (1975).

Iudin, P. 'Lzheprorok Ushurta [*sic!*]-Shikh Mansur (Iz Istorii Religioznykh Dvizhenii na Kavkaze) [The False Prophet Ushurma-Shaykh Mansur. (From the History of Religious Movements in the Caucasus)]', *Russkii Arkhiv*, 1914, No. 10, pp. 217-228.

Ivanov, A. I., 'Natsional'no-Osvoboditel'noe Dvizhenie v Chechne i Dagestane v 60-70kh GG. XIX V. [The National Liberation Movement in Chechnia and Daghestan in the 1860s and 1870s]', *Istoricheskie Zapiski*, No. 12 (1941), pp. 165-199.

-------- 'Sotsial'no-Ekonomicheskoe i Politicheskoe Polozhenie Dagestana do Zavoevaniia Tsarskoi Rossiei [The Socio-Economic and Political Situation of Daghestan Before the Conquest by Tsarist Russia]', *Istoricheskii Zhurnal*, 1940, No. 2, pp. 62-72.

-------- 'Vostanie v Chechne v 1877 G. [The Uprising in Chechnia in 1877]', *Istoricheskie Zapiski*, No. 10 (1941), pp. 280-294.

Jones, Stephen, 'Russian Imperial Administration and the Georgian Nobility. The Georgian Conspiracy of 1832', *Slavonic and East European Review*, Vol. LXV, No. 1 (January 1987), pp. 53-76.

Jorre, Georges, *The Soviet Union. The Land and Its People* Trans. E. D. Laborde, London: Longmans, 1961 (2nd edition).

Kafli, Kadircan, *Simali Kafkasya [The Northern Caucasus]*, Istanbul: Vakit Matbaasi, 1942.

Kalishevskii, An., 'Tri Nedeli Sredi Kavkazskikh Gortsev [Three Weeks Among the Caucasian Mountaineers]', *Voennyi Vestnik*, 1903, No. 12, pp. 182 -193.

Kaimarazov, G. Sh., *Ocherki Istorii Kul'tury Narodov Dagestana [Outline of the History of the Culture of Daghestan's Peoples]*, Moscow, 'Nauka', 1971.

Kartsov, P. P., 'K Istorii Pokoreniia Kavkaza [To the History of the Conquest of the Caucasus]', *Russkaia Starina* 1884, No. 7, pp. 203-214, No. 9, pp. 605-618.

Kapidzic, Hamdija, *Hercegovacki Ustanak 1882 Godine [The Uprising in Hercegovina of 1882]*, Sarajevo: Veselin Maslesa, 1973.

Kapiev, Efendi (ed.), *Dagestankaia Antologiia [A Daghestani Anthology]*, Moscow: Gosudarstvennoe Izdatel'stvo Khudozhestvennoi Literatury, 1934.

Kasday, Tzvi, *Mamlakhot Ararat. Parashat Mas'otaybe-Meshekh Kamma Shanim be-Aratsot Qawqaz ume-'Ever le-Hararey Qawqaz be'Ever Yam ha-Kaspi ve-Asiya ha-Tikhona ve-Khule ... [The Kingdoms of Ararath. The Story of My Journey during Several Years in the Caucasus and Beyond the Caucasus Mountains, Beyond the Caspian Sea and in Central Asia etc. ...]*, Odessa: Defus 'Moriya', 5672 [1912].

Katz, Albert, *Die Juden im Kaukazus*, Berlin: Verlag von Hugo Schilldberger, 1894.

Kaval, E., 'Sheikh Mansur', *United Caucasus*, No. 8 (25) (August 1953), pp. 23-27.

Kavkaz [The Caucasus], Moscow: 'Nauka', 1966.

Kavtaradze, Aleksandr Georg'evich, *General A. P. Ermolov*, 'Nashi Slavnye Zemliaki' Series, Tula: Priokskoe Knizhnoe Izdatel'stvo, 1977.

Kazemzadeh, Feriruz, 'Russian penetration of the Caucasus,' in: T. Hunczak (ed.), *Russian Imperialism from Ivan the Great to the Revolution*, New Brunswick, NJ.: 1974, pp. 239 - 264.

'K Diskussii o Kharaktere Dvizheniia Gortsev Dagestana pod Rukovodstvom Shamilia [On the Discussion on the Character of the Movement of the Mountaineers of Daghestan Under the Leadership of Shamil]', *Voprosy Istorii*, 1957, No. 1, pp. 195-196.

Keep, John Lesley Howard, *Soldiers of the Tsar. Army and Society in Russia, 1462 - 1874*, Oxford: Clarendon Press, 1985.

A Kempis, Thomas, *De Imitatione Christi*, London: William W. Gibbins, 1889 (The 'Museum' edition).

Kentmann, Paul, *Der Kaukazus. Hundertfünfzig Jahre Russische Herrschaft*, Leipzig: Wilhelm Goldmann Verlag, 1943.

Khachapuridze, G., *Guriis Ajankheba 1841 Tsels [The 1841 Revolt in Guriia]*, Tpilisi: Sakhelmtsipo Gamontseloba, 1931.

Khal'fin, Naftula Aronovich and Rassadina, Ekaterina Federovna, *N. V. Khanykov. Vostokoved i Diplomat [N. V. Khanykov. Orientalist and Diplomat]*, Moscow: 'Nauka', 1977.

Khalifov, Kh. (ed.), *Skazki Narodov Dagestana [Tales of the Peoples of Daghestan]*, Moscow: 'Nauka', 1961.

Khalilov, A. M., 'Shamil' v Istoriil i v Pamiati Noroda [Shamil in History and in the People's Memory]', *Sovetskii Dagestan*, 1988, No. 5 (September-October), pp. 31-37.

Kharuzin, N. N., 'Zametki o Iuridicheskom Byte Chechentsev i Ingushei [Notes on the Legal Mores of the Chechens and Ingush]', *Sbornik Materialov po Etnografii Izdavaemyi pri Dashkovskom Etnograficheskom Muzee*, Vol.III (1888), pp.115-142.

Khashaev, Khadzhi-Murat Omarovich, *Obshchestvennyi Stroi Dagestana v XIX Veke [The Social Structure of Daghestan in the Nineteenth Century]*, Moscow: Izdatel'stvo Akademii Nauk SSSR, 1961.

Khoursch, Baha Eddin, *Obrona Twierdzy Achulgo przez Imama Szamila [The Defence of the Fortress of Akhulgoh by Imam Shamil]*, Warsaw: Wydawnictwo Instytutu Wschodniego, 1939.

-------- 'Voennaia Operatsia v Dagestane v 1843 Godu [The Military Operation in Daghestan in 1843]', *Gortsy Kavkaza*, No. 39 (1931), pp. 7 -20, No. 40, pp. 10-14, No. 48 (1933), pp. 10-14, No. 49 (1934), pp. 12-20.

Khutsunov, Petr, 'Snosheniia Rossii s Severnoi Chastiiu Kavkaza [Russia's Relations with the Northern Part of the Caucasus]', *Sbornik Gazety Kavkaz*, 1846, pp. 203-219.

Kiernan, Victor G., *European Empires from Conquest to Collapse*, London: Fontana, 1982 (paperback).

Kiniapina, Nina Stepanovna, Bliev, Mark Maksimovich and Degoev, Vladimir Vladimirovich, *Kavkaz i Sredniaia Aziia vo Vneshnei Politike Rossii. Vtoraia Polovina XVIII - 80e Gody XIX V. [The Caucasus and Central Asia in Russia's Foreign Policy. The Second Half of the Eighteenth Century to the 1880s]*, Moscow: Izdatel'stvo Moskovskogo Universiteta, 1984.

Kiselev, P. (ed.), *Checheno-Ingushskii Folklor [Chechno-Ingush Folklore]*, Moscow: Gosudarstvennoe Izdatel'stvo 'Khudozhestvennaia Literatura', 1940.

'Kn. V. G. Madatov [Prince V. G. Madatov]', *Russkaia Srarina*, 1872, No. 12, p. 669.

'Konfersentsiia Chitatelei Zhurnala 'Voprosy Istorii' [Conference of the Readers of 'Voprosy Istorii']', *Voprosy Istorii*, 1956, No. 2, pp. 199-213.

Korol'kov, M. Ia., 'Sheikh Mansur Anapskii. (Epizod iz Pervykh Let Zavoevaniia Kavkaza) [Shaykh Mansur from Anapa (An Episode from the Early Years of the Conquest of the Caucasus)]', *Russkaia Starina*, 1914, No. 5, pp. 410-417.

Kortepeter, Carl Max, *Ottoman Imperialism during the Reformation. Europe and the Caucasus*, New York: New York University Press, 1972.

Korzun, Viktor Borisovich, *Folklor Gorskikh Narodov Severnogo Kavkaza. Dooktiabrskii Period [The Folklore of the Mountain Peoples of the Northern Caucasus. The Pre-Soviet Period]*. Groznyii: Checheno-Ingushskoe Knizhnoe Izdatel'stvo, 1966.

Kosven, Mark Osipovich, et al. (eds.), *Narody Kavkaza [The Peoples of the Caucasus]*, Moscow: Izdatel'stvo Akademii Nauk SSSR, 1960.

Kosven, Mark Osipovich and Khashaev, Khadzhi-Murad Omarovich (eds.), *Narody Dagestana. Sbornik Stat'ei [The Peoples of Daghestan. Collection of Articles]*, Moscow: Izdatel'stvo Akademii Nauk SSSR, 1955.

Kovalevskii, P. I., *Kavkaz [The Caucasus]*, Vol. II: *Istoriia Zavoevaniia Kavkaza [The History of the Conquest of the Caucasus]*, Petrograd: Tipografiia M. I. Akshevieva, 1915.

Kozubskii, E. I., 'Bibliograficheskaia Zametka o Grafe P. Kh, Grabbe i E. A. Golovine [A Bibliographical Remark About Count P. Kh. Grabbe and E, A. Golovin]', *Russkii Arkhiv*, 1893, No. 2, p. 281.

-------- 'Dagestanskii Konnyi Polk. (Ocherki Dagestanskoi Stariny) [The [[Irregular]] Daghestan Mounted Regiment. (Sketches of Daghestan's Past)]', *Russkii Arkhiv*, 1909, No. 1, pp. 98-118.

-------- 'K Istorii Dagestana [Contribution to the History of Daghestan]', *Russkii Arkhiv*, 1896, No. 9, pp. 101-131.

-------- *Pamiatnaia Knizhka Dagestanskoi Oblasti [The Commemorative Book of the Daghestan District]*, Temir-Khan-Shura: Russkaia Tipografiia V. M. Sorokina, 1895.

-------- '25-e Avgusta, 1859-1909 [25 August [[6 September]] 1859-1909]', *Russkii Arkhiv*, ,1909, No. 10, pp. 185-191.

Krachkovskii, Ignatii Iul'ianovich, 'Arabskaia Literatura na Severnom Kavkaze [Arabic Literature in the Northern Caucasus]', in: *Izbrannye Sochineniia*, Moscow and Leningrad: Izdatel'stvo Akademii Nauk SSSR, 1960, Vol. IV, pp. 609-622.

-------- 'Arabskaia Rukopis' Vospominanii o Shamile [An Arabic Manuscript of Memoirs About Shamil]', in: *Izbrannye Sochineniia*, Moscow and Leningrad: Izdatel'stvo Akademii Nauk SSSR, 1960, Vol. VII, pp. 559-570.

-------- 'Arabskie Materialy po Istorii Shamilia v Sobraniiakh Akademii Nauk [Arabic Sources on Shamil in the Collections of the Academy of Sciences]', in: *Izbrannye Sochineniia*, Moscow and Leningrad: Izdatel'stvo Akademii Nauk SSSR, 1960, Vol. VI, pp. 574-584.

-------- 'Dagestan i Iemen [Daghestan and the Yemen]', in: *Izbrannye Sochineniia*, Moscow and Leningrad: Izdatel'stvo Akademii Nauk SSSR, 1960, Vol. V1, pp. 574-584.

-------- 'Novye Arabskie Materialy po Istorii Shamilia v Institute Vostokovodenia Akademii Nauk SSSR [New Arabic Sources on Shamil in the Institute of Orientalism at the Academy of Sciences of the USSR]', *Istoricheskii Sbornik*, Vol. V (1936), pp. 239-246.

-------- 'Novye Rukopisi Istorii Shamilia Mukhamed Takhira al-Karakhi [New Manuscripts of Muhammad Tahir al-Qarakhi's History of Shamil]', *Istoricheskii Arkhiv*, Vol. II (1939), pp. 5-31.

Krivenko, Vasilii S., 'Vosstanie v Dagestane v 1877 Godu [The Uprising of 1877 in Daghestan]', *Russkii Vestnik*, 1892, No. 3, pp. 167-184.

Kuliev, K., Dzhusoita, N. and Registian, G. (eds.), *Pesni Narodov Severnogo Kavkaza [Songs of the Peoples of the Northern Caucasus]*, Leningrad: Izdatel'stvo 'Sovetskii Pisatel', 1976.

Kumykov, Tugan Kilabasovich, *Vovlechenie Severnogo Kavkaza vo Vserossiiskii Rynok v XIX V, (Po Materialam Kabardino-Balkarii, Severnoi Osetii i Checheno-Ingushetii [The Drawing of the Northern Caucasus into the All-Russian Market in the*

Nineteenth Century (Based on the Sources in Kabardino-Balkariia, Northern Ossetiia and Checheno-Ingushetiia)], Nal'chik: Kabardino-Balkarskoe Knizhnoe Izdatel'stvo, 1962.

Kundukh, Aytek, *Kafkasya Müridizmi (Gazavat Tarihi) [The Caucasian Murid Movement (The History of the Holy War)]*, Istanbul: Gözde Kitaplar Yayinevi, 1987.

Kushnerev, I. N. and Pirogov, A. N., *Russkaia Voennaia Sila. Istoriia Razvitiia Voennogo Dela ot Nachala Rusi do Nashego Vremeni [The Russian Military Might. The History of the Develpment of the Military Craft from the Beginning of Rus' until the Present Day]*, Moscow: I. N. Kushnerev and Co.,1892 (2nd edition).

Kutlu, Tarik Cemal, *Imam Mansur*, Istanbul: Bayrak Yayincilik, 1987.

Kuznetsova, Nina Alekseevna, *Iran v pervoi polovine XIX Veka [Iran in the First Half of the Nineteenth Century]*, Moscow: 'Nauka', 1983.

Kvinitadze, G., 'Khadzhi Murat', *Kavkaz* (Paris), 1934, No. 7, pp. 8-12.

-------- 'Sdacha Shamilia [Shamil's Surrenderl', *Kavkaz* (Paris), 1934, No. 2, pp. 10-12.

Lacinski [Latsinskii], A., 'Khronologiia Russkoi Voennoi Istorii. Khronologicheskii Ukazatel' Voin, Srazhenii i Del v Kotorykh Uchavtsvovali Russkie Voiska ot Petra Velikogo do Noveishego Vremeni [A Chronology of Russian Military History. A Chronological Guide to the Wars, Battles and Skirmishes in which Russian Troops Took Part, from Peter the Great to Recent Times]', Appendix to *Voennyi Sbornik*, 1891, No. 5.

Lane-Poole, Stanley, *The Life of the Right Honourable Stratford Canning, Viscount Stratford de Redcliffe,* London: Longmans, Green and Co., 1888.

Lang, David Marshal, *A Modern History of Georgia*, London: Weidenfeld and Nicolson, 1962.

-------- *The Last Years of the Georgian Monarchy, 1658 - 1832*, New York: Columbia University Press, 1957.

Lange, Olaf, *Kaukazus. Reiseminder ag Skildringer [The Caucasus. Travel Notes and Descriptions]*, Copenhagen: Gyldendalske Boghandels Ferlag, 1891.

Layton, Susan, 'The Creation of an Imagined Caucasian Geography,' *Slavic Review*, Vol.45, No. 3 (1986), pp. 470 - 485.

Lermontov, Mikhail Iur'evich, *Polnoe Sobranie Sochinenii [Complete Works]*, St. Petersburg: A. F. Markov, 1901 (second edition).

Lesure, Michel 'La France et le Caucase a l'Epoque de Chamil a la Lumiere des Depeches des Consuls Francais', *Cahiers du Monde Russe et Sovietique*, Vol. XIX, No. 1-2 (January-June 1978), pp. 5-65.

Levin, E. S., *Perevaly Tsentral'nogo Kavkaza [The Passes of the Central Caucasus]*, Moscow: Ogiz, 1938.

Lewis, Bernard, *The Middle East and the West*, New York: Harper and Row, 1966 (paperback).

Leyda, Jay, *Kino. A History of the Russian and Soviet Film*, London: George, Allen and Unwin, 1960.

Lockhart, Laurence, *Nadir Shah. A Critical Study Based upon Contemporary Sources*, London: Luzac & Co., 1938.

Luguev S. A. et al. (eds.), *Material'naia Kul'tura Narodov Dagestana v XIX - Nachale XX Veka [The Material Culture of the Peoples of Daghestan in the Nineteenth - Beginning of the Twentieth Centuries]*, Makhachqala: Dagestanskii Filiial AN SSSR, 1983.

-------- *Voprosy Obshchestvennogo Byta Narodov Dagestana v XIX - Nachale XX Veka [Qustions of the Social Mode of Life of the Peoples of Daghestan in the Nineteenth - Beginning of the Twentieth Centuries]*, Makhachqala: Dagestanskii Filiial AN SSSR, 1987.

Lutfi al-Sayyid Marsot, Afaf, *Egypt in the Reign of Muhammad Ali*, Cambridge: Cambridge University Press, 1984.

Luxenburg, Norman, 'England and the Caucasus during the Crimean War', *Jahrbücher für Geschichte Osteuropas*, Vol. 16, No. 4 (1968),pp. 499 - 504.

Luzbetac, Lewis J., *Marriage and Family in Caucasia. A Contribution to the Study of Notrh Caucasian Ethnology and Customary Law*, Viena-Modling: St. Gabriel' s Mission Press, 1951.

van der Maaten, K., *Snouck Hurgronje en de Atjeh Oorlog [Snouck Hurgronje on the Ache War]*, Leiden: Oostersch Institut, 1948.

Maclean, Fitzroy, *The Cuacasus -- the End of all Earth. An Illustrated Companion to the Caucasus and Transcaucasia*, London: Jonathan Cape, 1976.

Magoma [Mahoma], A., 'The Caucasus in the Path of Russian Expension', *The Caucasus*, No. 3 (8) (March 1952), pp. 6-8.

Mahomedov [Magomedov], Rasul M., *Dagestan v Period Tsarskogo Zavoevaniia [Dagheatn in the Times of the Tsarist Conquest]*, Makhachqala: Dagestanskoe Gosudarstvennoe Izdatel'stvo, 1940.

-------- *Shamil'*, Makhachqala: Dagestanskoe Gosudarstvennoe Izdatel'stvo, 1940.

Mahomedov [Magomedov], R. M., *Rossiia i Dagestan. Stranitsy Istorii [Russia and Daghestan. Pages of History]*, Makhachqala: Dagestanskoe Knizhnoe Izdatel'stvo, 1987.

Mahomedov [Magomedov], Ramazan Mahomedovich, *Khronologiia Istorii Dagestana [A Chronology of the History of Daghestan]*, Makhachqala: Dagestanskoe Knizhnoe Izdatel'stvo, 1959.

-------- 'Adaty Dagestanskikh Gortsev kak Istoricheskii Istochnik [The *'Adawat* of the Daghestani Mountaineers as an Historical Source]', in B. G. Gafurov et al. (eds.), *Trudy Dvatsat' Piatogo Mezhdunarodnogo Kongressa Vostokovedov, Moskva, 9 - 16 Avgusta 1960 G.*, Vol. III, Moscow: Izdatel'stvo Vostochnoi Literatury, 1963, pp. 639-645.

-------- *Obshchestvenno-Ekonomicheskii i Politicheskii Stroi Dagestana v XVIII - Nachalo XX Vekov [The Socio-Economic and Political Structure of Daghestan in the Eighteenth - the Beginning of the Twentieth Centuries]*, Makhachqala: Dagestanskoe Knizhnoe Izdatel'stvo, 1957.

Mahmudbekov, 'Miuridicheskaia Sekta na kavkaze [The *Murid* Sect in the Caucasus]', *Sbornik Materialov dlia Opisaniia Mestnostei i Plemen Kavkaza*, Vol. XXIV (1898), Part I, pp. 14-40.

Makievskii-Zubok, N. G., 'Kavkaz i Kavkazskie Namestniki [The Caucasus and the Caucasian Viceroys]', *Vestnik Evropy*, 1909, No. 2, pp. 613-653, No. 3, pp. 91-130.

Maksimov, Ev[genii], 'Chechentsy. Istoriko-Geograficheskii i Statistiko-Ekonomicheskii Ocherk [The Chechens. An Historical-Geographical and Statistical-Economic Sketch]', *Terskii Sbornik*, Vol. III, Book 2 (1893), Part I, pp. 3-100.

Maliavkin, G., 'Ocherki Obshchinnogo Zemlevladeniia v Chechne [An Outline of Communal Land Ownership in Chechnia]', *Terskie Vedomosti*, 25 November [7 December] (No. 141), p. 3, 27 November [9 December] (No. 142), p. 4, 4 [16] December 1892 (No. 1450, p. 4, 13 [25] January (No. 6), pp. 2-3, 15 [27] Janaury 1893 (No. 7), p. 3.

Markova, O1'ga Petrovna, *Rossiia, Zakavkaz'e i Mezhdunarodnye otnosheniia v XVIII Veke [Russia, Transcaucaia and International Relations in the Eighteenth Century]*, Moscow: 'Nauka', 1966.

-------- 'Vostochnyi Kritis 30kh-Nachala 40kh Godov XIX Veka i Dvizhenie Miuridizma [The Eastern Crisis of the 1830s and Early 1840s and the *Murid* Movement]', *Istoricheskie Zapiski*, No.42 (1953), pp. 202-237.

Marr, N. Ia., *Plemennoi Sostav Nasseleniia Kavkaza. Klassifikatsiia Narodov Kavkaza (Rabochii Prospect) [The Tribal Composition of the Population of the Caucasus. The Classification of the Peoples of the Caucasus (A Working Prospect)]*, Petrograd: Tipografiia Rossiiskoi Akademii Nauk, 1920.

Marriott, John Arthur Ronsourt, *The Eastern Question. An Historical Study in European Diplomacy*, Oxford: The Clarendon Press, 1956 (4th edition).

Maslov, E. P., Gozulov, A. I. and Riazantsev, S. N. (eds.), *Severnyi Kavkaz [The Northern Caucasus]*, Moscow: Gosudarstvennoe Izdatel'stvo Geograficheskoi Literatury, 1957.

Megrelidze, Shamshe Varfolomeevich,*Gruziia v Russko-Turetskoi Voine 1877 - 1878 GG. [Georgia in the Russo-Ottoman War of 1877* - 1878*]*, Batumi: Gosudarstvennoe Izdatel'stvo, 1955.

-------- *Zakavkaz'e v Russko-Turetskoi Voine 1877 - 1878 GG. [Transcaucasia in the Russo-Ottoman War of 1877* - 1878*]*, Tbilisi: 'Mitsniereba', 1972.

Melikoff, Irene, 'L'Ideologie Religieuse du Muridisme Caucasien', *Bedi Kartlisa*, Vol. XXV (1968), pp. 27-45.

Mercer, Samuel A. B., *The Tell El-Amarna Tablets*, Toronto: MacMillan, 1939.

Met, Çunatuka [Yusuf Izzet Pasa], *Kafkas Tarihi [The History of the Caucasus]*, Istanbul: Haris Matbaasi, 1330 [1912].

Mosely, Philip Eduard, *Russian Diplomacy and the Opening of the Eastern Question in 1838 and 1839,* Cambridge, Mass.: Harvard University Press, 1934.

Mufti (Habjoka), Shauket, *Heroes and Emperors in Circassian History*, Beirut: Librairie du Liban, 1972.

Murav'evy. Rodoslovnaia: 1488 - 1893, Revel': Tipografiia 'Revel'skikh Izvestii', 1893.

N. D., 'Ocherki Kavkazskoi Voiny [An Outline of the Caucasian War]', *Voennyi Sbornik*, 1890, No. 8, Part II, pp. 79-114, No. 10, Part II, pp. 93-119.

-------- 'Ocherki Voennyih Deistvii na Kavkaze [An Outline of the Military Operations in the Caucasus]', *Voennyi Sbornik*, 1866, No. 6, Part II, pp. 81-100, No. 7, Part II, pp. 1-34, No. 8, Part II, pp. 109-128, No. 9, Part II, pp. 1-13, No. 11, Part II, pp. 1-29, No. 12, Part II, pp. 109-138.

N. Sh., 'General Vel'iaminov i ego Znachenie dlia Istorii Kavkazskoi Voiny [General Vel'iaminov and his Significance to the History of the Caucasian War]', *Kavkazskii Sbornik*, Vol. VII (1883), pp. 1-155.

Nadezhdin, P. P., *Kavkazskii Krai. Priroda i Liudi [The Land of the Caucasus. Nature and People]*, Tula: E. I. Druzhinin, 1895 (2nd edition).

'Naib Magomet-Amgen [The *Na'ib* Muhammad Amin]', *Kavkazskii Gorets*, No. 23 (1925), pp. 46-47.

Nansen, Fridtjof, *Through the Caucasus to the Volga*, Trans. G. C. Wheeler, London: George Allen and Unwin, 1930.

Nazif, Suleyman, 'Seyh Samil', *Kuzey Kafkasya*, Vol. VIII, No. 47 (February-March 1978), p. 1.

Nietzsche, Friedrich, *Also Sprach Zarathustra*, New York: Frederic Ungar Publishing Co., [n. d.]

Norris, J. A., *The First Afghan War, 1838 - 1842*, Cambridge: Cambridge University Press, 1967.

Nortman, Henry Norman, *All the Russias. Travels and Studies in Contemporary European Russia, Finland, Siberia, the Caucasus and Central Asia*, London: William Heinemann, 1902.

'Obsuzhdenie 'Ocherkov Istorii Checheno-Ingushskoi ASSR': Konferentsiia v G. Groznom [Discussion of the 'Outline of the History of the Checheno-Ingush ASSR'. A Conference in Groznyi]', *Istoriia SSSR*, 1974, No. 1, pp. 232-238.

'Obsuzhdenie Voprosa o Kharakteve Dvizhenii Gorsiikh Narodov Severnogo Kavkaza v 20-50kh Godakh XIX Veka [Discussion of the Question of the Character of the Movements of the Mountain Peoples of the Northern Caucasus in the 1820s- 1850s]', *Voprosy Istorii*, 1956, No. 12, pp. 188-198.

Ocherki Istorii Dagestana [An Outline of the History of Daghestan], Makhachqala: Dagestanskoe Knizhnoe Izdatel'stvo, 1957.

'Ochevidets [Eyewitness]', 'Lezginskii Miatezh v Iuzhnom Dagestane [The Lesghian Mutiny in Southern Daghestan]', *Russkii Vestnik*, 1880, No. 12, pp. 663-700.

'O Grazhdanskikh, Voennykh i Dukhovnykh Postanovleniiakh Shamilia [About the Civil Military and Religious Legislation of Shamil]', *Voennyi Sbornik*, 1900, No. 3, pp. 210-213.

Oldenbourg, Zoe, *Catherine the Great*, Trans. Anne Carter, New York: Bantam Books, 1966 (paperback).

Oleinikov, Dmitrii Ivanovich, 'Shamil,' *Voprosy Istorii*, 1996, No. 5- 6, pp. 58 - 76.

Omarov, A. S., 'K Voprosu o Formakh Gosudarstvennosti i Prava, Slozhivshikhsia v Khode Dvizheniia Gortsev Dagestana i Chechni 20-50 GG. XIX V. [To the Question of the Forms of Statehood and Legislation which Developed during the Movement of the Mountaineers of Daghestan and Chechnia in the 1820s-1850s]', *Uchennye Zapiski*, Vol. XIX, Book II (1969), pp. 225-271.

'Otnoshenie Rossii k Kavkazu [Russia's Attitude to the Caucasus]', *Sbornik Gazety Kavkaz*, 1846, pp. 401-410.

Orazaev, G. M.-R. (ed.), *Istoriko-Literaturnoe Nasledie Gasana Alkadari. Sbornik Nauchnykh Trudov [The Hisorical and Literary Heritage of Hasan al-Alqadari. A collection of Scientific Papers]*, Makhachqala: Dagestanskii Filial AN SSSR, 1988.

Ortabaev, B. Kh. And Totoev, F. V., 'Eshche Raz o Kavkazskoi Voine: o ee Sotsial'nykh Istokakh i Sushchnosti [Once Again on the Caucasian War: on its Social Origins and Essance]', *Istoriia SSSR*, 1988, No. 4, pp. 78 - 96.

Özdes,Oguz, *Seyh Samil* [A Novel]. Ankara: Tekin Yayinevi, 1981.

P. 'O Posledstviiakh Ubiistv i Poranenii Mezhdu Gortsami Vostochnogo Kavkaza [About the Consequences of Killings and Woundings among the Mountainers of the Eastern Caucasus]', *Sbornik Svedenii o Kavkazskikh Gortsakh*, Vol. VIII (1875), 14 pp. (separate pagination).

Pereira, N. G. O., *Tsar-Liberator. Alexander II of Russia, 1818 - 1881*, Newtonville, Ma.: Oriental Research Partners, 1983.

Petrushevskii, Il'ia Pavlovich, *Dzharo-Belakanskie Vol'nye Obshchestva v Pervoi Tret'i XIX Stoletiia. Vnutrennyi Stroi i Bor'ba s Rossiiskim Kolonial'nym Nastuplaniem [The Free Communities of Chartalah in the First Third of the Nineteenth Century. [[Their]] Internal Structure and Struggle Against the Russian Colonial Offensive]*, Tiflis: Izdatel'stvo 'Zaria Vostoka', 1934.

-------- 'Sotsialnaia Struktura Dzharo-Belakanskikh Vol'nykh Obshchestv Nakanune Rossiiskogo Zavoevaniia [The Social Structure of the Free Communities of Chartalah on the Eve of Russian Conquest]', *Istoricheskii Sbornik*, No. 1 (1934), pp. 191-228.

Pikman, A. M., 'Kak Ispol'zovalis' Tsarskie Proklamatsii Protiv Dvizheniia Gortsev v XIX V. [How the Tsar's Proclamations Were Used Against the Movement of the Mountaineers in the Nineteenth Century]', *Istoriia* SSSR, 1969, No. 4, pp. 118-122.

-------- 'O Bor'be Kavkazskikh Gortsev s Tsarskimi Kolonizatorami [On the Struggle of the Caucasian Mountaineers Against the Tsarist Colonialists]', *Voprosy Istorii*, 1956, No. 3, pp. 75-84.

Plaetschke, Bruno, *Die Tschetschen . Forschungen zur Völkerkunde des Nordöstlichen Kaukazus auf Grund von Reisen in den Jahren 1918 - 1920 und 1927/28*, Hamburg: Friedrichson, de Gruyter und Co., 1929.

'Plenitel' Shamilia.(Pamiati General Fel'dmarshala Kniazia A. I. Bariatinskogo) [Shamil's Captor.(In Mameriam Fieldmarshal Prince A. I. Bariatinsiiii)]', *Istoricheskaia Letopis'*, 1914, Book III, pp. 934-942.

Pokhvisnev, M. N., 'Aleksei Petrovich Ermolov (Po Povodu Pomeshchennykh v 'Russkoi Starine' Materialov pod Zaglaviem: 'Ermolov, Dibich i Paskevich') [Aleksei Petrovich Ermolov. (A Reaction to the Documents Published in *Russkaia Starina* under the Title 'Ermolov, Diebitsch and Paskiewicz')]', *Russkaia Starina*, 1872, No. 11, pp. 475-492.

Pokorennyi Kavkaz. Ocherki Istoricheskogo Proshlogo i Sovremennogo Polozheniia Kavkaza po Povodu Stoletiia Geroiskoi Bor'by za Kavkaz i Sorokoletiia Zamireniia Kavkaza [The Subdued Caucasus. An outline of the Historical Past and the Present

State of the Caucasus on the Occasion of the Centenary of the Heroic Struggle for the Caucasus and the Fourtieth Anniversary of its Pacification], Free Appendix to *Rodina*, 1904.

Pokrovskii, M., N., 'Zavoevanie Kavkaza [The Conquest of the Caucasus]', in *Istoriia Rossii v XIX Veke,* Vol. V, Moscow: Izd. Brat'ev A. i I. Gratat i Ko., 1909, pp. 292 - 340.

Reprint in: *Diplomatiia i Voiny Tsarskoi Rossii v XIX Stoletii. Sbornik Stat'ei*, Moscow: Izdatel'stvo 'Krasnaia Nov'', 1923, pp. 179-229.

Pokrovskii, N. I., 'Miuridizm u Vlasti. ('Teokraticheskaia Derzhava' Shamilia) [Muridism in Power (Shamil's 'Theocratic State')]', *Istorik Marksist*, 1934, No. 2 (36), pp. 30-75.

-------- 'Obzor Istochnikov po Istorii Imamata [A Review of the Sources to the History of Shamil's State]', *Problemy Istocnikovedeniia*, Book II (1936), pp. 187-234.

Polikarpov, V., 'L. N. Tolstoi na Voennoi Sluzhbe [Tolstoy's Military Service]', *Voenno-Istoricheskii Zhurnal*, 1972, No. 4 , pp. 65 - 67.

Polonskii, L., 'Tragedia Talanta [The Tragedy of a Talent]', *Bakinskii Rabochii*, 22 September 1988.

'Po Povodu Vosstaniia v Zakatal'skom Okruge v 1863-m Godu [Concerning the Uprising in the District of Zakartalah in 1863]', *Kavkazskii Sbornik*, Vol. X (1886), pp. 585-607.

Popov. M. Ia., 'M. Iu. Lermontov -- Boevoi Ofitser [Lermontov as a Field Officer]', *Voenno-Istoricheskii Zhurnal*, 1989, No. 11, pp. 72 - 76.

Potto, Vasilii Aleksandrovich, 'Gadzhi Murat (Biograficheskii Ocherk [Hajimurad (A Biographical Sketch)]', *Voennyi Sbornik*, 1870, No. 11, Part I, pp. 159-187.

-------- *Kavkazskaia Voina v Otdel'nykh Ocherkakh, Epizodakh, Legendakh i Biografiiakh [The War in the Caucasus in Separate Sketches, Episodes, Tales and Biographies]*, St. Petersburg: Tipografiia R. Golike, 1885-1887.

Potto, Vasilii Aleksandrovich, and Beliavskii, N. N., (eds.), *Utverzhdenie Russkogo Vladychestva na Kavkaze [The Consolidation of Russian Rule in the Caucasus]*, Tiflis: Tipografiia la. K. Libermana, 190 I.

Pozhidaev, V. P, *Gortsy Severnogo Kavkaza. Ingushy, Chechentsy, Khevsury, Osetiny i Kabardintsy. Kratkii Istoriko-Etnograficheskii Ocherk [The Mountaineers of the Northern Caucasus. The Ingush, Chechens, Khevsurs, Ossets and Ghabarta. A short Historical and Ethnographic Outline]*, Moscow and Leningrad: Gosudarstvennoe Izdatel'stvo, 1926.

Prawdin, Michael (pseud. of Michael Charol) *The Mongol Empire. Its Rise and Legacy*, Trans. Eden and Cedar Paul, London: George Allen and Unwin, 1940.

'Predaniia o Khadzhi Murate [Traditions About Hajimurad]', *Dagestanskii Sbornik*, Vol. III (1927), pp. 7-49.

Prozritelev, G. N., 'Posol'stvo ot Shamilia k Abadzekham [An Embassy from Shamil to the Abadzekhs]', *Dagestanskii Sbornik*, Vol.. III (1927), pp. 125-129.

[Pushkin, Aleksandr Sergeevich,] *A. S. Pushkin o Kavkaze [A. S. Pushkin about the Caucasus]*, Piatigorsk: Severo-Kavkazskoe Kraevoe Gosudarstvennoe Izdatel'stvo, 1937.

Ramazani, Rouhollah K., *The Foreign Policy of Iran, 1500 - 1914. A Developing Nation in World Affairs*, Charlottesville: University Press of Virginia, 1966.

Rhinelander, Laurence Hamilton, 'The Creation of the Caucasian Viceregensy', *Slavonic and East European Review*, Vol. 59, No. 1 (1981), pp. 15 - 40.

-------- 'Russia's Imperial Policy. The Administration of the Caucasus in the First Half of the Nineteenth Century', *Canadian Slavonic Papers*, Vol. XVII, No. 2 (Summer 1975), pp. 218-235.

Robinson,Gertrude, *David Urquhart. Some Chapters in the Life of a Victorian Knight-Errant of Justice and Liberty*, Oxford: Basil Blackwel, 1920.

-------- *Some Account of David Urquhart.* Oxford: Basil Blackwel, 1921.

Romanowski [Romanovskii], Dmitrii Il'ich, *Kavkaz i Kavkazskaia Voina. Publichnye Lektsii Chitannye v Zale Pasazha v 1860 Godu [The Cuacasus and the Caucasus War. Lectures Delivered in 1860 in the Passage Hall]*, St. Petersburg: Tipografiia Tovarishchestva 'Obshchestvennaia Pol'za', 1860.

-------- 'GeneraI-Fel'dmarsbal Kniaz' Aleksandr Ivanovich Bariatinskfi i Kavkazskaia Voina, 1815-1879 GG. [Fieldmarshal Prince Alexander Ivanovich Bariatinskii and the War in the Caucasus, 1815- 1879]', *Russkaia Starina*, 1881, No. 2, pp. 247-318, 444.

Russkii Biograficheskii Slovar [The Russian Biographical Dictionary], St. Petersburg: I. N. Skorokhodov, 1896-1911.

Rustum, Asad Jibra'il, *The Royal Archives of Egypt and the Disturbances in Palestine, 1834*, Beirut: The American Press, 1938.

Rywkin, Michael, *Russia in Central Asia*, New York: Collier Books, 1963 (paperback).

Sabry, M., *L'Empire Egyptienne sous Mohamed-Ali et la Question d'Orient (1811 - 1849)*, Paris: Librairie Oientaliste Paul Geuthner, 1930.

Saidov, M., 'Dagestanskaia Literatura XVII-XIX VV. na Arabskom Iazyke [Dagbestan's Literature in Arabic between the Seventeenth and Nineteenth Centuries]', in: Gafurov, B. G. et al. (eds.), *Trudy Dvatsat' Piatogo*

Mezhdunarodnogo Kongressa Vostokovedov, Moskva, 9 - 16 Avgusta 1960 G.., Moscow: Iztdatel'stvo Vostochnoi Literatury, 1963, Vol. II, pp. 118-123.

Sanders, A. (pseud. of Alexander Nikuradze), *Kaukasien. Nordkaukasien, Aserbeidschan, Armenien, Georgien. Geschichtlicher Umriss,* Munich: Hoheneichen Verlag, 1944 (2nd edition).

Sarkisyanz, Emmanuel, *Geschichte der Orientalischen Völker Russlands bis 1917. Eine Erganzug zur Ostslawischen Geschichte Russlands*, Munich: R. 01denbourg Verlag, 1961.

Savinov, V. I., *Shikh Mansur* [A Historical Novel], St. Petersburg: Tipografiia A. Dmitrieva, 1853.

-------- *Teskol'skoe Ushchelie [The Gorge of Teskel]* [A Novel], St. Petersburg: Tipografiia Eduarda Veimara, 1853.

-------- *Znakhari* [A Novel], St. Petersburg: Tipograffia K. Kraia, 1854.

Schilder [Shil'der] N. K., *Graf Eduard Ivanovich Totleben. Ego Zhizn' i Deiatel'nost'. Biograficheskii Ocherk [Count Eduard Todtleben. His Life and Deeds. A Bigraphical Outline]*, St. Petersburg: Tipografiia 'Russkaia Skoropechatnaia', 1885.

-------- *Imperator Nikolai Pervyi. Ego Zhizn' i Tsarstvovanie [Emperor Nicholas I. His Life and Reign]*, St. Petersburg: Izdanie A. S. Suvorina, 1903.

von Seeger, Karl, *Imam Schamyl, Prophet und Feldherr*, Leipzig: Paul List Verlag, 1937.

Seif, Theodor, 'Beitrage zur Geschichte Scheich Schamyls', *Wiener Zeitschrift für die Kunde des Morgenlandes*, Vol.XXIX (1915), pp. 355 - 363.

Semenov, L. P., 'Khadzhi-Murat v Khudothestvennoi Literature. Bibliograficheskaia Zametka [Hajimurad in Literature. A Bibliographical Note]', in *idem* (ed.), *Kavkaz i Lev Tolstoi. Sbornik*, Vladikavkaz: Ingushskii Nauchno-Isledovatel'skii Institut Kraevedenia, 1928.

-------- 'Lev Tolstoi i Kavkaz [Leo Tolstoy and the Caucasus]', in: *idem* (ed.), *Kavkaz i Lev Tolstoi. Sbornik,* Vladikavkaz: Ingushskii Nauchno-Isledovatel'skii Institut Kraevedenia, 1928.

Semenov, N., 'Khronika Chechenskogo Vosstanniia 1877G. [A Chronicle of the Chechen Uprising of 1877]', *Terskii Sbornik*, Vol. I, Part I, pp. 1-92.

-------- *Tuzemtsy Severo-Vostochnogo Kavkaza. Razskazy, Ocherki, Issledovaniia. Zametki o Chechentsakh, Kumykakh i Nogaitsakh i Poezii Etikh Narodtsev[The Natives of the North-Eastern Caucasus. Stories, Sketches, Researches, Notes about the Chechens, Ghumuqs and Nogays and the Poetry of These Poeples]*, St. Petersburg: Tipografiia A. Khomskogo, 1895.

Sergeeva, Galina Aleksandrovna, *Archintsy [The Archis]*, Moscow: 'Nauka', 1965.

Serov, F., 'Naezdnik Beibulat Taimazov [The Raider Beybulat Taymaz]', *O Tekh Kogo Nazyvali Abrekami [About Those who were Called Abreks]*, [Groznyi:] Izdanie Otdela Chechenskogo Narodnogo Obrazovaniia, 1925, pp.125-139.

Shabad, Theodore, *Geography of the USSR. A Regional Survey*, New York: Columbia University Ptess, 1951.

'Al-Shaykh Shamuyil/ The Circassian Shaikh Shamyl, Father of the Actual Brigadier-General Muhammad Pasha Ghazi', *Al-Nahla/The Bee* (London), 1 August 1877, pp. 54-56 (Arabic and Englisb texts).

Shcherbatov, *General-Fel'dmarshal Kniaz' Paskevich. Ego Zhizn' i Deiatel'nost' [Fieldmarshal Prince Paskiewicz. His Life and Deeds]*, St. Petersburg: Tipografiia-Litografiia Postavshchika Dvora E. I. V., 1888-1904.

Shcherbinin, Mikhail Pavlovich, *Biografiia General-Marshala Kniazia Mikhaila Semenovicha Vorontsova [A biography of Field-Marshal Prince Mikhail Semenovich Vorontsov]*, St. Petersburg: Tipografiia Eduarda Veimara, 1858.

[Shaw, George Bernard,] *The Complete Works of Bernard Shaw*, London: Odham Press, 1937.

Shaw, D. J. B., 'Southern Frontiers of Muscovy, 1550- 1700', in Bater, James H. and French, R. A. (eds.), *Studies in Russian Historical Geography*, London: Academic Press, 1983, Vol. I, pp. 118-142.

Sheehy, Ann, 'Yet Another Rewrite of the History of the Caucasian War?' *Radio Liberty Research*, RL 39/84, 30 Janaury 1984.

Sheripov, Z., 'Sheikh Mansur (Kratkii Istoriko-Biograficheskii Ocherk) [Shaykh Mansur (A Short Historic-Biographical Sketch)]', *O Tekh Kogo Nazyvali Abrekami*, [Groznyi:] Izdanie Chechenskogo Otdela Narodnogo Obrazovaniia, 1925, pp. 151-158.

Shikhsaidov, Amri R., 'Pismennye Pamiatniki Dagestana XIX V. (Zhanr Biografii) [Writen Works from Daghestan of the Nineteenth Century (The Biographical Janre)]', in: Kh. A. Omarov (ed.), *Pis'menye Pamiatniki Dagestana XVIII -XIX VV.*, Makhachqala: Dagestanskii Filial AN SSSR, 1989, pp. 5 - 14.

von Siemens, Werner, *Kaukazus reisen*, Zeuleronda: Bernhardt Sporn Verlag, 1943.

Sineokow, Vladimir, *La Colonisation Russe en Asie*, Paris: Marcel Giard, 1929.

Sivkov, K. V., 'O Proektakh Okonchaniia Kavkazskoi Voiny v Seredine XIX V. [On Some Plans to End the War in the Caucasus in Mid-Nineteenth Century]', *Istoriia SSSR*, 1958, No. 3, pp. 191 - 196.

Skrine, Prancis Henry, *The Expansion of Russia, 1815 - 1900*, Cambridge:

Cambridge University Press, 1903.

Sluzhivyi (pseud.), *Ocherki Pokoreniia Kavkaza [An Outline of the Conquest of the Caucasus]*, St. Petersburg: Tipografiia M. M. Stasiulevicha, 1901.

Slovar' Kavkazskikh Deiatelei [Dictionary of [[Russian]] Personalities in the Cuacasus], Tiflis: Tipografiia M. Vartaniantsa, 1890.

Smirnov, Nikolai Aleksandrovich, *Miuridizm na Kavkaze [The Murid Movement in the Caucasus]*, Moscow: Izdatel'stvo Akademii Nauk SSSR, 1963.

-------- (ed.), *Ocherki Istorii Checheno-Ingushskoi ASSR [An Outline of the History of the Checheno-Ingush ASSR]*, Groznyi: Checheno-Ingushskoe Knizhnoe Izdatel'stvo, 1967.

-------- *Politika Rossii na Kavkaze v XVI - XIX Vekakh [Russia's Policy in the Caucasus in the Sixteenth to Nineteenth Centuries]*, Moscow: Izdatel'stvo Sotsial'no-Ekonomicheskoi Literatury, 1958.

-------- 'Sheikh Mansur i Ego Turetskie Vdokhnoviteli [Shaykh Mansur and His Turkish Inspirators]', *Voprosy Istorii*, 1950, No. 10, pp. 19-39,

Smirnov, V., 'Nepravil'noe Osveshchenie Vazhnogo Voprosa [A Wrong Elucidation of an Important Question]' *Pravda*, 20 November 1956.

Sollohub [Sollogub], Vladimir Aleksandrovich, *Biografiia Generala Kotliarevskogo [The Biography of General Kotliarevskii]*, St.Petersburg: Tipografiia K. Kraia, 1856 (2nd edition).

de Souchesmes, R., *Du Caucase a Vistule*, Nancy: Imprimerie de Berger-Levrault, 1897.

Sovetskaia Istoricheskaia Entsiklopediia [The Soviet Historical Encyclopedia], Moscow: 1965-1967.

Spencer, Edmund, *The Prophet of the Caucasus. An Historical Romanse of Krim-Tartary*, London: Whittaker and Co., 1840.

Starozhil (pseud.), *Kavkaz. Spravochnaia Kniga [The Caucasus. A Guide]*, Tiflis: Tipograffia L. G. Kramarenko, 1888.

Sumbatzade, A. S., *Kubinskoe Vosstanie 1837 G. [The Qubah Uprising of 1837]*, Baqu: Izdatel'stvo Akademii Nauk Azerbaidzhanskoi SSR, 1961.

Sumner, B. H., *Peter the Great and the Emergence of Russia*, London: English Universities Press, 1950.

Surkhay, 'Kavkaz i Derzhavy v XIX V. [The Caucasus and the [[Great]] Powers in the Nineteenth Gntury]', *Kavkaz* (Paris), 1938, No. 4 (52), pp. 17-21, No. 5 (53), pp. 13-

17, No. 7 (55), pp. 4-8 No. 10 (58), pp. 26-28, 1939, No. 1 (61), pp. 21-24, No. 2 (62), pp. 18-21, No. 5 (65), pp. 8-11.

Sviderskii, P. F., 'K Antropologii Archintsev [To the Anthropology of the Archis]', *Russkii Antropologicheskii Zhurnal*, Book XXXV-XXXVI (1913), pp. 32-44.

Sykes, Percy, *A History of Persia*, London: MacMillan and Co., 1921 (2nd edition).

Szczelnicki [Strshel'nitskii], 'Dva Uzdena [Story]',Trans. from Polish *Sbornik Gazety Kavkaz*, 1846, pp. 248-281, 312-315.

T., 'Razboi i Samorasprava na Kavkaze [Robbery and Lynch Law in the Caucasus]', *Vestnik Evropy,* 1885, No. 12, pp. 617-646.

Tansu, Samih Nafiz, *Çarlara Besegmeyen Dagli. Seyh Samil [The Mountaineer who Did not Kneel before the Tsars. Shaykh Shamil]*, Istanbul: Inkilap ve Aka Kitabevleri, 1963.

Tarnovskii, Konstantin Nikolaevich, *Sovetskaia Istoriografiia Rossiiskogo Imperializma [Soviet Historiography of Russian Imperialism]*, Moscow: 'Nauka', 1964.

Tatishchev, S. S., *Imperator Aleksandr II. Ego Zhizn' i Tsarstvovanie [Emperor Alexandre II. His Life and Reign]*, St. Petersburg: Izdanie A. S. Savorina, 1903.

Tatlock, T., 'The Centenial of the Capture or Shamil: A Shamil Bibliography', *Caucasian Review*, No. 8 (1959), pp. 83-91, 101 -102.

Temperley, Harold, *England and the Near East. The Crimea*, London: Longmans, Green and Co., 1936.

von Thielman, Freiherr Max, *Streifzuge im Kaukazus, in Persien und in der Asiatischen Türkei*, Leipzig: Duncker und Humblot, 1875.

Tillet, Lowell R., 'Shamil and Muridism in Recent Soviet Historiography', *American Slavic and East European Review*, Vol. XX (1961), pp. 253-269.

--------*The Great Friendship. Soviet Historians on the Non-Russian Nationalities*, Chapel Hill: The University of North Carolina Press, 1969.

Tkachev, G, A,, *Ingushi i Checentsy v Sem'e Narodnostei Terskoi Oblasti [The Ingush and Chechens in the Family of Peoples of the Terek District]*, Vladikavkaz: Elektropechatnaia Tipografiia Terskogo Oblastnogo Pravleniia, 1911.

Tolstoi, Iurii, 'Ocherk Zhizni i Sluzhby E. A. Golovina [An Outline of the Life and Service of E. A. Golovin]', in: Bartenev, Petr (ed.), *Deviatnadtsatyi Vek. Istoricheskii Sbornik*, Moscow: P. Iohanson, 1872, Vol. I, pp. 1-64.

Tolstov, S. P. et al (eds.), *Ocherki Obshchei Etnografii. Aziatskaia Chast' SSSR [An Outline of General Ethnography, The Asian Part of the USSR]*, Moscow: Izdatel'stvo Akademii Nauk SSSR, 1940.

Totoev, Mikhail Soslanbekovich, *K Istorii Doreformennoi Severnoi Osetii [Contribution to the History of Pre-Reform North Ossetiia]*, Ordzhonikidze: Severo-Osetinskoe Kniziinoe Izdatel'stvo, 1955.

Traho, Ramazan, 'Literature on Checheno-Ingushes and Karachay-Balkars', *Caucasian Review*, No. 5 (1957), pp. 76-96.

-------- 'The 'Rehabilitation' of Imam Sbamil', *Caucasian Review*, No. 1 (1955), pp. 145-162.

Trevisan, Alessandra, 'Shamil Tra Mill'ani in una Comedia di Sollogub (1854): Traduzione Annotata', *Oriente Moderno*, New Series, Vol. II, No. 1-12 (January-December 1983), pp. 97-123.

Trimingham, J. Spencer, 'The Formative Stages of the lslamic Religious Order', *Glasgow University Oriental Society, Transactions*, No. 18 (1959-1960), pp. 65-76.

-------- *A History of Islam in West Afrjca*, London: Oxford University Press, 1962.

-------- I*slam in East Africa*, Oxford: Oxford University Press, 1964.

-------- *Islam in the Sudan*, London: Oxford University Press, 1949.

-------- *The Sufi Orders in Islam*, Oxford: Calrendon and Oxford University Presses, 1971.

Troyat, Henri (pseud. of Lev Tarassov), *Pushkin. A Biography*, Trans Randolph T. Weaver, London: Victor Golancz, 1951 .

-------- *Tolstoy*, Trans. Nancy Amphoux, London: W. H. Allen, 1968.

Trubetskoi, Nikita Sergeevich, 'Dagestanskii Konnyi Polk [The Daghestan [[Irregular]] Mounted Regiment]', *Russkii Voenno-Istoricheskii Vestnik* (Paris), No. 2 (1948), pp.9 - 11.

-------- 'Osada Aula Chokh [The Siege of tbe *Awul* Chokha]'. *Russkii Voenno-Istoricheskii Vestnik* (Paris), , No. 6 (1950), pp. 9-12.

Ts--ov, Akhmet, 'Russkaia Biurokratiia i Kavkazskie Gortsy [The Russian Bureaucracy and the Caucasian Mountaineers]', *Vestnik Evropy*, 1909, No. 9, pp. 298-315.

Tumanskii, A, G., *Arabskii Iazyk i Kavkazovedenie [The Arabic Language and the Study of the Caucasus]*, Tiflis: Tipografiia A. I. Petrova, 1911.

Tutaeff, David, *The Soviet Caucasus*, London: G. G. Harrap and Co., 1942.

Uebersberger, Hans, *Russlands Orienpolitik in den Letzten Zwei Jahrhunderten*, Stuttgart: Deutsche Verlags-Anstadt, 1913.

Vertepov, G., 'Po Povodu Piatidesiatiletii Kreposti (Nyne Slobody) Vozdvizhenskoi [On the Occasion of the 50th Anniversary of the Fortress (Now Township) Vozdvizhenskaia]', *Terskie Vedomosti*, 6 [18] April (No. 41), pp. 3-4, 8 [20] April 1894 (no. 42), pp. 3-4.

-------- 'Sud'ba Religiozno-Politicheskikh Uchenii v Chechne [The Destiny of the Religio-Poliltical Teacbings in Chechnia]', *Terskie Vedomosti*, 1[13] May (No. 52), p.3, 6 [18] May 1892 (No. 54), pp. 2-3.

Viktorov, A. F., Himmelreich [Gimmel'reikh], P. L., L'vov, P. L., Mikulin, I. N. and El'darov, M. M., *Dagestanskaia ASSR. Fiziko-Geograficheskii i Ekonomiko-Geograficheskii Obzor [The Daghestan ASSR. A Survey of its Physical and Economic Geography]*, Makhachqala: Dagestanskoe Uchebno-Pedagogicheskoe Izdatel'stvo, 1958.

Vinogradov, Boris Stepanovich, *Kavkaz v Russkoi Literature 30kh Godov XIX Veka. Ocherki [The Caucasus in Russian Literature of the 1830s. An Outline]*, Groznyi: Checheno-Ingushskoe Knizhnoe Izdatel'stvo, 1966.

Vinogradov, V. B,, 'Rossiia i Severnyi Kavkaz (Obzor Literatury za 1971 - 1975 GG.) [Russia and the Northern Caucasus. (A Bibilographical Survey for 1971-1975)]', *Istorii SSSR*, 1977, No. 3, pp. 158-166.

Vladykin, M., *Putevodel' i Sobesednik v Puteshestvii po Kavkazu [A Guide and Phrase Book to the Caucasus]*, Moscow: I. Rodzevich and V.Islen'ev, 1874.

Voennaia Entsyklopediia [Military Encyclopedia], St. Petersburg: T-vo I. D. Syfina,1911-1914.

Volkova, Natal'ia Grigor'evna, *Etnicheskii Sostav Nasseleniia Severnogo Kavkaza v XVIII - Nachale XX Veka [The Ethnic Composition of the population of the Northern Caucasus in the Eighteenth to the Beginning of the Twentieth Centuries]*, Moscow: 'Nauka', 1974.

Wald, Alexander, *Kurze Biographie des Fürsten Michail Simeonowitsch Woronzow*, Odessa: Buchdrukerei von L. Nietsche, 1863.

Webster, Charles Kingsley, *The Foreign Policy of Palmerstone, 1830 - 1841*, London: G. Bell and Sons, 1951.

-------- 'Urquhart Ponsonby and Palmerstone', *English Historical Review*, Vol. LXII (July 1947), pp. 327-351.

Weidenbaum, Eugen [Veidenbaum, Evgenii G.],'Berengeim i Gordeev [Bergenheim and Gordeev]', in: *idem, Kavkazskie Etiudy. Issledovaniia i Zametki*, Tiflis: Skoropechatnaia M. Martirosiantsa, 1901, pp. 289-297.

-------- 'Ermolov i Paskevich [Ermolov and Paskiewicz]', in: *idem, Kavkazskie Etiudy. Issledovaniia i Zametki*, Tiflis: Skoropechatnaia M. Martirosiantsa, 1901, pp. 216-232.

-------- 'Kavkaz v Russkoi Poezi [The Caucasus in Russian Poetry]', in: *idem, Kavkazskie Etiudy. Issledovaniia i Zametki*, Tiflis: Skoropechatnaia M. Martirosiantsa, 1901, pp. 274-281.

-------- 'O Probyvanii Pushkina na Kavkaze v 1829 G. [About Pushkin's Stay in the Caucasus in 1829]', in: *idem, Kavkazskie Etiudy. Issledovaniia i Zametki*, Tiflis: Skoropechatnaia M. Martirosiantsa, 1901, pp. 233-260.

-------- 'Polkovnik, F. I. Gene [Colonel F. I. Hene]', in: *idem, Kavkazskie Etiudy. Issledovaniia i Zametki*, Tiflis: Skoropechatnaia M. Martirosiantsa, 1901, pp. 281-289.

-------- 'Prodelki na Kavkaze [Tricks in the Caucasus]', in: *idem, Kavkazskie Etiudy. Issledovaniia i Zametki*, Tiflis: Skoropechatnaia M. Martirosiantsa, 1901, pp. 308-320.

-------- *Putevoditel' po Kavkazu [A Guide to the Caucasus]*, Tiffis: Tipografiia Kantseliarii Glavnonachal'stvuiushchego Grazhdanskoi Chastiu na Kavkaze, 1888.

-------- 'V. T. Nerezhnyi i ego Kavkazskii Roman [V. T. Nerezhnyi and his Caucasian Novel]', in: *idem, Kavkazskie Etiudy. Issledovaniia i Zametki*, Tiflis: Skoropechatnaia M. Martirosiantsa, 1901, pp. 303-308.

Whittock, M., 'Ermolov: Proconsul of the Caucasus', *The Russian Review*, Vol. XVIII, No. 1 (January 1959), pp. 53-60.

Widerszal, Ludwik, *Sprawy Kaukazkie w Politice Europejskej w Latach 1834 - 1864 [Affairs of the Caucasus in European Politics 1834 - 1864]*, Warsaw: Naklad Tawarzystwa Naukowego Warszawskiego oraz Institutu Wschodniego w Warszawie, 1934.

Winckler, Hugo, *The Tell-El-Amarna Letters*, London: Luzac & Co., 1896.

Wolfe, Bertram D., 'Operation Rewrite: The Agony or Soviet Historians', *Foreign Affairs*, Vol. XXXI, No.1 (October 1951), pp. 39-57.

Yetik, Zubeyir, *Imam Samil*, Istanbul: Beyaz Yayinlari Zafer Matbaasi, 1986.

Yitshaqi [Yitshaqovich]. Ya'qov ben Yitshaq and Anisimov, Sharbat ben Nisim, *Sefer Toldot Yehudey Daghestan ha-Mada'im ha-Nimtsa'im be-Harey Qawqaz 'ad Henna [History of the Median Jews of Daghestan, who Have Been Living in the Caucasus Mountains until the Present]*, Jerusalem: Frumqin, 5654 [1894].

Yusufov, R. F., *Dagestan i Russkaia Literatura Kontsa XVIII i Pervoi Poloviny XIX V. [Daghestan and Russian Literature of the End of the 18th and the First Half of the 19th Centuries]*, Moscow: 'Nauka', 1964.

Z. N., *Dagestanskii Plennik ili Neumolimyi Mstitel' [The Daghestani Prisoner or the Inexorable Avanger]* [A Novel], Moscow: Tipografiia V. Got'e, 1852.

Zabitov, S. N., ''Krug Ucheniia' Saida iz Arakani [The 'Learning Circle' of Sa'id al-Harakani]', in: Kh. A. Omarov (ed.), *Pis'menye Pamiatniki Dagestana XVIII -XIX VV.*, Makhachqala: Dagestanskii Filial AN SSSR, 1989, pp.93 - 102.

Zajaczkowski [Zaionchkovskii], P. A., 'D. A. Miliutin. Biograficheskfi Ocherk [D. A. Miliutin. A Biographical Sketch]', Introduction to: *idem* (ed.), *Dnevnik D. A. Miliutina*, Moscow: Gosudarstvennaia Biblioteka SSSR Imeni V.I. Lenina, 1947, pp. 5-72.

Zakharin (Iakunin), Iv[an] N., *Kavkaz i ego Geroi [The Caucasus and its heroes]*, St. Petersburg: Tipografiia A. E. Kolpinskogo, 1902.

Zand, Michael, 'The Literature of the Mountain Jews of the Caucasus', *Soviet Jewish Affairs,* Vol. XV, No. 2 (May 1985), pp. 3-22, Vol. XVI, No. 1 (February 1986), pp. 35-51.

Zasedateleva, Lidiia Borisovna, *Terskie Kazaki (Seredina XVI - Nachalo XX V.) [The Terek Cossacks (Mid 16th to the Beginning of 20th Centuries)]*, Moscow: Izdatel'stvo Moskovskogo Universiteta, 1974.

Zhelikovskaia, V, P., *Ermolov na Kavkaze [Ermolov in the Caucasus]*, St. Petersburg: Tipografiia Tovarishchestva 'Obshcbestvennaia Pol'za', [n. d.]

Zhizn' General-Leitenanta Kniazia Madatova [The Life of Lieutenant-General Prince Madatov], St. Petersburg: Tipograffia Gaia. 1837.

Züssermann [Ziserman], Arnold B., *Fel'dmarshal Kniaz' Aleksandr Ivanovich Bariatinskii [Fieldmarshal Prince Aleksandr Ivanovich Bariatinskii]*, Moscow: Universitetskaia Tipografiia 1888-1891.

Also Serialised in: *Russkii Arkhiv*, 1888 - 1889.

-------- *Istoriia 80-go Pekhotnogo Kabardinskogo General-Fel'dmarshala Kniazia Bariatinskogo Polka (1726 - 1880) [History of the 80th Infantry the 'Ghabarta' Regiment named after General-Fieldmarshal Prince Bariatinskii]*, St. Petersburg: Tipografiia V. Gratsianskogo. 1881.

-------- 'Osada Kazy-Mulloi Burnoi i Derbenta v 1831 Godu [Ghazi Muhammad's Siege of Burnaia and Derbend in 1831]', *Russkii Vestnik*, 1864, No.12, pp. 698-732.

Index